John Willis

WITH ASSOCIATE EDITOR **Barry Monush**

SCREEN WORLD

2004 FILM ANNUAL

VOLUME 55

APPLAUSE
THEATRE & CINEMA BOOKS

SCREEN WORLD
Volume 55

Art Direction: Mark Lerner
Book design by Pearl Chang **Cover design** by Kristina Rolander

ISBN (hardcover): 1-55783-638-8
ISBN (paperback): 1-55783-639-6
ISSN: 1545-9020

Applause Theatre & Cinema Books
151 West 46th Street, 8th Floor
New York, NY 10036
Phone: (212) 575-9265
Fax: (646) 562-5852
Email: info@applausepub.com
Internet: www.applausepub.com

Applause books are available through your local bookstore, or you may order at www.applausepub.com or call Music Dispatch at 800-637-2852

Sales & Distribution
North America:
Hal Leonard Corp.
7777 West Bluemound Road
P.O. Box 13819
Milwaukee, WI 53213
Phone: (414) 774-3630
Fax: (414) 774-3259
Email: halinfo@halleonard.com
Internet: www.halleonard.com
Europe:
Roundhouse Publishing Ltd.
Millstone, Limers Lane
Northam, North Devon EX 39 2RG
Phone: (0) 1237-474-474
Fax: (0) 1237-474-774
Email: roundhouse.group@ukgateway.net

CONTENTS

EDITOR John Willis
ASSOCIATE EDITOR Barry Monush

ACKNOWLEDGEMENTS:

Anthology Film Archives, Artisan Entertainment, Bazan Entertainment,
Thomas Buxereau, Castle Hill Films, David Christopher, The Cinema Guild,
Columbia Pictures, Consolidated Poster Service, Samantha Dean and Associates,
DreamWorks, Brian Durnin, Film Forum, First Look Pictures, First Run Features,
Focus Features, Fox Searchlight, IFC Films, Kino International, Lions Gate Films,
Tom Lynch, MGM, Mike Maggiore, Magnolia Pictures, Menemsha Entertainment,
Milestone Films, Miramax Films, David Munro, New Line Cinema/Fine Line
Features, New Yorker Films, Newmarket Films, Susan Norget, Open City
Communications, Palm Pictures, Paramount Pictures, Paramount Classics,
7th Art Releasing, Shadow Distribution, Kallie Shimek, Sony Classics, Sony
Pictures Entertainment, Sheldon Stone, Strand Releasing, TLA Entertainment,
ThinkFilm, Twentieth Century Fox, Universal Pictures, Walt Disney Pictures,
Jeremy Walker & Associates, Wellspring, Zeitgeist Films

Nightfall

The Miracle Worker

The Pumpkin Eater

7 Women

Young Winston

The Turning Point

1981

Garbo Talks

'night, Mother

To **ANNE BANCROFT**

An impassioned, clever, and gifted actress who has been equally brilliant in both drama and comedy, emerging as one of the most enduring and respected performers of her generation.

FILMS: 1952: Don't Bother to Knock; **1953:** Treasure of the Golden Condor; Tonight We Sing; The Kid from Left Field; **1954:** Demetrius and the Gladiators; The Raid; Gorilla at Large; **1955:** A Life in the Balance; New York Confidential; The Naked Street; The Last Frontier; **1956:** Nightfall; Walk the Proud Land; **1957:** The Girl in Black Stockings; The Restless Breed; **1962:** The Miracle Worker (Academy Award for Best Actress); **1964:** The Pumpkin Eater (Academy Award nomination); **1965:** The Slender Thread; **1966:** 7 Women; **1967:** The Graduate (Academy Award nomination); **1972:** Young Winston; **1975:** The Prisoner of Second Avenue; The Hindenburg; **1976:** Lipstick; Silent Movie; **1977:** The Turning Point (Academy Award nomination); **1980:** Fatso (also director, writer); The Elephant Man; **1983:** To Be or Not to Be; **1984:** Garbo Talks; **1985:** Agnes of God (Academy Award nomination); **1986:** 'night, Mother; **1987:** 84 Charing Cross Road; **1988:** Torch Song Trilogy; **1989:** Bert Rigby, You're a Fool; **1992:** Honeymoon in Vegas; Love Potion No. 9; **1993:** Point of No Return; Malice; Mr. Jones; **1995:** How to Make an American Quilt; Home for the Holidays; Dracula: Dead and Loving It; **1996:** The Sunchaser; **1997:** G.I. Jane; Critical Care; **1998:** Great Expectations; Antz (voice); **2000:** Keeping the Faith; Up at the Villa; **2001:** Heartbreakers; In Search of Peace, Part 1: 1948–1967 (voice).

SCREEN HIGHLIGHTS OF 2003

BIG FISH
Right: Ada Tai, Arlene Tai
Below: Alison Lohman, Ewan McGregor

KILL BILL: VOLUME 1
Right: Uma Thurman
Below: Chiaki Kuriyama, Lucy Liu, Julie Dreyfus

PHOTOS COURTESY OF MIRAMAX

LOST IN TRANSLATION
Above: Scarlett Johansson, Bill Murray
Left: Mathew Minami, Bill Murray
PHOTOS COURTESY OF FOCUS FEATURES

SHATTERED GLASS
Right: Peter Sarsgaard
PHOTO COURTESY OF LIONS GATE

ELEPHANT
Below: Alex Frost
PHOTO COURTESY OF FINE LINE FEATURES

AMERICAN SPLENDOR
Above: Hope Davis, Paul Giamatti
PHOTO COURTESY OF FINE LINE FEATURES

21 GRAMS
Left: Naomi Watts
PHOTO COURTESY OF FOCUS FEATURES

THE LORD OF THE RINGS:
THE RETURN OF THE KING
Below: Viggo Mortensen
Top, right: Ian McKellen
Bottom, right: Liv Tyler
PHOTOS COURTESY OF NEW LINE CINEMA

COLD MOUNTAIN
Above: Nicole Kidman, Jude Law
PHOTO COURTESY OF MIRAMAX

MASTER & COMMANDER
Left: Max Benitz, Russell Crowe
PHOTO COURTESY OF 20TH CENTURY FOX/MIRAMAX/UNIVERSAL

UNDER THE TUSCAN SUN
Above: Diane Lane, Raoul Bova
PHOTO COURTESY OF TOUCHSTONE

IN AMERICA
Right: Sarah Bolger, Paddy Considine, Emma Bolger
PHOTO COURTESY OF FOX SEARCHLIGHT

**PIRATES OF THE CARIBBEAN:
THE CURSE OF THE BLACK PEARL**
Left: Johnny Depp
PHOTO COURTESY OF TOUCHSTONE

THE LAST SAMURAI
Above: Tom Cruise
PHOTO COURTESY OF WARNER BROS.

MYSTIC RIVER
Left: Sean Penn
PHOTO COURTESY OF WARNER BROS.

FINDING NEMO
Right: Squirt, Crush, Dory, Marlin
PHOTO COURTESY OF WALT DISNEY PICTURES

SOMETHING'S GOTTA GIVE
Below: Amanda Peet, Jack Nicholson
PHOTO COURTESY OF COLUMBIA/WARNER BROS.

THE SCHOOL OF ROCK
Above: Veronica Afflerbach, Miranda Cosgrove,
Jordan-Claire Green, Zachary Infante, Jack Black
PHOTO COURTESY OF PARAMOUNT

BRUCE ALMIGHTY
Left: Morgan Freeman, Jim Carrey
PHOTO COURTESY OF UNIVERSAL

THE BARBARIAN INVASIONS
Right: Toni Cecchinato, Louise Portal,
Marina Hands, Rémy Girard, Yves Jacques,
Pierre Curzi, Dorothee Berryman,
Stephane Rousseau, Dominique Michel

PHOTO COURTESY OF MIRAMAX

SEABISCUIT
Below: Tobey Maguire

PHOTO COURTESY OF UNIVERSAL/DREAMWORKS

BEND IT LIKE BECKHAM
Left: Keira Knightley, Parminder Nagra

PHOTO COURTESY OF FOX SEARCHLIGHT

MONSTER
Above: Christina Ricci, Charlize Theron

PHOTO COURTESY OF NEWMARKET

HOUSE OF SAND AND FOG
Left: Jennifer Connelly

PHOTO COURTESY OF DREAMWORKS

DOWN WITH LOVE
Left: Renée Zellweger, Tony Randall, Sarah Paulson
PHOTO COURTESY OF 20TH CENTURY FOX

INTOLERABLE CRUELTY
Below: George Clooney, Catherine Zeta-Jones
PHOTO COURTESY OF UNIVERSAL

A MIGHTY WIND
Above: Eugene Levy, Catherine O'Hara
PHOTO COURTESY OF WARNER BROS.

LOVE ACTUALLY
Right: Andrew Lincoln, Keira Knightley
PHOTO COURTESY OF UNIVERSAL

DOMESTIC FILMS
2003 RELEASES

JUST MARRIED

(20TH CENTURY FOX) Producer, Robert Simonds; Executive Producers, Tracey Trench, Joel Rosen, Lauren Shuler Donner; Director, Shawn Levy; Screenplay, Sam Harper; Photography, Jonathan Brown; Designer, Nina Ruscio; Costumes, Debra McGuire; Music, Christophe Beck; Editor, Don Zimmerman; Co-Producer, Ira Shuman; Casting, Sheila Jaffe, Georgianne Walken; a Robert Simonds production, presented in association with Mediastream 1. Productions; Dolby; Super 35 Widescreen; Color; Rated PG-13; 94 minutes; Release date: January 10, 2003

Cast

Tom Leezak **Ashton Kutcher**
Sarah McNerney **Brittany Murphy**
Peter Prentiss **Christian Kane**
Kyle **David Moscow**
Lauren McNerney **Monét Mazur**
Mr. McNerney **David Rasche**
Willie McNerney **Thad Luckinbill**
Paul McNerney **David Agranov**
Dickie McNerney **Taran Killam**
Mr. Leezak **Raymond J. Barry**
Yuan **Toshi Toda**
Father Robert **George Gaynes**
Fredo **Massimo Schina**
Wendy **Valeria**
Fred **Alex Thomas**
Henri Margeaux **Laurent Alexandre**

and Jill Parker-Jones (Nasty Stewardess), Sandy McCormack (Huge Man on Plane), Timmy Fitzpatrick (Kid in the Bathroom), Francesco Fantasia (Bernardo Salviati), Aled Ardenti (Bouncer), Robert Branco (Prison Guard), Joseph Vassallo (Customs Official), Roberto Tagliapietra (Gondolier), Clement von Franckenstein (Car Rental Clerk), Anderson Goncalves (Bell Boy), Guido Foehrweisser (Tow Truck Driver), Lorenzo Caccialanza (Italian Man), Veronica Cartwright (Mrs. McNerney).

Tom and Sarah fall instantly in love and quickly marry, their already beleaguered relationship being tested when they go on a hellish vacation to Italy.

Brittany Murphy, Ashton Kutcher

Ashton Kutcher, Brittany Murphy PHOTOS COURTESY OF 20TH CENTURY FOX

KANGAROO JACK

(WARNER BROS.) Producer, Jerry Bruckheimer; Executive Producers, Mike Stenson, Chad Oman, Barry Waldman, Andrew Mason; Director, David McNally; Screenplay, Steve Bing, Scott Rosenberg; Story, Steve Bing, Barry O'Brien; Photography, Peter Menzies, Jr.; Designer, George Liddle; Costumes, Daniel Orlandi, George Liddle; Music, Trevor Rabin; Music Supervisors, Kathy Nelson, Bob Badami; Editors, John Murray, William Goldenberg, Jim May; Visual Effects Supervisor, Hoyt Yeatman; Casting, Ronna Kress, Shauna Wolifson; Stunts, Glenn Boswell; a Castle Rock Entertainment presentation of a Jerry Bruckheimer production; Dolby; Panavision; Technicolor; Rated PG; 89 minutes; Release date: January 17, 2003

Cast

Charlie Carbone **Jerry O'Connell**
Louis Booker **Anthony Anderson**
Jessie **Estella Warren**
Sal Maggio **Christopher Walken**
Mr. Smith **Marton Csokas**
Anna Carbone **Dyan Cannon**
Frankie Lombardo **Michael Shannon**
Blue **Bill Hunter**
Mr. Jimmy **David Ngoombujarra**
Blasta **Mark Sellitto**
Baby J **Damien Fotiou**
Crumble **Christopher Baker**
Hoon **Ryan Gibson**
Tansy **Denise Roberts**
Toot **Antonio Vitiello**
Tommy **Mario Di Ienno**

and Tony Nikolakopoulos (Sal's Capo), Robert Reid (Young Charlie), Shawn Smith (Young Frankie), Emma-Jane Fowler (Outback Bartender), Helen Thomson (TV Announcer), John McNeill (Customs Officer), Paul Wilson (Interrogation Room Officer), David Walsman (Beach Lifeguard), Lara Cox (Cute Girl on Plane), Terrell Dixon (NY Cop), John Gibson, Nick Jasprizza (Sal's Goons), Adam Garcia (Voice of Kangaroo Jack)

Charlie and Louis, a pair of losers trying to get a break, are given an assignment by Charlie's stepfather, mob boss Sal Maggio, to deliver $50,000 in cash to one of Sal's associates in the Australian Outback, only to have a feisty kangaroo take off with the loot.

Kangaroo Jack, Anthony Anderson

Anthony Anderson, Jerry O'Connell

Jerry O'Connell, Anthony Anderson, Estella Warren

Christopher Walken, Jerry O'Connell PHOTOS COURTESY OF WARNER BROS.

NATIONAL SECURITY

(COLUMBIA) Producers, Bobby Newmyer, Jeff Silver, Michael Green; Executive Producers, Moritz Borman, Guy East, Nigel Sinclair, Martin Lawrence; Director, Dennis Dugan; Screenplay, Jay Scherick, David Ronin; Photography, Oliver Wood; Designer, Larry Fulton; Costumes, April Ferry; Editor, Debra Neil-Fisher; Music, Randy Edelman; Music Supervisor, Michelle Kuznetsky, Mary Ramos; Co-Executive Producers, Peaches Davis, Jeffrey Kwatinetz; Co-Producers, Andy Given, Scott Strauss, Sharon Dugan; Stunts, Mickey Gilbert, Stan Lee Rice; Casting, Mary Vernieu, Anne McCarthy, Felicia Fasano; an Outlaw/Intermedia/Firm Films production; Dolby; Rated PG-13; 88 minutes; Release date: January 17, 2003

Cast

Earl Montgomery **Martin Lawrence**
Hank Rafferty **Steve Zahn**
Detective Frank McDuff **Colm Feore**

and Bill Duke (Lieutenant Washington), Eric Roberts (Nash), Timothy Busfield (Charlie Reed), Robinne Lee (Denise), Matt McCoy (Robert Barton), Brett Cullen (Heston), Cleo King (Woman in Car), Gerry Del Sol (Booking Clerk), Ken Lerner (Hank's Lawyer), Mari Morrow (Lola), Stephen Tobolowsky (Billy Narthax), Joe Flaherty (Owen Fergus), Keith Cooke (Ang), Mike Brady (Smith), Troy Gilbert (Cain), Anthony Schmidt (Eddie), Joe Bucaro (Bratton), Carl Ciarfalio (Stanton), Bobby McLaughlin (Ashcroft), Robert Harvey, John Henry Binder (Cops at Impound Yard), Margaret Travolta (Judge), Wayne Morse (Bailiff), Terry Logan (LAPD Cops), Mark Lonow (Detective at Interrogation), Jeffrey Ross (Security Guard), Jocko Marcellino, Jonathan Loughran (Sarcastic Cops), Noel Guglielmi (Latino Convict), Hiep Thi Le (McDuff's Secretary), Leslie Jones (Trucker Woman), Dawn Lewis (Woman at Impound Yard), Jackie Flynn (Guard in Solitary), Hal Fishman (Himself), Andy Dugan (Student Driver), Mickey Gilbert (Driving Instructor), Richardson Morse, Ben Hernandez (Detectives), Tom Forrest (Obnoxious Guy), Amy Aquino (Councilwoman), Amanda Van Roberts (Rich Lady), Mike Grasso (Training Cop), Bruce Franklin, Dan Sudick (Training Facility Officers), Maia Danzinger (Jaguar Lady), Greg Serano (Carjacker)

A cocky police cadet and an uptight officer both wind up working for National Security where they uncover a smuggling operation and a possible police cover-up.

Martin Lawrence, Steve Zahn PHOTO COURTESY OF COLUMBIA

Lee Cormie, Emma Caufield PHOTO COURTESY OF COLUMBIA

DARKNESS FALLS

(COLUMBIA) Producers, John Hegeman, John Fasano, William Sherak, Jason Shuman; Executive Producers, Derek Dauchy, Lou Arkoff; Director, Jonathan Liebesman; Screenplay, John Fasano, James Vanderbilt, Joe Harris; Story, Joe Harris; Photography, Dan Laustsen; Designer, George Liddle; Costumes, Anna Borghesi; Music, Brian Tyler; Editors, Steve Mirkovich, Tim Alverson; Creature Designed and Created by Stan Winston Studio; Casting, Lynne Ruthven, Maura Fay & Associates; a Revolution Studios presentation of a Distant Corners/Blue Star Pictures production; Dolby; Super 35 Widescreen; Deluxe color; Rated PG-13; 85 minutes; Release date: January 24, 2003

Cast

Kyle Walsh **Chaney Kley**
Caitlin "Cat" Greene **Emma Caulfield**
Michael Greene **Lee Cormie**
Larry Fleishman **Grant Piro**
Officer Matt Henry **Sullivan Stapleton**
Dr. Peter Murphy **Steve Mouzakis**
Dr. Travis **Peter Curtin**
Nurse Lauren **Kestie Morassi**
Nurse Alex **Jenny Lovell**

and John Stanton (Captain Thomas Henry), Angus Sampson (Ray Winchester), Charlotte Rees (Marie Winchester), Joshua Anderson (Young Kyle), Emily Browning (Young Caitlin), Rebecca McCauley (Kyle's Mom), Daniel Daperis (Young Larry), Andrew Bayly (Officer Andy Batten), Aaron Gazzola (Billy, Little Boy), Cecelia Specht, Matt Robertson (Little Boy's Parents), Mark Blackmore (Bartender), Joshua Parnell (Store Clerk), Rayne Guest (Spilled Beer Girl), Andrew T. Dauchy (Drinking Buddy), Bruce Hughes (Medical Examiner), Roy Edmunds, Philip Reilley, Mark Wickham, Marnie Statkus (Police Officers), Gary Hecker (Tooth Fairy Vocal Effects), Antony Burrows (Tooth Fairy)

A young man plagued by nightmares hopes to put an end to the mysterious killer "tooth fairy" who has terrorized the town of Darkness Falls for years.

Bridget Moynahan, Colin Farrell

Colin Farrell

Al Pacino, Colin Farrell PHOTOS COURTESY OF TOUCHSTONE

THE RECRUIT

(TOUCHSTONE) formerly *The Farm*; Producers, Roger Birnbaum, Jeff Apple, Gary Barber; Executive Producers, Jonathan Glickman, Ric Kidney; Director, Roger Donaldson; Screenplay, Roger Towne, Kurt Wimmer, Mitch Glazer; Photography, Stuart Dryburgh; Designer, Andrew McAlpine; Costumes, Beatrix Aruna Pasztor; Editor, David Rosenbloom; Music, Klaus Badelt; Stunts, Steve Lucescu, Mike Russo; a Spyglass Entertainment presentation of a Birnbaum/Barber production; Distributed by Buena Vista Pictures; Dolby; Super 35 Widescreen; Technicolor; Rated PG-13; 105 minutes; Release date: January 31, 2003

Cast

Walter Burke **Al Pacino**
James Clayton **Colin Farrell**
Layla Moore **Bridget Moynahan**
Zack **Gabriel Macht**
Ronnie **Mike Realba**
Instructors **Dom Fiore, Steve Lucescu**
Dennis Slayne **Karl Pruner**
Dell Rep (Bill Rudolph) **Ron Lea**
Co-Ed #1 **Jeanie Calleja**
Brunette at Blue Ridge **Jessica Greco**
Cab Driver **Angelo Tsarouchas**
Polygraph Interrogator **Veronika Hurnick**
Husky Man **Eugene Lipinski**
Rob Stevens **Richard Fitzpatrick**
Guard **John Watson**
Art Wallis **Chris Owens**

and Janet Bailey, Scott McCord (Young Instructors), Sam Kalilieh (Eliot), Merwin Mondesir (Stan), Elsa Mollecherry (Lisa Sahadi), Sheldon Davis (Security Officer #1), Oscar Hsu, Arlene Mazerolle, Brian Rhodes (Psychiatrists), Steve Behal (Exam Procter), Janet Moffat (Polygraph Technician), Bart Bedford (Co-Worker), Tony Craig (Transit Cop), David Boyce (New Security Guard), Tova Smith (Beth), Michael Rubenfeld (Felix), Ken Mitchell (Alan), Mark Ellis (Test Instructor), Neil Crone, Ray Paisley (Farm Instructors), Jennifer Levine (Blonde), Shaun Verreault, Safwan Javed, Earl Pereira (Band Members), Conrad Bergshcneider (Firing Range Instructor), John Shafer (Langley Gate Guard), Stephen Lee Wright (Running Instructor)

After James Clayton is recruited to be a CIA agent and goes through the rigorous testing procedure, he is handed his first assignment: to root out a mole within the system.

THE GURU

(UNIVERSAL) Producers, Tim Bevan, Eric Fellner, Michael London; Executive Producers, Shekhar Kapur, Liza Chasin, Debra Hayward; Director, Daisy von Scherler Mayer; Screenplay, Tracey Jackson; Photography, John De Borman; Designer, Robin Standefer; Costumes, Michael Clancy; Editors, Cara Silverman, Bruce Green; Music, David Carbonara; Music Supervisor, Dawn Soler; Choreographer, Mary Ann Kellogg; Casting, Laura Rosenthal, Ali Farrell; a Studiocanal presentation of a Working Title production; U.S.-British; Dolby; Deluxe color; Rated R; 91 minutes; Release date: January 31, 2003

Jimi Mistry, Marisa Tomei

Cast

Ramu Gupta **Jimi Mistry**
Sharonna **Heather Graham**
Lexi **Marisa Tomei**
Dwain **Michael McKean**
Rusty **Dash Mihok**
Vijay **Emil Marwa**
Edwin **Ronald Guttman**
Father Flanagan **Malachy McCourt**
Sanjiv **Ajay Naidu**
Mrs. McGee **Anita Gillette**
Peaches, the Makeup Person **Dwight Ewell**
Chantal **Christine Baranski**

and Parul Shah (Indian Princess in Movie), Douglas Dolan (Boy With Mom), Omar Rahim (Indian Prince in Movie), Bina Sharif (Older Woman in Dance Class), Sakina Jaffrey (Young Woman in Dance Class), Susham Bedi (Lady in Glasses in Dance Class), Sinia Jane (Mrs. Gupta), Anoop Puri (Mr. Gupta), Kamla Sethi (Nana), Jeneva Talwar (Mira), Raahul Singh (Amit), Jed Sexton, Tommy Crudup (Rude Lunch Patrons), Damian Young (Hank, the Camera Man), Philip Levy (Sound Man), Sarah Stanley (Ramrod Production Assistant), Bobby Cannavale (Randy), Krista Bogetich (Party Planner), Thomas McCarthy (Lars), Sanjeev Bhaskar (Rasphal, the Cook), Ajay Mehta (Swami Bu), Rizwan Manji (Party Waiter), Carmen Dell'Orefice (Socialite), Georgia Creighton (Uptight Woman), Amanda

Hall Rogers (Amy), Tina Sloan (Kitty), Dominc Fumusa (Waldo Hernandez), Rebecca Thomas (Subway Passenger), Steven Randazzo (Tony, the Baker), Edythe Bronstein (Turned On Woman), Roger Kachel (Turned On Man), Don Fessman (Chatty Nude Guy), Margaret Hall (Mrs. Taylor), Bill Massof (Prof. Wank), Jason Harris (Josh's Assistant), Pat McNamara (Mr. McGhee), Wayne Gurman (Guy in Bar), Sally Jessy Raphaël (Herself), John Holyoke (Sally Jessy Audience Member), Becca Ayers, Robert Rod Barry, Nicole Barth, Rob Besserer, Gwendolyn Bucci, Dimitri Christy, Barry Ford, John-Charles Kelly, Richard Lear, Paul Liberti, Susan Malick, Joseph P. McDonnell, Frank Moran, Scott Rink, Jeanna Schweppe, Valda Setterfield, Alec Timerman, Judith Van Buren, Jennifer Way Rawe, Darlene Wilson (Lexi's Birthday Party Dancers), Cara Butler, Darrah Carr, Kim Cea, Colleen Hawks, Christopher LaMontagne, Henry Menendez, David O'Hanlon, Frank Root, Michelle West (Wedding Dancers), John Keane (Wedding Bagpiper), Nicki Cochrane, Jasmine Persad (Bombay Dance Class Dancers)

A struggling Indian dance teacher, hoping to make it in American show business, finds his fortunes changing for the better when he is mistaken for a guru and becomes an overnight sensation.

Heather Graham, Jimi Mistry PHOTOS COURTESY OF UNIVERSAL

SHANGHAI KNIGHTS

(TOUCHSTONE) Producers, Roger Birnbaum, Gary Barber, Jonathan Glickman; Executive Producers, Jackie Chan, Willie Chan, Solon So, Stephanie Austin, Edward McDonnell; Director, David Dobkin; Screenplay, Alfred Gough, Miles Millar; Photography, Adrian Biddle; Designer, Allan Cameron; Costumes, Anna Sheppard; Editor, Malcolm Campbell; Music, Randy Edelman; Action Choreographer, Jackie Chan; Stunts, Steve M. Davison, Jaroslav Peterka; Casting, Donna Morong, Priscilla John; a Spygalls Entertainment presentation of a Birnbaum/Barber production; Distributed by Buena Vista Pictures; Dolby; Panavision; Technicolor; Rated PG-13; 115 minutes; Release date: February 7, 2003

Cast
Chon Wang **Jackie Chan**
Roy O'Bannon **Owen Wilson**
Charlie Chaplin **Aaron Johnson**
Artie Doyle **Thomas Fisher**
Lord Nelson Rathbone **Aidan Gillen**
Chon Lin **Fann Wong**
Wu Chan **Donnie Yen**
Jack the Ripper **Oliver Cotton**
Prostitute **Alison King**
The Mayor **Constantine Gregory**
Fagins **Jonathan Harvey, Matthew Storey**
Street Preacher **Richard Haas**
Debutantes **Anna Louise Plowman, Georgina Chapman**
Server **John Owens**
Master at Arms **Richard Bremmer**
Chon Wang's Father **Kim S. Chan**
Queen Victoria **Gemma Jones**
Front Desk Clerk **Eric Meyers**

and Daisy Beaumont (Cigarette Girl), Stephen Fisher (Head Waiter), Matt Hill (Deputy), Terry Howson (Shotgun), Ryan James (Waiter), Barry Stanton (Lord Chancellor), Tom Wu (Lead Boxer Liu), Vincent Wang (Imperial Guard), Charlie G. Hawkins (Newspaper Boy), Gerard Whelan, René Hajek (Rathbone Guards), Le Ho Ban, Bui Van Hai (Palace Guards), Vladimir Hrbek (Old Man with Cane), Jiri Mojzis, Marta Andresová (Old Couple), David Listván (Palace Guard with Rifle), Petra Jezková (Toothless Flower Girl), Barbora Nedeljáková, Eva Ruzicka (Debutantes #3 & 4), Hanka Schudlova (Cleopatra Model), Hana Jouzová (Hapist), Tom Klár, Jan Petrik, Milolás Cech, Karel Urban (Quartet)

After his father is murdered, Chon Wang, sidekick Roy O'Bannon, and Wang's sister journey to London to find the killer and wind up discovering a plot to kill the royal family. Sequel to the 2000 Touchstone film *Shanghai Noon*, with Chan and Wilson repeating their roles.

Fann Wong, Jackie Chan, Owen Wilson

Owen Wilson, Jackie Chan

Donnie Yen, Aidan Gillen PHOTOS COURTESY OF TOUCHSTONE

HOW TO LOSE A GUY IN 10 DAYS

(PARAMOUNT) Producers, Lynda Obst, Robert Evans, Christine Peters; Executive Producer, Richard Vane; Director, Donald Petrie; Screenplay, Kristen Buckley, Brian Regan, Burr Steers; Based on the book by Michelle Alexander and Jeannie Long; Photography, John Bailey; Designer, Thérèse DePrez; Costumes, Karen Patch; Editor, Debra Neil-Fisher; Music, David Newman; Music Supervisor, Dana Millman-Dufine; Casting, Gail Levin, Andrew S. Brown; a Robert Evans/Christine Peters production and a Lynda Obst production; Dolby; Deluxe color; Rated PG-13; 115 minutes; Release date: February 7, 2003

Cast

Andie Anderson **Kate Hudson**
Benjamin Barry **Matthew McConaughey**
Michelle Rubin **Kathryn Kahn**
Jeannie Ashcroft **Annie Parisse**
Tony **Adam Goldberg**
Thayer **Thomas Lennon**
Spears **Michael Michele**
Green **Shalom Harlow**
Phillip Warren **Robert Klein**
Lana Long **Bebe Neuwirth**
Lori **Samantha Quan**
Mike **Justin Peroff**
Glenda **Celia Weston**
Jack **James Murtaugh**
Uncle Arnold **Archie MacGregor**

and John DiResta (Joey Sr.), Scott Benes, Zachary Benes (Joey Jr.), Rebecca Harris (Dora), Liliane Montevecchi (Mrs. DeLauer), James Mainprize (Mr. DeLauer), William Hill (DeLauer Security), Georgia Craig (Receptionist Candi), Tony Longo (Sensitive Moviegoer), Warner Wolf, Marvin Hamlisch (Themselves), Doug Murray (Mark Sawyer), Natalie Brown (Mrs. Sawyer), Andrew Moodie (Poker Pal Ronald), David MacNiven (Poker Pal Francis), Jeff Gruich (Poker Pal Joe), William Duell (Old Concession Worker), Ross Gallo (Young Concession Worker), Gina Sorell (Vegetarian Waitress), Diego Fuentes (Kitchen Worker), Ingrid Hart (Mullen's Hostess), Al Bernstein (Party Waiter), Collin Barrett, Bruce Farquhar, Rod MacDonald, Bob Reeves, Gery Soles, Jim Paris, Frank Perry (Orchestra), Marv Albert (Voice of the New York Knicks), Randy Kerdoon (Court Announcer), Harry & Izzy (Krull)

To write her article on bad dating habits, magazine journalist Andie Anderson is given the challenge of finding a boyfriend and having him end the relationship in ten days. Meanwhile, ad man Ben Barry is told that he can have a coveted account if he can make any woman fall in love with him in ten days.

Annie Parisse, Kate Hudson, Kathryn Kahn

Matthew McConaughey, Kate Hudson

Matthew McConaughey, Michael Michele, Robert Klein, Shalom Harlow

Adam Goldberg, Thomas Lennon, Matthew McConaughey

DELIVER US FROM EVA

(FOCUS) Producers, Len Amato, Paddy Cullen; Executive Producers, Paula Weinstein, Barry Levinson; Director, Gary Hardwick; Screenplay, James Iver Mattson, B.E. Brauner, Gary Hardwick; Story, James Iver Mattson, B.E. Brauner; Photography, Alexander Gruszynski; Designer, Edward T. McAvoy; Costumes, Debrae Little; Editor, Earl Watson; Music, Marcus Miller; Casting, Reuben Cannon, Kim Williams; a Baltimore/Spring Creek Pictures production; Dolby; Color; Rated R; 105 minutes; Release date: February 7, 2003

Mel Jackson, Dartanyan Edmonds, Duane Martin

Cast

Ray Adams **LL Cool J (James Todd Smith)**
Eva Dandridge **Gabrielle Union**
Kareenah Dandridge **Essence Atkins**
Bethany Dandridge **Robinne Lee**
Jacqui Dandridge **Meagan Good**
Mike **Duane Martin**
Tim **Mel Jackson**
Darrell **Dartanyan Edmonds**
Ormandy **Kym Whitley**
Telly **Royale Watkins**
Oscar **Matt Winston**
Rashaun **Ruben Paul**
Lucius Johnson **Dorian Gregory**
Renee Johnson **Kenya Moore**
Cynda **Yuri Brown**
Lori **Jazsmin Lewis**

and Mane R. Andrew (Thomas), Craig Anton (Theo Wilson), Aloma Wright (Reverend Washington), Kim Oja (Colette), Angela Bryant (Anita), Terry Crews (Big Bartender), Nicole Lyn (Margaritte), Henry Kingi, Jr., April Weeden Washington (Mounted Cops), Steve Stapenhorst (Mayor), Adam Lazzare-White (Security Officer), Lynn Ann Leveridge (Woman in Crowd), Bobby Hall (Husband), Mark Swenson (Earl), Tery Dexter (Valerie), Tony Wilkins (Choir Director), Tamiko Williams, Gina Taylor-Pickens, Sybil Harris, Debra Byrd, Hillary Wicht, G. Janee David, Nick Cooper, Cory Briggs (Choir Members)

Gabrielle Union, LL Cool J

Three men, who find their relationships with three Dandridge sisters constantly thwarted by the sisters' over-protective, feminist sibling Eva, pay Ray Adams $5,000 to seduce her.

Meagan Good, Gabrielle Union, LL Cool J, Robinne Lee, Essence Atkins

Gabrielle Union   PHOTOS COURTESY OF FOCUS

DAREDEVIL

(20TH CENTURY FOX) Producers, Arnon Milchan, Gary Foster, Avi Arad; Executive Producers, Stan Lee, Bernie Williams; Director/Screenplay, Mark Steven Johnson; Photography, Ericson Core; Designer, Barry Chusid; Costumes, James Acheson; Editors, Dennis Virkler, Armen Minasian; Music, Graeme Revell; Music Supervisor, Dave Jordan; Visual Effects Supervisor, Rich Thorne; Co-Producers, Kevin Feige, Becki Cross Trujillo; Casting, Donna Isaacson, Eyde Belasco; Stunts, Jeff Imada; a Regency Enterprises presentation in association with Marvel Enterprises, Inc., of a New Regency/Horseshoe Bay production; Dolby; Super 35 Widescreen; Deluxe color; Rated PG-13; 104 minutes; Release date: February 14, 2003

Ben Affleck

Michael Clarke Duncan, Colin Farrell PHOTOS COURTESY OF 20TH CENTURY FOX

Jennifer Garner, Ben Affleck

Cast

Matt Murdock (Daredevil) **Ben Affleck**
Elektra Natchios **Jennifer Garner**
Bullseye **Colin Farrell**
Wilson Fisk (Kingpin) **Michael Clarke Duncan**
Franklin "Foggy" Nelson **Jon Favreau**
Young Matt **Scott Terra**
Karen Page **Ellen Pompeo**
Ben Urich **Joe Pantoliano**
Wesley Owen Welch **Leland Orser**
Nick Manolis **Lennie Loftin**
Nikolas Natchios **Erick Avari**
Father Everett **Derrick O'Connor**
Quesada **Paul Ben-Victor**
Jack "The Devil" Murdock **David Keith**

and Frankie Jay Allison (Abusive Father), Joe J. Garcia (Meat Packer), John Rothman (Quesada Attorney), Jim FitzGerald (Ring Announcer), Casey McCarthy (Angela Sutton), Louis Bernstein (Judge #1), Josie Divincenzo (Josie), Jorge Noa (NY Cop #1), Levett M. Washington, Albert Gutierrez, Lakeith S. Evans (Kids), Stefanos Miltsakakis (Stavros), Pat Crawford Brown (Sweet Old Lady), Carrie Geiben (Flight Attendant), Luke Strode (Little Boy), Bruce Mibach (Rookie Cop), David Doty (Drunken Englishman), Ron Mathews (Sharpshooter), Kevin Smith (Forensic Assistant), Daniel B. Wing, Jeff Padilla, Sonya Didenko (Quesada's Friends), Dan Brinkle (Referee), Jackie Reiss (Boxing Referee #2), Stan Lee (Old Man at Crossing), Greg "Christopher" Smith (Swat Leader), Christopher Prescott (Policeman), Ari Randall (Waitress), John S. Bakas (Greek Priest), Greg Collins (Fisk Bodyguard), Robert Iler, Chad Christopher Tucker, Jamie Mahoney (Bullies), Jorn H. Winther (Stavros' Friend)

Blind attorney Matt Murdock, whose four other senses function with superhuman sharpness, devotes his life to battling crime, hoping to stop criminal kingpin, Wilson Fisk.

Karey Williams, Zooey Deschanel, Danny McBride

ALL THE REAL GIRLS

(SONY CLASSICS) Producer, Jean Doumanian, Lisa Muskat; Director/Screenplay, David Gordon Green; Photography, Tim Orr; Designer, Richard Wright; Costumes, Erin Aldridge Orr; Editors, Zene Baker, Steven Gonzales; Line Producer, Derrick Tseng; Associate Producer, Kim Jose; Music, Michael Linnen, David Wingo; Music Supervisor, Janice Ginsberg; Casting, Mali Finn; a Jean Doumanian production; Dolby; Widescreen; Deluxe Color; Rated R; 108 minutes; Release date: February 14, 2003

Cast
Paul **Paul Schneider**
Noel **Zooey Deschanel**
Elvira Fine **Patricia Clarkson**
Leland **Benjamin Mouton**
Bo **Maurice Compte**
Bust-Ass **Danny McBride**
Tip **Shea Whigham**
Geoff Seibanick **Bartow Church**
and Maya Ling Pruitt (Feng Shui), Heather McComb (Mary-Margaret), Eddie Rouse (Dancing Orderly), Karey Williams (Tammy Klinard), John Kirkland (Justin), James Marshall Case (Judge), Matt Chapman (Strong Bad), Amanda Chaney (Girl on Porch), Mary Beth Ayers, Summer Shelton (Noel's Friends), Tracie Dinwiddie (Tonya)

In a small North Carolina mill town, Paul, a 22-year-old with no prospects, falls in love with 18-year-old Noel, a self-assured girl who has spent 6 years away from her roots.

Zooey Deschanel, Paul Schneider PHOTOS COURTESY OF SONY CLASSICS

THE JUNGLE BOOK 2

(WALT DISNEY PICTURES) Producers, Mary Thorne, Chris Chase; Director, Steve Trenbirth; Screenplay, Karl Geurs; Additional Written Material, Carter Crocker, Evan Spiliotopoulos, David Reynolds, Roger S.H. Schulman, Tom Rogers; Unit Director, Andrew Collins; Voice Casting and Dialogue Director, Jamie Thomason; Music, Joel McNeely; Original Songs, Lorraine Feather, Paul Grabowsky; Art Director, Michael Peraza; Editors, Peter N. Lonsdale, Christopher Gee; Storyboard Supervisor, Douglas Murphy; Character Designer, Ritsuko Notani; Dolby; Color; Rated G; 72 minutes; Release date: February 14, 2003

Kaa, Shere Khan

Baloo, Mowgli PHOTOS COURTESY OF WALT DISNEY PICTURES

Voice Cast
Baloo **John Goodman**
Mowgli **Haley Joel Osment**
Shanti **Mae Whitman**
Ranjan **Connor Funk**
Bagheera **Bob Joles**
Shere Khan **Tony Jay**
Ranjan's Father **John Rhys-Davies**
Kaa/Colonel Hathi/M.C. Monkey **Jim Cummings**
Lucky **Phil Collins**

Mowgli, raised in the jungles, tries desperately to adjust to his new life among the humans, while the lure of the wild and his animals coax him back to his old ways. Sequel to the 1967 Disney film *The Jungle Book*.

THE LIFE OF DAVID GALE

(UNIVERSAL) Producers, Alan Parker, Nicolas Cage; Executive Producers, Moritz Borman, Guy East, Nigel Sinclair; Director, Alan Parker; Screenplay, Charles Randolph; Photography, Michael Seresin; Designer, Geoffrey Kirkland; Costumes, Renée Ehrlich Kalfus; Editor, Gerry Hambling; Music, Alex Parker, Jake Parker; Line Producer, David Wimbury; Co-Executive Producer, Norm Golightly; Casting, Juliet Taylor, Howard Feuer; an Intermedia Films presentation of a Saturn Films/Dirty Hands production; Dolby; Color; Rated R; 130 minutes; Release date: February 21, 2003

Cast

David Gale **Kevin Spacey**
Elizabeth "Bitsey" Bloom **Kate Winslet**
Constance Harraway **Laura Linney**
Zack Stemmons **Gabriel Mann**
Berlin **Rhona Mitra**
Dusty Wright **Matt Craven**
Braxton Belyeu **Leon Rippy**
Barbara Kreuster **Cleo King**
Reporter A.J. Roberts **Constance Jones**
Joe Mullarkey **Lee Ritchey**

and Brandy Little (Motel Waitress), Cindy Waite (Margie), Jim Beaver (Duke Grover), Jesse De Luna (Supervising Guard), Vernon Grote (Door Guard), Kimberly Tortorice (Grad Student), Katie Lott (Berlin's Classmate), Noah Truesdale (Jamie Gale), Larissa Wolcott (Babysitter), Chuck Cureau (Greer), Sean Jennigan (Ross), Charles Sanders (John), Michael Fontaine (TV Assistant Director), Marco Perella (TV Host), Michael Crabtree (Governor Hardin), Julio Cedillo (Officer Ramirez), Christopher Meister (Officer Hasermann), Melissa McCarthy (Goth Girl, Nico), Elizabeth Gast (Sharon Gale), Cliff Stephens (University President), Chris Drewy (Radio Shed Executive), Jeff Gibbs (Josh), Katina Potts (Rosie), Katherine James (Beth), James Huston (Death Watch Chief), Cindyu Michelle (Constance's Doctor), Chris Warner (Hospital Orderly), Jennifer Halverson (College Girl), Maurice Moore (Belyeu's Clerk), Brenda Sendejo (Belyeu's Assistant), Julia LaShae (New Homeowner), Rick Morrow (Section 1835 Guard), Mathew Posey (Inmate Cook), Julia Kay-Laskowsi (TV Soprano), Donald Braswell (TV Tenor), Jack Gould (Chaplain), Lynn Mathis (Warden), Jack Watkins (Photographer), Robert Lott, Mark Voges, Katherine Willis (Bullhorn Protesters), Gwyn Little (Religious Woman), Patrick Fries (News Cameraman), Pilar Ferreiro (Barcelona Neighbor), Amparo Moreno (Sharon's Maid), Claudia Parker (Mail Girl), Joan Gispert (Guillermo), Janis Kelly (Liu), Mark Richardson (Timur), Justin Lavender (Calaf), Barbara Petricini Buxton, David Dahl, Asia Demarcos, Amparo Garcia-Crow, James Huston, Catenya McHenry, Brian Orr, Kirk Sisco, Cassandra L. Small, Oliver Tull, Michelle Valen, Tanya Zieger (TV Reporters), Nick Dawson, Steve Flanagan, George Haynes, Kathy Lamkin, Evelyn Lindsey, T.J. McFarland (Interviewees)

Reporter Bitsey Bloom races against the clock to find the truth behind the murder that has placed death-penalty advocate David Gale on death row awaiting his own execution.

Kevin Spacey, Laura Linney

Kevin Spacey

Gabriel Mann, Kate Winslet

Rhona Mitra PHOTOS COURTESY OF UNIVERSAL

GODS AND GENERALS

(WARNER BROS.) Producer/Director/Screenplay, Ronald F. Maxwell; Based on the book by Jeffrey M. Shaara; Executive Producers, Ted Turner, Robert Katz, Robert Rehme, Moctesuma Esparza, Mace Neufeld; Co-Executive Producer, Ronald G. Smith; Co-Producer, Nick Grillo; Associate Executive Producer, Robert J. Wussler; Photography, Kees von Oostrum; Designer, Michael Z. Hanan; Editor, Corky Ehlers; Music, John Frizzell, Randy Edelman; Music Production and Supervision, David Franco; Visual Effects Producer, Thomas G. Smith; Casting, Joy Todd; a Ted Turner Pictures presentation of an Antietam Filmworks production; Dolby; Panavision; Color; Rated PG-13; 223 minutes; Release date: February 21, 2003

Stephen Lang, Robert Duvall PHOTOS COURTESY OF WARNER BROS.

Cast

Lt. Col. Joshua Lawrence Chamberlain **Jeff Daniels**
Gen. Stonewall Jackson **Stephen Lang**
Gen. Robert E. Lee **Robert Duvall**
Fanny Chamberlain **Mira Sorvino**
Sgt. Buster Kilrain **Kevin Conway**
Sgt. Thomas Chamberlain **C. Thomas Howell**
Jim Lewis **Frankie Faison**
Col. Adelbert Ames **Matt Letscher**
Capt. Alexander "Sandie" Pendleton **Jeremy London**
Gen. A.P. Hill **William Sanderson**
Anna Morrison-Jackson **Kali Rocha**
Gen. Winfield Scott Hancock **Brian Mallon**
Jane Beale **Mia Dillon**
Gen. James Longstreet **Bruce Boxleitner**
Gen. George Pickett **Billy Campbell**
Capt. James Power Smith **Stephen Spacek**
Maj. Walter Taylor **Bo Brinkman**

and Donzaleigh Avis Abernathy (Martha), Mark Aldrich (Adjutant), George Allen (Confederate Officer), Keith Allison (James J. White), Royce D. Applegate (Gen. James Kemper), Mac Butler (Gen. Joseph Hooker), Robert C. Byrd (Confederate General), Shane Callahan (Bowdoin Student), David Carpenter (Rev. Beverly Tucker Lacy), John Castle (Old Penn), Jim Choate (Gen. Bernard Bee), Martin Clark (Dr. George Junkin), Chris Clawson (Charles Beale), Chris Conner (John Wilkes Booth), Scott Cooper (Lt. Joseph Morrison), Devon Cromwell (Cadet Charlie Norris),

Ryan Cutrona (Gen. Marsena Patrick), Scott Davidson (Sam Beale), Justin Dray (George Jenkins), Robert Easton (John Janney), Miles Fisher (John Beale), Keith Flippen (Maj. Gilmore), Joseph Fuqua (Col. J.E.B. Stuart), James Garrett (Gen. John Curtis Caldwell), Bourke Floyd (Longstreet's Courier), David Foster (Capt. Ricketts), Dennis E. Frye (Griffin's Aide), Karen Goberman (Lucy Beale), Alexander Gordon (Martha's Older Son), Patrick Gorman (Gen. John Bell Hood), Phil Gramm (Virginia Delegate), Bo Greigh (Private Pogue), Fred Griffith (Gen. Robert Rodes), Karen Hochstetter (Roberta Corbin), James Horan (Col. Cummings), Con Horgan (Pvt. Dooley), Ben Hulan (A Lieutenant), Sam Hulsey (Julian Beale), Alex Hyde-White (Gen. Ambrose E. Burnside), Lydia Jordan (Jane Corbin), Les Kinsolving (Gen. William Barksdale), Damon Kirsche (Jackson's Courier), James Thomas Lawler (Another Looter), Matt Lindquist (Johann Heros Von Borcke), Doug Lory (Second Irishman), Dan Mannning (Maj. John Harman), Edward Markey (Irish Brigade Officer), Tom Mason (Old Man in Fredericksburg), Jonathan Maxwell (Capt. Ellis Spear), Malachy McCourt (Francis P. Blair), Terry McCrea (A Captain), Andrew McOmber II (Young Corporal), Rosemary Meacham (Hattie), Marquis Moody (Martha's Younger Son), Peter Neofotis (Wounded Main Man), Mark Nichols (Surgeon in Fredericksburg), Carsten Norgaard (Gen. Darius Nash Couch), Tim O'Hare (Lt. Col. Clair Mulholland), Sean Pratt (Dr. Hunter Holmes McGuire), Jasmyn Proctor (Martha's Daughter), John Prosky (Gen. Lewis Armistead), Kyle Prue (Wounded Maine Soldier), W. Joseph Quam (First Irishman), Ted Rebich (Looter #3), Dana Rohrabacher (20th Maine Officer), Tim Ruddy (Pvt. McMillan), Noel Schwab (Colston's Officer), W. Morgan Sheppard (Gen. Isaac Trimble), Christie Lynn Smith (Catherine Corbin), Michael Sorvino (Federal Soldier), Dana Stackpole (Lottie Estelle), Matthew Staley (Lt. Boswell), David Stifel (Rev. David S. Jenkins), James Patrick Stuart (Gen. Edward Porter Alexander), Stephen Leonard Sullivan (Federal Soldier), Buck Taylor (Gen. Maxcy Gregg), Tyler Trumbo (Young Wellford), R.E. Turner (Col. Tazewell Patton), Christopher Crutchfield Walker (A Looter), Trent Walker (Pvt. McClintock), Scott Watkins (Gen. Raleigh Colston)

A look at the military tactics and personal stories surrounding three key battles of the Civil War: Manassas, Fredericksburg, and Chancelorville. Prequel to the 1993 New Line film *Gettysburg*, with Jeff Daniels, C. Thomas Howell, Patrick Gorman, Bo Brinkman, Joseph Fuqua, Royce Applegate, and Brian Mallon repeating their roles. Stephen Lang, Matt Letscher, Tim Ruddy, and Con Horgan who appeared in the first film, return in different roles.

Scott Cooper, Jeremy London, Stephen Spacek, Matthew Staley

Michael Michele

Kurt Russell, Ving Rhames

DARK BLUE

(UNITED ARTISTS) Producers, James Jacks, Sean Daniel, Caldecot Chubb, David Blocker; Executive Producers, Moritz Borman, Guy East, Nigel Sinclair; Director, Ron Shelton; Screenplay, David Ayer; Story, James Ellroy; Photography, Barry Peterson; Designer, Dennis Washington; Costumes, Kathryn Morrison; Music, Terence Blanchard; Executive Music Producer, Joel Sill; Casting, Francine Maisler; an Intermedia Films presentation in association with IM Filmproduktion of an Alphaville production in association with Cosmic Pictures; U.S.-German; Dolby; Super 35 Widescreen; Fotokem color; Rated R; 118 minutes; Release date: February 21, 2003

Cast
Eldon Perry **Kurt Russell**
Jack Van Meter **Brendan Gleeson**
Bobby Keough **Scott Speedman**
Beth Williamson **Michael Michele**
Sally Perry **Lolita Davidovich**
Arthur Holland **Ving Rhames**
Gary Sidwell **Dash Mihok**
James Barcomb **Jonathan Banks**
Peltz **Graham Beckel**
Janelle Holland **Khandi Alexander**
Darryl Orchard **Kurupt**
Maniac **Master P**
Deena Schultz **Marin Hinkle**
Rico **Eloy Casados**
Sapin **William Utay**

and Dana Lee (Henry Kim), Chapman Russell Way (Eldon Perry III), Jim Cody Williams (Suspect), Joe McChesney (Lefty), Faleolo Alailima (Lucky 7 Bouncer), Eddie Mui (Lucky 7 Bartender), Kaila Yu (Lucky 7 Dancer), Wayne A. King, Sr. (Mr. Lewis), Cheryl Reeves (Nurse), Peter Weireter (SWAT Leader), Keith MacKechnie (Interrrogation Officer), Jamison Jones (Frank), Victor Prince II (Metro Cop), David Doty (Judge Russo), Alan Davidson (Leon Taggert), Ted Marcoux (J.R.), John Fadule (Shooting Board Officer), Darrell Foster (Sgt. Jakes), Heather Hutchins (Stenographer), Gregg Miller (Officer Charlie), Nigel Gibbs (Pastor

Scott Speedman, Kurt Russell PHOTOS COURTESY OF UNITED ARTISTS

Dennis), Carmen Twilee, Dorian Holley, Monalisa Young, Kudisan Kai (Church Choir Singers), Julius Rizzotti (New Lieutenant), Jordy Oakland (Waitress Tina), Michael A. Bentt (Officer Clay), Giovanni Antonio Guichard (Rastas), Tom Todoroff (Police Dispatcher), Robert Tur (Helicopter Reporter), Eric Spillman (Newscaster)

On the eve of the 1992 L.A. riots, Assistant Police Chief Holland suspects corruption in the ranks of the police department when detective Eldon Perry and his partner are exonerated on a shooting charge.

OLD SCHOOL

(DREAMWORKS) Producers, Daniel Goldberg, Joe Medjuck, Todd Phillips; Executive Producers, Ivan Reitman, Tom Pollock; Director, Todd Phillips; Screenplay, Todd Phillips, Scot Armstrong; Story, Court Crandall, Todd Phillips, Scot Armstrong; Photography, Mark Irwin; Designer, Clark Hunter; Costumes, Nancy Fisher; Editor, Michael Jablow; Music, Theodore Shapiro; Music Supervisor, Randall Poster; Co-Producer, Paul Deason; Casting, Joseph Middleton; a Montecito Pictures Company production; Dolby; Super 35 Widescreen; Technicolor; Rated R; 91 minutes; Release date: February 21, 2003

Cast

Mitch Martin **Luke Wilson**
Frank Ricard **Will Ferrell**
Beanie Campbell **Vince Vaughn**
Dean Gordon Pritchard **Jeremy Piven**
Nicole **Ellen Pompeo**
Heidi **Juliette Lewis**
Lara Campbell **Leah Remini**
Marissa Jones **Perrey Reeves**
Mark **Craig Kilborn**
Darcie **Elisha Cuthbert**
Peppers **Seann William Scott**
Walsh **Matt Walsh**

and Artie Lange (Booker), Patrick Fischler (Michael), Sara Tanaka (Megan Huang), Harve Presnell (Mr. Springbook), Kate Ellis (Amy), Phe Caplan (Julie), Sarah Shahi (Erica), Kristen Kerr (Lisa), Dan Finnerty (Wedding Singer), Greg Alan Williams (Therapist), Ashley Jones (Caterer), Bryan Callen (Waiter), James Carville, Snoop Dogg, Warren G, Archbishop Don Magic Juan, Jerry "Mr. Kane" Long (Themselves), Todd Phillips (Gang Bang Guy), Stuart Cornfeld (Taxi Driver), Corinne Kingsbury (Jenny), Lisa Donatz (Jeanie), David Moreland (Convention Speaker), Chris Hendrie (Priest), Rachel Winfree (Archer's Wife), Nathalie Fay (Mindy), Kristina Hughes (Naked Woman), Nicholas Hosking (Naked Man), Sara Bryan, Sydney Bryan (Amanda), Noel Guglielmi, Robert Baker (Students), Bob Lazar (Marissa's Dad), Arthur Taxier (Professor), Darryl Armbruster, Gene Reed, David Arana, David Hughes, Marc Thaldorf, Jimi Englund (The Dan Band); The Pledges: Patrick Cranshaw (Blue), Jerod Mixon (Weensie), Rick Gonzalez (Spanish), Matthew Carey (Hatch), Simon Helberg (Jerry), Abdul Goznobi (Abdul), Eddie Pepitone (Archer), Robert Corddry (Warren), Charles Noland (Beav), Raymond Ma (Mr. Ma), Jesse Heiman (Budnick), Jose Gonzales (Gonzo), Patrick Adams (Patch), Jake Jarvi (Jarvi), Andy Dick (Garry), Terry O'Quinn (Goldberg)

A real estate lawyer coming off a bad relationship moves into a house adjacent to a college campus, prompting his two best friends to suggest he open his own fraternity.

Luke Wilson, Will Ferrell, Jeremy Piven

Will Ferrell

Will Ferrell, Luke Wilson, Vince Vaughn PHOTOS COURTESY OF DREAMWORKS

CRADLE 2 THE GRAVE

(WARNER BROS.) Producer, Joel Silver; Executive Producers, Herbert W. Ganis, Ray D. Copeland; Director, Andrzej Bartkowiak; Screenplay, John O'Brien, Channing Gibson; Story, John O'Brien; Photography, Daryn Okada; Designer, David Klassen; Costumes, Ha Nguyen; Editor, Derek G. Brechin; Co-Producers, Susan Levin, Melina Kevorkian; Music, John Frizzell, Damon "Grease" Blackman; Casting, Mary Gail Artz, Barbara Cohen; Stunts, Dan Bradley; a Silver Pictures production; Dolby; Super 35 Widescreen; Technicolor; Rated R; 99 minutes; Release date: February 28, 2003

Cast

Su **Jet Li**
Tony Fait **DMX**
Tommy **Anthony Anderson**
Sona **Kelly Hu**
and Tom Arnold (Archie), Mark Dacascos (Ling), Gabrielle Union (Daria), Michael Jace (Odion), Chi McBride (Jump Chambers), Drag-On (Miles), Paige Hurd (Vanessa), Paolo Seganti (Christophe), Richard Trapp (Douglas), Ron Yuan (Laser Tech), Woon Young Park (Bald Enforcer), Johnny Nguyen, Marcus Young (Ling's Hitmen), Stephen Quadros (Prison Guard Vogel), Sean Cory (Willy Chickens), Theodore Ture Johnson, Jr. (Jewelry Security Guard), Beth Gains (911 Operator), Gwen McGee (Subway Driver), Roxana Brusso (Vanessa's Nanny), Maximilian Mastransgelo (Archie's Worker), Rasta (Chamber's Club Doorman), Doc Newmann (Odion's Bodyguard), Paolo Mastropietro (Fight Club Doorman), Martin Klebba (Fight Announcer), Shawn Hollinger (Fight Club Manager), Tim Storms (Referee), Randy Couture (Fighter #8), Hector Echavarria, Chuck Liddell, Tito Oritz (Ultimate Fighters), Tom McCleister (Fight Club Fan), Wiley Pickett (Police Officer), André Ware (Pinky Ring Man), Larry Joshua (Cop in Vault), Chic Daniel, John Dohle, James Hart II (Swat Cops), Jake Muxworthy (Paramedic), Matt Baker (Motorcycle Rider), Daniel Dae Kim (Visiting Expert), Doug Spearman (African Buyer), Michael Desante (Egyptian Buyer), Julie du Page (French Buyer), Harry Dillon (Pakistani Buyer), Peter J. Lucas (Russian Buyer)

Su, a Taiwanese government agent on the trail of his ruthless ex-partner Ling, joins forces with diamond thief Tony Fait to get back Tony's kidnapped daughter.

Jet Li PHOTO COURTESY OF WARNER BROS.

THE SAFETY OF OBJECTS

(IFC FILMS) Producers, Dorothy Berwin, Christine Vachon; Executive Producers, Pamela Koffler, Stephen Evans, Jody Patton, Angus Finney; Director/Screenplay, Rose Troche; Based on the book by A.M. Homes; Photography, Enrique Chediak; Designer, Andrea Stanley; Costumes, Laura Jean Shannon; Music, Barb Morrison, Nancy Nieland, Charles Nieland; Editor, Geraldine Peroni; Co-Producers, Eric Robison, Rose Troche; Associate Producers, Jon Marcus, Sophie Janson; Casting, Bonnie Finnegan, Steven Jacobs; a co-production of InFilm/Killer Productions, Renaissance Films, Vulcan Productions; Dolby; Super 35 Widescreen; Color; Rated R; 120 minutes; Release date: March 7, 2003

Patricia Clarkson, Joshua Jackson PHOTO COURTESY OF IFC FILMS

Cast

Esther Gold **Glenn Close**
Jim Train **Dermot Mulroney**
Julie Gold **Jessica Campbell**
Annette Jennings **Patricia Clarkson**
Paul Gold **Joshua Jackson**
Susan Train **Moira Kelly**
Howard Gold **Robert Klein**
Randy **Timothy Olyphant**
and Mary Kay Place (Helen Christianson), Kristen Stewart (Sam Jennings), Alex House (Jake Train), Charlotte Arnold (Sally Christianson), Andrew Airlie (Bruce Jennings), Stephanie Mills (Karen), Angela Vint (Tina), Aaron Ashmore (Bobby Christianson), C. David Johnson (Wayne Christianson), Haylee Wanstall (Rayanne Jennings), Carly Chalom (Emily Train), Guinevere Turner (Voice of Tani), Dwayne Hill (Bill McArthur), Kathryn Winslow (Catherine), Michael McMurtry (Contest Winner, Frankie), Katie Griffin (Contestant #1, Sue), Kristi Angus (Z-100 Employee), Aaron Poole (Z-100 Judge), Alex Poch-Goldin, Elisa Moolecherry (Contestants), Craig Eldridge (Hank), Andrea Pinnock (Marilyn), Derek McGrath (Mr. Peabody), Victoria Snow (Jill), Domenic Cuzzocrea (Appliance Salesman), Dmitry Chepovetsky (Bartender), Bill Lake (Baseball Coahc), Balazs Koós (Sports Store Employee), James Lafaznos (Adam), Lucas Denton (Johnny), Noam Jenkins (Patrick Green), Lori Nancy Kalamanski (Linda Green), Hunter Shannon (Audrey)

A look at four suburban families who are linked to a car accident that has left aspiring musician Paul Gold in a coma.

LAUREL CANYON

(SONY CLASSICS) Producers, Susan A. Stover, Jeffrey Levy-Hinte; Executive Producer, Scott Ferguson; Director/Screenplay, Lisa Cholodenko; Co-Producers, David McGiffert, Dara Weintraub; Photography, Wally Pfister; Designer, Catherine Hardwicke; Costumes, Cindy Evans; Editor, Amy Duddleston; Music, Craig Wedren; Music Supervisor, Karyn Rachtman; Casting, Deborah Aquila, Tricia Wood; an Antidote Films production, in association with Good Machine International; Dolby; Color; Rated R; 102 minutes; Release date: March 7, 2003

Frances McDormand

Natascha McElhone

Alessandro Nivola, Frances McDormand

Cast
Jane **Frances McDormand**
Sam **Christian Bale**
Alex **Kate Beckinsale**
Sara **Natascha McElhone**
Ian McKnight **Alessandro Nivola**
Fripp **Louis Knox Barlow**
Rowan **Russell Pollard**
Dean **Imaad Wasif**
Mickey **Mickey Petralia**
Claudia **Melissa De Sousa**
Darla **Alexandra Carter**
China **Michelle Demirjian**
Wyatt **Rick Gonzalez**
Mr. Elliot **Dennis Howard**

and Catherine McGoohan (Mrs. Elliot), Judith Montgomery, Patricia Place (Women), Willo Hausman, Greg Wolfson, Brandy Nightingale (Cambridge Party Guests), Catharine Scott (Stewardess), Marcus Ashley (Tom), Lyle Kanouse, Marcia Cholodenko (Hospital Patients), Gina Doctor (Gloria), Lauri Johnson (Landlord), Tom Griffiths (Manager), Reef Karim (ER Doctor), Lou Cutell (Elderly Man), Zeus (Elderly Man's Dog), Nick Kiriazis (Justin), Heidi Sulzman (Laura), Ariel Felix (Mark), Marie Blanco (Debby), Ted Koland (Room Service Guy), Philip Pavel (Concierge), Mark Rogerson (Doctor), Justin Meldal-Johnsen (Soft Rocker), Mark Linkous, Daniel Lanois (Themselves)

Sam and his fiancée, Alex, move to Los Angeles to complete their medical school studies and take up temporary residence with Sam's mother, Jane, a record producer whose loose and unconventional lifestyle shakes up the young couple's conservative ways.

Christian Bale, Kate Beckinsale PHOTOS COURTESY OF SONY CLASSICS

BRINGING DOWN THE HOUSE

(TOUCHSTONE) Producers, David Hoberman, Ashok Amritraj; Executive Producers, Jane Bartelme, Queen Latifah; Director, Adam Shankman; Screenplay, Jason Filardi; Photography, Julio Macat; Designer, Linda DeScenna; Costumes, Pamela Withers-Chilton; Editor, Jerry Greenberg; Music, Lalo Schifrin; Music Supervisor, Michael McQuarn; Co-Producer, Todd Lieberman; Choreographer, Anne Fletcher; Casting, Victoria Thomas; a David Hoberman/Ashok Amritraj production; Dolby; Panavision; Technicolor; Rated PG-13; 105 minutes; Release date: March 7, 2003

Cast

Peter Sanderson **Steve Martin**
Charlene Morton **Queen Latifah**
Howie Rottman **Eugene Levy**
Mrs. Arness **Joan Plowright**
Kate **Jean Smart**
Sarah Sanderson **Kimberly J. Brown**
Georgey Sanderson **Angus T. Jones**
Ashley **Missi Pyle**

and Michael Rosenbaum (Todd Gendler), Betty White (Mrs. Kline), Steve Harris (Widow), Jim Haynie (Ed Tobias), Aengus James (Mike), Jernard Burks, Bronzell Miller (Widow's Bodyguards), Matt Lutz (Aaron), Randy Oglesby (FBI Agent), Jesse Corti (Italian FBI Agent), Smalls (Doorman), Victor Webster (Glen), Teddy Lane, Jr., Vincent M. Ward (Big Men), Michael Ensign (Daniel Barnes), Tracey Cherelle Jones (Sofia), Josh Waters (College Party Boy), Anne Fletcher (Saleslady), John Prosky (Commentator), Alonzo Bodden (Bear), Seth Howard (Caddy), Diana Carreno, Tim Stevenson, Eddie Garcia (Hip Hoppers), Sundy Carter (Flygirl), Anne Bellamy (Hostess), Robin Michelle (McClamb), Walter Addison (Mr. Kline), Gina Morelli (Rosa), Seth Altschull (Waiter), Deezer D. (Heavy Guy), Kelly Price (Nightclub Singer), Candace Jackson, Erika Nuri (Backup Singers), Faida Amana Brigham, Aminah Abdul-Jillil, Barry Lee Youngblood, Cristian K. Judd, Oscar L. Orosoco, Garland R. Spencer (Dancers), Montrose Hagins (Charlene's Neighbor), Laura Grady Peterson (Hotel Hostess), Linus the Dog (William Shakespeare)

Peter Sanderson, a straight-laced attorney, finds his life shaken up by the appearance of fun-loving, outspoken Charlene, a prison escapee who wants Peter to help clear her name.

Michael Rosenbaum, Joan Plowright

Steve Martin, Queen Latifah, Eugene Levy

Missi Pyle, Queen Latifah

Steve Martin PHOTOS COURTESY OF TOUCHSTONE

Awaovieyi Agie, Monica Bellucci, Akosua Busia

Chad Smith, Paul Francis, Bruce Willis, Johnny Messner, Nick Chinlund,
Cole Hauser, Charles Ingram

Tom Skerritt

TEARS OF THE SUN

(COLUMBIA) Producers, Michael Lobell, Arnold Rifkin, Ian Bryce; Executive Producer, Joe Roth; Director, Antoine Fuqua; Screenplay, Alex Lasker, Patrick Cirillo; Photography, Mauro Fiore; Designer, Naomi Shohan; Costumes, Marlene Stewart; Music, Hans Zimmer; Editor, Conrad Buff; Casting, Mary Vernieu; Stunts/2nd Unit Director, Phil Neilson; a Revolution Studios presentation of a Michael Lobell production, a Cheyenne Enterprises production; Dolby; Panavision; Technicolor; Rated R: 118 minutes; Release date: March 7, 2003

Cast
Lieutenant A.K. Waters **Bruce Willis**
Dr. Lena Kendricks **Monica Bellucci**
James "Red" Atkins **Cole Hauser**
Ellis "Zee" Pettigrew **Eamonn Walker**
Kelly Lake **Johnny Messner**
Michael "Slo" Slowenski **Nick Chinlund**
Demetrius "Silk" Owens **Charles Ingram**
Danny "Doc" Kelley **Paul Francis**
Jason "Flea" Mabry **Chad Smith**
Captain Bill Rhodes **Tom Skerritt**
Colonel Idris Sadick **Malick Bowens**
Musa **Awaovieyi Agie**
Patience **Akosua Busia**
Amaka **Hadar Busia-Singleton**
Lasana **Ida Onyango**

and Fabrice Yahve Habimana, Jr. (Bujo), Sammi Rotibi (Arthur Azuka), Benjamin Ochieng (Colonel Emanuel Okeze), Jimmy Jean-Louis (Gideon), Fionnula Flanagan (Sister Grace), Cornelia Hayes O'Herlihy (Sister Siobhan), Pierrino Mascarino (Father Gianni), Peter Mensah (Terwase), Howard Mungo (President Samuel Azuka), Kanayo Chiemelu (General Mustafa Yakubu), Nikeonye Newankwo (Refugee Woman), Alpha Osman Davies (Alpha), Morris Sesay (Man with Goat), Cle Sloan (Mission Rebel), Kobby Dankyi (Rebel Officer), Lahai Fahnbulleh (Injured Old Man), Allison Dean (Rape Victim), Rodney Charles (Christopher Marwa), Jewel

Bruce Willis, Johnny Messner PHOTOS COURTESY OF COLUMBIA

McDonald (Village Woman), George Reid (Tortured Villager), Yannick Doth (Teenage Rebel Soldier), Ousmane Sall (Village Attacker), Harry Van Gorkum (Carrier Reporter), Michael Clossin (Rhodes' Aide), Anthony Vaughan (Rebel Squad Commander), Randall J. Gillet (Seahawk Pilot), William Wood (Carrier Corpsman), Chinyere A. Joyce, Martha Myles (Chanting Women)

When the Nigerian government collapses and is taken over by a dangerous military dictator, Navy SEAL A.K. Waters is ordered to retrieve Dr. Lena Kendricks, who begs the lieutenant to take the villagers safely to the border.

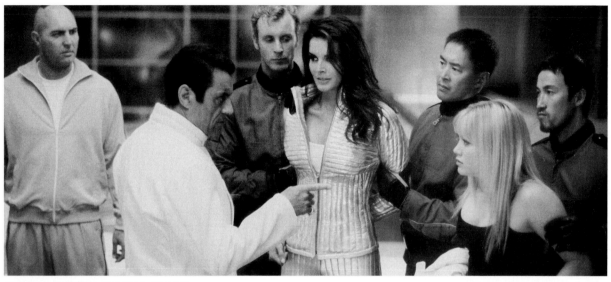

Arnold Vosloo, Ian McShane, Angie Harmon, Hilary Duff

AGENT CODY BANKS

(MGM) Producers, Dylan Sellers, David C. Glasser, Andreas Klein, Guy Oseary, David Nicksay; Executive Producers, Madonna, Jason Alexander, Jennifer Birchfield-Eick, Kerry David, Danny Gold, Michael Jackman, Mark Morgan, Bob Yari; Director, Harald Zwart; Screenplay, Ashley Edward Miller, Zack Stentz, Scott Alexander, Larry Karaszewski; Story, Jeffrey Jurgensen; Photography, Denis Crossan; Designer, Rusty Smith; Costumes, Suzanne McCabe; Music, John Powell; Music Supervisor, Julianne Jordan; Editor, Jim Miller; Co-Producer, Robert Meyer Burnett; Associate Producers, Veslemoey Ruud Zwart, Tom Gulbrandsen; Casting, John Papsidera; a Splendid Pictures, Maverick Films, Dylan Sellers production; Dolby; Panavision; Color; Rated PG; 102 minutes; Release date: March 14, 2003

Cast

Agent Cody Banks **Frankie Muniz**
Natalie Connors **Hilary Duff**
Agent Ronica Miles **Angie Harmon**
CIA Director **Keith David**
Mrs. Banks **Cynthia Stevenson**
Francois Molay **Arnold Vosloo**
Brinkman **Ian McShane**
Dr. Connors **Martin Donovan**
Mr.Banks **Daniel Roebuck**
Earl **Darrell Hammond**
Surveillance Agents **Marc Shelton, Chris Gauthier**

and Harry Van Gorkum (Double Agent), Connor Widdows (Alex Banks), Eliza Norbury (Mom), Justin Kalvari, Saul Kalvari (Baby), Andy Thompson (CIA Assistant), Benjmain Ratner (McAllister), Stephen E. Miller (Army Colonel), Miriam Smith (Cynical Agent), Alexandra Purvis (Amy), Chad Krowchuk, Jeffrey Ballard, Shayn Solberg, Anthony Quao (Jefferson Buddies), Dee Jay Jackson (Helicopter Agent), Peter New (Rosychuk), Jared Van Snellenberg (Earl's Intern), Natalie Sellers (Young Girl), Noel Fisher (Fenster), Andrew Francis, Branden Naden (Fenster Droogs), Jessica Harmon, Hayley Bouey (Natalie's Friends), Chang Tseng (Mr. Yip), Michael Cromien (Bug Man), Dan Zukovic (Disgruntled Agent), Fiona Hogan (Inept Agent), Eric Keenleyside (Kitchen Cleaning Agent), Scott Swanson (Bedroom Agent), Terence Kelly (Dog Walker), Gary Peterman (Gardener), Dennis Caughlan (Farting Agent), Xantha Radley (Animal Behavior Scientist), Prevail (Rapper), Alex Daikun (Intelligence Agent), Lisa Calder (Relationship Agent), Alan C. Peterson (Dark Agent), Moneca Delain (Hologram Babe), Sonja Bakker (School Nurse), Ty Olsson (Security Guard), Forbes Angus (Croupier), Lorena Gale (Waitress), Tyler Boissonnault (Kid), Annabel Kershaw (Parent), Andrew Johnston (Paranoid Agent)

Teenager Cody Banks, trained to be a special agent, is assigned the task of keeping an eye on Natalie Connors, whose father has developed a coveted formula to create a fleet of nanobots with the power to destroy mankind.

Frankie Muniz PHOTOS COURTESY OF MGM

Laura Elena Harring, Crispin Glover

Crispin Glover

WILLARD

(NEW LINE CINEMA) Producers, James Wong, Glen Morgan; Executive Producers, Bill Carraro, Toby Emmerich, Richard Brener; Director/Screenplay, Glen Morgan; Based upon the novel *Ratman's Notebooks* by Stephen Gilbert, and upon the screenplay by Gilbert Ralston; Photography, Robert McLachlan; Designer, Mark Freeborn; Editor, James Coblentz; Music, Shirley Walker; Special Effects Coordinator, Bob Comer; Visual Effects Supervisor, Stuart Robertson; Casting, John Papsidera; a Hard Eight Pictures production; Dolby; Super 35 Widescreen; Deluxe color; Rated PG-13; 100 minutes; Release date: March 14, 2003

Cast

Willard Stiles **Crispin Glover**
Mr. Martin **R. Lee Ermey**
Cathryn **Laura Elena Harring**
Mrs. Stiles **Jackie Burroughs**
Ms. Leach **Kimberly Patton**
Mr. Garter **William S. Taylor**
Colquitt **Edward Horn**
George Foxx **Gus Lynch**
Janice Mantis **Laara Sadiq**
Detective Boxer **David Parker**
Officer Salmon **Ty Olsson**

A painfully shy young man, living under the domineering thumb of his sickly mother and his abusive boss, gets his chance to inflict some vengence on the world that has mistreated him when he begins training a horde of rats. Remake of the 1971 film *Willard* (Cinerama), which starred Bruce Davison and Ernest Borgnine.

Crispin Glover PHOTOS COURTESY OF NEW LINE CINEMA

THE HUNTED

(PARAMOUNT) Producers, Ricardo Mestres, James Jacks; Executive Producers, James Griffiths, Peter Griffiths, Marcus Viscidi, Sean Daniel; Director, William Friedkin; Screenplay, David Griffiths, Peter Griffiths, Art Monterastelli; Photography, Caleb Deschanel; Designer, William Cruse; Costumes, Gloria Gresham; Music, Brian Tyler; Editor, Augie Hess; Co-Producer, Art Monterastelli; a Ricardo Mestres/Alphaville production, presented in association with Lakeshore Entertainment; Casting, Denise Chamian; Stunts, Buddy Joe Hooker; Dolby; Color; Rated R; 94 minutes; Release date: March 14, 2003

Cast

L.T. Bonham **Tommy Lee Jones**
Aaron Hallam **Benicio Del Toro**
Abby Durrell **Connie Nielsen**
Irene **Leslie Stefanson**
Ted Chenoweth **John Finn**
Moret **Jose Zuniga**
Van Zandt **Ron Canada**
Dale Hewitt **Mark Pellegrino**
Stokes **Aaron Brounstein**
Kohler **Carrick O'Quinn**
Zander **Lonny Chapman**
Powell **Rex Linn**
Richards **Eddie Velez**
Loretta **Jenna Boyd**
Sheriff **Alexander Mackenzie**

and Hank Cartwright (Construction Foreperson), Gary Taylor (Tactical Commander), Michael Williamson (Tactical Agent), Alisha Garric (Girl at Airport), Bobby Preston, Nathan Sabatka (Boys at Airport), Jeff Gianola (TV Reporter), Brent Braun, Steve Enfield (FBI Field Agents), Michael John White (Delta Colonel), Mio Drag Jakula (Serb Commander), Neno Pervan, Zoran Radanovich (Serb Guards), Caitlin Clements (Girl in Kosovo)

Professional tracker L.T. Bonham is called on to help stop a psychotic soldier whom Bonham had trained for the Special Forces operatives in Kosovo.

Tommy Lee Jones

Benicio Del Toro

Tommy Lee Jones, Benicio Del Toro PHOTOS COURTESY OF PARAMOUNT

Damian Lewis, Thomas Jane, Timothy Olyphant, Jason Lee   PHOTO COURTESY OF WARNER BROS.

DREAMCATCHER

(WARNER BROS.) Producers, Lawrence Kasdan, Charles Okun; Executive Producer, Bruce Berman; Director, Lawrence Kasdan; Screenplay, William Goldman, Lawrence Kasdan; Based on the novel by Stephen King; Photography, John Seale; Designer, Jon Hutman; Costumes, Molly Maginnis; Editors, Carol Littleton, Raul Davalos; Music, James Newton Howard; Co-Producers, Stephen Dunn, Casey Grant, Jon Huttman; Special Visual Effects & Animation, Industrial Light & Magic; Visual Effects Supervisor, Stefen Fangmeier; Creature Designer, Crash McCreery; Casting, Ronna Kress; a Castle Rock Entertainment presentation in association with Village Roadshow Pictures and NPV Entertainment of a Kasdan Pictures production; Dolby; Super 35 Widescreen; Color; Rated R; 131 minutes; Release date: March 21, 2003

Cast

Col. Abraham Curtis **Morgan Freeman**
Dr. Henry Devlin **Thomas Jane**
Joe "Beaver" Clarendon **Jason Lee**
Gary "Jonesy" Jones **Damian Lewis**

and Timothy Olyphant (Pete Moore), Tom Sizemore (Capt. Owen Underhill), Donnie Wahlberg (Douglas "Duddits" Cavell), Mikey Holekamp (Young Henry Devlin), Reece Thompson (Young Beaver), Andrew Robb (Young Duddits), Giacomo Baessato (Young Jonesy), Joel Palmer (Young Pete), Eric Keenleyside (Rick McCarthy), Rosemary Dunsmore (Roberta Cavell), Michael O'Neill (Gen. Matheson), Darrin Klimek (Maples), Campbell Lane (Old Man Gosselin), C. Ernst Harth (Barry Neiman), Ingrid Kavelaars (Trish Oservich), Chera Bailey (Rachel Mendol), Alex Campbell (Richie Grenadeau), T.J. Riley (Scottie), Ryan De Boer (Duncan), Susan Charest (Becky Shue), Ty Olsson (Sgt. Andy Janas), Michael Dingerfield (Conklin), Kevan Ohtsji (Technician), Marcy Goldberg, Dion Johnstone (EMTs), Colin Lawrence (Edwards), Malik McCall (Platoon Leader), Jordan Walker (Helicopter Sentry), Jonathan Kasdan (Defuniak), Michael Richard Dobson (Stranger on Curb), John Moore (Bad Driver), Carolyn Tweedle (Woman in Crowd), Christopher Ang, Chris Duggan, Daniel Merali, Matt Riley (Apache Crewmen), John Armstrong, Jack Crowston, Trenna Frandsen, John Gagne, Sue Hartley, John Hombach, Kat Kosiancic (Detainees)

A group of childhood friends, invested with paranormal abilities, find themselves snowbound in their cabin in the Maine woods where they are confronted by alien creatures searching for human bodies to possess.

PIGLET'S BIG MOVIE

(WALT DISNEY PICTURES) Producers, Michelle Pappalardo-Robinson; Direector, Francis Glebas; Unit Director, Masaki Sugiyama; Screenplay, Brian Hohlfeld; Adapted from and inspired by the works of A.A. Milne; Additional Screenplay Material, Ted Henning; Songs, Carly Simon; Additional Songs, Richard M. Sherman, Robert B. Sherman; Music, Carl Johnson; Voice Casting and Dialogue Director, Jamie Thomason; Art Director, Fred Warter; Supervising Film Editor, Ivan Bilancio; Technical Directors, Charlie Luce, Darren Clark; Associate Producers, Ferrell Barron, Yukari Kiso; Animation Director, Taekshi Atomura; Dolby; Technicolor; Rated G; 75 minutes; Release date: March 21, 2003

Voice Cast

Piglet **John Fiedler**
Winnie the Pooh/Tigger **Jim Cummings**
Owl **Andre Stojka**
Kanga **Kath Soucie**
Roo **Nikita Hopkins**
Eeyore **Peter Cullen**
Rabbit **Ken Sansom**
Christopher Robin **Tom Wheatley**

Told that he is too small in the Hundred Acre Woods' "honey harvest," a dejected Piglet takes off on his own.

Piglet, Winnie the Pooh

Eeyore, Tigger, Christopher Robin, Winnie the Pooh, Piglet   PHOTOS COURTESY OF WALT DISNEY PICTURES

VIEW FROM THE TOP

(MIRAMAX) Producers, Brad Grey, Matthew Baer, Bobby Cohen; Executive Producers, Alan C. Blomquist, Robbie Brenner, Amy Slotnick; Director, Bruno Barreto; Screenplay, Eric Wald; Photography, Affonso Beato; Designer, Dan Davis; Costumes, Mary Zophres; Music, Theodore Shapiro; Executive Music Producer, Randy Spendlove; Editors, Christopher Greenbury, Ray Hubley; Co-Producers, Laura Hopper, Francesca Silvestri, Elizabeth Zox Freidman; Casting, Marci Liroff; a Brad Grey Pictures/Cohen Pictures production; Dolby; Super 35 Widescreen; Color; Rated PG-13; 87 minutes; Release date: March 21, 2003

Rob Lowe

Cast

Donna Jensen **Gwyneth Paltrow**
Christine Montgomery **Christina Applegate**
Ted Stewart **Mark Ruffalo**
Sally Weston **Candice Bergen**
Randy Jones **Josh Molina**
Sherry **Kelly Preston**
Steve Bench **Rob Lowe**
John Witney **Mike Myers**
Tommy Boulay **Marc Blucas**
Angela **Stacey Dash**
Roy Roby **Jon Polito**

and Concetta Tomei (Mrs. Stewart), Robyn Peterson (Donna's Mom), Nadia Dajani (Paige), John Francis Daley (Rodney), Frederick Coffin (Mr. Stewart), Chelsey Cole (Donna, Six Years Old), Troy Evans (Customer), David Hayward (Pete), Jorge R. Hernandez (Spanish Man), Duane King (Royalty Operations Clerk), Christina Malpero (Rita), Merrilee McCommas (June), Mary McNeal (Ted's Study Partner), Stephanie Miller (TV Interviewer), Susan Mosher (Senior Flight Attendant), Emile Ohyaon (French First Class Man), Daniel Raymont (British Man), Donna-Marie Recco (Tammy), Matt Roth (Greg), Connie Sawyer (Grandma Stewart), Priscilla Lee Taylor (Janette), Jon Tenting (Donna's Co-Pilot), Jeff Yagher (Ghost Rider), Spiegel Anastacia (Runaway Model at Airport), Jessica Capshaw (Royalty International Flight Attendant), Andrew Chitko (Roulette Dealer), Roark Critchlow (Tennis Pro), Chad Everett (Jack Thorton), Wayne Federman (Whiskey Sour Man), Scott Ford, Victoria L. Kelleher (Clerks), Brad Hanson (Guy in 3-B), George Kennedy (Passenger Requesting Vodka), Christian Miller, Payton Miller (Twins), Paula M. Neiman, Amy Oberer, Amanda Wycoff (Trainees), Frank Novack (Gambler), Clarinda Ross (Diaper Woman), Ward Shrake (Fresno to Laughlin Passenger), Stephen Tobolowsky (Frank Thomas), Dawn Marie Whelan (Trainie #13, Annie)

Kelly Preston, Christina Applegate, Gwyneth Paltrow

Donna Jensen, hoping to escape her dead-end trailer park existence decides to become an airline stewardess.

Josh Molina, Gwyneth Paltrow PHOTOS COURTESY OF MIRAMAX

THE CORE

(PARAMOUNT) Producers, David Foster, Cooper Layne, Sean Bailey; Director, Jon Amiel; Screenplay, Cooper Layne, John Rogers; Photography, John Lindley; Designer, Philip Harrison; Costumes, Dan Lester; Editor, Terry Rawlings; Music, Christopher Young; Visual Effects Supervisor, Gregory L. Murphy; Co-Producer, David Householter; Casting, Deborah Aquila, Tricia Wood; a David Foster, Cooper Layne, Sean Bailey production; Dolby; Panavision; Deluxe color; Rated PG-13; 136 minutes; Release date: March 28, 2003

Aaron Eckhart, Hilary Swank, Delroy Lindo, Stanley Tucci, Bruce Greenwood, Tcheky Karyo

Cast
Dr. Josh Keyes **Aaron Eckhart**
Major Rebecca "Beck" Childs **Hilary Swank**
Dr. Ed "Braz" Brazzleton **Delroy Lindo**
Dr. Conrad Zimsky **Stanley Tucci**
Taz "Rat" Finch **DJ Qualls**
General Thomas Purcell **Richard Jenkins**
Dr. Serge Leveque **Tchéky Karyo**
Commander Robert Iverson **Bruce Greenwood**
Talma Stickley **Alfre Woodard**
Dave Perry **Christopher Shyer**
Paul **Ray Galletti**
Lynne **Eileen Pedde**
Danni **Rékha Sharma**
Acker **Tom Scholte**
FBI Agents **Glenn Morshower, Anthony Harrison**
Dad **Bart Anderson**
Mom **Nicole Leroux**
and Justin Callan (Little Boy), Chris Humphreys (GBTV Reporter, Trafalgar Square), Dion Johnstone (Flight Engineer Timmins), Fred Ewanvick (Endeavor Flight Engineer), Hrothgar Mathews (Chief Engineer Mission Control), Shawn Green (Himself), Ming-Tzong Hong (Scientist), Jennifer Spence (Zimsky's Assistant), Michael St. John Smith (Pentagon General), John Shaw (FBI Agent, Rat's Apartment), Nickolas Baric (Security Policeman, Tribunal), Fred Keating (Court Marshall Presiding Officer), Rosa Di Brigida, Roberto Roberto, Ermanno De Biagi, Marcello Laurentis

(Rome Cafe Patrons), Greg Bennett (Technician, Virgil Base), Matt Winston (Luke Barry), Claire Riley, Marke Driesschen (News Anchors), Laurie Murdoch, Costa Spanos (Project Destiny Engineers), Monique Martel, Lenie Scoffie (Paris Cafe Ladies), Nathaniel DeVeaux (U.S.S. *Constellation* Captain), Robert Manitopyes (U.S.S. *Constellation* Screen Ops)

When the Earth's inner core stops rotating, a team of scientists race against the clock to build a craft that will take them to the center of the planet where they will try to reactivate the core.

Aaron Eckhart, DJ Qualls

Delroy Lindo PHOTOS COURTESY OF PARAMOUNT

HEAD OF STATE

(DREAMWORKS) Producers, Ali LeRoi, Chris Rock, Michael Rotenberg; Executive Producer, Ezra Swerdlow; Director, Chris Rock; Screenplay, Chris Rock, Ali LeRoi; Photography, Donald E. Thorn; Designer, Steven Jordan; Costumes, Amanda Sanders; Editor, Stephen A. Rotter; Music, Marcus Miller, David "DJ Quik" Blake; Choreographer, Fatima Robinson; Casting, Victoria Thomas; a 3 Arts Entertainment production; Dolby; Technicolor; Rated PG-13; 95 minutes; Release date: March 28, 2003

Cast

Mays Gilliam **Chris Rock**
Mitch Gilliam **Bernie Mac**
Martin Geller **Dylan Baker**
Brian Lewis **Nick Searcy**
Debra Lassiter **Lynn Whitfield**
Kim **Robin Givens**
Lisa Clark **Tamala Jones**
Senator Bill Arnot **James Rebhorn**
Bernard Cooper **Keith David**
Meat Man **Tracy Morgan**
Nikki **Stephanie March**
Advisor **Robert Stanton**
Mr. Earl **Jude Ciccolella**
Himself **Nate Dogg**
Nate's Girls **Angie Mattson, Elizabeth Johnson**
Gaines **Kirk Penberthy**
Gen. Olson James **John Badila**
Mr. Hawkins **Ed Wheeler**
Kid **Jamil Shaw**
Miss Pearl **Gammy L. Singer**
Mike Blake **Ned Eisenberg**
Officer Waters **Reg E. Cathey**
Demolition Man **Brad Marshall**
Warren **Patrice O'Neal**
Lotto Man **Mario Joyner**

and Don Neal, Beau James, Doug Roberts (Senators), Charles Able (Charlie), Raymond Clark (Mays Decoy), Camille J. Thomas (Super Whore Drill Instructor), Mark Zeisler, Pat Moran (1st Fundraiser Issue People), Tad Ohta (Asian Man), Brad Strange (French Man), Clarke Peters (Fundraiser Demo-Tape Man), Delaney Williams, Wes Johnson (Teamsters), Madeline DeVan, Deborah S. Smith, Victoria Chapman (Singing Ladies), John Hall, Robin L. Hall, Barbara Suto, Thomas Bevans, Helaine Fonda, Sharon Savoy, David Savoy, Terry Chasteen, Robert J. Norman, Ann Haynsworth, James P. Bergdahl (Hip Hop Dancers), Linda Kenyon (Screaming Woman), Alan Chadsey (Falling Man), Irving Jacobs (1st Fundraiser Party Goer), Norman Seltzer, Patsy Grady Abrams (1st Fundraiser Couple), Ashton Marks, Michalel Munford, Michael Marceau, Akira Otsuka, Bob Perilla (Bob Berilla's Big Hillbilly Bluegrass Band), Cornell D. Thomas (Muhammad Muhammad Muhammad), Lee E. Cox (Players Ball Pimp), Jeremy Borash (Wrestling Announcer), Scott Armstrong (Referee), Michael Ahl (Klansman), Annika Pergament (Cable Anchorwoman), Gwendolyn Mulamba, Mike Hodge (2nd Fundraiser Issue

Chris Rock, Tamala Jones

People), Gabrielle Goyette (The Woman), Gustave Johnson (Chester Allen), Heather Alicia Simms (Tish), Kevin Witt (Secret Service Agent), Brenna McDonough (School Reporter), Cory Rosemeier (Helicopter Pilot), David DeBoy (Police Chief), Cailin Ray (Little Girl), Kate Guyton (Foot Lady), Jim Scopeletis (Pork Man), Billoah Greene (Musician), Mojo Gentry (Porter), Lucy Newman-Williams (Train Station Reporter), James Tingle, Ivan Scott, Doris E. McMillon (Talk Show Hosts), Sloane Brown (Roadside Repter), Steven Maurice (Shorty G), Lois Kelso Hunt (Lewis' Mother), Novella Nelson (Moderator), Nancy Ding, John F. Degen, H. Reneé, James G. Pasierb (Voters on Street), Ali LeRoi (Crazy Hostile Dreadlocked Voter), Sade Baderinwa (Transit Reporter), LeeAnna Saunders (Old Woman Transit Rider), Kevin Reese, Stan Stovall (Anchors), Peter Puglisi (California Screamer), Marilyn Getas, Bruce Elliott (National Anchors), Tony Harris, Jennifer Gilbert (Local Anchors), Donna Hamilton (Regional Anchor), DJ Funkmaster Flex (Inaugural Ball Announcer)

Struggling D.C. alderman Mays Gilliam is chosen by an ambitious senator to be his party's presidential candidate.

Bernie Mac, Chris Rock PHOTOS COURTESY OF DREAMWORKS

ASSASSINATION TANGO

(UNITED ARTISTS) Producers, Robert Duvall, Rob Carliner; Executive Producers, Francis Ford Coppola, Linda Reisman; Director/Screenplay, Robert Duvall; Photography, Felix Monti; Designer, Stefania Cella; Costumes, Beatriz De Benedetto; Music, Luis Bacalov; Editor, Stephen Mack; Co-Producers, Steven Brown, Raúl Outeda; Casting, Ed Johnston, Renee Rousselot; an American Zoetrope production in association with Butchers Run Films; Dolby; Color; Rated R: 114 minutes; Release date: March 28, 2003

Ruben Blades, Robert Duvall

Cast

John J. Anderson **Robert Duvall**
Miguel **Ruben Blades**
Maggie **Kathy Baker**
Manuela **Luciana Pedraza**
Frankie **Frank Glo**
Orlando **Julio Oscar Mechoso**
Whitey **James Keane**
Jenny **Katherine Micheaux Miller**
Jo Jo **Frank Cassavetes**
Cop **Michael Corrente**
Tony Manas **Raul Outeda**
Pirucha **Geraldine Rojas**
General Humberto Rojas **Evlio Nessier**
Intelligence Officer **Gregory Dayton**
Girl at Bar **Karen De Vuono**
Man at Bar **Gustavo Pastorini**
Girl at Table **Danay Wilson**

While in Argentina to assassinate a war criminal, hitman John J. becomes obsessed with the art of the tango, and a professional dancer.

Luciana Pedraza, Robert Duvall

Luciana Pedraza

Robert Duvall, Kathy Baker PHOTOS COURTESY OF UNITED ARTISTS

Brian Van Holt, Connie Nielsen

John Travolta

Connie Nielsen, John Travolta, Brian Van Holt, Tim Daly

BASIC

(COLUMBIA) Producers, Mike Medavoy, Arnie Messer, James Vanderbilt, Michael Tadross; Executive Producers, Moritz Borman, Nigel Sinclair, Basil Iwanyk, Jonathan Krane; Director, John McTiernan; Screenplay, James Vanderbilt; Photography, Steve Mason; Designer, Dennis Bradford; Costumes, Kate Harrington; Editor, George Folsey, Jr.; Co-Executive Producer, Bradley J. Fischer; Co-Producers, Andy Given, Louis Phillips; Music, Klaus Badelt; Executive Music Producer, Joel Sill; Casting, Pat McCorkle; an Intermedia Films presentation of a Phoenix Pictures production; Dolby; Panavision; Deluxe color; Rated R; 95 minutes; Release date: March 28, 2003

Cast

Tom Hardy **John Travolta**
Lt. Julia Osborne **Connie Nielsen**
Sgt. Nathan West **Samuel L. Jackson**
Col. Bill Styles **Tim Daly**
Levi Kendall **Giovanni Ribisi**
Raymond Dunbar **Brian Van Holt**
Pike **Taye Diggs**
Mueller **Dash Mihok**
Castro **Cristian de la Fuente**
Nunez **Roselyn Sanchez**
Pete Vilmer **Harry Connick, Jr.**

and Georgia Hausserman (Pilot), Margaret Travolta, Dena Johnston (Nurses), Nick Loren, Cliff Fleming (Helicopter Pilots), Steven Maye (CID Officer), Jonathan Rau (G.I. on the Tarmac), Tait Rupert (Jeep Driver), Timothy S. Wester (Doctor), Chris Byrne, Curtis Ricks, Charles L. Fails (MPs)

DEA agent and former Army Ranger, Tom Hardy, is summoned to help solve the murder of the much-hated Sergeant Nathan West during a training exercise in the jungles of Panama.

Dash Mihok, Samuel L. Jackson PHOTOS COURTESY OF COLUMBIA

Krystal Rodriguez, Victor Rasuk, Silvestre Rasuk, Altagracia Guzman

RAISING VICTOR VARGAS

(SAMUEL GOLDWYN FILMS) formerly *Long Way Home*; Producers, Alaine de la Mata, Peter Sollett, Robin O'Hara, Scott Macaulay; Executive Producer, Vincent Maravan; Director/Screenplay, Peter Sollett; Story, Peter Sollett, Eva Vives; Photography, Tim Orr; Designer, Judy Becker; Costumes, Jill Newell; Editor, Myron Kerstein; Music, Roy Nathanson, Bill Ware; Casting, Ulysses Torrero; a Fireworks Pictures presentation of a Studiocanal production in association with Forensic Films; Dolby; Color; Rated R: 88 minutes; Release date: March 28, 2003

Victor Rasuk, Judy Marte

Cast
Victor Vargas **Victor Rasuk**
Judy Ramirez **Judy Marte**
Melonie **Melonie Diaz**
Grandma **Altagracia Guzman**
Nino Vargas **Silvestre Rasuk**
Vicki Vargas **Krystal Rodriguez**
Harold **Kevin Rivera**
Carlos Ramirez **Wilfree Vasquez**
Donna **Donna Maldonado**
Al **Alexander Garcia**
Macho **John Ramos**
Judy's Mom **Theresa Martinez**
Pool Boys **Randy Luna, Jeff Asencio**
Israel **Juan I. Lebron**
Security Guard **Joe Rosario**
Social Worker **Gladys Austin**
Singer **Jacqueline Rosario**

In Manhattan's Lower East Side, Victor Vargas, a teenaged self-proclaimed ladies man, is brought down to earth when he pursues the popular Judy Ramirez.

Victor Rasuk, Judy Marte PHOTOS COURTESY OF SAMUEL GOLDWYN FILMS

WHAT A GIRL WANTS

(WARNER BROS.) Producers, Denise Di Novi, Bill Gerber, Hunt Lowry; Executive Producers, E.K. Gaylord II, Alison Greenspan, Casey La Scala; Director, Dennie Gordon; Screenplay, Jenny Bicks, Elizabeth Chandler; Based on the play *The Reluctant Debutante* by William Douglas Home; Photography, Andrew Dunn; Designer, Michael Carlin; Costumes, Shay Cunliffe; Music, Rupert Gregson-Williams; Music Supervisor, Debra A. Baum; Editor, Charles McClelland; Casting, Suzanne Crowley, Gilly Poole; a Di Novi Pictures/Gerber Pictures production, presented in association with Gaylord Films; Dolby; Super 35 Widescreen; Color; Rated PG; 100 minutes; Release date: April 4, 2003

Cast

Daphne Reynolds **Amanda Bynes**
Lord Henry Dashwood **Colin Firth**
Libby Reynolds **Kelly Preston**
Lady Jocelyn Dashwood **Eileen Atkins**
Glynnis Payne **Anna Chancellor**
Alastair Payne **Jonathan Pryce**
Ian Wallace **Oliver James**
Young Daphne **Soleil McGhee**
Sir John Dashwood **Peter Reeves**
Percy **James Greene**
Clarissa Payne **Christina Cole**

James Greene, Eileen Atkins, Colin Firth, Anna Chancellor, Christina Cole, Amanda Bynes

and Steven Osborne (Staff Member), Mike Toller, Tom Penn, Tom Goodfellow, James Bell (Libby's Band Members), Mindy Lee Raskin (Bride), Stanley Townsend (Bride's Father), Raffaello Dagruttola (Groom), Tara Summers (Noelle), Newton Boothe (Taxi Driver), Pieter Vodden (Sven), Nita Mistry (Girl in Hostel), Steven Anderson (Television Reporter), James Woolley, James Linton (Political Advisors), Jonah Russell (Policeman), Ella Desmond Oakley (Baby Daphne), Peter Hugo (Prince Charles), Matthew Turpin (Prince William), Chris Castle (Prince Harry), Ben Schofield (Armistead Stuart), Charlie Beall (Rufus), Tom Harper (Edward), Natalie Bromley (Jane), Stephanie Lane (Fiona), Bruno Tonioli (Fashion Emcee), Sylvia Syms (Princess Charlotte), Antony Carrick

Anna Chancellor, Amanda Bynes, Kelly Preston

(Prince Michael), Neville Phillips (Butler), Roger Ashton-Griffiths (Lord Orwood), Cassie Powney (Peach Orwood), Connie Powney (Pear Orwood), Luke Ferdericks, Tim Fornara, David Gyasi, Tom Hanna, David Temple, David Whitmey (Ian's Band Members), Andrew Clarke, Peter Clarke (Twins), Daniel Tuite, Sarah Mark (Newspaper Reporters), Victoria Wicks (Henry's Secretary), Vernon Preston (Duke of Edinburgh), Elizabeth Richard (Queen), Flaminia Cinque (Caterer), Matt Acheson (Country Club Wedding Singer), Judy Collins, Ethel Crichlow, Ash Croney, Malcolm Davey, Layla Ellison, Peter Jessup, Jafri Jobaid, Tony Kemp, Allan Laza, Anne Lucas, Count Prince Miller, George Miller, Susan Mills, Bharti Patel, Basil Patton, Barrington Shaw, Louis Saint-Juste, Jane Victory, Sian Todd, June Walker, Thomas Michael Voss, Maureen Waters (Dancers)

Hoping to forge a relationship with the father she has never known, teenager Daphne Reynolds flies off to London to hook up with her British dad, who happens to be a high profile politician. Previous adaptation of *The Reluctant Debutante* was released in 1958 by MGM and starred Rex Harrison, Kay Kendall, and Sandra Dee.

Amanda Bynes, Oliver James PHOTOS COURTESY OF WARNER BROS.

Colin Farrell, Arian Ash, Paula Jai Parker

Colin Farrell, Keith Nobbs PHOTOS COURTESY OF 20TH CENTURY FOX

Colin Farrell, John Enos, Arian Ash

PHONE BOOTH

(20TH CENTURY FOX) Producers, Gil Netter, David Zucker; Executive Producer, Ted Kurdyla; Director, Joel Schumacher; Screenplay, Larry Cohen; Photography, Matthew Libatique; Designer, Andrew Laws; Costumes, Daniel Orlandi; Editor, Mark Stevens; Music, Harry Gregson-Williams; Casting, Mali Finn; a Fox 2000 Pictures presentation of a Zucker/Netter production; Dolby; Super 35 Widescreen; Deluxe color; Rated R; 81 minutes; Release date: April 4, 2003

Cast

Stu Shepard **Colin Farrell**
The Caller **Kiefer Sutherland**
Captain Ramey **Forest Whitaker**
Kelly Shepard **Radha Mitchell**
Pamela McFadden **Katie Holmes**
Felicia **Paula Jai Parker**
Corky **Arian Ash**
Asia **Tia Texada**
Leon **John Enos III**
Sergeant Cole **Richard T. Jones**
Adam **Keith Nobbs**
Pizza Guy **Dell Yount**
Negotiator **James MacDonald**

and Josh Pais (Mario), Yorgo Constantine (ESU Commander), Colin Patrick Lynch (ESU Technician), Troy Gilbert (ESU Sniper), Richard Paradise (ESU Guy), Seth Meier (Officer McDuff), Svetlana Efremova (Erica), Billy Erb (Lars), Domenick Lombardozzi (Wyatt), Maile Flanagan (Lana), Tom Reynolds (Richard), Julio Oscar Mechoso (Hispanic Medic), Kahara Muhoro (Nigerian Vendor), Zidu Chen (Kirean Husband), Shu Lan Tuan (Korean Wife), Dean Cochran, Amy Kowallis, Tory Kittles, Bruce Roberts (Reporters), Tyree Simpson (Doorman), Dean Tarrolly (Newscaster #1), Mary Randle, Paul Fontana (Dispatchers)

Stu Shepard, a pretentious Manhattan media consultant, makes the mistake of answering a call in a phone booth, the anonymous caller on the other end threatening to kill Stu if he dares to hang up.

A MAN APART

(NEW LINE CINEMA) Producers, Tucker Tooley, Vincent Newman, Joseph Nittolo, Vin Diesel; Executive Producers, Michael De Luca, Claire Rudnick Polstein, F. Gary Gray, Robert J. Degus; Director, F. Gary Gray; Screenplay, Christian Gudegast, Paul Scheuring; Co-Producer, George Zakk; Line Producer, Michael Nelson; Photography, Jack N. Green; Designer, Ida Random; Costumes, Shawn Barton; Editors, Bob Brown, William Hoy; Music, Anne Dudley; Music Supervisor, Dana Sano; Casting, Jane Jenkins, Janet Hirshenson; a Vincent Newman & Tucker Tooley production and Joseph Nittolo Entertainment production; Dolby; Super 35 Widescreen; Color; Rated R; 109 minutes; Release date: April 4, 2003

Vin Diesel

Vin Diesel

Cast
Sean Vetter **Vin Diesel**
Demetrius Hicks **Larenz Tate**
Hollywood Jack Slayton **Timothy Olyphant**
Stacy Vetter **Jacqueline Obradors**
Memo Lucero **Geno Silva**
Mateo Santos **Juan Fernandez**
Ty Frost **Steve Eastin**
Big Sexy **George Sharperson**
Gustavo Leon **Mik Moroff**
Pomona Joe **Jeff Kober**
Garza **Emilio Rivera**
Overdose **Malieek Straughter**

Jacqueline Obradors, Vin Diesel PHOTOS COURTESY OF NEW LINE CINEMA

and Alice Amter (Marta), Jim Boeke (Bad Cop), Ken Davitian (Ramon Cadena), Robert Fraade (Counsel), Richard Gross (Old Agent), Richard Haje (Lucero's Bodyguard), Terri Hoyos (Lucero's Wife), Thomas Kopache (Chief Neal), Julia Lee (Spa Receptionist), Atiana Coons-Parker (Rachel Hicks), F. Valentino Morales (GT Commando), Aleane Fitz-Carter (Old Lady), Zachary John Gonzales (Lucero's Son), Joe Xavier Rodriguez (Mexican Bureaucrat), Marco Rodriguez (Hondo), Mik Scriba (Prison Guard), Scott Reitz (DEA Agent), Karin "Yizette" Stephens (Candice Hicks), Rachel Sterling (Assia), Rubelio Bracamonte (Santos Henchman), Ben Bray, Toby Holguin (Assassins), Norm Compton (Bat), Esteban Cueto (Federale), Diana Espen (Stripper), Paula Harrison (Dancer), Dawn Alane, Elizabeth Alvarez, Roslyn Benzanilla, Charlie Curtis, Azalea Davila, Kristin Eckert, Sonia Enriquez, Cristina LaMonica, Laura Salem (Nightclub Workers), Lamont Tyler (Tow Truck Driver)

Cop Sean Vetter joins forces with captured drug lord Lucero to take revenge on an even deadlier drug kingpin who has murdered Vetter's wife.

ANGER MANAGEMENT

(COLUMBIA) Producers, Jack Giarraputo, Barry Bernardi; Executive Producers, Todd Garner, John Jacobs, Adam Sandler, Allen Covert, Tim Herlihy; Director, Peter Segal; Screenplay, David Dorfman; Photography, Donald M. McAlpine; Designer, Alan Au; Costumes, Ellen Lutter; Editor, Jeff Gourson; Music, Teddy Castellucci; Music Supervisor, Michael Dilbeck; Co-Producers, Michael Ewing, Allegra Clegg, Derek Dauchy; Casting, Roger Mussenden; a Revolution Studios presentation of a Happy Madison production; Dolby; Panavision; Technicolor; Rated PG-13; 106 minutes; Release date: April 11, 2003

Jack Nicholson, Adam Sandler

Marisa Tomei, Adam Sandler

Adam Sandler PHOTOS COURTESY OF COLUMBIA

Jonathan Loughran, Luis Guzman, John Turturro

Cast

Dave Buznik **Adam Sandler**
Dr. Buddy Rydell **Jack Nicholson**
Linda **Marisa Tomei**
Lou **Luis Guzman**
Andrew **Allen Covert**
Judge Brenda Daniels **Lynne Thigpen**
Frank Head **Kurt Fuller**
Nate **Jonathan Loughran**
Stacy **Krista Allen**
Gina **January Jones**
Galaxia/Security Guard **Woody Harrelson**
Chuck **John Turturro**
Sam **Kevin Nealon**
Arnie Shankman **John C. Reilly**

and Heather Graham (Kendra), Harry Dean Stanton (Blind Man), Conrad Goode (Bailiff/Lexus Man), Gina Gallego (Bar Waitress), Nancy Walls, Marisa Chandler (Flight Attendants), Donald Diamont (Man in Seat), Isaac Singleton, Jr. (Air Marshal), Bobby Knight, John McEnroe, Rudy Giuliani, Judith Nathan, Tony Carbonetti, Robert Merrill, Roger Clemens, Derek Jeter (Themselves), Bob Sheppard (The Voice of the Yankees), Lori Heuring (Anger Management Receptionist), Stephen Dunham (Maitre d'), Jeff Morris (Porter), Tony Genaro (Cabbie), John Kirk (Bar Waitress's Lawyer), Ken Rosier (Buddy's Lawyer), Clint Black (Masseur), Rob Steiner (Dave's Co-Worker), Lorna Scott (Lady in Restroom), Bonnie Hellman (Wife at Table), Joe Howard (Husband at Table), Kevin Duniga, Paul Renteria (Men in Anger Group), Kevin Grady (Baseball Fan), Sid Ganis (Neighbor), Larry Morgan (Pool Player), Cody Arens (Boy at Yankee Stadium), Mike Arthur (Police Officer), Jonathan Osser (Young Dave), Melissa Mitchell (Sara), Alan James Morgan (Young Arnie), Lindsay Weber (Arnie's Sister), Halley Eveland (Wedgie Boy), Taylor Segal (Laughing Girl), Nicole Segal (Girl Playing in Water)

Due to a misunderstanding on an airplane, mild-mannered Dave Buznik is ordered to attend anger management sessions run by the eccentric Buddy Rydell.

James J. Tobin, Parry Shen, Roger Fan in *Better Luck Tomorrow* PHOTO COURTESY OF PARAMOUNT

XX/XY

(IFC FILMS) Producers, Isen Robbins, Aimee Schoof; Executive Producer, Mitchell Robbins; Associate Producers, Allen Bain, Richard J. Burns, Jesse Scolaro; Director/Screenplay, Austin Chick; Photography, Uta Brieswitz; Designer, Judy Becker; Costumes, Sarah Beers; Editor, William A. Anderson; Casting, Ellen Parks; a Robbins Entertainment production in association with Intrinsic Value; Dolby; Color; Rated R; 91 minutes; Release date: April 11, 2003

Cast

Coles **Mark Ruffalo**
Thea **Kathleen Robertson**
Sam **Maya Stange**
Sid **Kel O'Neill**
Nick **Zach Shaffer**
Mitchell **John A. MacKay**
Undercover Cop **Tommy Nohilly**
Miles **David Thornton**

and Ben Tolpin (Guy at College Party), Jeff Ward, Keith Siglinger (Cops), William Keeler (Boss), Evan Neuman (Guy Who Asks for His Money Back), Paula Roth (Mom), Lee Cobb (Stepfather), Petra Wright (Claire), T.J. Kenneally, Sam Zuckerman (Executives), Jenna Jolley (Lisa), Joey Kern (Tommy), Jordan Lage (Car Salesman), Joshua Spafford (Jonathan)

A trio of college friends who had indulged in a freewheeling threesome are reunited ten years later, reigniting passions and problems.

Mark Ruffalo, Kathleen Robertson, Maya Stange in *XX/XY* PHOTO COURTESY OF IFC FILMS

BETTER LUCK TOMORROW

(PARAMOUNT CLASSICS) Producers, Julie Asato, Ernesto M. Foronda, Justin Lin; Executive Producers, Gustavo Spoliansky, Michael Manshel, Michael Cole, Troy Craig Poon; Director/Editor, Justin Lin; Screenplay, Ernesto M. Foronda, Justin Lin, Fabian Marquez; Co-Producer, Joan Huang; Photography, Patrice Lucien Cochet; Costumes, Sandi Lieu; Music, Semiautomatic, Michael J. Gonazles; Casting, Donna Tina Charles; a Hudson River Entertainment, Cherry Sky Films, Day O Productions presentation of a Trailing Johnson production; Dolby; Color; Rated R; 101 minutes; Release date: April 11, 2003

Cast

Ben Manibag **Parry Shen**
Virgil Hu **Jason J. Tobin**
Han **Sung Kang**
Daric Loo **Roger Fan**
Steve Choe **John Cho**
Stephanie Vandergosh **Karin Anna Cheung**

and Shirley Anderson (Hot Dog Planet Customer), Nanette Matoba (Housewife), Kenji Matoba (Toddler), Ashley Arai, Danielle Conner, Karen DiToa, Smita Satiani, Kristen Stinson (Cheerleaders), Jeff DeJohn (Ryan), Robert Zepeda, Collin Kahey, Christopher J. Francis (Jocks), Ryan Cadiz (Jesus Navarro), Karin Anna Cheung (Stephanie Vandergosh), Jerry Mathers (Biology Teacher), Jessie S. Marion (Gina Nabham), A.J. Green (Mr. Farmer), Jaime S. Kelly (Nurse), Esthert "Tita" Mercado (Hospital Patient), Octavia Osby (Doctor), Beverly Sotelo, Scott McShane (Cashiers), Brandon Bain, Jesse Bustos, Troy Cartwright, Brandon Dennis, Ronald Dross, Christopher R. Edmonds, Jon Paul Lourenco, Anthony Moore, Jason Reyes, Dominique Ricks, Khalil Semaan, Jonathan Uyloan, Terry White, Chad Young (Basketball Players), Kenwood Jung (Basketball Coach), Jeff Russell (Assistant Basketball Coach), Aaron Takahashi (Takashi), Darian Weiss (Kenny Vandergosh), Alden Villaverde (Ulden), Emmie Hsu (Miriam), Lily Hu (Tina), Donna Tina Charles (Waitress), Crystal Keith (Karen), Laura Esposito (Camille), Juliet Wong (Mary), Justin Murphy (Adam), James Isaac Barry (Porn Jock), Wayne Ford (Student Buying Cheat Stamp), Kevin Alfoldy, Daniel R. Bonneau, Lisa Grant, David Laurence, Nate Petre, Ramona T. Ramirez (Steve's Decathalon Team), Stephanie Noel Little (Steve's Barbie), Tom Chalmers (Liquor Store Clerk), Bryan Baluyot, Mark Baluyot, Joseph Jaldon, Marc Montecillo (Gangsters), Joe Hernandez-Kolski (Scared Student), Jay Green, Denise Barnard (Assistant Vice Principals), Bruno Oliver (History Teacher), Fabian Marquez (Security Guard), Walter Butler (Peter), Christopher Monjoy (Student Buying Drugs), Ina Burke (Tracy), Jennifer Avelyn Wu (Ben's Admirer), Pauline Kanako Kamiyama (Party Girl), Leila Lee (Slapper), Evan Leong (Slapper Boyfriend), Suzanne Keilly (Salesgirl), Shane Kualapai (Casino Security Guard), Ariadne Shaffer (Rachel), Sean Alexander, Joey Barro, Ben Donaldson, Walker Edmondson, Chris Good (New Year's Party Band), Diana Bonilla (New Year's Party Flirt)

Honor student Ben Manibag endangers his future aspirations when he and his friends begin dabbling in petty crimes that spin out of control.

James Cameron, Bill Paxton PHOTO COURTESY OF WALT DISNEY PICTURES

GHOSTS OF THE ABYSS

(WALT DISNEY PICTURES) Producers, James Cameron, Chuck Comisky, Gig Rackauskas, Janace Tashjian; Director, James Cameron; Creative Producer, Ed W. Marsh; Line Producer, Andrew Wight; Photography, Vince Pace; Visual Effects Supervisor, Chuck Comisky; Editors, Ed W. Marsh, Sven Pape, John Refoua; Music, Joel McNelly; Music Supervisor, Randy Gerston; Jake and Elwood ROV Creators, Mike Cameron, Dark Matter LLC; an Earthship Production in association with Walden Media; Distributed by Buena Vista Pictures; Dolby; CFI Color; IMAX 3-D; Rated G; 60 minutes; Release date: April 11, 2003. Documentary in which director James Cameron travels with a team of marine experts and historians to the wreck of the Titanic.

With

Bill Paxton, Lewis Abernathy, John Bruno, Vince Pace (Observers), Dr. John Broadwater (NOAA Marine Archaeologist), Dr. Lori Johnston, Dr. Charles Pellegrino (Microbiologists), Don Lynch (Historian), Ken Marschall (Visual Historian), James Cameron, Mike Cameron, Jeffrey N. Ledda (ROV Pilots), Corey Jaskolski, Jason Pau, Eric Schmitz (ROV Technicians), Genya Chernaiev, Victor Nischeta, Dr. Anatoly Sagalevitch (MIR Pilots).

Cast

Miguel Wilkins (Quartermaster Hichens), Federico Zambrano (John Jacob Astor), Dale Ridge (Elizabeth Lines), Ken Marschall (J. Bruce Ismay), Judy Prestininzi (Molly Brown), Adriana Valdez (Helen Churchill Candee), Justin Shaw (John "Jack" Phillips), Thomas Kilroy (Poker Player), Charlie Arneson (1st Officer Murdoch), Piper Gunnarson (Madeleine Astor), John Donovan (Captain Smith), Janace Tashjian (Edith Russell), Don Lynch (Thomas Andrews), Jesse Baker (2nd Officer Lightoller), Justin Baker (Harold Bride)

BULLETPROOF MONK

(MGM) Producers, Charles Roven, Terence Chang, John Woo, Douglas Segal; Executive Producers, Kelley Smith-Wait, Michael Yanover, Gotham Chopra, Caroilne Macaulay; Director, Paul Hunter; Screenplay, Ethan Reiff, Cyrus Voris; Based on the Flypaper Press Comic Book; Co-Producer, Brent O'Connor, Alan G. Glazer; Photography, Stefan Czapsky; Designer, Deborah Evans; Costumes, Delphine White; Editor, Robert K. Lambert; Music, Eric Serra; Music Supervisor, Anita Camarata; Make-Up Effects Creators, Greg Cannom, Keith Vanderlaan; Visual Effects Supervisor, John E. Sullivan; Casting, Mindy Marin; Stunts, Branko Racki, John Stoneham, Jr., Guy Leslie Norris; a Lion Rock production, a Flypaper Press production, presented in association with Lakeshore Entertainment and Mosaic Media Group; Dolby; Clairmont-Scope; Deluxe Color; Rated PG-13; 104 minutes; Release date: April 16, 2003

Cast

Monk With No Name **Chow Yun-Fat**
Kar **Seann William Scott**
Jade/Bad Girl **Jaime King**

and Karel Roden (Struker), Victoria Smurfit (Nina), Marcus Jean Pirae (Mr. Funktastic), Mako (Mr. Kojima), Roger Yuan (Master Monk), Chris Collins (Sax), Sean Bell (Diesel), Kishaya Dudley (DV), Rob Archer (Buzz), Mauricio Rodas (Wicho), Bayo Akinfemi (Shade), Russell Yuen (Brother Tenzin), Albert Chung (Young Monk), Karis Han (Boy Monk), Angela Seto (Old Sho Girl), Paul Fauteux (Subway Cop), Raven Dauda (Young Mother), Isys McKoy (Little Girl), Peter Snider (Three Piece Suit), Suresh John (Cabbie), Geoff Williams (Breathless Cop), Michael Yanover (Hotdog Vendor), Chad Camileri, Steve Lucescu, James Acheson, John MacDonald, Danny Lima, Robert Racki, Kevin Rushton, Hadley Sandiford, Brian Jagersky, Matt Birman, Blair Johannes (Mercs), Regan Morre, Joel Harris, Patrick Mark, Henry Korhonen, Billy Oliver, Neil Davison, Bryan Thomas, Christopher McGuire (Kommandos), Lloyd Adams, Christopher D. Amos, Murray R. Croft (Transit Cops), Phil Chiu, Mike Gow, Allen Keng (Monastery Monks), Tommy Chang, Mike Chow, Fabian Choe, James Kim (Temple Monks), Alan Tang, Nathan Lam, Peter Wong, Feng Jun Weit, Lin Yi-Sheng (Wu Shu Monks)

The Monk, a Zen-calm martial arts master entrusted to protect a powerful ancient scroll, arrives in America where he searches out his successor who turns out to be the unlikely street thug Kar.

Chow-Yun Fat, Seann William Scott PHOTO COURTESY OF MGM

A MIGHTY WIND

(WARNER BROS.) Producer, Karen Murphy; Director, Christopher Guest; Screenplay, Christopher Guest, Eugene Levy; Photography, Arlene Donnelly Nelson; Designer, Joseph T. Garrity; Costumes, Durinda Wood; Music, Jeffrey C.J. Vanston; Songs, Christopher Guest, John Michael Higgins, Eugene Levy, Michael McKean, Catherine O'Hara, Annette O'Toole, Harry Shearer, Jeffrey C.J. Vanston; Editor, Robert Leighton; Casting, Richard Hicks; a Castle Rock Entertainment presentation; Dolby; Technicolor; Rated PG-13; 90 minutes; Release date: April 16, 2003

Michael Mantell, Jane Lynch, Fred Willard, Jennifer Coolidge

John Michael Higgins, Jane Lynch, Parker Posey, Chris Moynihan

Cast

Jonathan Steinbloom **Bob Balaban**
Lars Olfen **Ed Begley, Jr.**
Amber Cole **Jennifer Coolidge**
George Menschell **Paul Dooley**
Alan Barrows **Christopher Guest**
Terry Bohner **John Michael Higgins**
Lawrence F. Turpin **Michael Hitchcock**
Elliott Steinbloom **Don Lake**
Mitch Cohen **Eugene Levy**
Laurie Bohner **Jane Lynch**
Jerry Palter **Michael McKean**
Wally Fenton **Larry Miller**
Sean Halloran **Christopher Moynihan**
Mickey Devlin Crabbe **Catherine O'Hara**
Leonard Crabbe **Jim Piddock**
Sissy Knox **Parker Posey**
Mark Shubb **Harry Shearer**
Naomi Steinbloom **Deborah Theaker**
Mike LaFontaine **Fred Willard**

and Jim Moret (Newscaster), Stuart Luce (Irving Steinbloom), Mary Gross (Ma Klapper), Marty Belafsky (Ramblin' Sandy Pitnik), Michael Baser (Pa Klapper), Jared Nelson Smith (Young Chuck Wiseman), Ryan Raddatz (Bill Weyburn), Todd Lieberman (Fred Knox), Matthew Joy (Boy Klapper),

Laura Harris (Girl Klapper), Brian Riley (Young George Menschell), Rachel Harris (Steinbloom's Assistant), Tyler Forsberg (Young Jonathan Steinbloom), Jim Ortlieb (David Kantor), Andrew Dickler (1971 Dell Wiseman), Thom Lowry (1971 Howard Wiseman), Keva Rosenfeld (1971 Chuck Wiseman), Brian Allen (1960s Mitch & Mickey Bass), Danny Merritt (1960s Mitch & Mickey Guitar), Paul Benedict (Martin Berg), Floyd Vanbuskirk (Steve Lang), David Blasucci (Tony Pollono), Patrick Sauber (Jerald Smithers), Steve Pandis (Johnny Athenakis), Mark Nonisa (Mike Maryama), Cameron Sprague (Young Terry Bohner), Leshay Tomlinson (Steinbloom's Secretary), Mina Kolb (Dr. Mildred Wickes), Wendel Meldrum, Diane Delano, James Jennewein, Richard Hicks (Witches), Michael Mantell (Deputy Mayor), Bill Cobbs (Blues Musician), Freda Foh Shen (Melinda Barrows), Darlene Kardon (Shirley Steinbloom), Scott Williamson (PBN TV Director), Joe Godfrey (Mitch & Mickey Bass), Bruce Gaitsch (Mitch & Mickey Guitar), Diane Baker (Supreme Folk Defense Lawyer)

To pay tribute to their folk icon dad, Jonathan and Naomi Steinbloom put together a memorial concert, which brings together some of the reigning folk music favorites of the past.

This film received an Oscar nomination for song ("A Kiss at the End of the Rainbow").

Harry Shearer, Michael McKean, Christopher Guest PHOTOS COURTESY OF WARNER BROS.

HOLES

(WALT DISNEY PICTURES) Producers, Mike Medavoy, Andrew Davis, Teresa Tucker-Davies, Lowell Blank; Executive Producers, Marty Ewing, Louis Phillips; Director, Andrew Davis; Screenplay, Lousi Sachar, based on his novel; Photography, Stephen St. John; Designer, Maher Ahmad; Costumes, Aggie Guerard Rodgers; Editors, Tom Nordberg, Jeffrey Wolf; Music, Joel McNeely; Music Supervisor, Karyn Rachtman; Casting, Amanda Mackay Johnson, Cathy Sandrich Gelfond; a Chicago Pacific Entertainment/Phoenix Pictures production, presented in association with Walden Media; Dolby; Technicolor; Rated PG; 118 minutes; Release date: April 18, 2003

Shia LaBeouf, Khleo Thomas

Cast

CAMP GREEN LAKE
The Warden **Sigourney Weaver**
Mr. Sir **Jon Voight**
Dr. Pendanski **Tim Blake Nelson**
Stanley Yelnats IV **Shia LaBeouf**
Hector "Zero" Zeroni **Khleo Thomas**
Squid **Jake M. Smith**
Armpit **Byron Cotton**
X-Ray **Brenden Jefferson**
Magnet **Miguel Castro**
Zigzag **Max Kasch**
Twitch **Noah Poletiek**
Barfbag **Zane Holtz**
Lump **Steve Kozlowski**

and Ski Carr (Guard), Jim Wilkey (Bus Driver), Roma Mafia (Carla Morengo), Ray Baker (Asst. Attorney General), Alex Daniels, Tom Brainard (Texas Rangers), Haleigh Ann Trickett (Young Warden)

YELNATS' HOME
Stanley's Mother **Siobhan Fallon Hogan**
Stanley's Father **Henry Winkler**
Grandfather **Nathan Davis**

and Rick Worthy, Mary Jo Mecca (Officers), Shelley Malil (Nosy Landlord), Rick Fox (Clyde "Sweetfeet" Livingston), Nicole Pulliam (Mrs. Sweetfeet), Michael Cavanaugh (Judge), Bruce Ramsay (Prosecutor), Shirley Butler (Mrs. Zeroni), Conrad Palmisano (Private Investigator)

LATVIA
Madame Zeroni **Eartha Kitt**
Elya Yelnats **Damien Luvara**
Myra Menke **Sanya Mateyas**
Morris Menke **Ravil Isyanov**
Igor Barkov **Ken Davitian**

OLD GREEN LAKE
Kissin' Kate Barlow **Patricia Arquette**
Trout Walker **Scott Plank**
Sam **Dulé Hill**
Stanley the 1st **Allan Kolman**
Mr. Collingwood **Louis Sachar**
Sheriff **Eric Pierpoint**

and Brian Peck (Townsman in Classroom), Melissa Mitchell (Young Linda), Allison Smith (Linda), Brooke Eby (School Kid), Gary Bullock (Prospector), Jeff Ricketts (Partner), Paul Norwood (Doc), Benny Manning (Stage Coach Driver), Jim Wikley (Kissed Stage Coach Driver), Julian Reed Davis (Prisoner in Green Lake Jail)

Stanley Yelnats, the latest in his family to be victimized by an ancient curse, is falsely accused of theft and sent to Camp Green Lake, a prisonlike facility where he and the other boys are forced to endlessly dig holes in the desert.

Jon Voight, Sigourney Weaver, Tim Blake Nelson

Shia LaBeouf, Byron Cotton, Max Kasch, Miguel Castro, Jake M. Smith, Khleo Thomas, Brenden Jefferson PHOTOS COURTESY OF WALT DISNEY PICTURES

MALIBU'S MOST WANTED

(WARNER BROS.) Producers, Mike Karz, Fax Bahr, Adam Small; Executive Producer, Bill Johnson; Director, John Whitesell; Screenplay, Fax Bahr, Adam Small, Jamie Kennedy, Nick Swardson; Photography, Mark Irwin; Designer, Bill Elliott; Costumes, Debrae Little; Editor, Cara Silverman; Music, John van Tongeren, Damon Elliott; Themes, John Debney; Co-Producers, Russell Hollander, Josh Etting; Casting, Mary Vernieu; a Karz Entertainment production; Dolby; Clairmont Widescreen; Technicolor; Rated PG-13; 86 minutes; Release date: April 18, 2003

Anthony Anderson, Jamie Kennedy, Taye Diggs PHOTO COURTESY OF WARNER BROS.

Cast
Brad "B-Rad" Gluckman **Jamie Kennedy**
Sean **Taye Diggs**
PJ **Anthony Anderson**
Shondra **Regina Hall**
Tom Gibbons **Blair Underwood**
Tec **Damien Dante Wayans**
Bill Gluckman **Ryan O'Neal**
Bess Gluckman **Bo Derek**
Dr. Feldman **Jeffrey Tambor**
Hadji **Kal Penn**

and Nick Swardson (Mocha), Keili Lefkovitz (Monster), Kellie Martin (Jen), Greg Grunberg (Brett), J.P. Manoux (Gary), Howard Mann (Uncle Louie), Curtis Blanck (13-year-old Brad), Tristan Jarred (7-year-old Brad), Kody Coye (Toddler Brad), Niecy Nash (Gladys), Terry Crews (8 Ball), Tory Kittles (Deuce), Noel Guglielmi (Snuffy), Rey Gallegos (Loc), Damion Poitier (Tec's Crew), Jo Deodato Clark (Saleswoman), Suzy Nakamura (Reporter), Snoop Dogg (Ronnie Rizzat), James Kiriyama-Lem (Korean Man), Felli Fel, Hi-C, Young Dré, Bigg Steele, Drop Da Bomb, Hal Fishman, Big Boy (Themselves), Keesha Sharp, Rhona Bennett (Sisters), Ken Lawson (African American Aid), Sarah Thompson (Krista the Barista), Michael Quill (Mike the Reporter), Christa Campbell (Angry Feminist), Giuliana DePandi (Massage Therapist), Ecco Morgan (Sandy), Nikki Martinez, Mary Nelson (Escalade Dancers), Mike Epps (Rap Battle Host)

Worried that his son Brad's adopted hip-hop persona will hinder his chances to become governor, rich Malibu resident Bill Gluckman's campaign manager hires a pair of out-of-work actors to play thugs and kidnap Brad to show him what the real "hood" is like.

THE REAL CANCUN

(NEW LINE CINEMA) Producers, Mary-Ellis Bunim, Jonathan Murray; Executive Producers, A.J. Dix, Anthony Rhulen, Bill Shively, Richard Brener, Toby Emmerich, Matt Moore; Director, Rick de Oliveira; Co-Producers, Rick de Oliveira, Jamie Schutz; Line Producer, Tony Testa; Supervising Editor, Ben Salter; Supervising Story Editor, Eric Monsky; Music, Michael Suby; Music Supervisor, Dave Stone; Casting, Sasha Alpert; a Bunim-Murray/Film Engine production; Dolby; Deluxe Color; HD-to-35mm; Rated R; 96 minutes; Release date: April 25, 2003. Documentary follows sixteen college students as they spend spring break in Cancun, Mexico.

With

Benjamin "Fletch" Fletcher, Nicol Frilot, Roxanne Frilot, Britanny Brown-Hart, David Ingber, Jeremy Jazwinski, Amber Madison, Paul Malbry, Marquita "Sky" Marshall, Laura Ramsey, Matthew Slenske, Alan Taylor, Heidi Vance, Jorell Washington, Casey Weeks, Sarah Wilkins; and Chris Desanti, Jason Karlinski (Sun Splash Tours), Snoop Dogg, Simple Plan, Hot Action Cop (Themselves)

Alan Taylor, Laura Ramsey PHOTO COURTESY OF NEW LINE CINEMA

IDENTITY

(COLUMBIA) Producer, Cathy Konrad; Executive Producer, Stuart Besser; Director, James Mangold; Screenplay, Michael Cooney; Photography, Phedon Papamichael; Designer, Mark Friedberg; Costumes, Arianne Phillips; Music, Alan Silvestri; Editor, David Brenner; a Konrad Pictures production; Dolby; Panavision; Foto-Kem color; Rated R; 90 minutes; Release date: April 25, 2003

Cast
Ed **John Cusack**
Rhodes **Ray Liotta**
Paris **Amanda Peet**
Larry **John Hawkes**
Doctor Malick **Alfred Molina**
Ginny **Clea DuVall**
George York **John C. McGinley**
Lou **William Lee Scott**
Robert Maine **Jake Busey**
Malcolm Rivers **Pruitt Taylor Vince**
Caroline Suzanne **Rebecca DeMornay**
Defense Lawyer **Carmen Argenziano**
District Attorney **Marshall Bell**
Alice York **Leila Kenzle**
Assistant District Attorney **Matt Letscher**
Timmy York **Bret Loehr**
Judge Taylor **Holmes Osborne**
Detective Varole **Frederick Coffin**

and Joe Hart (Bailiff Jenkins), Michael Hirsch (Naked Businessman), Terence Bernie Hines (Bailiff), Stuart Besser (Frozen Body)

Ten strangers are brought together at a desolate motel during a torrential rainstorm where they are killed off one by one.

John Hawkes, Ray Liotta, Amanda Peet, John Cusack

John Cusack, Amada Peet

John Cusack, Ray Liotta PHOTOS COURTESY OF COLUMBIA

CONFIDENCE

(LIONS GATE) Producers, Marc Butan, Michael Paseornek, Michael Burns, Michael Ohoven; Executive Producers, Eric Kopeloff, Marco Mehlitz, Eberhard Kayser, Scott Bernstein; Director, James Foley; Screenplay, Doug Jung; Photography, Juan Ruiz-Anchia; Designer, Bill Arnold; Costumes, Michele Michel; Editor, Stuart Levy; Music, Christophe Beck; Music Supervisor, Joel High; Co-Producer, John Sacchi; Casting, Sheila Jaffe, Georgianne Walken; an Ignite Entertainment and Cinewhite production, presented in association with Cinerenta; Dolby; Widescreen; Color; Rated R; 98 minutes; Release date: April 25, 2003

Edward Burns, Dustin Hoffman

Dustin Hoffman

Dustin Hoffman, Rachel Weisz

Cast

Jake Vig **Edward Burns**
Lily **Rachel Weisz**
Gunther Butan **Andy Garcia**
Winston King **Dustin Hoffman**
Gordo **Paul Giamatti**
Officer Lloyd Whitworth **Donal Logue**
Officer Omar Manzano **Luis Guzman**
Mike **Brian Van Holt**
Lupus **Franky G**
Travis (Butch) **Morris Chestnut**
Bobby **Ethan Embry**
Harlin **Tommy "Tiny" Lister**
Grant Ashby **John Carroll Lynch**
Alphonse "Big Al" Moorley **Louis Lombardi**
Lionel Dolby **Leland Orser**
Mr. Lewis **Robert Pine**
Salesgirl **Elysia Skye**
Attractive Blonde **April O'Brien**
Morgan Price **Robert Forster**
Kitty **Michelle Ruben**
Marie **Mary Portser**

and Michael Dempsey (Special Agent Artie/IA Officer #1), Elle Alexander (Michelle Strigo), Steve Tom (Hamilton-Tan), Jay Giannone (Car Salesman), Melissa Lawner (Katie), Nicole Lenz (Ally)

After con man Jake Vig scams $150,000 from powerful mobster Winston King, he agrees to settle the score with him by setting up a $5 million scam on a corrupt banker.

Edward Burns, Rachel Weisz PHOTOS COURTESY OF LIONS GATE

IT RUNS IN THE FAMILY

(MGM/BUENA VISTA INTL.) formerly *A Few Good Years* and *Smack in the Kisser*; Producer, Michael Douglas; Executive Producers, Fred Schepisi, Kerry Orent; Director, Fred Schepisi; Screenplay, Jesse Wigutow; Co-Producer, Marcy Drogin; Associate Producer, Joel Douglas; Photography, Ian Baker; Designer, Patrizia von Brandenstein; Costumes, Ellen Mirojnick; Editor, Kate Williams; Music, Paul Grabowsky; Music Supervisor, Susan Jacobs; a Furthur Films production; Dolby; Rated PG-13; 109 minutes; Release date: April 25, 2003

Kirk Douglas, Michael Douglas, Cameron Douglas

Cast

Alex Gromberg **Michael Douglas**
Mitchell Gromberg **Kirk Douglas**
Eli Gromberg **Rory Culkin**
Asher Gromberg **Cameron Douglas**
Evelyn Gromberg **Diana Douglas**
Peg Maloney **Michelle Monaghan**
Malik **Geoffrey Arend**
Suzie **Sarita Choudhury**
Abby Staley **Irene Gorovaia**
Deb **Annie Golden**
Stephen Gromberg **Mark Hammer**
Sarah Langley **Audra McDonald**
Barney **Josh Pais**
Rebecca Gromberg **Bernadette Peters**

Michael Douglas, Bernadette Peters

and Louie Torrellas (Jeremy), Jonathan Mondel (Morgan), Wynter Kullman (Katie), Kelly Overton (Erica), Marc Damon Johnson (Professor Edwards), Carmen Lopez (Rosario), Stephen Singer (Dr. Kaplan), Keith Nobbs (Stein), Derek Kelly (Driver), Roy Milton Davis (Homeless Man), Lisa Ann Frisone (Homeless Woman), Adrian Martinez (Mitchell's Doorman), Cameron Boyd, Ian Boyd, Demetrius Kiprakis, Sho "Xiao" Ma (Skateboarders), Ray DeMattis (Italian Waiter), David Greenspan (Howard), Alvin Crawford (Male Nurse), Robert Montano (Officer Bane), Jerome Preston Bates (Officer McDonough), Adam Mucci (Officer Samms), Adam Grupper (Principal), Linda Johnson, Brenda Thomas Denmark (Teachers), Joel Rooks (Suit), Antonio Charity, Erik-Anders Nilsson, Sara Meyer (Joggers), Mark Ledbetter, Shantell Herndon (Young Joggers), Bob Kaliban (Jim Lindsay)

Kirk Douglas, Diana Douglas

Old wounds and misunderstandings arise in three generations of the Gromberg family.

Rory Culkin, Kirk Douglas PHOTOS COURTESY OF MGM/BUENA VISTA INTL.

PEOPLE I KNOW

(MIRAMAX) Producers, Michael Nozik, Leslie Urdang, Karen Tenkhoff; Executive Producers, Robert Redford, Kirk D'Amico, Philip von Alvensleben; Director, Dan Algrant; Screenplay, Jon Robin Baitz; Photography, Peter Deming; Co-Producer, Nellie Nugiel; Designer, Michael Shaw; Costumes, David Robinson; Editor, Suzy Elmiger; Music, Terence Blanchard; Music Supervisors, Robin Urdang, Christ Violette; Casting, Juliet Taylor, Laura Rosenthal; a Myriad Pictures presentation of a South Fork Pictures production in association with Galena/Greenstreet Films, Chal Productions, In-Motion AG and WMF V; Dolby; Color; Rated R; 95 minutes; Release date: April 25, 2003

Ryan O'Neal, Al Pacino

Cast

Eli Wurman **Al Pacino**
Victoria Gray **Kim Basinger**
Cary Launer **Ryan O'Neal**
Jilli Hopper **Téa Leoni**
Elliot Sharansky **Richard Schiff**
The Reverend Lyle Blunt **Bill Nunn**
Dr. Sandy Napier **Robert Klein**
Ross **Mark Webber**
Washroom Attendant **Eldon Bullock**
David Fielding **Ramsey Faragallah**
Jamie Hoff **Brian McConnachie**
Michael Wormly **Frank Wood**
Ms. Thuli Kani **Angelique Kidjo**
Mayor Nick Conlin **William J. Bratton**
Norris Volpe **Peter Gerety**

Kim Basinger, Al Pacino

and Ivan Martin (Serge), Keith Siglinger (Killer), Juliet Papa, Ben Shenkman (Voices of Radio Announcers), Lewis Dodley, Mr. G, Jon Hendricks, Pat Kiernan, Joy Philbin, Regis Philbin, Rex Reed, Cynthia Santana, Kaity Tong (Themselves), Daniel Whitner, William E. Corcoran (Lobby Guards), Jonathan Walker (Doorman at Party), Joe Duer (Michael Von Aelstrom), Laurine Towler (Julia Stone), Polly Adams (Mara Samuelson), Betsy Aidem (Talia Greene), Greg Stebner (Maitre'd), Tina Sloan (Dr. Napier's Receptionist), Paulina Porizkova (Dr. Anna Fahri), Sophie Dahl (Tillie in the Mink), Peter Van Wagner (Man in Limousine),

Al Pacino

Ajay Mehta, Tirlok Malik (Cab Drivers), Irina Pantaeva (Summerwear Showroom Receptionist), David Marshall Grant (Tom Silverton), Ted Neustadt (Man in Sharansky's Officer), Michael Graves (Harry Gould), Lisa Emery (Elsa Nye), Andrew Davoli (Romeo), Uzi Parnes (Berger), Shelley Kirk (Benefit Guest), William Hill (Paparazzi), Geraldine Bartlett (Sarah Niles), Steven Randazzo (Jack Pollan), Terry Urdang (Cokey), T. Scott Cunningham (Crispin), Roland Algrant (Rolly), Carl Charroux (Limo Driver)

Eli Wurman, a once-prominent publicist, is asked by his one remaining client, actor-turned-aspiring politican Cary Launer to tend to his drug-addicted girl-friend, only to have the woman end up murdered.

Richard Schiff <small>PHOTOS COURTESY OF MIRAMAX</small>

Matt Dillon, Natascha McElhone

CITY OF GHOSTS

(UNITED ARTISTS) Producers, Willi Baer, Michael Cerenzie, Deepak Nayar; Director, Matt Dillon; Screenplay, Matt Dillon, Barry Gifford; Line Producer, Rony Yakov; Co-Producers, J.B. Meyer, Olivier Granier; Photography, Jim Denault; Designer, David Brisbin; Editor, Howard E. Smith; Music, Tyler Bates; Music Supervisor, Dondi Bastone; Casting, Mary Vernieu, Anne McCarthy, Felicia Fasano; a Manline Productions and Banyan Tree presentation in association with Kintop Pictures; Dolby; Fotokem color; Rated R; 117 minutes; Release date: April 25, 2003

Cast

Jimmy Cremmins	**Matt Dillon**
Marvin	**James Caan**
Sophie	**Natascha McElhone**
Emile	**Gerard Depardieu**
Sok	**Sereyvuth Kem**
Kaspar	**Stellan Skarsgård**
Sabrina	**Rose Byrne**
Robbie	**Shawn Andrews**
Sideth	**Chalee Sankhavesa**
Larry Luckman	**Christopher Curry**
Simon	**Robert Campbell**
Gerard	**Bernard Merklen**

and Jack Shearer (Agent Burden), Kirk Fox (Agent Philips), Kyoza (Rocky), Abhijati Jusakul (Ming Chew), Gennady Fleyscher (Nevesky), Vladamir Epifanov, Jouni Johnanes Anttones (Nevesky Thugs), Rided Lardpanna (Heng), Michael Hayes (Harry, American Ex-Pat), Pok Panhavicyetr (Dr. Bopha), Suon Bou "Loto" (Red Tuxedo Man), Chim Sophal (Bar Kep Manager), Murray Wray, Dean B. Comish (Backpackers), Srai Lin (Buddhist Nun), Anvanith Gui (Mr. Fung), Peun Pad (Bo Tree Man), Ang Cheata (Bellvile Boy), Vanna (Buffalo Boy), Som Sophiak (Laughing Lotus Thug), Phoeuk Sokhen, Seth Sophiak (Laughing Lotus Girls), Sor Chandara (Laughing Lotus Mamasan), Kong Senghiene (Laughing Lotus Papasan), Ian Woodford "Snow" (Australian Ex-Pat), Jon Chan Lakana, Nuon Mony Rath, Pin Yatheam, Meng Bopha (Bar Kep Girls), Em Tepsophea (Sen), Polin (Mover), Bettina Schunter (Carol), Sa Eum (Somnang), Saichea Wongwivoj, Kawee Sirikanerat (Casino Men), Run Rosa (Orphanage Boy), Thou Soth (Wat Sarawan Pa Monk), Jadet (The Monkey)

Kyoza, Stellan Skarsgard, Matt Dillon

Journeying to Cambodia to track down his mentor, con man Jimmy Cremmins becomes involved in a plan to open a large scale casino with money from an insurance scam.

Gerard Depardieu, Matt Dillon PHOTOS COURTESY OF UNITED ARTISTS

SPELLBOUND

(THINKFILM) Producers, Sean Welch, Jeffrey Blitz; Director/Photography, Jeffrey Blitz; Music, Daniel Hulszier; Editor, Yana Gorskaya; Associate Producer, Ronnie Eisen; a Blitz/Welch production; Color; Rated G; 97 minutes; Release date: April 30, 2003. Documentary on the National Spelling Bee; featuring Harry Altman, Angela Arenivar, Ted Brigham, April DeGideo, Neil Kadakia, Nupur Lala, Emily Stagg, Ashley White, Alex Cameron, Dan Brigham, George Thampy

This film received an Oscar nomination for documentary feature (2002).

Spellbound PHOTO COURTESY OF THINKFILM

THE LIZZIE MCGUIRE MOVIE

(WALT DISNEY PICTURES) Producer, Stan Rogow; Executive Producers, David Roessell, Terri Minsky; Director, Jim Fall; Screenplay, Susan Estelle Jansen, Ed Decter, John J. Strauss; Photography, Jerzy Zielinski; Designer, Douglas Higgins; Costumes, Monique Prudhooome, David Robinson; Editor, Margie Goodspeed; Music, Cliff Eidelman; Music Supervisor, Elliot Lurie; Song, "Why Not" by Charlie Midnight, Matthew Gerrard/performed by Hilary Duff; Co-Producer, Susan Estelle Jansen; Casting, Robin Lippin; Dolby; Panavision; Technicolor; Rated PG; 93 minutes; Release date: May 2, 2002

Cast

Lizzie McGuire/Isabella **Hilary Duff**
David "Gordo" Gordon **Adam Lamberg**
Jo McGuire **Hallie Todd**
Sam McGuire **Robert Carradine**
Matt McGuire **Jake Thomas**
Kate Sanders **Ashlie Brillault**
Ethan Craft **Clayton Snyder**
Miss Ungermeyer **Alex Borstein**
Paolo Valisari **Yani Gellman**

and Brendan Kelly (Sergei), Carly Schroeder (Melina Bianco), Daniel Escobar (Mr. Escobar), Jody Racicot (Giorgio), Peter Kelamis (Dr. Comito), Terra C. MacLeod (Franca), Alessandro Cavalieri (Tour Bus Driver), Paolo Giovannucci (Florista #1), Riccardo Marino (Gelato Vendor), Katy Saunders, Silvia Caricato (Cute Girls), Michael Carrat, Giulio Maria Berruti, Matteo Perazzini (Italian Guys), Ona Grauer, Antonio Cupo (Models), Marcus Hondro (Janitor), Stefano Colacitti (Sound Engineer), Taylor Hoover (Taylor), Jackson Rogow (Curly Hair Kid), Brent Chapman, Christine Lippa, Dan Joffre (Parents), Chiara Tommasino, Ilaria Tommassino, Pierluigi Sambucci (Small Children), Jeremy Beck (Jeremy), Claude Knowlton (Stage Manager), John Ulmer (Airport Worker), Michael H. Fall (Italian Man at Airport), Peter Grasso, Aaron Douglas, Stefano Giulianetti (Paparazzi), Heather Gray, Kevin Mylrea, Chelsea Bate, Morgan Tanner (Background Dancers)

During a class trip to Rome, Lizzie McGuire is mistaken for a pop singer whose former boyfriend falls in love with her and plans to turn her into a singing sensation. Based on the Disney Channel series *Lizzie McGuire* with the stars repeating their roles.

Ashlie Brillaut, Hilary Duff

Hilary Duff

Hilary Duff (center)

Yani Gellman, Hilary Duff

Jake Thomas, Robert Carradine, Hallie Todd PHOTOS COURTESY OF WALT DISNEY PICTURES

BLUE CAR

(MIRAMAX) Producer, Peer J. Oppenheimer, Amy Sommer, David Waters; Director/Screenplay, Karen Moncrieff; Co-Producer, Gene Viglione; Associate Producers, Don Daniel, Kelly Simpson, John Mays; Photography, Rob Sweeney; Designer, Kristan Andrews; Music, Adam Gorgoni; Editor, Toby Yates; Casting, Wendy Weidman; a Peer J. Oppenheimer production; Dolby; Rated R; 96 minutes; Release date: May 2, 2003

Cast
Auster **David Strathairn**
Meg Dunning **Agnes Bruckner**
Diane **Margaret Colin**
Delia **Frances Fisher**
Pat **A.J. Buckley**
Lily **Regan Arnold**
Georgia **Sarah Buehler**
Rob **Dustin Sterling**
Dad **Mike Ward**
Don **Wayne Armstrong**
Boy in Class **Aftab Pureval**
Georgia's Mom **Wendy Lardin**
Blonde Girl **Jenn O'nofrio**
Priest **Greg Miller**
Mr. Kastran **Michael Raysses**
Diner Waitress **Amy Benedict**
Girl in the Yellow Dress **Jaime Scheingross**
Bank Teller **Julie Schuster**
Nurse **Jane Mowder**
Department Store Manager **David Carroll**
Pharmacist **Jacqueline Childs**
Cop **Dan Buran**
Pawn Shop Owner **Jeff Gage**
Florida Oasis Cocktail Waitress **Kristan Andrews**
Diner Customer **Peer J. Oppenheimer**

A troubled teenager is encouraged by her teacher to enter a poetry contest and finds herself entering into an unexpected relationship with the man.

Agnes Bruckner

Agnes Bruckner, David Strathairn PHOTOS COURTESY OF MIRAMAX

THE DANCER UPSTAIRS

(FOX SEARCHLIGHT) Producers, Andrés Vicente Gómez, John Malkovich; Executive Producers, Lianne Halfon, Russ Smith; Director, John Malkovich; Screenplay, Nicholas Shakespeare, based on his novel; Photography, José Luis Alcaine; Designer, Pierre-François Limbosh; Costumes, Bina Daigeler; Music, Alberto Iglesias; Editor, Mario Battisel; Line Producer, Yousaf Bokhari; Casting, Camilla-Valentine Isola, Katrina Bayonas; a LolaFilms presentation of a Mr. Mudd Production in association with Anetna 3 Televisión and VIA Digital; U.S.-Spanish, 2002; Dolby; Color; Rated R; 124 minutes; Release date: May 2, 2003

Javier Bardem

Laura Morante (right)

Cast

Agustín Rejas **Javier Bardem**
Sgt. Sucre **Juan Diego Botto**
Yolanda **Laura Morante**
Llosa **Elvira Mínguez**
Sylvina **Alexandra Lencastre**
Police Chief Merino **Oliver Cotton**
Calderón **Luís Miguel Cintra**
Ezequiel/Durán **Abel Folk**
Laura **Marie-Anne Berganza**
Gómez **Lucas Rodríguez**
Pascual **Xabier Elorriaga**
Marina **Natalia Dicenta**
Santiago **Wolframio Sinué**
Sgt. Pisac **Ramiro Jiménez**

and Montserrat Astudillo (Woman in Pick-Up/Edith Pusanga), Galo Urbina, Jairon Flores (Indians in Pick-Up), Lam Chuen (Major Kwan), José Antonio Izaguirre (Quesada), Isabel Prinz (Quesada's Wife), Ignacio Carreño (Quesada's Bodyguard), Benjamas Boonnak (Chinese Ambassadress), Tito García (Adrmial Prado), Verónica Noboa (Model), Luís Gaspar (Judge), Steve Emerson (TV Producer), Carlos Carrillo (TV

Technician), Eusebio Lázaro (Father Ramon), Paulina Aguilar (Shanty Girl), Esteban Salazar (Shanty Policeman), Germán Núñez (Manager), Pachacutic Chugchilan (Bomb Boy), Santiago Carlos Vellido (Soldier in Rejas' Office), Diego Naranjo (Captain Montesinos), Montse Iglesias (Student), Celina Casarai (María), Maribel Rivera (Patricia), Ignacio Durán (Theatre Manager), Frida Torresblanco (Woman in Theatre), Ana Lozano (Vera), Lola Peno (Nurse), Francisco Javier Paez (Army Colonel), David Aguilar (Boy with a Poster), Raquel Rocha (Woman in Convertible), Alexis Rodrigues (Man in Convertible), Daniel Aguilar (Cocacola Cap), Yousaf Bokhari, Monserrat Inglesias, Natalia Tarnawieck, Carlos Thiebaut (Radio Announcers), John Malkovich (Abimael Guzman)

Javier Bardem, Laura Morante   PHOTOS COURTESY OF FOX SEARCHLIGHT

While searching for the leader of a terrorist organization known as the Shining Path, determined detective Rejas falls in love with his daughter's ballet teacher.

X2

(20TH CENTURY FOX) Producers, Lauren Shuler Donner, Ralph Winter; Executive Producers, Avi Arad, Stan Lee, Tom DeSanto, Bryan Singer; Director, Bryan Singer; Screenplay, Michael Dougherty, Dan Harris; Story, Bryan Singer, David Hayter, Zak Penn; Photography, Newton Thomas Sigel; Designer, Guy Hendrix Dyas; Costumes, Louise Mingenbach; Editor, John Ottman; Co-Producer, Ross Fanger; Visual Effects Supervisor, Michael Fink; Special Makeup Design, Gordon Smith; Casting, Roger Mussenden; Stunts, Gary Jensen, Jacob Rupp, Melissa Stubbs, Ernie Jackson; Presented in association with Marvel Enterprises, Inc.; Dolby; Panavision; Deluxe color; Rated PG-13; 134 minutes; Release date: May 2, 2003

Cast

Professor Charles Xavier **Patrick Stewart**
Logan/Wolverine **Hugh Jackman**
Eric Lensherr/Magneto **Ian McKellen**
Storm/Ororo Munroe **Halle Berry**
Jean Grey **Famke Janssen**
Scott Summers/Cyclops **James Marsden**
Mystique **Rebecca Romijn-Stamos**
William Stryker **Brian Cox**
Kurt Wagner/Nightcrawler **Alan Cumming**
Senator Kelly **Bruce Davison**
Rogue **Anna Paquin**
Yuriko Oyama **Kelly Hu**
John Allerdyce/Pyro **Aaron Stanford**
Kitty Pryde **Katie Stuart**
Jason 143 **Michael Reid Mackay**
Little Girl 143 **Keely Purvis**
Bobby Drake/Iceman **Shawn Ashmore**
Jubilee **Kea Wong**
Colossus **Daniel Cudmore**
Jones **Connor Widdows**
Artie **Bryce Hodgson**
Siryn **Shauna Kain**

and Cotter Smith (President McKenna), Alfred E. Humphreys (Drake), Jill Teed (Madeline Drake) James Kirk (Ronny Drake), Ty Olsson (Mitchell Laurio), Glen Curtis, Greg Rikaart (Museum Teenagers), Mark Lukyn (Cop #1, Lead Cop), Kendall Cross (Cop #2), Michasha Armstrong (Plastic Prison Guard), Alfonso Quijada, Rene Quijada (Federal Bldg. Cleaning Twins); Peter Wingfield (Stryker Soldier Lyman), Stephen Spender (Stryker Soldier Smith), Aaron Douglas, Colin Lawrence, Jason S. Whitmer, Aaron Pearl (Stryker Soldiers), Dylan Kussman (Stryker Soldier Wilkins), David Kaye (TV Host), Charles Siegel (Dr. Shaw), Steve Bacic (Dr. Hank McCoy), Michael David Simms (White House Agent, Lead Agent), Roger R. Cross (Oval Office Agent Cartwright), David Fabrizio (Oval Office Agent Fabrizio), Michael Soltis (Whtie House Checkpoint Agent), Chiara Zanni (Whitehouse Tour Guide), Ted Friend, Mi-Jung Lee, Marrett Green, Jill Krop (News Reporters), Nolan Funk, Devin Douglas Drewitz, Jermaine Lopez, Sideah Alladice (X-Kids, Captured), Brad Loree (Stryker at Age 40), Sheri G. Feldman (Augmentation Room Doctor), Richard Bradshaw (Special Ops Agent), Lori Stewart (F-16 Fighter Pilot),

Ian McKellen, Ty Olsen

Kurt Max Runte (Chief of Staff Abrahams), Richard C. Burton, Michael Joycelyn (Loading Bay Stryker Soldiers), Benjamin Glenday (Cameraman), Jackie A. Greenbank (President's Secretary), Robert Hayley (Cop)

Patrick Stewart, Anna Paquin, James Marsden, Shawn Ashmore, Famke Janssen, Halle Berry, Hugh Jackman

After an attack on the White House by mutant Nightcrawler, Colonel Stryker makes it his mission to find Charles Xavier's school for mutants which contains Cerebo, a device that can locate any mutant in the world. Sequel to the 2000 film *X-Men* (20th Century Fox), with most of the principals repeating their roles.

Alan Cumming <small>PHOTOS COURTESY OF 20TH CENTURY FOX</small>

Steve Zahn, Jeff Garlin, Eddie Murphy

Khamani Griffin, Eddie Murphy

DADDY DAY CARE

(COLUMBIA) Producers, John Davis, Matt Berenson, Wyck Godfrey; Executive Producers, Joe Roth, Dan Kolsrud, Heidi Santelli; Director, Steve Carr; Screenplay, Geoff Rodkey; Co-Producer, Jack Brodsky; Photography, Steven Poster; Designer, Garreth Stover; Costumes, Ruth Carter; Music, David Newman; Music Supervision, Sprign Aspers; Editor, Christopher Greenbury; Casting, Juel Bestrop, Jeanne McCarthy; a Revolution Studios presentation of a Davis Entertainment production; Dolby; Deluxe color; Rated PG; 92 minutes; Release date: May 9, 2003

Cast

Charlie Hinton **Eddie Murphy**
Phil **Jeff Garlin**
Marvin **Steve Zahn**
Kim Hinton **Regina King**
Bruce **Kevin Nealon**
Mr. Dan Kubitz **Jonathan Katz**
Peggy **Siobhan Fallon Hogan**
Crispin's Mom **Lisa Edelstein**
Jenny **Lacey Chabert**
Sheila **Laura Kightlinger**
Kelli **Leila Arcieri**
Gwyneth Harridan **Anjelica Huston**
Ben Hinton **Khamani Griffin**
Max **Max Burkholder**
Nicky **Arthur Young**
Jamie **Elle Fanning**
Sean **Cesar Flores**
Becca **Hailey Johnson**

and Felix Achille (Dylan), Shane Baumel (Crispin), Jimmy Bennett ("The Flash"/Tony), Connor Carmody (Duncan), Kennedy McCullough (Jeannie), Alyssa Shafer (Juel), Bridgette Ho (Erin), Brie Arbaugh (Jaime's Mom), Susan Santiago (Sean's Mom), Annabelle Gurwitch (Becca's Mom), Mary Portser (Tony's Mom), Timmy Deters (Tony's Brother), McNally Sagal (Enraged Mom), Damani Roberts (German Speaking Boy), Tara Mercurio (SAT Teacher), Gary Owen (Mr. Carrott), Wallace Langham (Jim Fields), Fred Stoler (Job Counselor), Joan Blair (Day Care Lady), Bess Meisler (Old

Gypsy Woman), Sonya Eddy (Waitress), Paul Anthony Reynolds (Co-Worker Marty), Rachael Harris (Co-Worker Elaine), Mark Griffin (Co-Worker Steve), Dennis Cockrum, Don Winston (Marketing Guys), Lisa Oliva (Marketing Girl), Michelle Krusiec (English Teacher), Kris Cruz Toledo (Interested Mom), Brian Palermo (Skeptical Father), Roger Reid (Parks Employee), Nathaniel Carter (Focus Group Kid), Tracy Britton (Office Worker), Cheap Trick (Themselves)

Charlie and Phil, two workaholic ad men who are fired from their jobs, decide that the most profitable way to take care of their own kids is to open a day care center.

Steve Zahn

Jeff Garlin, Eddie Murphy, Steve Zahn, with kids PHOTOS COURTESY OF COLUMBIA

DOWN WITH LOVE

(20TH CENTURY FOX) Producers, Bruce Cohen, Dan Jinks; Executive Producers, Paddy Cullen, Arnon Milchan; Director, Peyton Reed; Screenplay, Eve Ahlert, Dennis Drake; Photography, Jeff Cronenweth; Designer, Andrew Laws; Costumes, Daniel Orlandi; Editor, Larry Bock; Music, Marc Shaiman; Song: "Here's to Love" by Marc Shaiman and Scott Wittman/performed by Renée Zellweger and Ewan McGregor; Music Supervisors, Chris Douridas, Laura Z. Wasserman; Visual Effects, Matte World Digital, Asylum; Casting, Francine Maisler; a Fox 2000 Pictures and Regency Enterprises presentation in association with Mediastream III of a Jinks/Cohen Company production; Dolby; Panavision; Deluxe color; Rated PG-13; 102 minutes; Release date: May 9, 2003

Renée Zellweger, Ewan McGregor

Renée Zellweger

Renée Zellweger, Tony Randall, Sarah Paulson

Sarah Paulson, Renée Zellweger

Cast
Barbara Novak **Renée Zellweger**
Catcher Block ("Zip Martin") **Ewan McGregor**
Vicki Hiller **Sarah Paulson**
Peter MacMannus **David Hyde Pierce**
Gladys **Rachel Dratch**
Maurice **Jack Plotnick**
Theodore Banner **Tony Randall**
E.G. **John Alyward**
C.B. **Warren Munson**
J.B. **Matt Ross**
J.R. **Michael Ensign**
R.J. **Timothy Omundson**
Gwendolyn **Jeri Ryan**
Yvette **Ivana Milicevic**
Elke **Melissa George**
Sally **Dorie Barton**
Receptionist **Laura Kightlinger**
TV Emcee **Chris Parnell**
Dry Cleaner **Robert Katims**
Dry Cleaner's Wife **Florence Stanley**
Maitre'D **John Christopher Storey**
Waiter **Peter Spruyt**
Beatnik **Turtle**
Beatnik Girl **Lynn Collins**
Doorman **David Doty**
Private Eye **Jude Ciccolella**
Ed Sullivan **Will Jordan**
Johnny Trementus **Brad Hanson**
CBS Switchboard Operators **Beth LaMure, Christie Cronenweth**
Photographer **Norman Fessler**
Piano Player **Marc Shaiman**
Bartender **Scott Whitman**
Waiter **Patrick Cusick**
Narrator **Rick Scarry**
Astronettes **Megan Denton, Melanie Lewis, Sybil Azur, Joanna Collins, Sandra C. McCoy, Sarah Christine Smith**

David Hyde Pierce, Sarah Paulson

David Hyde Pierce, Ewan McGregor

Renée Zellweger

Ewan McGregor, Renée Zellweger

Jeri Ryan

After Barbara Novak's book *Down With Love* makes her a symbol of independence for women everywhere, ladies man Catcher Block makes it his goal to seduce her on his terms.

Sarah Paulson, Renée Zellweger PHOTOS COURTESY OF 20TH CENTURY FOX

THE SHAPE OF THINGS

(FOCUS FEATURES) Producers, Neil LaBute, Gail Mutrux, Philip Steuer, Rachel Weisz; Executive Producers, Tim Bevan, Eric Fellner; Director/Screenplay, Neil LaBute; Based on his play; Photography, James L. Carter; Art Director/Costumes, Lynette Meyer; Editor, Joel Plotch; Songs, Elvis Costello; Casting, Fiona Weir; a StudioCanal presentation of a Working Title production in association with Pretty Pictures; U.S.-French; Dolby; FotoKem color; Rated R; 96 minutes; Release date: May 9, 2003

Cast
Jenny **Gretchen Mol**
Adam **Paul Rudd**
Evelyn **Rachel Weisz**
Phillip **Frederick Weller**

Gretchen Mol, Frederick Weller

Paul Rudd, Gretchen Mol

Rachel Weisz, Paul Rudd

Frumpy museum employee meets the very independent, very direct Evelyn and begins to alter his life and looks to her desires, an act that unnerves his close friends Phillip and Jenny.

Rachel Weisz, Paul Rudd

Frederick Weller, Paul Rudd PHOTOS COURTESY OF FOCUS FEATURES

Hugo Weaving, Keanu Reaves

THE MATRIX RELOADED

(WARNER BROS.) Producer, Joel Silver; Executive Producers, Andy Wachowski, Larry Wackowski, Grant Hill, Andrew Mason, Bruce Berman; Directors/Screenplay, Andy Wachowski, Larry Wachowski; Photography, Bill Pope; Designer, Owen Paterson; Costumes, Kym Barrett; Editor, Zach Staenberg; Music, Don Davis; Visual Effects Supervisor, John Gafta; Conceptual Designer, Geofrey Darrow; Supervising Stunt Coordinator, R.A. Rondell; Martial Arts Stunt Coordinator, Chad Stahelski; Casting, Mali Finn; a Silver Pictures production, presented in association with Village Roadshow Pictures and NPV Entertainment; Dolby; Panavision; Technicolor; Rated R; 138 minutes; Release date: May 15, 2003

Cast

Neo **Keanu Reeves**
Morpheus **Laurence Fishburne**
Trinity **Carrie-Anne Moss**
Agent Smith **Hugo Weaving**
Niobe **Jada Pinkett Smith**
The Oracle **Gloria Foster**
Persephone **Monica Bellucci**
Seraph **Collin Chou**
Zee **Nona Gaye**
Keymaker **Randall Duk Kim**
Commander Lock **Harry Lennix**
Link **Harold Perrineau**
The Twins **Neil Rayment, Adrian Rayment**
Merovingian **Lambert Wilson**
Ghost **Anthony Wong**
Concillor Hamann **Anthony Zerbe**

and Ray Anthony (Power Station Guard), Christine Anu (Kali), Andrew Valli, Andy Arness (Police), Alima Ashton-Sheibu (Girl, Link's Niece), Helmut Bakaitis (The Architect), Steve Bastoni (Soren), Don Batte (Vector), Daniel Bernhardt (Agent Johnson), Valerie Berry (Priestess), Ian Bliss (Bane), Liliana Bogatko (Old Woman at Zion), Michael Budd (Zion Controller), Stoney Burke (Bike Carrier Driver), Kelly Butler (Ice), Josephine Byrnes (Zion Virtual Control Operator), Noris Campos (Woman with Groceries), Paul Cotter (Corrupt), Marlene Cummins (Another Woman at Zion), Attila Davidhazy (Young Thomas Anderson, 12), Essie Davis (Maggie), Terrell Dixon (Wurm), Nash Edgerton (Security Guard #5), David Franklin (Maitre D'), Austin Galuppo (Young Thomas Anderson, 4), Daryl Heath (A.P.U. Escort), Roy Jones, Jr. (Ballard), Malcom Kennard (Abel), David A. Kilde (Agent Jackson), Christopher Kirby (Mauser), Peter Lamb (Colt), Nathaniel Lees (Mifune), Tony Lynch (Computer Room Technician), Robert Mammone (AK), Joshua Mbakwe (Boy, Link's Nephew), Matt McColm (Agent Thompson), John Walton, Scott McLean (Security Bunker Guards), Chris Mitchell (Power Station Guard), Steve Morris (Computer Room Guard), Tory Mussett (Beautiful Woman at Le Vrai), Rene Naufahu (Zion Gate Operator), Robyn Nevin (Councillor Dillard), David No (Cain), Genevieve O'Reilly (Officer Wirtz), Socratis Otto (Operator, Vigilant), Montaño Rain (Young Thomas Anderson, 8), Rupert Reid (Lock's Lieutenant), David Roberts (Roland), Shane C. Rodrigo (Ajax), Nick Scoggin ("Gidim" Truck Driver), Kevin C. Scott (18-Wheel Trucker), Tahei Simpson (Binary), Frankie Steens (Tirant), Nicandro Thomas (Young Thomas Anderson, 2), Gina Torres (Cas), Steve Vella (Malachi), Clayton Watson (Kid), Cornel West (Councillor West), Leigh Whannel (Axel), Bernard White (Rama-Kandra)

Neo, Trinity, and Morpheus return to the Matrix to do battle with the Machine Army who have unleashed 250,000 Sentinels to destroy mankind. Sequel to the 1999 Warner Bros. film *The Matrix* with Reeves, Fishburne, Moss, Weaving, and Foster repeating their roles. A third installment, *The Matrix Revolutions*, was released on November 5, 2003.

Randall Duk Kim, Carrie-Anne Moss

Adrian Rayment, Neil Rayment, Laurence Fishburne PHOTOS COURTESY OF WARNER BROS.

BRUCE ALMIGHTY

(UNIVERSAL) Producers, Tom Shadyac, Jim Carrey, James D. Brubaker, Michael Bostick, Steve Koren, Mark O'Keefe; Executive Producers, Gary Barber, Roger Birnbaum, Steve Oedekerk; Director, Tom Shadyac; Screenplay, Steve Koren, Mark O'Keefe, Steve Oedekerk; Story, Steve Koren, Mark O'Keefe; Photography, Dean Semler; Designer, Linda DeScenna; Costumes, Judy Ruskin Howell; Editor, Scott Hill; Music, John Debney; Music Supervisor, Jeff Carson; Visual Effects Supervisor, Bill Taylor; Casting, Junie Lowry-Johnson, Ron Surma; a Spyglass Entertainment presentation of a Shady Acres/Pit Bull production; Dolby; Deluxe color; Rated PG-13; 101 minutes; Release date: May 23, 2003

Cast

Bruce Nolan **Jim Carrey**
God **Morgan Freeman**
Grace Connelly **Jennifer Aniston**
Jack Keller **Philip Baker Hall**
Susan Ortega **Catherine Bell**
Debbie **Lisa Ann Walter**
Evan Baxter **Steven Carell**
Ally Loman **Nora Dunn**
Bobby **Eddie Jemison**
Dallas Coleman **Paul Satterfield**
Fred Donohue **Mark Kiely**
Anita **Sally Kirkland**
Himself **Tony Bennett**
Bruce's Cameraman **Timothy DiPri**
Bruce's Soundman **Brian Tahash**
Pete Fineman **Lou Felder**
Mama Kowolski **Lillian Adams**
Vol Kowolski **Christopher Darga**
Homeless Man **Jack Jozefson**
Zoe **Madeline Lovejoy**
Martin **Jovan & Koby Allie**
Bill (Ferry Owner) **Dan Desmond**
Irene Dansfield **Selma Stern**

Jim Carrey

Old Man **Alfred Dennis**
Pretty Woman **Rina Fernandez**
Phil Sidleman **Robert Curtis Brown**
Office Staffers **Christina Grandy, Jamison Yang**
Hazel **Bette Rae**
Teenagers **Andrew Hateley, Nick Huff**
Coach Tucker **Greg Collins**
Stalled Car Guy **Dougland Park**
Party Woman **Susan Ware**
Business Man **John Rosenfeld**
Heavyish Woman **Mary Pat Gleason**
Partying Sports Guy **Carey Scott**
Rioter **David A. Clemons**
College Rioter **Bradley Stryker**
Nurse **Laura Carson**
Paramedics **Zachary Aaron Krebs, Ben Livingston**
Doctor **Nelson Mashita**
Trainer **Glen Yrigoyen**

Jim Carrey, Jennifer Aniston

Jim Carrey, Jennifer Aniston

Morgan Freeman, Jim Carrey

Jim Carrey, Nora Dunn

Jim Carrey, Jennifer Aniston

Morgan Freeman

and Mark Adair-Rios, Enrique Almeida, Noel Guglielmi, Rolando Molina, Emilio Rivera, Albert P. Santos (Hoods), Michael Brownlee, Ted Garcia, Maria Quiban, Shaun Robinson, Saida Rodriguez-Pagan, Ken Rudulph, Gina St. John, Michael Villani (Newscasters), Dohn Norwood, Michael Olifiers (Police Training Center Officers), David Carrera (Phil's Cameraman), Howard S. Lefstein (Phil's Soundman), Miah Won (Connie, Masseuse), Darcy Fowers, Laura Shay Griffin (Attractive Woman at Restaurant), Darius Rose (Tyler), Micayla Bowden, Samantha Boyarsky, Dylan Ferguson, Cubbie Kile, Emily Needham, Alex Villiers (Day Care Kids), Moe Daniels (Day Care Teacher), Ara Celi, Jessica Leigh Mattson, Allison McCurdy, Patti O'Donnell, Janelle Perzina, Annie Wersching, Ashley Yegan (Women at Party), Micah Williams (Boy on Bike)

Recently fired from his job as a news reporter and feeling increasingly frustrated by his life, Bruce Nolan is summoned before God who offers Bruce the opportunity to play God for a while and see if he can carry out the responsibility.

Jim Carrey (center) PHOTOS COURTESY OF UNIVERSAL

THE IN-LAWS

(WARNER BROS.) formerly *The Wedding Party*; Producers, Bill Gerber, Elie Samaha, Bill Todman, Jr., Joel Simon; Executive Producers, Andrew Stevens, Tracee Stanley, Oliver Hengst; Director, Andrew Fleming; Screenplay, Nat Mauldin, Ed Solomon; Based on the screenplay by Andrew Bergman; Photography, Alexander Gruszynski; Designer, Andrew McAlpine; Costumes, Deborah Everton; Editor, Mia Goldman; Co-Producer, David Coatsworth; Executive Music Producer, Ralph Sall; Associate Producers, Ernst-August Schneider, Wolfgang Schamburg; Casting, Pam Dixon; a Franchise Pictures presentation of a Gerber Pictures production in association with Furthur Films and MHF Erste Academy Film GmBH & Co. Produktions KG; U.S.-German; Dolby; Technicolor; Rated PG-13; 98 minutes; Release date: May 23, 2003

Cast
Steve Tobias **Michael Douglas**
Jerry Peyser **Albert Brooks**
Angela Harris **Robin Tunney**
Mark Tobias **Ryan Reynolds**
Judy Tobias **Candice Bergen**
Jean-Pierre Thibodoux **David Suchet**
Melissa Peyser **Lindsay Sloane**
Katherine Peyser **Maria Ricossa**
Cherkasov **Vladimir Radian**
Cherkasov's Bodyguard **Michael Bodnar**
Patient **Boyd Banks**
Nurse **Susan Aceron**
Quan Lee **Chang Tseng**
Yadira **Tamara Gorski**
Agent at Restaurant **Matt Birman**
Agent Will Hutchins **Russell Andrews**
Agent Thorn **Richard Waugh**
Lecture Room Subject **Sergio di Zio**
Student **Aaron Abrams**
Gloria Rudnick **Emmy Laybourne**
and Novie Edwards, Tamara Levitt, Jeanie Calleja, Miranda Black (Bridesmaids), Gregory Vitale, Jeremy Mosier, Marcel Brouillet, Michel

Candice Bergen, Michael Douglas

Ryan Reynolds, Lindsay Sloane

Brouillet, Stefano Rocchetti, Billy Khoury, Luke Vitale (Thibodoux Guards), Paul Robbins (Thief at Thibodoux's), Mike Beaver (Rude Floral Consultant), Drew Lee (Buddhist Monk), Matthew Lantz (Dishwasher at the Marriott), KC (Himself), Maria de Crescenzo, Charlotte McKinnon (KC Background Singers), Jason Frost, Ralph Hunter, Stephen Lashley, Adjety Osekre, Peter Brewer (Sunshine Band Members), Kenner Ames (Janitor), Eric Fink (Uncle Ben), Cara Pifko (Rabbi), David Christo, Aaron Alexander, Perry Perlmutar (Frat Brothers), Jack Duffy (The Other Uncle)

A mild-mannered dentist is roped into a world of espionage with international arms smugglers after realizing that the father of his daughter's fiancé is a CIA operative. Remake of the 1979 WB film that starred Peter Falk and Alan Arkin.

Albert Brooks, Michael Douglas PHOTOS COURTESY OF WARNER BROS.

THE ITALIAN JOB

(PARAMOUNT) Producer, Donald De Line; Executive Producers, James R. Dyer, Wendy Japhet, Tim Bevan, Eric Fellner; Director, F. Gary Gray; Screenplay, Donna Powers, Wayne Powers; Based on the 1969 film written by Troy Kennedy Martin; Photography, Wally Pfister; Designer, Charles Wood; Costumes, Mark Bridges; Music, John Powell; Music Supervisors, Kathy Nelson, Julianne Jordan; Editors, Richard Francis-Bruce, Christopher Rouse; Casting, Sheila Jaffe; Stunts, Kurt Bryant, Ken Bates; a De Line Pictures production; Dolby; Panavision; Deluxe color; Rated PG-13; 111 minutes; Release date: May 30, 2003

Mos Def, Jason Statham

Cast
Charlie Croker **Mark Wahlberg**
Stella Bridger **Charlize Theron**
Steve **Edward Norton**
Lyle **Seth Green**
Handsome Rob **Jason Statham**
Left Ear **Mos Def**
Wrench **Franky G**
John Bridger **Donald Sutherland**
Italian Guard **Fausto Callegarini**
Garbagemen/Thugs **Stefano Petronelli, Fabio Scarpa, Cristiano Bonora, Tiberio Greco**
Detectives **Jimmy Shubert, Tammy Cubilette**
Stella's Receptionist **Mary Portser**
Himself **Shawn Fanning**
Young Left Ear **Christopher Moore, Jr.**
Kid on Left **Terrelle Jones**
Kid on Right **Valentine Ebunilo**
Young Charlie **Joel Homan**

and Erik Walker (Bully), Scott Adsit (Actor), Boris Krutonog (Yevhen), Julie Costello (Becky), Oscar Nuñez (Security Guard), Marty Ryan (ATSAC Supervisor), Aaron Speiser (Danielson), Olek Krupa (Mashkov), Peter Gawtti (Skinny Pete), Melanie Jayne (Skinny Pete's Girl), Gregory Scott Cummins (Ukranian), Thomas Alexander (Vance), Martin Morales (Valet), Dr. Frank Nyi (ATSAC Employee), Simon Rhee (Gold Truck Guard), Merritt

Mark Wahlberg, Charlize Theron, Jason Statham

Yohnka (Gold Truck Driver), Ryan Adams (Metro Conductor), John Alden (Motorcycle Guard), Gloria Fontenot (Handsome Rob's Policeman), Alfred Soltes (Left Ear's Butler), Kelly Brook (Lyle's Girlfriend)

Following a successful heist of $35 million in gold bullion from a safe in Venice, Charlie Croker and his team of criminals are left for dead by a traitorous member of the crew, on whom they plot their revenge. Remake of the 1969 Paramount film of the same name that starred Michael Caine.

Edward Norton (center) PHOTOS COURTESY OF PARAMOUNT

Jesse Friedman, Arnold Friedman, David Friedman, Seth Friedman, Elaine Friedman

CAPTURING THE FRIEDMANS

(MAGNOLIA) Producers, Andrew Jarecki, Marc Smerling; Director, Andrew Jarecki; Photography, Adolfo Doring; Additional Camera, Marc Smerling, Rosanna Rizzo, Aaron Phillips, Brian Jackson, Charlie Beyer; Editor, Richard Hankin; Music, Andrea Morricone; Associate Producer, Jennifer Rogen; a Hit the Ground Running Films presentation; Duart color; Not rated; 107 minutes; Release date: May 30, 2003. Documentary on how the seemingly average and happy life of the middle-class Long Island family of the Friedmans came crashing down in 1987 when father Arnold Friedman and son Jesse were arrested on charges of child pornography.

With

Arnold Friedman, Elaine Friedman, David Friedman, Seth Friedman, Jesse Friedman, Howard Friedman, John McDermott, Detective Frances Galasso, Anthony Sgeugloi, Joseph Onorato, Judd Maltin, Judge Abbey Boklan, Rob Georgalis, Scott Banks, Debbie Nathan, Jerry Bernstein, Peter Panaro, Lloyd Doppman, Jack Fallin.

This film received an Oscar nomination for documentary feature.

Jesse Friendman (center), Arnold Friedman (right) PHOTOS COURTESY OF MAGNOLIA

THE WEATHER UNDERGROUND

(SHADOW DISTRIBUTION) Producers, Sam Green, Bill Siegel, Carrie Lozano, Mark Smolowitz; Executive Producers, Christian Ettinger, Mary Harron, Sue Ellen McCann; Directors, Sam Green, Bill Siegel; Photography, Andrew Black, Federico Salsano; Editors, Sam Green, Dawn Logsdon; Music, Dave Cerf, Amy Domingues; Voice-Overs, Lili Taylor, Pamela Z; produced by the Free History Project; Color/black and white; Digital Video; Not rated; 92 minutes; Release date: June 4, 2003. Documentary about a late 1960s radical militant group, the Weather Underground, who engaged in numerous bombings to protest racism and the war in Vietnam.

Bernadine Dohrn

Bill Ayers PHOTOS COURTESY OF SHADOW DISTRIBUTION

With

Bernardine Dohrn, Mark Rudd, Brian Flanagan, David Gilbert, Bill Ayers, Naomi Jaffe, Todd Gitlin, Laura Whitehorn, Don Strickland, Kathleen Cleaver

This film received an Oscar nomination for documentary feature.

2 FAST 2 FURIOUS

(UNIVERSAL) Producer, Neal H. Moritz; Executive Producers, Lee R. Mayes, Michael Fottrell; Director, John Singleton; Screenplay, Michael Brandt, Derek Haas; Story, Michael Brandt, Derek Haas, Gary Scott Thompson; Photography, Matthew F. Leonetti; Designer, Keith Brian Burns; Costumes, Sanja Milkovic Hays; Editors, Bruce Cannon, Dallas Puett; Music, David Arnold; Co-Producer, Heather Lieberman; Stunts, Artie Malesci; Casting, Kimberly R. Hardin; a Neal H. Moritz production; Dolby; Panavision; Technicolor; Rated PG-13; 108 minutes; Release date: June 6, 2003

Cast

Brian O'Conner **Paul Walker**
Roman Pearce **Tyrese**
Monica Fuentes **Eva Mendes**
Carter Verone **Cole Hauser**
Tej **Chris "Ludacris" Bridges**
Agent Bilkins **Thom Barry**
Agent Markham **James Remar**
Suki **Devon Aoki**
Orange Julius **Amaury Nolasco**
Slap Jack **Michael Ealy**
Jimmy **Jin Auyeung**
Agent Dunn **Edward Finlay**

and Mark Boone Junior (Detective Whitworth), Matt Gallini (Enrique), Roberto "Sanz" Sanchez (Roberto), Eric Etebari (Darden), Johnny Cenatiempo (Korpi), Troy Brown (Paul Hackett), Corey Eubanks (Max Campisi), Sam Maloof (Joe Osborne), Troy Robinson (Feliz Vispone), Jose Perez (Jose), Sincerely A. Ward (Slap Jack's Girlfriend), Nievecita Dubuque, Tequilla Hill, Bettina Huffer, Phuong Tuyet Vo (Suki's Girls), Felecia Rafield, Mateo Herreros, Walter "Duke" Foster (Detectives), Zachary L. Mann (U.S. Customs Lead Agent), Marc Macaulay, Cobette Harper (Agents), Limary L. Agosto (Waitress), Tony Bolano (Gardener), Tara Carroll (Seductress), Neal Moritz (Swerving Cop), Marianne M. Arreaga (Police Chopper Pilot), Tamara Jones (Customs Technician)

In order to trap a crooked businessman running a money laundering cartel, Miami federal agents recruit disgraced former cop Brian O'Connor, who insists on his childhood friend, ex-con Roman Pearce, as his partner on the case. Sequel to the 2001 Universal film *The Fast and the Furious* with Paul Walker repeating his role.

Chris "Ludacris" Bridges, Tyrese, Paul Walker PHOTO COURTESY OF UNIVERSAL

Lil DeVille, Nigel Thornberry, Angelica Pickles, Dil Pickles, Chuckie Finster, Tommy Pickles
PHOTO COURTESY OF PARAMOUNT

RUGRATS GO WILD!

(PARAMOUNT) Producers, Arlene Klasky, Gabor Csupo; Executive Producers, Albie Hecht, Julia Pistor, Eryk Casemiro, Hal Waite; Directors, Norton Virgien, John Eng; Screenplay, Kate Boutillier; Based on the Rugrats Characters Created by Arlene Klasky, Gabor Csupo, Paul Germain, and on the Wild Thornberrys Characters Created by Arlene Klasky, Gabor Csupo, Steve Pepoon, David Silverman, Stephen Sustarsic; Designer, Dima Malanitchev; Music, Mark Mothersbaugh; Executive Music Producer, George Acogny; Editors, John Bryant, Kimberly Rettberg; Co-Produces, Tracy Kramer, Terry Thoren, Patrick Stapleton; Sequence Directors, Rick Farmiloe, Michael Girard, Raymie Muzquiz, Toni Vian, Frans Vischer; Casting, Barbara Wright; Voice Direction, Charlie Adler; a Nickelodeon Movies presentation of a Klasky Csupo production; Dolby; Widescreen; Deluxe color; Rated PG; 80 minutes; Release date: June 13, 2003

Voice Cast

E.G. Daily (Tommy Pickles), Nancy Cartwright (Chuckie Finster), Kath Soucie (Phil DeVille/Lil DeVille/Betty DeVille), Dionne Quan (Kimi Finster), Cheryl Chase (Angelica Pickles), Tim Curry (Nigel Thornberry), Joe Alaskey (Grandpa Lou), Tress MacNeille (Charlotte Pickles), Michael Bell (Drew Pickles/Chas Finster), Melanie Chartoff (Didi Pickles), Julia Kato (Kira Finster), Phil Proctor (Howard DeVille), Jack Riley (Stu Pickles), Tara Strong (Dil Pickles), Cree Summer (Susie Carmichael), Danielle Harris (Debbie Thornberry), Jodi Carlisle (Marianne Thornberry), Lacey Chabert (Eliza Thornberry), Flea (Donny Thornberry), Tom Kane (Darwin), Tony Jay (Dr. Lipschitz), Ethan Phillips (Toa), Chrissie Hynde (Siri), Bruce Willis (Spike)

The Rugrats clan gets stranded on a rainforest island where they encounter TV naturalist Nigel Thornberry and his family. Previous Paramount films involving these characters were *The Rugrats Movie* (1998), *Rugrats in Paris: The Movie* (2000), and *The Wild Thornberrys Movie* (2002).

HOLLYWOOD HOMICIDE

(COLUMBIA) Producers, Lou Pitt, Ron Shelton; Executive Producers, Joe Roth, David Lester; Director, Ron Shelton; Screenplay, Robert Souza, Ron Shelton; Photography, Barry Peterson; Designer, Jim Bissell; Costumes, Bernie Pollack; Editor, Paul Seydor; Music, Alex Wurman; Music Supervision, Dawn Solér, Kathy Nelson; Co-Producers, Robert Souza, Allegra Clegg, Scott Bernstein; Casting, Ed Johnston; Stunts, Jeff Dashnaw; a Revolution Studios presentation of a Pitt/Shelton production; Dolby; Panavision; Deluxe color; Rated PG-13; 115 minutes; Release date: June 13, 2003

Keith David

Cast

Joe Gavilan **Harrison Ford**
K.C. Calden **Josh Hartnett**
Ruby **Lena Olin**
Lt. Bennie Macko **Bruce Greenwood**
Antoine Sartain **Isaiah Washington**
Cleo Ricard **Lolita Davidovich**
Leon **Keith David**
Julius Armas **Master P**
Olivia Robidoux **Gladys Knight**
Wanda **Lou Diamond Phillips**
I.A. Det. Jackson **Meredith Scott Lynn**
I.A. Det. Zino **Tom Todoroff**
Danny Broome **James McDonald**
K-Ro **Kurupt**
Silk Brown **Andre Benjamin**
Commander Preston **Alan Dale**
Coroner Chung **Clyde Kusatsu**
Leroy Wasley **Dwight Yoakam**

and Martin Landau (Jerry Duran), Eric Idle (Celebrity), Frank Sinatra, Jr. (Marty Wheeler), Robert Wagner, Johnny Grant, Butch Cassidy, Kevin Law (Themselves), Smokey Robinson (Cabbie), Shawn Woods (Killer "Z"), Anthony Mackie (Killer "Joker"), Choppa, Krazy, Magic, T-Bo (H20Klick), Michael Bentt, Giovanni Guichard (Club Security Guards), Shalena Hughes (Club Girl), Eloy Casados (Det. Eddie Cruz), Gregg Daniel (Det. Mando Lopez), Jamison Jones (Det. Bobby Riley), Darrell Foster (Officer King), Christopher Wiehl (Cheeseburger Cop), Ramon Muniz (Station Cop), Dennis Burkley (Hank the Bartender), Slade Barnett (Bolt Cutter

Martin Landau

Cop), Malakai (Handcuffed Prisoner), Johnny Sneed, Joe Wandell (Arresting Officers), Anna Gasanova (Cleo's Girl), Regan Wallake (Hot Tub Brunette), Blake Gibbons, Jason Matthew Smith (Repo Guys), Valarie Rae Miller, Regina Russell (Sartain Receptionists), K.D. Aubert (Shauntelle), Victor Togunde (Chaplain), Kevin Daniels (Cuz), Ernest Harden, Jr. (Mixer), Brianna Lynn Brown (Shawna), Sonia Iris Lozada (Duran's Housekeeper), Shea Elmore (Yoga Girl), Luis Avalos (Det. Willie Palermo), Rudi Frenner (Autopsy Pathologist), Gretchen Becker (Venice Nanny), Frankie Jay Allison (Corrections Officer Meyers), Vincent Laresca (Corrections Officer Rodriguez), Gregg Donovan (Beverly Hills Ambassador), Jimmy Jean-Louis (Gianfranco Ferré Clerk), Brian Larkins (Beverly Hills Valet), John David Heffron (Van Family Dad), Kelly Lynn Warren (Van Family Mom), Jennette McCurdy (Van Family Daughter), Paul Butcher (Van Family Son), Leroy Michaux (S.U.V. Guy), Katie Boggs (Little Girl on Bike), May R. Boss (Taxi Lady), Lauren Sanchez, Jennifer York, Elvira Jimenez (Chopper Newscasters), Steve Stafford (Police Chopper Pilot), Tara Tovarek, Joan Farrell, Lisa Arning, Ali Elk (Women in Elevator), Chris Ulfand (Talent Agent), Freddy Lewis (Rooftop Cop Boudreau), Michael Merrins (Rooftop Cop Peterson), Brad Tiemann (Dumpster Cop), Gregg Miller (Sgt. Kelly), TJ Deline (Sgt. Davis), James E. Henderson (Playgoer Critic), Manny Suarez (*Streetcar* Pablo), Kathi Copeland (*Streetcar* Eunice), Steve Haase (*Streetcar* Mitch), Sarah Scivier (*Streetcar* Stella), Will McFadden (*Streetcar* Steve), K.D. Aubert (*Streetcar* Blanche)

Two cops, Joe Gavilan, a part-time realtor, and K.C. Calden, an aspiring actor, try to find out why a promising hip-hop group was slaughtered at a Hollywood nightclub.

Josh Hartnett, Lena Olin, Harrison Ford PHOTOS COURTESY OF COLUMBIA

Hulk

HULK

(UNIVERSAL) Producers, Gale Anne Hurd, Avi Arad, James Schamus, Larry Franco; Executive Producers, Stan Lee, Kevin Feige; Director, Ang Lee; Screenplay, John Turman, Michael France, James Schamus; Story, James Schamus; Based on the Marvel Comic Book Character created by Stan Lee and Jack Kirby; Photography, Frederick Elmes; Designer, Rick Heinrichs; Costumes, Marit Allen; Editor, Tim Squyres; Music, Danny Elfman; Animation Supervisor, Colin Brady; Visual Effects Supervisor, Dennis Muren; Visual Effects Producer, Tom Peitzman; Associate Producers, David Womark, Cheryl A. Tkach; Casting, Avy Kaufman; Stunts, Charlie Croughwell; a Valhalla Motion Pictures/Good Machine production, presented in association with Marvel Enterprises; Dolby; Technicolor; Rated PG-13; 138 minutes; Release date: June 20, 2003

Cast

Bruce Banner **Eric Bana**
Betty Ross **Jennifer Connelly**
General Ross **Sam Elliott**
Glenn Talbot **Josh Lucas**
David Banner **Nick Nolte**
Young David Banner **Paul Kersey**
Edith Banner **Cara Buono**
Young Ross **Todd Tesen**
Harper **Kevin Rankin**
Mrs. Krenzler **Celia Weston**
Teenage Bruce Banner **Mike Erwin**
Security Guards **Lou Ferrigno, Stan Lee, Regi Davis, Craig Damon**
President **Geoffrey Scott**
National Security Advisor **Regina McKee Redwing**

and Daniel Dae Kim (Aide), Daniella Kuhn (Edith's Friend), Michael & David Kronenberg (Bruce Banner as a Child), Rhiannon Leigh Wryn (Betty Ross as a Child), Lou Richards (Pediatrician), Jennifer Gotzon (Waitress), Louanne Kelley (Delivery Doctor), Toni Kallen (Delivery Nurse), Paul Hansen Kim (Officer), John Littlefield (Security NCO), Lorenzo Callender, Todd Lee Coralli, Johnny Kastl, Eric Ware (Soldiers), Jesse Corti, Rob Swanson (Colonels), Mark Atteberry, Eva Burkley, Rondda Holeman, John A. Maraffi, Michael Papajohn, David St. Pierre, Boni Yanagisawa (Technicians), David Sutherland (Tank Commander), Sean Mahon, Brett Thacher, Kirk B.R. Woller (Comanche Pilots), Randy Neville (F-22 Pilot), John Prosky (Atheon Technician), Amir Faraj (Boy), Ricardo Aguilar (Boy's Father), Victor Rivers (Paramilitary), Lyndon Karp (Davey)

After absorbing a normally deadly dose of gamma rays, research scientist Bruce Banner finds himself turning into an oversized, hulking, rampaging monster whenever he becomes enraged.

Eric Bana, Nick Nolte PHOTOS COURTESY OF UNIVERSAL

FROM JUSTIN TO KELLY

(20TH CENTURY FOX) Producers, Gayla Aspinall, John Steven Agoglia; Executive Producer, Simon Fuller; Director, Robert Iscove; Screenplay, Kim Fuller; Photography, Francis Kenny; Designer, Charles Rosen; Costumes, Bobbie Read; Editors, Casey O Rohrs, Tirsa Hackshaw; Co-Producers, Bob Engelman, Nikki Boella; Music, Michael Wandmacher; Music Supervisor, Michael Fey; Choreographer, Travis Payne; Casting, Roger Messenden, Lori S. Wyman; a 19 Entertainment production; Dolby; Deluxe color; Rated PG; 81 minutes; Release date: June 20, 2003

Justin Guarini, Brian Dietzen, Greg Siff

Cast
Kelly **Kelly Clarkson**
Justin **Justin Guarini**
Alexa **Katherine Bailess**
Kaya **Anika Noni Rose**
Brandon **Greg Siff**
Eddie **Brian Dietzen**
Carlos **Jason Yribar**
Officer Cutler **Theresa San Nicholas**
Greg **Justin Gorence**
Luke **Christopher Bryan**
Ashley **Kaitlin Riley**
Brianna **Renee Robertson**
Darren **Yamil Piedra**
Mr. O'Mara **Marc Macaulay**

and Toi Svane Stepp (Lizzie), Louis Smith "Tre Luv" & Michael Yo Simmons (Vee Jays), Sherman Roberts (Motel Clerk), Jessica Sutta (Bracelet Girl), Camila Quaresma (Hot Girl), Nancy Anderson (Insulted Girl/Dancer), Jeffrey C. Moore (Volleyball Athlete), Karin Freeland (Girl), Sam Surles (Bathroom Girl #2), Jonathan Sanchez (Salsa Band Leader), Laurie Sposit, Brandon Henschel, Kristin Denehy, Loe Moctezuma, Dondraico Johnson, Melanize Benz, Kato Bonner, Teresa Espinosa, Alison Faulk, Janina Garraway, Christian George, Kehynde Hill, Robert Hoffman, Melanie Lewis, Brook Lipton, Jesus Maldonado, Michael Morris, Brandi

Kelly Clarkson, Justin Guarini PHOTOS COURTESY OF 20TH CENTURY FOX

Olgesby, Nancy Omera, Misty Rascon, Eduardo Adrian Rozas, Gilbert Salvidar, Josh Eli Seffinger, Becca Sweitzer, Gustavo Vargas, Zach Woodlee (Dancers), Henry Herrera, Zumel Michel, Humberto A. Tous, Yohana Zaldivar, Petty Rivas, Abelacid Rodriguez (Salsa Dancers)

Texas singer Kelly and her best friends head off for spring break in Miami at the same time that Pennsylvania student Justin and his buddies arrive in the resort, all of them looking for fun, romance, and music.

Katherine Bailess, Laurie Sposit, Kelly Clarkson, Anika Noni Rose

Rob Reiner

Kate Huson, Luke Wilson

Kate Huson, Luke Wilson

ALEX & EMMA

(WARNER BROS.) Producers, Rob Reiner, Jeremy Leven, Alan Greisman, Todd Black, Elie Samaha; Executive Producers, Peter Guber, Jeffrey Stott, Jason Blumenthal, Steve Tisch; Director, Rob Reiner; Screenplay, Jeremy Leven; Photography, Gavin Finney; Designer, John Larena; Costumes, Shay Cunliffe; Editors, Robert Leighton, Alan Edward Bell; Music, Marc Shaiman; Co-Producers, Joseph Merhi, James Holt; Casting, Jane Jenkins, Janet Hirshenson; a Franchise Pictures presentation of a Reiner-Greisman/Escape Artists production; Dolby; Technicolor; Rated PG-13; 96 minutes; Release date: June 20, 2003

Cast

Emma Dinsmore/Ylva/Elsa/Edora/Anna **Kate Hudson**
Alex Sheldon/Adam Shipley **Luke Wilson**
Polina Delacroix **Sophie Marceau**
John Shaw **David Paymer**
Wirschafter **Rob Reiner**
Croupier **Francois Giroday**
Bobby/Flamenco Dancer #1 **Lobo Sebastian**
Tony/Flamenco Dancer #2 **Chino XL**
"Whistling" John Shaw **Paul Willson**
Andre Delacroix **Alexander Wauthier**
Michele Delacroix **Leili Kramer**
Polina's Father **Rip Taylor**
Madame Blanche **Gigi Bermingham**
Claude **Jordan Lund**
Bus Driver **Robert Costanzo**
Grandmother **Cloris Leachman**
Bernard Pompier **Earl Carroll**
Flamenco Dancer #3 **Jordi Caballero**
Casino Owner **Michael Rappaport**
Receptionist **Danica Sheridan**

Alex Sheldon, suffering from writer's block and threatened with death unless he can pay the $100,000 he owes two Cuban loan sharks, and knowing the only way he can come up with that amount of cash is to finish his new book, hires stenographer Emma Dinsmore to type his dictation of the story in time to meet the thirty-day deadline.

Sophie Marceau, David Paymer

CHARLIE'S ANGELS: FULL THROTTLE

(COLUMBIA) Producers, Leonard Goldberg, Drew Barrymore, Nancy Juvonen; Executive Producers, Jenno Topping, Patrick Crowley; Director, McG; Screenplay, John August, Cormac Wibberley, Marianne Wibberley; Photography, Russell Carpenter; Designer, J. Michael Riva; Costumes, Joseph G. Aulisi; Music, Edward Shearmur; Music Supervisor, John Houlihan; Visual Effects Supervisor, Mark Stetson; Casting, Justine Baddeley, Kim Davis-Wagner; Stunts, Tim Trella; a Leonard Goldberg/Flower Films/Tall Trees/Wonderland S&V production; Dolby; Panavision; Deluxe color; Rated PG-13; 111 minutes; Release date: June 27, 2003

Cast

Natalie Cook **Cameron Diaz**
Dylan Sanders **Drew Barrymore**
Alex Munday **Lucy Liu**
Jimmy Bosley **Bernie Mac**
Thin Man **Crispin Glover**
Seamus O'Grady **Justin Theroux**
Ray Carter **Robert Patrick**
Madison Lee **Demi Moore**

Lucy Liu, Bernie Mac, Drew Barrymore, Cameron Diaz PHOTO COURTESY OF COLUMBIA

and Rodrigo Santoro (Randy Emmers), Shia LaBeouf (Max), Matt LeBlanc (Jason), Luke Wilson (Pete), John Cleese (Mr. Munday), Ja'net DuBois (Momma Bosley), Cheung-Yan Yuen (Deranged Mongol), Daxing Zhang (Demented Mongol), John Chow (Eager Mongol), Bruce Comlois (Large Mongol), Khin-Kyaw Maung (Crooked-Tooth), Russell Bobbitt, Charles Townsend, Al Kahn (Madison's Minions), Bela Karolyi, Eve, Ricky Carmichael, Carey Hart, Jeremy McGrath (Themselves), Tanoai Reed (Wrestler), Joshua Miller (Chess Kid), Clifford Happy (Fleeing Suspect), Mushond Lee (FBI Agent), Robert Forster (Roger Wixon), Andrew Wilson (Cop), Eric Bogosian (Alan Caulfield), Travis Bobbitt (Surfer), Pink (Coal Bowl Starter), Guy Oseary (Restaurant Patron), Mark Cotone (Prison Guard), Carrie Fisher (Mother Superior), Zack Shada (Thin Boy), Ed Robertson (Sheriff), Jennifer Gimenez, Kate Hendrickson (Nuns), Josh Janowicz (Hot Priest), Shanti Lowry, Kasey Campbell, Nadine Ellis, Hannah Feldner-Shaw, Cyla Balten, Staci Flood, Carmit Bachar, Hayley Zeinker (Treasure Chest Dancers), Tommy Flanagan, Chris Pontius, Jones Barnes, Luke Massy (Irish Henchman), Big Boy, Anthony Griffith (Bosley's

Cousins), Wayne Federman, Steve Hylner (Bathroom Guys), Leo Moctezuma, Gabriel Paige (Reunion Dancers), Marc John Jefferies, Shawn Huang (Bus-Stop Kids), Michael Guarnera (Antonioni Crime Boss), Bob Stephenson (Crazed Fan), John Forsythe (Voice of Charlie), Ashley Olsen, Mary-Kate Olsen (Future Angels), Jaclyn Smith (Kelly Garrett), Bruce Willis (William Rose Bailey)

The Angels go undercover in an effort to retrieve a pair of valuable rings that contain encrypted information that could reveal the new identities of every person in the Federal Witness Protection Program. Sequel to the 2000 Columbia film *Charlie's Angels*, with Diaz, Barrymore, Liu, and Glover repeating their roles.

Sinbad, Marina PHOTO COURTESY OF DREAMWORKS

SINBAD: LEGEND OF THE SEVEN SEAS

(DREAMWORKS) Producers, Mireille Soria, Jeffrey Katzenberg; Directors, Tim Johnson, Patrick Gilmore; Screenplay, John Logan; Designer, Raymond Zibach; Music, Harry Gregson-Williams; Editor, Tom Finan; Head of Story, Jennifer Yuh Nelson; Head of Layout, Damon O'Beirne; Animation Supervisor, Kristof Serrand; Associate Producer, Jill Hopper; Art Directors, Seth Engstrom, David James; Digital Supervisor, Craig Ring; 3D Effects, Doug Ikeler; 2D Effects, Stephen Wood; Backgrounds/3D Paint, Desmond Downes; Color Stylist, Richard Daskas; Dolby; Technicolor; Rated PG; 86 minutes; Release date: July 2, 2003

Voice Cast

Sinbad **Brad Pitt**
Marina **Catherine Zeta-Jones**
Eris **Michelle Pfeiffer**
Proteus **Joseph Fiennes**
Kale **Dennis Haysbert**
Dymas **Timothy West**
Rat **Adriano Giannini**
Jin **Raman Hui**
Li **Chuang Chan**

and Jim Cummings (Luca/Additional Voices), Conrad Vernon (Jed), Andrew Birch (Grum and Chum), Chris Miller (Tower Guard)

Sinbad's good deed of returning the Book of Peace in order to save the life of his friend Proteus is challenged by Eris, the goddess of chaos.

Claire Danes, Nick Stahl, Arnold Schwarzenegger in *Terminator 3* PHOTO COURTESY OF WARNER BROS.

TERMINATOR 3: RISE OF THE MACHINES

(WARNER BROS.) Producers, Mario F. Kassar, Andrew G. Vajna, Joel B. Michaels, Hal Lieberman, Colin Wilson; Director, Jonathan Mostow; Screenplay, John Brancato, Michael Ferris; Story, John Brancato, Michael Ferris, Tedi Sarafian; Executive Producers, Moritz Borman, Guy East, Nigel Sinclair, Gale Anne Hurd; Photography, Don Burgess; Designer, Jeff Mann; Costumes, April Ferry; Music, Marco Beltrami; Editors, Neil Travis, Nicholas de Toth; Terminator Make-Up and Animatronic Effects, Stan Winston Studio; Special Visual Effects & Animation, Industrial Light & Magic; Digital Animation Supervisor, Dan Taylor; Visual Effects Supervisor, Pablo Helman; Executive Music Producer, Joel Sill; Casting, Randi Hiller, Sarah Halley Finn; a Mario F. Kassar and Andrew G. Vajna presentation of an Intermedia/IMF Production in association with C2 Picture and Mostow/Lieberman Productions; Dolby; Deluxe color; Panavision; Rated R; 110 minutes; Release date: July 3, 2003

Cast

Terminator **Arnold Schwarzenegger**
John Connor **Nick Stahl**
Kate Brewster **Claire Danes**
T-X **Kristanna Loken**
Robert Brewster **David Andrews**
and Mark Famiglietti (Scott Peterson), Earl Boen (Dr. Peter Silberman), Moira Harris (Betsy), Chris Lawford (Brewster's Aide), Chopper Bernet (Chief Engineer), Carolyn Hennesy (Rich Woman), Jay Acovone (Cop, Westside Street), M.C. Gainey (Roadhouse Bouncer), Susan Merson, Elizabeth Morehead, Kiki Gorton (Roadhouse Clubgoers), Jimmy Snyder (Stripper), Billy Lucas (Angry Man), Brian Sites (Bill Anderson), Alana Curry (Billy's Girlfriend), Larry McCormick (KTLA Anchorman), Robert Alonzo (Jose Barrera), Michael Papajohn (Paramedic #1), Tim Dowling (Paramedic Stevens), Jon Foster (Gas Station Cashier), Mark Hicks (Detective Martinez), Kim Robillard (Detective Edwards), Matt Gerald (SWAT Team Leader), William O'Leary (Mr. Smith), Rick Zief (Mr. Jones), Rebecca Tilney (Laura the CRS Tech), Chris Hardwick, Helen Eigenberg (Engineers), Walter von Huene (CRS Victim), Jerry Katell (CRS Executive) George E. Stack, Jr. (Semi Truck Driver)

A cyborg Terminator is sent from the future to protect John Connor and Kate Brewster from being killed by Skynet's hi-tech killing machine, T-X. Second sequel to Orion's 1984 film *The Terminator*, following *Terminator 2: Judgment Day* (TriStar, 1991), with Schwarzenegger repeating his role from both those films.

LEGALLY BLONDE 2: RED, WHITE & BLONDE

(MGM) Producers, Marc Platt, David Nicksay; Executive Producer, Reese Witherspoon; Director, Charles Herman-Wurmfeld; Screenplay, Kate Kondell; Story, Eve Ahlert, Dennis Drake, Kate Kondell; Based on characters created by Amanda Brown; Photography, Elliot Davis; Designer, Missy Stewart; Costumes, Sophie de Rakoff Carbonell; Music, Rolfe Kent; Music Supervisor, Anita Camaraa; Editor, Peter Teschner; a Marc Platt production, presented in association with Type A Films; Dolby; Deluxe color; Rated PG-13; 94 minutes; Release date: July 2, 2003

Cast

Elle Woods **Reese Witherspoon**
Congresswoman Victoria Rudd **Sally Field**
Grace Rossiter **Regina King**
Paulette Bonafonté-Parcelle **Jennifer Coolidge**
and Bruce McGill (Stanford Marks), Dana Ivey (Libby Hauser), Mary Lynn Rajskub (Reena Giuliani), Jessica Cauffiel (Margot), Alanna Ubach (Serena), J. Barton (Timothy McGinn), Stanley Anderson (Michael Blaine), Bruce Thomas (UPS Guy), Bob Newhart (Sid Post), Luke Wilson (Emmett Richmond), Ruth Williamson (Madeline Kroft), Jack McGee (Det. Finchley), Amir Talai (Associate), Zia Harris (Mailroom Guy), Sam Pancake (Kevin), Octavia L. Spencer (Security Guard), James Urbaniak (Lab Technician), Jan Devereaux (Partner), Lauren Cohn (Head Salsewoman/Amy), Melissa Wyler (Staff Member), Robert Peters (Guard), David Doty (Rob Cole), Clement E. Blake (Homeless Person), Josh Holland (Chief of Staff Ted Hall), Jackie Hoffman (Dog Spa Receptionist), JoBe Cerny (House Clerk), Michael A. Krawic (NIH Scientist), James Newman (Ray Fuchs), Jason Bushman (Fuchs' Aide), Bryan Cuprill (Different Aide), Matt Price (Cole's Aide), Karen Gordon (Kroft's Aide), Melissa Paull (Another Aide), Jeffrey Gelber (Yet Another Aide), George Simms (Speaker of the House), Lisa Long (Congresswoman), Carolyn Hennesy (Congresswoman with Haircut), Erin Cottrell (Delta Nu President), Jennie Vaughn (First Person in Line), Keone Young (Committee Clerk), Arianne Fraser (Secretary), Susan Bivens (Lady with Hair), Dale Waddington Horowitz (Seamstress), Wayne Edward Sherwood (Sound Technician), Brandon Smiley (Office Aide), James Read (Elle's Father), Tane McClure (Elle's Mother), Moondoggie (Bruiser)

Elle Woods arrives in Washington D.C. in order to effect legislation against cosmetics testing on animals. Sequel to *Legally Blonde* (MGM, 2001), with Witherspoon, Wilson, and Coolidge repeating their roles.

Sally Field, Reese Witherspoon, Dana Ivey, Bruce McGill PHOTO COURTESY OF MGM

PIRATES OF THE CARIBBEAN: THE CURSE OF THE BLACK PEARL

(TOUCHSTONE) Producer, Jerry Bruckheimer; Executive Producers, Mike Stenson, Chad Oman, Bruce Hendricks, Paul Deason; Director, Gore Verbinski; Screenplay, Ted Elliott, Terry Rossio; Screen Story, Ted Elliott, Terry Rossio, Stuart Beattie, Jay Wolpert; Based on Walt Disney's Theme Park Attraction "Pirates of the Caribbean;" Photography, Dariusz Wolski; Designer, Brian Morris; Costumes, Penny Rose; Music, Klaus Badelt; Editors, Craig Wood, Stephen Rivkin, Arthur Schmidt; Visual Effects Supervisor, John Knoll; ILM Visual Effects Producer, Jill Brooks; Casting, Ronna Kress; Stunts, George Marshall Ruge; Presented in association with Jerry Bruckheimer Films; Distributed by Buena Vista Pictures; Dolby; Panavision; Technicolor; Rated PG-13; 143 minutes; Release date: July 9, 2003

Jonathan Pryce, Jack Davenport

Johnny Depp, Orlando Bloom

Orlando Bloom

Kevin R. McNally, Zoe Saldana

Cast

Captain Jack Sparrow **Johnny Depp**
Captain Barbossa **Geoffrey Rush**
Will Turner **Orlando Bloom**
Elizabeth Swann **Keira Knightley**
Commodore Norrington **Jack Davenport**
Governor Weatherby Swann **Jonathan Pryce**
Pintel **Lee Arenberg**
Ragetti **Mackenzie Crook**
Lt. Gillette **Damian O'Hare**
Murtogg **Giles New**
Mullroy **Angus Barnett**
Cotton **David Bailie**
Twigg **Michael Berry, Jr.**
Bo'sun **Isaac C. Singleton, Jr.**
Joshamee Gibbs **Kevin R. McNally**
Koehler **Treva Etienne**
Anamaria **Zoe Saldana**
Harbormaster **Guy Siner**
Mr. Brown **Ralph R. Martin**
Estrella **Paula Jane Newman**
Butler **Paul Keith**
Young Will **Dylan Smith**
Young Elizabeth **Lucinda Dryzek**
Seedy Looking Prisoner **Michael Sean Tighe**
Officer **Greg Ellis**
Sentry **Dustin Seavey**
Steersman **Christian Martin**
Grapple **Trevor Goddard**
Jacoby **Vince Lozano**
Seedy Prisoners **Ben Wilson, Antonio Valentino, Mike Babcock**
Scarlett **Lauren Maher**
Mallot **Brye Cooper**
Town Clerk **Owen Finnegan**
Sailor **Ian McIntyre**
Giselle **Vanessa Branch**
Crying Boy **Sam & Ben Roberts**
Marty **Martin Klebba**

Will Turner reluctantly enlists the aide of oddball buccaneer Jack Sparrow to help him rescue Elizabeth Swann from the nefarious pirate Barbossa and his cursed crew of the *Black Pearl*.

This film received Oscar nominations for actor (Johnny Depp), sound, sound editing, makeup, and visual effects.

Johnny Depp, Orlando Bloom

Isaac C. Singleton Jr., Geoffrey Rush

Geoffrey Rush, Keira Knightley PHOTOS COURTESY OF TOUCHSTONE

Michele Hicks, Kyle MacLachlan

Duel Farnes

Mark Polish, James Woods PHOTOS COURTESY OF PARAMOUNT CLASSICS

NORTHFORK

(PARAMOUNT CLASSICS) Producers/Screenplay, Mark Polish, Michael Polish; Executive Producers, Paul F. Mayersohn, James Woods, Anthony Romano, Michel Shane, Janet Jensen, Damon Martin; Director, Michael Polish; Co-Producers, Todd King, Paul Torok; Co-Executive Producers, Bruce E. Jones, Barbara A. Jones, Gil Amaral; Photography, M. David Mullen; Designers, Ichelle Spitzig, Del Polish; Costumes, Danny Glicker; Editor, Leo Trombetta; Music, Stuart Matthewman; Casting, Tina Buckingham; a Romano/Shane Productions and Departure Entertainment presentation of a Probation Pictures production; Dolby; Panavision; Technicolor; Rated R; 103 minutes; Release date: July 11, 2003

Daryl Hannah

Cast

Eddie **Peter Coyote**
Happy **Anthony Edwards**
Irwin **Duel Farnes**
Flower Hercules **Daryl Hannah**
Father Harlan **Nick Nolte**
Willis O'Brien **Mark Polish**
Walter O'Brien **James Woods**
Matt **Joshuin Barker**
Marvin **Graham Beckel**
Arnold **Jon Gries**
Cod **Ben Foster**
Cup of Tea **Robin Sachs**
Mr. Stalling **Marshall Bell**
Mr. Hope **Kyle MacLachlan**
Mrs. Hope **Michele Hicks**

and Douglas Sebern (Mayor), Claire Forlani (Mrs. Hadfield), Rick Overton (Rudolph), Mike Regan (Flaco), Mae Fassett (Ursula), Perry Hofferber (Mr. Pillsbury), Mark Twogood (Jigger), Josh Olsen (Mr. Young), Julie MacAlister (Mrs. Young), Saralyn Sebern (Mrs. Stalling #1), Ginny Watts (Mrs. Stalling #2), Eli Kaufman (Cookie), Steve Kramer (Radio Announcer)

As the town of Northfork, Montana is about to be flooded for a dam-building project, a dying orphan named Irwin encounters a group of angels.

THE LEAGUE OF EXTRAORDINARY GENTLEMEN

(20TH CENTURY FOX) Producers, Don Murphy, Trevor Albert; Executive Producers, Sean Connery, Mark Gordon; Director, Stephen Norrington; Screenplay, James Dale Robinson; Based upon the graphic novel by Alan Moore, Kevin O'Neill; Photography, Dan Laustsen; Designer, Carol Spier; Costumes, Jacqueilne West; Editor, Paul Rubell; Co-Producer, Michael Nelson; Music, Trevor Jones; Creature Effects, Steve Johnson's Edge FX, Inc.; Special Effects Supervisor, Terry Glass; Special Visual Effects, Industrial Light & Magic; Casting, Donna Isaacson, Lucinda Syson; Stunts, Eddie Perez; a Don Murphy production; Dolby; Panavision; Deluxe color; Rated PG-13; 110 minutes; Release date: July 11, 2003

Nasseerudin Shah (right)

Sartaj Garewal (Rocket Room Crewman), Neran Persaud (Crewman Patel), Andrew Rajan (Headphones Crewman), Daniel Brown (Stunned Guard), Aftab Sachak (Breathless Crewman), Guy Singh Digpal (Signal Crewman), Harmage Singh Kalirai (Crewman Chandra), Brian Caspe (Guard #1), Robert Goodman (Valet), René Hajek (Flame Thrower), Semere-Ab Etmet Yohannes (Witch Doctor).

A team of the world's legendary superheroes travels to Venice to stop a madman called the Fantom from sabotaging a conference of world leaders by sinking the entire city.

Peta Wilson, Jason Flemyng, Shane West

Cast
Allan Quartermain **Sean Connery**
Captain Nemo **Naseeruddin Shah**
Mina Harker **Peta Wilson**
Rodney Skinner (The Invisible Man) **Tony Curran**
Dorian Gray **Stuart Townsend**
Tom Sawyer **Shane West**
Henry Jekyll/Edward Hyde **Jason Flemyng**
M **Richard Roxburgh**
Dante **Max Ryan**
Sanderson Reed **Tom Goodman-Hill**
Nigel **David Hemmings**
Ishmael **Terry O'Neill**
Draper **Rudolf Pellar**
Eva **Winter Ave Zoli**
Constable Dunning **Robert Willox**
Running Officer **Robert Orr**

and Michael McGuffie, Joel Kirby (Coppers), Marek Vasut (Soldier), Ewart James Walters (Toby), Michal Grün (Assassin #3), Robert Vahey (Elderly Hunter), Sylvester Morand (Old Traveler), Mariano Titanti (Edgar Shreave), Huggyeaver (Hanson Cab Driver), Pael Bezdek, Stanislav Adamickij, James Babson (Marksmen), San Shella (Terrified Crewman), Ellen Savaria (Recordist), Riz Meedin (Venice Conning Tower Crewman),

Shane West, Sean Connery, Peta Wilson

Shane West, Sean Connery PHOTOS COURTESY OF 20TH CENTURY FOX

Mandy Moore, Peter Gallagher, Mary Catherine Garrison

HOW TO DEAL

(NEW LINE CINEMA) Producers, William Teitler, Erica Huggins; Executive Producers, Ted Field, Chris van Allsburg, Scott Kroopf, David Linde, Toby Emmerich, Michelle Weiss; Director, Clare Kilner; Screenplay, Neena Beber; Based upon the novels *Someone Like You* and *That Summer* by Sarah Dessen; Photography, Eric Edwards; Designer, Dan Davis; Costumes, Alexandra Welker; Editors, Janice Hampton, Shawna Callahan; Music, David Kitay; Music Supervisor, Jon Leshay; Casting, Avy Kaufman; a Radar Pictures/Golden Mean production; Dolby; Deluxe color; Rated PG-13; 101 minutes; Release date: July 18, 2003

Cast

Halley Martin **Mandy Moore**
Lydia Martin **Allison Janney**
Macon Forrester **Trent Ford**
Scarlett Smith **Alexandra Holden**
Steve Beckwith **Dylan Baker**
Grandma Halley **Nina Foch**
Lewis Warsher **Mackenzie Astin**
Marion Smith **Connie Ray**
Ashley Martin **Mary Catherine Garrison**
Carol Warsher **Sonja Smits**
Len Martin **Peter Gallagher**
Lorna Queen **Laura Catalano**
Donald Sherwood **Ray Kahnert**
Buck Warsher **Andrew Gillies**
Michael Sherwood **John White**
Sharon Sherwood **Alison MacLeod**
Ed **Bill Lake**
Elizabeth Gunderson **Charlotte Sullivan**

and Philip Akin (Mr. Bowden), Claire Crawford (Seamstress), Enis Esmer (Ronnie), Thomas Hauff (Minister), Darryl Pring (Big Burly Guy), Audrey Gardiner (Ginny Tabor), Jayne Eastwood (Mrs. Toussaint), Jody Croon (Reporter), Sandi Ross (Marcella), Garbriell Ashry (Dixie Cup Girl), Dana Reznik (Nurse), Darrin Brown (Steely Dan Fan), Darrell Jordan Hicks (Soccer Coach), Jon Hyatt (Skanky Guy), Francois Klanfer (Guest), Sharlene Yuen (Fan), Jeff White (Die Hard Fan)

Disillusioned with the relationships around her, 17-year-old Halley Martin finds it hard to believe in love, until her skepticism is tested by Macon Forrester.

Mandy Moore, Trent Ford

Trent Ford, Mandy Moore, Allison Janney, Connie Ray

Mackenzie Astin, Mary Catherine Garrison PHOTOS COURTESY OF NEW LINE CINEMA

BAD BOYS II

(COLUMBIA) Producer, Jerry Bruckheimer; Executive Producers, Mike Stenson, Chad Oman, Barry Waldman; Director, Michael Bay; Screenplay, Ron Shelton, Jerry Stahl; Story, Marianne Wibberley, Comac Wibberley, Ron Shelton; Photography, Amir Mokri; Designer, Dominic Watkins; Costumes, Deborah L. Scott, Carol Ramsey; Music, Trevor Rabin, Dr. Dre; Editors, Mark Goldblatt, Thomas A. Muldoon, Roger Barton; Music Supervisors, Kathy Nelson, Bob Badami; Casting, Billy Hopkins, Suzanne Smith, Kerry Barden; Stunts, Steve Picerni, Andy Gill; a Don Simpson/Jerry Bruckheimer production; Dolby; Super 35 Widescreen; Technicolor; Rated R; 146 minutes; Release date: July 18, 2003

Cast

Detective Marcus Burnett **Martin Lawrence**
Detective Mike Lowrey **Will Smith**

and Jordi Mollà (Hector Juan Carlos "Johnny" Tapia), Gabrielle Union (Sydney "Syd" Burnett), Peter Stormare (Alexei), Theresa Randle (Theresa Burnett), Joe Pantoliano (Captain Howard), Michael Shannon (Floyd

Poteet), Jon Seda (Roberto), Yul Yázquez (Det. Mateo Reyes), Jason Manuel Olazábal (Det. Marco Vargas), Otto Sanchez (Carlos), Henry Rollins (TNT Leader), Antoni Corone (DEA Tony Dodd), Oleg Taktarov (Josef), Gary Nickens (TNT Fanuti), Charlie Johnson, Jr. (TNT Lockman), Paul Villaverde (TNT Dexter), Rick Gavreau (TNT Lunt), Ray Hernandez (TNT Zank), Mike Francis (Ice Van Driver), Kiko Ellsworth (Blond Dread), Veryl E. Jones (DEA Taylor), Timothy Adams (DEA Van), Keith Hudson, Rich Kelley (DEA Agents), Bianca Bethune (Megan Burnett), Scott Cumberbatch (Quincy Burnett), Tevarus Smalls (James Burnett), Edward Finlay (Skinny Kid), J. Michael Tiedelberg (Thug Sized Ambulance Guy), John Salley (Fletcher), Jay A. Boulwell, Anthony Correa (Mortuary Security Guys), Bill Erfurth (Alpha 12), Amanda Haworth (Alpha 23), Gloria Irizarry (Donna Maria Tapia), Emerson Froth (Boat Dock Guy), Nancy Duerr (Police Psychologist), Phil Owens (AC DEA), Treva Ellenne (Icepick), James Zelley (Klan Leader), Bubba Baker, Steve Gibb (Klansmen), Carlos de Leon (Old Mourner), Dennis Green (Reggie), Scott Charles (Swamp Rat), Terrence J. Corwley (Car Salesman), Jennifer Diaz (Alpha 77 Lupe), Reynaldo A. Gallegos (Alpha 66/Tito Vargas), Jon Beshara (Alpha/Fake Drunk), Timothy Powell (DEA Snell), R.E. Rodgers (CIA Delongpre), Dave Corey (FBI Eames), Alissa Mullins-Diaz (Tapia's Daughter), Christopher J. Cambell (Shadowy Figure), Renee Reilly, Cash Casia (Hot South Beach Women), Ivelin Giro (Hot Cuban Nurse), Pedro Telemaco (Baseball Cap Cuban), Gino Salvano, Ralph Navarro, Fernando Gaviria, Frank Uria, Carlos Rey del Castillo (Tapia Muscle Crew), Peter D. Badalamenti II (Guy in Holding Area), JD Walsh (Sales Tech), Anthony Giaimo (Gay Hairdresser), Sharon Wilkins (Heavy Black Woman), Alexandra Warren (Medical Examiner), Chris Charles Herbert (Coast Guard Operator), Dan Marino (Himself), Bryan Bottinelli (Little Boy), Damaris Justamante (Group Therapist), Michael Bay (Crappy Car Driver), Jessica Karr (Corpse), Sean Lampkin (Zook Pest Control Owner), Nelson J. Perez (Coast Guard Captain), Bobby Talbert (AWAC Techie), Michael McDonough (Store Manager), Tiara Harris (Haitian Girl), Jaica Carter (Gay Haitian Hairdresser), Alhia Chacoff (Maid), Dieudonne S. Abel, Gregory Bastien, Shannon Briggs, Greg Elam, Irwin Gould, Carlos Guity, Rodney Merdock Mercer, Reggie Pierre, Bruno Ramos, Reggie Stanley, Todd Rodgers Terry, Raymond Tong (Haitian Gang)

Miami narcotics detectives Mike Lowrey and Marcus Burnett join a high-tech task force to stop a ruthless drug lord from expanding his empire. Sequel to the 1995 Columbia film *Bad Boys*, with Lawrence, Smith, Pantoliano, and Randle repeating their roles.

Martin Lawrence, Gabrielle Union, Will Smith PHOTO COURTESY OF COLUMBIA

Djimon Hounsou, Angelina Jolie PHOTO COURTESY OF PARAMOUNT

LARA CROFT TOMB RAIDER: THE CRADLE OF LIFE

(PARAMOUNT) Producers, Lawrence Gordon, Lloyd Levin; Executive Producer, Jeremy Heath-Smith; Director, Jan De Bont; Screenplay, Dean Georgaris; Story, Steven E. de Souza, James V. Hart; Based on the EIDOS Interactive Game Series Developed by Core Design; Photography, David Tattersall; Designer, Kirk M. Petruccelli; Costumes, Lindy Hemmings; Music, Alan Silvestri; Music Supervisor, Peter Afterman; Co-Producer, Louis A. Stroller; 2nd Unit Director/Stunts, Simon Crane; a Lawrence Gordon/Lloyd Levin production in association with Eidos Interactive Limited, presented in association with Mutual Film Company & BBC Tele-München Toho-Towa; U.S.-British-German-Japanese; Dolby; Panavision; Deluxe color; Rated PG-13; 118 minutes; Release date: July 25, 2003

Cast
Lara Croft **Angelina Jolie**
Terry Sheridan **Gerard Butler**
Bryce **Noah Taylor**
and Ciarán Hinds (Jonathan Reiss), Djimon Hounsou (Kosa), Til Schweiger (Sean), Christopher Barrie (Hillary), Simon Yam (Chen Lo), Terence Yin (Xien), Daniel Caltagirone (Nicholas Petraki), Fabiano Martell (Jimmy Petraki), Jonathan Coyne (Gus Petraki), Robert Cavanah (M16 Agent Stevens), Lenny Juma, Raymond Offula, Hezron Ajuala (Village Leaders), Ronan Vilbert (M16 Agent Calloway), Alfred Kalipso, Vincent Mbaya (Tribesmen), Ace Shigeo Yonamine (Shay Ling Giant), Robert Atiko (Armin Kal), Shirley Cantrell (Shu Mei), Sang Lui (Shay Ling Messenger), Richard Ridings (Mr. Monza), Elisabeth Seal, Hajaz Akram, Daryl Kwan, Richard Woo, David Kershaw (Buyers), Marem Hernandez, Kate Loustau (Air Stewardesses), Ralf Beck, Tom Wu, Gerald Kyd (Sean's Men), Mark Sung (Tapei Father), Loan Tran (Taipei Mother), Charlotte Nguyen (Taipei Girl), Vincent Poon (Taipei Boy), Tom Yang, Jamie Cho, Khan Bonfils, Jose Cuenco, Jr., Andrew Joshi, Mark Hampton (Reiss' Guards), Michael Wagg (Lead Tech), Martin Gyn Murray (Submarine Medic), Graham McTavish (Submarine Captain)

Lara Croft travels to an area of Africa known as "the Cradle of Life" to find Pandora's Box, and prevent it from falling into the hands of evil scientist Jonathan Reiss. Sequel to the 2001 Paramount release *Lara Croft: Tomb Raider*, with Jolie, Taylor, and Barrie repeating their roles.

SEABISCUIT

(UNIVERSAL/DREAMWORKS) Producers, Kathleen Kennedy, Frank Marshall, Gary Ross, Jane Sindell; Executive Producers, Gary Barber, Roger Birnbaum, Tobey Maguire, Allison Thomas, Robin Bissell; Director/Screenplay, Gary Ross; Based on the book *Seabiscuit: An American Legend* by Laura Hillenbrand; Photography, John Schwartzman; Designer, Jeannine Oppewall; Costumes, Judianna Makovsky; Editor, William Goldenberg; Music, Randy Newman; Race Design, Chris McCarron; Co-Producer, Patricia Churchill; Technical Consultant, Laura Hillenbrand; Stunts, Dan Bradley; a Spyglass Entertainment presentation of a Larger Than Life–Kennedy/Marshall production; Dolby; Panavision; Technicolor; Rated PG-13; 140 minutes; Release date: July 25, 2003

William H. Macy

Tobey Maguire

Cast

Johnny "Red" Pollard **Tobey Maguire**
Charles Howard **Jeff Bridges**
Tom Smith **Chris Cooper**
Marcela Howard **Elizabeth Banks**
George "The Iceman" Woolf **Gary Stevens**
Tick-Tock McGlaughlin **William H. Macy**
Narrator **David McCullough**
Bicycle Supervisor **Paul Vincent O'Connor**
Steamer Owner **Michael Ensign**
Car Customer **James Keane**
Annie Howard **Valerie Mahaffey**
Land Broker **David Doty**
Sam **Kingston DuCoeur**
Mr. Pollard **Michael O'Neill**
Mrs. Pollard **Annie Corley**
Young Red Pollard **Michael Angarano**
Pollard Children **Cameron Bowen, Noah Luke, Mariah Bess, Jamie Lee Redmon**
Charles Strub **Ed Lauter**
Alberto Gianini **Gianni Russo**
Mr. Blodget **Sam Bottoms**
Dutch Doogan **Royce D. Applegate**
Bug Boy Jockeys **William Hollick, Joe Rocco, Jr.**
Frankie Howard **Dyllan Christopher**
Boxing Match Referee **Anthony Klingman**
Marcela's Friend **Michelle Arthur**
Young Jockey **Danny Strong**
White Horse Trainer **Hans Howes**
Molina Rojo Woman **Camillia Sanes**
Angry Trainer **Clif Alvey**
Saratoga Trainer **Dan Daily**
Farm Manager **Borden Flanagan**
Sunny Fitzsimmons **Shay Duffin**
Saratoga Jockey **Kevin Mangold**
Bugle Player **Jay Cohen**
Santa Anita Track Announcer **Frank Mirahmadi**
Speed Dual Jockey **Michael Hunter**
and Peter Jason (Reporter Max), John Walcutt (Reporter Roy), Tony Volu (Racing Tout), James Dumont (Reporter Lewis), Robin Bissell (Horace

Halsteder), Eddie Jones (Samuel Riddle), Paige King (Tick-Tock's Squeeze), Andrew Schatzberg (Newsboy), Chris McCarron (Charley Kurtsinger), Roger E. Fanter (Pimlico Night Watchman), Gary McGurk (Tractor Worker), Michael B. Silver (Baltimore Doctor), Richard Reeves (Radio Reporter Joe), Matt Miller (Pimlico Starter), Gary Ross (Pimlico Track Announcer), Pat Skipper (Seabiscuit's Vet), Ben Campisi (Clocker Man), Ken Magee (California Doctor), Jose Hernandez, Jesse Hernandez, Julio Hernandez, Jose Ramirez, Fernando Moreno, Pedro Hernandez, Dennis Meade, Javier Juarequi, Aerial Delarosa, Eric Hernandez, Raul Cuellar (Male Mariachi Band), Catherine M. Baeza, Gina A. Duran, Cynthia Reifler Flores, Monica Fogelquist, Maria Luisa Fregosa, Ruby Guiterrez, Sylvia N. Hinojosa, Mariana Nanez, Leticia Olmos, Laura Pena,

Tobey Maguire, Chris Cooper

Karla Tovar (Female Mariachi Band), George Baker, Matthew Gillies, Jacqui Larsson, Daniel Martinez, Joshua Stanley, Michael White, Ivan Wild (Salvation Army Band)

Elizabeth Banks

The true story of how jockey Red Pollard, trainer Tom Smith, and millionaire Charles Howard combined forces to turn Seabiscuit into a champion racehorse. Previous film on the subject was *The Story of Seabiscuit* (WB, 1949), starring Barry Fitzgerald, Shirley Temple, and Lon McCallister.

This film received Oscar nominations for picture, sound, cinematography, editing, costume design, screenplay (adaptation), and art direction.

Chris McCarron, Gary Stevens

Chris Cooper

Jeff Bridges, Elizabeth Banks

Tobey Maguire, Gary Stevens

Tobey Maguire PHOTOS COURTESY OF UNIVERSAL/DREAMWORKS

CAMP

(IFC FILMS) Producers, Katie Roumel, Christine Vachon, Pamela Keffler, Danny DeVito, Michael Shamberg, Stacey Sher, Jonathan Weisgal; Executive Producers, John Wells, Richard Klubeck, Jonathan Sehring, Caroline Kaplan, Holly Becker; Co-Producers, Allen Bain, Dan Levine; Director/Screenplay, Todd Graff; Photography, Kip Bogdahn; Designer, Dina Goldman; Costumes, Dawn Weisberg; Music, Stephen Trask; Music Supervisor, Linda Cohen; Choreographers, Michele Lynch, Jerry Mitchell; Associate Producers, Miriam Kazdin, Brad Simpson; Casting, Bernard Telsey, Victoria Pettibone; an IFC Prods. presentation of a Jersey Films, Killer Films, Laughlin Park Pictures production; DuArt color; Rated PG-13; 114 minutes; Release date: July 25, 2003

Daniel Letterle, Joanna Chilocoat

Anna Kendrick, Joanna Chilocoat, Robin De Jesus, Tiffany Taylor

Robin De Jesus, Joanna Chilocoat

Cast

Vlad Baumann	**Daniel Letterle**
Ellen Lucas	**Joanna Chilocoat**
Michael Flores	**Robin De Jesus**
Shaun	**Steven Cutts**
Spitzer	**Vince Rimoldi**
Petie	**Kahiry Bess**
Jenna	**Tiffany Taylor**
Dee	**Sasha Allen**
Jill Simmons	**Alana Allen**
Fritzi Wagner	**Anna Kendrick**
Bert Hanley	**Don Dixon**
Emil	**Robert Orosco**
Himself	**Stephen Sondheim**

and Stephen DiMenna (Glen), Omar Edwards (Alston), Camilla Millican Samuelson (Hillary), Julie Kleiner (Lisa), Dequina Moore (Dequina), Brittany Pollack (Brittany), Tracee Beazer (Tracee), Tony Melson (Tony), Patrick Cubbedge (Patrick), Mario Concepcion (Mario), Ryan Fitzgerald (Ryan), Caitlin Van Zandt (Ilana), Luke Stanhope (Buddy Miller), Melanna Gray (Shaun and Petie's Mom), Eddie Clark (Jenna's Father), Leslie Frye (Jenna's Mother), Bill Simmons (Pianist), Sean Hanley (Husband), Jill Goldhand (Wife), David Perlow (Ellen's Brother), Egle Petraityte (Julie, Vlad's Girlfriend), Bylly Fagen (Photographer), Steven Brinberg (Barbra), Mairi Dorman (Cello), Kenny Brescia (Guitar/Banjo), Jeff Potter (Drums), Daniel Weiss (Organ/Guitar), Tony Conniff (Bass), T.O. Sterett (Piano), Roger K. Wendt (Trombone), Kenny Leeper (Trumpet), Matthew Snyder (Saxophone/Clarinet)

A diverse group of youngsters converge at a musical camp where they bond, bicker, and fall in love while trying to encourage an embittered Broadway composer to stage his new work.

Tracee Beazer, Alana Allen, Dequina Moore PHOTOS COURTESY OF IFC FILMS

SPY KIDS 3-D: GAME OVER

(DIMENSION) Producers, Elizabeth Avellan, Robert Rodriguez; Executive Producers, Bob Weinstein, Harvey Weinstein; Director/Screenplay/Photography/Designer/Editor/Music, Robert Rodriguez; Costumes, Nina Proctor; Additional 3D Photography, Vince Pace; Visual Effects Supervisors, Robert Rodriguez, Daniel Leduc; Casting, Mary Vernieu; a Troublemaker Studios production of a Robert Rodriguez Digital File; Distributed by Miramax Films; Dolby; Deluxe Color; 3-Dimension; Rated PG; 89 minutes; Release date: July 25, 2003

Ryan Pinkston, Alexa Vegas, Robert Vito, Daryl Sabara, Bobby Edner

Cast

Gregorio Cortez **Antonio Banderas**
Ingrid Cortez **Carla Gugino**
Carmen Cortez **Alexa Vega**
Juni Cortez **Daryl Sabara**
Grandfather **Ricardo Montalban**
Grandmother **Holland Taylor**
Donnagon Giggles **Mike Judge**
Gary Giggles **Matt O'Leary**
Gerti Giggles **Emily Osment**
Felix Gumm **Cheech Marin**
Toymaker **Sylvester Stallone**

and Bobby Edner (Francis), Courtney Jines (Demetra), Ryan Pinkston (Arnold), Robert Vito (Rez), Danny Trejo (Machete), Alan Cumming (Fegan Floop), Tony Shalhoub (Alexander Minion), Salma Hayek (Cesca Giggles), Steve Buscemi (Romero), Bill Paxton (Dinky Winks), George Clooney (Devlin), Elijah Wood (The GUY), Selena Gomez (Waterpark Girl), Evan Sabara (Creepy Kid), Camille Chen (Processor), Steve Wertheimer (Agent Hot Rod), Alejandro Rose-Garcia (Edog), Lane Turney (Logos), Glen Powell, Jr. (Long-Fingered Boy), Bob Fonseca (Agent Damage Report), Peter Marquardt (OSS Agent 2), James Paxton (Dinky Winks, Jr.)

Sylvester Stallone PHOTOS COURTESY OF DIMENSION

Juni Cortez attempts to free his sister Carmen who has been trapped within the fourth level of a videogame programmed by the evil Toymaker. Third film in the Dimension-Miramax series following *Spy Kids* (2001) and *Spy Kids 2: The Island of Lost Dreams* (2002), with most of the principals repeating their roles.

Justin Bartha, Jennifer Lopez, Ben Affleck, Lainie Kazan PHOTO COURTESY OF COLUMBIA

GIGLI

(COLUMBIA) Producers, Casey Silver, Martin Brest; Executive Producer, John Hardy; Director/Screenplay, Martin Brest; Photography, Robert Elswit; Designer, Gary Frutkoff; Costumes, Michael Kaplan; Music, John Powell; Editors, Billy Weber, Julie Monroe; Casting, Ellen Lewis; a Revolution Studios presentation of a City Light Films/Casey Silver production; Dolby; Panavision; Deluxe color; Rated R; 124 minutes; Release date: August 1, 2003

Cast

Larry Gigli **Ben Affleck**
Ricki **Jennifer Lopez**
Brian **Justin Bartha**
Starkman **Al Pacino**
Det. Stanley Jacobellis **Christopher Walken**

and Lainie Kazan (Gigli's Mom), Missy Crider (Robin), Terrance Camilleri (Man in Dryer), David Backus (Laundry Customer), Lenny Venito (Louis), Robert Silver (Man in Debt), Luis Alberto Martinez (Adult Care Resident), Todd Giebenhain, Brian Sites, Brian Casey, Les Bradford, David Bonfadini, Dwight P. Ketchum (High School Kids), Peter Van Norden (Morgue Attendant), Alex Fatovich (Packing Store Clerk), David Pressman (Assistant Director), Shelby Fenner (Australian Dancer), Theresa Barbosa-Adams, Kelly Cooper, RJ Durell, Shaun Earl, Nadine Ellis, Samuel Luis Givens, Hunter Hamilton, Stacey Harper, Zach Hensler, Brandon Henschel, Scott Hislop, Robert Hoffman, Dondraico L. Johnson, Elaine Klimaszewski, Melanie Lewis, Brooke Long, Kim McSwain, Mark Meismer, Ross Mulholland, Jenni Osborne, Brandi Oglesby, Zeke Ruelas, Robert Schultz, Jenny Seeger, Matt Sergott, Jeri Slaughter, Megan Stephens, Jenny Lynn Suckling, Giggi Thesman, Lisa Thompson, Nikki Tuazno, Salvatore Vassallo, Robert Vinson, Kevin Wilson, Tara Wilson, Tovaris Wilson (Beach Dancers)

Larry Gigli, a low-level hood assigned to kidnap the mentally handicapped younger brother of a powerful federal prosecutor, is given assistance in his task by a beautiful enforcer named Ricki, with whom he falls in love.

THE SECRET LIVES OF DENTISTS

(MANHATTAN PICTURES) Producers, George VanBuskirk, Campbell Scott; Executive Producers, David Newman, Martin Garvey, Jonathan Filley; Director, Alan Rudolph; Screenplay, Craig Lucas; Based on the novella *The Age of Grief* by Jane Smiley; Photography, Florian Ballhaus; Designer, Ted Glass; Costumes, Amy Westcott; Editor, Andy Keir; Music, Gary DeMichele; Music Supervisor, Jonathan McHugh; Casting, Pam Dixon Mickelson; a Holedigger Films presentation of a Readymade Film; Dolby; Color; Rated R: 105 minutes; Release date: August 1, 2003

Hope Davis, Campbell Scott

Hope Davis, Campbell Scott, Denis Leary

Robin Tunney

Cast
David Hurst **Campbell Scott**
Dana Hurst **Hope Davis**
Slater **Denis Leary**
Laura **Robin Tunney**
Larry **Peter Samuel**
Mark **Jon Patrick Walker**
Lizzie Hurst **Gianna Beleno**
Stephanie Hurst **Lydia Jordan**
Leah Hurst **Cassidy Hinkle**
Carol **Adele D'Man**
Virgins **Kathleen Kinhan, Sara Lerch, Lori Mirabal**
Conductor **Mark Ethan**
Patients **Flora Martinez, Herbert Ade**
Handsome Patient **J. Tucker Smith**
Dr. Danny **Kevin Carroll**
Elaine **Kate Clinton**
Policewoman **Aisha De Haas**
Nurse **Susie Essman**

A stressed dentist begins to suspect his wife and fellow dentist of having an affair.

Denis Leary PHOTOS COURTESY OF MANHATTAN PICTURES

AMERICAN WEDDING

(UNIVERSAL) Producers, Warren Zide, Craig Perry, Chris Moore, Adam Herz, Chris Bender; Executive Producers, Paul Weitz, Chris Weitz, Louis G. Friedman; Director, Jesse Dylan; Screenplay, Adam Herz, based on his characters; Photography, Lloyd Ahern; Designer, Clayton Hartley; Costumes, Pamela Withers Chilton; Music, Christophe Beck; Editor, Stuart Pappé; a Zide/Perry-Liveplanet production; Dolby; Panavision; Deluxe color; Rated R; 97 minutes; Release date: August 1, 2003

Cast

Jim Levenstein **Jason Biggs**
Steve Stifler **Seann William Scott**
Michelle Flaherty **Alyson Hannigan**
Paul Finch **Eddie Kaye Thomas**
Kevin Myers **Thomas Ian Nicholas**
Cadence Flaherty **January Jones**
Jim's Dad **Eugene Levy**
Jim's Mom **Molly Cheek**
Mary Flaherty **Deborah Rush**
Harold Flaherty **Fred Willard**
Grandma **Angela Paton**
Bear **Eric Allen Kramer**
Fraulein Brandi **Amanda Swisten**
Officer Krystal **Nikki Schieler Ziering**
Head Coach **Lawrence Pressman**

and Antoinette Levine (Cultured Saleswoman), Alexis Thorpe (Jennifer), Reynaldo A. Gallegos (Leslie Summers), Kate Hendrickson (Florist), Rob

Eugene Levy, Fred Willard, Deborah Rush, Molly Cheek

Nagle (Floral Assistant), Corinne Reilly-Elfont (Caterer), Loren Lester (Celebrant), Justin Isfeld (Justin), John Cho (John), James Reese (Concierge), Michael Garrity Coleman (Maitre'd), Patrick Gallo (Dress Salesman), Golde Starger (Elderly Woman in Restaurant), Max Goudsmit (Football Guy at Altar), Logan Bartholomew (Football Guy), Neal Flaherty (Football Team Captain), Jennifer Coolidge (Stifler's Mom), Julie Payne (Mrs. Zyskowski), Peter Reinert (Bartender), Chris Bender (Scared Guy in Bathroom), Tony Gatto (Elderly Man with Walker), William Belli (Butch Queen), Ryan Rubin, Brad Hammer (Gay Males), Frank Roessler (Gay Bar Back)

Jim Levenstein nervously prepares for his wedding to Michelle Flaherty, with the help of his buddies Steve and Paul, who are more interested in scoring with Michelle's gorgeous sister Cadence. Second sequel to Universal's 1999 film *American Pie*, following 2001's *American Pie 2*, with Biggs, Scott, Hannigan, Thomas, Nicholas, Levy, Cheek, and Coolidge returning in their roles.

Seann William Scott, January Jones, Jason Biggs, Alyson Hannigan, Eddie Kaye Thomas, Thomas Ian Nicholas PHOTOS COURTESY OF UNIVERSAL

FREAKY FRIDAY

(WALT DISNEY PICTURES) Producer, Andrew Gunn; Executive Producer, Mario Iscovich; Director, Mark Waters; Screenplay, Heather Hach, Leslie Dixon; Based on the book by Mary Rodgers; Photography, Oliver Wood; Designer, Cary White; Costumes, Genevieve Tyrrell; Music, Rolfe Kent; Music Supervisor, Lisa Brown; Editor, Bruce Green; Co-Producer, Ann Marie Sanderlin; a Gunnfilms production; Dolby; Technicolor; Rated PG; 96 minutes; Release date: August 6, 2003

Cast

Tess Coleman **Jamie Lee Curtis**
Anna Coleman **Lindsay Lohan**
Ryan **Mark Harmon**
Grandpa **Harold Gould**
Jake **Chad Michael Murray**
Mr. Bates **Stephen Tobolowsky**
Maddie **Christina Vidal**
Harry Coleman **Ryan Malgarini**
Peg **Haley Hudson**
Pei-Pei **Rosalind Chao**
Pei-Pei's Mom **Lucille Soong**
Evan **Willie Garson**
Dottie Robertson **Dina Waters**
Stacey Hinkhouse **Julie Gonzalo**
Same Shirt Girl **Christina Marie Walter**
Detention Monitor **Lu Elrod**
Gym Teacher **Heather Hach**
Butcher Woman **Lorna Scott**

and Chris Carlberg (Ethan—Drummer), Danny Rubin (Scott—Bass Player), Hayden Tank, Cayden Boyd (Harry's Friends), Marc McClure (Boris), Chris Heuisler (Mr. Waters), Jeffrey Marcus (Depressed Patient), Jacqueline Heinze (Crying Patient), Mary Ellen Trainor (Diary Reading Patient), Erica Gimpel (Harry's Teacher), William Caploe (Talk Show P.A.), Daniel Raymont (Makeup Artist), Veronica Brooks (Champagne Waitress), Lee Burns (Bouncer), Amir Derakh (House of Blues Emcee), Zoe Waters (Wedding Baby)

Thanks to a mystical fortune cookie, overworked single mom Tess Coleman and her rebellious teenaged daughter Anna wind up in each other's bodies. Remake of the 1977 Disney film of the same name that starred Barbara Harris and Jodie Foster; Marc McClure repeats his role from that film.

Haley Hudson, Lindsay Lohan, Christina Vidal

Jamie Lee Curtis, Lindsay Lohan

Jamie Lee Curtis, Mark Harmon

Lindsay Lohan, Chad Michael Murray PHOTOS COURTESY OF WALT DISNEY PICTURES

LE DIVORCE

(FOX SEARCHLIGHT) Producers, Ismail Merchant, Michael Schiffer; Executive Producers, Ted Field, Scott Kroopf, Erica Huggins; Director, James Ivory; Screenplay, Ruth Prawer Jhabvala, James Ivory; Based on the novel by Diane Johnson; Line Producer, Rahila Bootwala; Co-Producers, Paul Bradley, Richard Hawley; Photography, Pierre Lhomme; Designer, Frédéric Bénard; Costumes, Carol Ramsey; Music, Richard Robbins; Editor, John David Allen; Casting, Annette Trumel; a Merchant Ivory/Radar Pictures production; U.S.-French; Dolby; Panavision; Color; Rated PG-13; 117 minutes; Release date: August 8, 2003

Cast

Isabel Walker **Kate Hudson**
Roxeanne "Roxy" de Persand **Naomi Watts**
Maitre Bertram **Jean-Marc Barr**
Suzanne de Persand **Leslie Caron**
Margreeve Walker **Stockard Channing**
Olivia Pace **Glenn Close**
Yves **Romain Duris**
Piers Janely **Stephen Fry**
Antoine de Persand **Samuel Labarthe**
Roger Walker **Thomas Lennon**
Edgar Cosset **Thierry Lhermitte**
Louvre Expert **Daniel Mesguich**
Tellman **Matthew Modine**
Julia Manchevering **Bebe Neuwirth**
Charles-Henri de Persand **Melvil Poupaud**
Charlotte de Persand **Nathalie Richard**
Madame Florian **Catherine Samie**
Chester Walker **Sam Waterston**

and Jean-Marie Lhomme (Immigration Officer), Gennie de Persand (Esmée Buchet-Deàk), Jean-Jacques Pivert (Talkative Shopkeeper), Samuel Gruen, Peter Wyckoff (de Persand Children), Marianne Borgo (Ballet Mistress), Elie Axas (Television Interviewer), Humbert Balsan (Maitre Doisneau), Arnaud Borrel (Photographer), Rona Hartner (Magda Tellman), Marie-Louise Sellman (Bookstore Fan), Françoise Brion (Bookstore Owner), Philip Tabor (Bouncer), Alan Ewing (Singer), Sébastien Pascaud, Gérard Couchet (Television Talking Heads), Hélène Surgère, Fanny Brett (Lingerie Saleswomen), Pierre Aussedat, Anne Canovas

(Appraisers), Marc Tissot (Medic), Christian Erickson (Judith Burnett), David Applefield (Museum Curators), Marie-Christine Adam (Améie), Joaquina Belaunde (Chanel Assistant), Valérie Lang (Policewoman), Pierre-Olivier Brändli (Young Policeman), Christophe Vienne, Emmanuel Broche, Graziella Delerm (Eiffel Tower Security), Keiko Yoshiyama (Japanese Tour Guide), Jean-Pierre Bouvier (Police Inspector), Georges Delettrez (Auctioneer), Frederick Chanoit (Drouot Expert), Nelson (Matheiu)

Isabel Walker arrives in Paris to spend time with her pregnant stepsister Roxy, only to find out that Roxy's husband has abandoned her without explanation.

Stockard Channing

Naomi Watts, Sam Waterston, Kate Hudson, Thomas Lennon

Leslie Caron

Kate Hudson, Romain Duris PHOTOS COURTESY OF FOX SEARCHLIGHT

S.W.A.T.

(COLUMBIA) Producers, Neal H. Moritz, Dan Halstead; Executive Producer, Louis D'Esposito; Director, Clark Johnson; Screenplay, David Ayer, David McKenna; Story, Ron Mita, Jim McClain; Co-Producers, George Huang, Amanda Cohen; Co-Executive Producers, Todd Black; Photography, Gabriel Beristain; Designer, Mayne Berke; Costumes, Christopher Lawrence; Music, Elliot Goldenthal; Music Supervision, Evyen Klean; Editor, Michael Tronick; Casting, Sarah Halley Finn, Randi Hiller; Stunts, M. James Arnett; an Original Film/Camelot Pictures/Chris Lee production; Dolby; Arriflex Widescreen; Deluxe color; Rated PG-13; 116 minutes; Release date: August 8, 2003

Olivier Martinez

Samuel L. Jackson, Colin Farrell, LL Cool J

Cast

Sgt. Dan "Hondo" Harrelson **Samuel L. Jackson**
Jim Street **Colin Farrell**
Chris Sanchez **Michelle Rodriguez**
Deacon "Deke" Kaye **James Todd Smith (LL Cool J)**
T.J. McCabe **Josh Charles**
Brian Gamble **Jeremy Renner**
Michael Boxer **Brian Van Holt**
Alex Montel **Olivier Martinez**
Lt. Greg Velasquez **Reginald E. Cathey**
Capt. Thomas Fuller **Larry Poindexter**
Travis **Page Kennedy**
GQ **Domenick Lombardozzi**
Gus **James DuMont**
Sgt. Howard **Denis Arndt**
Agent Hauser **Lindsey Ginter**
Kathy **Lucinda Jenney**
Agent Kirkland **E. Roger Mitchell**
Lear Jet Pilot **Jay Acovone**
Beat-up Latino Thug **Mario Aguilar**
Bistro Gangsters **Peter Allas, Alexander Lyras**
Robbers **Gregory Sporleder, Frankie Jay Allison, Joey Bucaro**
Lee **Brad Crosby**
Uncle Martin Gascoigne **Kevin Davitian**
Officer David Burress **Reed Diamond**
Hip Cop **Martin Dorsla**
S.W.A.T. Truck Driver **Steve Forrest**
Latino Woman **Maria Galvez**
Newscaster #2 **Willie Gault**

Dispatchers **Sheri Goldner, Audra Platz**
Mr. Richard Segerstrom **Bruce Gray**
Paramedic **Michael Guanera**
Latino Thug **Noel Guglielmi**
Injured Bank Manager **Steven Hack**
Motorcycle Cop **Krista Hartling**
Sgt. Yamoto **Daniel Ichikawa**
Deke's Handsome Partner **Clark Johnson**
Waitress at Pub **Tricia Kelly**
Monique **Jenya Lano**
Cashier **Brian Leckner**

and Iris Little-Thomas (Bank Supervisor), Nicholas Vachon, Ricki Lopez (Agusta Pilots), Elio Lupi (Hot Dog Vendor), Larry McCormick (Himself), Jay Montalvo (Spanish Newscaster), Neal H. Moritz (Luxury Car Driver), Devika Parikh (Jail Intake Reporter), Rod Perry (Deke's Dad), Stephen Ramsey (Lear Jet Co-Pilot), Ken Rudolph (Reporter), Heather Salmon (Wounded Bank Teller), Ashley Scott (Lara), Richard Steinmetz (S.W.A.T. Negotiator), David St. James (Polish Hostage), Arlow Stewart (Homeboy), Shannon Sturges (Mrs. Segerstrom), Andy Umberger (Deputy Chief), Jeffrey Wincott (Ed Taylor)

Michelle Rodriguez PHOTOS COURTESY OF COLUMBIA

Jim Street, a disgraced cop, gets his chance to redeem himself when he is asked to join Hondo Harrelson's new Special Weapons and Tactics team which must escort an arrogant drug lord out of L.A., after the criminal has offered a $100 million bounty to anyone willing to free him from custody. Based on the television series that ran on ABC from 1975 to 1976. The star of that show, Steve Forrest, makes a cameo here.

AMERICAN SPLENDOR

(FINE LINE FEATURES) Producer, Ted Hope; Directors/Screenplay, Robert Pulcini, Shari Springer Berman; Based on the comic book series *American Splendor* by Harvey Pekar and *Our Cancer Year* by Harvey Pekar and Joyce Brabner; Photography, Terry Stacey; Line Producer, Christine Kunewa Walker; Associate Producer, Julia King; Designer, Thérèse DePrez; Music, Mark Suozzo; Music Supervisor, Linda Cohen; Editor, Robert Pulcini; Casting, Ann Goulder; an HBO Films in association with Fine Line Features presentation of a Good Machine production; Dolby; Deluxe Color; Rated R; 100 minutes; Release date: August 15, 2003

Cast

Harvey Pekar **Paul Giamatti**
Joyce Brabner **Hope Davis**
Robert Crumb **James Urbaniak**
Toby Radloff **Judah Friedlander**
Mr. Boats **Earl Billings**
Danielle **Madylin Sweeten**
Marty **Danny Hoch**
Real Harvey **Harvey Pekar**
Real Toby **Toby Radloff**
Real Joyce **Joyce Brabner**
Real Danielle **Danielle Batone**
Superman **Chris Ambrose**
Batman **Joey Krajcar**
Robin **Josh Hutcherson**
Green Lantern **Cameron Carter**
Young Harvey **Daniel Tay**
Housewife **Mary Faktor**
Interviewer **Shari Springer Berman**
Throat Doctor **Larry John Myers**
Lana **Vivienne Benesch**
Nurse **Barbara Brown**
Pahls **Eli Ganias**
Old Jewish Lady **Sylvia Kauders**
Cashier **Rebecca Borger**
Mattress Guys **Nick Baxter, Allen Branstein**
WWII Patient **Dick Prochaska**
Doctor **Charles Eduardos**
Bob the Director **Robert Pulcini**
Counter Girl **Bianca Santos**
Alice Quinn **Maggie Moore**
Rand **Mike Rad**
Cheery Waitress **Amy K. Harmon**
Stage Actor Harvey **Donal Logue**
Stage Actor Joyce **Molly Shannon**
Guitarist **Eytan Mirsky**
Stage Manager **Rob Grader**
Letterman Regular **Terrence Sullivan**
MTV Director **Ebon Moss-Bachrach**
Yuppie **Patrick Lafferty**
Miguel **Jesse Perez**

Paul Giamatti, Sylvia Kauders

and Jeff Peters (Talk Show Host), Ola Creston (PA #1), Robert J. Williams (Cancer Doctor), James McCaffrey (Fred), Jason Stevens (Letterman Regular Voice), Todd Cummings (Talk Show Host Voice)

The true story of underground comic writer Harvey Pekar and his relationship with fan and eventual wife Joyce Brabner.

This film received an Oscar nomination for screenplay (adaptation).

Hope Davis, Paul Giamatti

Joyce Brabner, Harvey Pekar PHOTOS COURTESY OF FINE LINE FEATURES

OPEN RANGE

(TOUCHSTONE) Producers, David Valdes, Kevin Costner, Jake Eberts; Executive Producers; Craig Storper, Armyan Bernstein; Director, Kevin Costner; Screenplay, Craig Storper, based on the novel *The Open Range Men* by Lauran Paine; Photography, James Muro; Designer, Gae Buckley; Costumes, John Bloomfield; Music, Michael Kamen; Editor, Michael J. Duthie, Miklos Wright; Visual Effects Supervisor, David J. Negron Jr.; Casting, Mindy Marin; a Tig Production, presented in association with Cobalt Media Group; Dolby; Super 35 Panavision; Technicolor; Rated R; 138 minutes; Release date: August 15, 2003

Cast
Boss Spearman **Robert Duvall**
Charley Waite **Kevin Costner**
Sue Barlow **Annette Bening**
Denton Baxter **Michael Gambon**
Percy **Michael Jeter**
Button **Diego Luna**
Sheriff Poole **James Russo**
Mose **Abraham Benrubi**
Doc Barlow **Dean McDermott**
Butler **Kim Coates**

Robert Duvall, Annette Bening, Kevin Costner

Diego Luna, Abraham Benrubi PHOTOS COURTESY OF TOUCHSTONE

Cafe Man **Herb Kohler**
Mack **Peter MacNeil**
Ralph **Cliff Saunders**
Ralph's Wife **Pat Stutz**
Wylie **Julian Richings**
Tom **Ian Tracey**
Gus **Rod Wilson**
Ballester **Diego Del Mar**
Cafe Woman **Patricia Benedict**
Bartender Bill **Tim Koetting**
Ray **Tom Carey**
Cory **Kurtis Sanheim**
Junior **Billy Morton**
Chet **Alex Zahara**
Ace **Chad Camilleri**
Pete **Greg Schlosser**
Roy **Guy Bews**
Mack's Wife **Lorette Clow**
Mack's Daughter **Alexis Cerkiewicz**

Boss and Charley, a pair of drifting, freerange cattlemen, run afoul of a greedy land baron.

Kevin Costner

UPTOWN GIRLS

(MGM) Producers, John Penotti, Fisher Stevens, Allison Jacobs; Executive Producers, Joe Caracciolo, Jr., Tim Williams, Boaz Yakin; Director, Boaz Yakin; Screenplay, Julia Dahl, Mo Ogrodnik, Lisa Davidowitz; Story, Allison Jacobs; Photography, Michael Ballhaus; Designer, Kalina Ivanov; Costumes, Sarah Edwards; Editor, David Ray; Music, Joel McNeely; Music Supervisor, Maureen Crowe; Casting, Laura Rosenthal, Ali Farrell; a GreeneStreet Films production; Dolby; Deluxe color; Rated PG-13; 93 minutes; Release date: August 15, 2003

Cast

Molly Gunn **Brittany Murphy**
Lorraine "Ray" Schleine **Dakota Fanning**
Ingrid **Marley Shelton**
Huey **Donald Faison**
Neal **Jesse Spencer**
Mr. McConkey **Austin Pendleton**
Roma Schleine **Heather Locklear**

and Will Toale (Briefs Model), Marceline Hugot (Nurse), Pell James (Julie), Benjamin Quddus Philippe, Russell Steinberg (Party Guys), Fisher Stevens (Funeral Guest), Susanna Frazer (Ballet Teacher), Wynter Kullman (Holly), Amy Korb (Kelli), Geraldine Bartlett (Woman), Mark McGrath, Dave Navarro (Rock Stars), Peter James Kelsch (Auction Hippie), Edmond Genest (Auctioneer), Greg Baglia (Burly Man), Angelina Hong (Cashier), Rocco Musacchia (Hot Dog Vendor), Edward Hibbert (Christies' Rep), David Wells (Celebrity Date), Ramsey Faragallah (Limo Driver), Tania Deighton (Elke), Tom Reilly, Reed Birney, Polly Adams (Executives), Laurine Towler (Admissions Counsellor), Martin Shakar (Mr. Feldman), Valentina McKenzie (Housemaid), Wayne Gurman (Moving Man), Susan Willis (Old Lady), A.D. Miles (Phone Rep), Maria Finglas (Store Manager), Philip Levy (Street Sweeper), Anthony J. Ribustello (Tony, Doorman), Brian Friedman, Nasir Jones, Carmen Electra, Duncan Sheik (Celebrities), Dana Klein, Samantha Toohey (Screaming Teens), Jeremy Petardi ($2,500 Man)

After her accountant steals her inheritance, Molly Gunn, an irresponsible, free-wheeling staple of the New York social scene, takes a job looking after an uptight 8-year-old girl.

Brittany Murphy, Marley Shelton, Dakota Fanning PHOTO COURTESY OF MGM

Robert Englund, Ken Kirzinger PHOTO COURTESY OF NEW LINE CINEMA

FREDDY VS. JASON

(NEW LINE CINEMA) Producer, Sean S. Cunningham; Executive Producers, Robert Shaye, Stokely Chaffin, Renee Witt, Douglas Curtis; Director, Ronny Yu; Screenplay, Damian Shannon, Mark Swift; Based on characters created by Wes Craven and Victor Miller; Photography, Fred Murphy; Designer, John Willett; Costumes, Gregory B. Mah; Editor, Mark Stevens; Music, Graeme Revell; Visual Effects Supervisor, Ariel Velasco Shaw; Casting, Matthew Barry, Nancy Green-Keyes; Stunts, Monty L. Simons, Scott Ateah; a Sean S. Cunningham production; Dolby; Super 35 Widescreen; Deluxe color; Rated R; 97 minutes; Release date: August 15, 2003

Cast

Freddy Krueger **Robert Englund**
Jason Voorhees **Ken Kirzinger**
Lori **Monica Keena**
Will Rollins **Jason Ritter**
Kia Waterson **Kelly Rowland**
Gibb **Katharine Isabelle**
Charlie Linderman **Christopher George Marquette**
Mark Davis **Brendan Fletcher**
Dr. Campbell **Tom Butler**
Deputy Scott Stubbs **Lochlyn Munro**

and Kyle Labine (Bill Freeburg), Zack Ward (Mark's Brother), Paula Shaw (Jason's Mother), Gary Chalk (Sheriff), Jesse Hutch (Trey), David Kopp (Blake), Brent Chapman (Blake's Father), Spencer Stump (Young Jason), Joelle Antonissen (Little Girl), Alistair Abell (Sheriff's Officer), L.E. Moko (Principal Shaye), Chris Gauthier (Shack), Colby Johannson (Teammate), Kimberley Warnat (Beer Line Girl), Kevin Hansen (Beer Line Guy), Alex Green (Glowing Raver), Odessa Munroe (Girl at Lake), Jamie Mayo (Dead Girl on Tree), Blake Mawson (Dead Boy on Tree), Viv Leacock (Male Nurse), Tony Willett (Asylum Guard), Claire Riley (TV Reporter), Sharon Peters (Lori's Mother), Sarah Anne Hepher, Kirsti Forbes, Taryn McCulloch (Skipping Girls), Eileen Pedde (School Nurse), Tyler Foley, Jacqueline Stewart, Laura Boddington (Counselors), Colton Schock, Spencer Doduk, Anysha Berthot (Cruel Children)

Psychopath Freddy Krueger resurrects fellow-madman Jason Voorhees to cause further destruction and murder on Elm Street.

D.W. Moffett, Evan Rachel Wood

Nikki Reed, Holly Hunter, Jeremy Sisto PHOTOS COURTESY OF FOX SEARCHLIGHT

Nikki Reed, Evan Rachel Wood

THIRTEEN

(FOX SEARCHLIGHT) Producers, Jeffrey Levy-Hinte, Michael London; Executive Producers, Tim Bevan, Eric Fellner, Liza Chasin, Holly Hunter; Director, Catherine Hardwicke; Screenplay, Catherine Hardwicke, Nikki Reed; Photography, Elliot Davis; Designer, Carol Strober; Costumes, Cindy Evans; Co-Producer, Rosemary Marks; Editor, Nancy Richardson; Music, Mark Mothersbaugh; Music Supervisor, Amy Rosen, Michelle Morrell; Casting, Jakki Fink, Shani Ginsberg; an Antidote Films production, presented in association with Michael London Productions and Working Title Films; Dolby; Fotokem Color; Rated R; 100 minutes; Release date: August 20, 2003

Cast
Melanie Freeland **Holly Hunter**
Tracy Freeland **Evan Rachel Wood**
Evie Zamore **Nikki Reed**
Brady **Jeremy Sisto**
Mason Freeland **Brady Corbet**
Brooke LaLaine **Deborah Kara Unger**
Luke **Kip Pardue**
Birdie **Sarah Clarke**
Travis **D.W. Moffett**
Noel **Vanessa Anne Hudgens**
Astrid **Jenicka Carey**
Rafe **Ulysses Estrada**
Medina **Sarah Cartwright**
Kayla **Jasmine Salim**
Yumi **Tessa Ludwick**
Businesswoman **CeCe Tsou**
Science Teacher **Jamison Yang**

and Frank Merino (Tattoo Artist), Cynthia Ettinger (Cynthia), Charles Duckworth (Javi), Steven Kozlowski (Skanky Guy), Java Benson, Mo (Rappers), Brandy Rainey (Tough Girl), Yasmine Delawari (English Teacher), Hampton (Himself)

Thirteen-year-old Tracy finds her life spinning out of control when she befriends fellow high schooler Evie, who's intent on having a good time no matter how dangerous the cost.

This film received an Oscar nomination for supporting actress (Holly Hunter).

THE BATTLE OF SHAKER HEIGHTS

(MIRAMAX) Producers, Jeff Balis, Chris Moore; Executive Producers, Ben Affleck, Matt Damon, Joel Hatch, Rick Schwartz; Directors, Efram Potelle, Kyle Rankin; Screenplay, Erica Beeney; Photography, Thomas E. Ackerman; Designer, Lisa K. Sessions; Costumes, Bega Metzner; Music, Richard Marvin; Editor, Richard Nord; Casting, Stacie Goodman-Binder; a LivePlanet production; Dolby; Fotokem Color; Rated PG-13; 78 minutes; Release date: August 22, 2003

Cast

Kelly Ernswiler **Shia LaBeouf**
Bart Bowland **Elden Henson**
Tabby **Amy Smart**
Lance **Billy Kay**
Eve **Kathleen Quinlan**
Sarah **Shiri Appleby**
Abe **William Sadler**
Harrison **Ray Wise**
Winer Weber **Anson Mount**
Mr. Norway **Michael McShane**
Principal Holmstead **Hattie Winston**
Xiou-Xiou Ling **France Nuyen**
Maurice/German Soldier **Philipp Karner**
Todd/German Soldier **Dale R. Simonton**
Mr. Thomas/German Officer **Rick Cramer**

and Ellis E. Williams (Charlie Hayes), Kate Hendrickson (A.D.), Dana Wheeler-Nicholson (Mathilda), Max Van Ville (Infantryman #1), Michael Reid MacKay (Skinny Guy), John Prosky (Director), Justin Thomsno (Infantryman #2/Gunter), Rachel Winfree (Angry Woman), Merritt Yoknka, Pete Turner, Gary Hymes (Attackers)

A troubled teen who dabbles in war reenactments finds himself falling in love with his new best friend's sister, who is scheduled to be married in a few days.

Shia LaBeouf, Amy Smart

Shiri Appleby, Shia LaBeouf

Shia LaBeouf, Elden Henson

Shia LaBeouf PHOTOS COURTESY OF MIRAMAX

Richard Benjamin, Lisa Kudrow

MARCI X

(PARAMOUNT) Producer, Scott Rudin; Executive Producers, Steve Nicolaides, Adam Schroeder; Director, Richard Benjamin; Screenplay, Paul Rudnick; Photography, Robbie Greenberg; Designer, Thérèse DePrez; Costumes, David C. Robinson; Editor, Jacqueline Cambas; Music, Mervyn Warren; Original Songs, Marc Shaiman, Mervyn Warren; Casting, Ilene Starger; a Scott Rudin production; Dolby; Color; Rated R; 84 minutes; Release date: August 22, 2003

Cast
Marci Feld **Lisa Kudrow**
Dr. S **Damon Wayans**
Ben Feld **Richard Benjamin**
Lauren Farb **Jane Krakowski**
Mary Ellen Spinkle **Christine Baranski**
Yolanda Quinones **Paula Garcés**
Lane Strayfield **Charles Kimbrough**

and Veanne Cox (Caitlin Mellowitz), Sherie Rene Scott (Kristen Blatt), Gano Grills (Freekazoid), Nashawn Kearse (Quantrelle), Myron Primes (T-Bill), Billy Griffith (Tubby Fenders), Andrew Keenan Bolger (Chip Spinkle), Adam Fleming, Matthew J. Morrison, Manley Pope, Michael Seelbach (Boys R Us), Gerry Becker (Dr. Skellar), Ebony Jo-Ann (Nurse in Ben's Hospital), Bruce Altman (Stan Dawes), Walter Bobbie (Walt Seldon), Henry Strozier (Drake Winship), Mustafa Shakir (Engine Trouble), Dell Maara (J-Smack), Lordikim (Chopped Sirloin), Brice McMillon (711), Capital Jay (Ill Will), R.L. Brazil (Bone Papa), Kaity Tong, Jim Watkins, Mary Murphy (News Anchors), Jolie Peters (Girl), Zachary Tyler (Boy), Mary Catherine Wright (Nurse at Auction), Maeve McGuire, Delphi Harrington, Vicki Nathan, Alexandra Neil, Gloria Barnes, Marie Wallace, Shelley Kirk, Elisa Scolamieri, Mimi Weddell, Sheila Smith, Bonnieben Pilar, Sybil Lines, Rita Gardner, Joann Cunningham, Jacqueline Betrand, Jane Altman (Women at Auction), John C. Vennema (Matron's Husband), Mary Hart (Herself), Hassan Johnson (Tinfoil), Jade Yorker, Alioune Badu Dieng, Kute Tonge (Teenagers), Lanette Ware, Nadine Mozon (Single Women), Queen Esther, Twinkle Burke, Universal, Sandra Daley, Dean Edwards, Barshem (Audience Members), Kevin Rennard (Drag Queen in Audience), Sheila Kay Davis, Monet Dunham, Daria Hardeman, Rachel L. Hollingsworth, Gabrielle Lee, Lynne Matthew, Khanya Mkhize, Lisa Tharps (Women in Audience), Ann Duquesnay (Singer), Aisha De Haas,

Capathia Jenkins (Gospel Singers), Big Tank (Scratcher), Jennifer Dempster (Reporter at Music Awards), Jodi Ross (Reporter, Feldco), Wally Dunn, Lisa Emery (Parents), Cynthia Tornquist (Reporter, Congress), Ted Sutton (Chuck Farley), Eric LaRay Harvey (Stage Manager), Vanessa Lake (Carlita), Myk Watford (Police Officer, Bad Medicine), Nancy Opel, Christine Toy Johnson, Jack Koenig, John Sloman (Reporter, Feld House), Raymond Seiden (Guard), Albert Macklin (Executive Security), Maureen Langan (Reporter), Shaun Kelly (Percusionist, Bad Medicine), Peter Appel (Officer at Prison), Vivian Sarnof (Sheila Feld), Todd Alan Etelson (Security Guard), Steven E. Wishnoff (Drag Queen)

When a controversial hip-hop CD causes a protest against the record label, its owner Ben Feld ends up hospitalized, prompting his spoiled and clueless daughter Marci to confront the rapper who caused it all, Dr. S.

Damon Wayans, Lisa Kudrow

Damon Wayans (center)

PARTY MONSTER

(STRAND) Producers, Jon Marcus, Bradford Simpson, Christine Vachon, Fenton Bailey, Randy Barbato; Executive Producers, Michael J. Werner, Wouter Barendrecht, John Wells, Edward R. Pressman, John Schmidt, Sofia Sondervan; Directors/Screenplay, Fenton Bailey, Randy Barbato; Based on the book *Disco Bloodbath* by James St. James; Photography, Teodoro Maiaci; Designer, Andrea Stanley; Costumes, Michael Wilkinson; Editor, Jeremy Simmons; Music, Jimmy Harry; Make-up Design, Kabuki; Line Producer, Derrick Tseng; a ContentFilm presentation in association with Fortissimo Film Sales of a Killer Films/John Wells production, a World of Wonder production; Dolby; CFI color; Rated R; 98 minutes; Release date: September 5, 2003

Macaulay Culkin, Chloë Sevigny

Macaulay Culkin

Cast

Michael Alig **Macaulay Culkin**
James St. James **Seth Green**
Gitsie **Chloë Sevigny**
Brooke **Natasha Lyonne**
DJ Keoki **Wilmer Valderamma**
Angel Melendez **Wilson Cruz**
Elke Alig **Diana Scarwid**
Peter Gatien **Dylan McDermott**
Christina **Marilyn Manson**
Young James **Dillon Woolley**
Natasha **Mia Kirshner**
Cabbie **Elliot Kriss**
TV Reporter **Janis Dardaris**
Johnny **Manny Perez**

and Justin Hagan (Freez), Brendan O'Malley (Young Michael), Phillip Knasiak (Young Wrestler), John Summerour (Rodney), John Stamos (Talk Show Host), Daniel Franzese (Dallas Stage Hand/Tiresias the Rat), Michael Kaycheck (Ben), Steven Marcus (Bill), Sofia Lamar, Amanda Lepore, Walt Paper, Arman Ra, Sacred, Astroearle, Aphodita, Keda (Themselves)

The true story of how Michael Alig's superficial and hedonistic lifestyle of club hopping and party going resulted in murder.

Wilson Cruz

Seth Green, Macaulay Culkin PHOTOS COURTESY OF STRAND

DICKIE ROBERTS: FORMER CHILD STAR

(PARAMOUNT) Producers, Adam Sandler, Jack Giarraputo; Executive Producer, Fred Wolf; Director, Sam Weisman; Screenplay, Fred Wolfe, David Spade; Photography, Thomas Ackerman; Designer, Dina Lipton; Costumes, Lisa Jensen; Music, Christophe Beck, Waddy Wachtel; Music Supervisor, Michael Dilbeck; Co-Producer, Blair Breard; Editor, Roger Bondelli; Casting, John Papsidera; a Happy Madison production; Dolby; Panavision; Deluxe color; Rated PG-13; 99 minutes; Release date: September 5, 2003

Scott Terra, David Spade, Jenna Boyd

Cast
Dickie Roberts **David Spade**
Grace Finney **Mary McCormack**
Sidney Wernick **Jon Lovitz**
George Finney **Craig Bierko**
Cyndi **Alyssa Milano**
Sam Finney **Scott Terra**
Sally Finney **Jenna Boyd**
Himself **Rob Reiner**
Peggy Roberts **Doris Roberts**
Young Dickie **Nicholas Schwerin**

and Michelle Ruben (Ring Girl), John Farley (Referee), Bobby Slayton (Commentator), Fred Wolf (Dickie's Corner Man), Joey "Coco" Diaz, Kevin Grevioux (Emmanuel's Entourage), Brian Clark (Guy in Car), Emily Harrison, Nancy M. Pimental (Girls), Alan Blumenfeld (Mr. Rollins), Sasha Mitchell (Angry Driver), Blair Breard (Alcoholic Speaker), Kathleen Lambert (Counselor), Peggy Mannix (Lamaze Group Leader), Rachel Dratch (Reiner's Secretary), Spencer Garrett, Hal Sparks (Publishers), Rob Elk (Biker), Retta (Sad Eye Sadie), Ian Gomez (Strange Man), Edie McClurg (Mrs. Gertrude), John Kirk (Passing Man with Camera), Alexander Slanger (Map Seller), Oliver Kindred, Brandon DePaul, Evan Lee Dahl (Bullies), Wyatt Smith (Boy in Crowd), Patrick Thomas O'Brien (Mr. Gertrude), Colin Ryan (Gertrude Kid), Christopher Johnson, Brandon Michael DePaul, Evan Lee Dahl (Bullies), Ambyr Childers (Barbie), Valerie Perri-Lipson (Teacher at Microphone), Ashley Edner (Heather Bolan), Michael McDonald (Maitre D'), Kevin Farley, Miko C. Brando (Valets), Mindy Burbano (News Correspondent), Lindsay Dann (Reporter), Erin Murphy (Brittany), Meghan Faye Gallagher (Janice), Dick Van Patten,

Jon Lovitz, David Spade

Michael Buffer, Emmanuel Lewis, Leif Garrett, Tom Arnold, Barry Williams, Danny Bonaduce, Corey Feldman, Dustin Diamond, Jann Carl, Lisa Joyner, Willie Aames, Fred Berry, Todd Bridges, Gary Coleman, Jeff Conaway, Tony Dow, Corey Haim, Florence Henderson, Chris Knight, Barry Livingston, Mike Lookinland, Maureen McCormick, Eddie Mekka, Jeremy Miller, Erin Moran, Hawyood Nelson, Jay North, Ron Palillo, Butch Patrick-Lilly, Jonathan Loughran, Peter Dante, Paul Petersen, Adam Rich, Rodney Allen Rippy, Marion Ross, Ernest Thomas, Charlene Tilton, Brendan Fraser (Themselves)

Dickie Roberts, the child star of a long-canceled '70s sitcom now reduced to parking cars for a living, makes it his goal to try to live the childhood he missed out on.

David Spade, Mary McCormack PHOTOS COURTESY OF PARAMOUNT

MATCHSTICK MEN

(WARNER BROS.) Producers, Jack Rapke, Ridley Scott, Steve Starkey, Sean Bailey, Ted Griffin; Executive Producer, Robert Zemeckis; Director, Ridley Scott; Screenplay, Nicholas Griffin, Ted Griffin; Based on the book by Eric Garcia; Photography, John Mathieson; Designer, Tom Foden; Costumes, Michael Kaplan; Music, Hans Zimmer; Co-Producers, Charles J.D. Schlissel, Giannina Facio; Editor, Dody Dorn; Casting, Debra Zane; an Imagemovers/Scott Free production in association with Rickshaw Productions and Liveplanet; Dolby; Panavision; Technicolor; Rated PG-13; 116 minutes; Release date: September 12, 2003

Cast

Roy Waller **Nicolas Cage**
Frank Mercer **Sam Rockwell**
Angela **Alison Lohman**
Dr. Klein **Bruce Altman**
Chuck Frechette **Bruce McGill**
Mrs. Schaffer **Jenny O'Hara**
Mr. Schaffer **Steve Eastin**
Laundry Lady **Beth Grant**
Kathy **Sheila Kelley**
Slacker Boyfriend **Fran Kranz**
Bishop **Tim Kelleher**
Holt **Nigel Gibbs**
Pharmacists **Bill Saito, Tim Maculan**
Man in Line **Stoney Westmoreland**
Bank Clerk **Lynn Ann Leveridge**
Bank Teller **Giannina Facio**

and Sonya Eddy (Parking Garage Cashier), Michael Clossin (Long Winded Parking Booth Driver), Kim Cassidy (Stripper), Paul Hubbard (Store Clerk),

Nicolas Cage, Alison Lohman

Monnae Michaell (Carpet Store Manager), Dennis Anderson (Cashier), Marco Kyris (Pizza Boy), Jerry Hauck (Taxi Tab Driver), Jim Zulevic (Airport Bartender), Ramsey Malouky (Hospital Intern), Andi Sherrill (Pharmacy Cashier), Kate Steele (Strip Club Waitress), Adam Clark (Strip Club Bouncer), Daniel Villarreal (Car Wash Employee), Marco Assante (Valet Parker)

Roy Waller, an obsessive-compulsive con man discovers that he has a 14-year-old daughter, who wants to meet the father she never knew.

Nicolas Cage, Sam Rockwell

Nicolas Cage

Nicolas Cage, Alison Lohman PHOTOS COURTESY OF WARNER BROS.

Bill Murray, Scarlett Johansson

Anna Faris

LOST IN TRANSLATION

(FOCUS FEATURES) Producers, Ross Katz, Sofia Copppola; Executive Producers, Francis Ford Coppola, Fred Roos; Director/Screenplay, Sofia Coppola; Photography, Lance Acord; Designers, Anne Ross, K.K. Barrett; Costumes, Nancy Steiner; Associate Producer, Mitch Glazer; Line Producer, Callum Greene; Music Producer, Brian Reitzell; Song: "More Than This" by Bryan Ferry/performed by Bill Murray; an American Zoetrope/Elemental Films production; Dolby; Color; Rated R; 102 minutes; Release date: September 12, 2003

Bill Murray

Cast

Bob Harris **Bill Murray**
Charlotte **Scarlett Johansson**
John **Giovanni Ribisi**
Kelly **Anna Faris**
Charlie **Fumihiro Hayashi**
Ms. Kawasaki **Akiko Takeshita**
Press Agents **Kazuyoshi Minamimagoe, Kazuko Shibata, Take**
Concierge **Ryuichiro Baba**
Bellboy **Akira Yamaguchi**
Jazz Singer **Catherine Lambert**
Sausalito Piano **Francois du Bois**
Sausalito Guitar **Tim Leffman**
American Businessmen **Gregory Pekar, Richard Allen**
Commercial Director **Yutaka Tadokoro**
Suntory Client **Jun Maki**
Premium Fantasy Woman **Nao Asuka**
Stills Photographer **Tetsuro Naka**
Make-Up Person **Kanako Nakazato**
Hiroko **Hiroko Kawasaki**
Bambie **Daikon**
Kelly's Translator **Asuka Shimuzu**
Ikebana Instructor **Ikuko Takahashi**
Bartender (NY Bar) **Koichi Tanaka**
Aerobics Instructor **Hugo Codaro**
P Chan **Akiko Monou**
French Japanese Club Patron **Akimitsu Naruyama**
Bartender (Nightclub) **Hiroshi Kawashima**
Hiromix **Hiromix**

Anna Faris, Scarlett Johansson, Giovanni Ribisi

Scarlett Johansson, Bill Murray

and Nobuhiko Kitamura (Nobu), Nao Kitman (Nao), Hans (Akira), Kunichi Nomura (Kun), Yasuhiko Hattori (Charlie's Friend), Shigekazu Aida (Mr. Valentine), Kazuo Yamada (Hospital Receptionist), Akira Motomura (Old Man), Osamu Shigematu (Doctor), Mathew Minami (TV Host), Kei Takyo (TV Translator), Ryo Kondo (Politician), Yumi Ikeda, Yumika Saki, Yuji Okabe (Politician's Aides), Diedrich Bollman, Georg O. P. Eschert (German Hotel Guests), Mark Willms (Carl West), Lisle Wilkerson (Sexy Businesswoman)

Bob Harris, an actor in Tokyo to shoot a whiskey commercial, and Charlotte, the wife of a workaholic photographer, are drawn together by their loneliness while staying at a luxury hotel.

2003 Academy Award–winner for Best Original Screenplay. This film received additional nominations for picture, actor (Bill Murray), and director.

Scarlett Johansson

Bill Murray (center)

Scarlett Johansson, Bill Murray

Mathew Minami, Bill Murray

Bill Murray, Scarlett Johansson PHOTOS COURTESY OF FOCUS FEATURES

ONCE UPON A TIME IN MEXICO

(COLUMBIA) Producers, Elizabeth Avellán, Carlos Gallardo, Robert Rodriguez; Director/Screenplay/Photography/Editor/Music, Robert Rodriguez; Co-Producers, Tony Mark, Sue Jett, Luz Maria Rojas; Costumes, Graciela Mazón; Visual Effects Supervisors, Robert Rodriguez, Daniel Leduc; Casting, Mary Vernieu; Stunts, Jeff Dashnaw, Troy Robinson; a Dimension Films presentation of a Troublemaker Studios production; Dolby; HD 24P Widescreen; Deluxe color; Digital Video-to-35mm; Rated R; 101 minutes; Release date: September 12, 2003

Cheech Marin

Cast
El Mariachi **Antonio Banderas**
Carolina **Salma Hayek**
Sands **Johnny Depp**
Billy **Mickey Rourke**
Ajedrez **Eva Mendes**
Cucuy **Danny Trejo**
Lorenzo **Enrique Iglesias**
Fideo **Marco Leonardi**
Belini **Cheech Marin**
Jorge FBI **Rubén Blades**
Barillo **Willem Dafoe**
Marquez **Gerardo Vigil**
President **Pedro Armendariz**
Advisor **Julio Oscar Mechoso**
Cab Driver **Tito Larriva**
Dr. Guevera **Miguel Couturier**
Chicle Boy **Tony Valdes**

Antonio Banderas, Salma Hayek

and Jose Luis Avendano (Alvaro), Rodolfo D'Alejandre (Omar), Natalia Torres (Mariachi's Girl), Steven Constancio (Right Hand), Troy Robinson (Romero), Ermahn Ospina (Qui-Que), Luz Maria Rojas (Pistolera), Mario Simon (Cook), Bernard Hacker (Blascoe), Cecilia Tijerina (Waitress), Carola Vazquez (Hospital Administrator), René Gatica (Chief Federale), Silvia Santoyo (Bachelorette), Juan Pablo Llaguno (Bull Fighter), Ignacio Torres (Teacher), Rogelio Gonzalez Grau (Manny), Jorge Becerril (Taco), Victor Carpinteiro (Left Nut), Dagoberto Gama (Que Pasa)

A corrupt FBI Agent recruits El Mariachi to help stop an assassination plot against the President of Mexico. Third in the Columbia *El Mariachi* series, following *El Mariachi* (1993) and *Desperado* (1995).

Danny Trejo

Johnny Depp PHOTOS COURTESY OF COLUMBIA

DUMMY

(ARTISAN) Producers, Richard Temtchine, Bob Fagan; Director/Screenplay, Greg Pritkin; Line Producer, Valerie Romer; Photography, Horacio Marquínez; Designer, Charlotte Bourke; Costumes, Marie Abma; Music, Paul Wallfisch; Songs, Mike Ruekberg; Executive Music Producer, Jellybean Benitez; Editors, Bill Henry, Michael Palmiero; Castign, Amanda Mackey Johnson, Cathy Sandrich Gelfond; a Quadrant Entertainment presentation; Dolby; Color; Rated R; 90 minutes; Release date: September 12, 2003

Adrien Brody, Illeana Douglas PHOTO COURTESY OF ARTISAN

Cast
Steven **Adrien Brody**
Fangora **Milla Jovovich**
Heidi **Illeana Douglas**
Lorena **Vera Farmiga**
Fern **Jessica Walter**
Lou **Ron Leibman**
Micheal **Jared Harris**
Bonnie **Mirabella Pisani**
Mrs. Gurkel **Helen Hanft**

and Richmond Hoxie (Sorensen), Adam LeFevre (Director), Joanne Bayes (Actress), Lou Martini, Jr. (Unemployed Italian), Gabor Morea (Unemployed Frottager), Edward Hibbert (Unemployed Actor), Robert Larkin (Pharmacist), Alan Semok (Ventriloquism Teacher), John Elsen (Cop), Debbie Ross (Le Bagel Waitress), Tom Plotkin (Magic Shop Clerk), Paul Wallfisch (Elmo), Andy Senor (Caterer)

A timid New Jersey clerk takes up ventriloquism and finds that his dummy possesses all the traits he needs to become indepedent adult.

CABIN FEVER

(LIONS GATE) Producers, Eli Roth, Lauren Moews, Sam Froelich, Evan Astrowsky; Executive Producer, Susan Jackson; Director/Story, Eli Roth; Screenplay, Randy Pearlstein, Eli Roth; Co-Executive Producer, Jeffrey D. Hoffman; Photography, Scott Kevan; Designer, Franco Giacomo-Carbone; Costumes, Paloma Candelaria; Music, Nathan Barr; Editor, Ryan Folsey; Special Make-Up FX, Robert Kurtzman, Greg Nicotero. Berger EFX Group; a Black Sky Entertainment in association with Deer Path Films presentation of a DownHome Entertainment/Tonic Films production; Dolby; Panavision; Deluxe color; Rated R; 94 minutes; Release date: September 12, 2003

Cast
Paul **Rider Strong**
Karen **Jordan Ladd**
Jeff **Joey Kern**
Marcy **Cerina Vincent**
Bert **James DeBello**

and Arie Verveen (The Hermit), Giuseppe Andrews (Deputy Winston), Christy Ward (The Hog Lady), Michael Harding (Shotgun Casey), Julie Childress (Beautiful Wife), David Kaufbird (Justin), Rock (Doctor Mambo, the dog), Robert Harris (Old Man Cadwell), Hal Courtney (Tommy), Matthew Helms (Dennis), Richard Boone (Fenster), Tim Parati (Andy), Dalton McGuire (Lemonade Boy), Jana Farmer (Lemonade Girl), Dante Walker (Shemp), Jeff Rendell (Fake Shemp), Brandon Johnson (Ray Shawn), Cherie Rodgers (Cadwell's Crush), Bill Terrell, Richard Terrell, Jeff Evans, Mike Hill, J.K. Godbold (Happy Wednesday Band), Richard Fullerton (The Sheriff), Phil Fox (Evil Deputy), Gabriel Roth, Donald Lee Hall, Jr., Jeremy A. Metcalf (Shooters), Noah Belson (Guitar Man), Doug McDermott (Harmonica Man), Matt Cappiello (Troubadour), Jessica Masserman (Winston's Date), Paige Hunter (Underage Girl), Gino Vincent (Marcy's Brother), Shiloh Strong (Paul's Brother), Jay Aaseng (Sir Chug-a-lot), Matthew Schwarz (The Bad Influence), Jessica Shortkoff (Cat Hat Girl), Mark Morse (Shocked Guy), Heather Simmons (Shocked Girl), Dean Masserman (Mr. Mom), Sam Froelich, Tom Terrell (Doctors), The Bunny Man (We Will Never Tell), Evan Astrowsky (Helpless Bystander), Mark Schwarz (Hospital Attendant), Shana Schwarz (Hospital Hottie), Joe Adams (Bowling Alley Killer), Adam Roth (The Happy Bald Guy), Jeff Hoffman, Dean Masserman, John Neff, Nancy Neff, Michael Reardon, Glenn Weisberger, Roy Wood (The Victims)

A group of college students, vacationing at a secluded cabin in the woods, find themselves plagued by a mysterious, contagious skin disease.

Cerina Vincent PHOTO COURTESY OF LIONS GATE

THE FIGHTING TEMPTATIONS

(PARAMOUNT) Producers, David Gale, Loretha Jones, Jeff Pollack; Executive Producer, Van Toffler, Benny Medina; Director, Jonathan Lynn; Screenplay, Elizabeth Hunter, Saladin K. Patterson; Story, Elizabeth Hunter; Photography, Affonso Beato; Designer, Victoria Paul; Costumes, Mary Jane Fort, Tracey A. White; Editor, Paul Hirsch; Music, Jimmy Jam, Terry Lewis, James "Big Jim" Wright; Music Supervisor, Spring Aspers; Executive Music Producers, Jimmy Jam, Terry Lewis, James "Big Jim" Wright, Loretha Jones; Co-Producers, Susan Lewis, Momita Sengupta; Casting, Robi Reed-Humes; an MTV Films production in association with Handprint Films; Dolby; Super 35 Widescreen; Deluxe color; Rated PG-13; 122 minutes; Release date: September 19, 2003

Cast

Darrin Hill **Cuba Gooding, Jr.**
Lilly **Beyoncé Knowles**
Lucius **Mike Epps**
Miles Smoke the DJ **Steve Harvey**
Paulina Pritchett **LaTanya Richardson**
Aunt Sally Walker **Ann Nesby**
Maryann Hill **Faith Evans**

and Melba Moore (Bessie Cooley), Nigel Washington (Little Darin), Chloe Bailey (Little Lilly), Demetress Long (Church Usher), Rosalie Washington (Faye Jenkins), Ricky Dillard (Choir Director), Reverend Shirley Caesar (Herself), Wendell Pierce (Reverend Lewis), Lou Myers (Homer T.), Lourdes Benedicto (Rosa Lopez), Richie Dye (Private Investigator), Dakin

Cuba Gooding Jr., Mike Epps

Angie Stone, Rue McClanahan, Cuba Gooding Jr., Melba Moore, Beyoncé Knowles, LaTanya Richardson

Cuba Gooding Jr., Montell Jordan, T-Bone, Chris Cole

Matthews (Mr. Fairchild), Wilbur Fitzgerald (L&G Rep), Daphne Duplaix (Tiffany), Joanie Fox (Waitress), Enoch King (Man Playing Poker), Jill Jane Clements (Train Attendant), James E. Gaines (Lilly's Grandfather), Mitchah Williams (Jimmy B), Vince Canlas (Simon), Nicky Buggs (Sarah), Rue McClanahan (Nancy Stringer), Angie Stone (Alma), Gene Conyers (Funeral Choir Director), Dave Sheridan (Bill), Lou Walker (Man in Church), Mechelle McCain (Girl in Nightclub), Bilal (Nightclub Singer), Kioka Hampton Carter ("Amazing Grace" Auditioner), Justin Mark Caudill, Steven Patrick Huie (Goofy Auditoners), Chuck Larkin (Saw & Nose Flute Auditioner), Roger Greene, Jr. (Gangsta Rapper), Karl D'Wayne Gardner ("Isn't She Lovely" Auditioner), Eddie Levert, Sr. (Joseph), Udoka Valentine Ndubisi (Kano), Darrell Vanterpool (Dean), Walter Williams, Sr. (Frank), Eric Nolan Grant (Samuel), John Wesley Chatham (Cashier), Mickey Jones (Scooter), Mae Middleton (Tasha), L. Warren Young (Guard), Faizon Love (Prison Warden), Rashawn Worthen (First Prison Guard), T-Bone (Bee-Z Briggs), Montel Jordan (Johnson), Chris Cole (Johnson), James Van Harper (Prison Guard at Church), Stephanie Bonner, Tracy Bryant, Delaurian Burton, Sherise Staten (Ramiyah), Debra Calloway Duke (Gospel Explosion Page), Yolanda Adams, Donnie McClurkin (Themselves), Clarence Fountain, Jimmy Carter, George Scott, Eric McKinnie, Joey Williams, Caleb Butler, Tracy Pierce (The Blind Boys of Alabama), Erica Campbell, Trecina Campbell (Mary Mary)

Hot shot Manhattan ad executive Darrin Hill travels back to his boyhood home in Georgia to claim an inheritance from his aunt only to be told that he must fulfill her final wish, to create a successful gospel choir.

Cuba Gooding Jr., Beyoncé Knowles PHOTOS COURTESY OF PARAMOUNT

Haley Joel Osment

Robert Duvall, Haley Joel Osment, Michael Caine

SECONDHAND LIONS

(NEW LINE CINEMA) Producers, David Kirschner, Scott Ross, Corey Sienega; Executive Producers, Toby Emmerich, Mark Kaufman, Janis Rothbard Chaskin, Karen Loop, Kevin Cooper; Director/Screenplay, Tim McCanlies; Co-Producer, Amy Sayres; Photography, Jack Green; Designer, David J. Bomba; Costumes, Gary Jones; Editor, David Moritz; Music, Patrick Doyle; Casting, Ed Johnston, Emily Schweber; a David Kirschner production in association with Digital Domain productions; Dolby; Super 35 Widescreen; Deluxe Color; Rated PG; 109 minutes; Release date: September 19, 2003

Cast

Garth McCann **Michael Caine**
Hub McCann **Robert Duvall**
Walter **Haley Joel Osment**
Mae **Kyra Sedgwick**
Stan **Nicky Katt**
Adult Walter **Josh Lucas**
Ralph **Michael O'Neill**
Helen **Deirdre O'Connell**
Sheik's Grandson **Eric Balfour**
Young Hub **Christian Kane**
Young Garth **Kevin Haberer**
Jasmine **Emmanuelle Vaugier**
The Shiek **Adam Ozturk**
Martha **Jennifer Stone**

Robert Duvall, Michael Caine

and Mitchel Musso, Marc Musso (Boys), Joe Stevens (Insurance Salesman), Charles Sanders (Gold Salesman), Morgana Shaw (Receptionist), Adrian Pasdar (Skeet Machine Salesman), Dameon Clarke (Animal Truck Driver), Jason Douglas (Helper), Rick Dial (Feed Store Owner), George Haynes (Farmer), Jo Harvey Allen (Woman in Hospital), Nadia Shihab (Handmaiden), Eugene Osment (Doctor), Jace Pitre (Frankie), Travis Willingham, Brian Stanton, Kanin Howell (Hoods), Billy Joe Shaver (Biplane Truck Driver), Dennis Letts (Sheriff), Daniel Brooks (Shiek's Great Grandson), Charles E. Gray (Turkish Soldier), Christa Kimlicko-Jones (Can Can Dancer)

A lonely, introverted boy is sent by his flighty mother to live in Texas with his two eccentric uncles.

Michael Caine, Haley Joel Osment, Robert Duvall PHOTOS COURTESY OF NEW LINE CINEMA

CASA DE LOS BABYS

(IFC FILMS) Producers, Lemore Syvan, Alejandro Springall; Executive Producers, Alison Bourke, Jonathan Shering, Caroline Kaplan; Director/Screenplay/Editor, John Sayles; Photography, Mauricio Rubinstein; Designer, Felipe Fernandez del Paso; Costumes, Mayes C. Ruben; Music, Mason Daring; Casting, Cindy Tolan, Lizzie Martinez; a Syvan/Springall production; Dolby; Color; Rated R; 95 minutes; Release date: September 19, 2003

Cast

Jennifer **Maggie Gyllenhaal**
Nan **Marcia Gay Harden**
Skipper **Daryl Hannah**
Eileen **Susan Lynch**
Gayle **Mary Steenburgen**
Leslie **Lili Taylor**
Senora Muñoz **Rita Moreno**
Asunción **Vanessa Martinez**
Doña Mercedes **Angelina Peláez**
Sor Juana **Lizzie Martinez**
Blanca **Amanda Álvarez**
Eusebio **Said Martinez**

and Abel Salas, Marco Mondragon (Bus Drivers), Jose Reyes (Van Driver), Claudia Benitez (Woman on Bus), Juan Ignacio de Anda (Tito), Jose Reyes, Jr. (Grande), Emmanuel Gonzalez (Chico), Dave Ortiz (Rufino),

Mary Steenburgen

Maggie Gyllenhaal

Blanca Loaria (Socorro), Bruno Bichir (Diomedes), Fredi Bogota (Gustavo), Héctor Mújica (Ruben), Guillermo Iván (Reynaldo), Juan Carlos Vives (Búho), Martha Higareda (Celia), Tony Marcin (Celia's Mother), Lourdes Echevarría, Lourdes Perez (Vendedora), Norma Moreno, Priscilla Corral (Dependienta), Isalas Ramirez (Boletero), Hilário Silva, Ceasar Rodriguez, Rad Wolf, Arturo Salazar (Guides), Pedro Armendáriz, Jr. (Ernesto), Victor Jauregui (Wilfrido), Alejandro Basurto (Vincente), Leonel Rendon (Hermino), Fernando Cervantes (Felix), Miguel Rodarte (Oscar), David Hevia (Iván), Felipe Ferández del Paso (Don Mercurio), Isabel Herrera (Number Girl), Ramoncita Lopez (Caseworker), Guillermo Iván Dueñas (Reynaldo)

Six American women bide their time living in South America while awaiting the okay allowing them to adopt babies.

Daryl Hannah

Rita Moreno PHOTOS COURTESY OF IFC FILMS

Jimmy Fallon, Jason Biggs

ANYTHING ELSE

Christina Ricci, Stockard Channing, Woody Allen

(DREAMWORKS) Producer, Letty Aronson; Executive Producer, Stephen Tenenbaum; Director/Screenplay, Woody Allen; Co-Executive Producers, Jack Rollins, Charles H. Joffe; Co-Producer, Helen Robin; Photography, Darius Khondji; Designer, Santo Loquasto; Costumes, Laura Jean Shannon; Editor, Alisa Lepselter; Casting, Juliet Taylor, Laura Rosenthal; a Perdido Production, presented in association with Gravier Productions; Dolby; Panavision; Technicolor; Rated R; 108 minutes; Release date: September 19, 2003

Cast
David Dobel **Woody Allen**
Jerry Falk **Jason Biggs**
Paula **Stockard Channing**
Harvey **Danny DeVito**
Bob **Jimmy Fallon**
Amanda **Christina Ricci**
Manager **Fisher Stevens**
Pip's Comic **Anthony Arkin**
Brooke **KaDee Strickland**
Herself **Diana Krall**
Psychiatrist **William Hill**
Movie Theatre Patron **Maurice Sonnenberg**
Hotel Desk Clerk **Kenneth Edelson**
Dr. Reed **David Conrad**
Bill **Joseph Lyle Taylor**
Connie **Erica Leerhsen**
Ray Polito **Adrian Grenier**
Car Thugs **Anthony J. Ribustello, Ray Garvey**
Emily **Wynter Kullman**
Ralph **Zach McLarty**
Cab Driver **Ralph Pope**

Jerry Falk, an aspiring writer, falls in love with the unconventional Amanda, while receiving advice on life and love from the neurotic David Dobel.

Christina Ricci, Jason Biggs PHOTOS COURTESY OF DREAMWORKS

Dennis Quiad, Kristen Stewart, Sharon Stone, Ryan Wilson PHOTO COURTESY OF TOUCHSTONE

COLD CREEK MANOR

(TOUCHSTONE) Producers, Annie Stewart, Mike Figgis; Executive Producers, Lata Ryan, Richard Jefferies; Director/Music, Mike Figgis; Screenplay, Richard Jefferies; Photography, Declan Quinn; Designer, Leslie Dilley; Costumes, Marie-Sylvie Deveau; Editor, Dylan Tichenor; Casting, Amanda Mackey Johnson, Cathy Sandrich Gelfond; a Red Mullet production; Dolby; Technicolor; Rated R; 119 minutes; Release date: September 19, 2003

Cast

Cooper Tilson **Dennis Quaid**
Leah Tilson **Sharon Stone**
Dale Massie **Stephen Dorff**
Ruby **Juliette Lewis**
Kristen Tilson **Kristen Stewart**
Jesse Tilson **Ryan Wilson**
Sheriff Ferguson **Dana Eskelson**
Mr. Massie **Christopher Plummer**
Ray Pinski **Simon Reynolds**
Ellen Pinski **Kathleen Duborg**
Stephanie Pinski **Paual Brancati**

and Aidan Devine (Skip Linton), Wayen Robson (Stan Holland), Jordan Pettle (Declan), Ray Paisley (Dink), Shauna Black (Janice), Peter Outerbridge (Dave Miller), Karen Glave (Tina), Leslie Dilley, George Buza (Antique Dealers), Paulette Sinclair (Crossing Guard), Shawn Korson, Robert Maratta, Tommy Brewster (Gang Members), John Bayliss (Team Eliminator), Daniel Kash, Timm Zemanek, Stephanie Morgenstern, Raoul Bhaneja, J. Bogdan (Locals), Stan Coles (Preacher), Jill Fleischmann (Clerk), Gary Johnson, Brian Kaulbeck, John C. Warwick (Police Officers)

The Tilsons purchase a crumbling house in New York State where they are plagued by a series of terrifying incidents.

DUPLEX

(MIRAMAX) Producers, Ben Stiller, Stuart Cornfeld, Jeremy Kramer, Nancy Juvonen, Drew Barrymore; Executive Producers, Bob Weinstein, Harvey Weinstein, Meryl Poster, Jennifer Wachtell, Richard N. Gladstein, Alan C. Blomquist; Director, Danny DeVito; Screenplay/Co-Producer, Larry Doyle; Photography, Anastas S. Michos; Designer, Robin Standefer; Costumes, Joe Aulisi; Music, David Newman; Editor, Lynzee Klingman; Casting, Margery Simkin; a Red Hour Films/Flower Films production; Dolby; Deluxe color; Rated PG-13; 89 minutes; Release date: September 26, 2003

Cast

Alex Rose **Ben Stiller**
Nancy Kendricks **Drew Barrymore**
Mrs. Connelly **Eileen Essel**
Kenneth **Harvey Fierstein**
Coop **Justin Theroux**
Chick **James Remar**
Officer Dan **Robert Wisdom**
Jean **Swoosie Kurtz**
Herman **Wallace Shawn**

and Maya Rudolph (Tara), Amber Valletta (Celine), Cheryl Klein (Ginger), Tim Maculan (Terrence), Jackie Titone (Bartender), Eugene Lazarev (Mr. Dzerzhinsky), Kumar Pallana (Indian Restaurant Owner), Philip Perlman (Phil), Gary Riotto (Drug Dealer), Michelle Krusiec (Dr. Kang), Margie Loomis, Linda Porter (Old Biddies), Edward Edwards (Antique Dealer), Louis Giambalvo (Pharmacist), Tracey Walter (Pharmacy Customer), John Hamburg (Mr. Friedman), Christina Kirk (Mrs. Friedman), Jenette Goldstein (Moderator), Leyna Nguyen (Newscaster), Chuma Hunter-Gault (Mailroom Guy), Jim Castillo (Weatherman), Michael Fahn (Sneezer on Train), Robert R. Deen (Caterer), Christopher Doyle (Tavern Bartender), Christine La Fontaine (Don Piper Fan #1), Joey Banks (Police Officer), Geraldine Hughes (Receptionist), Danny DeVito (Narrator)

Newlyweds Alex and Nancy move into a spacious Brooklyn brownstone where they are driven so crazy by the demanding, elderly lady living in a rent-controlled apartment upstairs that they plot to get rid of her.

Ben Stiller, Drew Barrymore PHOTO COURTESY OF MIRAMAX

The Rock, Seann William Scott, Ernie Reyes Jr.

THE RUNDOWN

(UNIVERSAL/COLUMBIA) Producers, Kevin Misher, Marc Abraham, Karen Glasser; Director, Peter Berg; Screenplay, R.J. Stewart, James Vanderbilt; Story, R.J. Stewart; Executive Producers, Vincent McMahon, Ric Kidney; Photography, Tobias Schliessler; Designer, Tom Duffield; Costumes, Louise Mingenbach; Editor, Richard Pearson; Music, Harry Gregson-Williams; Stunts/Fight Coordinator, Andy Cheng; Casting, Lynn Kressel; a Misher Films/Strike Entertainment production, presented in association with WWE Films, in association with IM3 Entertainment; Dolby; Super 35 Widescreen; Color; Rated PG-13; 104 minutes; Release date: September 26, 2003

Cast

Beck **The Rock**
Travis **Seann William Scott**
Mariana **Rosario Dawson**
Hatcher **Christopher Walken**
Declan **Ewan Bremner**
Harvey **Jon Gries**
Walker **William Lucking**
Manito **Ernie Reyes, Jr.**
Swenson **Stuart Wilson**
Naylor **Dennis Keiffer**
Henshaw **Garrett Warren**
Head Indian Tracker **Toby Holguin**
Martin **Paul Power**
Knappmiller **Stephen Bishop**
Mullaire **Chuck Norman**
Jamal **Jamal Duff**
Coggeshall **John Duff**
Kambui **Jeff Chase**
Rudy **Jackson Price**

and Anthony Diaz-Perez (Paymaster), Todd Stashwick (Quadrant Manager), Marcio Moraes (Guard), Tony Lima (Whipped Miner), James K. Miranda (Supply Unimog Passenger), David Prak (Rebel), Ron Cummings (Quadrant Captain), Bruno Serrano (Quadrant Captain), Donald R.

The Rock, Seann William Scott

Jankiewicz, Patrick A. Jankiewicz (Goons), Filpe Teixeira, Albertto Teixeira, Reginaldo Santana (Kontiki Rebels), Mary Joy (Professor), Arnold Schwarzenegger (Guy Leaving Club)

A hired debt collector, Beck, is sent to South America to retrieve a wise-ass double dealer named Travis, who holds the key to a valuable treasure and is therefore an asset to millionaire miner Hatcher.

Rosario Dawson, The Rock PHOTOS COURTESY OF UNIVERSAL/COLUMBIA

UNDER THE TUSCAN SUN

(TOUCHSTONE) Producers, Tom Sternberg, Audrey Wells; Executive Producers, Laura Fattori, Sandy Kroopf, Mark Gill; Director/Screen Story and Screenplay, Audrey Wells; Based on the book by Frances Mayes; Photography, Geoffrey Simpson; Designer, Stephen McCabe; Costumes, Nicoletta Ercole; Editors, Andrew Marcus, Arthur Coburn; Music, Christophe Beck; Casting, Linda Lowy, John Brace (U.S.), Beatrice Kruger (Italy); a Tinnick Films production, a Blue Gardenia production; Dolby; Panavision; Technicolor; Rated PG-13; 113 minutes; Release date: September 26, 2003

Cast

Frances Mayes **Diane Lane**
Patti **Sandra Oh**
Katherine **Lindsay Duncan**
Marcello **Raoul Bova**
Martini **Vincent Riotta**
Old Man with Flowers **Mario Monicelli**
Placido **Roberto Nobile**
Fiorella **Anita Zagaria**
Nona Cardinale **Evelina Gori**
Chiara **Giulia Steigerwalt**
Pawel **Pawel Szajda**
Jerzy **Valentine Pelka**
Zbigniew **Sasa Vulicevic**
Nino **Massimo Sarchielli**
Signora Raguzzi **Claudia Gerini**
Contessa **Laura Pestellini**
Ed **David Sutcliffe**
Grace **Kate Walsh**
Nasty Man **Don McManus**
Colleague **Matt Salinger**
Author **Elden Henson**
San Francisco Guy **John Radzik**
Head Mover **Geoffrey Rivas**
Apartment Manager **Jack Kehler**
Tour Member Rodney **Dan Bucatinsky**
David Tour Guide **Kristoffer Winters**
Seat Mate **Sean Kaplan**
Gianni **Nuccio Siano**
Gianni's Daughter **Malva Guicheney**
German Woman **Marit Nissen**
German Man **Ralph Palka**
Dinner Guest **Marco Bonini**
Marcello's Cousin **Domenico Gennaro**
Marcello's Niece **Romina Cansanella**
Positano Policeman **Emiliano Novelli**
Choir Singer **Francesca Petrucci**
Signor Martini's Wife **Chiara Porti**

and Jeffery Jones, Giuseppe Buondonno, Vittorio Pecchillo, Andrea Saran, Giulia Bernardini (Gay Tourists), Marco Fubini, Davide Paganini, Pierfilippo Macchiavelli (Rome Men), Salvatore Lazzaro, Sandro Dori, Marcello Marzialli (Contractor), Jeffrey Tambor (Divorce Lawyer)

Diane Lane, Raoul Bova

San Francisco writer Frances Mayers, trying to recover from a messy divorce, impulsively buys a run-down villa while on vacation in Tuscany, with the intention of fixing it up and making it her new home.

Diane Lane, Giulia Steigerwalt, Pawel Szajda

Sandra Oh, Kate Walsh, Diane Lane

Lindsay Duncan, Diane Lane PHOTOS COURTESY OF TOUCHSTONE

Denzel Washington, John Billingsley

Dean Cain, Sanaa Lathan

Eva Mendes, Denzel Washington PHOTOS COURTESY OF MGM

OUT OF TIME

(MGM) Producers, Neal H. Moritz, Jesse B'Franklin; Executive Producers, Kevin Reidy, Damien Saccani, Jon Berg, Alex Gartner; Director, Carl Franklin; Screenplay, Dave Collard; Photography, Theo Van de Sande; Designer, Paul Peters; Costumes, Sharen Davis; Editors, Carole Kravetz, Aykanian; Music, Graeme Revell; Casting, Mali Finn; an Original Film/ Monarch Pictures production, Dolby; Panavision; Deluxe color; Rated PG-13; 105 minutes; Release date: October 3, 2003

Sanaa Lathan

Cast

Matt Lee Whitlock **Denzel Washington**
Alex Diaz Whitlock **Eva Mendes**
Ann Merai Harrison **Sanaa Lathan**
Chris Harrison **Dean Cain**
Chae **John Billingsley**
Tony Dalton **Robert Baker**
Cabot **Alex Carter**
Deputy Baste **Antoni Corone**
Agent Stark **Terry Loughlin**
Dr. Donovan **Nora Dunn**
Dr. Frieland **James Murtaugh**
Judy Anderson **Peggy Sheffield**
Judy's Mom **Evelyn Brooks**
Hotel Clerk **Eric Hissom**
Living Gift Salesman **Tom Hilmann**
Dr. Shider **Parris Buckner**
Dental Assistant **Arian Ash**

and Mike Pniewski (Agent White), Veryl E. Jones (Agent Fetzer), Tim Ware (Fire Chief), Jesse B'Franklin (Ramona), Edward Amatrudo (Arson Investigator), Neil Brown, Jr. (Morgue Attendant), Elena Maria Garcia (Bartender), David Negron (Sketch Artist), O.L. Duke (Detective Bronze), Sharlene Garcia (Sharlene), Ronald J. Madoff (Detective), Steve Raulerson (Man Serving Divorce Papers), Suzanne Grant (Screaming Woman), Dorothy A. Healy (Woman in Lobby)

After a double homicide, Florida police chief Matt Whitlock comes to the realization that as the details of the case begin to surface, all of the evidence points to him.

THE SCHOOL OF ROCK

(PARAMOUNT) Producer, Scott Rudin; Executive Producers, Steve Nicolaides, Scott Aversano; Director, Richard Linklater; Screenplay, Mike White; Photography, Rogier Stoffers; Designer, Jeremy Conway; Costumes, Karen Patch; Editor, Sandra Adair; Music, Craig Wedren; Music Supervisor, Randall Poster; Song: "School of Rock" by Mike White and Sammy James Jr./performed by School of Rock; Casting, Ilene Starger; a Scott Rudin production; Dolby; Deluxe color; Rated PG-13; 108 minutes; Release date: October 3, 2003

Maryam Hassan, Caitlin Hale, Jack Black

Jack Black

Jack Black

Cast

Dewey Finn ("Mr. Schneebly") **Jack Black**
Rosalie Mullins **Joan Cusack**
Ned Schneebly **Mike White**
Patty Di Marco **Sarah Silverman**
Zack Mooneyham, the Lead Guitar Player **Joey Gaydos, Jr.**
Tomika, the Shy Singer **Maryam Hassan**
Freddy Jones, the Drummer **Kevin Clark**
Katie, the Bass Player **Rebecca Brown**
Lawrence, the Keyboard Player **Robert Tsai**
Marta, the Backup Singer **Caitlin Hale**
Alicia, the Backup Singer **Aleisha Allen**
Summer Hathaway, the Band Manager **Miranda Cosgrove**
Billy, the Band Stylist **Brian Falduto**
Gordon, the Special Effects Wiz **Zachary Infante**
Marco, the Computer Genius **James Hosey**
Frankie, the Band's Head of Security **Angelo Massagli**
Leonard, Band Security **Cole Hawkins**
Eleni, the Groupie **Veronica Afflerbach**
Michelle, the Groupie **Jordan-Claire Green**
Theo **Adam Pascal**
Neil **Lucas Papaelias**
Doug **Chris Stack**
Spider **Lucas Babin**

Joey Gaydos Jr., Kevin Clark, Jack Black, Rebecca Brown

Joan Cusack, Jack Black

Robert Tsai, Joey Gaydos Jr., Jack Black, Kevin Clark, Rebecca Brown

and Suzzanne Douglas (Tomika's Mother), Eron Otcasek, Carlos Velazquez (Musicians), Kimberly Grisby (Mrs. Sheinkopf), Lee Wilkof (Mr. Green), Kate McGregory-Stewart (Mrs. Lemmons), Wally Dunn (Gym Teacher), Tim Hopper (Zack's Father), Michael Dominguez-Rudolph (Art Student), Crash Cortez (Max), Nicky Katt (Razor), John E. Highsmith (Tony), Heather Goldenhersh (Sheila), Timothy "Speed" Levitch (Waiter), Scott Graham (Punk Rock Guy), Sharon Washington (Alicia's Mother), Kim Brockington (Leonard's Mother), Marty Murphy (Concerned Father), Kathleen McNenny (Freddy's Mother), Joanna P. Adler (Summer's Mother), Robert Lin (Lawrence's Father), Barry Shurchin (Cop), MacIntyre Dixon (Bus Driver), Amy Sedaris (Mrs. Haynish), Mary Fortune (Teacher's Assistant), Mandy Siegfried (Employee), Elsa Pugliese (Concert Goer), Carlos J. Da Silva (Security Guard), Ian O'Malley (Radio Exec), Chris Line (Radio DJ), Kyle Meaney (Toby), Frank Whaley (Event Coordinator)

Mike White, Sarah Silverman

Badly in need of some cash, Dewey Finn impulsively accepts a substitute position using the name of his best friend Ned and proceeds to turn his classroom of kids into a rock group so he can enter them in a Battle of the Bands competition.

Jack Black, Barry Shurchin, Mike White, Joan Cusack, Sarah Silverman

Veronica Afflerbach, Jordan-Claire Green, Jack Black PHOTOS COURTESY OF PARAMOUNT

THE STATION AGENT

(MIRAMAX) Producers, Mary Jane Skalski, Robert May, Kathryn Tucker; Director/Screenplay, Tom McCarthy; Photography, Oliver Bokelberg; Designer, John Paino; Costumes, Jeanne Dupont; Music, Stephen Trask; Music Supervisor, Mary Ramos, Michelle Kuznetsky; Editor, Tom McArdle; Casting, Hopkins, Smith and Barden; a SenArt Films Production in association with Next Wednesday; Dolby; Color; Rated R; 88 minutes; Release date: October 3, 2003

Cast

Finbar McBride **Peter Dinklage**
Olivia Harris **Patricia Clarkson**
Joe Oramas **Bobby Cannavale**
Emily **Michelle Williams**
Chris **Jayce Bartok**
Henry Styles **Paul Benjamin**
Store Customer **Jase Blankfort**
Cashier **Paula Garcés**
Carl **Josh Pais**
Louis Tiboni **Richard Kind**
Patty at the Good to Go **Lynn Cohen**
Cleo **Raven Goodwin**
Janice **Marla Sucharetza**
Danny **Joe Lo Truglio**
David **John Slattery**
Pappy's Waitress **Maile Flanagan**
Girl in Bar **Sarah Bolger**
Mrs. Kahn **Ileen Getz**
Jacob **Jeremy Bergman**
"What About Blimps" Girl **Annie Del Moro**
"Blimps Are Cool" Boy **Carlos Rosas**

After inheriting a train depot in a far off corner of New Jersey, Finbar McBride sets up house in the building, hoping to be left alone, only to find himself becoming unlikely friends with a troubled woman and an affable roadside vendor.

Peter Dinklage, Patricia Clarkson, Bobby Cannavale

Bobby Cannavale, Patricia Clarkson

Michelle Williams, Peter Dinklage PHOTOS COURTESY OF MIRAMAX

WONDERLAND

(LIONS GATE) Producers, Holly Wiersma, Michael Paseornek; Executive Producers, Tom Ortenberg, Peter Block, Marc Butan, Michael Burns, Randall Emmett, George Furla, Julie Yorn Kleidman; Director, James Cox; Screenplay, James Cox, Captain Mauzner, Todd Samovitz, Loriston Scott; Co-Producers, Scott Putman, Ali Forman; Photography, Michael Grady; Designer, Franco-Giacomo Carbone; Costumes, Maryam Malakpour, Kate Healey; Music, Cliff Martinez; Music Supervisors, Matt Aberle, David Falzone, Joel C. High; Editor, Jeff McEvoy; Casting, Barbara Fiorentino, Rebecca Mangieri; a Holly Wiersma/Lions Gate Films production; Dolby; Color; Rated R; 99 minutes; Release date: October 3, 2003

Eric Bogosian, Val Kilmer

Kate Bosworth, Lisa Kudrow

Josh Lucas, Dylan McDermott

Cast
John Holmes **Val Kilmer**
Sharon Holmes **Lisa Kudrow**
Dawn Schiller **Kate Bosworth**
David Lind **Dylan McDermott**
Ron Launius **Josh Lucas**
Louis Cruz **Franky G**
Billy Deverell **Tim Blake Nelson**
Sally Hansen **Carrie Fisher**
Eddie Nash **Eric Bogosian**
Sam Nico **Ted Levine**
Billy Ward **M.C. Gainey**
Greg Diles **Faizon Love**

Val Kilmer

and Christina Applegate (Susan Launius), Natasha Gregson Wagner (Barbara Richardson), Janeane Garofalo (Joy Miller), Louis Lombardi (Slim Jim), Chris Ellis (Captain Nimziki), Tess Parker (Chrissy), Julianne Steiger (Janet), Kim Mariner (Reporter), Michelle Borth (Sonia), George Leonardopoulas (Tracy), Joliegh Pulsonetii (Alexa), Joel Michaely (Bruce), Stephanie Roth (Biker Girl), Russell Sams (Cherokee), Chris Cioffi (Letterman Meathead), David Solomini (Guy at Party), Scott McNairy (Jack), Michael Pitt (Gopher), Alexis Dziena (Gopher's Girlfriend), Karen Lakritz (Bartender), Steve Cox (Guy at Bar), Paris Hilton (Barbie)

The true story of how former porn star John Holmes became involved in an ill-fated robbery that led to murder.

Kate Bosworth, Val Kilmer PHOTOS COURTESY OF LIONS GATE

MYSTIC RIVER

(WARNER BROS.) Producers, Robert Lorenz, Judie G. Hoyt, Clint Eastwood; Executive Producer, Bruce Berman; Director/Music, Clint Eastwood; Screenplay, Brian Helgeland; Based on the novel by Dennis Lehane; Photography, Tom Stern; Designer, Henry Bumstead; Costumes, Deborah Hopper; Editor, Joel Cox; a Malpaso production, presented in association with Village Roadshow Pictures and NPV Entertainment; Dolby; Panavision; Technicolor; Rated R; 137 minutes; Release date: October 8, 2003

Cast

Jimmy Markum	**Sean Penn**
Dave Boyle	**Tim Robbins**
Sean Devine	**Kevin Bacon**
Whitey Powers	**Laurence Fishburne**
Celeste Boyle	**Marcia Gay Harden**
Annabeth Markum	**Laura Linney**
Val Savage	**Kevin Chapman**
Brendan Harris	**Thomas Guiry**
Katie Markum	**Emmy Rossum**
Silent Ray Harris	**Spencer Treat Clark**
John O'Shea	**Andrew Mackin**
Nick Savage	**Adam Nelson**
Kevin Savage	**Robert Wahlberg**
Esther Harris	**Jenny O'Hara**
Driver	**John Doman**
Young Dave	**Cameron Bowen**
Young Jimmy	**Jason Kelly**
Young Sean	**Connor Paolo**
Jimmy's Father	**Bruce Page**
Sean's Father	**Miles Herter**
Michael Boyle	**Cayden Boyd**
Lauren Devine	**Tori Davis**
Pete	**Jonathan Togo**
Funeral Director	**Shawn Fitzgibbon**
FBI Agent Birden	**Will Lyman**
Nadine Markum	**Celine du Tertre**
Eve Pigeon	**Ari Graynor**
Diane Cestra	**Zabeth Russell**
Drew Pigeon	**Joe Stapleton**

Sean Penn (center)

Mrs. Prior	**Susan Willis**
Lt. Friel	**Jose Ramon Rosario**
CSS Tech	**Tom Kemp**
Medical Examiner	**Charles Broderick**
Lab Technician	**Lonnie Farmer**
Trooper Jenny Coughlin	**Celeste Oliva**
Loud Mouth Cop	**Bates Wilder**
Cop at Barricade	**Douglass Bowen Flynn**
Neighbor at Barricade	**Bill Thorpe**
Cop in Park	**Matty Blake**
Dave's Friend in Bar	**Ken Cheeseman**
Detective	**Scott Winters**
Headstone Salesman	**Thomas Derrah**
Reporter	**Jim Smith**
Handcuffed Man	**Patrick Shea**
Solicitor in Car	**Duncan Putney**
Communion Priest	**Ed O'Keefe**
'75 Police Officer	**Dave Zee Garison**
'75 Reporter	**Michael McGovern**
Liquor Store Owner	**Eli Wallach**
Theo	**Kevin Conway**

Three men, haunted by a past incident during their childhood in which one of them was abducted and molested, are thrown together years later by a brutal murder.

2003 Academy Award–winner for Best Actor (Sean Penn) and Best Supporting Actor (Tim Robbins). This film received additional Oscar nominations for picture, director, supporting actress (Marcia Gay Harden), and screenplay (adaptation).

Sean Penn, Tim Robbins

Tim Robbins, Marcia Gay Harden

Laurence Fishburne

Kevin Bacon, Laurence Fishburne

Kevin Bacon, Sean Penn, Laura Linney

Laura Linney, Marcia Gay Harden

Emmy Rossum, Sean Penn

Adam Nelson, Kevin Chapman, Sean Penn

Sean Penn, Kevin Bacon

Tim Robbins PHOTOS COURTESY OF WARNER BROS.

Liam Aiken, Brittany Moldowan

GOOD BOY!

(MGM) Producers, Lisa Henson, Kristine Belson; Executive Producer, Stephanie Allain; Director/Screenplay, John Hoffman; Screen Story, Zeke Richardson, John Hoffman; Based on *Dogs From Outer Space* by Zeke Richardson; Photography, James Glennon; Designer, Jerry Wanek; Music, Mark Mothersbaugh; Editor, Craig P. Herring; Co-Producer, Bill Bannerman; Casting, Deborah Aquila, Tricia Wood; Stunts, Randy Lee; a Jim Henson Pictures production; Rated PG; 88 minutes; Release date: October 10, 2003

Cast

Mrs. Baker **Molly Shannon**
Owen Baker **Liam Aiken**
Mr. Baker **Kevin Nealon**
Connie Fleming **Brittany Moldowan**
Mr. Leone **George Touliatos**
Ms. Ryan **Patti Allan**
Frankie **Hunter Elliot**
Fred **Mikhael Speidel**

and Benjamin Ratner (Wilson's Dad), Peter Fleming (Wilson's Other Dad), Paul C. Vogt (Bob the Dog Catcher), Brenda M. Crichlow (Mrs. Fleming), D. Harlan Cutshall (Mr. Fleming), Chaka White, Nicola Anderson (Women at the Pound), Ted Friend (TV Anchorman), Susan Bain (House Bidder),

Voice Cast

Hubble **Matthew Broderick**
Barbara Ann **Delta Burke**
Wilson **Donald Faison**
The Greater Dane's Henchman **Cheech Marin**
Nelly **Brittany Murphy**
The Greater Dane **Vanessa Redgrave**
Shep **Carl Reiner**

and the Dogs: Flynn, Mallie, Defford (Hubble), Lita, Lexi (Wilson), Banner, Scandal (Barbara Ann), Motif, Imp (Nelly), Odie, Willie (Shep), Valentino (The Greater Dane), Spiri (The Greater Dane's Henchman)

Kevin Nealon, Molly Shannon, Hubble, Liam Aiken

A lonely 12-year-old boy finds a lost dog and discovers that the pooch can not only talk, but also has been sent to Earth from the Dog Star Sirius to make sure that all canines have fulfilled their mission to colonize and dominate the planet.

Liam Aiken, Hubble PHOTOS COURTESY OF MGM

INTOLERABLE CRUELTY

(UNIVERSAL) Producers, Ethan Coen, Brian Grazer; Executive Producers, James Jacks, Sean Daniel; Director, Joel Coen; Screenplay, Robert Ramsey, Matthew Stone, Ethan Coen, Joel Coen; Story, Robert Ramsey, Matthew Stone, John Romano; Photography, Roger Deakins; Designer; Leslie McDonald; Costumes, Mary Zophres; Co-Producers, John Cameron, James Whitaker; Music, Carter Burwell; Editor, Roderick Jaynes; Casting, Ellen Chenoweth; an Imagine Entertainment presentation of a Brian Grazer production inassociation with Alphaville; Dolby; Technicolor; Rated PG-13; 100 minutes; Release date: October 10, 2003

Paul Adelstein, Edward Herrmann, George Clooney

Billy Bob Thornton, Catherine Zeta-Jones

Cast

Miles Massey **George Clooney**
Marilyn Rexroth **Catherine Zeta-Jones**
Donovan Donaly **Geoffrey Rush**
Gus Petch **Cedric the Entertainer**
Rex Rexroth **Edward Herrmann**
Freddy Bender **Richard Jenkins**
Howard D. Doyle **Billy Bob Thornton**
Wrigley **Paul Adelstein**
Sarah Sorkin **Julia Duffy**
Heinz, the Baron Krass von Espy **Jonathan Hadary**
Herb Myerson **Tom Aldredge**
Bonnie Donaly **Stacey Travis**
Ollie Olerud **Jack Kyle**
Wheezy Joe **Irwin Keyes**
Mrs. Gutman **Judith Drake**
Mr. Gutman **Royce Applegate**
Mrs. Gutman's Lawyer **George Ives**

and Booth Colman (Gutman Trial Lawyer), Kristin Dattilo (Rex's Young Woman), Wendle Josepher (Miles' Receptionist), Mary Pat Gleason (Nero's Waitress), Mia Cottet (Ramona Barcelona), Kiersten Warren (Claire O'Mara), Rosey Brown, Ken Sagoes, Dale E. Turner (Gus's Pals), Douglas Fisher (Maitre d'), Nicholas Shaffer (Waiter), Isabell Monk O'Connor (Judge Marva Munson), Mary Gillis (Court Reporter), Colin Linden (Father Scott), Julie Osburn (Stewardess), Gary Marshal (Las Vegas Waiter), Blake Clark (Convention Secretary), Allan Trautman (Convention Lawyer), Kate Luyben, Kitana Baker, Camille Anderson, Tamie Sheffield, Bridget Marquardt, Emma Harrison (Santa Fe Tarts), John Bliss (Mr. MacKinnon), Patrick Thomas O'Brien, Sean Fenton (Bailiffs), Bruce Campbell (Soap Opera Actor)

Geoffrey Rush

Miles Massey, a cunning divorce attorney famous for winning cases even for the most guilty of clients, meets his match in the beautiful Marilyn Rexroth, who is set on getting back at Miles after being deprived of money in her divorce settlement.

George Clooney, Catehrine Zeta-Jones PHOTOS COURTESY OF UNIVERSAL

KILL BILL VOL. 1

(MIRAMAX) Producers, Lawrence Bender, Quentin Tarantino; Executive Producers, Harvey Weinstein, Bob Weinstein, Erica Steinberg, E. Bennett Walsh; Director/Screenplay, Quentin Tarantino; Photography, Robert Richardson; Designer, Yohei Taneda, David Wasco; Costumes, Kumiko Ogawa, Catherine Marie Thomas; Editor, Sally Menke; Music, The RZA; Visual Effects, Centro Digital Pictures; Special Makeup Effects, K.N.B. EFX Group; Anime Sequence, Production I.G.; Martial Arts Advisor, Yuen Woo-ping; Fight Choreographer, Sonny Chiba; Stunts, Keith Adams; Casting, Johanna Ray; a Band Apart production; Dolby; Panavision; Deluxe color; Rated R; 110 minutes; Release date: October 10, 2003

Cast

The Bride **Uma Thurman**
O-Ren Ishii **Lucy Liu**
Vernita Green **Vivica A. Fox**
Budd **Michael Madsen**
Elle Driver **Daryl Hannah**
Bill **David Carradine**
Hattori Hanzo **Sonny Chiba**

Uma Thurman

Daryl Hannah, Vivica A. Fox, Michael Madsen, Lucy Liu

Uma Thurman, Daryl Hannah

Gordon Liu (center)

Gogo Yubari **Chiaki Kuriyama**
Johnny Mo **Gordon Liu Chia-hui**
Sheriff **Earl McGraw**
Earl McGraw **Michael Parks**
Sofie Fatale **Julie Dreyfus**
Buck **Michael Bowen**
Boss Tanaka **Jun Kunimura**
Bald Guy **Kenji Oba**
Proprietor **Yuki Kazamatsuri**
Edgar McGraw **James Parks**
Boss Ozawah **Akaji Maro**
Boss Honda **Goro Daimon**
Boss Benta **Shun Sugata**
The Deadly Viper Assassination Squad **The 5, 6, 7, 8's (Sachiko Fujii, Yoshiko Yamaguchi, Ronnie Yoshiko Fujiyama)**
Charlie Brown **Sakichi Sato**
Trucker **Jonathan Loughran**
Tokyo Businessman **Yoshiyuki Morishita**
Miki (Crazy 88 #1) **Tetsuro Shimaguchi**
Boss Orgami **Zhiang Jin Zhan**
Nikki Bell **Ambrosia Kelley**
Okinawa Airline Ticket Agent **Shu Lan Tuan**

and Kazuki Kitamura, Yoji Boba Tanaka, Issei Takahashi, So Yamanaka, Juri Manase (Crazy 88s), Chao Ren, Li Guo Hai, Qing Peng, Chen Jia Hu, Li Qu, Wang Guo Quan, Dai Wei Nan, Li Xiang, Wang Xia, Deng Guo Qing, Li Xiao Qiang, Wang Xiao Wen, Gao Fei, Ling Fei, Wang Young Xin, Gong Xiao Li, Liu Hong Ling, Xiao Hong, Hai Shan, Liu Ruo Xian, Xiao Hui, Hao Wan Jun, Liu Rui, Zhao Yun, Kang Jiang Qi, Qu Cheng Wei, Zhou Jie, Li Feng Mei, Ning Qing Feng, Zhuang Yuan Zhang (Crazy 88 Fight Team)

Chiaki Kuriyama, Lucy Liu, Julie Dreyfus

Vivica A. Fox

Uma Thurman (center)

Uma Thurman PHOTOS COURTESY OF MIRAMAX

Uma Thurman, Chiaki Kuriyama

Left for dead at her wedding by her former cohorts, the Deadly Viper Assassination Squad, the Bride sets out to eliminate those responsible for the carnage. This is the first half of a two-part film, with *Kill Bill Vol. 2* premiering on April 16, 2004.

PIECES OF APRIL

(UNITED ARTISTS) Producers, John Lyons, Gary Winick, Alexis Alexanian; Executive Producers, Jonathan Sehring, Caroline Kaplan, John Sloss; Director/Screenplay, Peter Hedges; Photography, Tami Reiker; Designer, Rick Butler; Costumes, Laura Bauer; Music, Stephin Merritt; Music Supervisor, Linda Cohen; Casting, Bernard Telsey, David Vaccari, Will Cantler; an IFC Productions presentation of an InDiGent production in association with Kalkaska Productions; Dolby; Color; Rated PG-13; 81 minutes; Release date: October 17, 2003

Cast

April Burns **Katie Holmes**
Joy Burns **Patricia Clarkson**
Bobby **Derek Luke**
Beth Burns **Alison Pill**
Timmy Burns **John Gallagher, Jr.**
Grandma Dottie **Alice Drummond**
Evette **Lillias White**
Latrell **SisQo**
Eugene **Isiah Whitlock, Jr.**
Tyrone **Armando Riesco**
Jim Burns **Oliver Platt**
Wayne **Sean Hayes**
Half Asleep Man **Vitali Baganov**
Man in Mohair Sweater **Adrian Martinez**
Tish **Susan Bruce**
Boy on Bicycle **Jamari Richardson**
Woman in Stairwell **Leila Danette**

and Stephen Chen (Lee Luong Tan), Sally Leung Bayer (Lee Quong Tan), Marcus Lovett (Parade Announcer), Jack Chen (Lee Quong), Jacqueline Dai (Lee Lang), Rosa Luo (Lee Wai Yam), Birdie M. Hale (Woman Outside Bodega), Christine Todino (Waitress), Anney Giobbe (Young Mother), Elizabeth Douglass (Young Girl), Rusty DeWees (Joy's Biker Guy), Vincent Roselli (Timmy's Biker Guy)

Katie Holmes, Sean Hayes

Derek Luke

Patricia Clarkson, Rusty DeWees

The Burns family travels to New York City to attend the Thanksgiving dinner their quirky daughter April is preparing in her West Village apartment.

This film received an Oscar nomination for supporting actress (Patricia Clarkson).

Oliver Platt   PHOTOS COURTESY OF UNITED ARTISTS

RUNAWAY JURY

(20TH CENTURY FOX) Producers, Arnon Milchan, Gary Fleder, Christopher Mankiewicz; Executive Producer, Jeffrey Downer; Director, Gary Fleder; Screenplay, Brian Koppelman, David Levien, Rick Cleveland, Matthew Chapman; Based on the novel *The Runaway Jury* by John Grisham; Photography, Robert Elswit; Designer, Nelson Coates; Costumes, Abigail Murray; Music, Christopher Young; Music Supervisor, Peter Afterman; a Regency Enterprises presentation of a New Regency production; Dolby; Super 35 Widescreen; Deluxe color; Rated PG-13; 127 minutes; Release date: October 17, 2003

Marguerite Moreau, Gene Hackman

Cast

Nick Easter **John Cusack**
Rankin Fitch **Gene Hackman**
Wendall Rohr **Dustin Hoffman**
Marlee **Rachel Weisz**
Durwood Cable **Bruce Davison**
Judge Harkin **Bruce McGill**
Lawrence Green **Jeremy Piven**
Doyle **Nick Searcy**
Garland Jankle **Stanley Anderson**
Frank Herrera **Cliff Curtis**
Janovich **Nestor Serrano**
Lamb **Leland Orser**
Vanessa Lembeck **Jennifer Beals**
Herman Grimes **Gerry Bamman**
Celeste Wood **Joanna Going**

Dustin Hoffman, Rachel Weisz

Jacob Wood **Dylan McDermott**
Lonnie Shaver **Bill Nunn**
Loreen Duke **Juanita Jennings**
Amanda Monroe **Marguerite Moreau**
Stella Hullic **Nora Dunn**
Eddie Weese **Guy Torry**
Millie Dupree **Rusty Schwimmer**
Jerry Hernandez **Luis Guzman**
Kaufman **Margo Moorer**
Birk **David Dwyer**
Raines **Michael Arata**
Rikki Coleman **Rhoda Griffis**
Sylvia Deshazo **Fahnlohnee R. Harris**

and Corri English (Lydia Deets), Jason Davis (Phillip Savelle), Xuan Van Nguyen (Henry Wu), Douglas M. Griffin (Terry Docken), Carol Sutton (Lou Dell), Deneen D. Tyler (Receptionist), Zach Hanner (Ted), Andrea Powell (Deborah), Ted Manson (Pulaski), David E. Jensen (Shamburg), Lori Heuring (Maxine), Adella Gauthier (Voodoo Shopkeeper), Afemo Omilami (SUV Driver), Barret O'Brien (Techie), Ned Bellamy (Jerome), Orlando Jones (Russell), Michelel M. Miller, Eric Paulsen, Margaret Lawhon (Reporters), Gary Grubbs (Dobbs), Lark Marie Fall (Singing Woman), Marco St. John (Daley), Henry Darrow (Sebald), Don Hendersno Baker (Thernstrom), Daniel T. Kamin (Cash), Lance E. Nichols (Agent Shield), Deacon Dawson (Hoppy Dupree), Elliott Street (Rignwald), Mike Pniewski (Strode), Joe Chrest (Owens), David Ramsey (Jimmy Hoke), Marcus Hester (Kyle Murphy), Lara Grace (Londe Decoy), Loren Kinsella (Cafe Waitress), Mark Jeffrey Miller (Vaughn), Wayne Roberts (Clerk), Harvey Reaves (Agent Crowley), Wayne Ferrera (Agent Novecki), Peter Jurasik (Professor Phelan), Shannon Eubanks (Phyllis), Celia Weston (Mrs. Brandt), Irene Ziegler (Peg Grimes), Ed Nelson (George Dressler), Bernard Hocke (Mason Foley), Mark Krasnoff (Aggressive Reporter), Christopher Mankiewicz (Bartender), Cedric Pendleton (Homeboy), Perry Brown, Don Hood, Elizabeth Omilami (Potential Jurors), Claudia Coffee, Charlie Detraz (Reporters), Sally Ann Roberts (Reporter with Cable), Stuart Greer (Kincaid), Kathy Seiden (Kathy), Jack Massey (Henry Wood)

A ruthless "jury consultant" does his best to chose the ideal jury in order to make sure that a powerful corporation will not be obliged to pay a multimillion dollar suit a widow has brought against them for providing the firearms responsible for the death of her husband.

John Cusack PHOTOS COURTESY OF 20TH CENTURY FOX

THE TEXAS CHAINSAW MASSACRE

(NEW LINE CINEMA) Producers, Michael Bay, Mike Fleiss; Executive Producers, Ted Field, Andrew Form, Brad Fuller, Guy Stodel, Jeffrey Allard; Director, Marcus Nispel; Screenplay, Scott Kosar; Based on the screenplay by Kim Henkel and Tobe Hooper; Photography, Daniel C. Pearl; Designer, Gregory Blair; Costumes, Bobbie Mannix; Editor, Glen Scantlebury; Music, Steve Jablonsky; Co-Producers, Kim Henkel, Tobe Hooper; Stunts, Anthony P. Cecere; Special Effects Coordinator, Rocky Gehr; Special Effects Makeup Artist, Scott Stoddard; a Platinum Dunes/Next Entertainment production, presented in association with Michael Bay and Radar Pictures; Dolby; Deluxe color; Rated R; 95 minutes; Release date: October 17, 2003

Cast
Erin **Jessica Biel**
Morgan **Jonathan Tucker**
Pepper **Erica Leerhsen**
Andy **Mike Vogel**
Kemper **Eric Balfour**
Thomas Hewitt (Leatherface) **Andrew Brynarski**
Sheriff Hoyt **R. Lee Ermey**

and David Dorfman (Jedidiah), Laura German (Teenage Girl), Terrence Evans (Old Monty), Marietta Marich (Luda May), Heather Kafka (Henrietta), Kathy Lamkin (Tea Lady in Trailer), Brad Leland (Big Rig Bob), Mamie Meek (Clerk), John Larroquette (Narrator)

A group of unsuspecting teens stumbles upon an insane family who take sport in butchering human beings. Remake of the 1974 film of the same name.

Jessica Biel, Mike Vogel, Erica Leerhsen, Jonathan Tucker, Eric Balfour

Eric Balfour, Jonathan Tucker, Jessica Biel, Mike Vogel, Erica Leerhsen
PHOTOS COURTESY OF NEW LINE CINEMA

Mark Ruffalo, Meg Ryan PHOTO COURTESY OF SCREEN GEMS

IN THE CUT

(SCREEN GEMS) Producers, Laurie Parker, Nicole Kidman; Executive Producers, Effie T. Brown, François Ivernel; Director, Jane Campion; Screenplay, Jane Campion, Susanna Moore; Based on the novel by Susanna Moore; Photography, Don Beebe; Designer, David Brisbin; Costumes, Beatrix Aruna Pasztor; Muisc, Hilmar Örn Hilmarsson; Music Supervisor, Laurie Parker; Casting, Billy Hopkins, Suzanne Smith, Kerry Barden, Mark Bennett; a Pathé Productions Ltd. presentation of a Laurie Parker production; U.S.-Australian; Dolby; Technicolor; Rated R; 118 minutes; Release date: October 22, 2003

Cast
Frannie Avery **Meg Ryan**
Detective Malloy **Mark Ruffalo**
Pauline **Jennifer Jason Leigh**
John Graham **Kevin Bacon**
Detective Rodriguez **Nick Damici**
Cornelius Webb **Sharrieff Pugh**
Frannie's Young Mother **Sunrise Coigney**
Frannie's Young Father **Micheal Nuccio**
Young Father's Fiance **Alison Nega**

and Dominick Aries (Attentive Husband), Susan Gardner (Perfect Wife), Heather Litteer (Angela Sands), Daniel T. Booth (Red Turtle Bartender), Patrice O'Neal (Hector, Baby Doll Dancer), Upendran Paniker (Taxi Driver), Kendra Zimmerman (Cafe Waitress), Michelle Hurst (Teacher at Frannie's School), Hal Sherman (Forensic Detective), Yaani King, Frank Harts, Sebastian Sozzi, Zach Wegner (Frannie's Students), Funda Duyal, Theo Kogan (Baby Doll Bartenders), Sandy Vital, Sharon Riggins, Karen Riggins, Nancy La Scala, Ami Goodheart (Baby Doll Dancers), Dana Lubotsky (Laundry Room Murder Witness), Jacinto Taras Riddick (Detective in Precinct), Arthur Nascarella (Captain Crosley), James Firo (Detective Halloran), Cordell Clyde (Informer), Tim House (Baby Doll Bar Customer), Julius Le Flore (Cursing Motorist), Vinny Vella, Sr. (Concerned Bystander)

Frannie Avery develops an intense sexual relationship with a detective investigating a series of brutal murders and begins to wonder just how deeply he is involved in the crimes.

RADIO

(COLUMBIA) Producers, Mike Tollin, Brian Robbins, Herbert W. Gains; Executive Producers, Todd Garner, Caitlin Scanlon; Director, Mike Tollin; Screenplay, Mike Rich; Photography, Don Burgess; Designer, Clay A. Griffith; Costumes, Denise Wingate; Music, James Horner; Music Supervisor, Laura Z. Wasserman; Editors, Chris Lebezon, Harvey Rosenstock; Casting, Margery Simkin; a Revolution Studios presentation of a Tollin/Robbins production; Dolby; Deluxe color; Rated PG; 109 minutes; Release date: October 24, 2003

Ed Harris, Cuba Gooding Jr.

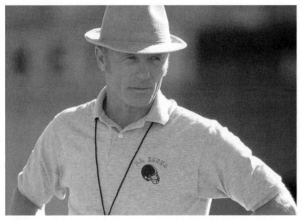
Ed Harris

Cast
James Robert "Radio" Kennedy **Cuba Gooding, Jr.**
Coach Howard Jones **Ed Harris**
Principal Daniels **Alfre Woodard**
Maggie Kennedy **S. Epatha Merkerson**
Honeycutt **Brent Sexton**
Frank **Chris Mulkey**
Mary Helen **Sarah Drew**
Johnny **Riley Smith**
Tucker **Patrick Breen**
Linda Jones **Debra Winger**
Del **Bill Roberson**
Don **Kenneth H. Callender**
Irv the Cop **Michael Harding**
Clive **Charles Garren**
Waitress **Rebecca Koon**
School Receptionist **Hi Bedford Roberson**
Young Cop **Michael Kroeker**
Football Referee **Mark Ellis**
Cop #2 **Shelley Reid**
Danny **Evan Aldrich**
Melodee **Megan Coffman**
and Benjamin L. Peters, Jr. (Hallway Kid), Leonard Wheeler (Hoop Referee), Therond Justin Adams (Laird), Othello Coleman III (Hanna Player), Bert Beatson (Hoop Player), Ty O'Farrell (Ron Wilborn), Dorothy

McDowell (Joyce Ann Yearwood), James Gooden (Teacher), Joseph Barrett (Autograph Kid), Deborah McTeer (Linda's Friend), Jamie Murdaugh (Student), William E. Lykes (Assistant Coach), Tammy Christine Arnold (Woman in Stands), Kasheem J. Peterson (Football Player), Kate Powell (Honeycutt's Squeeze), Michael Flippo (Bus Driver), James Robert "Radio" Kennedy, Harold Jones, Mike Anthony (Themselves), Rev. Eugene Cryer, Jr. (Pastor Wickland)

The true story of how a lonely, mentally handicapped man, nicknamed "Radio," found his life enriched when he was befriended by town's high school football coach and became a team mascot.

Ed Harris, Alfre Woodard

Riley Smith, Cuba Gooding Jr. PHOTOS COURTESY OF COLUMBIA

BEYOND BORDERS

(PARAMOUNT) Producers, Dan Halsted, Lloyd Phillips; Executive Producers, J. Geyer Kosinski; Director, Martin Campbell; Screenplay, Caspian Tredwell-Owen; Photography, Phil Meheux; Designer, Wolf Kroeger; Costumes, Norma Moriceau; Editor, Nicholas Beauman; Music, James Horner; Executive Music Producer, Budd Carr; Casting, Pam Dixon Mickelson; a Mandalay Picture presentation of a Camelot Pictures production; Dolby; JDC Widescreen; CFI color; Rated R; 127 minutes; Release date: October 24, 2003

Cast

Sarah Jordan **Angelina Jolie**
Dr. Nick Callahan **Clive Owen**
Charlotte Jordan **Teri Polo**
Henry Bauford **Linus Roache**
Elliott Hauser **Noah Emmerich**
Steiger **Yorick Van Wageningen**
Lawrence Bauford **Timothy West**

and Kate Trotter (Mrs. Bauford), Johnathan Higgins (Philip), John Gausden (Jimmy Bauford), Isabelle Horler (Anna Bauford), Iain Lee (Master of Ceremonies), Keelan Anthony (Jojo), John Bourgeois (Rolly), Kalyane Tea (Steiger's Girlfriend), Julian Casey, Norm Berketa (Police Officers), Aidan Pickering (TV Reporter), Nambitha Mpumlwana (Tuula), Fikile Nyandeni (Gemilla), Tony Robinow (Art Dealer), Andrew French (Meles), Jamie Bartlett (Jess), Tumisho Masha (Hamadi), Kate Ashfield (Kat), Faye Peters (Monica), John Matshikiza (Dawit Ningpopo), Zaa Nkweta (Titus), Sahajak Boonthanakit, Dennis Tan (Port Officials), Doan Jarden-Ngarm Mackenzie (Tao), Burt Kwouk (Colonel Gao), Teerawat Muvilai (Ma Sok), Bertrand A. Henri (Speaker), Jasmin Geljo (Truck Driver), Francis Xavier McCarthy (Strauss), Manuel Tadros (Chechen Mobster), Joseph Antaki (Rebel), Vladimir Radian (Muslim Warlord), Elizabeth Whitmere (Beatrice), Emma Stevens, Rob Burns, Matthew Tiffin, Robin Wilcock (Journalists), Mark Anthony Krupa, Roman Chtinov (Russian Soldiers), Donovan Ganeb (Abraha), Sam Roberts (Charity Ball Band Singer), Melissa Auf Der Maur, Steve Durand, Jordan Zadorozny, Kelli Scott, Eric Digras (Charity Ball Band)

Sarah Jordan, a pampered American living in London, is inspired by the passionate efforts of Dr. Nick Callahan and joins him to help starving children in Third World countries.

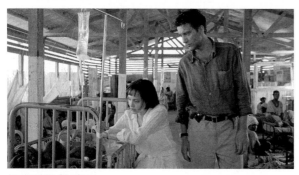

Angelina Jolie, Clive Owen PHOTO COURTESY OF PARAMOUNT

Anna Faris, Eddie Griffin, Queen Latifah PHOTO COURTESY OF DIMENSION

SCARY MOVIE 3

(DIMENSION) Producer, Robert K. Weiss; Executive Producers, Bob Weinstein, Harvey Weinstein, Andrew Rona, Brad Weston; Director, David Zucker; Screenplay, Craig Mazin, Pat Proft; Based on characters created by Shawn Wayans, Marlon Wayans, Buddy Johnson, Phil Beauman, Jason Friedberg, Aaron Seltzer; Co-Producer, Grace Gilroy; Photography, Mark Irwin; Designer, William Elliott; Costumes, Carol Ramsey; Editors, Malcolm Campbell, Jon Poll; Music, James L. Venable; Casting, John Papsidera; a Brad Grey Pictures production; Distributed by Miramax Films; Dolby; Technicolor; Rated PG-13; 88 minutes; Release date: October 24, 2003

Cast

Cindy Campbell **Anna Faris**
Mahalik **Anthony Anderson**
President Harris **Leslie Nielsen**
Trooper Champlin **Camryn Manheim**
George **Simon Rex**

and Pamela Anderson (Becca), Jenny McCarthy (Kate), Darrell Hammond (Father Muldoon), Kevin Hart (CJ), D.L. Hughley (John Wilson), Ja Rule (Agent Thompson), Drew Mikuska (Cody), Jeremy Piven (Ross Giggins), George Carlin (The Architect), Queen Latifah (Aunt ShaNeequa), Eddie Griffin (Orpheus), Denise Richards (Annie), Regina Hall (Brenda Meeks), Charlie Sheen (Tom), Ajay Naidu (Sayaman), Simon Cowell, Fat Joe, Master P, Marcy Gray, Method Man, Redman, Raekwon, The Rza, U-God (Themselves), Tim Stack (Carson Ward), Diane Klimaszewski (Diane), Elaine Klimaszewski (Elaine), Dame Lee, Doron Bell, Jr. (Rappers), Marny Eng (Tabitha), Jianna Ballard (Sue), Dexter Bell (Toilet Guy), William B. Taylor (Mr. Meeks), Patricia Idlette (Mrs. Meeks), David Edwards (Ralph), Frank C. Turner (Mr. Meek's Brother), Monica Dillon (Brenda's Grandmother), Lori Stewart (Tabitha's Mother), Jim Bremner (Guy in Chair), Phil Dornfeld (Tabitha's Voice), Edward Moss (MJ), Dee Jay Jackson (Zubie), Troy Yorke, Marco Soriano (Aliens), Cliff Solomon, Byron Chief-Moon, Dolly Madsen (Native Americans), John Hainsworth (Tracheotomy Man), Beverly Breuer (Tracheotomy Wife), Jessie Young (Girl Scout), Deanne Henry (Tammy Fae Baker), Eric Breker (Secret Serviceman Jones), Naomi Lawson-Baird (Sweet Tabitha), Abigail Adams (Wedding Guest)

A widowed priest and his apisiring rapper brother discover that their farm is the target for alien invaders, who may have some connection to the video tape that has been causing unexplained deaths. Third in the spoof series following *Scary Movie* (Dimension, 2000) and *Scary Movie 2* (Dimension, 2001).

ELEPHANT

(FINE LINE FEATURES) Producer, Dany Wolf; Executive Producers, Bill Robinson, Diane Keaton; Associate Producers, J.T. LeRoy, Jay Hernandez; Director/Screenplay/Editor, Gus Van Sant; Photography, Harris Savides; Casting, Mali Finn, Danny Stoltz; an HBO Films presentation in association with Blue Relief; Dolby; Color; Rated R; 81 minutes; Release date: October 24, 2003

Alex Frost

Elias McConnell

Cast
Alex **Alex Frost**
Eric **Eric Deulen**
John McFarland **John Robinson**
Elias **Elias McConnell**
Jordan **Jordan Taylor**
Carrie **Carrie Finklea**
Nicole **Nicole George**
Brittany **Brittany Mountain**
Acadia **Alicia Miles**
Michelle **Kristen Hicks**
Benny **Bennie Dixon**
Nathan **Nathan Tyson**
Mr. McFarland **Timothy Bottoms**
Mr. Luce **Matt Malloy**
GSA Teacher **Ellis E. Williams**

and Chantelle Chriestenson (Noelle), Kim Kenney (Assistant Principal's Secretary), Marci Buntrock (Assistant Secretary), Roman Ostrovsky (Red Haired Kid), Vana O'Brien (P.E. Instrucotr), Michael Paulsen (Bully), Alfred Ono (Mr. Fong), Larry Laverty (Teacher #3), Jason Seitz (Nate), Sarah Bing (GSA Student), Elisa De La Motte, Kathleen Mattice (Students)

A seemingly normal day at a high school examines the mundane occurances of various students who are unaware that violence is about to errupt.

Alicia Miles, John Robinson PHOTOS COURTESY OF FINE LINE FEATURES

BROTHER BEAR

(WALT DISNEY PICTURES) Producer, Chuck Williams; Directors, Aaron Blaise, Robert Walker; Screenplay, Tab Murphy, Lorne Cameron, David Hoselton, Steve Bencich, Ron J. Friedman; Music, Mark Mancina, Phil Collins; Songs by Phil Collins; Associate Producer, Igor Khait; Editor, Tim Mertens; Art Director, Robh Ruppel; Background Stylist, Xiangyuan Jie; Story Supervisor, Stephen Anderson; Layout Supervisor, Jeff Dickson; Backgrounds Supervisor, Barry R. Kooser; Clean-Up Supervisors, Philip Scott Boyd, Christine Lawrence Finney; Visual Effects Supervisor, Garrett Wren; Artistic Coordinator, Kirk Bodyfelt; Character Design, Rune Brandt Bennicke; Casting, Mary Hidalgo, Matthew Jon Beck; Distributed by Buena Vista Pictures; Dolby; Widescreen; Technicolor; Rated G; 85 minutes; Release date: October 24, 2003

Voice Cast

Kenai **Joaquin Phoenix**
Koda **Jeremy Suarez**
Denahi **Jason Raize**
Rutt **Rick Moranis**
Tuke **Dave Thomas**
Sitka **D.B. Sweeney**
Tanana **Joan Copeland**
Tug **Michael Clarke Duncan**
Old Denahi **Harold Gould**
Rams **Paul Christie, Daniel Mastrogiorgio**
Old Lady Bear **Estelle Harris**
Male Lover Bear **Greg Proops**
Female Lover Bear **Pauley Perrette**
Foreign (Croatian) Bear **Darko Cesar**
Chipmunks **Bumper Robinson**
Narrator (Inuit) **Angayuqaq Oscar Kawagley, Ph.D**

Kenai, a selfish young man, is transformed into a bear and finds himself on the run from his vengeful brother, who believes the man-bear is responsible for Kenai's death.

This film received an Oscar nomination for animated feature.

Koda, Kenai

Koda, Kenai

Tuke, Rutt, Kenai   PHOTOS COURTESY OF WALT DISNEY PICTURES

Koda (center)

THE HUMAN STAIN

(MIRAMAX) Producers, Gary Lucchesi, Scott Steindorff, Tom Rosenberg; Executive Producers, Bob Weinstein, Harvey Weinstein, Ron Bozman, Andre Lamal, Rick Schwartz, Steve Hutensky, Michael Ohoven, Eberhard Kayser; Director, Robert Benton; Screenplay, Nicholas Meyer; Based on the novel by Philip Roth; Photography, Jean Yves Escoffier; Designer, David Gropman; Costumes, Rita Ryack; Music, Rachel Portman; Music Supervisor, Dondi Bastone; Editor, Christopher Tellefsen; Casting, Deborah Aquila, Avy Kaufman, Tricia Wood; a Lakeshore Entertainment presentation of a Lakeshore Entertainment/Stone Village production in association wtih Cinerenta-Cineepsilon; Dolby; Panavision; Color; Rated R; 106 minutes; Release date: October 31, 2003

Wentworth Miller, Jacinda Barrett

Cast

Coleman Silk **Anthony Hopkins**
Faunia Farley **Nicole Kidman**
Lester Farley **Ed Harris**
Nathan Zuckerman **Gary Sinise**
Young Coleman **Wentworth Miller**
Steena Paulsson **Jacinda Barrett**
Mr. Silk **Harry Lennix**
Nelson Primus **Clark Gregg**
Mrs. Silk **Anna Deavere Smith**
Ernestine **Lizan Mitchell**
Ellie **Kerry Washington**
Iris Silk **Phyllis Newman**
Psychologist **Margo Martindale**
Herb Keble **Ron Canada**
Young Iris **Mili Avital**
Walter **Danny Blanco Hall**

and Kristen Blevins (Young Ernestine), Anne Dudek (Lisa Silk), Mimi Kuzyk (Professor Delphine Roux), John Finn (Louie Borero), Jeff Perry, Rick Snyder, Danny Stone (Tennis Players), Vito DeFilippo (Mark Silk), Robert Higden (Jeff Silk), Vlasta Vrana (Solly Tabak), Richard Mawe (Doc Chizner), Tom Rack (Bobcat), Bill Rowat (Swift), Richard Russo, Andrew Forge, Stella Arroyave (Faculty Committee Members), Jude Beny (Sally), Peter Cunningham, John Centiempo (Boxers), Frank Proctor (Announcer), Deano Clavet (Boxing Coach), Sylvain Dore (St. Nicholas Referee), Neville

Nicole Kidman, Anthony Hopkins

Edwards (Coleman's Cornerman), Phillip Collete Gervais (Train Conductor), Allison Davis (Diner on the Train), Charles W. Gray (Minister), Edward Lafferty, Steven Grise, Kim Gandol Ferenczi (Rally Protesters), Terry Haig (Police Officer #2), Laurent Imbault (Administrative Officer), Sylvain Landry (Maitre D), Pierre LeBlanc (Naval Recruiter), Nwamiko Madden (Young Man on the Porch), Luc Morisette (Street Photographer), Philip Pretten (Record Store Manager), Jessica Shutle (Student), Kate Whitney (Mrs. Primus), Brea Asher (Primus' Secretary), Russell Yuen (Chinese Waiter), Jimmy Chang (Chinese Restaurant Owner), Lydia Zadel (Nature Center Girl)

An elderly college professor, who resigns from his position after accusations of racism, begins an affair with a troubled younger woman.

Gary Sinise

Anthony Hopkins, Gary Sinise PHOTOS COURTESY OF MIRAMAX

SHATTERED GLASS

(LIONS GATE) Producers, Craig Baumgarten, Adam Merims, Gaye Hirsch, Tove Christensen; Executive Producers, Michael Paseornek, Tom Ortenberg, Tom Cruise, Paula Wagner; Director/Screenplay, Billy Ray; Based on the article written by H.G. Bissinger; Photography, Mandy Walker; Designer, Francois Séguin; Costumes, Renée April; Editor, Jeffrey Ford; Music, Mychael Danna; Casting, Cassandra Kulukundis; a Cruise/Wagner production, a Baumgarten Merims production, in association with Forest Park Pictures; Dolby; Super 35 Widescreen; Deluxe Color; Rated PG-13; 95 minutes; Release date: October 31, 2003

Hayden Christensen, Chloë Sevigny, Melanie Lynskey

Rosario Dawson, Cas Anvar, Steve Zahn

Kim Taschereau (Stout Woman), Phillip Cole (Security Guard), Mark Camocho (Glass' Lawyer), Ian Blouin (Chuck's Son), Lynne Adams (Kelly's Colleague), Caroline Goodall (Mrs. Duke), Brittany Drisdell (Megan)

Hayden Christensen, Peter Sarsgaard

The true story of how it was discovered that the *New Republic* reporter Stephen Glass had fabricated in whole or part more than two dozen articles he had managed to get published.

Cast

Stephen Glass **Hayden Christensen**
Charles "Chuck" Lane **Peter Sarsgaard**
Caitlin Avey **Chloë Sevigny**
Andy Fox **Rosario Dawson**
Amy Brand **Melanie Lynskey**
Michael Kelly **Hank Azaria**
Adam Penenberg **Steve Zahn**
Lewis Estridge **Mark Blum**
Catarina Bannier **Simone-Elise Girard**
David Bach **Chad Donella**
Aaron Bluth **Jamie Elman**
Rob Gruen **Luke Kirby**
Kambiz Foroohar **Cas Anvar**
Gloria **Linda E. Smith**
Marty Peretz **Ted Kotcheff**
Ian Restil **Owen Rotharmel**
George Sims **Bill Rowat**
Ian's Mother **Michele Scarabelli**
Joe Hiert **Terry Simpson**
Suit #1 **Howard Rosenstein**
Michael **Louis-Philippe Dandenault**

and Morgan Kelly (Joe), Christian Tessier (Cade), James Berlingieri (Jason), Brett Watson (Seth), Andrew Airlie (Alec Shumpert), Russell Yuen (Emmit Rich), Pierre LeBlanc, Pauline Little (Monica Merchants),

Hayden Christensen PHOTOS COURTESY OF LIONS GATE

DIE MOMMIE DIE!

(SUNDANCE) Producers, Dante Di Loreto, Anthony Edwards, Bill Kenwright; Executive Producer, Lony Dubrofsky; Director, Mark Rucker; Screenplay, Charles Busch, based on his play; Photography, Kelly Evans; Designer, Joseph B. Tintfass; Costumes, Thomas G. Marquez, Michael Bottari, Ronald Case; Co-Producer, Frank Pavich; Co-Executive Producer, Neil Ellman; Editor, Philip Harrison; Music, Dennis McCarthy; Casting, Jeff Greenberg, Collin Daniel; an Aviator Films, Ken Kenwright Ltd. presentation; Dolby; Color; Rated R; 90 minutes; Release date: October 31, 2003

Natasha Lyonne, Philip Baker Hall, Stark Sands

Jason Priestley, Natasha Lyonne

Cast

Angela Arden/Barbara Arden **Charles Busch**
Edith Sussman **Natasha Lyonne**
Tony Parker **Jason Priestley**
Bootsie Carp **Frances Conroy**
Sol Sussman **Philip Baker Hall**
Lance Sussman **Stark Sands**
Sam Fishbein **Victor Raider-Wexler**
Shatzi Van Allen **Nora Dunn**
Angela's Fan **Angela Paton**
Policeman **Josh Hutchinson**
Moving Men **Chris McDaniel, Tom Hughes**
Tuchman **Stanley DeSantis**
Leather Daddy **Paul Vinson**

Natasha Lyonne, Frances Conroy, Stark Sands, Charles Busch

In this spoof of Technicolor soap operas, aging actress Angela Arden will allow nothing to interfere with her extra-marital affair with hunky tennis instructor Tony Parker and plots to kill off her well-to-do producer husband.

Chris McDaniel, Charles Busch, Tom Hughes PHOTOS COURTESY OF SUNDANCE

THE MATRIX REVOLUTIONS

(WARNER BROS.) Producer, Joel Silver; Executive Producers, Andy Wachowski, Larry Wachowski, Grant Hill, Andrew Mason, Bruce Berman; Directors/Screenplay, The Wachowski Brothers; Photography, Bill Pope; Designer, Owen Paterson; Costumes, Kym Barrett; Editor, Zach Staenberg; Music, Don Davis; Visual Effects Supervisor, John Gaeta; Supervising Stunt Coordinator, R.A. Rondell; Martial Arts Stunt Coordinator, Chad Stahelski; Fight Choreographer, Yuen Wo Ping; a Silver Pictures production in association with Village Roadshow Pictures and NPV Entertainment; Dolby; Panavision; Technicolor; Rated R; 130 minutes; Release date: November 5, 2003

Laurence Fishburne, Jada Pinkett Smith

Lambert Wilson, Monica Belucci

Cast

Neo **Keanu Reeves**
Morpheus **Laurence Fishburne**
Trinity **Carrie-Anne Moss**
Agent Smith **Hugo Weaving**
Niobe **Jada Pinkett Smith**
The Oracle **Mary Alice**
Sati **Tanveer K. Atwal**
Persephone **Monica Bellucci**
Bane **Ian Bliss**
Seraph **Collin Chou**
Zee **Nona Gaye**
Mifune **Nathaniel Lees**
Commander Lock **Harry Lennix**
Link **Harold Perrineau**
The Trainman **Bruce Spence**
The Kid **Clayton Watson**
Rama Kandra **Bernard White**
Merovingian **Lambert Wilson**
Ghost **Anthony Wong**

and Helmut Bakaitis (The Architect), Kate Beahan (Coat Check Girl), Francine Bell (Councillor Grace), Rachel Blackman (Charra), Henry Blasingame (Deus Ex Machina Voice), David Bowers, Dion Horstmans (Q-Bail Gang Members), Zeke Castelli (Operations Officer Mattis), Essie

Davis (Maggie), Nona Gaye (Zee), Lachy Hulme (Sparks), Chris Kirby (Mauser), Peter Lamb (Colt), Robert Mammone (AK), Joe Manning, Kittrick Redmond (Operators at Command), Maurice Morgan (Tower Soldier), Tharini Mudaliar (Kamala), Rene Naufahu (Zion Gate Operator), Robyn Nevin (Councillor Dillard), Genevieve O'Reilly (Officer Wirtz), Rupert Reid (Lock's Lieutenant), Kevin M. Richardson (Deus Ex Machina), David Roberts (Roland), Richard Sydenham (Dock Sergeant), Che Timmins (Radio Bunker Man), Gina Torres (Cas), Clayton Watson (Kid), Cornel West (Councillor West), Bernard White (Rama-KAndra), Anthony Zerbe (Councillor Hamann)

Neo, Niobe and Trinity travel into the heart of Machine City in order to stop Agent Smith from destroying the real world and the Matrix. Third installment in the Warner Bros. series following *The Matrix* (1999) and *The Matrix Reloaded* (released earlier in the year on May 15, 2003).

Carrie-Anne Moss PHOTOS COURTESY OF WARNER BROS.

MY ARCHITECT: A SON'S JOURNEY

(NEW YORKER) Producers, Nathaniel Kahn, Susan Rose Behr, Director/Screenplay, Nathaniel Kahn; Co-Producer, Yael Melamede; Photography, Robert Richman; Music, Joseph Vitarelli; Editor, Sabine Krayenbühl; a Louis Kahn Project; Dolby; Color; Not rated; 116 minutes; Release date: November 7, 2003. Documentary in which filmmaker Nathaniel Kahn explores the life of his father, noted architect Louis Kahn, who died in bankruptcy in 1974.

Nathaniel Kahn, Louis Kahn

Louis Kahn, Nathaniel Kahn

With

Edmund Bacon, Edwina Pattison Daniels, B.V. Doshi, Frank O. Gehry, Philip Johnson, Nathaniel Kahn, Sue Ann Kahn, Harriet Pattison, Priscilla Pattison, I.M. Pei, Moshe Safdie, Robert A.M. Stern, Alexandra Tyng, Anne Tyng, Shamsul Wares

This film received an Oscar nomination for documentary feature.

Louis Kahn

PHOTOS COURTESY OF NEW YORKER

ELF

(NEW LINE CINEMA) Producers, Jon Berg, Todd Komarnicki, Shauna Robertson; Executive Producers, Toby Emmerich, Kent Alterman, Cale Boyter, Jimmy Miller, Julie Wixson Darmody; Director, Jon Favreau; Screenplay, David Berenbaum; Photography, Greg Gardiner; Designer, Rusty Smith; Costumes, Laura Jean Shannon; Music, John Debney; Co-Producer, David Householter; Visual Effects Supervisor, Joe Bauer; Casting, Susie Farris; a Guy Walks Into a Bar production; Dolby; Deluxe color; Rated PG; 97 minutes; Release date: November 7, 2003

Will Ferrell (right)

Will Ferrell, Peter Billingsley

Cast

Buddy **Will Ferrell**
Walter **James Caan**
Papa Elf **Bob Newhart**
Santa **Edward Asner**
Emily **Mary Steenburgen**
Jovie **Zooey Deschanel**
Michael **Daniel Tay**
Gimbel's Manager **Faizon Love**
Miles Finch **Peter Dinklage**
Deb **Amy Sedaris**
Fulton **Michael Lerner**
Morris **Andy Richter**
Eugene **Kyle Gass**
Gimbel's Santa **Artie Lange**
Voice of Leon the Snowman **Leon Redbone**
Voice of Polar Bear Cub **Ray Harryhausen**
NY 1 Reporter **Claire Lautier**
NY 1 Anchor **Ted Friend**
Security Guards **Patrick Ferrell, Patrick McCartney**
Doctor **Jon Favreau**

and Lydia Lawson (Carolyn), Brenda MacDonald (Nun), Annie Brebner, Luke Paul (Elf Students), Peter Billingsley, Meghan Black, Patrick Baynham (Elves), Michael Roberds (Disgruntled Cobbler Elf), Peter Hulne, Patrick Hulne (Elf Twins), Richard Side (Elf Teacher), David Paul Grove (Pom Pom), Kristian Ayre (Foom Foom), Lorion Heath (Perfume Clerk),

Bob Newhart

Edward Asner

Will Ferrell, Daniel Tay

Will Ferrell, Zooey Deschanel

Edward Asner

Dillard Brinson (Printer), Brad Turner, David Berenbaum, Brenda Crichlow (Officer Co-Workers), Oscar Goncalves (Francisco), Mary Black (Nurse), Murray Jack (Man in Elevator), Mark Acheson (Mailroom Guy), Robin Mossley (Chuck), Paul Schofield (Kid with Santa), Will McCormack, Gus Michael (Witnesses), Alexandra Michael (Child), Terry J. Scarlatos (Police Officer), Jonathan Bruce (Biker), Akeem A. Smith, Michael Christopher Fischetti (School Kids), Jane Bradbury (Susan Welles)

A full-sized human, raised by elves after accidentally ending up in Santa's bag, travels to New York City in search of his real father.

Zooey Deschanel

Will Ferrell

James Caan

Will Ferrell, James Caan

Will Ferrell

Russell Crowe

Max Pirkis

Max Benitz, Russell Crowe

MASTER AND COMMANDER: THE FAR SIDE OF THE WORLD

(20TH CENTURY FOX/MIRAMAX/UNIVERSAL) Producers, Samuel Goldwyn, Jr., Peter Weir, Duncan Henderson; Executive Producer, Alan B. Curtiss; Director, Peter Weir; Screenplay, Peter Weir, John Collee; Based upon the novels *Master and Commander* and *The Far Side of the World* by Patrick O'Brian; Photography, Russell Boyd; Designer, William Sandell; Costumes, Wendy Stites; Music, Iva Davies, Christopher Gordon, Richard Tognetti; Co-Producers, Meyer Gottlieb; Editor, Lee Smith; Visual Effects Supervisors, Stefen Fangmeier, Nathan McGuinness; Casting, Mary Selway, Fiona Weir; a Samuel Goldwyn Films production; Dolby; Super 35 Widescreen; Deluxe color; Rated PG-13; 139 minutes; Release date: November 14, 2003

Russell Crowe

Max Benitz

Paul Bettany, Russell Crowe

Paul Bettany, Robert Pugh, James D'Arcy, Russell Crowe

Cast

Captain Jack Aubrey **Russell Crowe**
Dr. Stephen Maturin **Paul Bettany**

OFFICERS
1st Lt. Thomas Pullings **James D'Arcy**
2nd Lt. William Mowett **Edward Woodall**
Captain Howard, Royal Marines **Chris Larkin**

MIDSHIPMEN
Lord Blakeney **Max Pirkis**
Boyle **Jack Randall**
Peter Calamy **Max Benitz**
Hollom **Lee Ingleby**
Williamson **Richard Pates**

WARRANT OFFICERS
Mr. Allen, Master **Robert Pugh**
Mr. Higgins, Surgeon's Mate **Richard McCabe**
Mr. Hollar, Boatswain **Ian Mercer**
Mr. Lamb, Carpenter **Tony Dolan**

CREW
Preserved Killick, Captain's Steward **David Threlfall**
Barrett Bonden, Coxswain **Billy Boyd**
Joseph Nagle, Carpenter's Mate **Bryan Dick**
William Warley, Cpt. of Mizzentop **Joseph Morgan**
Joe Plaice, Able Seaman **George Innes**
Faster Doudle, Able Seaman **William Mannering**
Awkward Davies, Able Seaman **Patrick Gallagher**
Nehemiah Slade, Able Seaman **Alex Palmer**
Mr. Hogg, Whaler **Mark Lewis Jones**
Padeen, Loblolly Boy **John De Santis**
Black Bill, Killick's Mate **Ousmane Thiam**

and Thierry Segall (French Captain)

Russell Crowe

After the HMS *Surprise* is badly damaged after a sudden attack by a French ship, Captain Jack Aubrey makes the decision to repair the ship at sea and pursue the enemy.

2003 Academy Award–winner for Best Sound Editing and Best Cinematography. This film received additional Oscar nominations for picture, director, sound, editing, costume design, makeup, art direction, and visual effects.

LOONEY TUNES: BACK IN ACTION

(WARNER BROS.) Producers, Paula Weinstein, Bernie Goldmann; Executive Producers, Chris deFaria, Larry Doyle; Director, Joe Dante; Screenplay, Larry Doyle; Photography, Dean Cundey; Designer, Bill Brzeski; Costumes, Mary Vogt; Editors, Marshall Harvey, Rick W. Finney; Music, Jerry Goldsmith; Choreographer, Marguerite Derricks; Animation Producer, Allison Abbate; Casting, Mary Gail Artz, Barbara Cohen; Associate Producer—Animation, Steven Wilzbach; Visual Effects Supervisor, Chris Watts; Visual Effects Supervisors—Animation, Michael D. Kanfer, Brad Kuehn; a Baltimore/Spring Creek/Goldmann Pictures production; Dolby; Panavision; Technicolor; Rated PG; 91 minutes; Release date: November 14, 2003

Cast

DJ Drake/Himself/Voice of Tazmanian Devil/Voice of Tazmanian She-Devil **Brendan Fraser**
Kate Houghton **Jenna Elfman**
Damien Drake **Timothy Dalton**
Mother **Joan Cusack**
Mr. Smith **Bill Goldberg**
Dusty Tails **Heather Locklear**
Mr. Chairman **Steve Martin**
Acme VP, Stating the Obvious **Marc Lawrence**
Acme VP, Nitpicking **Bill McKinney**
Acme VP, Unfairly Promoted **George Murdock**
Acme VP, Never Learning **Ron Perlman**
Acme VP, Rhetorical Questions **Robert Picardo**
Acme VP, Climbing to the Top **Leo Rossi**
Acme VP, Child Labor **Vernon G. Wells**
Acme VP, Bad Ideas **Mary Woronov**

and Don Stanton (Mr. Warner), Dan Stanton (Mr. Warner's Brother), Dick Miller (Security Guard), Roger Corman (Hollywood Director), Kevin McCarthy (Mr. Bennell), Jeff Gordon, Matthew Lillard (Themselves), Archie Hahn (Stunt Director), Allan Graf (Interrogator), Austyn Cuccia (Tour Bus Girl), Marie-Claude Jacques (Flower Vendor), Michael Azria (Paris Cafe Waiter), Dan Romanelli (Studio Executive), Ryan O'Dell (Bugs Bunny's Driver), Kevin Thompson, Arturo Gil, Gabriel Pimentel, Steve Babiar, Martin Klebba (Dancing Yosemite Sams), Tara Wilson, Gelsey Weiss, Liz Ramos, Becca Sweitzer, Alysha Wheeler, Chi Johnson, Shanti

Daffy Duck, Jenna Elfman, Brendan Fraser, Bugs Bunny

Lowry, Erica Gudis, Tanee McCall, Brenda Mae Hamilton, Emily Rose Zachary, Janina N. Garraway, Micki Duran, Shealan Spencer, Brandon Henschel (Dancers)

Heather Locklear

Voice Cast:

Joe Alaskey (Bugs Bunny/Daffy Duck/Beaky Buzzard/Sylvester/Mama Bear), Jeff Glenn Bennett (Yosemite Sam/Foghorn Leghorn/Nasty Canasta), Billy West (Elmer Fudd/Peter Lorre), Eric Goldberg (Tweety Bird/Marvin the Martian/Speedy Gonzalez), Bruce Lanoil (Pepe Le Pew), June Foray (Granny), Bob Bergen (Porky Pig), Casey Kasem (Shaggy), Frank Welker (Scooby-Doo), Danny Chambers (Cottontail Smith), Stan Freberg (Baby Bear), Will Ryan (Papa Bear), Danny Mann (Robo Dog/Spy Car), Mel Blanc (Gremlin Car)

Fired Warner Bros. security guard DJ Drake and Daffy Duck set out to find the Blue Monkey Diamond, with studio executive Kate Houghton and Bugs Bunny in hot pursuit.

Wile E. Coyote, Steve Martin PHOTOS COURTESY OF WARNER BROS.

Naomi Watts, Clea DuVall

21 GRAMS

(FOCUS FEATURES) Producers, Alejandro González, Robert Salerno; Executive Producer, Ted Hope; Director, Alejandro González Iñárritu; Screenplay/Associate Producer, Guillermo Arriaga; Story, Guillermo Arriaga, Alejandro González Iñárritu; Photography, Rodrigo Prieto; Designer, Brigitte Broch; Costumes, Marlene Stewart; Editor, Stephen Mirrione; Music, Gustavo Santaolalla; Casting, Francine Maisler; a This is That production, a Y Productions production; Dolby; Deluxe Color; Rated R; 125 minutes; Release date: November 21, 2003

Sean Penn, Naomi Watts

Cast

Paul Rivers **Sean Penn**
Jack Jordan **Benicio Del Toro**
Cristina Peck **Naomi Watts**
Mary Rivers **Charlotte Gainsbourg**
Marianne Jordan **Melissa Leo**
Rev. John **Eddie Marsan**
Claudia Williams **Clea DuVall**
Michael **Danny Huston**
Brown **Paul Calderon**
Trish **Annie Corley**
Doctor Rothberg **Denis O'Hare**

Gynecologist **John Rubinstein**
Katie **Carly Nahon**
Laura **Claire Pakis**
Boy **Nick Nichols**
Fat Man **Loyd Keith Salter**
Basketball Guy **Antef A. Harris**
Freddy Jordan **Marc Thomas Musso**
Gina Jordan **Teresa Delgado**
Guards **Terry Dee Draper, Tony Guyton**
Inmates **Wayne E. Beech, Jr., Keith Lamont Johnson**
Caddies **David Chattam, Jr., John Boyd West, Jeff Schmidt**
Al **Tony Vaughn**
Dolores **Anastasia Herin**
Lucio **Carlo Alban**
Cashier **Quang Hai Tran**
Receptionist **Sharon Bishop**
Cristina's Father **Jerry Chipman**
Doctor Jones **Tom Irwin**
Doctor Molina **Roberto Medina**
Doctor Badnews **Arita Trahan**
Barman **Rodney Ingle**
Ana **Catherine Dent**
Alan **Kevin Chapman**
Friends **Randall Hartzog, Verda Davenport-Booher, Dorothy Armstrong Miles, Barclay Roberts**
Wife **Lisa Sanchez**
P.J. **Stephen Bridgewater**

and Michael Finnell (Fat Prisoner), Juan Corrigan (Valet), Charlie B. Brown (Night Guard), Arron Shiver (Young Doctor), Pamela Blair (Doctor), Jennifer Pfalzgraff (Nurse), Lew Temple (County Sheriff), Tricia Branch (Skinny Woman)

A tragic accident brings together the disparate lives of an ex-con who has turned to religion, a college professor awaiting a heart transplant, and a housewife who must cope with an unbearable loss.

This film received Oscar nominations for actress (Naomi Watts) and supporting actor (Benicio Del Toro).

Melissa Leo, Teresa Delgado, Benicio Del Toro, Marc Thomas Musso

Spencer Breslin, Mike Myers, Dakota Fanning PHOTO COURTESY OF UNIVERSAL/DREAMWORKS

DR. SEUSS' THE CAT IN THE HAT

(UNIVERSAL/DREAMWORKS) Producer, Brian Grazer; Executive Producers, Eric McLeod, Gregg Taylor, Karen Kehela Sherwood, Maureen Peyrot; Director, Bo Welch; Screenplay, Alec Berg, David Mandel, Jeff Schaffer; Based on the book by Dr. Seuss; Photography, Emmanuel Lubezki; Designer, Alex McDowell; Costumes, Rita Ryack; Editor, Don Zimmerman; Music, David Newman; Songs by Marc Shaiman, Scott Wittman; Special Makeup Effects Creator, Steve Johnson; Visual Effects Supervisor, Douglas Hans Smith; Associate Producer, Aldric La'auli Porter; Casting, Juel Bestrop, Jeanne McCarthy; a Universal Pictures/DreamWorks Pictures/Imagine Entertainment presentation of a Brian Grazer production; Dolby; Super 35 Widescreen; Technicolor; Rated PG; 82 minutes; Release date: November 21, 2003

Cast

The Cat **Mike Myers**
Quinn **Alec Baldwin**
Mom **Kelly Preston**
Sally **Dakota Fanning**
Conrad **Spencer Breslin**
Mrs. Kwan **Amy Hill**
Mr. Humberfloob/The Fish **Sean Hayes**
Thing 1 **Danielle Ryan Chuchran, Taylor Rice**
Thing 2 **Brittany Oaks, Talia Prairie**
Voices of Thing 1 & Thing 2 **Dan Castellaneta**
Narrator **Victor Brandt**
Announcer **Daran Norris**
Nevins **Bugsy**
Nevins (Voice) **Frank Welker**
Kate the Caterer **Clint Howard**
Dumb Schweitzer **Steven Anthony Lawrence**
Club-Goer **Paris Hilton**
and Candace Dean Brown (Secretary), Stephen Hibbert (Jim McFlinnigan), Roger Morrissey (Mr. Vompatatat)

Sally and Conrad Walden, left with their sleeping babysitter, are visited by a six-foot-tall cat in a red-and-white striped, stovepipe hat, who shows them how to have fun.

GOTHIKA

(WARNER BROS./COLUMBIA) Producers, Joel Silver, Robert Zemeckis, Susan Levin; Executive Producers, Steve Richards, Gary Ungar, Don Carmody; Director, Mathieu Kassovitz; Screenplay, Sebastian Gutierrez; Co-Producer, Richard Mirsich; Photography, Matthew Libatique; Designer, Graham "Grace" Walker; Music, John Ottman; Editor, Yannick Kergoat; a Dark Castle Entertainment production; Dolby; Technicolor; Rated R; 96 minutes; Release date: November 21, 2003

Cast

Miranda Grey **Halle Berry**
Pete Graham **Robert Downey, Jr.**
Dr. Douglas Grey **Charles S. Dutton**
Sheriff Ryan **John Carroll Lynch**
Phil Parsons **Bernard Hill**
Chlöe Sava **Penélope Cruz**
Teddy Howard **Dorian Harewood**
Irene **Bronwen Mantel**
Rachel Parsons **Kathleen Mackey**
Turlington **Matthew G. Taylor**
Joe **Michel Perron**

and Andrea Sheldon (Tracey Seavers), Anana Rydvald (Glass Cell Nurse), Laura Mitchell, Amy Sloan (Inmates), Noël Burton (Prison Doctor), Benz Antoine, Andy Bradshaw, Jason Cavalier, Jasson Finney, Terry Simpson, Kwasi Songui (Guards), Caroline van Vlaardingen, Al Vandecruys (Reporters), Noah Bernett (Tim)

Halle Berry, Robert Downey Jr. PHOTO COURTESY OF WARNER BROS./COLUMBIA

Criminal psychologist Miranda Grey awakens after a nightmarish encounter with a mysterious young girl to discover that she is charged with having brutally murdered her husband, an act that has caused her to be confined to the psychiatric ward at which she worked.

THE COOLER

(LIONS GATE) Producers, Sean Furst, Michael Pierce; Executive Producers, Edward R. Pressman, John Schmidt, Alessandro Camon, Robert Gryphon, Brett Morrison, Joe Madden; Director, Wayne Kramer; Screenplay, Frank Hannah, Wayne Kramer; Co-Producers, Elliot Lewis Rosenblatt, Bryan Furst; Photography, James Whitaker; Designer, Toby Corbett; Costumes, Kristin M. Burke; Editor, Arthur Coburn; Music, Mark Isham; Executive Music Producer, Billy Gottlieb; Casting, Amanda Mackey Johnson, Cathy Sandrich Gelfond, Wendy Weidman, Sig de Miguel; a Content Film presentation of a Pierce/Williams/Furst Films production in association with Gryphon Films and Dog Pond Productions; Dolby; Panavision; Deluxe Color; Rated R; 101 minutes; Release date: November 26, 2003

Cast

Bernie Lootz **William H. Macy**
Shelly Kaplow **Alec Baldwin**
Natalie Belisario **Maria Bello**
Mikey **Shawn Hatosy**
Larry Sokolov **Ron Livingston**
Buddy Stafford **Paul Sorvino**
Charlene **Estella Warren**
Nicky "Fingers" Bonnatto **Arthur J. Narscarella**

Ron Livingston, Alec Baldwin

Johnny Capella **Joey Fatone**
Highway Officer **M.C. Gainey**
Doris **Ellen Greene**
Lou **Don Scribner**
Tony **Tony Longo**
Marty Goldfarb **Richard Israel**
The Player **Timothy Landfield**
Bulldog **T.J. Giola**
Hooker **Jewel Shepard**
Mr. Pinkerton **Gordon Michaels**

and Doc Watson (Morrie), Dan Lemieux (Suburbanite), Larry Elliott (Floor Manager), Joe Conti (Pit Boss), Chris Platt, Frank Hannah (Dealers), Norbert Ganska, Andrew Simbeck, Danny Grossen, Jeff Hill, Monet Beaman, Bryon Baker (Stickmen), Charlie Carr (Boxman), Kanie Kastroll (Croupier), John T. Kozeluh (Man), Cherilyn Hayres (Woman), James McCarthy (Televangelist), Monica White, Heather McHenry (Johnny Capella's Girls)

Unlucky Bernie Lootz, whose job it is to jinx the players at a gambling casino, finds his "midas touch" reversing when he falls in love.

This film received an Oscar nomination for supporting actor (Alec Baldwin).

Maria Bello, Alec Baldwin, William H. Macy

Maria Bello

William H. Macy PHOTOS COURTESY OF LIONS GAATE

Eddie Murphy, Marc John Jeffries PHOTO COURTESY OF WALT DISNEY PICTURES

THE HAUNTED MANSION

(WALT DISNEY PICTURES) Producers, Don Hahn, Andrew Gunn; Executive Producers, Barry Bernardi, Rob Minkoff; Director, Rob Minkoff; Screenplay, David Berenbaum; Based on Walt Disney's Haunted Mansion theme park attraction; Photography, Remi Adefarasin; Designer, John Myhre; Costumes, Mona May; Editor, Priscilla Nedd Friendly; Music, Mark Mancina; Visual Effects Supervisor, Jay Redd; Special Make-Up Effects, Rick Baker; Casting, Marcia Ross, Donna Morong, Gail Goldberg; Distributed by Buena Vista; Dolby; Super 35 Widescreen; Technicolor; Rated PG; 88 minutes; Release date: November 26, 2003

Cast

Jim Evers **Eddie Murphy**
Ramsley **Terence Stamp**
Master Gracey **Nathaniel Parker**
Sara Evers **Marsha Thompson**
Madame Leota **Jennifer Tilly**
Ezra **Wallace Shawn**
Emma **Dina Waters**
Michael Evers **Marc John Jefferies**
Megan Evers **Aree Davis**
Mr. Coleman **Jim Doughan**
Mrs. Coleman **Rachel Harris**
Mr. Silverman **Steve Hytner**
Mrs. Silverman **Heather Juergensen**
Hitchhiking Ghosts **Jeremy Howard, Deep Roy, Clay Martinez**
Tiki Lounge Customers **Bridget Brno, Gregg London**
Boy on Bicycle **Zach Minkoff**
The Singing Busts **The Dapper Dans: Shelby Grimm, Harry J. Campbell, William T. Lewis, Tim Reeder, Bob Hartley**

Realtor Jim Evers and his family are summoned to the mysterious and presumably haunted Gracey Mansion, where they are forced to spend the night.

BAD SANTA

(DIMENSION) Producers, John Cameron, Sarah Aubrey, Bob Weinstein; Executive Producers, Joel Coen, Ethan Coen; Director, Terry Zwigoff; Screenplay, Glenn Ficarra, John Requa; Co-Executive Producers, Harvey Weinstein, Brad Weston; Co-Producer, David Crockett; Photography, Jamie Anderson; Designer, Sharon Seymour; Costumes, Wendy Chuck; Editor, Robert Hoffman; Music, David Kitay; Casting, Mary Vernieu, Felicia Fasano; Dolby; Deluxe Color; Rated R; 91 minutes; Release date: November 26, 2003

Cast

Willie T. Stokes **Billy Bob Thornton**
Marcus **Tony Cox**
The Kid **Brett Kelly**
Sue **Lauren Graham**
Lois **Lauren Tom**
Gin **Bernie Mac**
Bob Chipeska **John Ritter**
Hindustani Troublemaker **Ajay Naidu**
Milwaukee Mother **Lorna Scott**
Milwaukee Boy **Harrison Bieker**
Milwaukee Mom with Photo **Alex Borstein**
Milwaukee Bratty Kid **Dylan Charles**
Milwaukee Security Guard **Billy Gardell**
Milwaukee Bartender **Lisa Ross**

and Bryan Callen (Miami Bartender), Tom McGowan (Harrison), Grace Calderon (Woman in Tight Pants), Christine Pichardo (Photo Elf), Max Van Ville (Skateboard Bully), Bucky Dominick (Deer Hunter 3 Boy), Georgia Eskew (Barbie Girl), Hayden Bromberg (Fraggle-Stick Boy), Briana Norton (Pinball Girl), Octavia L. Spencer (Opal), Ryan Pinkston (Shoplifter), Hallie Singleton (Woman in Food Court), Matt Walsh (Herb), Natsuko Ohama (Pedicurist), Dave Adams (Prison Guard), Ethan Phillips (Roger Merman), Joey Saravia (Pokemon Child), Cody Strauch (Watching Boy), Curtis Taylor (Phoenix Security Guard), Sheriff John Bunnell (Police Chief), Chloe Colville (Crying Girl), Joey Bucaro (Sergeant), Alexandra Korhan (Girl on Santa's Lap), Cloris Leachman (Grandma)

A foul-mouthed drunk gets a job as a department store Santa in order to carry out robberies.

Billy Bob Thornton, Lauren Graham PHOTO COURTESY OF DIMENSION

THE MISSING

(COLUMBIA) Producers, Brian Grazer, Daniel Ostroff, Ron Howard; Executive Producers, Todd Hallowell, Steve Crystal; Director, Ron Howard; Screenplay, Ken Kaufman; Based on the novel *The Last Ride* by Thomas Eidson; Photography, Salvatore Totino; Art Director, Guy Barnes; Costumes, Julie Weiss; Editors, Mike Hill, Dan Hanley; Music, James Horner; Co-Producers, Thomas Eidson, Sue Berger Ramin; Associate Producers, Louisa Velis, Aldric La'auli Porter, Kathleen McGill; Casting, Jane Jenkins, Janet Hirshenson; a Revolution Studios and Imagine Entertainment presentation of a Brian Grazer production in association with Daniel Ostroff productions; Dolby; Super 35 Widescreen; Deluxe color; Rated R; 135 minutes; Release date: November 26, 2003

Jenna Boyd, Evan Rachel Wood

In the 1885 American Southwest, Maggie Gilkeson's estranged father returns after spending 20 years living with the Apaches and is dismissed by his angry daughter until she realizes she needs him to help find her abducted daughter.

Jay Tavare

Tommy Lee Jones

Cast

Samuel Jones **Tommy Lee Jones**
Maggie Gilkeson **Cate Blanchett**
Lilly Gilkeson **Evan Rachel Wood**
Dot Gilkeson **Jenna Boyd**
Brake Baldwin **Aaron Eckhart**
Lt. Jim Ducharme **Val Kilmer**
Emiliano **Sergio Calderon**
Chidin **Eric Schweig**
Two Stone **Steve Reevis**
Kayitah **Jay Tavare**
Honesco **Simon Baker**

and Ray McKinnon (Russell J. Wittick) Max Perlich (Isaac Edgerly), Ramon Frank (Grummond), Elizabeth Moss (Anne), Josephine Schawn, Alexandra Elich (Sally), Deryle J. Lujan (Naazhaao—Hunter), Matthew Montoya (Tsi Beoyuao—Blowing Tree), Joe Saenz (Mba'tsu Naabitin—Wolf Trail), Gandi Shaw (Izhase—Bird), Rod Rondeaux (Hudluo—The One Who Laughs), Juddson Linn (Chauaiao—Evening Tim), Dutch Lunak (Aii sionzilo—Wild Horse), Yolanda Nez (aii Dahit-eeo—Dancing Horse), Heather Gulas, Scarlett McAlister, Aura Jensen-Curtis, Shelby Kocurek, Molly McAlister (Captive Girls), Angelina C. Torres (Esmeralda Nunez), Deborah Martinez (Maria Nunez), Clint Howard (Sheriff Purdy), Rance Howard (Telegraph Operator), Arron Shiver (Rancher), David Midthunder (Apache Scout), Paul Scallan (Stokley), Jerry King, Jim Tarwater (Drunk Soldiers), David Garver (Barker), Clemente Spottedhorse (Captured Apache), Brian Bronw, Toby Holguin, Eddie Fernandez, Jason Rodriguez (Mexican Slave Traders)

Tommy Lee Jones, Cate Blanchett PHOTOS COURTESY OF COLUMBIA

HONEY

(UNIVERSAL) Producers, Marc Platt, Andre Harrell; Executive Producer, Billy Higgins; Director, Bille Woodruff; Screenplay, Alonzo Brown, Kim Watson; Photography, John R. Leonetti; Designer, Jasna Stefanovich; Costumes, Susan Matheson; Music, Mervyn Warren; Executive Music Producer, Rodney Jerkins; Choreographers, Laurie Ann Gibson, Luther A. Brown; Editors, Mark Helfrich, Emma E. Hickox; Casting, Aisha Coley, Michelle Morris Gertz; a Marc Platt/Nuamerica production; Dolby; Fotokem color; Rated PG-13; 94 minutes; Release date: December 5, 2003

Cast
Honey Daniels **Jessica Alba**
Chaz **Mekhi Phifer**
Gina **Joy Bryant**
Benny **Lil' Romeo**
Michael Ellis **David Moscow**
Darlene Daniels **Lonette McKee**
Raymond **Zachary Isaiah Williams**
Themselves **Missy Elliott, Jadakiss & Sheek, Ginuwine, Harmonica Sunbeam, Silkk, 3rd Storee, Tweet**
Bar Customers **Christian Monzon, Al Shearer**
Joey **Jull Weber**
Katrina **Laurie Ann Gibson**
Katrina's Friend **O'Neal McNight**
Otis **Kevin Duhaney**
Beat Boxer **William Omar Tobar**
Neighborhood Guys **Damien Luvara, Sean Newman**
Letitia **Sarah Francis**

Jessica Alba, Lil' Romeo

and Ivan "Flipz" Velez, Jeremy Cedeno, Nicole Neal, Suga May (Street Dancers), Anthony Sherwood (Mr. Daniels), Lee Smart (Casting Director), Scott Neil (Lenny), Wes Maestro Williams (B.B.), Tracy Dawson (Assistant Director), Brandy Marie Ward (Choreographer), Jordan Madley, Natalie Johnson (Honey's Friends), Richard Fagon (Bouncer), Derek J. Watkins, Alicia Bruce, Lyriq Bent (Barbers), Alison Sealy-Smith (Marisol), Dwayne Morgan (Poet), Judy Embden (Mrs. Strom), Edney Hendrickson (2nd Assistant Director), Roy Anderson (Undercover Cop)

Jessica Alba

Dancer Honey Daniels is spotted doing her moves by a video director at a dance club and gets her big break, becoming a choreographer for some of the top acts in hip-hop and R&B.

Mekhi Phifer, Jessica Alba PHOTOS COURTESY OF UNIVERSAL

THE LAST SAMURAI

(WARNER BROS.) Producers, Edward Zwick, Marshall Herskovitz, Tom Cruise, Paula Wagner, Scott Kroopf, Tom Engelman; Executive Producers, Ted Field, Richard Solomon, Vincent Ward, Charles Mulvehill; Director, Edward Zwick; Screenplay, John Logan, Marshall Herskovitz, Edward Zwick; Photography, John Toll; Designer, Lilly Kilvert; Costumes, Ngila Dickson; Music, Hans Zimmer; Editor, Steven Rosenblum, Victor du Bois; Associate Producers, Graham J. Larson, Michael Doven, Yoko Narahashi; Visual Effects Supervisor, Jeffrey A. Okun; Casting, Victoria Thomas; Stunts, Nick Powell; a Radar Pictures/Bedford Falls Company/Cruise-Wagner production; Dolby; Panavision; Technicolor; Rated R; 154 minutes; Release date: December 5, 2003

Cast

Captain Nathan Algren **Tom Cruise**
Simon Graham **Timothy Spall**
Katsumoto **Ken Watanabe**
Zebulon Gant **Billy Connolly**
Colonel Bagley **Tony Goldwyn**
Ujio **Hiroyuki Sanada**
Taka **Koyuki**

Shichinosuke Nakamura, Ken Watanabe

Emperor Meiji **Shichinosuke Nakamura**
Nakao **Shun Sugata**
The Silent Samurai **Seizo Fukumoto**
Omura **Masato Harada**
Nobutada **Shin Koyamada**
Winchester Rep **William Atherton**
Winchester Rep's Assistant **Chad Lindberg**
Convention Hall Attendee **Ray Godshall, Sr.**
Omura's Companion **Masashi Odate**
Omura's Bodyguard **John Koyama**
General Hasegawa **Togo Igawa**
N.C.O. **Satoshi Nikaido**
Young Recruit **Shintaro Wada**
Higen **Sosuke Ikematsu**

and Aoi Minato (Magojiro), Shoji Yoshihara (Sword Master), Kosaburo Nomura IV, Takashi Noguchi, Noguchi Takayurki (Kyogen Players), Sven Toorvald (Omura's Secretary), Yuki Matsuzaki, Mitsuyuki Oishi, Jiro Wada (Soldiers in Street), Hiroshi Watanabe (Guard), Yusuke Myochin (Sword Master's Assistant)

Tom Cruise PHOTOS COURTESY OF WARNER BROS.

Koyuki, Tom Cruise

A disillusioned former war hero, Captain Nathan Algren, agrees to travel to Japan to train Japan's first modern, conscript army, and ends up forming an alliance with Katsumoto, the last leader of an ancient line of samurai warriors.

This film received Oscar nominations for supporting actor (Ken Watanabe), sound, costume design, and art direction.

BIG FISH

(COLUMBIA) Producers, Richard D. Zanuck, Bruce Cohen, Dan Jinks; Executive Producer, Arne L. Schmidt; Director, Tim Burton; Screenplay, John August; Based on the novel by Daniel Wallace; Photography, Philippe Rousselot; Designer, Dennis Gassner; Costumes, Colleen Attwood; Editor, Chris Lebenzon; Music, Danny Elfman; Special Visual Effects, Sony Pictures Imageworks, Inc.; Casting, Denise Cahmian; a Jinks/Cohen Company—a Zanuck Company production; Dolby; Deluxe color; 125 minutes; Release date: December 10, 2003

Cast

Ed Bloom (young) **Ewan McGregor**
Ed Bloom (senior) **Albert Finney**
Will Bloom **Billy Crudup**
Sandra Bloom (senior) **Jessica Lange**
Jenny (young & senior)/The Witch **Helena Bonham Carter**
Sandra Bloom (young) **Alison Lohman**
Dr. Bennett (senior) **Robert Guillaume**
Josephine **Marion Cotillard**
Karl the Giant **Matthew McGrory**
Don Price (age 18-22) **David Denman**
Mildred **Missi Pyle**
Beamen **Loudon Wainwright**
Ping **Ada Tai**
Jing **Arlene Tai**
Norther Winslow **Steve Buscemi**
Amos Calloway **Danny DeVito**
Mr. Soggybottom **Deep Roy**
Ed Bloom (age 10) **Perry Walston**
Jenny (age 8) **Hailey Anne Nelson**
Will Bloom (age 6-8) **Grayson Stone**
Ed's Father **R. Keith Harris**
Ed's Mother **Karla Droege**
Zacky Price (age 10) **Zachary Gardner**
Don Price (age 12) **John Lowell**
Wilbur (age 10) **Darrell Vanterpool**
Ruthie (age 8) **Destiny Cyrus**
Little Brave **Joseph Humphrey**
Will's Date **Morgan Grace Jarrett**

Ewan McGregor, Hailey Anne Nelson, Missi Pyle, Loudon Wainwright, Steve Buscemi

Helena Bonham Carter

Ewan McGregor, Hailey Anne Nelson

Albert Finney, Jessica Lange

Matthew McGrory, Ewan McGregor

Billy Crudup, Marion Cotillard

Ewan McGregor

Steve Buscemi, Ewan McGregor

Danny DeVito PHOTOS COURTESY OF COLUMBIA

Pretty Girl **Sallie Hedrick**
Mayor **Charles McLawhorn**
Sharecropper **Frank Hoyt Taylor**
Little Girl **Savanna James**
Banjo Man **Billy Redden**
Shotgun Toter **James DeForest Parker**
Some Farmer **Russell Hodgkinson**

and Don Young (Shephard), Jayne Morgan, David Ramsey, Greg Hohn (Townsfolk), Zach Hanner (Cashier), George McArthur (Colossus), Jeff Campbell (Jump Leader), Lawrence Sykkmon (Chinese Emcee), Bonnie Johnson (Teller Woman), Howard Houston, Jr. (Piano Student), Joanne Pankow (Heavy Set Nurse), Trevor Gagnon (Will's Son), Jacob Radford (Kid), Karlos Walkes (Dr. Bennett, young), Cathy Berry (Lobster Woman), John Fugate (Side Show Barker), Daniel Wallace (Econ Professor), Metz Duites (Ventriloquist), Vincent Ybiernas (Asian Officer), Barry C. Harvard (Chicken Plant Owner), Edward Aldag (Municipal Dump Owner), Michael Garnet Stewart (Auctioneer), Alan Rawlins (Pretty Man), Jake Brake (Old Zacky), Bevin Kaye (River Woman)

Edward Bloom, who has alienated his son with his tall tales about his life, looks back on the many odd people and strange occurances that may or may not have made up his colorful life.

This film received an Oscar nomination for original score.

SOMETHING'S GOTTA GIVE

(COLUMBIA/WARNER BROS.) Producers, Nancy Meyers, Bruce A. Block; Director/Screenplay, Nancy Meyers; Photography, Michael Ballhaus; Designer, Jon Hutman; Costumes, Suzanne McCabe; Co-Producer, Suzanne Farwell; Editor, Joe Hutshing; Music, Hans Zimmer; Casting, Jane Jenkins, Janet Hirshenson; a Waverly Films production; Dolby; Deluxe color; Rated PG-13; 128 minutes; Release date: December 12, 2003

Jack Nicholson, Diane Keaton

Frances McDormand

Diane Keaton, Keanu Reeves

Amanda Peet, Jack Nicholson

Cast

Harry Sanborn **Jack Nicholson**
Erica Barry **Diane Keaton**
Dr. Julian Mercer **Keanu Reeves**
Zoe Barry **Frances McDormand**
Marin **Amanda Peet**
Leo **Jon Favreau**
Dave **Paul Michael Glaser**
Dr. Martinez **Rachel Ticotin**
Beauties **Paige Butcher, Tanya Sweet, Kristine Szabo, Daniella Von Graas, Tamara Spoelder, Sonja Francis, Vanessa Haydon, Kathy Tong**
French Girl in Market **Marjie Gum**
Ladies in Market **Beatrice Quinn, Connie Sawyer**
Young Woman in Market **Jennifer Siebel**
Older Guy in Market **Robert Frank Telfer**
Paramedic **Ara Anton**
Hamptons Nurses **Melette Le Blanc-Cabot, Susan Dizon, Audrey Wasilewski, Roxanne Beckford, Robin Pearson Rose**
Harry's Assistants **Tania Deighton, Nicki Norris**
Mrs. Gimble **Lorna Scott**
Hamptons Waiter **TJ Thyne**
Kristen **KaDee Strickland**
Harry's Dinner Date **Tayrene Mugridge**
NYC Nurses **Elayn Taylor, Conroe Brooks**
Young Patient **Taylor Block**
Party Guests **Melissa Keller, Genelle Frenoy**
Harry's Lunch Date **Nichole Hiltz**
Broadway Actress **Leslie Upson**
Stage Manager **Patrick Fischler**
Danny Benjamin **Peter Spears**
Harry's Old Flames **Cindy Joseph, Alexandra Neil, Susan Misner**
and Michelle Fabiano, Catherine McGoohan, Blaine Allen, Julia Rose, Joan Adelle Nelson (Door Slammers), Sean Smith (Maitre'd), Maria Esquivel (Hostess)

Forced to play host to her daughter's much older lover after he suffers a heart attack, divorcee Erica Barry finds herself becoming strangely attracted to him.

This film received an Oscar nomination for actress (Diane Keaton).

Keanu Reeves, Jack Nicholson

Diane Keaton, Jack Nicholson

Frances McDormand, Diane Keaton, Amanda Peet

Keanu Reeves

Diane Keaton, Keanu Reeves, Jack Nicholson

Diane Keaton, Jack Nicholson, Amanda Peet

Frances McDormand, Diane Keaton PHOTOS COURTESY OF COLUMBIA/WARNER BROS.

STUCK ON YOU

(20TH CENTURY FOX) Producers, Bradley Thomas, Chrales B. Wessler, Bobby Farrelly, Peter Farrelly; Executive Producer, Marc S. Fischer; Director/Screenplay, Bobby Farrelly, Peter Farrelly; Story, Charles B. Wessler, Bennett Yellin, Peter Farrelly, Bobby Farrelly; Photography, Dan Mindel; Designer, Sidney J. Bartholomew, Jr.; Costumes, Deena Appel; Editors, Christopher Greenbury, Dave Terman; Music Supervisors, Tom Wolfe, Manish Raval; Co-Producers, Mark Charpentier, Garrett Grant, Kris Meyer; Makeup Effects Designer, Tony Gardner; Casting, Rick Montgomery; a Condundrum Entertainment/Charles B. Wessler production; Dolby; Panavision; Deluxe color; Rated PG-13; 118 minutes; Release date: December 12, 2003

Wen Yann Shih, Matt Damon, Greg Kinnear PHOTO COURTESY OF 20TH CENTURY FOX

Cast
Bob Tenor **Matt Damon**
Walt Tenor **Greg Kinnear**
April **Eva Mendes**
Herself **Cher**
Morty O'Reilly **Seymour Cassel**
May **Wen Yann Shih**

and Pat Crawford Brown (Mimmy), Ray "Rocket" Valliere (Rocket), Tommy Songin (Tommy), Terence Bernie Hines (Moe), Jackie Flynn (Howard), Meryl Streep, Griffin Dunne, Jay Leno, Sergio Garcia, Jesper Parnevik, Billy Andrade, Luke Wilson, Frankie Muniz (Themselves), Bridget Tobin (Vineyard Cutie), Danny Murphy (Dicky), Malcolm G. Chace, Jr. (Vineyard Buddie), Steve Cerrone (Dart in Head Guy), Docky (Short-Fuzed Geezer), Will Coogan (Eddie), Skyler Stone (George), Leslie Munroe (Vineyard Patron), Mike Cerrone (Hockey Stud), Michael Lee Merrins, Jonathan Cauff (Umpires), Sean P. Gildea (Baseball Coach), Michael Callan (Fox Prexy), Dane Cook (Officer Fraioli), Steve Tyler (Officer Reney), Peter Dante (Officer J.J. Hill), Ben Koldyke (Officer Tommy Johnson), Jessica Cauffiel (Bar Hottie), Roger Fan, Jennifer Azar Burnham (Executives), Elaine Curtis (Cher's Assistant), Gary Valentine (Wes), Mariann Neary, Terez Kocsis (Purse Babes), Benjamin S. Carson Sr., M.D. (Head Surgeon), Sayed Badreya (Assisting Surgeon), Hilary Matthews Thomas (Nurse's Aide), Dan Geraci (Handsome Hospital Orderly), Bob Mone (Hospital Heartthrob), Brian Mone (Tall Man), Catherine McCord, Kelly Albanese, Paulina Neely (Jogger Babes), Daniel Greene (Mr. Tourist), Kristen Trucksess (Mrs. Tourist), Brian Hayes Currie (Laughing Director), Ann Stocking, Tracy Ashton, Joe Steilen, Nate Steilen, Lisa Jouet Mosenson, Joni Friedman, Ellen Jacoby, Carrei Yazel-Steilen, Steve Cohen (Casting Agents), Pat Battistini, Doug Jones (Space Aliens), Lin Shaye (Makeup Babe), John Woodin (Porno Stage Hand), Johnny Cicco (Porno Director), Rene C. Kirby (Phil Rupp), Erica Lookadoo (Marianna Trench), Justin Alioto, Will Dunn, Terry Nicholson, Robyn MK Brooks (Beaze Fans), Ernie Garrett (Bar Thug), Bennett Leyllin, Gregory Wyler (SPFX Guys), Jeff Ross (Beaze Security Guard), Googy Gress (Pete Peterson), Gene Feldman (1st AD), Kiele Sanchez (Pepper Spray Cutie), Lenny Clarke (Jailhouse Comic), Michael Edward Thomas (Convenience Store Guy), Carolyn Stotes (Pretty Hostess), Anna Byers (Cute Autograph Girl), Gary M. Baker (Dave the Bartender), Colin Kenrick (Nine-Year-Old Walt), Dennis Kravchenko (Nine-Year-Old Bob), Galen Schrick (Brimstone Preacher), Otis Walter Albert, Elizardo Del Rio, Robert F. Smith (Outta Sight Singers), Jesse Peter (Bully Kid), Fred Burns (Street Comic), Niki Tyler-Flynn (Double Bubble Casting Agent), Tom Brady, Laweyr Milloy (Computer Geeks), George Christy (Beaze Stagehand), Caryl West (Oak Bluffs Theatre Women), Stephen Saux (Drive-by Heckler), Nancy Byers (Gorgeous Hostess), Ricky Blitt (Mobster), Pete Peterson (Piano Player), Larry Grant (Coffee Shop Patron), Tracey Ruggiero (Barney's Waitress), Artie Granfield (Barney's Patron), Rhona Mitra (Bus Stop Bombshell), Kevin Civale (Boxing Corner Man), John Mulcahy (Boxing Referee), Peter Grundy (Boxing Trainer), Joel B. Hayden (Piano Bar Patron), Ashley B. Howard, Monika Kramlik (Double Bubble Babes), Tiffany Anne Marie Lucich (Hottie Highlands Waitress), Ricky Williams (Martha's Vineyard Football Coach), Michael Burton (Beaze Executive), Gino Torretta, Bruce Armstrong (Beaze Thugs), Keith A. Hoffman (School Principal), John Chan (Incessant Photographer), Adam Shankman (Choreographer/Waiter), Bob Kocsis (Four-Year-Old Bob), Charlie Thomas (Four-Year-Old Walt), Stephen Mone (MV Cabbie), Brian Peterson (MV Villager), Gerry Harrington (MV Hockey Coach), Michael Cerrone, Jr. (MV First Baseman), Delwyn "Peewee" Young (Yarmouth Batter), Kevin Barnett (Yarmouth Runner), Michael "The Cannon" Gannon (Boxer "Red Trunks"), Ashley Millan (Boxing Fan), Katharine Patrikios, Mary Patrikios (Prom Queens), Greg Lubin (Prom King), Francesca Beale (Prom Night Teacher), Margo Murphy (Portuguese American Club Waitress), Mary & Michael Murphy (Halloween House Folks), Emily O'Donnell, Keegan O'Donnell, Madison Turner, Kelsie Turner (Halloween Trick O'Treaters), Joseph Martini (Robin Hood Stage Crew Member), Michael Lyons (Michael Lyons), Freddy "The Commissioner" Hildreth (Tinsel-Town Shuffleboard Pro), Peter Grossman, Clem Franek (Meryl Streep's Posse), Beth Jordan, Andrea Palm (Studio Executives), Joanne Wolfe (Babe in Red Car), Natasha Kassyutina (LA Restaurant Babe), Candy Carson (Emergency Room Nurse), Gary Reis (Hospital Orderly), Harold Olofsson (Bonnie & Clyde Mobster)

A pair of conjoined twins travel to Hollywood in hopes that one of them, Walt, will make it in show business.

MONA LISA SMILE

(COLUMBIA) Producers, Elaine Goldsmith-Thomas, Deborah Schindler, Paul Schiff; Director, Mike Newell; Screenplay, Lawrence Konner, Mark Rosenthal; Executive Producer, Joe Roth; Photography, Anastos Michos; Designer, Jane Musky; Costumes, Michael Dennison; Music, Rachel Portman; Music Supervisor, Randall Poster; Editor, Mick Audsley; Casting, Ellen Chenoweth, Susie Farris; a Revolution Studios presentation of a Red Om Films production; Dolby; Deluxe color; Rated PG-13; 117 minutes; Release date: December 19, 2003

Laura Allen, Maggie Gyllenhaal, Julia Stiles

Cast

Katherine Ann Watson **Julia Roberts**
Betty Warren **Kirsten Dunst**
Joan Brandwyn **Julia Stiles**
Giselle Levy **Maggie Gyllenhaal**
Connie Baker **Ginnifer Goodwin**
Bill Dunbar **Dominic West**
Amanda Armstrong **Juliet Stevenson**
Nancy Abbey **Marcia Gay Harden**
Paul Moore **John Slattery**

and Marian Seldes (President Jocelyn Carr), Donna Mitchell (Mrs. Warren), Terence Rigby (Dr. Edward Staunton), Jennie Eisenhower (Girl at the Station), Leslie Lyles (Housing Director), Laura Allen (Susan Delacorte), Topher Grace (Tommy Donegal), Lily Lodge (House Matron), Jordan Bridges (Spencer Jones), Ebon Moss-Bacharach (Charlie Stewart), Christopher Braden Jones (Bartender), Chuck Montgomery (Tall Man), Taylor Roberts (Louise), John Scurti (Stan Sher), Ed Peed (Taxi Driver), Rony Clanton (Porter), Becky Veduccio (Blue Ship Hostess), Paul Vincent Black (Joseph O'Neill), Lisa Roberts Gillan (Miss Albini), June Miller (Cape Cod Hostess), Aleksa Palladino (Frances the Girl in Italian Class), Charles Techman (Harvard Dorm Monitor), Lauren Adler, Daisy Baldwin, Janine Barris, Emily Bauer, Kirstie Bingham, Jennifer Bowen, Angelique Claire, Nikki Coble, Kristen Connolly, Kristyn Coppola, Kimberly Ehly, Megan Marie Ford, Lauren Fruchter, Kate Glass, Amanda Gruss, Stella Hao, Walker Hays, Michele Hillen, Annika Marks, Amy Montminy, Lily Rabe, Katherine Reilly, Krysten Ritter, Brandy Tipton, Trisha Trokan, Megan Tropea, Maja Walpvszyl (Art History Students), Mary S. Pascoe (Photographer), Elise Passamani (Phyllis), Laura M. Flahive, Devon Jencks, Erin E. Richardson, Emily R. See (Wet Girls), Rob Buntzen (Wedding Planner Host), Richard O'Rourke (Igor), Chris Bonomo

(Groomsman), Katherine Argo, Shelby Bond, Lou Brock, Michael Choi, Melissa Deles, John D. Fowler, Nicole Frydman, Noelle Gibson, Maria Vicens Girau, Natalie Gomez, Sid Grant, Madeleine Hackney, Betina Hershey, Yuval Hod, Richard Jones, Jerry Jordan, Nickolay Khazanov, Nadai Kravets, Maria Levinstein, Kellydawn Malloy, Annette Nicole, Lance Olds, Joe Palmer, Christian Perry, Daniel Ponickly, Tony Scheppler, Solomon Singer, Gabriel Vaughan, Kim Villanueva, Dan Weltner, Sarah Billings Wheeler, Denise Zadroga (Dancers), Peter J. Rowan (Wedding Photographer), Tori Amos (Singer), Kevin Osborne (Band Announcer), Brad Mehldau (Pianist), Larry Grenadier (Bass Player), Julie Wagner (Bartender), Jennifer Anderson, Lindsey White (Projectionists), Chris Burke (Custodian), Dorothy Dwyer (Faculty), Melanie Angelique Moyer, Canedy Knowles, Kristen Marie Holly, Carrie Ann Kaye (Christmas Students), Lilliane Thomas (Woman on Train), Jackie Sanders (Band Announcer)

Julia Roberts, Julia Stiles, Topher Grace

Katherine Watson, a free-thinking art history professor, arrives at Wellesley College in 1953 and is shocked to find that her female students are being taught that becoming a wife and mother are more important goals than a well-rounded education.

Julia Roberts, Dominic West PHOTOS COURTESY OF COLUMBIA

HOUSE OF SAND AND FOG

(DREAMWORKS) Producers, Michael London, Vadim Perelman; Director, Vadim Perelman; Screenplay, Vadim Perelman, Shawn Lawrence Otto; Based on the novel by Andre Dubus III; Co-Producer, Jeremiah Samuels; Photography, Roger Deakins; Designer, Maia Javan; Music, James Horner; Editor, Lisa Zeno Churgin; Casting, Deborah Aquila, Tricia Wood; a Michael London production, presented in association with Cobalt Media Group; Dolby; Technicolor; Rated R; 126 minutes; Release date: December 19, 2003

Ben Kingsley, Ron Eldard, Jonathan Ahdout

Cast

Kathy Nicolo	**Jennifer Connelly**
Massoud Amir Behrani	**Ben Kingsley**
Lester Burdon	**Ron Eldard**
Connie Walsh	**Frances Fisher**
Carol Burdon	**Kim Dickens**
Nadi	**Shohreh Aghdashloo**
Esmail	**Jonathan Ahdout**
Soraya	**Navi Rawat**
Lt. Alvarez	**Carlos Gomez**
Ali	**Kia Jam**
Yasmin	**Jaleh Modjallal**
Little Soraya	**Samira Damavandi**
Little Esmail	**Matthew Simonian**

Jennifer Connelly PHOTOS COURTESY OF DREAMWORKS

Shohreh Aghdashloo, Jennifer Connelly, Ben Kingsley

Ben Kingsley

and Namrata S. Gujral-Cooper, Al Faris, Mark Chaet (Wedding Guests), Marco Rodriguez (Mendez), Al Rodrigo (Torez), Aki Aleong (Tran), Joyce Kurtz (Kathy's Mom), Scott N. Stevens (County Official), Ken Kerman (Locksmith), Scott Kinworthy (Deputy Trainee), Tom Benick (Hotel Security), Samuel Hart (Elevator Man), Jackie Ahdout (Elevator Woman), Spencer Garrett (Auctioneer), Cooper Thornton (Gary), Isabelle James (Teenage Girl), Bonita Friedericy (Motel Manger), David Carrera, Michael Papajohn (Carpenters), Joe Howard (Appraiser), Aaron Frazier (Courier), Dan Brinkle (Husband, Buyer), Yan Lin (Wife, Buyer), Andre Dubus III (Myers), Max Jansen Weinstein (Nate), Ashley Louise Edner (Bethany), Ray Abruzzo (Frank), Tom Reynolds (Gas Station Worker), Jose Vasquez, Matt Waite (Arresting Officers), Pamela Shaddock (Nurse), Frank Gallego (Prison Guard), Karl Makinen (Officer at End), Zoran Radanovich (Sergei), Markus Baldwin (Young Husband), Brian Reed Garvin (Fat Man), Dennison Samaroo (Doctor), Elton Ahi, Shani Rigsbee, Andy Madadian (Wedding Singers)

When a bureaucratic error forces Kathy Nicolo to be evicted from her home, former Iranian officer Massoud Amir Behrani buys it at auction, starting a battle for ownership of the house.

This film received Oscar nominations for actor (Ben Kingsley), supporting actress (Shohreh Aghdashloo), original score.

MONSTER

(NEWMARKET) Producers, Charlize Theron, Mark Damon, Clark Peterson, Donald Kushner, Brad Wyman; Executive Producers, Sammy Lee, Meagan Riley-Grant, Stewart Hall, Andreas Grosch, Andreas Schmid; Director/Screenplay, Patty Jenkins; Photography, Steven Bernstein; Designer, Edward T. McAvoy; Music, BT; Music Supervisor, Howard Paar; Editors, Jane Kurson, Arthur Coburn; Casting, Ferne Cassel; presented in association with Media 8 Entertainment/DEJ Productions, a K/W Productions and Denver & Delilah Films production in association with VIP Medienfonds 2/MDP Filmproduktion; U.S.-German; Dolby; Color; Rated R; 109 minutes; Release date: December 24, 2003

Christina Ricci, Charlize Theron

Charlize Theron

Cast

Aileen Wuornos **Charlize Theron**
Selby Wall **Christina Ricci**
Thomas **Bruce Dern**
Horton (Last "John") **Scott Wilson**
Gene (Stuttering "John") **Pruitt Taylor Vince**
Vincent Corey **Lee Tergesen**
Donna Tentler **Annie Corley**
Evan (Undercover "John") **Marco St. John**
Will (Daddy "John") **Marc Macaulay**
Cop **Rus Blackwell**
Chuck **Tim Ware**
Lawyer **Stephan Jones**
Charles **Brett Rice**
Teenage Aileen **Kaitlin Riley**
7-Year-Old Aileen **Cree Ivey**
Justy **Catherin Mangan**
Bar Lap Girl **Magdelena Manville**
Bartender **T. Robert Pigott**
and Romonda Shaver (Employment Agent), Glenn R. Wilder (Restaurant Manager), Elaine Stebbins (Wife at Accident), Kane Hodder, Christian Stokes (Undercover Cops), Lyllian Barcaski, Nonalee Davis (Bar Girls), Bubba Baker (Cubby), Al Cannonball (Himself), Chad Vaccarino (Trevor), Honorable Gene R. Stephenson (Judge), Jesse Stern (Skate Rink Attendant), Bill Boylan (Police Chief), Jim R. Coleman (Newscaster), Chandra Leigh (Cute Teenage Attendant), Lori McDonald, Adam Brown (Attendants)

The true story of how Aileen Wuornos fell into a life of prostitution and eventual murder, which led to her capture and execution.

Charlize Theron received the 2003 Academy Award for Best Actress.

Bruce Dern PHOTOS COURTESY OF NEWMARKET

PAYCHECK

(PARAMOUNT/DREAMWORKS) Producers, John Davis, Michael Hackett, John Woo, Terence Chang; Executive Producers, Stratton Leopold, David Solomon; Director, John Woo; Screenplay, Dean Georgaris; Based on the short story by Philip K. Dick; Photography, Jeffrey L. Kimball; Designer, William Sandell; Costumes, Erica Edell Phillips; Music, John Powell; Editors, Kevin Stitt, Christopher Rose; Co-Producers, Caroline Macaulay, Arthur Anderson; Visual Effects Supervisor, Gregory L. McMurry; Stunts, Gregg Smrz, Owen Walstrom; Casting, Mandy Marin; a Davis Entertainment Company/Lion Rock production, in association with Solomon/Hackett Productions; Dolby; Super 35 Widescreen; Deluxe color; Rated PG-13; 118 minutes; Release date: December 25, 2003

Ben Affleck, Paul Giamatti

Aaron Eckhart, Uma Thurman

Cast

Michael Jennings **Ben Affleck**
James Rethrick **Aaron Eckhart**
Dr. Rachel Porter **Uma Thurman**
Shorty **Paul Giamatti**
John Wolfe **Colm Feore**
Agent Dodge **Joe Morton**
Agent Klein **Michael C. Hall**
Attorney General Brown **Peter Friedman**
Rita Dunne **Kathryn Morris**
Maya-Rachel **Ivana Milicevic**
Stevens **Christopher Kennedy**
Agent Fuman **Fulvio Cecere**
Agent Mitchell **John Cassini**
Judge (Guard) **Callum Keith Rennie**
Jane **Michelle Harrison**
Sara Rethrick **Claudette Mink**
Street Kid **Ryan Zwick**
Guard **Dee Jay Jackson**
Dekker **Serge Houde**

and Calvin Finlayson (Balloon Boy), Kendall Cross, Catherine Lough Haggquist (Scientists), Darryl Scheelar (Plain Clothes Federal Agent), Mark Brandon (Lottery Host), Roger Kashett (Lottery Official), Steve Wright (Allcom Helicopter Pilot), Craig Hosking (FBI Helicopter Pilot),

Emily Holmes (Betsy, Salesgirl), Krista Allen (Holographic Woman), Barclay Hope, Peter Shinkoda, David Lewis (Suits), Robert Clark, Andrea Siradze, Isabelle Roland, Peter Caton (String Quartet), Ryan Robbins (Husband), Benita Ha (Wife), Chelah Horsdal (Young Mother), Craig March (Janitor), Jason Calder, Mike Godenir, Brad Kelly, Brent Connolly (Wolfe Goons), Michelle Anderson, Lori Berlanga (Nursery Customers)

Agreeing to have his memory erased after working on a top secret project for three years, Jennings discovers that he has been denied access to the payment for his participation. He has left himself an envelope full of objects that seem to have been thought out in advance with the intention of providing him with assistance to solve his current dilemma.

Joe Morton, Michael C. Hall PHOTOS COURTESY OF PARAMOUNT/DREAMWORKS

THE COMPANY

(SONY CLASSICS) Producers, David Levy, Joshua Astrachan, Neve Campbell, Robert Altman, Christine Vachon, Pamela Koffler; Executive Producers, Jane Barclay, Sharon Harel, Hannah Leader, John Wells, Roland Pellegrino, Dieter Meyer; Director, Robert Altman; Screenplay, Barbara Turner; Story, Neve Campbell, Barbara Turner; Photography, Andrew Dunn; Designer, Gary Baugh; Costumes, Susan Kaufman; Editor, Geraldine Peroni; Music, Van Dyke Parks; Associate Producer, Jocelyn Hayes; Joffrey Ballet Artistic Director, Gerald Arpino; Casting, Pam Dixon Mickelson; a Killer Films/John Wells production in association with First Snow Productions and Sandcastle 5 Productions, presented in association with CP Medien and Capitol Films; U.S.-German; Dolby; HD 24P Widescreen; Color; Rated PG-13; 112 minutes; Release date: December 25, 2003

Malcolm McDowell, Domingo Rubio, Neve Campbell

Jennifer Goodman

Cast

Ry **Neve Campbell**
Alberto Antonelli **Malcolm McDowell**
Josh **James Franco**
Harriet **Barbara Robertson**
Edouard **William Dick**
Susie **Susie Cusack**
Ry's Mother **Marilyn Dodds Frank**
Ry's Father **John Lordan**
Stepmother **Mariann Mayberry**
Stepfather **Roderick Peeples**
Justin's Mentor **Yasen Peyankov**
THE JOFFREY DANCERS
Alec **Davis Robertson**
Deborah **Deborah Dawn**
John **John Gluckman**
Justin **David Gombert**

Suzanne **Suzanne L. Prisco**
Domingo **Domingo Rubio**
Noel **Emily Patterson**
Maia **Maia Wilkins**
Frankie **Sam Franke**
Trinity **Trinity Hamilton**
Julianne **Julianne Kepley**
Veronica **Valerie Robin**
Dana **Deanne Brown**
Michael **Michael Smith**
Colton **Matthew Roy Prescott**

and Lar Lubovitch, Robert Desrosiers (The Choreographers), Charthel Arthur, Cameron Basden (The Ballet Mistresses), Mark Goldweber, Pierre Lockett, Adam Sklute (The Ballet Masters), Heather Aagard, Michael Anderson, Erica Lynette Edward, Jennifer Goodman, Stacy Joy Keller, Calvin Kitten, Peter Kozak, Britta Lazanga, Michael Levine, Brian McSween, Elizabeth Mertz, Masayoshi Onuki, Samuel Pergande, Willy Shives, Erin Smith, Kathleen Thielhelm, Mauro Villanueva, Yukari Yasui (The Company), Tristan Alberda, Bobby Briscoe, Orlando Julius Canova, Angelina Sansone, Jacqueline Sherwood, Jessica Wyatt (The Apprentices), Michael Andrew Currey, Katherine Selig (Stage Managers), Paul Lewis (Company Pianist), Julie O'Connell (Physical Therapist), George Darveris (Production Manager), Marc Grapey (Toast Master), Keith Prisco (Bridegroom), Emma Harrison (Neo Waitress), Dwayne Whitmore (Neo Bouncer), Danny McCarthy (Bartender), Robert Breuler (Barfly), Larry Glazer (Grant Park Cellist), Mark Hummel (Grant Park Pianist)

A look at one season of the Joffrey Ballet of Chicago.

James Franco, Neve Campbell PHOTOS COURTESY OF SONY CLASSICS

Nicole Kidman, Jude Law

Brendan Gleason

Natalie Portman

COLD MOUNTAIN

(MIRAMAX) Producers, Sydney Pollack, William Horberg, Albert Berger, Ron Yerxa; Executive Producers, Iain Smith, Bob Weinstein, Harvey Weinstein, Bob Osher; Director/Screenplay, Anthony Minghella; Based on the novel by Charles Frazier; Photography, John Seale; Designer, Dante Ferretti; Costumes, Ann Roth, Carlo Poggioli; Executives in Charge of Production, Colin Vaines, Steve Hutensky; Music, Gabriel Yared; Editor, Walter Murch; Casting, David Rubin, Ronna Kress; a Mirage Enterprises/Bona Fide production; U.S.-British-Romanian-Italian; Dolby; Super 35 Widescreen; Deluxe color; Rated R; 155 minutes; Release date: December 25, 2003

Cast

W.P. Inman **Jude Law**
Ada Monroe **Nicole Kidman**
Ruby Thewes **Renée Zellweger**
Maddy **Eileen Atkins**
Stobrod Thewes **Brendan Gleason**
Reverend Veasey **Philip Seymour Hoffman**
Sara **Natalie Portman**
Junior **Giovanni Ribisi**
Reverend Monroe **Donald Sutherland**
Teague **Ray Winstone**
Sally Swanger **Kathy Baker**
Esco Swanger **James Gammon**
Bosie **Charlie Hunnam**
Georgia **Jack White**
Pangle **Ethan Suplee**
Ferry Girl **Jena Malone**

and Melora Walters (Lila), Lucas Black (Oakley), Taryn Manning (Shyla), Tom Aldredge (Blind Man), James Rebhorn (Doctor), Emily Deschanel (Mrs. Morgan), Robin Mullins (Mrs. Castlereagh), Ben Allison (Rourke), Trey Howell (Butcher), Alex Hassell (Orderly), Jay Tavare (Swimmer), William Boyer (Confederate Officer), Chris Fennell (Acton Swanger), Erik Smith (Ellis Swanger), Cillian Murphy (Bardolph), Richard Brake (Nym), Sean Gleeson (Pistol), Rasool J'han (Rebecca), Hank Stone (Brown), Mark Jeffrey Miller (Sheffield), Afemo Omilami (Joshua), Chet Dixon (Vesey

Charlie Hunnam, Ray Winstone

Nicole Kidman, Jude Law

Town Guard), Jamie Lee (Guard), Jen Apgar (Dolly), Katherine Durio (Mae), Martin Pemberton (Mo), Leonard Woodcock (Jo), William Roberts (Grayling), Dean Whitworth (Barber), Kristen Nicole La Prade (Grace Inman)

In 1864, following the bloody siege at Petersburg, Virginia, W.P. Inman, a Confederate soldier fed up with the inhumanity of war, vows to make his way back to Cold Mountain in North Carolina where Ada Monroe waits anxiously for his return.

2003 Academy Award–winner for Best Supporting Actress (Renée Zellweger). This film received additional nominations for actor (Jude Law), cinematography, editing, original score, original song ("The Scarlet Tide"), and original song ("You Will Be My Ain True Love").

Renée Zellweger

Lucas Black

Renée Zellweger, Nicole Kidman

Jude Law

Jack White PHOTOS COURTESY OF MIRAMAX

CHEAPER BY THE DOZEN

(20TH CENTURY FOX) Producers, Robert Simonds, Michael Barnathan, Ben Myron; Director, Shawn Levy; Screenplay, Sam Harper, Joel Cohen, Alec Sokolow; Screen Story, Craig Titley; Based upon the book by Frank Bunker Gilbreth, Jr. and Ernestine Gilbreth Carey; Photography, Jonathan Brown; Designer, Nina Ruscio; Costumes, Sanja Milkovic Hays; Music, Christophe Beck; Music Supervisor, Dave Jordan; Editor, George Folsey, Jr.; Co-Producer, Ira Shuman; Casting, Nancy Klopper; a Robert Simonds production; Dolby; Deluxe color; Rated PG; 98 minutes; Release date: December 25, 2003

BEHIND COUCH: Piper Perabo, Alyson Stoner, Tom Welling, Kevin G. Schmidt, Hilary Duff; SITTING ON COUCH: Forrest Landis, Steve Martin, Bonnie Hunt, Morgan York, Liliana Mumy; ON FLOOR: Jacob Smith, Shane Kinsman, Brent Kinsman, Blake Woodruff

Steven Anthony Lawrence, Steve Martin

Piper Perabo, Steve Martin, Bonnie Hunt

Cast

Tom Baker **Steve Martin**
Kate Baker **Bonnie Hunt**
Nora Baker **Piper Perabo**
Charlie Baker **Tom Welling**
Lorraine Baker **Hilary Duff**
Henry Baker **Kevin G. Schmidt**
Sarah Baker **Alyson Stoner**
Jake Baker **Jacob Smith**
Jessica Baker **Liliana Mumy**
Kim Baker **Morgan York**
Mark Baker **Forrest Landis**
Mike Baker **Blake Woodruff**
Nigel Baker **Brent Kinsman**
Kyle Baker **Shane Kinsman**
Hank **Ashton Kutcher**
Tina Shenk **Paula Marshall**
Dylan Shenk **Steven Anthony Lawrence**

and Alan Ruck (Bill Shenk), Richard Jenkins (Shake), Wayne Knight (Chandelier Installer), Holmes Osborne (Nick Gerhard), Vanessa Bell Calloway (Diana Phillips), Rex Linn (Coach Bricker), David Kelsey (Assistant Coach), Dax Shepard, Elon Gold (Camera Crew Members), Cody Linley (Quinn), Adam Taylor Gordon (Cooper), Julie Kay Araskog (Radio Talk Show Host), Benjamin Fitch, Kevin Carey (Reporters), Antonio Vega (Police Officer), David Bowe (TV Interviewer), Ossie Mair (Cabbie), Amy Hill (Miss Hozzie), Ted Rooney (Principal), Joel McCrary (Gil), Tiffany

Dupont (Beth), Shawn Levy (Press Room Reporter), Dylan S. Shults (Party Kid), Regis Philbin, Kelly Ripa (Themselves)

Tom Baker gets his dream job of becoming a university football coach but must contend with moving his huge family of 12 children. Previous film version of the Gilbreth-Carey book starred Clifton Webb and Myrna Loy and was released by 20th Century-Fox in 1950.

Tom Welling, Hilary Duff PHOTOS COURTESY OF 20TH CENTURY FOX

PETER PAN

(UNIVERSAL/COLUMBIA) Producers, Lucy Fisher, Douglas Wick, Patrick McCormick; Executive Producer, Mohamed Al Fayed, Gail Lyon, Jocelyn Moorhouse; Director, P.J. Hogan; Screenplay, P.J. Hogan, Michael Goldenberg; Based upon the original stageplay and books written by J.M. Barrie; Co-Executive Producer, Charles Newirth; Co-Producers, Gary Adelson, Craig Baumgarten; Photography, Donald M. McAlpine; Designer, Roger Ford; Costumes, Janet Patterson; Editors, Garth Craven; Music, James Newton Howard; Visual Effects Supervisor, Scott Farrar; Casting, Billy Hopkins, Suzanne Smith, Kerry Barden, Deborah Maxwell Dion; Stunts, Conrad E. Palmisano; Fight Coordinator, Brad Allan; a Revolution Studios presentation of a Douglas Wick-Lucy Fisher/Allied Stars production; U.S.-Australian; Dolby; Panavision; Technicolor; Rated PG; 113 minutes; Release date: December 25, 2003

Jason Isaacs, Richard Briers

Bruce Myles (Bank Manager), Maya Barnaby, Tory Mussett, Ursula Mills, Nadia Pirini, Vij Kaewsanan (Mermaids), Janet Strauss (Medicine Woman), Sam Morely (Fairy Bride), Brendan Shambrook (Fairy Groom), Saffron Burrows (Story Narrator), Rebel (Nana)

Peter Pan, a boy who refuses to grow up, transports Wendy Darling and her brothers to Neverland where they battle the nefarious Captain Hook. Previous film versions of the Barrie story include the animated *Peter Pan* (Walt Disney-RKO, 1953) and *Hook* (TriStar, 1991) with Robin Williams as Peter and Dustin Hoffman as Captain Hook.

Harry Newell, Freddie Popplewell, Rachel Hurd-Wood

Cast

Mr. Darling/Captain Hook **Jason Isaacs**
Peter Pan **Jeremy Sumpter**
Wendy Darling **Rachel Hurd-Wood**
Aunt Millicent **Lynn Redgrave**
Smee **Richard Briers**
Mrs. Darling **Olivia Williams**
Sir Edward Quiller Couch **Geoffrey Palmer**
John Darling **Harry Newell**
Michael Darling **Freddie Popplewell**
Tink **Ludivine Sagnier**
Slightly **Theodore Chester**
Tootles **Rupert Simonian**

and George MacKay (Curly), Harry Eden (Nibs), Patrick Gooch, Lachlan Gooch (Twins), Carsen Gray (Tiger Lily), Maggie Dence (Lady Quiller Couch), Kerry Walker (Miss Fulsom), Matthew Waters (Messenger Boy), Alan Cinis (Skylights), Frank Whitten (Starkey), Bruce Spence (Cookson), Daniel Wyllie (Alf Mason), Brian Carbee (Albino), Don Batte (Giant Pirate), Frank Gallacher (Alsation Fogarty), Septimus Caton (Noodler), Jacob Tomuri (Bill Jukes), Venant Wong (Quang Lee), Phil Meacham (Bollard), Darren Mitchell (Mullins), Michael Roughan (Cecco), Bill Kerr (Fairy Guide), Celeste MacIlwaine, Spike Hogan, Patrick Hurd-Wood, Brooke Duncan, Themora Bourne, Alexander Bourne (Sleeping Children),

Jeremy Sumpter, Rachel Hurd-Wood

Lachlan Gooch, George MacKay, Patrick Gooch, Harry Newell, Jeremy Sumpter, Rupert Simonian, Theodore Chester, Harry Eden PHOTOS COURTESY OF UNIVERSAL/COLUMBIA

THE SLAUGHTER RULE

(COWBOY) Producers, Gavin O'Connor, Greg O'Connor, Michael A. Robinson, David O. Russell; Executive Producer, Jerry McFadden; Co-Producers, Christopher Cronyn, Josh Fagin, Robert Hawk; Directors/Screenplay, Alex Smith, Andrew J. Smith; Photography, Eric Alan Edwards; Designer, John Johnson; Costumes, Kristin M. Burke; Editor, Brent White; Music, Jay Farrar; Casting, Felicia Fasano, Anne McCarthy, Mary Vernieu; Ranchwater Productions; Color; Rated R; 117 minutes; Release date: January 8, 2003. Cast: Ryan Gosling (Roy Chutney), David Morse (Gideon "Gid" Ferguson), Clea DuVall (Skyla), David Cale (Floyd "Studebaker"), Eddie Spears (Tracey Two Dogs), Kelly Lynch (Evangeline Chutney), Amy Adams (Doreen), Ken White (Russ Colfax), Noah Watts (Waylon Walks Along), Kim DeLong (Lem Axelrod), Geraldine Kearms (Gretchen Two Dogs), Douglas Seybern (Uncle Peyton), Cody Harvey (Coach Motlow), Melkon Andonian (Devo), J.P. Gabriel (Jute), Chris Offcut (Charlie), John Henry Marshall (Kibbs), Juliana Clayton (Fran), Volley Reid (Forfeit Referee), H.A. Smith (Slick Higgins), Michael Mahony (Nelson Chutney), Alison Tatlock (Jolene Chutney), Betty Ann Conard (Jailer), Michael Dunlap (Football Announcer), Wylie Gustafson (Wylie), Perle Weisman (Keno Lady), David Wiater (Male Nurse), Tim Boggs, Matt Cornelius, Nate McClure, Matt Pipinich, Paul Pipinich, Jesse Sidor, Michael Smart, Ben Snipes (Renegades), Miles Gravage (Tyke), Philip Heron (Stumpy), The Wild Wild West (Trails End House Band)

BLUE COLLAR COMEDY TOUR: THE MOVIE

(WARNER BROS.) Producers, Alan C. Blomquist, Casey La Scala, Hunt Lowry, J.P. Williams, Joseph Williams; Executive Producer, E.K. Gaylord; Director, C.B. Harding; Photography, Bruce L. Finn; Designer, Jeff Hall; Editor, Tony Hayman; Music, James S. Levine; Gaylord Films, Pandora Cinema, Parallel Entertainment; Dolby; Color; Rated PG-13; 105 minutes; Release date: January 10, 2003. Four comedians in concert: Jeff Foxworthy, Bill Engvall, Ron White, Larry The Cable Guy; and Heidi Klum (Victoria's Secret Saleswoman), David Alan Grier (Limo Driver)

A GUY THING

(MGM) Producers, David Ladd, David Nicksay; Director, Chris Koch; Screenplay, Greg Glienna, Pete Schwaba, Matt Tarses, Bill Wrubel; Story, Greg Glienna; Photography, Robbie Greenberg; Designer, Pamela Withers; Music, Mark Mothersbaugh; Music Supervisor, Maureen Crowe; Editor, David Moritz; Co-Producers, Danielle Sterling, David Kerwin; Casting, Risa Bramon Garcia, Brennan DuFresnse; a David Ladd Films production; Dolby; Deluxe color; Rated PG-13; 101 minutes; Release date: January 17, 2003. Cast: Jason Lee (Paul), Julia Stiles (Becky), Selma Blair (Karen), James Brolin (Ken), Shawn Hatosy (Jim), Lochlyn Munro (Ray), Diana Scarwid (Sandra), David Koechner (Buck), Julie Hagerty (Dorothy), Thomas Lennon (Pete), Jackie Burroughs (Aunt Budge), Jay Brazeau (Howard), Matthew Walker (Minister Green), Fred Ewanuick (Jeff), Lisa Calder (Tonya), Dan Joffre (Larry), Michael Teigen (Lou), Will Sanderson, Dave McGowan, Jonathon Young, Daniel McKellar (Bachelor Party Guys), Scott Williams, Josef Pelletier, Joe Sather (The Buddy Scott Trio), Alex Farquharson (Nephew), Brody Smith (Leo Ferris), Miriam Smith (Mrs. Ferris), John Destry (Angry Driver), Paul McGillion (Curt), Gina Stockdale (Gladys), Michael Sunczyk (Tony), Zahf Paroo (Ahmed), Noel Fisher (Acne-Faced Teen), Enid-Raye Adams (Maid of Honor), Benjamin Ratner, Dee Jay Jackson (Officers), Keith Dallas

David Morse, Ryan Gosling in *The Slaughter Rule* PHOTO COURTESY OF COWBOY

(Spend Mart Clerk), Donavon Stinson (Mouthy Bar Guy), Victor Varnado (Hansberry), Larry Musser (Ernie), Ron Selmour (Doc), Gus Lynch (Agent Harris), Fiona Hogan (Agent Roberts), Xantha Radley (Ken's Secretary), Leslie Jones (Sales Employee), Chris Wilding (Beaten Suspect), Andy Thompson (Guy in Washroom), Colin Foo (Phil), Lina Teal (Melanie), Shawn Bordoff (Guy on Sofa), Anita Brown (Laundramat Girl), Doris Blomgren (Elderly Shopper), Benjamin Ettenberg (Zulu Patron), Bonnie Kean, Jean Kean (Drug Store Twins), Stephanie Thorpe (Shopper), Clayton Watmough (Police Officer), Peter New (Guy in Tiki Bar Bathroom), Jared von Snellenberg (Guy on Moped), Larry Miller (Minister)

P.S. YOUR CAT IS DEAD

(TLA) Producers, Steve Guttenberg, Kyle A. Clark; Director, Steve Guttenberg; Screenplay, Steve Guttenberg, Jeff Korn; Based on the play and novel by James Kirkwood, Jr.; Photography, David A. Armstrong; Designer, Mark Harper; Costumes, Carlie Tracey; Editor, Derek Vaughn; Music, Dean Grinsfelder; Casting, Kim Coleman; from Mr. Kirby Productions; Dolby; Color; Rated R; 92 minutes; Release date: January 17, 2003. Cast: Steve Guttenberg (Jimmy Zoole), Lombardo Boyar (Eddie Tesoro), Cynthia Watros (Kate), Shirley Knight (Aunt Claire), Tom Wright (Fred), A.J. Benza (Carmine), Paul Dillon (Pidgeon), Kenneth Moskow (Stewart), Fred Medrano (Stanley), Anne Guttenberg (Lady at Party), Stanley Guttenberg (Man on Bus), Kim Mariner (TV Announcer), Patsy Fitzgerald, Christopher Vogler (Veterinarians), Lisa Popeil (Voice of 911 Operator), Frederick Lawrence (Fireman), Tom Mesmer (Carlos), Dan Rosenberg (Policeman)

Julia Stiles, Selma Blair, Jason Lee in *A Guy Thing* PHOTO COURTESY OF MGM

7TH STREET

(PARADISE ACRES PRODS.) Executive Producer, Catherine Scheinman; Director/Screenplay, Josh Pais; Photography, Elia Lyssy, Josh Pais; Editor, Linda Hattendorf; Color; Not rated; 71 minutes; Release date: January 17, 2003. Documentary in which actor-filmmaker Josh Pais takes a loving look at the neighborhood he grew up in and returned to as an adult, East 7th Street, between Avenues C & D in the Lower East Side of Manhattan.

90 MILES

(INDEPENDENT) Producers, Juan Carlos Zaldívar, Nicole Betancourt; Director, Juan Carlos Zaldívar; Photography, Nicole Betancourt, Juan Carlos Maciquez; Music, José Conde; Editor, Zelda Greenstein; Black and white/color; Not rated; 75 minutes; Release date: January 24, 2003. Documentary in which filmmaker Juan Carlos Zaldívar charts his journey from Cuba to America.

Steve Guttenberg, Lombardo Boyar in *P.S. Your Cat is Dead* PHOTO COURTESY OF TLA

THE R.M.

(Halestorm) Producer, Dave Hunter; Executive Producers, Dave Hunter, Kurt Hale; Director, Kurt Hale; Screenplay, Kurt Hale, John E. Moyer; Photography, Ryan Little; Designer, Doug Ellis; Editor, Wynn Hougaard; Music, Cody Hale; Casting, Michelle Wright; Dolby; Color; Rated PG; 101 minutes; Release date: January 24, 2003. Cast: Kirby Heyborne (Jared Phelps), Will Swenson (Kori Swenson), Britani Bateman (Kelly Power), Tracy Ann Evans (Emma Phelps), Merrill Dodge (Brigham Phelps), Michael Birkeland (Dewey), Maren Ord (Sariah Phelps), Leroy Te'o (Humu), Curt Dousett (Defense Attorney), Wally Joyner (Brother Jensen), Gary Crowton (Bishop Andrews), Rulon Gardner (Good Samaritan), Larry H. Miller (Car Dealer), Jimmy Chunga (Phat Cop), Ruth Hale (Church Organist), Ruth Todd (News Woman), Randall Carlisle (News Man), Scott Christopher (District Attorney), Lincoln Hoppe (Steve), Mitch English (Lloyd Finderlyon), Jeremy Hoover (Frat Guy), Adam Johnson (Tucker), Sherry Leigh (Julie Jensen), Patrick Livingston (Telemarketer), John E. Moyer (Would-Be Home Teacher), Jake Suazo (Tommy), Michelle Wright (Attorney), Micah Young, Daryn Tufts (Basketball Players), Jericho Road (Prison Band)

SUPER SUCKER

(PURPLE ROSE FILMS) Producer, Tom Spiroff; Executive Producer, Bob Brown; Director/Screenplay, Jeff Daniels; Photography, Richard Brauer; Editor, Robert L. Tomlinson; Dolby; Color; Rated R; 90 minutes; Release date: January 24, 2003. Cast: Jeff Daniels (Fred Barlow), Sandra Birch (Rhonda), Matt Letscher (Howard Butterworth), Harve Presnell (Winslow Schnaebelt), Dawn Wells (Herself), Guy Sanville (Leonard), Kate Peckham (Darlene), Will Young (Clifford), Michelle Mountain (Bunny Barlow), John Seibert (Shelby), Suzi Regan (Jill), Phil Powers (Jack), Aaron Toronto (AASAHA Agent), Lora Vatalaro (Beef-Eating Wife)

L'CHAYIM, COMRADE STALIN!

(CINEMA GUILD) Producer/Screenplay, Elizabeth Schwartz; Director/Music, Yale Strom; Photography, Nils Kenaston; Editor, Yefim Gribov; Narrator, Ron Perlman; Black and white/color; Not rated; 93 minutes; Release date: January 31, 2003. Documentary chronicling Yale Strom's journey to Birobidzhan, the capitol of the Jewish Autonomous Region of Siberia.

BIKER BOYZ

(DREAMWORKS) Producers, Stephanie Allain, Gina Prince-Bythewood, Erwin Stoff; Executive Producer, Don Kurt; Director, Reggie Rock Bythewood; Screenplay, Craig Fernandez, Reggie Rock Byethewood; Based on the *NY Times* article by Michael Gougis; Photography, Gregory Gardiner; Designer, Cecilia Montiel; Music, Camara Kambon; Music Supervisor, John Houlihan; Editors, Terilyn A. Shropshire, Caroline Ross; Casting, Kimberly R. Hardin, Chemin Sylvia Bernard; Stunts, Gary M. Hymes; Dolby; Technicolor; Rated PG-13; 110 minutes; Release date: January 31, 2003. Cast: Laurence Fishburne (Smoke), Derek Luke (Kid), Orlando Jones (Soul Train), Djimon Hounsou (Motherland), Lisa Bonet (Queenie), Brendan Fehr (Stuntman), Larenz Tate (Wood), Kid Rock (Dogg), Rick Gonzalez (Primo), Meagan Good (Tina), Salli Richardson-Whitfield (Half & Half), Vanessa Bell Calloway (Anita), Dante Basco (Philly), Dion Basco (Flip), Tyson Beckford (Donny), Titus Welliver (Max), Kadeem Hardison (T.J.), Terrence DaShon Howard (Chu Chu), Aysia Polk (Cee Cee), George Lovell Jefferson IV (Little Willie), Wren T. Brown (Rev. Maxwell), Jonas Chaka (Kamera Man), Lisa Duvernay (Young Woman), Keith Diamond (Jerome), Dena Cali (Nikki), Juliette Jeffers (Waitress), Nadine E. Velazquez (Allison), Pokey/aka Manuel Galloway (Pokey), Dondiel Smith (DJ), Troy Thomas (Dre), David Boyd (Prospect #2), Cole M. McLarty (Life), Tameka Settle (Racer), Eriq LaSalle (Slick Will)

Salli Richardson, Laurence Fishburne, Orlando Jones in *Biker Boyz* PHOTO COURTESY OF DREAMWORKS

FINAL DESTINATION 2

(NEW LINE CINEMA) Producers, Warren Zide, Craig Perry; Executive Producers, Toby Emmerich, Richard Brener, Matt Moore, Jeffrey Reddick; Director, David R. Ellis; Screenplay, J. Mackye Gruber, Eric Bress; Story, J. Mackye Gruber, Eric Bress, Jeffrey Reddick; Based on characters created by Jeffrey Reddick; Photography, Gary Capo; Designer, Michael Bolton; Music, Shirley Walker; Co-Producer, Justis Greene; Casting, John Papsidera; a Zide/Perry production; Dolby; Deluxe Color; Rated R; 90 minutes; Release date: January 31, 2003. Cast: Ali Larter (Clear Rivers), A.J. Cook (Kimberly Corman), Michael Landes (Thomas Burke), David Paetkau (Evan Lewis), James Kirk (Tim Carpenter), Lynda Boyd (Nora Carpenter), Keegan Connor Tracy (Kat), Jonathan Cherry (Rory), T.C. Carson (Eugene Dix), Justina Machado (Isabella Hudson), Tony Todd (Mr. Bludworth), Sarah Carter (Shaina), Alex Rae (Dano), Shaun Sipos (Frankie), Andrew Airlie (Mr. Corman), Christina Jastrzembska (Administrator), Eileen Pedde (Anesthesiologist), Jill Krop (Anchorwoman), Marrett Green (Anchorman), Don Bell (Biker), Odessa Munroe (Biker's Girlfriend), Noel Fisher (Brian Gibbons), Benita Ha (Dental Receptionist), Aaron Douglas (Deputy Steve), Eric Kennleyside (Det. Suby), Enid-Raye Adams (Dr. Kalarjian), Fred Henderson (Dr. Lees), Veena Sood (ER Nurse), David Purvis (Guest), Marke Driesschen (Host), Darcy Laurie (Man in Elevator), John R. Taylor (Man with Hooks), Alfred E. Humphreys (Mr. Gibbons), Chilton Crane (Mrs. Gibbons), Sarah Kattingh (Nurse in Delivery Room), Klodyne Rodney (Obstetrician), Rheta Hutton (On-Ramp Lady), John Stewart (Paramedic at Farm), Cam Cronin (Paramedic at Hospital), Alison Matthews (Physician), Mark Lukyn (Rescue Worker), Lorne Stewart (Skate Rat), Jenny Lang (Young Woman)

GOD HAS A RAP SHEET

(SCORE ON FOUR PRODS.) Producers, Paul Goodrich, Theo Armorios, Salvatore Argano; Executive Producers, N.J. Lenders, Kamal Ahmed; Director/Screenplay, Kamal Ahmed; Photography, Tom Agnello; Costumes, Wendy Winters; Editor, Alex Kopit; Dolby; Color; Not rated; 118 minutes; Release date: February 5, 2003. Cast: John Ford Noonan (God), William Smith (Devil), Peter Appel (Josh Zmirov), Bonz Malone (Big Rolla Bills), Shane Franklin (Ian), Mark Love (Anthony), Andre De Leon (Oscar), Mohamed Djellouli (Mohamed Aziz), Ken Lin (John), Tommy Houlihan (Patrick), Stu Alson (Guy with Date), Sal Argano (Italian Toughguy), Salvatore Argano (Mob Boss), Jimmy Coonan (Irish Rouge), Michael Harkins (Tranny), Artie Lange (Fat Guy), Rick Li (Gay Guy), Coati Mundi (Oscar's Father), Justine Noelle, Laura San Luis (Strippers), Anthony Peralo, Gus Sofroniou (Toughguys), "Lee" George Quinones (Dope Addict), Scott Sherratt (Cop)

Ali Larter, A.J. Cook, Michael Landes in *Final Destination 2* PHOTO COURTESY OF NEW LINE CINEMA

Mark Moskowitz in *Stone Reader* PHOTO COURTESY OF JET FILMS

STONE READER

(JET FILMS) Producers, Mark Moskowitz, Robert Goodman; Director/Screenplay, Mark Moskowitz; Photography, Joseph Vandergast, Jeffrey Confer, Mark Moskowitz; Editors, Mark Moskowitz, Kathleen Soulliere; Music, Michael Mandrell; Color; Rated PG-13; 127 minutes; Release date: February 12, 2003. Documentary about filmmaker Mark Moskowitz's efforts to track down Dow Mossman, the author of the 1972 novel *The Stones of Summer*; featuring Carl Brandt, Frank Conroy, Bruce Dobler, Robert C.S. Downs, Robert Ellis, Leslie Fiedler, Robert Gottlieb, Dan Guenther, John Kashiwabara, William Cotter Murray, John Seelye

GERRY

(THINKFILM) Producer, Dany Wolf; Director, Gus Van Sant; Screenplay, Casey Affleck, Matt Damon, Gus Van Sant; Photography, Harris Savides; Associate Editor, Paul Zucker; Music, Arvo Part; Associate Producer, Jay Hernandez; a My Cactus Inc. presentation; Dolby; Arriscope; Technicolor; Rated R; 103 minutes; Release date: February 14, 2003. Cast: Matt Damon (Gerry), Casey Affleck (Gerry)

MAY

(LIONS GATE) Producers, Scott Sturgeon, Marius Balchunas; Executive Producers, Eric Koskin, John Veague; Director/Screenplay, Lucky McKee; Photography, Steve Yedlin; Designer, Leslie Keel; Costumes, Mariano Diaz, Marcelo Pequeno; Music, Jaye Barnes-Luckett; Editors, Debra Goldfield, Rian Johnson, Chris Sivertson; Special Makeup Effects Artists, Eva Lohse, Randy Westgate; Casting, Shannon Makhanian; from 2 Loop Films; Dolby; Color; Rated R; 93 minutes; Release date: February 7, 2003. Cast: Angela Bettis (May Dove Canady), Jeremy Sisto (Adam Stubbs), Anna Faris (Polly), James Duval (Blank), Nichole Hiltz (Ambrosia), Kevin Gage (Papa Canady), Merle Kennedy (Mama Canady), Chandler Riley Hecht (Young May), Rachel David (Petey), Nora Zehetner (Hoop), Will Estes (Adam's Roommate), Roxanne Day (Buckle), Samantha Adams (Lucille), Brittney Lee Harvey (Diedre), Connor Matheus (Young School Boy), Mike McKee (Dr. Wolf, Optometrist), Ken Davitian (Foreign Doctor), Bret Roberts (Distraught Man at Vet Clinic), Traci Burr (Short Girl), Jude McVay (Zombie), Tricia Kelly (Amy), Norwood Cheek (Girl on Bench), Jesse Hlubik (Jack in *Jack and Jill*), Jennifer Grant (Jill in *Jack and Jill*), Lucky McKee (Guy Making Out in Elevator)

LOCKDOWN

(PALM PICTURES) Producers, Oren Koules, Mark Burg, Stevie "Black" Lockett, Jeff Clanagan; Director, John Luessenhop; Screenplay, Preston A. Whitmore II; Photography, Chris Chomyn; Designer, Billy Jett; Costumes, Nicole L. Schroud; Music, John Frizzell; Editor, Joseph Gutowski; Casting, Stevie "Black" Lockett; an Evolution Management, No Limit Films production; Dolby; Color; Rated R; 105 minutes; Release date: February 14, 2003. Cast: Richard T. Jones (Avery Montgomery), Gabriel Casseus (Cashmere), De'aundre Bonds (Dre), Master P (Clean Up), Melissa De Sousa (Krista), Bill Nunn (Charles), Clifton Powell (Malachi Young), Sticky Fingaz (Broadway), David "Shark" Fralick (Graffiti), Lloyd Avery II (Nate), Anna Maria Horsford (Saunders), Chrystale Wilson (Dana), Paulette Braxton (Marisa), Mike Butters (Barkley), Joe Torry (Alize), Mary Evans (Anderson), Anthony Boswell (Ruckus), Dwayne Macopson (Gains), Courtney McLean (Nuke), Antonio Lewis Todd (Hill), David Nickey (Lefty), Tait Fletcher (Shaz), Tracy Hightower (Clark), Jesus Gonzalez (Hector), Devon Lumpkin (Jordan), Mikel Lumpkin (Jordan), Darrell Young (Little G), Dianna St. Hilaire (Martina), Debra Johns (Mrs. Wells), Bud White (Judge), Doug Berryman (Bus Driver), Darrold Morris (Arresting Officer), Mark Fourte (Board Officer), Amy Lawrence (Ming), Edward Sisneros (Roberto), Dorsey Ray, La Wanda Johnson, Harriett Levine (Committe Members), Forrest Fyre (State Official), Kevin Kennedy (Visiting Guard #1), Gary D. Williams (Minister), Timothy Richard Hopper (Coach), Frederick Deane (Time Keeper), Angelo Dimascio (Prison Guard)

ORDINARY SINNER

(JOUR DE FETE) Producers, Chris Bongrine, John Henry Davis, J.B. White; Executive Producer/Screenplay, William Mahone; Director, John Henry Davis; Story, William Mahone, John Henry Davis, J.B. White; Photography, Mathieu Roberts; Designer, Henry Dunn; Costumes, Christianne Myers; Editor, Paul Zehrer; Music, Brian Adler; Casting, Vince Liebhart, Tom Alberg; a Magic Lantern Inc., Shorelands Productions, The Thief Company production; Color; Not rated; 91 minutes; Release date: February 14, 2003. Cast: Brendan P. Hines (Peter), Joshua Harto (Scott), Kris Park (Alex), Elizabeth Banks (Rachel), A. Martinez (Father Ed), Peter Onorati (Mike), Chris Messina (Silvio), Daniel Sherman (Edgar), Nathaniel Marston (Robert), Kia Joy Goodwin (Deborah), Jesse Tyler Ferguson (Ogden), Rusty DeWees (Bill Parish), Annie Davidson (Young Mother), Parker White (Boy), Lynn Bowman (Mrs. Sherm), Brian Hammer (Gas Attendant), William Mahone (Detective Arcudi), John Wilson (Prison Guard), Trevor Lavine (Police Officer)

The band Bering Strait in *The Ballad of Bering Strait* PHOTO COURTESY OF EMERGING PICTURES

THE BALLAD OF BERING STRAIT

(EMERGING PICTURES) Producer, Nina Gilden Seavey; Director, Nina Gilden Seavey; Photography, Erich Roland; Editor, Jeff Consiglio; a co-production of NHK and the Documentary Center, Georgetown University; Color; Not rated; 98 minutes; Release date: February 19, 2003. Documentary follows the journey of the aspiring rock band Bering Strait as they travel from Russia to Nashville in hopes of landing a record contract; featuring Natasha Borzilova, Ilya Toshinsky, Lydia Salnikova, Alexander Ostrovsky, Sergei Passov, Sergei Olkhovsky, Andrei Misikhin (Bering Strait); Alexander Arzamastev, Tim DuBois, Mike Kinnamon, Brent Maher, Ray Johnson, Valery Salnikov, Phil O'Donnell, Lee Bach.

Hugh Masekela in *Amandla!* PHOTO COURTESY OF ARTISAN

AMANDLA! A REVOLUTION IN FOUR PART HARMONY

(ARTISAN) Producers, Lee Hirsch, Sherry Simpson; Director, Lee Hirsch; Photography, Clive Sacke, Brand Jordaan, Ivan Leathers; Editor, Johanna Demetrakas; an ATO Pictures, Kwela Productions Ltd production; U.S.-South African; Dolby; Color; Rated PG-13; 108 minutes; Release date: February 19, 2003. Documentary about the part music has played in the fight against apartheid in South Africa; with Hugh Masekela, Abdullah Ibrahim, Miriam Makeba, Vusi Mahlasela, Sibongile Khumalo, Sophie Mgcina, Dolly Rathebe, Sifiso Ntuli, Duma Ka Ndlovu, Sibusiso Nxumalo, Thandi Modise, Lindiwe Zulu.

Matt Damon, Casey Affleck in *Gerry* PHOTO COURTESY OF SAVIDES/VAN SANT

Michele Greene, Helen Lesnick in *A Family Affair* PHOTO COURTESY OF SMALL PLANET

A FAMILY AFFAIR

(SMALL PLANET) Producer, Valerie Pichney; Executive Producers, Helen Lesnick, Dolores E. Lesnick; Director/Screenplay, Helen Lesnick; Photography, Jim Orr; Designer/Costumes, Lorrie Blackard; Music, Danny De La Isla, Robert Westlind, Kelly Neill; Casting, Helen Lesnick, Valerie Pichney; from Atta Girl Productions; Technicolor; Not rated; 107 minutes; Release date: February 21, 2003. Cast: Helen Lesnick (Rachel Rosen), Erica Shaffer (Christine Peterson), Arlene Golonka (Leah Rosen), Barbara Stuart (Sylvia Peterson), Michele Greene (Reggie Abravanel), Suzanne Westernhoefer (Carol Rosen), Michael Moerman (Sam Rosen), David Radford (Joe), Don Loper (Matthew Rosen), Keith E. Wright (Rob), Mark DeWhitt (Danny), Tracy Hughes (Nancy), Joel Hepner (Stanley Peterson), Sue Wakefield (Kathi), Michael McGee (Barry), Jack Silbaugh (Steve), Kelly Neill (Debi), Ellen Lawler (Suzi), Suzi Miller (Teri)

Sander Hicks, J.H. Hatfield in *Horns and Halos* PHOTO COURTESY OF RUMOR INC.

HORNS AND HALOS

(RUMOR INC.) Producers, Suki Hawley, David Bellinson, Michael Galinsky; Executive Producer, Sheila Nevins; Directors, Michael Galinsky, Suki Hawley; Photography, Michael Galinsky, Suki Hawley, Bob Ray; Music, DJ Angola; Editor, Suki Hawley; an HBO/Cinemax Documentary Films, RumuR Inc. production; Color; Not rated; 79 minutes; Release date: February 28, 2003. Documentary about the tell-all biography *Fortunate Son: George W. Bush and the Making of an American President* by J.H. Hatfield; featuring J.H. Hatfield, Sander Hicks, Peter Slover, Mark Crispin Miller, Stewart Bagwell, Randall Beek, Jay Butterman, David Cogswell, Todd Colby, Pam Colloff, Nick Colt, Richard Curtis, Ron English, Zack Exley, Jim Fitzgerald, Don Goede, Amy Goodman, David Greenberg, Nick Mamatas, Dale Miller, Colin Moynihan, Richard Eoin Nash, Cynthia Nelson, Dan O'Brien, Tara Jane O'Neil, Toby Rogers, Mary Lou Rosen, Bob Rosen, Tom Shaw, Sparrow, Seth Tobocman, Cat Tyc, William "Upski" Wimsatt

Annunziata Gianzero, Andrew Borba, Thomas Jay Ryan in *Dischord* PHOTO COURTESY OF ARTISTIC LICENSE

DISCHORD

(ARTISTIC LICENSE) Producers, Mark Wilkinson, Nancy Trombacco; Director/Screenplay/Editor, Mark Wilkinson; Photography, Ernst Kubitza; Designers, Erica Switzer, Natcha Alpert; Music, John McCarthy; Casting, Michael Scott Myers, Pam Lyles; from Ivy Films, Rudolph and Beer Productions; Color; Not rated; 102 minutes; Release date: February 28, 2003. Cast: Thomas Jay Ryan (Jimmy), Annunziata Gianzero (Gypsy), Dick Bakalyan (Det. Dunbarton), Andrew Borba (Lucian), Rick Wessler (The Beachcomber), Michael DeLuise (Billy Dunbarton), Tom Crawford (Patrolman Swenson), Alex McArthur (Recording Studio Exec), Will Lyman (Capt. Jack), Kent Burnham (Scott), Erik Parillo (Agent Croix), Elizabeth Callahan (Mrs. Detective), Jeanette O'Connor (Mrs. Hirshenson), Dean Regan (Stephan), Lisa Dinkins (Sandra), Dane Petersen (Jenna), Emma Shaw (Raya), Patrick Donnelly (Record Store Dude), Brownyn Sims (Recording Studio Assistant), Clark Tufts (Recording Mixer), Wayne Hinkley (Cop), Michael Wyle (Wannabe), Edna Page (Quincy Diner Waitress), Dorothy Brodesser-Platt (Dolly the Waitress), Richard Mitrani (Flirting Man), Willy O'Donnell (Kyle), Tommy Pellegrino (Perce), Robin Jones (Janet), Charlotte Gilkman (Young Gypsy), Erol Zeybekoglu (Young Jimmy), Ben Slade (Young Lucian), Jeff Zinn (Jimmy's Dad), Sarah Newhouse (Jimmy's Mom), Scott Jacobs (Dealer), Ryan Landry (Hustler), Mike Zammito (Beachcomber Doorman), Timothy Sawyer (Golf Pro), Lou Richards (Voice of Radio DJ)

POOLHALL JUNKIES

(GOLDWYN/GOLD CIRCLE) Producers, Tucker Tooley, Vincent Newman, Karen Beninati; Executive Producer, Norm Waitt; Director, Mars Callahan; Screenplay, Mars Callahan, Chris Corso; Photography, Robert Morris; Designer, Robert La Liberte; Costumes, Kristin Persson; Music, Richard Glasser; Editor, James E.

Tooley; Co-Producer, Nancy Lanham; Casting, Roe Baker; a Vincent Newman & Tucker Tooley production; Dolby; Color; Rated R; 94 minutes; Release date: February 28, 2003. Cast: Chazz Palminteri (Joe), Rick Schroder (Brad), Rod Steiger (Nick), Michael Rosenbaum (Danny Doyle), Mars Callahan (Johnny Doyle), Alison Eastwood (Tara), Christopher Walken (Mike), Glenn Plummer (Chico), Ernie Reyes, Jr. (Tang), Peter Mark Richman (Phillip Stein), Orien Richman (Brett), Shannon Engemann (Beth), Kristina Santoro (Scarlet), Michelle Ainge (Party Girl), Jerry North (Red), Bojesse Christopher (Noah), Nathan Stevens (Kid), Mick E. Jones (Rags), Billy Lamb (Bill), John-Paul Salisbury (Moose), Chato (Spaniard), Stephen Book (Laurence), Michael Aronin (Jack Caine), Gino Dentie (Merv), Robert Scott McCloud (Teenager), Dimitrius Deslis (Greek), Chris Corso (Houseman), Phillip Glasser (Max), Mike Massey (St. Louie Louis), Anson Mount (Chris), Lissa Pallo (Pool Pro), Richard Porntow (Toupe Jay), Steve Short (Boston Shorty)

Chazz Palminteri, Rick Schroder in *Poolhall Junkies* PHOTO COURTESY OF GOLDWYN/GOLD CIRCLE

THE SCOUNDREL'S WIFE

(MIRACLE ENTERTAINMENT) a.k.a. *Homefront*; Producers, Peggy Rajski, Jerry Daigle; Executive Producers, Michael Donaldson, Steven Stull; Co-Producer, Michael Arata; Director, Glen Pitre; Screenplay, Michelle Benoit, Glen Pitre; Photography, Uta Briesewitz; Designer, Kelly Curley; Costumes, Astrid Brucker; Music, Ernest Troost; Editor, Peter B. Ellis; Casting, Sharon Howard-Field, Douglas Wright; a co-production of Advantage Partners Pictures, Circle in the Sky Prods., Cote Blanche, Heritage Entertainment; Dolby; Color; Rated R; 99 minutes; Release date: February 28, 2003. Cast: Tatum O'Neal (Camille Picou), Julian Sands (Dr. Lenz), Tim Curry (Father Antoine), Lacey Chabert (Florida Picou), Eion Bailey (Ens. Jack Burwell), Rudolf Martin (Neg), Patrick McCullough (Blue), Lance Spellerberg (Klaus), Kurt Gerard (Dieter), John McConnell (Norbert), Michael Arata (Commander), Jade Galliano (Wounded Soldier), David P. Kufner (German Soldier)

JOURNEYS WITH GEORGE

(HBO FILMS) Producer/Editor, Aaron Lubarsky; Directors, Alexandra Pelosi, Aaron Lubarsky; Screenplay/Photography, Alexandra Pelosi; Purple Monkey Prods.; Color; Not rated; 79 minutes; Release date: March 14, 2003. Documentary following George W. Bush's campaign for the presidency.

Jason Schwartzman in *Spun*

SPUN

(NEWMARKET) Producers, Chris Hanley, Timothy Wayne Peternel, Fernando Sulichin, Danny Vinik; Executive Producers, Ash R. Shah, Brad L. Schlei, Mark Mower, Kiki Miyake, Nicola Doring, Yves Chevalier, Mark Boone Junior; Supervising Producer, Terry Spazek; Director, Jonas Åkerlund; Screenplay, Creighton Vero, Will De Los Santos; Photography, Eric Broms; Designer, Richard LaSalle; Costumes, B.; Editors, Jonas Åkerlund, Johan Söderberg; Music, Billy Corgan; Casting, Renita Whited; a Brink Films, Little Magic Films, Muse Productions, Muse/Blacklist Films, Saggitaire, Silver Nitrate Films, Spun Inc., Stone Canyon Entertainment production; Dolby; Color; Not rated; 98 minutes; Release date: March 14, 2003. Cast: Jason Schwartzman (Ross), Mickey Rourke (The Cook), Brittany Murphy (Nikki), John Leguizamo (Spider Mike), Patrick Fugit (Frisbee), Mena Suvari (Cookie), Chloe Hunter (April Love), Elisa Bocanerga (Giggles), Julia Mendoza (La Sadgirl), China Chow (Escort), Nicholas Gonzalez (Angel), Deborah Harry (Neighbor), Josh Peck (Fat Boy), Charlotte Ayanna (Amy), Eric Roberts (The Man), Larry Drake (Dr. K), Rob Halford (Porn Clerk), Peter Stormare (Mullet Cop), Alexis Arquette (Moustache Cop), Jorge Cottini (Doorman), Annie O'Donnell (Vet Receptionist), Ericka Lesa (Cocktail Waitress), Billy Dorgan (Doctor), Tony Kaye (Emcee), Ron Jeremy (Bartender), Tom Knickerbocker (Jail Cop), Lisa Brounstein (Frisbee's Mother), Marji Martin (Truck Stop Clerk)

Mena Suvari in *Spun* PHOTOS COURTESY OF NEWMARKET

DECASIA

(HYPNOTIC) Producer/Director/Screenplay/Editor, Bill Morrison; Music, Michael Gordon; Dolby; Black and white; Not rated; 70 minutes; Release date: March 19, 2003. Visual collage of burnt and decaying films.

BOAT TRIP

(ARTISAN) Producers, Andrew Sugerman, Brad Krevoy, Gerhard Schmidt, Frank Hübner; Exeecutive Producer, Sabine Müller; Director, Mort Nathan; Screenplay, Mort Nathan, William Bigelow; Photography, Shawn Maurer; Designer, Charles Breen; Costumes, Tim Chappel; Editor, John Axmess; Music, Robert Folk; Casting, Roger Mussenden; a Motion Picture Corporation of America and International West Pictures and Apollo Media presentation of a Brad Krevoy and Germund Films production; U.S.-German; Dolby; Deluxe color; Rated PG-13; 94 minutes; Release date: March 21, 2003. Cast: Cuba Gooding, Jr. (Jerry), Horatio Sanz (Nick), Vivica A. Fox (Felicia), Roselyn Sanchez (Gabriella), Maurice Godin (Hector), Lin Shaye (Sonya), Bob Gunton (Captain), Victoria Silvstedt (Inga), Richard Roundtree (Felicia's Dad), Roger Moore (Lloyd), Ken Campbell (Tom), Zen Gesner (Ron), William Bumiller (Steven), Noah York (Perry), Jennifer Gareis (Sheri), Steven M. Porter (Marshall), Li Hagman (Pia), Jerry Collins (Larry), Artie Lange (Brian), Philip Krevoy (Man on Deck), Eddie Driscoll (Steward), Steve Hudson (Contestant), Andrew Whelan, Brian Pollack (Bachelors), Norman Krevoy (Grandpa), Cecile Krevoy (Grandma), Glenn D. Feig

Cuba Gooding Jr., Vivica A. Fox in *Boat Trip* PHOTO COURTESY OF ARTISAN

(Man at Railing), Mort Rich (Lloyd's Date), Erika Johnson (Hawaiian Tropic Girl), Donte Calarco (Massage Client), Thomas Lennon (Minister), Brad Krevoy (Pilot), Christoph Quest (Inga's Dad), Wieslawa Wesolowska (Inga's Mother), Martin Richert (Masseuse), Roger Mussenden (S&M Guy), Norbert Heisterkamp (Andre), Jami Ferrell (Bridgit), Jack Baldwin, John Baldwin, Shawn Scott (Hydra Tourists), Clara May Beasley, Margo Castor, Jami Ferrell, Evangelia Geovandekou, Katharine Maassen, Sandra Martellotta, Barbara Matziris, Diana Pink, Michelle Ruben, Jennifer Stehr, Katie Vigers, Anja Weber (Swedish Sun Tanning Team), Sterling Rice, Erika Johnson, Cheryl Connell, Bjorg Lovstad, Linda Mitchell, Nofit Shevach, Tatjana Tutan, Veroniqa Wallens (Hawaiian Tropic Team), Will Ferrell (Brian's Boyfriend)

DOWN AND OUT WITH THE DOLLS

(INDICAN) Producers, Matt Hill, Nanda Rao; Executive Producers, Stephen Hill, Peter Hill; Director/Screenplay, Jurt Voss; Photography, Tony Croll; Designer, Nalini "DD" Cheriel; Costumes, Jill Lucas; Editors, Mick Erausquin, Clayton Halsey; Music, Zoe Poledouris; Songs, Coyote Shivers; Whyte House Productions; Color; Not rated; 88 minutes; Release date: March 21, 2003. Cast: Zoe Poledouris (Fauna), Kinnie Starr (Reggie), Nicole Barrett (Kali), Melody Moore (Lavender), Coyote Shivers (Levi), Brendan O'Hara (Mulder), Mikael Jehanno (Paulo), Jennifer Shepard (Alcoholly), Shawn Robinson (Clark), Sierra Feldner-Shaw (Heather), Lemmy Klimister (Joe), Alan Charing (Bill Black), Kate Merril (Zoe), Janis Tanaka (Trudie), Inger Lorre (Shade)

Nicole Barrett, Zoe Poledouris, Kinnie Starr, Melody Moore in *Down and Out with the Dolls*
PHOTO COURTESY OF INDICAN

STEVIE

(LIONS GATE) Producers, Adam Singer, Gordon Quinn, Steve James; Executive Produce, Robert May; Director, Steve James; Photography, Gordon Quinn, Dana Kupper, Peter Gilbert; Music, Dirk Powell; Editors, William Haugse, Steve James; from Kartemquin Films, SenArt Films; Dolby; Color; Rated R; 140 minutes; Release date: March 28, 2003. Filmmaker Steve James' documentary about his effort to reconnect with Stephen Fielding, a troubled youth to whom he had been an "Advocate Big Brother" in the 1980s; featuring Steve James, Stephen Fielding, Tonya Gregory, Bernice Hagler, Verna Hagler, Brenda Hickam, Doug Hickam, Judy James

FATAL FALLOUT

(INDEPENDENT) Producer/Editor, Liza Koch; Director, Gary Null; Photography, Barry Markowitz, Derek Ramsey, Robert Kehoe; Music, Killer Track; Color; Not rated; 86 minutes; release date: April 3, 2003. Documentary on the vulnerability of nuclear reactors in the United States; featuring Michio Haku, Helen Caldicott, Ernest J. Sternglass, Joseph Mangano.

DYSFUNKTIONAL FAMILY

(MIRAMAX) Producers, Eddie Griffin, David Permut, Paul Brooks; Executive Producers, Norm Waitt, Peter Safran; Director, George Gallo; Original Comedy Material Written by Eddie Griffin; Photography, Theo van de Sande; Co-

Eddie Griffin (left) in *DysFunktional Family* PHOTO COURTESY OF MIRAMAX

Producers, Steven A. Longi, Jeff Levine, Larry Katz; Co-Executive Producer, Scott Niemeyer; Music, Andrew Gross; Editor, Michael R. Miller; Music Supervisor, Randy Gerston; a Permut Presentations production, presented in assocation with Gold Circle Films and Heartland Productions; Dolby; Color; Rated R; 89 minutes; Release date: April 4, 2003. Concert documentary of comedian Eddie Griffin, combined with footage of Griffin in his hometown of Kansas City, Missouri; featuring Joe Howard, Matthew Brent, Robert Noble.

LEVITY

(SONY CLASSICS) Producers, Richard N. Gladstein, Adam J. Merims, Ed Solomon; Executive Producers, Morgan Freeman, Lori McCreary, Fred Schepisi, Andrew Spaulding, James Burke, Doug Mankoff; Director/Screenplay, Ed Solomon; Photography, Roger Deakins; Designer, François Séguin; Costumes, Marie-Sylvie Deveau; Music, Mark Oliver Everett; Music Supervisor, Liza Richardson; Co-Producer, Irene Litinsky; Editor, Pietro Scalia; a Studio Canal presentation of a Filmcolony Prroduction in association with Revelations Entertainment, Echo Lake Productions and Entitled Entertainment; Dolby; Deluxe Color; Rated R; 100 minutes; Release date: April 7, 2003. Cast: Billy Bob Thornton (Manuel Jordan),

Morgan Freeman (Miles Evans), Holly Hunter (Adele Easley), Kirsten Dunst (Sofia Mellinger), Manuel Aranguiz (Senor Aguilar), Geoffrey Wigdor (Abner Easley), Luke Robertson (Young Abner Easley), Dorian Harewood (Mackie Whittaker), Catherine Colvey (Claire Mellinger), Billoah Greene (Don), Sadiki Burke (Sadiki), Abede Burke (Abede), Diego Abella (Raul), Brent Rogers (Ty), Cordell Clyde (Cleve), Fabio Lopez (Samuel), Chris D'Arienzo (Waffle Boy)

HOUSE OF 1000 CORPSES

(LIONS GATE) Producer, Andy Goul; Director/Screenplay/Music, Rob Zombie; Photography, Tom Richmond, Alex Poppas; Designer, Greg Gibbs; Costumes, Amanda Friedland; Editors, Kathryn Himoff, Robert K. Lambert, Sean Lambert; Executive Producers, Andy Given, Guy Oseary; Special Effecst Co-ordnators, David Blitstein, M. Kam Cooney; Special Make-up Effects, Wayne Toth; Casting, Donald Paul Pemrick, Dean E. Fronk; Dolby; Fotokem color; Rated R; 88 minutes; Release date: April 11, 2003. Cast: Sid Haig (Captain Spaulding), Bill Moseley (Otis Driftwood), Sheri Moon (Baby), Karen Black (Mother Firefly), Chris Hardwick (Jerry Goldsmith), Erin Daniels (Denise Willis), Jennifer Joslyn (Mary Knowles), Rainn Wilson (Bill Hudley), Walton Goggins (Deputy Steve Naish), Tom Towles (Lt. George Wydell), Matthew McGrory (Tiny), Robert Mukes (Rufus), Dennis Fimple (Grampa Hugo), Harrison Young (Don Willis), William H. Bassett (Sheriff Huston), Irwin Keyes (Ravelli), Michael J. Pollard (Stucky), Chad Bannon (Killer Karl), Judith Drake (Skunk Ape Wife), Greg Gibbs (Dr. Wolfenstein), Ken Johnson (Skunk Ape Husband), Jake McKinnon (The Professor), Walter Phelan (Dr. Satan), David Reynolds (Richard Wick), Rob Zombie (Wolfenstein's Assistant)

THE YOUNG UNKNOWNS

(INDICAN) Producers, Catherine Jelski, Eric M. Klein, Kimberly Shane O'Hara; Director/Screenplay, Catherine Jelski; Inspired by the play *Magic Afternoon* by Wolfgang Bauer; Photography/Editor, Gabor Szitanyi; Costumes, Merrie Lawson; Music, Hypnogaja; Co-Producers/Casting, Dan Shaner, Michael Testa; a Wit's End Productions presentation in association with Yellow Duck Productions; Dolby; Color; Not rated; 87 minutes; Release date: April 11, 2003. Cast: Devon Gummersall (Charlie), Arly Jover (Paloma), Eion Bailey (Joe), Leslie Bibb (Cassandra), Dale Godboldo (Franklin), Simon Templeman (Voice of Sebastian)

Morgan Freeman, Billy Bob Thornton in *Levity* PHOTO COURTESY OF SONY CLASSICS

Devon Gummersall, Eion Bailey, Leslie Bibb in *The Young Unknowns* PHOTO COURTESY OF INDICAN

Love Hinson, Donyaeh Hinson in *Love & Diane* PHOTO COURTESY OF WOMEN MAKE MOVIES

LOVE & DIANE

(WOMEN MAKE MOVIES) Producer/Director, Jennifer Dworkin; Executive Producer, Jennifer Fox; Consulting Producer, Doug Block; Photography, Tsuyoshi Kimoto; Editor, Mona Davis; a presentation of the Independent Television Service; Color; Not rated; 155 minutes; Release date: April 16, 2003. Documentary in which Love Hinson and her siblings, the children of former crack addict Diane Hazzard, are reunited with their mother; with Love Hinson, Donyaeh Hinson, Diane Hazzard, Trenise "Tootie" Arnold, Morean Arnold, Willie Hazzard, Courtney White, Tameka Arnold, Lauren Shapiro, Antonia Diaz, Charles Modiano, Charles Hazzard

CHASING PAPI

(20TH CENTURY FOX) Producers, Forest Whitaker, Tracey Trench, Laura Angelica Simón; Executive Producer, Tajamika Paxton; Director, Linda Mendoza; Screenplay, Laura Angelica Simón, Steven Antin, Alison Balian, Elizabeth Sarnoff; Story, Laura Angelica Simón, Steven Antin; Photography, Xavier Pérez Grobet; Designer, Candi Guterres; Editor, Maysie Hoy; Music, Emilo Estefan, Jr.; Music Supervisor, Frankie Pine; Co-Producers, Elaine Dysinger, Nellie Nugiel; Casting, Chemin Sylvia Bernard; a Fox 2000 Pictures presentation of a Spirit Dance Entertainment production; Dolby; Deluxe color; Rated PG; 80 minutes;

Jaci Velasquez, Sofia Vergara, Roselyn Sanchez in *Chasing Papi* PHOTO COURTESY OF 20TH CENTURY FOX

Release date: April 16, 2003. Cast: Roselyn Sanchez (Lorena), Sofia Vergara (Cici), Jaci Velasquez (Patricia), Eduardo Verástegui (Papi), Lisa Vidal (Carmen), Freddy Rodríguez (Victor), D.L. Hughley (Rodrigo), Maria Conchita Alonso (Maria), Walter Mercado, Carlos Ponce, Mariette Areco Detotto (Themselves), Joy Enriquez (Mary), Ian Gomez (Dr. Chu), Diana Maria Riva (Fala), Ivette Sosa (Gloria), Barbar Bermudo (Miami TV Reporter), Henriette Mantel (Desk Clerk), Bryce Johnson (Bellboy), Nicole Scherzinger (Miss Puerto Rico), Sandra Ramírez (Miss Mexico), Nadine E. Velazquez (Attractive Woman at Conga Club), Linda Mendoza Kahle (Lorena's Office Receptionist), Bunnie Rivera (Patricia's Maid), Ed Marques (Flight Attendant), Mildred Dumas (Airport Woman), Amy French (Novice Nun), Bret Roberts (Biker), Tony Denison (Agent Quinn), Lucy Butler (Ms. James), Laurie Carrasco (La Llorona), Christina Vidal (Festival Singer), Sheila E. and the E Train: Sheila E., Pete Escovedo, Peter Michael Escovedo (Latin Festival Band Members), Theresa Barbosa-Adams, Nicole Pantenburg, Joaquín Escamilla, Marcos Santana, Carlos Marín, Marie Frances Pérez, Ariana Muratti, Tita Guerrero (Club Dancers), Paul Rodriguez (Costas Delgado)

Joseph Gordon-Levitt, Cody Lightning, Sara Rivas, Zooey Deschanel, Don Cheadle in *Manic* PHOTO COURTESY OF IFC FILMS

MANIC

(IFC FILMS) Producers, Trudi Callon, Kirk Hassig; Executive Producers, Chuck Reeder, Joanne Hoffman, Peter Broderick; Director, Jordan Melamed; Screenplay, Michael Bacall, Blayne Weaver; Photography, Nick Hay; Designer, Carol Strober; Costumes, Dolores Ybarra, Dahlia Foroutan; Music, David Wingo, Michael Linnen; Editors, Gloria Rosa Vela, Madeleine Gavin; Casting, Mali Finn; a Manic production; Dolby; Color; Rated R; 100 minutes; Release date: April 25, 2003. Cast: Joseph Gordon-Levitt (Lyle), Michael Bacall (Chad), Zooey Deschanel (Tracy), Cody Lightning (Kenny), Elden Henson (Michael), Sara Rivas (Sara), Don Cheadle (Dr. David Monroe), Adrienne Rollo (Emergency Room Nurse), Maggie Baird (Rebecca), Lydell M. Cheshier (J.C.), Roxie Fuller (Roxie), Bree Nogueira (Bree), Kathy Paradise, Joey Hernandez (Nurses), Lauren Shubert (Lauren), William Richert (Diego), Ben Markham (Card Kid), Travis Sutton (High School Baseball Catcher/Eddie), Nic Henley (Nic), Julia Remala (Night Nurse), Van Epperson (Night Staff), Jamielyn Kane (Dairy Girl), Michael O'Neil (Harold), Victoria Scott (Kid #3), Portia Medina (Group Kid), Swede Adamson, Stephan Maloney, Sean Tippins (Orderlies)

JERSEY GUY

(CASTLE HILL) Producer, Roosey Khawly; Executive Producer, Jay Cannold; Director, Elia Zois; Screenplay, Christ Zois, Elia Zois; Photography, Terry Stacey; Designer, Lisa Mareiniss; Costumes, Dee Pool; Editor, Charlie Sadoff; Casting,

Meredith Jacobson; a Jersey Guy Films production; Dolby; Color; Rated R; 90 minutes; Release date: April 25, 2003. Cast: Steve Parlavecchio (Jack), Arthur Nascarella (Father), Stacy Mistysyn (Susan), Ralph Caputo (Merle), Jill Wolfe (Samantha), Tom Borrillo (George), Vincent Tufariello (Hal), Roosey Khawly (Dr. Kay), David Stepkin (Harry Watkins), Vickie Thaw (Mom), Andrew Berry (Alex), Mazdack Rassi (Robert), Nur Khan (Brad), Benjamin Liu (Salesman), Shannon Burkett (Ingrid), Lauren Ezersky (Fashion Editor), Doris Brent (Helen), Greta Cazzoni, Lea Kelmann, Daniella Rotelli (Dinner Models), Margareth Lahoussaye, Valerie Celis (Photo Shoot Models), Margaret Scarpa (Receptionist), Pamela Bramsin (Roommate), Paul James, Jr. (Bouncer), Trish Zocchi (Girl in Pool), Irma St. Paule (Mrs. Rappaport), Joseph Borlo (Himself), Jason Hollias, Bevan Meyers, Michel Nafziger (Photo Shoot Assistants)

Jersey Guy PHOTO COURTESY OF CASTLE HILL

A DECADE UNDER THE INFLUENCE

(IFC FILMS) Producers, Gini Reticker, Jerry Kupfer, Richard LaGravenese, Ted Demme; Executive Producers, Alison Bourke, Caroline Kaplan, Jonathan Sehring; Directors, Richard LaGravenese, Ted Demme; Photography, Clyde Smith, Anthony Janelli; Editor, Meg Reticker; Music, John Kimbrough; Interviewers: Ted Demme, Richard LaGravenese, Alexander Payne, Neil LaBute, Scott Frank, Michael De luca, Mark Riley, James V. Hart, Robert Mark Kamen, Steven Schiff; an IFC presentation of a Written in Stone, Constant Communications production; Color; Not rated; 109 minutes; Release date: April 25, 2003. Documentary on the countercultural filmmaking wave of the late 1960s–early 1970s; with Robert Altman, John G. Avildsen, Peter Bogdanovich, Marshall Brickman, Ellen Burstyn, John Calley, Julie Christie, Francis Ford Coppola, Roger Corman, Bruce Dern, Clint Eastwood, Milos Forman, William Friedkin, Pam Grier, Monte Hellman, Dennis Hopper, Sidney Lumet, Paul Mazursky, Mike Medavoy, Polly Platt, Sydney Pollack, Jerry Schatzberg, Roy Scheider, Paul Schrader, Martin Scorsese, Sissy Spacek, Robert Towne, Jon Voight

RETURNING MICKEY STERN

(METROSCAPE ENTERTAINMENT) Producers, Michael Prywes, Jason Akel, Victor Erdos, Joseph Bologna; Executive Producers, Barry J. Charles, Joseph Brad

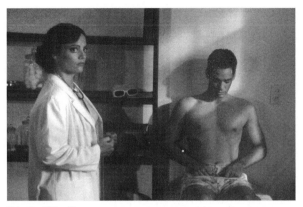
Returning Mickey Stern PHOTO COURTESY OF METROSCAPE ENTERTAINMENT

Kluge; Director/Screenplay, Michael Prywes; Photography, Mark Smith; Art Director, Nicole Pressly; Costumes, Jocelyn Worrell; Music, Jeff Jones; Editor, Suzanne Pillsbury; Casting, Liz Lewis; 2 Life! Films; DuArt Color/black and white; PG-13; 91 minutes; Release date: April 25, 2003. Cast: Joseph Bologna (Mickey Stern), Tom Bosley (Harry Mankelbaum), Joshua Fishbein (Young Mickey), Brett Tabisel (Young Harry), Kylie Delre (Young Leah), Charlotte Prywes (Nurse), Arnie Prywes (Doctor), Joan Garnock (Older Leah), Sarah Schoenberg (Dina), John Sloan (Joe), Bernard Furmanski (Jogger), Michael Oblerander (Ben), Kristina Sisco (Pretty Teen), Josh Bitton (Soda Jerk), NaAma Ginat (Sales Woman), Ray Bressingham (Bouncer), Robert Bressingham (Lush), Renée Taylor (Jeannie), Connie Stevens (Dr. Eloise Vanderwild), Jennifer Jenei (Pick-up Artist)

AFGHAN STORIES

(SEVENTH ART) Producer/Director/Screenplay, Taran Davies; Co-Producer, Walied Osman; Music, Andre Fratto; Editor, Penelope Falk; a Wicklow Films production; Color; Not rated; 60 minutes; Release date: April 30, 2003. Documentary on the people of Afghanistan, made shortly after the September 11, 2002, attacks on the United States.

Afghan Stories PHOTO COURTESY OF SEVENTH ART

Marisa Coughlan, Jordan Bridges in *New Suit* PHOTO COURTESY OF TRILLION ENTERTAINMENT

NEW SUIT

(TRILLION ENTERTAINMENT) Producers, Christina Zilber, Laurent Zilber; Director, François Velle; Screenplay, Craig Sherman; Line Producer, Doug Blake; Photography, David Mullen; Designer, Nava; Costumes, Alix Friedberg; Music, Daniel J. Nielsen; Editor, Kris Cole; Casting, Nancy Nayor; an Unbrilled Pictures presentation ofa Hungry Eye Lowlands Pictures production; Dolby; Color; HD Video; Rated R; 94 minutes; Release date: May 2, 2003. Cast: Jordan Bridges (Kevin Taylor), Marisa Coughlan (Marianne Roxbury), Heather Donahue (Molly), Mark Setlock (Smokey), Benito Martinez (Juan), Charles Rocket (Del Strontium), Paul McCrane (Braggy Shoot), Dan Hedaya (Muster Hansau), Dan Montgomery, Jr. (Andy), James Marsh (Trey), Danny Strong (Greg), Jere Burns (Dixon Grain), Branton Boxer (Nick Chafe), Andrew Ableson (Girard), Amber Smith (Jennifer), Jenya Lano (Barbie), Jodi Long (Feng Shui Woman), Michael Dow (Phil), Melissa Marsala (Plastic Productions Receptionist), Deirdre Quinn (Big Agency Receptionist), Nancy Fish (Small Time Agent), Paul Korver (Player-Type), Dale Godboldo, Eric Matheny (Power Agents), Jessica Maider (Susan), Portia Dawson (Lana), Elise Ballard (Glaze), Craig Sherman (Baskin Robbins Guy)

RENO: REBEL WITHOUT A PAUSE

(SEVENTH ART) Producer, Richard Guay; Executive Producers, Nancy Savoca, Reno; Director, Nancy Savoca; Screenplay, Reno; Photography, Lisa Leone; Editor, Suzanne Spangler; a co-production of Exile Films and The Reno Co.; Color; Not rated; 75 minutes; Release date: May 2, 2003. A filmed version of stand-up comedian Reno's 2001 act.

Reno in *Reno: Rebel without a Pause* PHOTO COURTESY OF SEVENTH ART

CHARLOTTE SOMETIMES

(VISIONBOX PICTURES) Producers, Eric Byler, Marc Ambrose; Executive Producers, Michael Kastenbaum, John Bard Manulis; Director/Screenplay, Eric Byler; Story, Eric Byler, Jeff Liu; Photography, Robert Humphreys; Designer, Robert Shinso; Costumes, Marianne Kai; Editors, Eric Byler, Kenn Kashima, Tom Moore; Music, Michael Brook; Casting, Stacey V. Herman; a Hart Sharp Video, Small Planet Pictures, The Sundance Channel production; Color; Rated R; 85 minutes; Release date: May 2, 2003. Cast: Jacqueline Kim (Darcy/Charlotte), Eugenia Yuan (Lori), Michael Idemoto (Michael), Matt Westmore (Justin), Shizuko Hoshi (Aunt), Kimberly-Rose Wolter (Annie), Jon Jacobs (Jason on TV), Michael A. Krawic (Nightclub Owner), Andrew J. Turner (Andrew)

Eugenia Yan, Matt Westmore, Jacqueline Kim, Michael Idemoto in *Charlotte Sometimes* PHOTO COURTESY OF VISIONBOX PICTURES

Rufus Thomas, Carla Thomas in *Only the Strong Survive* PHOTO COURTESY OF MIRAMAX

ONLY THE STRONG SURVIVE

(MIRAMAX) Producer, Roger Friedman; Executive Producers, Harvey Weinstein, Bob Weinstein; Associate Producer, Rebecca Marshall; Directors, Chris Hegedus, D.A. Pennebaker; Photography, James Desmond, Chris Hegedus, Erez Laufer, Jehane Noujaim, D.A. Pennebaker; Editors, Roger Friedman, Chris Hegedus, Erez Laufer, D.A. Pennebaker; a Pennebaker Hegedus Films production; Dolby; Color; Rated PG-13; 95 minutes; Release date: May 9, 2003. Concert documentary featuring several veteran soul artists and the music of Stax Records; featuring William Bell, Jerry Butler, The Chi-Lites, Issac Hayes, Sam Moore, Ann Peebles, Wilson Pickett, Sir Mack Rice, Carla Thomas, Rufus Thomas, Mary Wilson

Steve Braun, Larry Sullivan in *The Trip* PHOTO COURTESY OF TLA RELEASING

THE TRIP

(TLA RELEASING) Producers, Miles Swain, Houston King; Executive Producer, Tom Blount; Director/Screenplay, Miles Swain; Photography, Charles L. Barbee, Scott Kevan; Designers, Donna Willinsky, David Touster; Costumes, Kristen Anacker, Renee Raphael, Sevilla Granger; Music, Steven Chesne; Editor, Carlo Gustaff; Casting, Gale Salus; a Falcon Lair Films production; Dolby; Color; Rated R; 95 minutes; Release date: May 9, 2003. Cast: Larry Sullivan (Alan Oakley), Steve Braun (Tommy Ballenger), Ray Baker (Peter Baxter), James Handy (Hal), Faith Salie (Ignored Woman), Dennis Bailey (Larry Jenkins), Alexis Arquette (Michael), Sirena Irwin (Beverly), Zoe "Joshua Tree" Logan (1973 Jogger), Jill St. John (Mary Oakley), Art Hindle (Ted Oakley), Christina Cameron Mitchell (TV Reporter), Julie Brown (OutLoud Receptionist), David Mixner (Himself), Alfred Dennis (George Baxter), Connie Sawyer (Barbara Baxter), Rosemary Alexander (Ticket Agent), Al Rondon (Motel Manager), Alejandro Patino (Gas Station Owner), Geoffrey Rivas (Police Officer), Cy Carter (Young Fan at Bookstore), John Harnagel (Middle Aged Man), Brian Leckner (Man One), Doug Lee (Stoner), Miles Swain (Mark)

ALMOST SALINAS

(CURB ENTERTAINMENT) Producer, Wade W. Danielson; Executive Producer, Anna Marie Crovetti; Director/Screenplay, Terry Green; Photography, David Garden; Designer, Jay Pelissier; Costumes, Lisa Davis; Editor, Jennifer Krouse; Music, David Reynolds; Casting, Richard S. Kordos; from Stratia Productions, Inc.; Color; Rated PG; 92 minutes; Release date: May 9, 2003. Cast: John Mahoney (Max Harris), Linda Emond (Nina Ellington), Lindsay Crouse (Allie), Virginia Madsen (Clare), Ian Gomez (Manny), Nathan Davis (Zelder Hill), Tom Groenwald (Leo Quinlan), Ray Wise (Jack Tynan), Amanda Pitera (Billie), Glenn Dunk (Jason), Lucy Reeves (Moira), Adrian Neil (Dante), Eric Wrye (Buz)

WASHINGTON HEIGHTS

(MAC RELEASING) Producers, Alfredo de Villa, Luis Dantas, Manny Perez, Tom Donahue; Executive Producers, Peter Newman, Jon Rubenstein, Joseph La Morte, Greg Johnson; Director, Alfredo de Villa; Screenplay, Alfredo de Villa, Junot Diaz, Manny Perez, Nat Moss; Photography, Claudia Chea; Designer, Charlotte Bourke; Costumes, Chasia Kwane, Natalie Johnson, Carla Tenorio; Music, Leigh Roberts; Editor, Tom Donahue; Casting, Brett Goldstein; from Heights Productions; Color; Rated R; 80 minutes; Release date: May 9, 2003.

Cast: Tomas Milian (Eddie Ramirez), Manny Perez (Carlos Ramirez), Danny Hoch (Mickey Kilpatrick), Jude Ciccolella (Sean Kilpatrick), Andrea Navedo (Maggie), Bobby Cannavale (Angel), David Zayas (David), Callie Thorne (Raquel), Roberto Sanchez (Tito), Judy Reyes (Daisy), Jaime Tirelli (Guillermo), Michael Hyatt (Michelle), Darien Sills-Evans (Danny), Sara Ramirez (Belkis), Joseph Lyle Taylor (Gunman), Josh Stamberg (Dr. Field), Denia Brache (Flirting Woman), Anna McDonough (Mary Kilpatrick), Gloria Irizarry (Senora Marquez), Jose Ramon Rosario (Bodega Guy), Gary Perez (Comic Store Owner), Brian DeJesus (Steven), Lisa Hammer (Berna), Michelle Zangara (Overnight Woman), Yvette Mercedes (Tenant), Melissa Delaney-Del Valle (Janeanne), Luis Jimenez, Moon Shadow (Radio Djs), Marcos Palma (Rafael), Martin Zapata (Martin), Randy Rodriguez (Groom), Don Juarez (Congo Player), Fernando Baez (Man on Street), El "Cuba" (Domino Player)

ATTITUDE

(9 @ NIGHT FILMS/TENDERLOIN GROUP) Producers, Jon Sajetowski, Terry Forgette; Director/Screenplay, Rob Nilsson; Photography, Mickey Freeman; Editor, Chikara Motomura; Black and white; Not rated; 100 minutes; Release date: May 14, 2003. Cast: Michael Disend (Spoddy), Marion Christian (Big E), Vernon Medearis (Blackie), Robert Viharo (Modisco), Gabriela Maltz Larkin (Francesca), John Hunsaker (Chuckles), David Fine (Salowitz), Paige Olson (St. Tre), Cory Duval (Bid), Hernan Peña (Assault Victim), Bruce Marovich (Qually), Brian Danker (Sgt. Danker), Scott Cooper (Rails), Maria Mastroyannis-Zaft (Mapel), Edwin Johnson (Johnny), Teddy Weiler (Phil), Marianne Heath (Jane), Irit Levi (Lulu), Adan J. Faudoa (Butch), Chie Uchida (Chie), Karoi Nakata (Kaori), Keith Hemmerling (Guitar Man), Dean Adams (Henry), Johnny Holiday (Homeless Old Man), Pat Wallace (Lily Jo), Kevin Woodruff (Lil F), Anya Luchitskaia (Anya), David Dror (Smoke Shop Owner), Matt Gonzalez (Matty), Stephen Maul (Craig)

BEYOND VANILLA

(STRAND) Producers, Rob Dunlap, Claes Lilja; Director/Screenplay/Editor/Narrator, Claes Lilja; Photography, Claes Lilja, Rob Dunlap; Music, Jay Rando, Nancy Engelken; Associate Producers, Hays Holmes, John Robertson; from Hanky Code Productions, Inc.; Color; Not rated; 91 minutes; Release date: May 16, 2003. Documentary on extreme sex practices; featuring Mitch Banning, Bud Cockerham, Chloe, Kevin Dailey, Alex Del Rosario, Antonio Ferrelli, Lady Green, Nina Hartley, Richard Hunter, ChiChi LaRue, Mark Masterson, Gauge McLeod, Sasha Michaels, Chris Passanisi, Carol Queen, Randi Rage, Cole Tucker.

Nina Hartley in *Beyond Vanilla* PHOTO COURTESY OF STRAND

SECRET LIVES: HIDDEN CHILDREN AND THEIR RESCUERS DURING WWII

(CINEMA GUILD) Producers, Aviva Slesin, Ann Rubenstein Tisch; Co-Producer/Screenplay, Toby Appleton Perl; Director, Aviva Slesin; Photography, Anthony Forma, Itamar Hadar; Music, John Zorn; Editor, Ken Eluto; a Film Transit International production; Black and white/Color; Not rated; 72 minutes; Release date: May 16, 2003. Documentary about the people who risked their lives hiding Jewish children during World War II.

Secret Lives: Hidden Children and Their Rescuers PHOTO COURTESY OF CINEMA GUILD

FRIENDS AND FAMILY

(REGENT ENTERTAINMENT) Producers, Linda Moran, Kristen Coury, Joseph Triebwasser; Director, Kristen Coury; Screenplay, Joseph Triebwasser; Line Producer, Valerie Romer; Photography, John Leuba; Designer, Sonya Gropman; Costumes, Michelle Martini; Music, Kurt Hoffman; Editors, Tom Swartwout, Hector Venegas; Casting, Judy Henderson; a Belladonna Productions, Charleston Pictures production; Dolby; Color; Not rated; 87 minutes; Release date: May 16, 2003. Cast: Tony Lo Bianco (Victor Patrizzi), Greg Lauren (Stephen Torcelli), Christopher Gartin (Danny Russo), Tovah Feldshuh (Alma Jennings), Rebecca Creskoff (Jenny Patrizzi), Beth Fowler (Ada Torcelli), Edward Hibbert (Richard Grayson), Meshach Taylor (Bruno), Brian Lane Green (Damon Jennings), Anna Maria Alberghetti (Stella Patrizzi), Louis Zorich (Marvin Levine), Frank Pellegrino (Mr. Torcelli), Patrick Collins (Matt Jennings), Danny Mastrogiorgio (Vito Patrizzi), Lou Carbonneau (Frankie Patrizzi), Allison Mackie (Cheryl), Bruce Winant (Senator Pete Bloomer), Michael Squicciarini (Ray), Frank Minucci (Leo), Victor Colicchio (Sammy), Garry Pastore (Chuck), Richard Petrocelli (Eddie), Sam Coppola (Carlo Ricci), Elisa Heinsohn (Tanya, Singer at

Christopher Gartin, Greg Lauren in *Friends and Family* PHOTO COURTESY OF REGENT ENTERTAINMENT

That's My Face PHOTO COURTESY OF CHIMPANZEE PRODUCTIONS

Banquet), Max Chalawsky (Tim), Greg Kachejian (Restaurant Waiter), Larry Nathanson (David Levine), Flotilla DeBarge (Darnay), Jesse Volt (Saffron), Brian Donahue (Morris), Tina Bruno (Little Old Lady), Breein Sweeney (Mary), Sara Moon (Sophie Patrizzi), Kenneth Solarino (Policeman), Ralph Cole, Jr. (Gay Man), Johnny Russo (Max), Mike Arotsky (Unruly Customer), Richard DeGasperis (Ricky), Jeremy Kuszel (Joey)

Annabeth Gish, Patrick Van Horn, Jenn Gross in *Pursuit of Happiness* PHOTO COURTESY OF MTI

PURSUIT OF HAPPINESS

(MTI) Producers, Alex Hyde-White, John R. Zaring; Co-Producer, Daryl Taja; Associate Producers, Shelly Hyde-White, Jerry P. Jacobs; Director, John Putch; Screenplay, John R. Zaring; Photography, Ross Berryman; Designer, Mara A. Spear; Costumes, Bonnie Stauch; Editor, Vanick Moradian; Music, Alexander Baker, Clair Marlow; Casting, Cathy Henderson-Martin, Dori Zuckerman-Mentzer; from TMG Productions; Color; Rated R; 93 minutes; Release date: May 16, 2003. Cast: Frank Whaley (Alan), Annabeth Gish (Marissa), Alex Hyde-White (Paul), Amy Jo Johnson (Tracy), Dawn Eason (Janet), Adam Baldwin (Chad Harmon), Jean Stapleton (Lorraine), Patrick Van Horn (Mike), Liz Vassey (Renee), Cress Williams (Ace), Jenn Gross (Sally), Kieran Mulroney (Calvin), Anne-Marie Johnson (Devin Quinn), Michelle Krusiec (Miko), Megan Blake (Minister), Jessica Randle (Coffee Shop Manager), Tom Wright (Thom), Tudi Roche (Receptionist), Amy Tinkham (Flight Attendant), Michael Raysses (Seattle Limo Driver), Michael Harrity (Bartender), Ernest Harden, Jr. (Moving Guy), Ken Kerman (Moving Supervisor)

THAT'S MY FACE

(CHIMPANZEE PRODUCTIONS) Producer, Thomas Allen Harris; Line Producer, Sasha Dees; Director, Thomas Allen Harris; Screenplay, Thomas Allen Harris, Don Perry; Photography, Thomas Allen Harris, Albert Sidney Johnson, Jr.; Music, Vernon Reid, Jason Stanyek; Editors, Thomas Allen Harris, Emir Lewis; Black and white/color; Not rated; 60 minutes; Release date: May 23, 2003.

GIGANTIC (A TALE OF TWO JOHNS)

(COWBOY PICTURES) Producer, Shirley Moyers; Director, AJ Schnack; Photography, Yon Thomas; Music, John Flansburgh, John Linnell; Editors, Jason Kool, Alisa Lipsitt; from Bonfire Films of America; Color; Not rated; 102 minutes; Release date: May 23, 2003. Documentary about the rock group They Might Be Giants; featuring John Flansburgh, John Linnell, Gina Arnold, Michael Azerrad, Adam Bernstein, David Bither, Frank Black, Linwood Boomer, Brian Cohen, Pat Dillett, Sue Drew, Dave Eggers, Jake Fogelnest, Joe Franklin, Janeane Garofalo, Ira Glass, Jonathan Gregg, Dan Hickey, Kurt Hoffman, Mark Hoppus, Al Houghton, John Houlihan, William Ingoglia, Mike Kelly, Jamie Kitman, Jamie Lincoln Kitman, Josh Kornbluth, Bill Krauss, Robert Krulwich, Michael McKean, Dan Miller, Glenn Morrow, Alex Noyes, Conan O'Brien, Annette O'Toole, Gary Ray, Andy Richter, Raoul Rosenberg, Harry Shearer, Paul Simon, Michael Small, Jim Stabile, Jon Stewart, Syd Straw, Sarah Vowell, Danny Weinkauf

John Flansburgh, John Linnell in *Gigantic (A Tale of Two Johns)* PPHOTO COURTESY OF COWBOY PICTURES

WRONG TURN

(20TH CENTURY FOX) Producers, Erik Feig, Robert Kulzer, Stan Winston, Brian Gilbert; Executive Producers, Mitch Horwits, Patrick Wachsberger, Don Carmody, Aaron Ryder; Director, Rob Schmidt; Screenplay, Alan McElroy; Photography, John S. Bartley; Designer, Alicia Keywan; Costumes, Georgina Yarhi; Editor, Michael Ross; Music, Elia Cmiral; Music Supervisor, Randy Gerston; Make-Up Effects Supervisor, Shane Mahan; Special Make-Up Effects Creator & Designer, Stan Winston Studio, Inc.; Casting, Anya Colloff, Jennifer Fishman Pate, Amy McIntyre Britt; a Summit Entertainment and Constantin Film presentation of a Constantin Film/Summit Entertainment/McOne/Stan Winston Production in association with Newmarket Capital Group; Dolby; Deluxe color; Rated R; 84 minutes; Release date: May 30, 2003. Cast: Desmond Harrington (Chris Finn), Eliza Dushku (Jessie Burlingame), Emmanuelle Chriqui (Carly),

Jeremy Sisto (Scott), Kevin Zegers (Evan), Lindy Booth (Francine), Julian Richings (Three Finger), Garry Robbins (Saw-Tooth), Ted Clark (One-Eye), Yvonne Gaudry (Halley), Joel Harris (Rich), David Huband (Trooper), Wayne Robson (Old Man), James Downing (Trucker)

Eliza Duskhu, Desmond Harrington in *Wrong Turn* PHOTO COURTESY OF 20TH CENTURY FOX

AMERICA SO BEAUTIFUL

(B GOOD FILMS) Producer/Director, Babak Shokrian; Screenplay, Babak Shokrian, Brian Horiuchi; Executive Producer, Jane Reardon; Photography, Thom Ryan; Designer, Leora Lutz; Costumes, Chris Kreiling; Music, Ramin Torkian; Editor, Andrew M. Somers, Mary Stephen; Casting, John Cato; Corey Tong, Epicentre Films, Filmmakers Alliance productions; Color; Not rated; 91 minutes; Release date: May 30, 2003. Cast: Mansour (Houshang), Alan De Satti (Hamid), Houshang Touzie (Sahmi), Diane Gaidry (Lucy), David Fairborz Davoodian (Parviz), Atossa Leoni (Maryam), Shohreh Aghdashloo (Exiled Actress), Belinda Waymouth (Kathy), Steven Zlotnick (Club Door Manager)

CONTROLLED CHAOS

(LOVESTREAKS PRODS.) Producer/Director/Screenplay/Designer/Casting, Azita Zendel; Photography, Brian Booth, Lila Javan, Brendon Phillips; Music, Pinar Toprak; Editors, Azita Zendel, Eric Chase; Color; Not rated; 93 minutes; Release date: June 4, 2003. Cast: Amy Blomquist (Elsie), Erik Engstrom (Slick), Charley Izabella (Pam), Kurt Hall (Doc), Lori Enterline (Tara), Tara John (Michelle), Markus Nash (Steve), Tim Nistler (Franzino), Ginny Kunz (Madeline), Ty Auston Rainey (Paul), Ron De Shay (Robert), Matthew Vinci (Jack), David Moradzadeh (Martin), Joel Bond (Ned), Deborah Joy (Rebeca), Masami Okada (Agnes), Jason Allen (Nathan), John Tye (Aaron), Dwight R. Williams (Hector), Jayne Armstrong (Margaret), Robert Jolly (Editor), Stefen Malone (Gustave), McLaurin Jackson (Stan), Charley Marean (Professor), Kris Jacobs (Ray), Jeffrey D. Carter (Mac), Cindy Kimmel (Nurse), Marshall J. Keyes (Doctor), Bahman Ezzati (Bouncer), Guy Blews (Monroe), Elaine Burns (Betsy), Azita Zendel (Bailarina), Nicole Halimi, Timothy Halimi, Corey Rainey, Alan Raouf (Fans), Dolat Melamed (Guest), Pat Toma, Patrick Martens (Medics), Scott Wunno (New 2nd A.D.), Claudia Patton (Antoinette), Dave Shelton (Photographer)

Saundra Santiago, Poncho Ramirez in *Garmento* PHOTO COURTESY OF SPANISH MOSS PRODS.

GARMENTO

(SPANISH MOSS PRODS.) Producer/Director/Screenplay, Michele Maher; Photography, Mark Schwartzbard; Designer, Henry Dunn; Costumes, Amy Westcott; Music, Ed Tomney; Editor, Andrew Malenda; Associate Producer, Ruth Thomas-Suh; Casting, Susan Shopmaker; Technicolor; Rated R; 90 minutes; Release date: June 6, 2003. Cast: Katie MacNichol (Grindy Malone), David Thornton (Ronnie Grossman), Juan Carlos Hernandez (Poncho Ramirez), Saundra Santiago (Franca Fortuna), Jerry Grayson (Ira Gold), Gretchen Cleevely (Rimi Stone), Jason Butler Harner (Jasper Judson), Geoffrey Cantor (Fred Macmoudi), Matt Servitto (Louie Purdaro), P.J. Minnick (Shawn), Heather Magee, Christine Bosco, Cristen Elmore, Peter Kress, David Ley, Mark Neveldine, Krysten Ritter, Scot Schwartz, Yasha Young (Poncho Models), Cassidy Ladden (Young Grindy), Sara McGovern (Grindy's Mother), Danny Darron (Salesman), Larry Marx (Jobber), Joey Kern (Tye), Kevin Sussman (Caesar), Ben Wang (Shoji), Howard Spiegel (Mel), Maggie Burke (Miriam), Bruce Turk (Sage), Jeff Whitty (Tim), Jennifer Wrubel (Tammy), Michaela Conlin (Marcy), Alyson Silverman (Jeanine), Christian Baskous (Guy), Glenn Fleshler (Tony), Croix Lazzara (Thomas), Rohan Quine (Lee), T.R. Knight (Daniel), Michele Maher (Reporter), Kevin Geer (Jack Kearns), Carol Tammen (News Reporter), Christine Perkins, Larry Block (Discount Store Manager), Gil Rogers (Detective), Dean Obeidallah (Policeman), Denny Dillon (Sylvia Walsh), Uzi Parnes, Brandon Jenkins, Jonathan Klein, Jason Pabon, Christian Pabon, Adam Ramirez, Cruise Russo (Poncho Commercial Actors)

LOVE THE HARD WAY

(KINO) Producer, Wolfram Tichy; Supervising Producer, Marco Mehlitz; Director, Peter Sehr; Screenplay, Peter Sehr, Marie Noelle; Based on the novel by Shuo Wang; Photography, Guy Dufaux; Designer, Debbie DeVilla; Costumes, Kathryn Nixon; Editor, Christian Nauheimer; Associate Producers, Jayne Belliveau, Kevin J. Moore; Casting, Ellen Parks, Sabine Schroth; a Daybreak Pictures, Open City Films, P'Artisan Filmproduktion GmbH, TiMe Film-und TV-Productions GmbH, Wif Filmproduction GmbH; U.S.-German; Rated R; 104 minutes; Release date: June 6, 2003. Cast: Adrien Brody (Jack), Charlotte Ayanna (Claire), Jon Seda (Charlie), August Diehl (Jeff), Pam Grier (Linda Fox), Liza Jessie Peterson (Pamela), Elizabeth Regen (Sue), Katherine Moennig (Debbie), Joey Kern (Fitzgerald), Jonathan Hadary (Boris), Michael G. Chin, Ben Wang (Asian Men), Ned Stresen-Reuter (Brian), Michaela Conlin (Cara), Lee Sellars (Dennis), Sylvia Kauders (Mrs. Rosenberg), Jose Rabello (Cook), Dave Simonds (Librarian), Jeffrey Marchetti (Biggest Guy), John Elsen (Interrogating Detective), Miguel

Sierra (Car Mechanic), Andy Dupping (Precision Driver #1), Bobby J. Brown (Man in Video Arcade), Steven Goldstein (The John), Sara Klingebiel (Jill), Francisco Lorite (Barry), Kris Eivers (Bartender, Tunnel), Eric Kornfeld (Claire's Trick), Amber Gross (Hooker #3), Gregor Manns, Kevin Merrill-Wilson (Large Men), James Saito (Akiri), Robert G. McKay (Louis), Chaz Menendez, Charles Santy, Mick O'Rourke, Washington Mitchell (Prisoners), Peter McRobbie (Prison Doctor), Tod Engle (Lucky Guy), Grace Garland (Port Authority Official), Amy Laughlin (Vendor at Hotel Dior), David Ross, Slava Schoot (Russian Guys), Jack Lotz (John in Bedroom), Charles Duval (Waiter)

Adrien Brody, Pam Grier in *Love the Hard Way* PHOTO COURTESY OF KINO

MANITO

(FILM MOVEMENT) Producers, Jesse Scolaro, Allen Bain; Executive Producers, John P. McGrath, Paul Corvino, Neil Davis, Peggy Fry; Director/Screenplay, Eric Eason; Photography, Didier Gertsch; Designer, Christine Darch; Music, Saundi Wilson; Editor, Kyle Henry; a Seventh Floor in association with Smashing Entertainment presentation Dolby; Color; Not rated; 76 minutes; Release date: June 13, 2003. Cast: Franky G (Junior Moreno), Leo Minaya (Manny Moreno), Manuel Jesus Cabral (Oscar Moreno), Julissa Lopez (Miriam Moreno), Jessica Morales (Marisol), Hector Gonzalez (Abuelo), Panchito Gomez (Rodchenko), Lavidaria Ramirez (Anita), Casper Martinez (Enrique), Lou Torres (Bartender), Adeal Irizarry (Hercules), Edwin Morel DeLeon (Roberto), Jeff Ascencio (Ignacio), Jay Dog, Gilly Delgado (Muggers), Yovanna Jose (Nena), Tiffany Yates (Mrs. Wendorf), John P. McGrath (Detective), Petra Quinones (Aunt Aida), Monique Vasquez (Miriam's Friend), Haydee Rivera (Marisol's Abuela), Barbara Resnick (Public Defender), Mark Anthony (Lawyer), Anthony Desio (Bail

Eric Christian Olsen, Derek Richardson in *Dumb & Dumberer* PHOTO COURTESY OF NEW LINE CINEMA

Bondsman), C.J. Rodriguez (Junior's Son), Mark Anthony, Jr. (Nena's Son), Charlton Lamar (Parole Officer), Fulantino (The Band)

THE NAZI OFFICER'S WIFE

(SEVENTH ART) Producers, Laurent M. Zilber, Christina Zilber; Director, Liz Garbus; Screenplay, Jack Youngelson; Photography, Daniel B. Gold; Music, Sheldon Mirowitz; Editor, Eric Seuel Davies; a Moxie Firecracker Films, Trillion Entertainment production; Black and white/color; Not rated; 90 minutes; Release date: June 13, 2003. Documentary on Edith Han, a law student forced into a Jewish ghetto along with her mother. Voices: Susan Sarandon (Narrator), Julia Ormond (Edith Hahn)

The Nazi Officer's Wife PHOTO COURTESY OF SEVENTH ART

DUMB AND DUMBERER: WHEN HARRY MET LLOYD

(NEW LINE CINEMA) Producers, Oren Koules, Charles B. Wessler, Brad Krevoy, Steve Stabler, Troy Miller; Executive Producers, Toby Emmerich, Richard Brener, Cale Boyter, Bennett Yellin; Director, Troy Miller; Screenplay, Robert Brener, Troy Miller; Story, Robert Brener; Based on characters created by Peter Farrelly, Bennett Yellin, Bobby Farrelly; Co-Producer, Carl Mazzocone; Photography, Anthony Richmond; Art Director, Paul Huggins; Costumes, Susanna Puisto; Music, Eban Schletter; Music Supervisors, Joonathan McHugh, Matthew Sullivan; Editor, Lawrence Jordan; Casting, John Papsidera; a Brad Krevoy/Charles B. Wessler/Steve Stabler and a Burg/Koules and Dakota Pictures production; Dolby; Deluxe color; Rated PG-13; 85 minutes; Release date: June 13, 2003. Cast: Eric Christian Olsen (Lloyd Christmas), Derek Richardson (Harry Dunne), Rachel Nichols (Jessica), Cheri Oteri (Ms. Heller), Luis Guzman (Ray), Elden Henson (Turk), William Lee Scott (Carl), Mimi Rogers (Mrs. Dunne), Eugene Levy (Principal Collins), Lin Shaye (Margie), Shia LaBeouf (Lewis), Josh Braaten (Toby), Teal Redmann (Terri), Julia Duffy (Jessica's Mom), Michelle Krusiec (Ching Chong), Timothy Stack (Doctor), Wayne Federman (Officer Dave), Lucas Gregory (8 Year-Old Harry), Holly Towne (Preppy Student), Vahe Manoukian (Security Guard), Carl Mazzocone (Football Coach), Tally Barr (Nice Jugs Girl), Brian Posehn (Cale, Store Clerk), Lawrence Jordan (Man), Dawn M. Gerrior (Woman), Nancy M. Pimental (Museum Docent), Bob Saget (Jessica's Dad), Kevin Centazzo (Boyfriend), Tess Brewer (Little Girl), Jill Talley (Mom), Aaron Kaplan (Ten-year-old Kid), Stacey Hill (Dog Driver), Nathan Wright (Nebbish Guy), Dana Gould (Mr. Moffitt), Roger Eschbacher (Superintendent Zimmer), Julie Costello, Shawnie Costello (Twins), Jeff Cesario (P.A. Announcer)

LOCO LOVE

(ARTISAN/PATHFINDER) a.k.a. *Mi Casa, Su Casa;* Executive Producer, Charlie Bravo; Line Producer, Lara Blasingame; Director, Bryan Lewis; Screenplay, Steven Baer; Photography, Thaddeus Wadleigh; Designer, Robin Kirk; Costumes, Carol Nolan; Music, Jon McCallum; Editor, Sherril Schlesinger; from Enigma Entertainment, Three Spring Productions; Dolby; Color; Rated PG; 94 minutes; Release date: June 13, 2003. Cast: Laura Harring (Catalina), Roy Werner (Donald), Gerardo Mejia (Miguel Sanchez), Margaret Scarborough (Barbara), Victoria Ramirez (Juanita), Frank Gallegos (Tobias), Barbara Eden (Jackie), Erick Carrillo (Pedro), Paul Keith (Mr. Hurley), Michael Kuka (Norm), Rhonda Le (Eli), Miguel Mas (Hector), Debbie McLeod (Mrs. Hurley), Ken Perkins (Maitre D'), Tara Price (Carla the Bartender), Dominique Reino (Honeymooner), Dan Twyman (INS Agent)

BONHOEFFER

(FIRST RUN FEATURES) Producer/Director/Screenplay/Narrator, Martin Doblmeier; Associate Producers, Adele Schmidt, Kristin Fellows, Janna Morishima; Photography, Dennis Boni, David Goulding, Jörg Pilca, Peter V. Schultz; Music, John D. Keltonic; Editors, Tim Finkbiner, Matthew B. Kelly; a Journey Films production; Black and white/color; Not rated; 91 minutes; Release date: June 20, 2003. Documentary on Dietrich Bonhoeffer, a German pacifist who defied the Nazi regime and died tragically as a result; featuring Eberhard Bethge, John De Gruchy, Geffrey Kelly, Bishop Desmond Tutu, Ruth Alice von Bismarck, Otto Dudzes, Marianne Libeholz, Victoria Barnett, John Conway, Christian Gremmels, Clifford Green, Bishop Wolfgang Huber, Inge Sembritzki, Rev. Henry Mitchell, Josiah Youing, Winifried Maechler, Peter Hoffmann, Christoph von Dohnanyi, Bishop Albrecht Schonherr (Themselves); Voices: Klaus Maria Brandauer (Dietrich Bonhoeffer), Richard Mancini (Bishop Bell), Adele Schmidt (Sabine)

Bonhoeffer PHOTO COURTESY OF FIRST RUN FEATURES

HELL'S HIGHWAY: THE TRUE STORY OF HIGHWAY SAFETY FILMS

(KINO) Producers, Bret Wood, Felicia Feaster, Tommy Gibbons; Director/Screenplay/Editor, Bret Wood; Photography, Steve Anderson; Music Supervisors, Alan Licht, Tim Barnes; Narrator, Helena Reckitt; from Livin' Man Productions; Black and white/color; Rated R; 91 minutes; American release date: June 27, 2003. Documentary on highway safety films; featuring John F. Butler, Earle J. Deems, John R. Domer, David Krug, Eric Krug, Rick Prelinger, Mike Vraney, James Waller, Martin Yant.

ON_LINE

(INDICAN) Producers, Adam Brightman, Tanya Selvaratnam; Executive Producers, Claude Arpels, Richard D. Titus, Tavin Marin Titus; Director, Jed Weintrob; Screenplay, Jed Weintrob, Andrew Osborne; Photography, Toshiaki Ozawa; Designer, Jory Adam; Costumes, Mia Morgan; Editor, Stephanie Sterner; Music, Roger Neil; Casting, Adrienne Stern; an Internet Stories production; Dolby; Color; Rated R; 97 minutes; Release date: June 27, 2003. Cast: Josh Hamilton (John Roth), Harold Perrineau (Moe Curley), Isabel Gillies (Moira Ingalls), John Fleck (Al Fleming), Vanessa Ferlito (Jordan Nash), Eric Millegan (Ed Simone), Liz Owens (Angel)

THE JOURNEY

(INDEPENDENT) Producers/Screenplay, Edwin Avaness, Emy Hovanesyan, Anghela Zograbyan; Executive Producer, Krikor Tatoyan; Directors, Edwin Avaness, Emy Hovanesyan; Photography/Editor, Edwin Avaness; Designer, Anghela Zorgrabyan; Music, Alan Derian; JF Productions; Color; HD Video; Not rated; 96 minutes; Release date: July 11, 2003. Cast: Sona Tatoyan (Eve), Varduhi Vardéresyan (Eve's Grandmother), Tigran Nersesyan (David), Anoush Stepanyan (Emma), Zenda Tatoyan (Eve's Mother), Roupen Harmandayan (Eve's Dad), Sohrab Bek-Gasparents (Ruben), Hasmik Ter-Hayrapetyan (Arman's Mother), Gayane Mardirosian (Young Eve)

THIS THING OF OURS

(SMALL PLANET) Producers, Daniel Farash, Ted A. Bohus, Michael DelGaizo; Supervising Producer, Gerry Brynes; Director, Danny Provenzano; Screenplay, Danny Provenzano, Ted A. Bohus; Photography, George Mitas; Music, Lawrence Manchester, Jack Douglas; Editor, Andy Kier; Casting, Stephanie Reggio; an Austin Film Group production; Dolby; Color; Not rated; 100 minutes; Release date: July 18, 2003. Cast: Frank Vincent (Danny Santini), Vincent Pastore (Skippy), Danny Provenzano (Nicholas Santini), Edward Lynch (Johnny Irish), Louis Vanaria (Austin Palermo), Christian Maelen (Robert Biaggio), Chuck Zito (Chuck), Michael DelGaizo (Patsy DeGrazio), Pat Cooper (John Bruno), James Caan (Jimmy "The Con"), Vinny Vella, Sr. (Carmine), Joe Regano (Joe), Tony Ray Rossi (Anthony Russo), Paul Vario (Big Paul), Danny Musico (Guy wheeling Jimmy), Bobby Pantoliano (Sally), Lou Silver (Santini Soldier), Ted A. Bohus (Teddy Alexander), Johnny Speciale (Jimmy S.), Anthony Castelli (Anthony), Michael Gerardi (Johnny), Dan Conte (Guy Who Didn't Get Joke), Jon Doscher (Agent Clark), Robert Nathna (FBI Guy), Felix Valentine (Chin), Boby Cassidy (Joey), Frank Bonsuange (Office Cleaner), Anthony Corozzo, P.B. Jr. (Soldiers), Gaetano LoGiudice (Tommy), Phil Faicco (Phil), Shawn Stailworth (Agent Jason Black), Ricky Lucchese III (Guy in Restroom with DeGrazio), Alket Adini (Nino the

Zip), Brad Whitford (Brad), Joe Abbate (DeGrazio Soldier outside Warehouse), Rolando Millet (Cuban Boss), Stephanie Reggio (Stephanie)

Hell's Highway   PHOTO COURTESY OF KINO

THE ANARCHIST COOKBOOK

(Innovation) Producers, Amy Greenspun, Jordan Susman, Robert Latham Brown; Director/Screenplay, Jordan Susman; Photography, Brown Cooper; Designer, Jeff Knipp; Music, Josh Kramon; Editor, Alan Edward Bell; Casting, Liz Kiegley, Sari E. Keigley; from Freedonia Productions; Dolby; Color; Rated R; 101 minutes; Release date: July 18, 2003. Cast: Devon Gummersall (Puck), Dylan Bruno (Johnny Black), Katharine Towne (Jody), Steve Van Wormer (Double D), Johnny Whitworth (Sweeney), Gina Philips (Karla), John Savage (Johnny Red), Travis Willingham (Tour Leader), Richard Jackson (Campus Security Guard), Sabine Singh (Gin), Amy Greenspun (News Reporter), Bo Barron (Cool Teen), Marcus Moziek (Golden Chick Dude), Todd Terry (Judge William Haversford), Matt Morton (Shoplifting Dude), Ryan Thomas Brockington (Clean-cut Basketball Player), Nancy Drotning (Businesswoman), Sean Hennigan (Businessman), Montre Bible (Bike Messenger), Larry Johnson (Fur Store Guard), Justin Howard (Davy Crockett), Julio Cedillo (Santa Ana), Willie Minor (Willie), Irene Cortez (Latina), R. Bruce Elliot (Coffee Shop Manager), Brent Anderson (Another Businessman), Gail Cronauer (Woman in Book Store), Jordan Wall (Straight-Laced Teen), Collin David (Bam Bam), Laurel Whitsett (Sweet Thing), Kinna McInroe (Rollerskating Waitress), Cliff Stephens (Officer Roger), Jack Watkins (Sergeant at Arms), Kim Terry (Mrs. Gold), Darryl Cox (Mr. Gold), Brooke Leslie (Susie/Hannah), Morgana Shaw (Mother in Supermarket), Jerry Cotton (Boss), Scarlett McAlister (Caroline), Jeff Hartman (Sales Guy), Richard Black (Milo), Bob Hess (Dale), Sonny Franks (Rich), Cynthia Dorn (FBI Agent), Brad Leland (Truck Driver)

MASKED AND ANONYMOUS

(SONY CLASSICS) Producer, Nigel Sinclair, Jeff Rosen; Executive Producers, Anatoly Fradis, Joseph Cohen, Vladimir Dostal, David M. Thompson, Guy East, Marie Cantin, Pietro Scalia; Director, Larry Charles; Screenplay, Rene Fontaine (Larry Charles), Sergei Petrov (Bob Dylan); Photography, Rogier Stoffers; Music, Bob Dylan; Editors, Luis Alvarez y Alvarez, Pietro Scalia; Casting, Irene Cagen; Liberman/Patton; BBC Films and Marching Band Productions presentation of a Spitfire Pictures and Grey Water Park Production; U.S.-British; Dolby; Color;

Rated PG-13; 112 minutes; Release date: July 24, 2003. Cast: Jeff Bridges (Tom Friend), Penélope Cruz (Pagan Lace), Bob Dylan (Jack Fate), John Goodman (Uncle Sweetheart), Jessica Lange (Nina Veronica), Luke Wilson (Bobby Cupid), Angela Bassett (Mistress), Steven Bauer (Edgar), Bruce Dern (Editor), Ed Harris (Oscar Vogel), Val Kilmer (Animal Wrangler), Cheech Marin (Prospero), Christian Slater, Chris Penn (Crew Guys), Giovanni Ribisi (Soldier), Mickey Rourke (Edmund), Richard Sarafian (President), Susan Tyrrell (Ella the Fortuneteller), Tracey Walter (Desk Clerk), Fred Ward (Drunk), Robert Wisdom (Lucius), Larry Campbell, Tony Garnier, George Receli, Charlie Sexton (Members of Jack Fate's Band), Michael Paul Chan (Guard), Alex Désert (Valentine), Treva Etienne (Percy), Dan Frichman (Eddie Quicksand the Ventriloquist), Eddie Gorodestsky (Bacchus), Noel Guglielmi (The Inmate), Shawn Michael Howard (Nestor), Shirley Jones (Third-World Prostitute), Tinashe Kachungwe (Mrs. Brown's Daughter), Bruce Kirschbaum (Dion), Reggie Lee (Armed Man), Antonio David Lyons (Government Soldier), Davenia McFadden (Bus Driver), Sam Sarpong (Blunt), Jon Sklaroff (Young Jack Fate), Susan Traylor (Mrs. Brown), Perla Walter (The Caretaker)

John Goodman, Luke Wilson, Bob Dylan in *Masked and Anonymous*
PHOTO COURTESY OF SONY CLASSICS

BOYS LIFE 4: FOUR PLAY

(STRAND) Executive Producers, Bill Kirkner, Brian Sloan; Color; Not rated; 83 minutes. Release date: August 1, 2003. *L.T.R.:* Producer/Director/Screenplay, Phillip J. Bartell. Cast: Cole Williams (Michael), Weston Mueller (Riley), Aimee Garcia (Caitlan), Michael Azria (Tobias), Phillip J. Bartell (Voice of Interviewer), Jonathan Alberts (Blurred Boy in Coffee Shop), David Feldman, Barry Gellis, Rich Rennessy, Michael Peters, Howard Simsno, Tobias Trost (Boys in Line). *O Beautiful:* Producer/Director/Screenplay, Alan Brown. Cast: Jay Gillespie (Brad), David Rogers (Andy). *Bumping Heads:* Producer, Robert Ahrens; Director/Screenplay, Brian Sloan. Cast: Craig Chester (Craig), Andersen Gabrych (Gary), Nora Burns (Doctor), Ned Stresen-Reuter (Robert), Katherine Carlson (Vanessa), John Spencer (Cowboy), David Martin (Hospital Orderly), Tashya Valdevit (Gary's Counselor), Mike Albo (Craig's Therapist). *This Car Up:* Producer, Julie Hartley; Director, Eric Mueller; Screenplay, Andrew Peterson. Cast: Michael Booth (Pete), Brent Doyle (Adrian), Carol Vnuk (Receptionist), Derek Meeker (Hunky Lawyer), Patricia Nieman (Kissing Woman), David Anderson (Kissing Man), Trevor Collis (Other Messenger), Melissa Miller (Dog Owner)

ENEMIES OF LAUGHTER

(OUTRIDER) Producers, Joey Travolta, Richard Salvatore; Executive Producers, Ray Gaspard, Carmen M. Miller, Marc Sferrazza; Director, Joey Travolta; Screenplay, Glen Merzer; Photography, Kristian Bernier; Designer, Joe Lemmon; Costumes, Lexi Nikitas; Music, Barry Coffing; Editor, Will Wuorinen; Casting, Robin Libben, Lisa London; from Two Sticks Prods.; Color; Not rated; 90 minutes; Release date: August 1, 2003. Cast: David Paymer (Paul Halpern), Judge Reinhold (Sam), Rosalind Chao (Carla), Beatrice Arthur (Paul's Mother), Peter Falk (Paul's Father), Vanessa Angel (Jennifer), Kristina Fulton (Regina), Kathy Griffin (Cindy), Marilu Henner (Dani), Paul Sampson (Waiter), Daphne Zuniga (Judy Kravitz), Glen Merzer (Josh), Leila Kenzle, Melody Krell (Women), Shera Danese (Helen), Melissa Greenspan (Erica), Doyle McCurley (The Chef), Rick Otto (Comedy Writer #1)

Keala Kennelly in *Step into Liquid* PHOTO COURTESY OF ARTISAN

STEP INTO LIQUID

(ARTISAN) Producer, John-Paul Beeghly; Executive Producers, Bruce Brown, Ray Willenberg, Jr.; Director/Screenplay, Dana Brown; Photography, John-Paul Beeghly; Music, Richard Gibbs; Associate Producer, Scott Waugh; a New Visual Entertainment presentation of a Top Secret production; Dolby; FotoKem color; Super 16mm/24P HD Video; 87 minutes; Release date: August 8, 2003. Documentary on surfing; with Jim Knost, Alex Knost, Dan Malloy, Chris Malloy, Keith Malloy, Laird Hamilton, Rob Machado, Kelly Slater, Dale Webster.

Weston Mueller, Cole Williams in *Boys Life 4: Four Play* PHOTO COURTESY OF STRAND

PASSIONADA

(SAMUEL GOLDWYN) Producer, David Bakalar; Executive Producer, Jim Jermanok; Associate Producer, Lori Keith Douglas; Director, Dan Ireland; Screenplay, Jim Jermanok, Steve Jermanok; Photography, Claudio Rocha; Designer, John Frick; Costumes, Rudy Dillon; Music, Harry Gregson-Williams; Editor, Luis Colina; Casting, Amanda Mackey Johnson, Sig De Miguel; a Fireworks Pictures and Sandyo Productions presentation of a David Bakalar production; Dolby; Panavision; Fotokem Color; Rated PG-13; 108 minutes; Release date: August 8, 2003. Cast: Jason Isaacs (Charles Beck), Sofia Milos (Celia Amonte), Emmy Rossum (Vicky Amonte), Theresa Russell (Lois Vargas), Seymour Cassel (Daniel Vargas), Lupe Ontiveros (Angelica Amonte), Chris Tardio (Gianni Martinez), Luis Colina (Anthony, The Lobster Man), Marion Eaton (Betsy), John Freus (Escort for Women), J. Patrick George (Gambler Cashing Out Chips), Tom Kemp (Bartender), Robert Montano (Father Emmanuel), Anthero Montenegro (Joseph Amonte), Benjamin Mouton (Pit Boss), Stephen O'Neil Martin (Poker Dealer), Joe Simon (Michael), Russ Vigilante (Roberto), Matt Blake (Security Guard #1), Charley Broderick (Club Owner)

Sofia Milos, Jason Isaacs in *Passionada* PHOTO COURTESY OF SAMUEL GOLDWYN

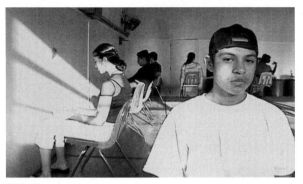

OT: Our Town PHOTO COURTESY OF FILM MOVEMENT

OT: OUR TOWN

(FILM MOVEMENT) Producer/Director/Photography, Scott Hamilton Kennedy; Executive Producer, Mark Pellington; Music, Doug DeAngelis, Kevin Haskins, Messy; Editors, Scott Hamilton Kennedy, Chris Figler; a Stressbox Inc., OT Films production; Color; Not rated; 76 minutes; Release date: August 15, 2003. Documentary about how two teachers and twenty-four students at Dominguez High in Compton, CA, attempt to put on a production of Thornton Wilder's *Our Town*; featuring Catherine Borek, Karen Greene (Teachers/Directors), Ebony Starr Norwood-Brown (The Stage Manager), Archie Posada ("George Gibbs"), Armia Robinson ("Emily Webb"), Jackie Oliver ("Mrs. Soames"), Christopher Patterson ("Mr. Webb"), Jose Perez ("Simon Stimson")

GRIND

(WARNER BROS.) Producers, Bill Gerber, Hunt Lowry, Casey La Scala; Executive Producers, K. Gaylord II, Morgan Stone; Director, Casey La Scala; Screenplay/Executive Music Producer, Ralph Sall; Photography, Richardo Crudo; Designer, Perry Andelin Blake; Costumes, Tangi Crawford; Editor, Eric Strand; Co-Producers, Betsy Mackey, Lance Sloane; Casting, Nancy Nayor; a Pandora

presentation of a Gaylord Films/Gerber Pictures production in association with 900 Films; Dolby; Color; Rated PG-13; 105 minutes; Release date: August 15, 2003. Cast: Mike Vogel (Eric Rivers), Vince Vieluf (Matt Jensen), Adam Brody (Dustin Knight), Joey Kern (Sweet Lou), Jennifer Morrison (Jamie), Jason London (Jimmy Wilson), Summer Altice (Winona), Bam Margera (Bam), Erin Murphy (Hot Mama), Baron La Scala (In Utero), Stephen Root (Cameron), Wee Man (Little Timmy), Brian Posehn (Orville the Scraggly Guy), Christopher McDonald (Mr. Rivers), Donte Calarco, Mercedes Brito (Buxom Girls), Lanna Taskey (Woman with List), Chad Fernandez, Alfred Briere, Ehren McGhehey (Rival Skaters), Jake Muxworthy (Pro), Julia Lee (Another Hot Girl), Shonda Farr (Sandy), Bob Goldthwait (Bell Clerk), Ryan Sheckler (Rod St. James), Brandon Smith, Dylan Rieder (Kids), Don Gibb (Scabby Security Guy), Bucky Lasek (Touring Pro), Preston Lacy (Hefty Man), Rolando Molina (Show Security), Christine Estabrook (Sarah Jensen), Randy Quaid (Jock Jensen), David Bowe (Registration Clerk), Tom Green (Colorado Skate Shop Owner), Karen McDougal, Dalene Kurtis (Playmates), Dave Foley (Tour Manager), Shazia (Native American Girl), Mike Carter (MC), Shane Hunter (Mark), Rick Martins (Concert Security Guy), Lindsay Marie Felton (Dawn Jenson), Sasha Jensen (Greg), Kane Hodder (Sweet Lou's "Girlfriend's" Dad), Brian Sumner (Himself)

Adam Brody, Vince Vieluf, Jennifer Morrison, Joey Kern, Mike Vogel in *Grind*
PHOTO COURTESY OF WARNER BROS.

CATCHING OUT

(SEVENTH ART) Producer/Director, Sarah George; Photography, Pallas Weber, Shane F. Kelly; Time Lapse Photography, John Nonnemacher; Editor/Associate Producer, Casey P. Chinn; Music, Pete Droge; Color; Not rated; 80 minutes; Release date: August 20, 2003. Documentary on modern day hobos who ride freight trains to travel the country; featuring Switch & Baby Girl, Jessica, Lee, North Bank Fred, Duffy Littlejohn, Luther the Jet

Switch, Baby Girl in *Catching Out* PHOTO COURTESY OF SEVENTH ART

Ashton Kutcher, Tara Reid in *My Boss's Daughter* PHOTO COURTESY OF DIMENSION

MY BOSS'S DAUGHTER

(DIMENSION) Producers, Gil Netter, John Jacobs; Executive Producers, Paddy Cullen, Bob Weinstein, Harvey Weinstein, Andrew Rona, Brad Weston; Director, David Zucker; Screenplay, David Dorfman; Co-Producer, Ashton Kutcher; Photography, Martin McGrath; Designer, Andrew Laws; Costumes, Daniel Orlandi; Music, Teddy Castelluci; Music Supervisors, Madonna Wade-Reed, Jennifer Pyken; Editors, Patrick Lussier, Sam Craven; Casting, John Papsidera; a Gil Netter and a John Jacobs production; Distributed by Miramax Films; Dolby; Deluxe Color; Rated PG-13; 86 minutes; Release date: August 22,

2003. Cast: Ashton Kutcher (Tom Stansfield), Tara Reid (Lisa Taylor), Terence Stamp (Jack Taylor), Jeffrey Tambor (Ken), Andy Richter (Red Taylor), Molly Shannon (Audrey Bennett), Michael Madsen (T.J.), Carmen Electra (Tina), Mark Aisbett (Commuter), Jon Abrahams (Paul), Tyler Labine (Spike), Ryan Zwick (Delivery Boy), Patrick Cranshaw (Old Man), Angela Little (Sheryl), David Koechner (Speed), Ronald Selmour (Darryl), Kenan Thompson (Hans), Charlotte Zucker (Gertrude), Jim Byrnes (George), Ever Carradine (Julie), Dan Joffre (Smith), Tim Henry (Jones), Link Baker (Paramedic), Carmen Aguirre, Mark McConchie, Susan Breslau (Executives), Betty Linde (Coffee Customer), Tongo Ma (Thai Bus Driver), Henry Mah (Thai Bus Passenger), Dave Foley (Henderson)

Purva Bedi, Vikram Dasu in *Green Card Fever* PHOTO COURTESY OF NET EFFECT MEDIA

GREEN CARD FEVER

(NET EFFECT MEDIA) Producer, Vijay Vaidyanathan; Supervising Producer, Sheena Vaidyanhathan; Director/Screenplay, Bala Rajasekharuni; Photography, Joe M. Johnston, Scott Spears; Art Director, Michael Tipka; Costumes, Crystal Parzik, Vidhya Bhaskaran; Music, Pete Sears; Editor, Robert Komatsu; Casting, Kathy Smith; a Vijay Vaidyanathan presentation; Color; Not rated; 100 minutes; Release date: August 22, 2003. Cast: Vikram Dasu (Murali), Purva Bedi (Bharathi), Deep Katdare (Omjeet Singh Purewal), Chayton Arvin (Ram), Robin Lin (Chan), Subash Kundanmal (Dada), Srinath Sampath (Patel), Aatif Khan (Shubho), Cyrstal Parzik (Nicki), Lynn Oh (Chinese Agitator #1), Nick Baldasare (Patrick), Miguel Baldoni (Interpreter), Sunder Bhatia (Surgit, Omjeet's Dad), Kelsey Carter (Cousin Ann), Arunda Chowdry (Bharathi's Mom), Kair Cogswell (Cousin Ellie), Michael Coleman (Mayor), Peter Comerford (Detention Officer), Jagdish Davda (AC President), Shobhana Davda (Omjeet's Mom), Karam Dhillon (Young Omjeet), Pamela Dooley (Sarah), Timothy Fulton (Cousin Frank), Jessica Hamlin (Deborah), Joseph Hite (Cousin Derek), Akilah Holloway (Babysitter), Brant Jones (Cousin Bill), Rajesh Kanumaury (Rajender), Kaizaad Kotwal (Parvesh), Paul Liu (Chinese Association President), Robert M. Maines (Robert Tandy), Johnny Ray Miller (Gene), Pamela Murphy (Judge's Girlfriend), Ratna Palakodeti (Bharathi's Dad), Sarvabhaum Parikh (Venkat Rao), Gnanesh Patel (Rusi), Dovie Pettitt (License Examiner), Veeraraghavan Pirumalai (Gandi), Kamal Punjabi (Rana), Peter John Ross (Director), Satish Sattanathan (Ramachandra Rao), Cristina Shoemaker (Cousin Carol), Sam Snavley (Aaron), Adit Vakil (Vamsi), Sewell Whitney (Aaron's Dad), Jacques Barnes (Serious INC Cop), David Alan Shaw (INS Judge)

Tilda Swinton in *Teknolust* PHOTO COURTESY OF THINKFILM

TEKNOLUST

(THINKFILM) Producers, Lynn Hershman-Leeson, Youssef Vahabzadeh, John Bradford King, Oscar Gubernati; Executive Producer, Amy Sommer; Director/Screenplay, Lynn Hershman-Leeson; Photography, Hiro Narita; Designer, Chris Farmer; Costumes, Yohji Yamamoto, Marianna Astrom-DeFina; Music, Klaus Badelt, Marc Tschanz; Editor, Lisa Fruchtman; Makeup: Tonya Crooks; Special Effects Supervisor: Megan I. Carlson; Casting, Nancy Hayes; from Blue Turtle, Epiphany Productions, Hotwire Productions, ZDF Productions; U.S.-German-U.K.; Dolby; Color; Rated R; 85 minutes; Release date: August 22, 2003. Cast: Tilda Swinton (Rosetta Stone/Ruby/Marinne/Olive), Jeremy Davies (Sandy), James Urbaniak (Agent Hopper), John O'Keefe (Prof. Crick), Karen Black (Dirty Dick), Al Nazemian (Dr. Bea), S.U. Violet (Dr. Aye), Josh Kornbluth (Tim), Thomas Jay Ryan (Preacher), Howard Swain (Alex), Diana Demar (Dana), John Pirruccello (Hair Dresser), Abigail Van Alyn (Sandy's Mom), Dick Bright (Phil), Brad King (Nathan), Paul Barnett (Sam), Benton Greene (Frank), Diane Luby Lane (Sales Clerk), Paula West (Herself), Andrea Zomber (Leonora)

STOKED: THE RISE AND FALL OF GATOR

(PALM PICTURES) Producer/Director/Screenplay, Helen Stickler; Associate Producer, Zachary Mortensen; Photography, Helen Stickler, Peter Sutherland, Dag Yngvesson; Editor, Ana Esterov; Black and white/color; Rated R; 80 minutes; Release date: August 22, 2003. Documentary on 1980's skateboarding leg-

Stoked: The Rise and Fall of Gator PHOTO COURTESY OF PALM PICTURES

end Mark "Gator" Rogowski; featuring Mark "Gator" Rogowski, Tony Hawk, Jason Jessee, John Brinton Hogan, Steve Olson, Brandi McClain, Stacy Peralta, Lance Mountain, Steve Caballero, John Hogan, Kevin Staab, Michelle Chaves, Harry Jumonji, Carol Leggett, Krist Markovich, MoFo, Billy Smith, Tod Swank, Ed Templeton, Mike Valley

JEEPERS CREEPERS 2

(UNITED ARTISTS) Producer, Tom Luse; Executive Producers, Francis Ford Coppola, Bobby Rock, Kirk D'Amico, Lucas Foster; Director/Screenplay, Victor Salva, based on his characters; Co-Executive Producer, Philip von Alvensleben; Photography, Don E. FauntleRoy; Designer, Peter Jamison; Costumes, Jana Stern; Editor, Ed Marx; Music, Bennett Salvay; Special Effects Makeup, Brian Penikas; Visual Effects Supervisor, Jonathan Rothbart; Casting, Aaron Griffith, Linda Phillips-Palo; an American Zoetrope production, presented in association with Myriad Pictures; Dolby; Panavision; Deluxe color; Rated R; 104 minutes; Release date: August 29, 2003. Cast: Ray Wise (Jack Taggart Sr.), Jonathan Breck (The Creeper), Garikayi Mutambirwa (Deaundre "Double D" Davis), Eric Nenninger (Scott Braddock), Nick Aycox (Minxie Hayes), Travis Schiffner (Izzy Bohen), Lena Cardwell (Chelsea Farmer), Billy Aaron Brown (Andy "Bucky" Buck), Marieh Delfino (Rhonda Truitt), Diane Delano (Bus Driver Betty), Thom Gossom, Jr. (Coach Charlie Hanna), Tom Tarantini (Coach Dwayne Barnes), Al Santos (Dante Belasco), Josh Hammond (Jake Spencer), Kasan Butcher (Kimball "Big K" Ward), Drew Tyler Bell (Jonny Young), Luke Edwards (Jack Taggart, Jr.), Shaun Fleming (Billy Taggart), Justin Long (Darry Jenner), Bob Papenbrook (Man in Station Wagon), Jon Powell (Older Jack Jr.), Marshall Cook, Joe Reegan (Boys), Stephanie Denise Griffin (Girl)

The Backyard PHOTO COURTESY OF HIQI MEDIA

THE BACKYARD

(HIQI MEDIA) Executive Producers, Geza Decsy, John Hough, Steve Tzirlin; Director, Paul Hough; Music, Seth Jordan; a Paul Hough Entertainment production; Color; Not rated; 80 minutes; Release date: August 29, 2003. Documentary about boys who stage wrestling bouts in their backyards; featuring The Lizard, Scar, Chaos, Heartless, Bongo, The Retarded Butcher, Nympho, Sic, Rob Van Dam, James Weston.

Luke Edwards, Ray Wise in *Jeepers Creepers 2* PHOTO COURTESY OF UNITED ARTISTS

NOLA

(GOLDWYN/FIREWORKS) Producers, Jill Footlick, Rachel Peters; Director/Screenplay, Alan Hruska; Photography, Horacio Marquínez; Designer, Sharon Lomofsky; Costumes, Melissa Toth; Music, Edmund Choi; Editor, Peter C. Frank; Casting, Lina Todd, Alison E. McBryde; an Archer Entertainment production; Color; Rated PG-13; 97 minutes; Release date: August 29, 2003. Cast: Emmy Rossum (Nola), Mary McDonnell (Margaret), Steven Bauer (Leo), James Badge Dale (Ben), Thom Christopher (Niles), Michael Cavadias (Wendy), Joe Ambrose (Homeless Man), Lou Cantres (Marshal), Sam Coppola (Gus), Taj Crown (Van Vendor), Janis Dardaris (Nola's Mother), Robert Kabakoff (Reporter), Adam LeFevre (Sam), LeDonna Mabry (Leo's Secretary), Dominic Marcus (Slick), Lynne Matthew (Judge Belfray), Bernie McInerney (Prof. Cummings), Michael Medeiros (Flanders), Stephanie Mnookin (Classified Ad Rep), Al Nazemian (Young East Indian Man), Sasha Peters (Dog), Larry Pine (Max), James Ransone (Neo-Gothboy), Matt Servitto (Nola's Stepfather), Timothy Owen Waldrip (Clerk), Jerry Walsh (Bailiff), Damian Young (Maitre D')

CIVIL BRAND

(LIONS GATE) Producers, Neema Barnette, Steve Lockett, Carl Petragal, Jeff Clanagan; Director, Neema Barnette; Screenplay, Preston Whitmore; Photography, Yuri Neyman; Editors, David Beatty, Zene Baker; Casting, Monica R. Cooper; a Mandalay Sports Entertainment, Neena Films production; Dolby; Color; Rated R; 95 minutes; Release date: August 29, 2003. Cast: Lisa Raye (Frances Shepard), N'Bushe Wright (Nikki Barnes), Mos Def (Michael Meadows), Da Brat (Sabrina), Monica Calhoun (Wet), Clifton Powell (Capt. Deese), Reed R. McCants (Warden Nelson), Tichina Arnold (Aisha), Lark Voorhies (Little Momma), MC Lyte (Sgt. Cervantes), Robert Lynn (John Banks)

Monica Calhoun, N'Bushe Wright, Lisa Raye, Lark Voorhies in *Civil Brand*
PHOTO COURTESY OF LIONS GATE

HEY! IS DEE DEE HOME?

(INDEPENDENT) Producers, Odile Allard, Ronni Raygun; Director, Lech Kowalski; Editor, Jay Bones; Extinkt Films; Color; Not rated; 63 minutes; Release date: September 3, 2003. Documentary on the Ramones' bass player Dee Dee Ramone.

ZERO DAY

(AVATAR) Executive Producers, Richard Abramowitz, Adam Brightman; Producer/Director/Photography, Ben Coccio; Screenplay, Ben Coccio, Chris Coccio; Editors, Ben Coccio, David Shuff; Designer, Courtney Jordan; Color; Digital Video; Not rated; 92 minutes; Release date: September 3, 2003. Cast: Rachel Benichak (Rachel Laurie), Christopher Coccio (Chris Kriegman), Andre Keuck (Andre Kriegman), Gerhard Keuck (Andre's Father), Johanne Keuck (Andre's Mother), Samantha Philips (911 Operator), Calvin Robertson (Calvin Gabriel)

Heath Ledger in *The Order* PHOTO COURTESY OF 20TH CENTURY FOX

THE ORDER

(20TH CENTURY FOX) a.k.a. *Sin Eater*; Producers, Brian Helgeland, Craig Baumgarten; Executive Producers, Michael Kuhn, Thomas M. Hammel; Director/Screenplay, Brian Helgeland; Photography, Nicola Pecorini; Designer, Miljen "Kreka" Kljakovic; Costumes, Caroline Harris; Music, David Torn; Editor, Kevin Stitt; Co-Producer, Giovanni Lovatelli; Casting, Donna Isaacson; a Baumgarten Merims production; Dolby; Technovision; Cinecitta Color; Rated R; 102 minues; Release date: September 5, 2003. Cast: Heath Ledger (Alex Bernier), Shannyn Sossamon (Mara), Benno Fürmann (William Eden, The Sin Eater), Mark Addy (Thomas), Peter Weller (Driscoll), Francesco Carnelutti (Dominic), Mattia Sbragia (Apathetic Bishop), Mirko Casaburo (Little Boy), Giulia Lombardi (Little Girl), Richard Bremmer (Bookstore Owner), Cristina Maccá (Sister Franca), Paola Emilia Villa (Sister Marie), Rosalinda Celentano (Faraway Eyes Girl), Alessandro Costanzo (Eden's Maid), Paolo Lorimer (Englishman), Davide Odore (Young Eden), John Karlsen (Eden's Manservant), Fabrizio Lozzi (Eden's Driver), David Ambrosi (Demon), Adam Levy (Master Builder), Bruno Bilotta (Bigger Bouncer), Leagh Conwell (Alex, Ten Years Old), John Schwab (American Bureaucrat), Jon Laurimore (Bumham—British Aristocrat), Steve Toussaint (New York Detective), James Greene (British Doctor), Luigi Basagaluppi (Father of Eden), Michele Melega (Morgue Attendant), Emanuele Carucci Viterbi (Priest at St. Peter's), Richard Leaf (Sin Eater at St. Peter's), Clive Riche (Towncar Driver), Alex Van Damme (Club Bartender), Barbara Pastrovich (Irish Whore)

HOME ROOM

(DEJ/INNOVATION FILM GROUP) Producer, Ben Ormand; Co-Producers, Russ Matthews, Paul F. Ryan; Director/Screenplay/Editor, Paul F. Ryan; Photography, Rebecca Baehler; Designer, Johanna Vivstam; Costumes, Julia Bartholomew; Music, Michael G. Shapiro; Casting, Cecily Adams; a DEJ Prods. presentation in conjunction with MOP Pictures of a Benjamin Ormand production; Dolby; Fotokem Color; Rated R; 132 minutes; Release date: September 5, 2003. Cast: Busy Philipps (Alicia Amanda Browning), Erika Christensen (Deanna Cartwright), Victor Garber (Det. Martin van Zandt), Raphael Sbarge (Det. Macready), Ken Jenkins (Police Captain), Holland Taylor (Dr. Hollander), Arthur Taxier (Browning), James Pickens, Jr. (Pincipal Robbins), Constance Zimmer (Assistant Kelly), Richard Gilliland (Mr. Cartwright), Roxanne Hart (Mrs. Cartwright), Agnes Bruckner (Cathy), Nathan West (James), Theodore Borders (Terrance), Ben Gould (Doug), Jenette Goldstein (Main Nurse), Vernee Watson-Johnson (Duty Nurse), Rick Lenz (Bereaved Father), Joan McMurtrey (Bereaved Mother), Harper Johnston (Tactical Officer), Joshua H. Hayes (Driving Police Officer), Jay Mitchell (Escort Police Officer), John Beard (Voice of Newscaster)

Erika Christensen, Busy Philipps in *Home Room* PHOTO COURTESY OF DEJ/INNOVATION FILM GROUP

WHERE'S THE PARTY YAAR?

(MUSIC MASALA FILMS) Producer, Sunil Thakkar; Executive Producer, Sandhya Thakkar; Director, Benny Mathews; Screenplay, Benny Mathews, Sunil Thakkar, Soham Mehta; Photography, Anthony Fennell; Designer, Randy Cole; Costumes, Fiona McDougal; a Farid Virani presentation; Fotokem Color; Not rated; 107 minutes; Release date: September 5, 2003. Cast: Kal Penn (Mohan Bakshi), Sunil Malhotra (Harishkumar Patel), Prem Shah (Ramesh Kumar), Tina Cherian (Priya Varghese), Serena Varghese (Janvi Valia), Sunil Thakkar (Shyam Sunder Balabhadrapatramukhi), Mousami Dave (Poonam Mehta), Ulka Amin (Mrs. Bakshi), Arun Bakshi (Dr. Bakshi), Subodh Buchar (Lele), Datta Dave (Bobby D), Prakash Desai (Mr. Kumar), Kal Gejera (Satyam Shah), Zarina Khan (Sheetal), Kurun Magon (Bouncer #1), Ankur Mehta (Video Store Clerk), Bobby Moon (Kash), Ankur Patel (Hash), Mital Patel (Possession Eyes), Shaan Puri (Deepu Bakshi), Mohinder Singh (Mr. Valia), Ravi Waghmare (Shivi), Indi Wijay (Rajoo Mathews)

The Same River Twice PHOTO COURTESY OF PARADIGM

THE SAME RIVER TWICE

(PARADIGM) Producer/Director/Cinematographer, Robb Moss; Editor, Karen Schmeer; a Next Life Films production; Color, 16mm/HD-to-HD Video); Not rated; 78 minutes; Release date: September 10, 2003. Documentary catching up with the participants of a 1978 Colorado River rafting/kayaking trip, which was filmed in 1982 for Moss's documentary *Riverdogs*.

NO GOOD DEED

(MAC RELEASING) a.k.a. *The House on Turk Street*; Producers, David Braun, Maxime Remillard, Peter Hoffman, Herb Nanas, Sam Perlmutter, André Rouleau, Barry M. Berg; Executive Producers, Jan Fantl, David E. Allen, Peter Hoffman, Julian Rémillard, Frank Hübner; Director, Bob Rafelson; Screenplay, Steve Barancik, Christopher Canaan; Based on the short story *The House on Turk Street* by Dashiell Hammett; Photography, Juan Ruiz Anchia; Designer, Paul Peters; Costumes, Mary Claire Hannan; Music, Jeff Beal; Editor, William S. Scharf; Casting, Victoria Burrows, Scot Boland; a co-production of Apollo Media, Kismet Entertainment Group, Remstar Corp., Seven Arts Pictures; U.S.-German; Dolby; Color; Rated R; U.S.-German; 103 minutes; Release date: September 12, 2003. Cast: Samuel L. Jackson (Jack Friar), Milla Jovovich (Erin), Stellan Skarsgård (Tyrone), Doug Hutchison (Hoop), Grace Zabriskie (Mrs. Quarre), Joss Ackland (Mr. Quarre), Jonathan Higgins (David Brewster), Shannon Lawson (Amy), Joris Jarsky (Ruby Jones), Robert Welch (Willy), Terence Bowman (Postman), Tony Calabretta (Cadillac Owner), Richard Jutras (Clarevoyant), John Sanford Moore (Weatherman), Emily Van Camp (Connie)

Michael Taliferro, Allen Payne, William Johnson, Aaron D. Spears in *Blue Hill Avenue*
PHOTO COURTESY OF ARTISAN

FORBIDDEN PHOTOGRAPHS: THE LIFE AND WORK OF CHARLES GATEWOOD

(LITTLE VILLA FEATURES) Director, Bill MacDonald; Music, Peter Stone; Narrator, Daniel Lapin; Color; Not rated; 90 minutes; Release date: September 12, 2003. Documentary featuring Charles Gatewood, Jameson Black, Annie Sprinkle.

LUSTER

(TLA RELEASING) Producer, Robert Shulevitz; Director/Screenplay, Everett Lewis; Photography, Humberto De Luna; Art Director, Alex Brewer-Disarufino; Costumes, Mimi Maxmen; Associate Producer, Garrett Scullin; Casting, Nicole Arbusto, Joy Dickson; a Film Research Unit, Form A 2042 Films production; Color; Not rated; 90 minutes; Release date: September 12, 2003. Cast: Justin Herwick (Jackson), Shane Powers (Sam), B. Wyatt (Jed/Orgy Body), Pamela Gidley (Alyssa), Susannah Melvoin (Sandra), Jonah Blechman (Billy), Sean Thibodeau (Derek), Willie Garson (Sonny Spike), Gabriel Dell, Jr. (Private Investigator), Henriette Mantel (Sam's Mom), Norman Reedus (Sextools Delivery Boy), Chris Freeman (Kurt Domain), J.D. Cullum (Ned Smythe), Brian Grillo (Bartender), Mikee McCraine (Orgy Girl), Beth Lapides (Gallery Owner), BunBoy (Herman/Orgy Body), Steve Berra (Skaterboy), Chad Kula (Pressure Zone Photographer), Justin Bloomenthal (Impressionable Customer), Nicole Dillenberg, Lesa Carlson (Pressure Zone Editors), Tra-Mi Callahan (No Life Content Customer), Patti Scanlon (Stoned Customer), Shon Greenblatt (Blowdogg), Peter Taylor (Madonna Customer), Nick Hyman (Bribed Customer), Tim Taylor (Scooterboy), Adana Gardner, Mark Gardner (Orgy Bodies)

B. Wyatt, Justin Herwick in *Luster* PHOTO COURTESY OF TLA RELEASING

BLUE HILL AVENUE

(ARTISAN) Producer, Mike Erwin, J. Max Kirishma, Brian "Killa B" Hinds; Executive Producers, Rand Chortkoff, Craig Ross Jr., Mark Holdon; Director/Screenplay/Editor, Craig Ross, Jr.; Photography, Carl Bartles; Designer, Heather Young; Costumes, Lauda Swan; Casting, Cathy Henderson Martin, Dori Zuckerman; Presented in association with Cahoots Prods., Asiatic Associates, Glen Shaffer, Den Pictures; Dolby; Deluxe color; Rated R; 128 minutes; Release date: September 19, 2003. Cast: Allen Payne (Tristan), Angelle Brooks (Martine), William Johnson (E-Bone), Aaron D. Spears (Money), Andrew Divoff (Det. Tyler), Clarence Williams III (Benny), William Forsythe (Det. Torrance),

Michael "Bear" Taliferro (Simon), Myquan Jackson (Wren), Marlon Young (Twinkie), Richard Lawson (Uncle Rob), Latamra Smith (Nicole)

Beck in *Southlander*

Rossie Harris, Rory Cochrane in *Southlander* PHOTOS COURTESY OF POP TWIST

SOUTHLANDER

(POP TWIST) Director, Steve Hanft; Screenplay, Steve Hanft, Ross Harris, Robert J. Stephenson; Photography, Lance Acord; Editor, Haines Hall; a Propaganda Films production; Color; Not rated; 80 minutes; Release date: September 19, 2003. Cast: Rory Cochrane (Chance), Rossie Harris (Ross Angeles), Lawrence Hilton-Jacobs (Motherchild), Beck (Himself), Beth Orton (Rocket), Hank Williams III (Hank III), Laura Prepon (Seven=Five), Richard Edson (Thomas), Mark Gonzales (Vince), Gregg Henry (Lane Windbird), Ione Skye (Miss Highrise), Pat Matthews (Chuckles Martin)

TIBET: CRY OF THE SNOW LION

(ARTISTIC LICENSE) Producers, Tom Peosay, Sue Peosay, Mario Florio, Victoria Mudd; Executive Producer, Bruce Hayse; Director/Photography, Tom Peosay; Screenplay, Sue Peosay, Victoria Mudd; Music, Nawang Khechog, Jeff Beal; Editor, Kathryn Himoff; Narrator, Martin Sheen; an Earthworks Films-Zambuling Pictures production; Dolby; Color; Digital Video; Not rated; 104 minutes; Release date: September 19, 2003. Documentary on China's invasion of Tibet.

RED BETSY

(LANG FILMS) Producer, James Calabrese; Executive Producer, Andrew Lang; Director/Screenplay, Chris Boebel; Story, Charles E. Boebel; Photography, David Tumblety; Designer, Mark White; Costumes, Patricia Sarnataro; Music, Michael Bacon, Sheldon Mirowitz; Editor, David Leonard; Casting, Adrienne Stern; Dolby; Color; Rated PG; 98 minutes; Release date: September 19, 2003. Cast: Alison Elliott (Winifred Rounds), Leo Burmester (Emmet Rounds), Lois Smith (Helen Rounds), Chad Lowe (Orin Sanders), William Wise (Grandpa Charles), Isa Thomas (Grandma K), Brent Crawford (Dale Rounds), Courtney Jines (Jane Rounds), Kyle Gallner (Charlie), Simon Jacobs (Richard), Carrie Van Deest (Edna), Nathan Connor (Charles, Jr.), John Filmanowicz (Charlie, age 3), Mary Kabaik (Florence), Heather Ullsvik (Katie), Brian Sheridan, Chad Grote (Gravediggers), Ed Amor (Justice of the Peace), Peder Melhuse (Horace the Mailman), Paul Kennedy (Western Union Man), Patricia Whitely (Mrs. Breckler), Michelle Towey (Theatre Ticket Taker), JoAnna Beckson (School Administrator), Amanda Arnold (Dorothy)

Alison Elliott, Brent Crawford in *Red Betsy* PHOTO COURTESY OF LANG FILMS

HOW IT ALL WENT DOWN

(THE ASYLUM) a.k.a. *The Way It All Went Down*; Executive Producer, Andy Chu; Director/Screenplay, Silvio Pollio; Editor, Jimi Stewart; U.S.-Canadian; Color; Not rated; 93 minutes; Release date: September 19, 2003. Cast: Silvio Pollio, Joe Pascual, Kristina Copeland, Daniella Evangelista, Chris J. Clayton, Alistair Abell, Luisa Cianni

7 YEAR ZIGZAG

(NEXT STEP STUDIOS) Producers/Directors of Storyteller Sequences, Donna Dubain, Richard Green; Executive Producer, Gloria Green; Director/Screenplay, Richard Green; Photography, Dermott Downs, Cynthia Pushek, Alexander Szuch; Music, Dinah & Green; Editor, Michael Wargo; a Had to Be Made Films production; Color; Not rated; 90 minutes; Release date: September 24, 2003. Cast: Richard Green (Storyteller/Nick), Robin Banks (Dreamgirl), Caroline Davis (Lily), Leslie Macker (Kitchen Girl/Hedy), Victoria Davis (Boston Widow), Joe Torcello (Boston Millionaire), Chris Leavens (Young Producer), Aurora Cravens (Brooklyn Brunette), Molly Neylan (Bluegrass Girl), Cheyenne Day (Taxi Driver), Donna Du Bain (Witch), Jay Lay (Al Gonquin), Diane Perry (Bar Lady), Harry Lee (Producer), Alex Blanc (Producer's Friend), Greg Collins (The Husband), John Achorn (Biz

Manager), Audrey Moore (Debutante), Paul Bennett (Bartender), Tessa Wood, Miriam Cutler, Lee Thornburg, Sam Green (Themselves); *Storyboard* Characters: John Russell (Louie), Kevin Cross (Henway), David Fletcher (Burley Cop), Toby Sali (Sax/Apple), Lih Russell (Trumpet Guy), Ralf Tomandl (Guitar Guy), Ted Hamilton (Bass Guy), Wendy Ann De Ryke (Trombone Gal)

7 Year Zig Zag PHOTO COURTESY OF NEXT STEP STUDIOS

CAMERA OBSCURA

(FISH EYE FILMS) Producer, Tassos Kazinos; Executive Producer, Albertino Abela; Director/Screenplay, Hamlet Sarkissian; Photography, Haris Zambarloukos; Music, Tigran Mansuryan; Editor, Andrea Zondler; Dolby; Deluxe Color/black and white; Not rated; 99 minutes; Release date: September 24, 2003. Cast: Adam Trese (Jimmy), Adriana Gil (Maria), Cully Fredricksen (Flowers), V.J. Foster (Russo), Molly Bryant (Coroner, Mo Donahue), Kate Mulligan (Hooker), Kirk Ward (Fish), Eiko Nijo (Model)

Adriana Gill, Adam Trese in *Camera Obscura* PHOTO COURTESY OF FISH EYE FILMS

BUBBA HO-TEP

(VITAGRAPH) Producers, Don Coscarelli, Jason R. Savage; Executive Producer, Dac Coscarelli; Director/Screenplay, Don Coscarelli; Based on the short story by Joe R. Lansdale; Photography, Adam Janeiro; Designer, Daniel Vecchione; Costumes, Shelley Kay; Music, Brian Tyler; Editors, Donald Milne, Scott J. Gill;

Special Makeup Effects Supervisor, Robert Kurtzman; Casting, Jerry Whitworth; a Silver Sphere Corporation production; Dolby; Color; Rated R; 92 minutes; Release date: September 26, 2003. Cast: Bruce Campbell (Elvis Presley/Sebastian Haff), Ossie Davis (Jack Kennedy), Reggie Banister (Rest Home Administrator), Ella Joyce (Nurse), Heidi Marnhout (Callie), Bob Ivy (Bubba Ho-tep), Edith Jefferson (Elderly Woman), Timothy E. Goodwin, James Maley, "Two-Gun" Tyler, Chuck Williams (Elvis's Boys), Larry Pennell (Kemosabe), Gigi Fast Elk Porter (Trailer Trash), Daniel Roebuck, Daniel Schweiger (Hearse Drivers), Harrison Young (Bull Thomas)

Gina Gershon in *Prey for Rock & Roll* PHOTO COURTESY OF MAC RELEASING

Bruce Campbell, Ossie Davis in *Bubba Ho-Tep* PHOTO COURTESY OF VITAGRAPH

NATIONAL LAMPOON'S DORM DAZE

(120 DEGREE FILMS) Producers/Directors, David Hillenbrand, Scott Hillenbrand; Executive Producers, Mike McBride, James Henrie; Screenplay, Worm Miller, Patrick Casey; Photography, Philip D. Schwartz; Designer, Jack Cloud; Costumes, Darryle Johnson; Music, David Berrel; Editor, Dave O'Brien; Casting, Aaron Griffith, Richard DeLancy, Iris Hampton; Dolby; Color; Rated R; 96 minutes; Release date: September 26, 2003. Cast: Tatyana Ali (Claire), Boti Bliss (Dominique the Hooker), James DeBello (Cliff), Marieh Delfino (Gerri), Tony Denman (Newmar), Danielle Fishel (Marla), Courtney Gains (Lorenzo), Edwin Hodge (Tony), Jennifer Lyons (Lynne), Chris Owen (Booker McFee), Cameron Richardson (Adrienne), Patrick Renna (Styles McFee), Randy Spelling (Foosball), Gable Carr (Rachel), Patrick Casey (Man on Tour), Patrick Cavanaugh (Pete), Scott Brandon (Campus Security Officer), Gregory Hinton (Ted), Rob G. Kahn, Choice Skinner, Francine Sama (Police Officers), Paul Hansen Kim (Wang), Katie Lohmann (Dream Girl), Marie Noelle Marquis (Dominique the Student), Worm Miller (Brady the R.A.), Lindsey Talbott (Britney "The Snake"), Michelle Warren (Woman on Tour)

PREY FOR ROCK & ROLL

(MAC RELEASING) Producers, Donovan Mannato, Gina Gershon, Gina Resnick; Executive Producer, Robin Whitehouse; Line Producer, Pat Scanlon; Director, Alex Steyermark; Screenplay, Cheri Lovedog, Robin Whitehouse; Photography, Antonio Calvache; Designer, John Chichester; Costumes, Vanessa Vogel; Music, Stephen Trask; Songs, Cheri Lovedog; Editor, Allyson C. Johnson; Casting, Sheila Jaffe; Dolby; Color; Rated R; 103 minutes; Release date: September 26, 2003. Cast: Gina Gerhson (Jacki), Drea de Matteo (Tracy), Lori Petty (Faith), Shelly Cole (Sally), Marc Blucas (Animal), Ivan Martin (Nick), Eddie Driscoll (Chuck), Ashley Drane (Punk Rock Girl), Shakara Ledard (Jessica), Texas

Terri (Herself), Sandra Seacat (Jacki's Mom), Nancy Pimental (Natalie), Greg Rikaart (Scott), Francois Harold (Johnny), Joannah Portman, Hallie King (Sorority Girls), Benjamín Benítez (Drug Dealer)

GANG OF ROSES

(DEJ PRODUCTIONS) Producers, Jean-Claude Le Marre, Timothy Swan, Larry Rattner, Doug Schwab; Director/Screenplay, Jean-Claude La Marre; Photography, Ben Kufrin; Designer, Charlotte Newman; Costumes, Kara Saun; Music, Michael Cohen; Casting, Reno Logan; a Sleeping Giant Films presentation; Dolby; CFI Color; Rated R; 88 minutes; Release date: October 3, 2003. Cast: Bobby Brown (Left Eye Watkins), Monica Calhoun (Rachel), Stacey Dash (Kim), Charity Hill (Little Suzy), Lil' Kim (Chastity), Jean-Claude La Marre (Baby Face Malone), Brian "Skinny B" Lewis (Paco), LisaRaye (Maria), Marie Matiko (Ming Li), Licia L. Shearer (Sally), Louis Mandylor, Glenn Plummer, Macy Gray

STEALING TIME

(NICKEL PALACE) Producers, Michael Shane, Mike Gabrawy, Michael Garrity, Anthony Romano; Director, Marc Fusco; Screenplay, Marc Fusco, Michael Garrity; Photography, Stephen Sheridan; Designer, Macie Vener; Costumes, Nadine Haders; Music, Joey Newman; Editor, Peter Fandetti; Casting, Rita VanderWaal; a Magellan Filmed Entertainment presentation; Dolby; Deluxe Color; Rated R; 98 minutes; Release date: October 3, 2003. Cast: Charlotte Ayanna (Samantha Parkes), Ethan Embry (Trevor Logan), Peter Facinelli (Alec Nichols), Scott Foley (Casey Shepard), Jennifer Garner (Kiley Bradshaw), Jeff Anderson (Buddy), Debra Christofferson (Roselyn Hatchett), Gabriel Olds (Larry), Charles Walker (Mr. Freeman), Gary Werntz (Mr. Johnson), Kiele Sanchez (Emily the Bank Teller), Victor McCay (Immigration Lawyer), Annalouise Paul (Olina Menka), Paul Dooley (Hank), Lenny Goldsmith (George), Jan Bartlett (Registration Clerk), Candace Kita (Social Services Receptionist), Mike Gabrawy (Soccer Referee), Kiesha McCorry (Law Firm Receptionist), Diane Hudock (Angry Woman in Car), Parker Swanson (First A.D.), Stefane Zamorano (Pharmacist), Sarah Zinsser (Nurse), David Aronson (Doctor), Michael Garrity, Aaron Shalka (Gay Cowboys), Deeonna Lanay (Clara Menka), Brandon Johnson (Account Service Man), Frank Novak (Bank Manager), Ben Falcone, Keesia Kordelle (Bank Tellers), Eugene Wells, Laura Wells (Bank Customers), Callan White (Diner Waitress), Tom McComas, Rick Payne, Sean Patrick Murphy (Police Officers), Annie Abbott (Casting Director), Lorraine Montgomery (Outlaw's Waitress), Andy Greenberg (Outlaw's Bartender), Debra Snell (Newscaster)

EXORCISM

(INDEPENDENT) Producers, William A. Baker, Bubacarr A. Batchilly; Executive Producers, William A. Baker, Lisa Amorim; Director/Screenplay/Casting, William A. Baker; Photography, Christophe Gosch; Designer, Madia Kruza; Costumes, Marianne Parker; Music, Earl Wooten; Editor, John Allen; Visual Effects Supervisor, Bob Morgenroth; an Exorcism the Movie presentation; Technicolor; Rated PG-13; 98 minutes; Release date: October 3, 2003. Cast: Brian Patrick Clarke (Jerry Lansing), Jack Donner (Father Lansing), Tony Burton (Bishop Harris), Eddie Applegate (Archbishop), Eileen Dietz (Evil Nurse), Karen Knotts (Mrs. Lansing), Nicole Dionne (Sarah Lansing), Dwayne Chattman (Daniel), Alice Amter (Katherine Miller), Kimberly Atkinson (ER Doctor), Robert Axelrod (Dark Prince), William A. Baker (Priest), Stephanie Cheeva (Pat), Anita Marie Curran (Possessed Girl), Ernest Hardin, Jr. (Evil Messenger), Iva Hasperger (Jessica Andrew), Paul Jefferson (Policeman), William Knight (Father Donovan), Masami Kosaka (Coroner), Maia (Daniel's Mom), Jeff Marchelletta (Gene), Miyuki Matsunaga (Nurse), Patrick M. O'Connor (Father Deloid), Chelsea Rendon (Connie), Reva Rose (Sister Vera), Ken Rosier (Det. Ross), Flora Santiago (Coroner's Assistant), Jessica Slating (Emergency Room Nurse), Tony Tanner (Dr. Lewis), David Thomas (Oscar), Ashley Tucker (Jason Morris), Courtney Black (Angela), Stephen Wozniak (Jack)

DOPAMINE

(SUNDANCE) Producers, Tad Fettig, Debbie Brubaker; Executive Producer, Eric Kovisto; Co-Producers, Liz Decena, Brian Benson, Timothy Breitbach; Director, Mark Decena; Screenplay, Mark Decena, Timothy Breitbach; Photography, Rob Humphreys; Designer, S. Quinn; Costumes, Deirdre Scully; Music, Eric Holland; Music Supervisor, Jonathan McHugh; Editor, Jess Congdon; a Kontent Films presentation; Dolby; Color; 24 P HD Video; Rated R; 79 minutes; Release date: October 10, 2003. Cast: John Livingston (Rand), Sabrina Lloyd (Sarah McCaulley), Bruno Campos (Winston), Reuben Grundy (Johnson), Kathleen Antonia (Tammy), Nicole Wilder (Machiko), Ivan Kraljevic (Sleazy Guy), William Windom (Rand's Father)

GIRLS WILL BE GIRLS

(IFC FILMS) Producers, Michael Warwick, Richard Ahren; Executive Producer, Jack Plotnick; Director/Screenplay, Richard Day; Photography, Nicholas Hutak; Designer, Shannon Schweibert; Music, Steve Edwards; Editor, Chris Conlee; Casting, Collin Daniel; an SRO Pictures production; Dolby; Color; HD; Not rated; 79 minutes; Release date: October 10, 2003. Cast: Jack Plotnick (Evie), Clinton Leupp (Coco), Jeffery Roberson (Varla/Marla), Ron Mathews (Stevie), Eric Stonestreet (Dr. Benson), Hamiton von Watts (Laurent), Dana Gould (Jeff), Chad Lindsey (Dr. Perfect), Greg Whitney (Asteroid Actor), Dennis Hensley (Specimercial Director), Sam Pancake (Brad), Jamie Malone (Young Stevie), Lurie Poston (Young Varla), Mike Stoyanov (Michael), Jay Fuentes (Nurse), Richard Ahren (Burn Victim), Mark Cirillo (Diner Waiter), Kris Andersson (Receptionist), Edward Tunney (Guy on Street), Cliff Curry (Student), Nathan LePage (Priest), Michael Warwick (Clown), Chris Isaacson (Waitress), Just Jan (Whore at Restaurant), Richard Day (John at Restaurant), Sir Tony (John in Alley), Mort Kessler (Mort), Aaron Emmett (Mover), Pat Towne (Announcer Voices), Ginger Snaps (Magazine Cover Cher), Raphael Louis Marino (Magazine Cover Madonna)

John Livingston, Sabrina Lloyd in *Dopamine* PHOTO COURTESY OF SUNDANCE

THE BEST TWO YEARS

(MAELSTROM) Producer/Director/Screenplay, Scott S. Anderson; Executive Producer, Fred C. Danneman; Photography, Gordon Lonsdale; Editor, Wynn Hougaard; Music, John Batdorf, Michael McLean, Scott McLean; from Harvest Films; Color; Rated PG; 90 minutes; Release date: October 10, 2003. Cast: K.C. Clyde (Elder John Rogers), Kirby Heyborne (Elder Hezekiah Calhoun), David Nibley (Elder Emmit Johnson), Cameron Hopkin (Elder Steven Van Pelt), Andrea Anderson, Jaime Anderson, Alice Lonsdale (Elder Van Pelt's Girlfriends), Scott Christopher (Kyle Harrison), Ineke den Hollander (Woman on Train), Michael Flynn (President Sandburg)

FLESH FOR THE BEAST

(MEDIA BLASTERS) Producer, Carl Morano; Executive Producer, John Sirabella; Director/Screenplay, Terry West; Photography, Richard Siegel; Art Director, Stew Noack; Special Effects, Pete Gerner, Stephen R. Hicks, Brian Spears; Editor, Andrew Sterling; from Fever Dream productions; Color; Rated R; 90 minutes; Release date: October 10, 2003. Cast: Jane Scarlett (Erin Cooper), Sergio Jones (John Stoker), Clark Beasley, Jr. (Ted Sturgeon), Jim Coope (Jack Ketchum), David Runco (Joseph Monks), Arron Clayton (Douglas Clegg), Michael Sinterniklaas (Martin Shelly), Caroline Hoermann (Pauline), Ruby Larocca (Cassandra), Barbara Joyce (Irene), Kevin G. Shinnick (Jimmy/Zombie), Keith Leopard, Kelly Troy Howard, Zoe Moonshine, Michael Roszhart, Jonathan Lees (Zombies), Isadora Edison (Shower Silhouette), Caroline Munro (Carla the Gypsy), Aldo Sambrell (Alfred Fischer)

Aldo Sambrell, Caroline Munro in *Flesh for the Beast* PHOTO COURTESY OF MEDIA BLASTERS

KHACHATURIAN

(SEVENTH ART) Producer/Director/Photography, Peter Rosen; Screenplay, Bill Van Horn, based on the writings of Aram Khachaturian; Executive Producers, Serviarian-Kuhn, Robert Lawrence Kuhn; Music, Aram Khachaturian; Editor, Aaron Kuhn; Narrator, Eric Bogosian; a Kuhn Foundation presentation of a Peter Rosen Prods. production; Color/Black and white; DV-to-35mm; Not rated; 76 minutes; Release date: October 17, 2003. Documentary on Soviet artist Aram Khachaturian; featuring Solmon Volkov, Karen Khachaturian, Mstislav Rostropovich, Vladimir Vasiliev, Tikon Khrennikov, Alexander Hartoian, Emin Khachaturian.

HIGH TIMES' POTLUCK

(POTLUCK) Producers, James Scura, Paul F. Bernard; Executive Producers, Alison Thompson, Robert Agueli, Jeri Carroll-Colicchio, John A. Gallagher; Director, Alison Thompson; Screenplay, Victor Colicchio, Nicholas Iacovino; Photography, Michael Green; Designer, Jordan Jacobs; Costumes, Yasmine Mustaklim Savoia; Music, Mark Bryan, John Nau; Editor, Marie-Pierre Renaud; Color; Rated R; 90 minutes; Release date: October 17, 2003. Cast: Frank Adonis (Frank), Theo Kogan (Jade), Charles Malik Whitfield (Malik), Victor Colicchio (Vic), Nick Iacovino (Mickey), Leif Riddell (Ryan), Jason Isaacs (Armeau), Dan Lauria (Carmine), Sylvia Miles (Ma), Jason Mewes (Guy), Jackie Martling

Aram Khachaturian in *Khachaturian* PHOTO COURTESY OF SEVENTH ART

(Mercury), Tommy Chong (Hippie), Frank Gorshin (The Slim Man), Kim Chan (Saki), Christopher Kenney (Edie/Anthony), Bryant Carroll (Jack), Ivan Martin (Jim), Joseph Rigano (Rigano), Vinny Vella (Vinny), David Peel (Himself), Paul Borghese (Joey Pots), Erik Van Wyck (Young Slim Man)

MORNING SUN

(LONG BOW GROUP) Producer/Directors, Carma Hinton, Richard Gordon, Geramie Barmé; Screenplay, Carma Hinton, Geramie Barmé; Music, Mark Pevsner; Editor, David Carnochan; Color; Not rated; 117 minutes; Release date: October 22, 2003. Documentary about the violence behind the Chinese Cultural Revolution.

Morning Sun PHOTO COURTESY OF LONG BOW GROUP

THE PARTY'S OVER

(FILM MOVEMENT) a.k.a. *The Last Party 2000*; Producers, Donovan Leitch, Stanley Buchthal, Rebecca Chaiklin; Executive Producers, Henri Kessler, Jon Kilik, Mark Severini, Vincent Roberti; Director, Donovan Leitch, Rebecca Chaiklin; Photography, Carter Smith, Kevin Ford, Ben Weinstein, Luke Geissbuhler; Music, Sabina Sciubba; Editors, Eric Bruggeman, Sabine Hoffmann; Dolby; Color; Not rated; 90 minutes; Release date: October 24, 2003. Documentary follows actor Philip Seymour Hoffman as he covers the final sixth months of the 2000 presidential election; featuring Ben Harper, Noam Chomsky, Harold Ford Jr., Tim Robbins, John Sellers, Susan Sarandon, Chrsitopher Shays, Bill Maher, Rosie O'Donnell, Melissa Etheridge, Courtney Love, Dr. Antonia Novella, Rudolph Giuliani, The Interpreters, Ralph Reed, Cheri Honkala, Rev. Jesse Jackson, Rev. Pat Robertson, Patricia Ireland, Ralph Nader, Newt Gingrich, Jim Reese, Barney Frank, Tim Hutchinson, Jeff Johnston, Barenaked Ladies, Ed Robertson, Willie Nelson, Arlo Guthrie, Julia Butterfly Hill, Bonnie Raitt, Floyd Red Crow Westerman, Rage Against the Machine, Ben Cohen, Michael Moore, Gary Johnson, Stone Temple Pilots, Scott Weiland, Adora Obi Nweze, Robert Muhammad, Steve Earle, Greg Ladden, Bianca Jagger, John Kerry, Campbell Brown, Eddie Vedder, Mark Fritz, Rabbi Goldstein, Rosalyn Brodsky, Jesse Jackson Jr., Barbara Bush, George Bush, George W. Bush, Laura Bush, Bill Clinton, Chelsea Clinton, Hillary Rodham Clinton, Karenna Gore, Tipper Gore, Lee Greenwood, Katherine Harris, Tom Hayden, Charlton Heston, Larry King, Joseph Lieberman, Rick Schroeder, Arnold Schwarzenegger

SISTER HELEN

(HBO FILMS) Producers/Directors, Rob Fruchtman, Rebecca Cammisa; Photography, Rebecca Cammisa, Rob Fruchtman, Peter Pearce, Alex Aurichio, Andrew Holbrooke, Scott Sinkler; Music, Simon Gentry; Editors, Jonathan Oppenheim, Juliet Weber; from R&R Films; Color; Not rated; 90 minutes; Release date: October 24, 2003. Documentary about Sister Helen Travis, a Benedictine nun who opened a shelter for recovering alcoholics and drug addicts in the Mott Haven section of the South Bronx.

THE SINGING DETECTIVE

(PARAMOUNT CLASSICS) Producers, Mel Gibson, Steve Haft, Bruce Davey; Executive Producer, Stan Wlodkowski; Director, Keith Gordon; Screenplay, Dennis Potter, based on his television series; Photography, Tom Richmond; Designer/Costumes, Patricia Norris; Editor, Jeff Wishengrad; Associate Producer, Kevin Lake; Co-Producers, Jane Potter, Sarah Potter, Robert Potter; Makeup Effects Creators, Greg Cannom, Keith Vanderlaan; Choreographers, Jacqui & Bill Landrum; Music Supervisor, Ken Weiss; a Haft Enterprises production, an Icon Production; Dolby; Super 35 Widescreen; Color; Rated R; 109 minutes; Release date: October 24, 2003. Cast: Robert Downey, Jr. (Dan Dark), Robin Wright Penn (Nicola/Nina/Blonde), Mel Gibson (Dr. Gibbon), Jeremy Northam (Mark Binney), Katie Holmes (Nurse Mills), Carla Gugino (Betty Dark/Hooker), Adrien Brody, Jon Polito (Hoods), Saul Rubinek (Skin Specialist), Alfre Woodard (Chief of Staff), Amy Aquino (Nurse Nozhki), David Dorfman (Young Dan Dark), Eddie Jones (Moonglow Bartender), Lily Knight (Physiotherapist), Clyde Kusatsu (Visiting Japanese Doctor), Earl C. Poitier (Orderly), Don Fischer (Intern), Andy Umberger (Mr. Dark), David Denman (Soldier With Betty Dark), Alec Puro (Dark's Drummer), Renn Hawkey (Dark's Bass Player), Bryan Law (Dark's Guitar Player), Carla Anderson, Sandahl Bergman, Rita Bland, Billy Bonsangue, Sergio Carbajal, Leonard Crofoot, Erin Crouch, Kiva Dawson, Richard Dorton, Brenda Hamilton, Gordon Hart, Famisha La Pree, Suzie Lonergan, Eva Mikita, Tara Nicole, Regan Patno, Randi Pareira, Sandra Plazinic, Sheldon Robins, Deanna Steele, Tasha Tae, Elle Taylor, Jessica Vallot, Dee Dee Weathers, Spice Williams, Darrel Wright, Dani Wylie (Dancers)

GIRLHOOD

(WELLSPRING) Producers, Liz Garbus, Rory Kennedy; Director, Liz Garbus; Photography, Tony Hardmon; Editor, Mary Manhardt; Music, Theodore Shapiro; Color; Not rated; 82 minutes; Release date: October 29, 2003. Documentary on two female inmates serving time in a Maryland juvenile detention cetner.

Shanae Owens, Megan Jensen in *Girlhood* PHOTO COURTESY OF WELLSPRING

Robert Downey Jr. in *The Singing Detective* PHOTO COURTESY OF PARAMOUNT CLASSICS

SUSPENDED ANIMATION

(FIRST RUN FEATURES) Producers, John Hancock, Robert J. Hiler; Executive Producer, Carey Westberg; Director, John Hancock; Screenplay, Dorothy Tristan; Co-Producers, Dean Jacobson, Ken Kitch; Photography, Misha Susluv; Designer, Don Jacobson; Costumes, Richard E. Donnelly; Music, Angelo Badalamenti; Editor, Dennis O'Connor; a Robert J. Hiler presentation of a Filmacres production; Dolby; Color; Rated R; 114 minutes; Release date: October 31, 2003. Cast: Alex McArthur (Tom Kempton), Laura Esterman (Vanessa Boulette), Sage Allen (Ann Boulette), Rebecca Harrell (Hilary Kempton), Fred Meyers (Sandor Hansen), Maria Cina (Clara Hansen), Jeff Puckett (Cliff Modjeska), Daniel Riordan (Jack Starr), J.E. Freeman (Philip Boulette), Sean Patrick Murphy (Fred Phelps), Daniel Mooney (Arnold Mann), Gary J. Mion (Sheriff Montaigne), Joe Forbrich (Production Manager), Robert Breuler (Dr. Leo Sagan), Denise Bohn, Faith Krycka (Correspondents), Mike McCalmet (Joe Moss), Andrew Tallackson (Production Designer), Glenn Huchinson (Bar Customer)

Suspended Animation PHOTO COURTESY OF FIRST RUN FEATURES

BILLABONG ODYSSEY

(ARENAPLEX LLC) Producer, Vincent Leone; Executive Producers, Ivan Cheah, Alvaro Otero; Director, Philip Boston; Co-Producers, Will Taylor, Jay van Joy; Associate Producers, Rosaldo Cavalcanti, Jorge Guimaraes; Editors, Todd Busch, Andrew Marcus, Lars Woodruff; Photography, Mike Prickett; Music, Dorian Cheah; Music Supervisor, Niki Gascon; presented in association with Estudios Mega; Color; Digital Video; Not rated; 87 minutes; Release date: November 7, 2003. Documentary on surfing; featuring Shawn "Barney" Barron, Layne Beachley, Ken Bradshaw, Brad Gerlach, Brian Keaulana, Josh Loya, Mike Parsons, Rush Randle, Bill Sharp, Darryl "Flea" Virostko.

TUPAC: RESURRECTION

(PARAMOUNT) Producers, Preston Holmes, Karolyn Ali, Lauren Lazin; Executive Producers, Afeni Shakur, Van Toffler, David Gale; Director, Lauren Lazin; Co-Producers, Michael Cole, Dina Laplot; Photography, Jon Elise; Editor, Richard Calderon; Senior Associate Producer, Richard Calderon; Associate Producers, Azon Juan, Katy Garfield, Barion Grant; Music Supervisor, Afeni Shakur; an MTV Films/Amaru Entertainment, Inc. production; Dolby; Deluxe Color; Rated R; 100 minutes; Release date: November 14, 2003. Documentary on late hip-hop performer Tupac Shakur, as told in his own words.

Tupac Shakur in *Tupac: Resurrection* PHOTO COURTESY OF PARAMOUNT

HIDDEN IN PLAIN SIGHT

(SEVENTH ART) Producer, Vivi Letsou; Director, John Smihula; Photography, Chip Holley; Music, Luis Perez Villegas; Editor, Andrea Zondler; Narrator, Martin Sheen; Stereo; Color; Not rated; 90 minutes; Release date: November 7, 2003. Documentary about the School of the Americas, a training ground for Latin soldiers on U.S. soil; featuring Noam Chomsky, Christopher Hitchens, Eduardo Galeano, Barbara Lee, Mac Collins, Maj. Gen. John LeMoyne, Sister Dianna Ortiz.

MARTIN & ORLOFF

(SPIT & GLUE) Producers, Lawrence Blume, Linda Moran, Rene Bastian, Gill Holland; Director, Lawrence Blume; Screenplay, Matt Walsh, Ian Roberts, Katie Roberts; Photography, David Phillips; Designer, Dina Goldman; Costumes, Christopher Del Coro; Music, Bill Ware, Roy Nathanson; Editor, Jay Freund; Casting, Adrienne Stern; a Belladonna, Cineblast production; Dolby; Widescreen; Color; Not rated; 87 minutes; Release date: November 7, 2003. Cast: Ian Roberts (Martin Flam), Matt Walsh (Dr. Eric Orloff), H. Jon Benjamin (Keith), Amy Poehler (Patty), Kim Raver (Kashia), Matt Besser (Ron), David Cross (Dan Wasserman), Les Mau (Mr. Chan), Katie Roberts (Donna), Sal Graziano (Jimbo), Miriam Tolan (Linda), Andy Richter (Maitre D), Rachel Dratch, Tina Fey (Southern Ladies), Janeane Garofalo (Hairdresser), Sean Conroy (Frankie), Marylouise Burke (Mrs. Flam), Teddy Coluca (Petros), Marie O'Reilly (M. Force Secretary), Billy Chang, Terrence Bae (China Chef Thugs), Nolan Carley (Old Man in Theater), Jennifer Jai (Waitress)

JUST AN AMERICAN BOY

(COWBOY PICTURES) Director, Amos Poe; Music, Steve Earle; Black and white/color; Not rated; 95 minutes; Release date: November 7, 2003. Documentary on musician/activist Steve Earle and his controversial album *Jerusalem*

A HOUSE ON A HILL

(ABRAMORAMA ENTERTAINMENT) Producers, Ronald Colby, Chuck Workman; Executive Producers, Michael Clofine, Marc Sperling; Director/Screenplay, Chuck Workman; Photography, Theodore Cohen; Designer, Hans Pfleiderer; Architectural Design, Melinda Gray; Costumes, Astrid Brucker; Assistant Editor, E. Scott Tremblay; Line Producer, Lon Casler Bixby; Casting, Rosemary Welden; Calliope Films; Color; Not rated; 89 minutes; Release date: November 14, 2003. Cast: Philip Baker Hall (Harry Mayfield), Laura San Giacomo (Gaby), Shirley Knight (Mercedes Mayfield), Rebecca Staab (Kate), Henry Rollins (Arthur, the Dentist), James Karen (Sy, the Lawyer), Paul Mazursky (A Former Mayfield House Owner), Daphna Kastner (The Gas Station Owner's Daughter), Jack Conley (Richard), Charles Lucia (The Contractor), Domenica Scorses (Jennifer, the Assitant), Darryl E. Smith (Danny, the Cameraman), Robert Harders (A Friendly Neighbor)

Hidden in Plain Sight PHOTO COURTESY OF SEVENTH ART

Ian Roberts, Matt Walsh in *Martin & Orloff* PHOTO COURTESY OF SPIT & GLUE

Isabel Rose in *Anything but Love* PHOTO COURTESY OF GOLDWYN

ANYTHING BUT LOVE

(GOLDWYN) a.k.a. *Standard Time*; Producers, Aimee Schoof, Isen Robbins; Director, Robert Cary; Screenplay, Isabel Rose, Robert Cary; Photography, Horacio Marquínez; Designer, Cecil Gentry; Costumes, Sarah Beers; Music, Andrew Hollander, Steve Lutvak; Editor, Bob Reitano; Music Supervisor, Janice Ginsberg; Casting, Ricki G. Maslar, James Calleri; a Jubilee Productions and Intrinsic Value presentation; Dolby; Color; Rated PG-13; 102 minutes; Release date: November 14, 2003. Cast: Isabel Rose (Billie Golden), Cameron Bancroft (Greg Ellenbogen), Eartha Kitt (Herself), Ilana Levine (Marcy), Andrew McCarthy (Elliot Shephard), Alix Korey (Laney Golden), Sean Arbuckle (T.J.), Victor Argo (Sal), Michael J. Burg (Amboise), Josh Stamberg (Steve), Matthew Lawler (Ted), Shannon Lewis (Suzy), Leslie Bell (Annette), Angela Pietropino (Peggy), Caroline Hall (Kyra), Jesse Doran (Ronald Salzman), Buzz Bovshow (Casting Director), Lisa LeGuillou (Toddler's Mother), Dawn Ouellette (Monitor), Peter Maloney (Cliff Mendelson), Joseph Murphy (Doctor), Frank Senger (Limo Driver), Peter Appel (Man), Tom Fenaughty, Gene Burke (Senior Gay Men), Craig Wroe (Minister), Bart DeFinna (Handsome Man)

THE SINGING FOREST

(HOLLYWOOD INDEPENDENTS) Director/Screenplay, Jorge Ameer; Music, Pedro Bromfman; Editor, Richard Oldfield; from A.J. Productions; Color; Not rated; 95 minutes; Release date: November 14, 2003. Cast: Jon Sherrin (Christopher), Erin Leigh Price (Destiny), Craig Pinkston (Alexander/Ben), Erik Morris (Jo), David Guzzone (Young Christopher), Shelley Price (Savannah), Jorge Ameer (Charlie), Toni Zobel (Psychic), Lance Black (Bill), Sal Roman (Stephen), Marc Ambrose, Randal Craig, Nolo Ortiz, Justin Huddleston, Gregory Saites (Nazi Guards), Emire Ozpirincci, Skyler Thomas (Holocaust Victims), Lisa Marx (Television Guest), Renae Plant (Television Host), Louis Perez (Pastor), Jean Carol (Emily), Gerry Rand (Fred), Colin Campbell (Heinz)

ACTS OF WORSHIP

(MANIFESTO) Producers, Rosemary Rodriguez, Annie Flocco, Nadia Leonelli, Fredrik Sundwall; Director/Screenplay, Rosemary Rodriguez; Photography, Luke Geissbuhler; Designer, Johnn Hardesty; Costumes, Jan Bohan; Music, Jim Coleman; Editor, Elizabeth Downer; Casting, Susan Shopmaker; Dolby; Technicolor; Not rated; 94 minutes; Release date: November 21, 2003. Cast:

Ana Reeder (Alix), Michael Hyatt (Digna), Nestor Rodriguez (Anthony), Christopher Kadish (Mark), Kelly Cole (Carl), James Joseph O'Neil (Louis), Shawn M. Richardz (Prostitute)

MAIL ORDER BRIDE

(SMALL PLANET) Producer, Sergey Konenkov; Executive Producers, Mark Settembre, Alexander Zavaruec; Directors, Robert Capelli Jr., Jeffrey Wolf; Screenplay, Robert Capelli Jr., Sergey Konenkov, Doug Bollinger; Photography, Ly Bolia; Designer, Michele Ferentinos; Costumes, Cynthia Lahiff; Music, The Red Elvises; Editor, Martin Levenstein; Casting, Michele Ortlip; a Relativity Pictures production; Dolby; Color; Rated R; 84 minutes; Release date: November 21, 2003. Cast: Danny Aiello (Tony Santini), Robert Capelli, Jr. (Anthony Santini), Ivana Milicevic (Nina), Artie Lange (Tommy), Slava Schoot (Ivan), Vinnie Pastore (Tootie), Raymond Serra (Robber), Frankie Bongiorno (Willie the Whiner), Marilyn Papa (Gina), Jackie Martling (Jackie the Viking), Steven Ogg (Pavel), Aleksandr Yakovlev (No. 1 Guy in the Russian Mafia), Liza Zavaruyeva (Nina's Sister), Yuri Dumchev (Driver), Kamal Ahmed (Buddha), Alex Corrado (Ernie the Biker), Michael Squicciarini (Gina's Father), Frank Gorshin (Russian Doctor), Aleksandr Lazarev, Valentin Smirnitsky, Roman Madyanov (Gamblers), Nikolai Chindyajkin (Uncle Peter), Yana Nikolayeva (Oxana), Charles Grady, Igor Shafranov (FBI Guy), Kirill Dvorsky (Russian Accountant), Misha Dvortsov (Michael), Vince Viverito (Larry), Tony Del Salvatore (Angie), Rich D'Ellasandro (Nick), Andrei Gorbushin (Big Guy), Robert Capelli, Sr. (Mob Guy), David Orifice (Young Anthony), Charlie Saxton (Young Tommy), Tony Ray Rossi, Charles Sammarco (How You Doing Guys), Jeff Kovatch (Manny the Mute), Chris Spina (Louis the Leprechaun), Tom Patti (Coach), Sergei Yushkevich (Vladimir), Sergei Ruben (Guard Guy), Maksim Malinin (Banker), Aleksandr Pashutin (Taxi Driver), Anthony Russo (Anthony's Father), Margo Singaliese (Anthony's Mother), Vladimir Starodub (No. 1 Guy in Russian Government)

AMERICAN STORYTELLERS

(INDICAN) Producer/Director/Editor, Kevin Mukherji; Photography, Michael C. Clark; Music, Penka Kouneva; a Clearwater Pictures, Magnum Independent Pictures production; Color; Not rated; 90 minutes; Release date: November 21, 2003. Documentary in which filmmakers John McNaughton, Harold Ramis, John Sayles, and Forest Whitaker talk about their work.

Kelsey Grammer, Jon Favreau in *The Big Empty* PHOTO COURTESY OF ARTISAN

BLINDNESS

(PATHFINDER) Producer, Karen Koch; Executive Producers, Anna Chi, Federico Faggin; Director, Anna Chi; Screenplay, Anna Chi, Jared Rappaport; Photography, Rico Sands; Designer, Gary Meyers; Costumes, Joseph A. Porro; Music, Mark Governor; Editors, Michael A. Stevenson, Brian Johnson; from Park Avenue Productions; Color; Not rated; 88 minutes; Release date: November 21, 2003. Cast: Vivian Wu (Natalie), Joe Lando (Patrick), Lisa Lu (Mrs. Hong), Han Chin (Daniel Hong)

EL LEYTON

(SAHARA FILMS) Producers, Carlo Bettin, Gonzalo Justiniano; Director, Gonzalo Justiniano; Screenplay, Gonzalo Justiniano, Fernando Aragón, based on the book by Luis Acuña; Photography, Inti Briones; Art Director, Polin Garbizu; Music, Cuti Aste; Editor, Carolina Quevedo; Chilean-French; Color; Not rated; 95 minutes; American release date: November 21, 2003. Cast: Siboney Lo, Francisca Arze, Gabriela Hernández, Carolina Jérez, Ramón Llao, José Martín, Juan Pablo Sáez, Luis Wigdorsky, Pilar Zderich

THE BIG EMPTY

(ARTISAN) Producers, Doug Mankoff, Gregg L. Daniel, Andrew Spaulding, Keith Resnick; Executive Producers, Steven Bickel, Jeffrey Kramer, Steven G. Kaplan, Peter Wetherell; Director/Screenplay, Steve Anderson; Photography, Chris Manley; Designer, Aaron Osborne; Costumes, Kristin M. Burke; Music, Brian Tyler; Editor, Scot Scalise; Line Producer, Rich Cowan; Casting, Jory Weitz; Dolby; Alpha Cine Color; DV-to-35mm; 94 minutes; Release date: November 21, 2003. Cast: Jon Favreau (John Person), Kelsey Grammer (Agent Banks), Joey Lauren Adams (Grace), Bud Cort (Neely), Jon Gries (Elron), Daryl Hannah (Stella), Adam Beach (Randy), Gary Farmer (Indian Bob), Rachael Leigh Cook (Ruthie), Brent Briscoe (Dan), Melora Walters (Candy), Sean Bean (Cowboy), Larry Mill (Asshole Eddie), Bona Potenta (Waitress), Alejandra Aguilan, Jay Brothers, Sara Fouts, Britney Gillum, Martin Gluhar, Jessie Jenkins, Steven G. Kaplan, Mamie Powell, Gerald Smith, Maria Smith, Patti Smith, Brian Tippett, Anthony Vallejos, Gordon Vallejos (The Travelers)

TIMELINE

(PARAMOUNT) Producers, Lauren Shuler Donner, Jim Van Wyck, Richard Donner; Director, Richard Donner; Screenplay, Jeff Maguire, George Nolfi; Based on the novel by Michael Crichton; Executive Producers, Michael Ovitz, Gary Levinsohn, Don Granger; Photography, Caleb Deschanel; Designer, Daniel T. Dorrance; Costumes, Jenny Beavan; Editor, Richard Marks; Music, Brian Tyler; Visual Consultant, Tom Sanders; Special Effects Coordinator, Neil Corbould; ILM Visual Effects Supervisor, Roger Guyett; Casting, Sarah Halley Finn, Randi Hiller; a Mutual Film Company and Cobalt Media Group presentation of a Donners' Company/Artists Production Group production; Dolby; Super 35 Widescreen; DeLuxe color; Rated PG-13; 116 minutes; Release date: November 26, 2003. Cast: Paul Walker (Chris Johnston), Frances O'Connor (Kate Ericson), Gerard Butler (Andre Marek), Billy Connolly (Prof. Johnston), David Thewlis (Robert Doniger), Anna Friel (Lady Claire), Neal McDonough (Frank Gordon), Matt Craven (Steven Kramer), Ethan Embry (Josh Stern), Michael Sheen (Lord Oliver), Lambert Wilson (Lord Arnaut), Marton Csokas (De Kere), Rossif Sutherland (François Dontelle), Steve Kahan (Baker), David La Haye (Arnaut's

Rossif Sutherland, Frances O'Connor, Paul Walker, Gerard Butler, Neal McDonough in *Timeline* PHOTO COURTESY OF PARAMOUNT

Deputy), Richard Zeman (Oliver's Lieutenant), Patrick Sabongui (Jimmy Gomez), Mike Chute (Bill Baretto), Jayson Merrill (Taub), Vlasta Vrana, Marc Oliver, Jerry Moss (Monks), Danny Blanco-Hall (Sheriff), Paul Tuerpe (News Reporter), Cas Anvar, Stephanie Biddle (E.R. Doctors), Lois Dellar, Lynne Adams (E.R. Nurses), Christian Tessier (MRI Technician), Millie Tresierra, Amy Sloan, Ryan J. Wulff (Undergraduates), Christian Paul, Marian Collier, Edward J. Rosen (Archaeologists), Kathryn Stanleigh (Doniger's Secretary), Stephen Liska, Cecile Cristobal, Stefanie Buxton, Bruce Ramsay (ITC Techs), Hilary Porter (ITC Prep Room Nurse), Marie-Josée D'Amours (Oliver's Wife), Alicia Wininger (Oliver's Daughter), Luke Létourneau (Oliver's Son)

MY FLESH AND BLOOD

(STRAND) Producer, Jennifer Chaiken; Director, Jonathan Karsh; Photography, Amanda Micheli; Music, Hector H. Perez, B. Quincy Griffin; Editor, Eli Olson; a Chaiken Films, Cinemax, Home Box Office production; Color; Not rated; 83 minutes; Release date: November 28, 2003. Documentary on Susan Tom and her eleven adopted, special-needs children, Anthony Tom, Faith Tom, Joe Tom, Margaret Tom, Xenia Tom.

Xenia Tom in *My Flesh and Blood* PHOTO COURTESY OF STRAND

VALLEY OF TEARS

(SEVENTH ART) Producer/Director/Photography, Hart Perry; Screenplay, Juan Gonzales; Editor, Richard Lowe; Music, Estavio Jordan, Maria Guardiana, Phil Marsh; a David Sandeval and Perry Films presentation; DuArt Color; Digital Video; Not rated; 80 minutes; Release date: November 28, 2003. Documentary on a workers' strike in the Texas town of Raymondville; featuring Juanita Valdez, Jesus Moya, Juan Guerra, Marcial Silva, Oscar Correa, Winnie Wetegrove, Paul Whitworth, Tocho Almendarez, Barbara Savage, Norris McGee, Mike Crowell, Larry Spence, Othal Brand, Adriana Flores, Pete Moreno, Fred Klosterman, Quina Flores, Peter Flores, Joe Herrod.

WHAT ALICE FOUND

(CASTLE HILL) Producer/Photography, Richard Connors; Director/Screenplay, A. Dean Bell; Executive Producers, Don Wells, J.C. Chmiel, Rita Fredricks, A.P. Feurerman; Costumes, Michell Teague; Editor, Chris Houghton; Casting, Kristine Bulakwoski; a Factory Films presentation in association with Highland Entertainment; Color; Digital Video; Not rated; 96 minutes; Release date: December 5, 2003. Cast: Judith Ivey (Sandra), Bill Raymond (Bill), Emily Grace (Alice), Jane Lincoln Taylor (Sally), Justin Parkinson (Sam), Tim Hayes (Danny), Lucas Papaelias (Alex), Katheryn Winnick (Julie), Tom Tumminello (Pete), John Knox (Trooper), David Rose (Rough Trucker), Rita Fredricks (Judge), Clint Jordan, Martin Pfefferkorn (Lot Truckers), Matt Campbell (Clerk), Michael C. Maronna (Alice's Boyfriend), Laura Poe (Julie's Mom), Greg Jackson (Irv), Lisa Balkun (Young Alice), Brian De Benedictus (John at the Bar)

Judith Ivey, Emily Grace in *What Alice Found* PHOTO COURTESY OF CASTLE HILL

PRIDE AND PREJUDICE

(EXCELL ENTERTAINMENT GROUP) Producer, Jason Faller; Executive Producer, Daniel Shanthakumar; Director, Andrew Black; Screenplay, Anne K. Black, Katherine Swigert, Jason Faller; Based on the novel by Jane Austen; Photography, Travis Cline; Designer, Anne K. Black; Editor, Alexander Vance; Casting, Kate Kennedy; a Camera 40 Production in association with Bestboy Pictures; Dolby; Color; Rated PG; 104 minutes; Release date: December 5, 2003. Cast: Kam Heskin (Elizabeth Bennet), Orlando Seale (Darcy), Lucila Sola (Jane), Kelly Stables (Lydia), Honor Bliss (Anna Darcy), Ben Gourley (Charles Bingley),

Nicole Hamilton (Kitty), Kara Holden (Caroline Bingley), Rainy Kerwin (Mary), Henry Maguire (Jack Wickham), Hubbel Palmer (Collins), Carmen Rasmusen (Charlotte), Jared Hess (Rev. Steve "Two Trees" Green)

Power Trip PHOTO COURTESY OF INDEPENDENT-FILM FORUM

POWER TRIP

(INDEPENDENT-FILM FORUM) Producer/Director/Editor, Paul Devlin; Co-Producers, Valery Odikadze, Claire Missanelli; Photography, Paul Devlin, Valery Odikadze; a Paul Devlin production; Color; Digital Video; Not rated; 85 minutes; Release date: December 10, 2003. Documentary about AES, an American power company, and its involvement with the impoverished, corrupt country of Georgia; with Piers Lewis, Dennis Bakke, Butch Mederos, Bill O'Reilly, Michael Scholey

WAY PAST COOL

(EMERGING PICTURES) Producer, Ira Deutchman; Executive Producers, Milos Forman, Norman Lear, Paul Rassam; Line Producer, Michael Jackman; Director, Adam Davidson; Screenplay, Jess Mowry, Yule Caise; Based on the novel by Jess Mowry; Photography, Amy Vincent; Designer, William McAllister; Costumes, Darryle Johnson, Sharon Childress; Music, Zen Amen; Editor, Stuart Emanuel; Casting, Jaki Brown-Karman; a Price 1/Act II Prods./Redeemable Features production; Color; Rated R; 101 minutes; Release date: December 10, 2003. Cast: Wayne Collins (Deek), Luchisha Evans (Markita), Terrence Williams (Ty), Kareem Woods (Danny), Wes Charles, Jr. (Lyon), D'andre Jenkins (Rac), D'esmond Jenkins (Ric), Partap Khalsa (Curtis), Jonathan Roger Neal (Gordon), Lawrence Ball (Gameboy), Calvin Hall (Turbo), Ritchie Holliman (Tunk), Dejuan D. Turrentine (Wesley), John Webb (Ajay), Melvyn Hayward, Sr. (Officer Washington), Adam Davidson (Officer Hoover), Marshon Williams, Benjamin Mills (Big Boys), Courtney D. Howe, Jr. (Stanley), Melody Garrett (Ty & Danny's Mother), Arthur Reggie, Sr. (Justin), Dajon Maize (Marcus), Julian Richardson (J'Row), Christina Gibbs (Tom Boy), Debra D. Holt (Gordon's Mother), Quehannes Jones (Leroy), Marcus Salgado (Junkie), Edward Turner (Preacher), Harold Johnson, Sr., Talitha Manor, Olivia Foster Reese, Janet F. Kyle, Greg Floyd (Choir)

Nick Cannon, Steve Harvey in *Love Don't Cost a Thing* PHOTO COURTESY OF WARNER BROS.

LOVE DON'T COST A THING

(WARNER BROS.) Producers, Mark Burg, Reuben Cannon, Andrew A. Kosove, Broderick Johnson; Executive Producer, Oren Koules; Director, Troy Beyer; Screenplay, Troy Beyer, Michael Swerdlick; Based upon the screenplay *Can't Buy Me Love* by Michael Swerdlick; Photography, Chuck Cohen; Designer, Cabot McMullen; Costumes, Christine Peters, Jennifer Mallini; Editor, David Codron; Music, Richard Gibbs; Music Supervisor, Michael McQuarn; Co-Producers, Nava Levin, Kira Davis, Steven P. Wegner; Choreographers, Chonique Sneed, Lisette Bustamante; Casting, Reuben Cannon, Kim Williams; an Alcon Entertainment presentation of a Burg/Koules production; Dolby; Technicolor; Rated PG-13; 100 minutes; Release date: December 12, 2003. Cast: Nick Cannon (Alvin Johnson), Christina Milian (Paris Morgan), Steve Harvey (Clarence Johnson), Kenan Thompson (Walter Colley), Kal Penn (Kenneth Warman), Kevin Christy (Chuck Mattock), Nichole Robinson (Yvonne Freeman), Melissa Schuman (Zoe Parks), Al Thompson (Ted), Jordan Burg (Little Boy), Jackie Benoit (Old Lady), George Cedar (Old Man), Gay Thomas Wilson (Judy Morgan), Sam Sarpong (Kadeem), Imani Parks (Mia), Ian Chidlaw (Eddie), JB Guhman (JB), Russell Howard (Anthony), Elimu Nelson (Dru Hilton), Stuart Scott (Himself), Vanessa Bell Calloway (Vivian Johnson), Ashley Monique Clark (Aretha Johnson), Michael Davis (Junior), Nicole Scherzinger (Champagne Girl), Peter Siragusa (Ben), Maria Carmen (Chemistry Teacher), Damon Butler (Martial Arts Mambo Instructor), Shani Pride (Jasmine), Raistalla, Kelly Becerra, Lindsey Blaufarb, Crystal Colar, Rocio Mendoza (Drill Team Members), Ben Stephens (Jock #1), Dante Basco (Spoken Word Artist), Charles Owen (Jazz Musician), Mayte Garcia (Dancer), Ralph Scherer (Poetry Reader), Ernestine Parks (Singer), Shvona Lavette Williams (Guitar Playing Vocalist), Reagan Gomez-Preston (Olivia)

THE HEBREW HAMMER

(STRAND) Producers, Josh Kesselman, Sofia Sondervan, Lisa Fragner; Executive Producers, Edward R. Pressman, John Schmidt; Director/Screenplay, Jonathan Kesselman; Photography, Kurt Brabbée; Designer, Cabot McMullan; Costumes, Alysia Raycroft, Michelle Phillips; Music, Michael Cohen; Editor, Dean Holland; Casting, Valerie McCaffrey; a Content Film presentation of a Jericho Entertainment, Content Film production; Dolby; Panavision; Color; Rated R; 85 minutes; Release date: December 19, 2003. Cast: Adam Goldberg (Mordechai

Jefferson Carver), Judy Greer (Esther Bloomenbergansteinthal), Andy Dick (Damian), Mario Van Peebles (Mohammed Ali Paula Abdul Rahiem), Peter Coyote (J.J.L. Chief), Sean Whalen (Tiny Tim), Tony Cox (Jamal), Nora Dunn (Mrs. Carver), Richard Riehle (Santa), Melvin Van Peebles (Sweetback), Rachel Dratch (Tikva), Harrison Chad (Shlomo), Jim Petersmith (Skinhead Bartender), Annie McEnroe (Mrs. Highsmith), Grant Rosenmeyer (Young Mordechai), Elaine Hendrix (Blonde Bombshell), Ayelet Ben-Hur (Israeli Rental Agent), Alex Corrado (Tony), Brad Duck (Jimmy), Jason Fuchs (Adolescent Hasidic Boy), Edward I. Koch (Himself), Gary Pratt (Head Elf), Woodraw Asai (Mun Chi), Daryl Wein (Teenage Gentile), Michael J. Mylett, T.J. Sullivan, Audrey Twitchell, Alexa Eisenstein (Gentiles), Evelyn Page (Old Woman), George Hosmer (Chairman of the Worldwide Jewish Media Conspiracy), Ronald Schultz (ADL Chairman), Leslie Shenkel, Alan Nebelthau (JDL Members), Jerome Richards (Council Elder), C.P. Lacey (Sammy Davis Jr. Jr./MC Hammer), Ephraim Benton (Black Teen), David Lee (White Accoutant), Adam Rose (Addict Jewish Child), Devin Rene Burns (Blonde Gentile Girl), Jimmy Walsh (Freckle Faced Gentile), Chris McGinn (Samples Woman), Kathryn Gordon (Bambi), Anna Berger (Harriet Tubbleman), Ivan Sandro (Carnival Worker), Jeff Marlowe (Joshua), Ronald Shore (Bandleader), Tom Chalmers (Chaim Feygele), David Joseph Steinberg (Elf Flunky), Mylika Davis (Sassy Black Prostitute), Moshe Kesselman (Hatcheck Guy), David Kesselman (Macabee)

Adam Goldberg, Judy Greer in *The Hebrew Hammer* PHOTO COURTESY OF STRAND

FOREIGN FILMS

RELEASED IN THE U.S. IN 2003

THE SON

(NEW YORKER) Producers, Jean-Pierre Dardenne, Luc Dardenne, Denis Freyd; Director/Screenplay, Jean-Pierre Dardenne, Luc Dardenne; Photography, Alain Marcoen; Set Designer, Igor Gabriel; Costumes, Monic Parelle; Editor, Marie-Hélène Dozo; Line Producer, Olivier Bronckart; Les Films du Fleuve, Archipel 35, RTBF (Belgian TV); Belgian-French, 2002; Dolby; Color; Not rated; 103 minutes; American release date: January 10, 2003

Morgan Marinne, Olivier Gourmet

Cast

Olivier **Olivier Gourmet**
Francis **Morgan Marinne**
Magali **Isabella Soupart**
Philippo **Rémy Renaud**
Omar **Nassim Hassaïni**
Raoul **Kevin Leroy**
Steve **Félicien Pitsaer**

and Annette Closset (Training Center Director), Fabian Marnette (Rino), Jimmy Deloof (Dany), Anne Gerard (Dany's Mother), Pierre Nisse, Stephan Barbason, David Manna, Abdellah Amarjouf (Apprentice Welders), Dimitri Legros (Cafe Customer), Leon Michaux (Tutor), Colette Hobsig (Cook), Anne Dortu (Baker), Sandro Scariano (Hot Dog Seller), Isabelle Comte (Cafe Waitress)

Olivier Gourmet

Olivier, a divorced carpentry instructor, becomes interested in a mysterious 16-year-old student, unaware of the teen's connection to his own troubled past.

Morgan Marinne   PHOTOS COURTESY OF NEW YORKER

CITY OF GOD

(MIRAMAX) Producers, Andréa Barata Ribeiro, Mauricio Andrade Ramos; Director, Fernando Meirelles; Screenplay, Braulio Mantovani; Based on the novel by Paulo Lins; Photography, Cesar Charlone; Art Director, Tulé Peake; Music, Antonio Pinto, Ed Córtes; Editor, Daniel Rezende; a Walter Salles and Donald K. Ranvaud presentation of an Oz Filmes and VideoFilmes production; Brazilian-German-French, 2002; Dolby; Panavision; Color; Rated R; 131 minutes; American release date: January 17, 2003

Cast
Buscapé (Rocket) **Alexandre Rodrigues**
Zé Pequeño (Li'l Ze) **Leandro Firmino da Hora**
Bené (Benny) **Phellipe Haagensen**
Dadinho (Li'l Dice) **Douglas Silva**
Cabeleira (Shaggy) **Jonathan Haagensen**
Sandro Cenoura (Carrot) **Matheus Nachtergaele**
Mané Galinha (Knockout Ned) **Sou Jorge**
Alicate (Clipper) **Jefechander Suplino**
Angélica **Alice Braga**
Barbantinho **Emerson Gomes**
Adult Barbantinho **Edson Oliveira**
Bené as a Child **Michel de Souza Gomes**
Berenice **Roberta Rodrigues**
Buscapé as a Child **Luis Otávio**
Cabeção **Mauricio Margques**
Newspaper Editor **Gustavo Engracia**
Filé com Fritas **Darlan Cunha**
Gelson **Robson Rocha**
Lampião **Thiago Martins**
Lúcia Maracanã **Leandra Miranda**
Marina Cintra **Graziella Moretto**
Marreco (Goose) **Renao de Souza**
Paraíba's Wife **Karina Falcão**
Galinha's Girlfriend **Sabrina Rosa**
Neguinho **Rubens Sabino**
Otavio **Marcos Junqueira (Kikito)**
Buscapé's Father **Edson Montenegro**
Paraíba **Gero Camilo**
Rafael **Felipe Silva**
Thiago **Daniel Zettel**
Tio Sam **Charles Paraventi**
Touro **Luiz Carlos Ribeiro Seixas**
Tuba **Paulo César (Jacaré)**
Paraiba's Neighbor **Danielle Ornellas**
Aristóstles **Julio César Siqueira**
Ba **Denise Fonseca**
Exu **Adão dos Santos Thiago**
Addicted Kid **Edward Boggiss Lustosa**
Supermarket Manager **Gutti Fraga**
Grande **Alexandre Santana**
Mané Galinha's Brothers **Marcelo Costa, Marcos Coutinho**
Jabá **João Soares**
Young Worker **Rafael Fontenele**
Buscapé's Mother **Rosangela Rodrigues**

and Jota Farias (Driver of DKW), Mary Sheyla de Paula (Neguinho's Wife), Gil Torres (Woman on Bus), Paulo Lins (Church Priest), Christian Duurvoort (Guy from Sao Paulo), Olivia Araujo (Motel Receptionist)

Alexandre Rodrigues, Alice Braga

Alexandre Rodrigues PHOTOS COURTESY OF MIRAMAX

During the 1960s and '70s, in a poverty stricken area of Rio de Janeiro known as Cidade de Deus, young Rocket watches the inhabitants of his world descend into a nightmare of violence, drugs and murder.

This film received Oscar nominations for director, screenplay adaptation, cinematography, and film editing.

AMEN.

(KINO) Producer, Claude Berri; Executive Producer, Michèle Ray; Director, Costa-Gavras; Screenplay, Costa-Gavras, Jean-Claude Grumberg; Based on the play *The Representative* by Rolf Hochhuth; Designer, Ari Hantke; Costumes, Edith Verspérini; Music, Armand Amar; Editor, Yannick Kergoat; French-German, 2002; Dolby; Color; Not rated; 130 minutes; American release date: January 24, 2003

Cast

Kurt Gerstein **Ulrich Tukur**
Riccardo Fontana **Mathieu Kassovitz**
The Doctor **Ulrich Mühe**
The Cardinal **Michel Douchaussoy**
The Count Fontana **Ion Caramitru**
The Pope **Marcel Iures**
Gerstein's Father **Friedrich von Thun**
Mrs. Gerstein **Antje Schimdt**
Grawitz **Hanns Zischler**
Hoess **Sebastian Koch**
Von Rutta **Erich Hallhuber**
The Director **Burkhard Heyl**
Tittman **Angus MacIness**
Bishop von Galen **Bernd Fischerauer**
Pastor Wehr **Pierre Franckh**

and Taylor Richard Durden (The Ambassador), Monika Bleibtreu (Ms. Hinze), Justus von Dohnanyi (Baron von Otter), Günther-Maria Halmer

Mathieu Kassovitz

Bernd Fischerauer (center)

Ulrich Tukur PHOTOS COURTESY OF KINO

(Priest Dibelius), August Zirner (Von Weizsäcker), Horatiu Malaele (Fritsche), Ovidiu Cuncea (Stephan Lux), Markus Hering (Karl), Susanne Lothar (Alexandra Baltz), Alexander Geringas (Helmut Franz), Theodor Danetti (The Old Cardinal)

The true story of how SS Officer Kurt Gerstein tried to alert the outside world to the atrocities taking place in the Nazi deathcamps.

BLIND SPOT: HITLER'S SECRETARY

(SONY CLASSICS) Producers, Danny Krausz, Kurt Stocker; Line Producer, Manfred Fritsch; Directors/Concept, André Heller, Othmar Schmiderer; Photography, Othmar Schmiderer; Editor, Daniel Pöhacker; Production Coordinator, Gerd Huber; Interviews by André Heller; a Dor Film production in association with the Heller Werkstatt; German, 2002; Dolby; Color; Not rated; 90 minutes; American release date: January 24, 2003. Documentary in which Traudl Junge tells about work as one of the private secretaries to Adolf Hitler from 1943 until his suicide in 1945.

Traudi Junge in *Blind Spot* PHOTO COURTESY OF SONY CLASSICS

Rachida Brakni in *Chaos*

CHAOS

(NEW YORKER) Producer, Alain Sarde; Director/Screenplay, Coline Serreau; Photography, Jean-François Robin; Designer, Michèle Abbe; Costumes, Karen Serreau; Line Producer, Christine Gozlan; Editor, Catherine Renault; Music, Ludovic Navarre; Casting, Bruno Levy, Olivier Carbone, Dan Berthier; a Les Films Alain Sarde—France 2 Cinema—ENILOC co-production with the participation of Canal+; French, 2001; Dolby; Color; Not rated; 109 minutes; American release date: January 29, 2003

Cast
Hélène **Catherine Frot**
Paul **Vincent Lindon**
Noémie/Malika **Rachida Brakni**
Mamie **Line Renaud**
Fabrice **Aurélien Wiik**
Touki **Ivan Franek**
Florence **Chloé Lambert**
Charlotte **Marie Denarnaud**
Marsat **Michel Lagueyrie**
Pali **Wojtek Pszoniak**

and Eric Poulain (Young Cop), Omar-Echériff Attalah (Tarek), Hajar Nouma (Zora), Jean-Marc Stehlé (Blanchet), Léa Drucker (Nicole), Nicolas Serreau (Barman), Jean-Loup Michou (1st Guy), Julie Durand (Zoriza), Simon Bakhouche (Henri), Delphine Bibet, Sylvie Raboutet, Nicolas Lartigue (Sitcom Cast)

Rachida Brakni in *Chaos* PHOTOS COURTESY OF NEW YORKER

Wracked with guilt after seeing a young woman beaten and left for dead, Hélène decides to devote her time to helping the woman and finds that she must recscue her from the pimps responsible for the attack.

LOST IN LA MANCHA

(IFC FILMS) Producer, Lucy Darwin; Directors/Screenplay, Keith Fulton, Louis Pepe; Photography, Louis Pepe; Associate Producers, Andrew Curtis, Rosa Bosch; Music, Miriam Cutler; Editor, Jacob Bricca; *The Story of Don Quixote* animated by Stefan Avalos, from sketches by Gustave Doré; *Terry Gilliam's Picture Show* animated by Chaim Bianco; Narrator, Jeff Bridges; a Quixote Films and Low Key Pictures production in association with Eastcroft Productions; British-U.S., 2002; Color; Not rated; 93 minutes; American release date: January 31, 2003. Documentary on director Terry Gilliam's valiant but ultimately unsuccessful attempt to make the movie *The Man Who Killed Don Quixote*.

Terry Gilliam

With

Terry Gilliam (writer/director), Jean Rochefort, Johnny Depp (actors), Tony Grisoni (co-writer), Philip Patterson (1st assistant director), Rene Cleitman (producer), Nicola Pecorini (director of photography), Jose Luis Escolar (line producer), Barbara Perez-Solero (assistant set decorator), Benjamin Fernandez (production designer), Andrea Calderwood (former head of production, Pathé), Ray Cooper (longtime Gilliam colleague), Gabriella Pescucci (costume designer), Bernard Douix (executive producer), Fred Milstein (completion guarantor)

Johnny Depp

Johnny Depp, Terry Gilliam

Jean Rochefort, Terry Gilliam

Terry Gilliam, Jean Rochefort PHOTOS COURTESY OF IFC FILMS

ZUS & ZO

(LIFE SIZE ENTERTAINMENT) a.k.a. *Hotel Paraiso*; Producer, Jacqueline de Goeij; Director/Screenplay, Paula van der Oest; Photography, Bert Pot; Designer, Harry Ammerlaan; Costumes, Mariella Kallenberg; Music, Fons Merkies; Editor, Sander Vos; Casting, Job Gosschalk; from Filmprodukties de Luwte; Dutch, 2002; Color; Not rated; 100 minutes; American release date: February 7, 2003

Cast

Nino **Jacob Derwig**
Bo **Halina Reijn**
Sonja **Monic Hendrickx**
Wanda **Anneke Blok**
Michelle **Sylvia Poorta**
Hugo **Theu Boermans**
Jan **Jaap Spijkers**

and Annet Nieuwenhuyzen (Mother), Pieter Embrechts (Felix Delicious), Lore Dijkman (Young Wanda), Jeroen van Koningsbrugge (Police Officer)

Three sisters are worried when their gay brother announces that he is going to marry a woman, which, according to the stipulations in their father's will, will prevent them from inheriting the family's waterfront hotel. This film received an Oscar nomination for foreign language film (2002).

Zus & Zo

Jacob Derwig, Halina Reijn in *Zus & Zo*

Samuel Le Bihan, Audrey Tautou

HE LOVES ME...HE LOVES ME NOT

(SAMUEL GOLDWYN FILMS) Producer, Charles Gassot; Director, Laetitia Colombani; Screenplay, Laetitia Colombani, Caroline Thivel; Photography, Pierre Aim; Art Director, Jean-Marc Kerdelhue; Costumes, Jacqueline Bouchard; Editor, Veronique Parnet; Music, Jerome Coullet; Casting, Pierre-Jacques Benichou; a Charles Gassot presentation of a Telema, TF1 Films production with the participation of TPS Cinema, Cofimage 12; French, 2002; Dolby; Color; Not rated; 92 minutes; American release date: February 14, 2003

Cast

Angélique **Audrey Tautou**
Loïc **Samuel Le Bihan**
Rachel **Isabelle Carré**
David **Clément Sibony**
Héloïse **Sophie Guillemin**
Julien **Eric Savin**
Claire Belmont **Michèle Garay**

and Elodie Navarre (Anita), Catherine Cyler (Jeanne), Mathilde Blache (Léa), Charles Chevalier (Arthur), Michael Mourot (Jean-Louis), Yannick Alnet (Jean Timbault), Nathalie Krebs (Sonia Jasmin)

An art student, obsessively in love with a married cardiologist, hopes her lover will leave his pregnant wife for her, only to find out that he has been accused of assaulting a patient. Once this series of events is played out from the woman's point of view, we then witness these occurances as seen through his eyes.

Audrey Tautou

OPEN HEARTS

(NEWMARKET) Producer, Vibeke Windelov; Executive Producer, Peter Aalbaek, Anders Thomas Jensen; Director, Susanne Bier; Screenplay, Anders Thomas Jensen, based on an idea by Susanne Bier; Photography, Morten Soborg; Designer, William Knuttel; Costumes, Stine Gudmundsen Holmgreen; Editors, Pernille Bech Christensen, Thomas Krag; Music, Jesper Winge Leisner; Casting, Jette Termann, Lene Seested; a Zentropa Entertainment production; Danish; Dolby; Color; Rated R; 114 minutes; American release date: February 21, 2003

Sonja Richter, Nikolaj Lie Kaas

Paprika Steen   PHOTOS COURTESY OF NEWMARKET

Cast
Cecilie **Sonja Richter**
Joachim **Nikolaj Lie Kaas**
Niels **Mads Mikkelsen**
Marie **Paprika Steen**
Stine **Stine Bjerregaard**
Hanne **Birthe Neumann**
and Niels Olsen (Finn), Ulf Pilgaard (Thomsen), Ronnie Hiort Lorenzen (Gustav), Pelle Bang Sorensen (Emil), Anders Nyborg (Robert), Ida Dwinger (Sanne), Philip Zanden (Tommy), Michel Castenholt (Furniture Store Assistant), Birgitte Prins (A&E Doctor), Susanne Juhasz (Cashier at Iso), Hans Henrik Clemensen (Chef), Jens Basse Dam (Waiter), Hane Windfeld, Tina Gylling Mortensen (Nurses)

Joachim and Cecilie, a young couple on the verge of getting married, find their happiness shattered when he is paralyzed after being struck by a car.

Helena Bonham Carter, Guy Pearce   PHOTO COURTESY OF PARAMOUNT CLASSICS

TILL HUMAN VOICES WAKE US

(PARAMOUNT CLASSICS) Producers, Shana Levine, Dean Murphy, Nigel Odell, David Redman, Thomas Augsberger, Matthias Emcke; Executive Producers, Beau Flynn, Yoram Pelman, Stefan Simchowitz; Co-Executive Producers, Andrew Deane, Gareth Wiley; Director/Screenplay, Michael Petroni; Photography, Roger Lanser; Designer, Ralph Moser; Costumes, Jeanie Cameron; Music, Amotz Plessner; Editor, Bill Murphy; Casting, Stewart Faichney, Maura Fay; an Instict Entertainment production, presented by the Australian Film Commission and Key Entertainment; Australian, 2002; Dolby; Super 35 Widescreen; Cinevex Color; Rated R; 97 minutes; American release date: February 21, 2003

Cast
Dr. Sam Franks **Guy Pearce**
Ruby **Helena Bonham Carter**
Maurie Lewis **Frank Gallacher**
Young Sam Franks **Lindley Joyner**
Silvy Lewis **Brooke Harman**
Dr. David Franks **Peter Curtin**
Dorothy Lewis **Margot Knight**
Russ **Anthony Martin**
Mrs. Sacks **Dawn Klingberg**
Lawyer **David Ravenswood**
Reverend Mortenbury **Stewart Faichney**
Mrs. Pickford **Diana Greentree**
and Ian Swan (Police Sergeant), Mark Perren Jones (Police Constable), Sally Plant (Student #1), Andrea Swifte, Josephine Keen (Patients), Fred Barker (Train Conductor), Reville Smith (Undertaker), Joanie Thomas (Lady on Train), Roger O'Conner (Man on Train), Amanda Douge (Katherine), Kathy Bedford (Nurse)

A psychoanyalst, haunted by a childhood tragedy, meets up with an enigmatic woman who develops amnesia after trying to drown herself.

LAWLESS HEART

(FIRST LOOK PICTURES) Producer, Martin Pope; Executive Producers, Francesca Barra, Steve Christian, Jim Reeve, Roger Shannon; Directors/Screnplay, Neil Hunter, Tom Hunsinger; Photography, Sean Bobbitt; Designer, Lynne Whiteread; Costumes, Linda Alderson; Music, Adrian Johnson; Editor, Scott Thomas; an MP Production, presented in association with Isle of Man Film Commission, Film Council and October Productions, with the participation of British Screen and BSKY8; British, 2002; Dolby; Color; Rated R; 86 minutes; American release date: February 21, 2003

Josephine Butler

Josephine Butler, Douglas Henshall

Bill Nighy, Clémentine Célarié PHOTOS COURTESY OF FIRST LOOK PICTURES

Cast

Tim Marsh **Douglas Henshall**
Nick **Tom Hollander**
Corinne **Clémentine Célarié**
Dan **Bill Nighy**
David **Stuart Laing**
Leah **Josephine Butler**
Judy **Ellie Haddington**
Charlie **Sukie Smith**
Darren **Dominic Hall**
Stuart **David Coffey**
Mrs. Marsh, Tim's Mother **June Barrie**
Mr. Marsh, Tim's Father, **Peter Symonds**
Justin **Will Hunter**
Georgia **Jessica Napier**
Michelle **Sally Hurst**
Michael **Richard Cant**

and Barney Lark (James), Alasdair Craig (Tim's Friend Giles), Hari Dillon (Will), Henie Lewis (Steve), Zoe Shipway (Jeweller), Jim McManus (Chef), Howard Gossington (Waiter)

At a seaside English village, three men are brought together by the funeral of a mutual friend.

Monica Bellucci, Vincent Cassel

Albert Dupontel, Monica Bellucci, Vincent Cassel

Monica Bellucci PHOTOS COURTESY OF LIONS GATE

IRREVERSIBLE

(LIONS GATE) Producers, Christophe Rossignon, Richard Grandpierre; Director/Screenplay, Gaspar Noé; Photography, Benoît Debie; Art Directors, Alan Juteau Soler, Bayart Costello; Costumes, Fred Cambier Calandre, Eric Bigot, Ly Cheng Born Tea; Editors, Gaspar Noé, Araud Gauchy; Casting, Jacques Grant Leroux; Produced by Nord-Ouest Production and Eskwad in co-production with StudioCanal, 120 Films and Les Cinemas de la Zone with the participation of Canal+; French, 2002; Dolby; Color; Not rated; 98 minutes; American release date: March 7, 2003

Monica Bellucci

Cast

Alex **Monica Bellucci**
Marcus **Vincent Cassel**
Pierre **Albert Dupontel**
Le Tenia **Jo Prestia**
Philippe **Philippe Nahon**
Stéphane **Stéphane Drouot**
Maso, Man Beaten to Death in Club **Jean-Louis Costes**
Tapeworm **Mike Gondoin**
Mourad **Mourad Khima**
Dancer with Hawaiian Shirt **Christopher Lemaire**
Clients **Stéphane Derdérian, Gaspar Noé**

The police arrest a pair of teachers, Marcus and Pierre, at a gay S&M club, and the reason for their crime becomes apparent as the story unfolds in reverse order.

Juliane Köhler, Lea Kurka

Silas Kerati, Karoline Eckertz

Lea Kurka, Sidede Onyulo

Juliane Köhler, Merab Nikidze PHOTOS COURTESY OF ZEITGEIST

NOWHERE IN AFRICA

(ZEITGEIST) Producers, Peter Herrmann; Executive Producer, Andreas Bareisss; Co-Producers, Michael Weber, Thilo Kleine, Bernd Eichinger, Sven Ebeling; Director/Screenplay, Caroline Link, based on the novel by Stephanie Zweig; Photography, Gernot Roll; Designers, Uwe Szielasko, Susann Bieling; Costumes, Barbara Grupp; Music, Niki Reiser, Jochen Schmidt-Hambrock; Editor, Patricia Rommel; Casting, Uwe Bunker, An Dorthe Braker; a co-production of Bavaria Film, Constantin Film Produktion, Media Cooperation One, MTM Medien & Television Munchen; German, 2001; Dolby; Arriscope Color; Not rated; 140 minutes; American release date: March 7, 2003

Lea Kurka, Sidede Onyulo

Cast

Jettel Redlich **Juliane Köhler**
Walter Redlich **Merab Ninidze**
Susskind **Matthias Habich**
Owuor **Sidede Onyulo**
Young Regina **Lea Kurka**
Older Regina **Karoline Eckertz**
Max **Gerd Heinz**
Ina **Hildegard Schmahl**
Liesel **Maritta Horwarth**
Kathe **Regine Zimmermann**
Maid **Gabrielle Odinis**
Mrs. Sadler **Bettina Redlich**
Inge **Julia Leidl**
Elsa Konrad **Mechthild Grossman**
Young Jogona **Peter Lenaeku**
Older Jogona **Silas Kerati**

and Kanyaman (Kimani), Andrew Rashleigh (Captain Caruther), Anthony Bate (Mr. Brindley), David Michaels (Robert Green), Steve Weston (Mr. Morrison), Diane Keen (Mrs. Rubens), Andrew Sachs (Mr. Rubens), Joel Wajsberg (Hubert), Miriam Wajsberg (Ruth), Marian Losch (Johannes), Bela Klenze (Sad Boy), Steven Price (British Officer in Norfolk), Ken Brown (Bure), M.M. Sha (Patel)

A Jewish family escapes from Nazi Germany in 1938 and relocates in the wild of Kenya.

2002 Academy Award winner for Best Foreign Language Feature.

BEND IT LIKE BECKHAM

(FOX SEARCHLIGHT) Producers, Deepak Nayar, Gurinder Chadha; Executive Producers, Ulrich Feslberg, Zygi Kamasa, Simon Franks, Haneet Vaswani, Russel Fischer; Director, Gurinder Chadha; Screenplay, Gurinder Chadha, Guljit Bindra, Paul Mayeda Berges; Photography, Jong Lin; Designer, Nick Ellis; Costumes, Ralph Holes; Line Producer, Paul Ritchie; Editor, Justin Krisch; Music, Craig Pruess; Music Supervisor, Liz Gallacher; Casting, Liora Reich, Carrie Hilton; a Kintop Pictures presentation in association with The Film Council and Filmfoerderung Hamburg with the participation of BSKYB and British Screen and in association with Helkon SK, The Works, Future Film Financing, of a Kintop Pictures/Bend It Films/Roc Media/Road Movies co-production; British-German, 2002; Dolby; Color; Rated PG-13; 112 minutes; American release date: March 12, 2003

Parminder Nagra, Jonathan Rhys-Meyers

Parminder Nagra

Cast

Jess Bhamra	**Parminder Nagra**
Jules Paxton	**Keira Knightley**
Joe	**Jonathan Rhys-Meyers**
Mr. Bhamra	**Anupam Kher**
Pinky Bhamra	**Archie Panjabi**
Mel	**Shaznay Lewis**
Alan Paxton	**Frank Harper**
Paula Paxton	**Juliet Stevenson**
Mrs. Bhamra	**Shaheen Khan**
Tony	**Ameet Chana**
Meena	**Poojah Shah**
Bubbly	**Paven Virk**
Monica	**Preeya Kalidas**
Taz	**Trey Farley**
Sonny	**Saraj Chaudhry**
Gary	**Imran Ali**
Teetu	**Kulvinder Ghir**
Teetu's Mom	**Harvey Virdi**
Teetu's Dad	**Ash Varrez**
Themselves	**Gary Lineker, Alan Hansen, John Barnes**
Elderly Aunt	**Adlyn Ross**
Polly	**Shobu Kapoor**
Biji	**Zohra Sehgal**

and Ahsen Bhatti (Nairobi Grandson), Tanveer Ghani (Video Man), Nina Wadia (Wedding Guest), Jenni Birch, Olivia Scholfield, Natasha Lee, Louise Walker, Danielle Richards, Suzanna Keeka, Tanya Beverly, Sally Kirkbride, Maki Okumurakami, Nav Bopari (Hounslow Harriers), Sudha Buchar, Mr. and Mrs. Tarlochan, Singh Bindra, Bujinder Bindra, Ezme Bushell, Ajay Chhabra, Balwant Kaur Chadha, Sheran Chadha, Mr. and Mrs. Kulwant, Singh Chowdhary, Amerjit Deo, Satpal Kaur Mahajan, Kaval Mahajan, Harvir Mahajan, Tripat Mahajan, Mr. and Mrs. Taywant Singh, Mohindru, Parminder Sekhon (Bhamra Family)

In Hounslow, England, 18-year-old Jess Bharma dreams of becoming a professional soccer player while her more traditional Punjabi Sikh parents have decided that she will earn a law degree and marry.

Keira Knightley, Parminder Nagra PHOTOS COURTESY OF FOX SEARCHLIGHT

Wu Qiong, Zhao Tao PHOTO COURTESY OF NEW YORKER

UNKNOWN PLEASURES

(NEW YORKER) Producers, Shozo Ichiyama (T-Mark, Japan), Lit Kit-ming (Hu Tong Comm., China), Masayuki Mori (Officer Kitano, Japan); Executive Producers, Hengameh Panahi (Lumen Films, France), Paul Yi (E-Pictures, Korea); Director/Screenplay, Jia Zhang-Ke; Photography, Yu Lik Wai; Art Director, Liang Jiang Dong; Editor, Chow Keung; Chinese-Japanese-French-Korean, 2002; Dolby; Color; Not rated; 113 minutes; American release date: March 26, 2003

Cast

Qiao Qiao **Zhao Tao**
Bin Bin **Zhao Wei Wei**
Xiao Ji **Wu Qiong**
Yuan Yuan **Zhou Qing Feng**
Xiao Wu **Wang Hong Wei**
Bin Bin's Mother **Bai Ru**
Xiao Ji's Father **Liu Xi An**
Sister Zhu **Xu Shou Lin**
The Hairdresser **Ren Ai Jun**
Mr. Ren **Xiao Dao**
The Concubine **Ying Zi**
Karaoke Customer **Wang Li Min**

A group of alienated and restless teens drift through their daily lives with little future before them.

FELLINI: I'M A BORN LIAR

(FIRST LOOK PICTURES) Director, Damian Pettigrew; Screenplay, Damian Pettigrew, Olivier Gal; Photography, Paco Wiser; Editor, Florence Ricard; French-Italian-British, 2002; Color; Not rated; 105 minutes; American release date: April 2, 2003. Documentary on Italian filmmaker Federico Fellini.

With

Roberto Benigni, Luigi "Titta" Benzi, Italo Calvino, Federico Fellini, Dante Ferretti, Rinaldo Geleng, Tullio Pinelli, Giuseppe Rotunno, Terence Stamp, Donald Sutherland, Daniel Toscan du Plantier

Marcello Mastroianni, Federico Fellini on the set of *8 1/2*

Fellini: I'm a Born Liar PHOTOS COURTESY OF FIRST LOOK PICTURES

CET AMOUR-LÀ

(NEW YORKER) Producer, Alain Sarde; Director/Screenplay, José Dayan; Dialogue in Collaboration With, Yann Andréa, Maren Sell, Gilles Taurand; Based on the novel by Yann Andréa; Photography, Caroline Champetier; Designer, Sylvie Fennee; Costumes, Mimi Lempika; Associate Producer, Christine Gozlan; Music, Angelo Badalamenti; Editor, Anne Boissel; Casting, Sarah Tepper; Produced by Les Films Alain Sarde/Arte France Cinema; French, 2001; Dolby; Color; Not rated; 98 minutes; American release date: April 2, 2003

Cast

Marguerite Duras **Jeanne Moreau**
Yann Andréa **Aymeric Demarigny**
Woman in a Smock **Christiane Rorato**
Night Nurse **Sophie Mileron**
Hospital Employee **Justine Levy**
Oyster Stall Kid **Adrien Guilbert**
Buffet Waiter **Stanislas Sauphanor**
Barman **Didier Lesour**
The Ambassador's Wife **Tanya Lopert**

The true story of the love affair between French author Marguerite Duras and her much younger muse and apprentice, Yann Andrea.

Jeanne Moreau, Aymeric Demarigny

Jeanne Moreau, Marguerite Duras

Jeanne Moreau PHOTOS COURTESY OF NEW YORKER

THE GOOD THIEF

(FOX SEARCHLIGHT) Producers, Stephen Woolley, John Wells, Seaton McLean; Executive Producers, Neil Jordan, Kristin Harms, Thierry de Navacelle; Director/Screenplay, Neil Jordan; Based on the film *Bob Le Flambeur* by Jean Pierre Melville, with screenplay by Auguste Le Breton and Jean Pierre Melville; Photography, Chris Menges; Designer, Anthony Pratt; Costumes, Penny Rose; Editor, Tony Lawson; Co-Producer, Tracey Seaward; Music, Elliot Goldenthal; Makeup/Hair Designer, Jenny Shircore; Casting, Susie Figgis; an Alliance Atlantis presentation; British-French-Irish; Dolby; Fujicolor; Rated R; 109 minutes; American release date: April 2, 2003

Nick Nolte, Tchéky Karyo

Nutsa Kukhianidze, Nick Nolte

Cast

Bob Mantagnet **Nick Nolte**
Roger **Tchéky Karyo**
Paulo **Saïd Taghmaoui**
Anne **Nutsa Kukhianidze**
Raoul **Gérard Darmon**
Remi **Marc Lavoine**
Vladimer **Emir Kusturica**
Said **Ouassini Embarek**
Yvonne **Patricia Kell**
Petit Louis **Warren Zavatta**
Luigi **Nicolas Dromard**
Philippa **Sarah Bridges**
Fernandez **Sergio Candiota**
Philippe **Julien Maurel**
Bill **Theo Trifard**
Chief Security Man **Frederico Scotto**
Casino Manager **Laurent Grevill**

and Roland Munter (Spanish Night Club Heavy), Damien Arnone (Security Guard), Mark Polish (Albert), Mike Polish (Bertram), Jean M'Bale (Monitor Security Guard), Ralph Fiennes (Tony Angel), Enzo Iovino (Croupier)

Nutsa Kukhianidze, Nick Nolte

Gambler Bob Mantagnet brings together a team of thieves to help him heist a batch of valuable paintings, while leading the police to believe they are robbing a casino. Remake of the 1955 French film *Bob le Flambeur*.

Nutsa Kukhianidze, Nick Nolte PHOTOS COURTESY OF FOX SEARCHLIGHT

Markku Peltola, Marko Haavisto, Jouni Saarnio, Jyrki Telila, Jukka Teerisaari

THE MAN WITHOUT A PAST

(SONY CLASSICS) Producer/Director/Screenplay, Aki Kaurismaki; Photography, Timo Salminen; Set Designers, Markku Pätilä, Jukka Salmi; Wardrobe, Outi Herjupatana; Editor, Timo Linnasalo; Finnish-German-French; Dolby; Color; Rated PG-13; 97 minutes; American release date: April 4, 2003

Cast
The Man **Markku Peltola**
Irma **Kati Outinen**
Nieminen **Juhani Niemelä**
Kaisa Nieminen **Kaija Pakarinen**
Anttila **Sakari Kuosmanen**
Flea Market Manageress **Annikki Tähti**
Bar Owner **Anneli Sauli**
Shipyard Clerk **Elina Salo**
Bank Clerk **Outi Mäenpää**

and Esko Nikkari (Bank Robber), Perlti Swehoim (Investigating Officer), Matti Wuori (Lawyer), Aino Seppo (Ex-Wife), Janne Hyytiäinen (Ovaskainen), Antti Reini (Electrician), Tähti (Hannibal), Marko Haavisto, Jouni Saarnio, Jukka Teerisaari, Jyrki Telilä (The Salvation Army Band), Risto Korhonen, Panu Vauhkonen, Tom Wahlroos (Muggers)

A man left for dead after being beaten by thugs, awakens in the hospital with no memory and makes a new life for himself living among the destitute along the Helsinki waterfront.

Kati Outenin, Markku Peltola PHOTOS COURTESY OF SONY CLASSICS

LILYA 4-EVER

(NEWMARKET) Producer, Lars Jonsson; Director/Screenplay, Lukas Moodysson; Photography, Ulf Brantàs; Art Director, Josefin Asberg; Costumes, Denise Ostholm; Editors, Michal Leszczylowski, Oleg Morgunov, Bernhard Winkler; Music, Nathan Larson; Co-Producers, Peter Aalbæk Jensen, Gunnar Carlsson, Tomas Esliksson; Line Producer, Malte Forssell; Casting, Jesper Kurlandsky; Produced by Memfis Film in co-production with Zentropa Entertainments5 ApS, Film i Vast, Sveriges Television Goteborg, Nordic Film & TV Fund/Svend Abrahamsen; Swedish-Danish, 2002; Dolby; Color; Rated R; 109 minutes; American release date: April 18, 2003

Oksana Akinshina, Elina Benenson PHOTO COURTESY OF NEWMARKET

Cast
Lilya **Oksana Akinshina**
Volodya **Artiom Bogucharskij**
Lilya's Mother **Ljubov Agapova**
Aunt Anna **Lilia Sinkarjova**
Natasha **Elina Benenson**
Andrei **Pavel Ponomarjov**
Witek **Tomas Neumann**
Neighbor **Anastasia Bedredinova**
Sergei **Tönu Kark**
Natasha's Boyfriend **Nikolai Bentsler**

and Aleksander Dorosjkevitch, Jevgeni Gurov, Aleksandr Sokolenko (Friends), Margo Kostelina, Veronika Kovtun (Cashiers), Jelena Jakovleva (Teacher), Tamara Solodnikova (Social Worker), Nikolai Kütt (Man on the Bridge), Oleg Rogatchov (Natasha's Dad), Aleksadr Okunev (Volodya's Dad), Herardo Kontreras (Anna's Neigbor), Madis Kalmet (Man in Hotel Room), Bo Christer Hjelte (Lonely Man), Sten Erici (BMW Man)

Hoping to move to America, 16-year-old Lilya is left behind by her mother and stepfather in the Soviet Union where she moves into her aunt's squalid apartment and begins hanging out with a group of wayward teens.

WINGED MIGRATION

(SONY CLASSICS) Producers, Christophe Barratier, Jacques Perrin; Executive Producer, Jean de Trégomain; Director/Narrator, Jacques Perrin; Screenplay, Stéphane Durand, Jacques Perrin; Co-Directors, Jacques Cluzaud, Michel Debats; Associate Producers, Reinhard Brundig, Danièle Delorme, Jean-Marc Henchoz, Jean Labadie, José María Morales, Andrea Occhipinti, Yves Robert; Photography, Michael Benjamin, Sylvie Carcedo-Dreujou, Laurent Charbonnier, Luc Drion, Laurent Fleutot, Philippe Garguil, Dominique Gentil, Bernard Lutic, Thierry Machado, Stéphane Martin, Fabrice Mondrot, Ernst Sasse, Michael Terrasse, Thierry Thomas; Designer, Régis Nicolino; Editor, Marie-Josèphe Yoyotte; Music, Bruno Coulais; English Narrator, Philippe Labro; French, 2002; Dolby; Color; Rated G; 89 minutes; American release date: April 18, 2003. Documentary charting the movements of birds along their migration routes.

2002 Oscar nominee for feature documentary.

Winged Migration

Winged Migration PHOTOS COURTESY OF SONY CLASSICS

HOUSE OF FOOLS

(PARAMOUNT CLASSICS) Producers, Andrei Konchalovsky, Felix Kleiman; Director/Screenplay, Andrei Konchalovsky; Photography, Serguei Kozlov; Designer, Lubov Skorina; Costumes, Svetlana Volter; Music, Edward Artemiev; Editor, Olga Grinshpun; Casting, Alexander Aronin; a Hachette Premiere from Persona Productions; Russian, 2002; Dolby; Color; Rated R; 104 minutes; American release date: April 25, 2003

Cast
Zhanna **Julia Vysotsky**
Officer **Evgeni Mironov**
Akhmed **Sultan Islamov**
Ali **Stanislav Varkki**
Lucy **Elena Fomina**
Vika **Marina Politseimako**
Makhmud **Rasmi Jabrailov**
Karlusha **Vladimir Federov**
Doctor **Vladas Bagdonas**
Fucue **Anatoly Adoskin**

and Georgy Ovakimyan (Goga), Rusian Naurbiev (Chechen Commander Vakhid), Bryan Adams (Himself), Cecelia Thomson (Lithuanian Sharpshooter), Tigranui Chakrian (Karapetovna), Margarita Zykova (Baba Vera), Jonas Baublis (Bibika), Viktoras Baublis (Buka), Anatoly Zhuraviev (Boxer), Alexander Seleznev (Feodor the Drunk), Magomed Zurabov (Afgani), Ibragim Bekov (Yusouff), Temerian Dzeitov (Askhab), Denis Nadtochi (Vitek the Male Nurse)

The inmates at a small psychiatric hospital in the Russian republic of Ingushetia find themselves temporarily abandoned by the staff as the Chechen conflict draws nearer.

Julia Vysotsky

Julia Vysotsky (center) PHOTOS COURTESY OF PARAMOUNT CLASSICS

MAN ON THE TRAIN

(PARAMOUNT CLASSICS) Producer, Philippe Carcassonne; Executive Producer, Christophe Audeguis; Director, Patrice Leconte; Screenplay, Claude Klotz; Photography, Jean-Marie Dreujou; Designer, Ivan Maussion; Costumes, Annie Périer; Music, Pascal Esteve; Editor, Joelle Hache; Line Producer, Brigitte Faure; Co-Producer, Carl Clifton; a Philippe Carcassonne presentation of a Ciné B—Zoulou Films—Rhone-Alpes Cinéma—FCC Tubedale Films—Pandora Film Produktion—Cinema Parisien—Media Suits co-production, in association with the Film Council; French-German-British-Swiss, 2002; Dolby; Super 35 Widescreen; Color; Rated R; 90 minutes; American release date: May 9, 2003

Jean Rochefort, Johnny Hallyday

Johnny Hallyday

Johnny Hallyday, Jean Rochefort

When a bank robber and a retired school teacher cross paths, both men start to wish they had chosen the other's way of life

Cast

Manesquier **Jean Rochefort**
Milan **Johnny Hallyday**
Luigi **Jean-François Stevenin**
Max **Charlie Nelson**
Sadko **Pascal Parmentier**
Viviane **Isabelle Petit-Jacques**
The Sister of Manesquier **Edith Scob**
Hairdresser **Maurice Chevit**
Burly Guy **Riton Liebman**
Schoolboy **Olivier Fauron**
Baker **Véronique Kapoian**
Waitress **Elsa Duclot**
Gardener **Armand Chagot**
Pharmacist **Michel Laforest**
Surgeon **Alain Guellfaff**
Radiologist Nures **Hélèn Chambon**
Operating Room Nurse **Sophie Durand**
Verlin **Jean-Louis Vey**
Friend of the Burly Guy **Sébastien Bonnet**
Bank Manager **Jean-Jacques Cronillon**

Jean Rochefort   PHOTOS COURTESY OF PARAMOUNT CLASSICS

L'AUBERGE ESPAGNOLE

(FOX SEARCHLIGHT) a.k.a. *Pot Luck*; Producer, Bruno Levy; Executive Producer, Luisa Matienzo; Director/Screenplay, Cédric Klapisch; Photography, Dominique Colin; Designer, Francois Emmanuelli; Costumes, Anne Schotte; Editor, Francine Sandberg; Music, Loïk Dury, Mathieu Dury; Co-Producers, Mate Cantero, Stephane Sorlat, Julio Fernandez; Casting, Pep Armengol (Spain), Lucy Boulting (UK), Annette Borgmann (Germany), Toni Tommasi (Italy), Tine Saetter Lassen (Denmark), Emmanuelle Gaborit, Jeanne Millet, Guillaume Malandrin (France); French-Spanish, 2002; Dolby; Color; Rated R; 116 minutes; American release date: May 16, 2003

Cast
Xavier **Romain Duris**
Anne-Sophie **Judith Godrèche**
Martine **Audrey Tautou**
Isabelle **Cécile de France**
Wendy **Kelly Reilly**
Soledad **Cristina Brondo**
Alessandro **Fédérico D'Anna**
Tobias **Barnaby Metschurat**
Lars **Christian Pagh**
William **Kevin Bishop**
Jean-Michel **Xavier de Guillebon**
Jean-Charles Perrin **Wladimir Yordanoff**
Neus **Irène Montala**
Juan **Javier Coromina**
Alistair **Iddo Goldberg**
Xavier's Mother **Martine Demaret**
Bruce **Olivier Raynal**
Flamenco Teacher **Paulina Gálvez**
Xavier's Father **Jacno**
Faculty Secretary **Sylvie Lachat**
Air Hostess **Magali Roze**
Miralpeix Nurse **Shilpa Baliga**
Miralpeix Neighbor **Nadala Batista**

Judith Godreche, Romain Duris

and Pere Sagrista (Catalan Professor), Pere Abello (Patron), Babou Cham, Dani Grao, Ivan Morales (Catalan Students), Jacques Royer (Erasmus), Mira Herfort Wanting (Mira), Arsene Royer (Lars' Son), Sophie Delin (Inn Neighbor), Zinedine Soualem (Barman), Pablo Klapisch (Xavier as a Child), Cédric Klapisch (Stressed-Out Teacher)

Encouraged to study Spanish economics, 24-year-old Parisian Xavier agrees to spend a year in Barcelona as part of the Erasmus program, ending up sharing an apartment with a diverse group of students from various countries.

Christian Pagh, Frederico d'Anna, Cristina Brondo, Cecile de France, Barnaby Metschurat, Romain Duris

Romain Duris, Cecile de France

Romain Duris, Audrey Tautou PHOTOS COURTESY OF FOX SEARCHLIGHT

SWEET SIXTEEN

(LIONS GATE) Producer, Rebecca O'Brien; Director, Ken Loach; Screenplay, Paul Laverty; Photography, Barry Ackroyd; Designer, Martin Johnson; Costumes, Carole K. Millar; Editor, Jonathan Morris; Music, George Fenton; Co-Producers, Ulrich Felsberg, Gerardo Herrero; Line Producer, Peter Gallagher; a Sixteen Films production with Road Movies Filmproduktion and Tornasol.Alta Films; a Scottish Screen and BBC films presentation with the support of Filmstifung Nordrhein-Westfalen and the Glasgow Film Office; British-Scottish-German, 2002; Dolby; Deluxe color; Not rated; 106 minutes; American release date: May 16, 2003

Annmarie Fulton, Martin Compston

Cast
Liam **Martin Compston**
Chantelle **Annmarie Fulton**
Pinball **William Ruane**
Suzanne **Michelle Abercromby**
Jean **Michelle Coulter**
Stan **Gary McCormack**
Rab **Tommy McKee**
Calum **Calum McAlees**
Scullion **Robert Rennie**
Tony **Martin McCardle**
Tony's Gang **Robert Harrison, George McNeilage, Rikki Traynor**
Douglas **Jon Morrison**
Night-Time **Junior Walker**
Side-Kick **Gary Maitland**
Davi-Vampire **Scott Dymond**
Pizza Boys **Mark Dallas, Stephen McGivern, Robert Muir**
Motorbike Policeman **Matt Costello**
Truck Driver **Sandy Hewitt**
Barmaid **Lily Smart**
Caravan Site Manager **Bruce Sturrock**
Muggers **William Cassidy, Robert McFadyen, Stephen Purdon**
Cold Pizza Man **Tony Collins**
Woman on Stairs **Marie Shankley**

Martin Compston

In Greenock, Scotland, 15-year-old Liam vows to buy a caravan for his mother once she is released from prison and sets out to earn money as a drug runner.

Martin Compston PHOTOS COURTESY OF LIONS GATE

THE SEA

(PALM PICTURES) Producers, Baltasar Kormákur, Jean-François Fonlupt; Director/Screenplay, Baltasar Kormákur; Based on the play by Olafur Haukur Símonarson; Photography, Jean-Louis Vialard; Designer, Tonie Zetterström; Costumes, Thorunn Elisabet Sveinsdóttir; Music, Jón Ásgeirsson; Editor, Valdís Óskarsdottir; a co-production of Blueeyes Productions, Emotion Pictures, Filmhuset; Icelandic-French-Norwegian, 2002; Dolby; Color; Not rated; 109 minutes; American release date: May 16, 2003

Cast

Thórdur **Gunnar Eyjólfsson**
Ágúst **Hilmir Snær Gudnason**
Françoise **Hélène de Fougerolles**
Kristín **Kristbjörg Kjeld**
Morten **Sven Nordin**
Raghnheidour **Gudrún Gísladóttir**
Haraldur **Sigurdur Skúlason**
Áslaug **Elva Ósk Ólafsdóttir**
María **Nína Dögg Filippusdóttir**
Kata **Herdís Thorvaldsdóttir**
Teenager **Thórir Gunnar Jónsson**
Bóbó **Theódor Júlíusson**

Gudrún Gísladóttir, Nína Dögg Filippusdóttir

The Sea PHOTOS COURTESY OF PALM PICTURES

and Hjalti Rögnvaldsson (Bensó), Ellert Ingimundarson (Hannes), Magnús Ragnarsson (Agent), Erlingur Gíslason (Mangi Bö), Thröstur Leó Gunnarsson (Kalli Bumba), Kristjana Samper (Sunna), Ármann Hjörleifsson (Young Ágúst), Annetta Rut Kristjánsdóttir (Haraldur's daughter), Bjarki Birkisson, Gísli Gunnarsson (Haladur's Sons), Maria Theresa Michelsen, Heideleta A. Thorgrimsson (Cosmo Customers), Bjarni Adalsteinsson (Liquor Store Clerk), Stella I. Steinthórsdóttir (Naked Woman)

A dysfunctional family gathers at a remote Icelandic fishing village where the father hopes to convince his disinterested children to carry on his fishery after he is gone.

Vincenzo Amato, Valeria Golino, Francesco Casisa in *Respiro* PHOTO COURTESY OF SONY CLASSICS

RESPIRO

(SONY CLASSICS) Producer, Domenico Procacci; Director/Screenplay, Emanuele Crialese; Photography, Fabio Zamarion; Art Director, Beatrice Scarpato; Costumes, Eva Coen; Music, John Surman; Editor, Didier Ranz; Co-Producer, Anne-Dominique Toussaint; Associate Producer, Raphael Berdugo; a co-production of Eurimages, Fandango, Les Films des Tournelles, Medusa Produzione, Roissy Films, Rouse Films, TPS Cinema, Telepiu; Italian-French, 2002; Dolby; Color; Rated PG-13; 90 minutes; American release date: May 23, 2003

Cast

Grazia **Valeria Golino**
Pietro **Vincenzo Amato**
Pasquale **Francesco Casisa**
Marinella **Veronica D'Agostino**
Filippo **Filippo Pucillo**
Grandmother **Muzzi Loffredo**
Pier Luigi **Elio Germano**
Olivier **Avy Marciano**

In an Italian fishing village the erratic behavior of a manic depressive woman causes her husband to seek treatment, prompting the woman to run off.

TOGETHER

(UNITED ARTISTS) Producers, Ton Gang, Chen Hong; Executive Producers, Yang Buting, Yan Xiaoming, Li Bolun, Chen Kaige; Director, Chen Kaige; Screenplay, Chen Kaige, Xue Xiaolu; Co-Producers, Han Sanping, Huang Jianxin; Photography, Kim Hyungkoo; Designers, Cao Jiuping, Liu Luyi; Costumes, Hah Yongsoo; Music, Zhao Lin; Editor, Zhou Ying; Violin Solos, Li Chuanyun; a Moonstone Entertainment presentation of a Four Production Company of China Film Group Corporation, Century Hero Film Investment Co. Ltd., China Movie Channel, 21st Century Shengkai Film Company production; Chinese, 2002; Dolby; Color; Rated PG; 118 minutes; American release date: May 30, 2003

Cast
Xiaochun **Tang Yun**
Liu Cheng **Liu Peiqi**
Lili **Chen Hong**
Professor Jiang **Wang Zhiwen**
Professor Yu **Chen Kaige**
Lili's Lover **Cheng Qiang**
Lin Yu **Zhang Qing**
Debao **Liu Bing**
Mrs. Yu **Kim Hairi**
Tang Rong **Li Chuanyun**

Liu Peiqui, Tang Yun

Tang Yun, Chen Kaige

Liu Cheng moves to Beijing, determined to get the best teachers for his son, a 13-year-old violin prodigy for whom he is ready to sacrifice all.

Tang Yun

Tang Yun, Chen Hong   PHOTOS COURTESY OF UNITED ARTISTS

WHALE RIDER

(NEWMARKET) Producers, Tim Sanders, Frank Hübner, John Barnett; Executive Producers, Bill Gavin, Linda Goldstein Knowlton; Director/Screenplay, Niki Caro; Based on the novel by Witi Ihimaera; Co-Producer, Reinhard Brundig; Associate Producer, Witi Ihimaera; Photography, Leon Narbey; Designer, Grant Major; Costumes, Kristy Cameron; Music, Lisa Gerard; Editor, David Coulson; Casting, Diana Rowan; a co-production of ApolloMedia, New Zealand Film Commission, New Zealand Film Production Fund, New Zealand On Air, Pandora Filmproduktion GmbH, South Pacific Pictures; New Zealand-German; Dolby; Super 35 Widescreen; Color; Rated PG-13; 101 minutes; American release date: June 6, 2003

Rawiri Paratene

A young girl defies her stubborn grandfather to fulfill her destiny.

This film received an Oscar nomination for actress (Keisha Castle-Hughes).

Keisha Castle-Hughes

Cliff Curtis

Cast

Paikea "Pai" Apirana **Keisha Castle-Hughes**
Koro Apirana **Rawiri Paratene**
Nanny Flowers Apirana **Vicky Haughton**
Porourangi Apirana **Cliff Curtis**
Uncle Rawiri Apirana **Grant Roa**
Hemi **Mana Taumaunu**
Shilo **Rachel House**
Willie **Taungaroa Emile**
Dog **Tammy Davis**
Maka **Mabel Wharekawa-Burt**
Miro **Rawinia Clarke**
Miss Parata **Tahei Simpson**
Rewi **Roimata Tamana**
Rehua Apirana **Elizabeth Skeen**
Jake **Tyronne White**
Ropata **Taupua Whakataka-Brightwell**

and Tenia McClutchie-Mita (Wiremu), Peter Patuwai (Bubba), Rutene Spooner (Parekura), Riccardo Davis (Maui), Apiata Whangaparita-Apanui (Henare), John Sumner (Obstetrician), Sam Woods (Young Rawiri Apirana), Pura Tangira (Ace), Jane O'Kane (Anne), Aumuri Parata-Haua (Baby Paikea)

Lawrence Chou, Lee Sin-Je PHOTO COURTESY OF PALM PICTURES

THE EYE

(PALM PICTURES) Producers, Lawrence Cheng, Peter Chan Ho-sun; Executive Producers, Eric Tsang, Allan Fung, Daniel Yun; Co-Producer, Udom Piboonlapudom; Associate Producer, Jojo Hui; Directors/Editors, Pang Brothers (Danny Pang, Oxide Pang); Screenplay, Jojo Hui, Pang Brothers; Photography, Decha Srimantra; Art Directors, Simon So, Kritapas Suttinet; Costumes, Jittima Kongsri; Music, Orange Music; Digital Visual Effects Supervisor, Frankie Chung; an Applause Pictures/Raintree Pictures presentation of an Applause Pictures production; Hong Kong, 2002; Dolby; Color; Not rated; 98 minutes; American release date: June 6, 2003

Cast
Wong Ka-man **Lee Sin-je**
Lo Wah **Lawrence Chou**
Chiu Wai-Ling **Chutcha Rujinanon**
Mun's Sister **Candy Lo**
Dr. Eak **Pierre Png**
Dr. Lo **Edmund Chen**
Ying Ying **So Yut-Lai**
Mun's Grandmother **Ko Yin-Ping**
Ling's Mother **Wang Sue-Yuen**
Mr. Ching **Ben Yuen**

and Florence Wu (Nurse), Miyuki Lau (Wah's Secretary), Poon Ming (Boy with Cap), Cub Chin (Boy's Father), Winson Yip (Taoist), Wu Tian-Nan (Calligraphy Teacher), Ho Si-Won (Ghost in the Restaurant), Lau Yuk-Ha (Waitress), Jim Pui-Ho (Boy in the Car Accident), Sungwien Cummee (Ghost in the Elevator), Tassanana Nuntasaree (Ling, aged 4), Damrongwiseeatpanich (Ling, aged 8)

After a violinist undergoes a corneal transplant to restore the sight she lost as a child she begins experiencing terrifying visions.

THE HARD WORD

(LIONS GATE) Producer, Al Clark; Executive Producers, Gareth Jones, Hilary Davis; Director/Screenplay, Scott Roberts; Photography, Brian Breheny; Designer, Paddy Reardon; Costumes, Terry Ryan; Editor, Martin Connor; Music, David Thrussell; Casting, Ann Robinson; an Alibi Films International and Australian Film Finance Corporation presentation of a Wildheart production; Australian-British; Dolby; Super 35 Widescreen; Cinevex; Color; Rated R; 102 minutes; American release date: June 13, 2003

Rachel Griffiths, Guy Pearce PHOTO COURTESY OF LIONS GATE

Cast
Dale Twentyman **Guy Pearce**
Carol **Rachel Griffiths**
Frank **Robert Taylor**
Shane Twentyman **Joel Edgerton**
Mal Twentyman **Damien Richardson**
Jane **Rhondda Findleton**
Pamela **Kate Atkinson**
Kelly **Vince Colosimo**
O'Riordan **Paul Sonkkila**
Paul **Kim Gyngell**
Tarzan **Dorian Nikono**

and Stephen Whittaker (Rawson), Torquil Neilson (Mick), Don Bridges (Mick), Don Bridges (Doug), Doug Bowles (Bill), Greg Fleet (Tony), Ross Daniels (Dave), Peter Regan (Governor), Roger Neave (Doctor), Jason Gilchrist (Weightlifter), Jasper Bagg (Prisoner in Visiting Room), Niniane Le Page (Prisoner's Wife), Beth Buchanan (Nurse), Frank Kennedy (Sick Prisoner), Tony Jones (Newsreader), Louise Crawford, Mischelle Radford (Waitresses), Kerry Coyle (Norbert), Colwyn Roberts (Bookie), Georgie Bax (Sheryl), Leanne McCulloch (Massage Woman), Nash Edgerton (Bank Guard), Aris Gounaris, James Shaw, James Charters (Hotel Security Guards), Gary Rens, Wasim Sabra, Phil Pollard, Tahu Marumaru (Security Guards), Marc Calderazzo (Prison Guard)

A trio of imprisoned criminal brothers are enlisted by a corrupt lawyer and two crooked cooks to help them carry out robberies while still behind bars.

Helena Bonham Carter, Paul Bettany PHOTO COURTESY OF THINKFILM

THE HEART OF ME

(THINKFILM) Producer, Martin Pope; Executive Producers, David M. Thompson, Tracey Scoffield, Steve Christian, Keith Evans, Paul Federbush, Shebnem Askin; Director, Thaddeus O'Sullivan; Screenplay, Lucinda Coxon; Based on the novel *The Echoing Grove* by Rosamond Lehmann; Photography, Gyula Pados; Designer, Michael Carlin; Costumes, Sheena Napier; Music, Nicholas Hooper; Editor, Alex Mackie; Casting, Kate Rhodes James; an MP production, presented in association with Take 3, Isle of Man Film Commission, Pandora; British-German; Dolby; Deluxe color; Rated R; 96 minutes; American release date: June 13, 2003

Cast

Dinah **Helena Bonham Carter**
Madeleine **Olivia Williams**
Rickie **Paul Bettany**
Mrs. Burkett **Eleanor Bron**
Anthony **Luke Newberry**
Jack **Tom Ward**
Betty **Gillian Hanna**
Charles **Andrew Havill**
Bridie **Alison Reid**
Sylvia **Kathryn Tennant-Maw**

and Rebecca Charles (Miss Matthews), John Rowe (Drysdale), Shaughan Seymour (Jeweller), Simon Day (Hospital Doctor), Jenny Howe (Nurse), Rosie Ede (Landlady), Rosie Bonham-Carter (Clarissa), Paul Ridley (Policeman)

Rickie falls in love with his wife Madeleine's younger sister Dinah and embarks on an affair with the free-spirited bohemian that has dire repercussions for all.

JET LAG

(MIRAMAX) Producer, Alain Sarde; Executive Producer, Christine Gozlan; Director, Danièle Thompson; Screenplay, Danièle Thompson, Christopher Thompson; Photography, Patrick Blossier; Designer, Michéle Abbé; Costumes, Elisabeth Tavernier; Music, Eric Serra; Editor, Sylvie Landra; Casting, Gérard Moulévrier; a co-production of Les Films Alain Sarde, TF1 Films Production, Pathe Ltd. with the participation of Canal+; French-British; Dolby; Super 35 Widescreen; Color; Rated R; 91 minutes; American release date: June 13, 2003

Cast

Rose **Juliette Binoche**
Félix **Jean Reno**
Sergio **Sergi López**
The Doctor **Scali Delpeyrat**
Air France Attendant **Karine Belly**
Félix's Father **Raoul Billerey**
Roissy Passenger **Nadège Beausson-Diagne**
Ground Hostess **Alice Taglioni**
The Concierge **Jérôme Keen**

and Sébastien Lalanne (The Barman), Michel Lepriol (The Waiter), M'bembo (Post Office Employee), Laurence Colussi, Lucy Harrison, Rebecca Steele, Thiam (Hostesses)

Rose, a flaky beautician, and Félix, a wearied businessman, meet and fall in love during a flight delay at the Roissy-Charles de Gaulle Airport in Paris.

Juliette Binoche, Jean Reno

Jean Reno, Juliette Binoche PHOTOS COURTESY OF MIRAMAX

Cillian Murphy

28 DAYS LATER...

(FOX SEARCHLIGHT) Producer, Andrew MacDonald; Director, Danny Boyle; Screenplay, Alex Garland; Photography, Anthony Dod Mantle; Designer, Mark Tildesley; Costumes, Rachel Fleming; Music, John Murphy; Editor, Chris Gill; Make-Up Designer, Sallie Jaye; Line Producer, Robert How; Casting, Gail Stevens; Presented in association with DNA Films and The Film Council; British-U.S.-French, 2002; Dolby; Deluxe color; Rated R; 112 minutes; American release date: June 27, 2003

Cast
Jim **Cillian Murphy**
Selena **Naomie Harris**
Major Henry West **Christopher Eccleston**
Hannah **Megan Burns**
Frank **Brendan Gleeson**
Infected Priest **Toby Sedgwick**
Mark **Noah Huntley**
Jim's Father **Christopher Dunne**
Jim's Mother **Emma Hitching**
Mr. Bridges **Alexander Delamere**
Mr. Bridges' Daughter **Kim McGarrity**
Infected Kid **Justin Hackney**
Private Clifton **Luke Mably**
Sergeant Farrell **Stuart McQuarrie**
Corporal Mitchell **Ricci Harnett**
Private Jones **Leo Bill**

and Junior Laniyan (Private Bell), Ray Panthaki (Private Bedford),Alex Palmer, Bindu de Stoppani, Jukka Hiltunen (Activists), Sanjay Rambaruth (Private Davis), Marvin Campbell (Private Mailer), Adrian Christopher, Richard Dwyer, Nick Ewans, Terry John, Paul Kasey, Sebastian Knapp, Nicholas James Lewis, Jenni Lush, Tristan Matthiae, Jeff Rann, Joelle Simpson, Al Stokes, Steen Young (Featured Infected)

28 days after a deadly virus has wiped out most of the population, a cycle courier awakens from a coma in a deserted hospital and begins to search for other survivors, trying to avoid contact with the zombie-like "infected."

Cillian Murphy, Naomie Harris   PHOTOS COURTESY OF FOX SEARCHLIGHT

Ludivine Sagnier, Charlotte Rampling

SWIMMING POOL

(FOCUS) Producers, Olivier Delbosc, Marc Missonnier; Co-Producer, Timothy Burrill; Director, François Ozon; Screenplay, François Ozon, Emmanuele Bernheim; Photography, Yorick Le Saux; Art Director, Wouter Zoon; Costumes, Pascaline Chavanne; Music, Philippe Rombi; Editor, Monica Coleman; Casting, Sarah Bird, Antoinette Boulat; a Canal+, Fidelite Productions, France 2 Cinema, Gimages, Headforce production; French-British; Dolby; Color; Rated R; 102 minutes; American release date: July 2, 2003

Cast

Sarah Morton **Charlotte Rampling**
Julie **Ludivine Sagnier**
John Bosload **Charles Dance**
Marcel **Marc Fayolle**
Franck **Jean-Marie Lamour**
Marcel's Daughter **Mireille Mossé**
First Man **Michel Fau**
Second Man **Jean-Claude Lecas**
Waitress at Cafe **Emilie Gavois-Kahn**
Old Man **Erarde Forestali**
Julia **Lauren Farrow**
Terry Long **Sebastian Harcombe**
Lady on Train **Frances Cuka**
Sarah's Father **Keith Yeates**
Bosload's Secretary **Tricia Aileen**
Pub Barman **Glen Davies**

Experiencing writer's block, mystery author Sarah Morton borrows her publisher's summer house in the South of France to work on her latest novel, only to have this serene atmosphere disrupted by the arrival of her publisher's reckless, neglected daughter Julie.

Charles Dance, Charlotte Rampling

Ludivine Sagnier

Jean-Marie Lamour, Charlotte Rampling, Ludivine Sagnier PHOTOS COURTESY OF FOCUS

MADAME SATÃ

(WELLSPRING) Produces, Mauricio Andrade Ramos, Isabel Diegues; Executive Producers, Walter Salles, Donald K. Ranvaud; Co-Producers, Juliette Renaud, Marc Beauchamps, Vincent Marval; Director/Screenplay, Karim Ainouz; Photography, Walter Carvalho; Designer, Marcos Pedroso; Costumes, Rita Murtinho; Music, Marcos Suzano, Sacha Ambak; Editor, Isabela Monteiro de Castro; Casting, Luiz Henrique Norueira; a Dominant 7, Lumiere, VideoFilmes, Wild Bunch production; Brazilian-French, 2002; Dolby; Color; Not rated; 105 minutes; American release date: July 9, 2003

Cast
Joao Francisco dos Santos (Madame Satã) **Lazaro Ramos**
Laurita **Marcelia Cartaxo**
Taboo **Flavio Bauraqui**
Renatinho **Felipe Marques**
Amador **Emiliano Quieroz**
Vitoria dos Anjos **Renata Sorrah**

and Giovana Barbosa (Firmina), Ricardo Blat (Jose), Guilherme Piva (Alvaro), Marcelo Valle (Commissioner), Floriano Peixoto (Gregario), Gero Camilo (Agapito), Ora Figueiredo (Policeman)

The true story of Brazilian drag performer and hustler Joao Francisco dos Santos and the denizens of the notorious Lapa district of Rio de Janeiro.

Albert Illuz, Tchelet Semel

THE HOLY LAND

(CAVU PICTURES) Producers, Ran Bogin, Udi Yerushalmi; Executive Producers, Michael Sergio Isil Bagdadi; Director/Screenplay, Eitan Gorlin; Photography, Nils Kenaston; Costumes, Laura Dinolsky; Editors, Josh Apter, Yair Elazar; Music, Chris Cunningham; Associate Producer, Arnon Regular; Co-Producer, Saul Stein; Casting, Bruria Albeck; a Romeo Salta Films production; Israeli, 2001; Color; Not rated; 96 minutes; American release date: July 11, 2003

Lazaro Ramos in *Madame Satã* PHOTO COURTESY OF WELLSPRING

Cast
Mendy **Oren Rehany**
Sasha **Tchelet Semel**
Mike **Saul Stein**
The Exterminator **Arie Moskuna**
Razi **Albert Illuz**
Mendy's Mother **Liat Bayn**
Mendy's Father **Yehoyachim Friedlander**
Prof. Milan **Mosko Alkalay**
Daryl **Lupo Berkowitz**
Reuven **Harel Nof**
Icho **Icho Avital**

and Jenny Flysher (Stanislav, the Boss), Gregury Tai (Boris, the Goon), Igor Mirkorbanov (Vladimir, the Piano Teacher), Julia Gilinski (Monika), Reb Nochom (Alon Dahan), Arie Hasfari (Jamal), Rav Shmuel (Singing Rabbi)

A 19-year-old yeshiva student becomes infatuated with a lap dancer at a Tel Aviv strip club.

Tchelet Semel, Oren Rehany PHOTOS COURTESY OF CAVU PICTURES

THE CUCKOO

(SONY CLASSICS) Producer, Sergei Zhegalov; Director/Screenplay, Alexander Rogozhkin; Photography, Andrei Zhegalov; Designer, Vladimir Svetorzarov; Costumes, Marina Nikolaeva; Music, Dmitry Pavlov; Editor, Julia Roumyantseva; a CTB Film Company production; Russian, 2002; Dolby; Color; Rated PG-13; 104 minutes; American release date: July 11, 2003

Cast
Anni **Anni-Kristiina Juuso**
Veiko **Ville Haapasalo**
Ivan **Viktor Bychkov**

In Northern Finland during World War II, a Finnish private, a Russian captain, and a Saami woman are all thrown together by circumstances, forcing them to try to get along and communicate although they don't speak each others' languages.

Ville Haapasalo, Anni-Kristiina Juuso in *The Cuckoo* PHOTO COURTESY OF SONY CLASSICS

Jean-Pierre Bacri, Émilie Dequenne

Émilie Dequenne

THE HOUSEKEEPER (UNE FEMME DE MÉNAGE)

(PALM PICTURES) Producer/Director/Screenplay, Claude Berri; Based on the novel by Christian Oster; Executive Producer, Pierre Grunstein; Photography, Eric Gautier; Designer, Joang Than At; Costumes, Corinne Jorry; Music, Frederic Botton; Editor, Francois Gedigier; Casting, Gerard Moulevrier; a co-production of Hirsch, Pathe, Renn Productions; French, 2002; Dolby; Super 35 Widescreen; Color; Not rated; 91 minutes; American release date: July 11, 2003

Cast
Jacques **Jean-Pierre Bacri**
Laura **Émilie Dequenne**
Claire **Brigitte Catillon**
Ralph **Jacques Frantz**
Helene **Axelle Abbadie**

and Catherine Breillat (Constance), Apollinaire Louis-Philippe Doge (Ernest), Almaric Gérard (Julien), Nathalie Boutefeu (Young Girl at Concert), Djura (Chanteuse), Xavier Maly (Jacques' Assistant)

Jacques, still trying to recover from a breakup with his wife, goes looking for a housekeeper to put his apartment in order and gets a reply from an attractive young woman, who asks if she can move in as well.

Jean-Pierre Bacri, Émilie Dequenne PHOTOS COURTESY OF PALM PICTURES

KM.0

(TLA) Producer, Gianni Ricci; Executive Producers, Stefan Nicoll, Marc Cases, Pastora Delgado, Rafael Alvero; Directors/Screenplay, Juan Luis Iborra, Yolanda García Serrano; Photography, Ángel Luis Fernández; Art Director, Ana Alvargonzález; Costumes, Josune Lasa; Editor, José Salcedo; Music, Joan Bibiloni; a co-production of Cuarteto Producciones Cinematográficas, Media Park, Universal Pictures Spain; Spanish, 2000; Dolby; Color; Rated R; 108 minutes; American release date: July 11, 2003

Miguel García, Víctor Ullate

Elisa Matilla, Carlos Fuentes

Silke Hornillos Klein, Tristan Ulloa PHOTOS COURTESY OF TLA

Concha Velasco, Jesus Cabrero

Merce Pons, Georges Corraface

Cast

Marga **Concha Velasco**
Gerardo **Georges Corraface**
Amor **Silke**
Pedro **Carlos Fuentes**
Silvia **Mercè Pons**
Sergio **Alberto San Juan**
Tatiana **Elisa Matilla**

and Armando del Río (Máximo), Miguel García (Benjamín), Jesús Cabrero (Miguel), Víctor Ullate, Jr. (Bruno), Cora Tiedra (Roma), Tristán Ulloa (Mario), Roberto Álamo, Roberto Álvarez (Marido Marga), Julia Altares (Mujer Carterista), Carmen Balagué (Girl at Km.0), José Bernal (Joven Religioso), Carlos Blanes (Attractive Girl at Km.0), Gonzalo Garralda (Coach Train Conductor), Silvia Gil (Another Attractive Girl), Juan Luis Iborra (Tatiana's Client), José Mellado (Ladron Copilot), María Eugenia Mur (Friend of Girl at Km.0), Joaquín Oristrell, Claudio Sierra (Dependente Joyeria), Ana Pascual (Mujer Joyeria), José Salcedo (Taxista), Rosario Santesmases (Silvia's Friend)

The love lives of fourteen different people interconnect during one August afternoon around Madrid's Plaza del Sol.

Rose Byrne, Romola Garai

Marc Blucas, Rose Byrne

Bill Nighy, Sinéad Cusak PHOTOS COURTESY OF SAMUEL GOLDWYN FILMS

I CAPTURE THE CASTLE

(SAMUEL GOLDWYN FILMS) Producer, David Parfitt; Executive Producers, David M. Thompson, Anant Singh; Director, Tim Fywell; Screenplay, Heidi Thomas; Based on the novel by Dodie Smith; Co-Producer, Mark Cooper; Photography, Richard Greatrex; Designer, John-Paul Kelly; Costumes, Charlotte Walter; Editor, Roy Sharman; Music, Dario Marianelli; Casting, Kate Rhodes James; a Distant Horizon, BBC Films presentaiton in association with The Isle of Man Film Commission and Baker Street/Take 3 Partnerships of a Trademark Films/BBC Films production; British; Dolby; Super 35 Widescreen; Color; Rated R; 97 minutes; American release date: July 11, 2003

Romola Garai, Henry Thomas

Cast

Simon Cotton **Henry Thomas**
Nei Cotton **Marc Blucas**
Rose Mortmain **Rose Byrne**
Cassandra Mortmain **Romola Garai**
James Mortmain **Bill Nighy**
Topaz Mortmain **Tara Fitzgerald**
Stephen Colley **Henry Cavill**
Mrs. Cotton **Sinéad Cusack**
Vicar **David Bamber**
Aubrey Fox-Cotton **James Faulkner**
Leda Fox-Cotton **Sarah Woodward**
Cassandra (aged 7) **Sophie Stuckey**
Mother **Helena Little**

and Florence Jones (Rose, aged 10), Harrison Ward (Thomas, aged 7) Joe Sowerbutts (Thomas), Ray De-Haan (Neighbor), Sorel Johnson (Lady in Simpsons), Dolly Wells (Fur Department Vendeuse), James Warrior (Station Master), Christopher Ettridge (Station Bystander), Jean Warren (Waitress in Cafe), Bernadette Windsor (Girl in Cafe)

Seventeen-year-old Cassandra and her family reside in a dilapitated castle, isolated from the outside world until a pair of American brothers show up claiming to have inherited the structure.

Audrey Tautou, Chiwetel Ejiofor

Audrey Tautou

Chiwetel Ejiofor, Audrey Tautou PHOTOS COURTESY OF MIRAMAX

DIRTY PRETTY THINGS

(MIRAMAX) Producers, Tracey Seaward, Robert Jones; Executive Producers, Paul Smith, David M. Thompson, Tracey Scoffield, Allon Reich, Teresa Moneo, Julie Goldstein; Director, Stephen Frears; Screenplay, Steven Knight; Photography, Chris Menges; Designer, Hugo Luczyc-Wyhowski; Costumes, Odile Dicks-Mireaux; Editor, Mick Audsley; Music, Nathan Larson; Casting, Leo Davis; a BBC Films presentation of a Celador Films production; British, 2002; Dolby; Color; Rated R; 97 minutes; American release date: July 18, 2003

Cast
Okwe **Chiwetel Ejiofor**
Senay **Audrey Tautou**
Sneaky **Sergi López**
Juliette **Sophie Okonedo**
Guo Yi **Benedict Wong**
Ivan **Zlatko Buric**
Asian Businessman **Kriss Dosanjh**
Cab Controller **Jeffery Kissoon**
Cafe Owner **Kenan Hudaverdi**
Punter **Damon Younger**
Mohammed **Paul Bhattacharjee**
Immigration Officer **Darrell D'Silva**
Shinti **Sotigui Kouyaté**
Shinti's Son **Abi Gouhad**
Hospital Cleaning Lady **Jeillo Edwards**
Pharmacy Nuse **Rita Hamill**
Pharmacist **Ron Stenner**

Audrey Tautou, Sergi López

and Jemanesh Solomon (Shinti's Daughter-in-Law), Naomi Simpson (Shinti's Granddaughter), Barber Ali (Sweatshop Foreman), Jean-Philippe Ecoffey (Jean-Luc), Yusuf Altin (Sweatshop Boy), Fisun Burgess (Factory Worker), Sabina Michael (German Woman), Michael Mellinger (German Man), Norma Dumezweni (Celia), Adrian Scarborough (The Doctor)

Okwe, an immigrant doctor in London who earns extra money as a receptionist at London's Hotel Baltic, is horrified to discover that the manager is running a trade in illegal human organs.

JOHNNY ENGLISH

(UNIVERSAL) Producers, Tim Bevan, Eric Fellner, Mark Huffam; Director, Peter Howitt; Screenplay, Neal Purvis, Robert Wade, William Davies; Photography, Remi Adefarasan; Designer, Chris Seagers; Costumes, Jill Taylor; Editor, Robin Sales; Music, Edward Shearmur; Song "A Man for All Seasons" by Robbie Williams, Zimmer/performed by Robbie Williams; Co-Producers, Debra Hayward, Liza Chasin, Jo Burn; Associate Producer, Chris Clark; Hair & Makeup Designer, Graham Johnston; Visual Effects Supervisor, Peter Chiang; Casting, Priscilla John; a Studiocanal presentation of a Working Title production; Dolby; British-U.S.; Dolby; Color; Rated PG; 86 minutes; American release date: July 18, 2003

Ben Miller, Rowan Atkinson, Natalie Imbruglia

An inept junior intelligence worker is called on to fill in for the British Secret Service's late Agent Number One in order to stop a criminal mastermind from stealing the crown jewels.

Rowan Atkinson

Cast

Johnny English **Rowan Atkinson**
Lorna Campbell **Natalie Imbruglia**
Bough **Ben Miller**
Pacal Sauvage **John Malkovich**
Exotic Woman **Tasha de Vasconcelos**
Agent One **Greg Wise**
Carlos Vendetta **Douglas McFerran**
Dieter Klein **Steve Nicolson**
Official at Funeral **Terence Harvey**
Prime Minister **Kevin R. McNally**
Pegasus **Tim Pigottt-Smith**
Pegasus' Secretary **Nina Young**
Sir Anthony Chevenix **Rowland Davies**
Snobby Woman **Philippa Fordham**
Roger **Tim Berrington**
Assailant **Simon Bernstein**
Hearse Driver **Martin Lawton**

John Malkovich, Rowan Atkinson

and Neville Phillips (Priest), Oliver Ford Davies (Archbishop of Canterbury), Takuya Matsumoto (Sushi Waiter), Peter Tenn (Sushi Bar Customer), Sam Beazley (Elderly Man), Kevin Moore (Doctor), Faruk Pruti (Truth Serum Guard), Marc Danbury (Guard), Jack Raymond (French Reception Waiter), Jenny Galloway (Foreign Secretary), Bond (String Quartet), Chris Tarrant (Radio Announcer), James Greene (Scottish Bishop), Clive Graham (Welsh Bishop), Trevor McDonald (Newscaster)

Rowan Atkinson, Oliver Ford Davies PHOTOS COURTESY OF UNIVERSAL

THE EMBALMER

(FIRST RUN FEATURES) Producer, Domenico Procacci; Executive Producer, Luigi Lagrasta; Director, Matteo Garrone; Screenplay, Ugo Chiti, Matteo Garrone, Massimo Gaudioso; Photography, Marco Onorato; Art Director, Paolo Bonfini; Costumes, Francesca Leoneff; Music, Banda Osiris; Editor, Marco Spolenti; a Fandango production; Italian, 2002; Dolby; Cinemascope; Technicolor; Not rated; 104 minutes; American release date: July 18, 2003

Cast

Peppino **Ernesto Mahieux**
Diego **Valerio Foglia Manzillo**
Deborah **Elisabetta Rocchetti**
Deborah's Mother **Lina Bernardi**
Deborah's Father **Pietro Biondi**
Patron **Bernardino Terracciano**
Manuela **Marcella Granito**

Peppino, a short, homely taxidermist, develops a crush on handsome young Diego and invites him to join his business, only to find his new partner's attention diverted by the strong-willed Deborah.

Elisabetta Rocchetti, Valerio Foglia Manzillo, Ernesto Mahieux in *The Embalmer*
PHOTO COURTESY OF FIRST RUN FEATURES

Russell Dykstra, Kick Gurry, Pia Miranda in *Garage Days* PHOTOS COURTESY OF FOX SEARCHLIGHT

Pia Miranda, Kick Gurry, Russell Dykstra, Chris Sadrinna, Brett Stiller in *Garage Days*

GARAGE DAYS

(FOX SEARCHLIGHT) Producers, Alex Proyas, Topher Dow; Director, Alex Proyas; Screenplay, Alex Proyas, Dave Warner, Michael Udesky; Story, Alex Proyas, Dave Warner; Co-Producer, Adrienne Read; Photography, Simon Duggan; Designer, Michael Philips; Costumes, Jackline Sassine; Music, Anthony Partos, David McCormack, Andrew Lancaster; Editor, Richard Learoyd; Casting, Greg Apps; an Australian Film Finance Corp., Mystery Clock Cinema; Australian; Dolby; Color; Rated R: 105 minutes; American release date: July 18, 2003

Cast

Freddy **Kick Gurry**
Kate **Maya Stange**
Tanya **Pia Miranda**
Bruno **Russell Dykstra**
Joe **Brett Stiller**
Lucy **Chris Sadrinna**
Kevin **Andy Anderson**

and Marton Csokas (Shad Kern), Yvette Duncan (Angie), Tiriel Mora (Thommo), Holly Brisley (Scarlet), Matthew Le Nevez (Toby), Dave Cotsios, Chris "Skinner" MacGuire, Scott Ryper (Sprimp), Natalie Jain (Destiny), Gunther Berghofer (Tanya's Father), Anne Grigg (Tonya's Mother), William Sayer (Little Freddie), Rashpal Singh (Swami), Peter Cudlipp, Sandra Campbell (Music Teachers), Vanessa Williams (Freddy's Mum), James Lugton (Freddy's Dad), Johnaton Devoy, Ian "Cut Snake" Thomas, April Hind, Kurt Eckhart (Punk Band), Emma Lung (Freddy's Babysitter), Benjamin O'Reilly (Impatient Yuppie), Nicholas Gibbs (Freddy's Co-Worker), Greg Apps (Unversity Professor), Ben Fletcher (Student), Shirley Sheppard (Granny), Derek Tong (Pharmacist), Ali Mutch (Busty Young Blonde), Jimmy Costas (Very Large Boyfriend), Bill Bader (Elderly Neighbor), Kimble Rendall (Suicidal Man), Tanya Ginori (Cyring Woman), Michael Kazonis (Dumpy Guy), Rohan Nichol (Young Pub Manager), David McCormack, Andrew Lancaster, Dylan McCormack, Emma Tom, Ivan Jordan (York Pub Band), Petrina Buckley (Young Woman), Sigourney Gray (Lucy's Woman), Jabba (Rockumentarian)

A second-rate garage band from Sydney, Australia, attempts to break into the big-time music scene.

Emmanuelle Laborit in Segment #2 of *September 11*

SEPTEMBER 11

(EMPIRE) Artistic Director, Alain Brigan; : Producers, Jacques Perrin, Nicolas Mauvernay; Executive Producer, Jean de Tregomain; from Galatée Films, Studio Canal; French, 2002; Dolby; Color; Not rated; 135 minutes; American release date: July 18, 2003. Eleven short films, each 11 minutes, nine seconds and one frame long, commenting on the September 11, 2001 terrorist attacks on the United States.

#1: Director/Screenplay, Samira Makhmalbaf; Photography, Ebrahim Ghafori; Editor, Mohsen Makhmalbaf; Music, Mohamad Rezadarvishi.

Cast: Maryam Karimi (The School Teacher), Mohamada Dolati, Agelem Habibi, Esmat Vahedi, Ameneh Banizaden, Razieh Jafari, Hassan Rezai, Najbeh Habibi (The Children)

#2: Executive Producer, Tania Zazulinsky; Director/Screenplay, Claude Lelouch; Photography, Pierre Uytterhoeven; Music, Jean-Charles Martel; Editor, Pierre-William Glenn.

Cast: Emmanuelle Laborit (Deaf and Dumb Woman), Jérome Horry (Tour Guide)

#3: Executive Producers, Gabriel Khoury, Mariane Khoury; Director/Screenplay, Youssef Chahine; Photography, Mohsen Nasr; Editor, Rashida Abd Elsalam.

Cast: Nour Elsherif (Youssef Chahine), Ahmed Seif Eldine (Donald "Danny" Donahue, the GI), Sanaa Younes (Mother), Ahmed Fouad Selim (Father), Maher Essam (Palestinian), Eveline Selim (Reporter)

#4: Executive Producer, Cedomir Kolar; Director/Screenplay, Danis Tanovic; Photography, Mustafa Mustafic; Music, "Sto te Nema"; Editor, Monique Rysselnick.

Cast: Dzana Pinjo (Selma), Aleksandar Seksan (Nedim), Tatiana Sojic (Hanka), Ejla Bavcic (Lecturer)

#5: Executive Producer, Nicolas Cand; Director/Screenplay, Idrissa Ouedrago; Photography, Luc Drion; Music, Salif Keita, Manu Dibango; Editor, Julia Gregory.

Cast: Lionel Zizreel Guire (Adama), René Aimé Bassinga (Ibrahim), Lionel

Ga'l Folikoue (Ga'l), Rodrigue Andre Idani (Rodrigue), Alex Matial Traore (Alex), Marc (Bin Laden), Hypolite T. Ouangrawa (Adama's Uncle), Justine Sawadogo (Adama's Aunt), Haoua Ouatara (Adama's Mother), Milla S. Saturnin (Airport Policeman), Oumar Barou Quedraogo (Rodrigue's Father)

#6: Executive Producer, Rebecca O'Brien; Director, Ken Loach; Screenplay, Paul Laverty, Vladimir Vega; Photography, Noel Willoughby, Peter Hellmich, Jorge Muller Silva; Music, Vladimir Vega; Editor, Jonathan Morris.

Cast: Vladimir Vega.

#7: Executive Producers, Palayo Gutierrez, Shelly Townsend; Director/Screenplay, Alejandro González Iñárritu; Music, Gustavo Santaolalla, Osvaldo Golijov; Editors, Robert Duffy, Kim Bica.

#8: Executive Producer, Laurent Truchot; Director, Amos Gitai; Screenplay, Amos Gitai, Marejos Sanselme; Photography, Yoav Kosh; Editor, Kobi Netanel.

Cast: Keren Mor (The Reporter), Liron Levo (Liron Liboh) Tomer Russo (The Ambulance Man)

#9: Executive Producers, Lydia Dean Pilcher, Emily Gardiner; Director, Mira Nair; Screenplay, Sabrina Shawan; Photography, Declan Quinn; Music, "Ali Maula Ali"; Editor, Allyson C. Johnson.

Cast: Tanvi Azmi (Talat Hamdani), Kapil Bawa (Salim Hamdani), Taleb Adlah (Adnaan Hamdani), Talat Hamdani (Taani), Robert Reardon (Mr. Bonner), Neil Mooney (Sylvia Franko), George Sheffey, Maryann Towne (FBI Agents), Suleman Din (Salman Hamdani)

#10: Executive Producer, Jon C. Scheide; Director/Screenplay, Sean Penn; Photography, Samuel Bayer; Music, Heitor Pereira, Michael Brook; Editor, Jay Cassidy.

Cast: Ernest Borgnine (Old Man).

#11: Executive Producers, Nobuyuki Kaiikawa, Catherine Dussart, Masato Shinada, Masamishi Sawada; Director, Shohei Imamura; Screenplay, Daisuke Tengan; Photography, Masakazu Oka, Toshihiro Seino; Music, Tara Iwashiro; Editor, Hajime Okayasu.

Cast: Tomoro Taguchi (Yukichi Furuhashi), Kumiko Aso (Sae Furuhashi), Akira Emoto (Sakichi Furuhashi), Mitsuko Baisho (Kayo Furuhashi), Kazuo Kitamura (Village Mayor), Testuro Tanba (Bonze)

Segment #5 of *September 11* PHOTOS COURTESY OF EMPIRE

Leon Robinson, Joaquin Phoenix, Michael Pena

BUFFALO SOLDIERS

(MIRAMAX) Producers, Rainer Grupe, Ariane Moody; Executive Producers, Paul Webster, James Schamus, Reinhard Klooss; Director, Gregor Jordan; Screenplay, Gregor Jordan, Eric Axel Weiss, Nora MacCoby; Based on the novel by Robert O'Connor; Photography, Oliver Stapleton; Designer, Steven Jones-Evans; Costumes, Odile Dicks-Mireaux; Editor, Lee Smith; Music, David Holmes; Co-Producer, Chris Thompson; Casting, Laura Rosenthal, Ali Farrell; a FilmFour presentation with Odeon Pictures in association with Good Machine International and Grosvenor Park; British-German, 2002; Dolby; Super 35 Widescreen; Technicolor; Rated R; 98 minutes; American release date: July 25, 2003

Cast

Ray Elwood **Joaquin Phoenix**
Colonel Berman **Ed Harris**
Sergeant Lee **Scott Glenn**
Robyn Lee **Anna Paquin**
Mrs. Berman **Elizabeth McGovern**
Garcia **Michael Peña**
Stoney **Leon Robinson**
Knoll **Gabriel Mann**
General Lancaster **Dean Stockwell**
Colonel Marshall **Brian Delate**
Sergeant Saad **Sheik Mahmud-Bey**
Kirschfield **Amani Gethers**
Rothfuss **Noah Margetts**
Squash **Tom Ellis**
Video **Kick Gurry**
The Turk **Haluk Bilginer**
Kimbrough **Idris Elba**
Hicks **Glenn Fitzgerald**
Walters **Kimo Wills**
Johnnie **Enoch Frost**

and Jimmie Ray Weeks (Colonel Armstrong), Roger Griffiths (Simmons), Alexis Rodney (Parsons McCovey), Josef Ostendorf (Herman), Tom George (Nerdy Young Soldier), Lars Rudolph (Courier), Paul Conway (Frank), Martin Cole (MP), Ilhami Terzi (Davood), Alexander Theodossiadis

Leon Robinson, Joaquin Phoenix, Michael Pena

Anna Paquin, Joaquin Phoenix

(Bouncer), Derek Lea, Mark Newman (Truck Drivers), David Crow (Private), Jason Rayford (Young Soldier), Gary Washington, James Battles, Leon Deavers, Gerald Jacy, Michael Johnson, John Lovett, Antonio Ruffin, Glenn Stephens, Terrence Packer (Sergeant Saad's Men)

A new top sergeant at a U.S. army base in Germany makes it his mission to trap Ray Elwood, a batallion clerk and black marketeer who has taken a shine to the sergeant's daughter.

Ed Harris, Joaquin Phoenix PHOTOS COURTESY OF MIRAMAX

MONDAYS IN THE SUN

(LIONS GATE) Producers, Elías Querejeta, Jaume Roures; Co-Producers, Jérôme Vidal, Andrea Occhipinti; Director, Fernando León de Aranoa; Screenplay, Ignacio del Moral, Fernando León Aranoa; Photography, Alfredo F. Mayo; Art Director, Julio Esteban; Costumes, Maiki Marín; Editor, Nacho Ruiz Capillas; Music, Lucio Godoy; Casting, Luis San Narciso; a Sogepaq presentation of an Elias Quarejetam and Juame Roures production, a co-production with Quo Vadis Cinema (France), Eyescreen S.R.L. (Italy), Television de Galicia S.A.; Spanish-French-Italian, 2002; Dolby; Color; Rated R; 113 minutes; American release date: July 25, 2003

Luis Tosar, Javier Bardem

Cast
Santa **Javier Bardem**
José **Luis Tosar**
Lino **José Ángel Egido**
Ana **Nieve de Medina**
Reina **Enrique Villén**
Amador **Celso Bugallo**
Rico **Joaquín Climent**
Nata **Aida Folch**
Seguei **Serge Riaboukine**
Ángela **Laura Domínguez**
Samuel **Pepo Olivia**
Lazaro **Fernando Tejero**

and Andrés Lima (Lawyer), César Cambeiro (Prosecutor), Antonio Durán (Bank Manager), Luis Castro (Shipyard Employment Officer), María Luisa Martínez (Employment Office Clerk), Casilda García (Boarding House Owner), Mónica García (Monica), Luisa Merelas (Lino's Wife), Pablo de la Fuente (Lino's Son), Belén López (Lino's Daughter), Denis Gómez (Boy on Ferry), Miguel Barines (Canning Factory Manager), Gracia Mestre (Woman in Supermarket), Lois Seaxe (Ana's Workmate), Isabel Cervino (Court Secretary), Pablo Vázquez (Child in House), Talco (Bizco)

Javier Bardem PHOTOS COURTESY OF LIONS GATE

A group of friends, left unemployed by the closing of the shipyards, find themselves becoming increasingly despondent as they attempt to find work and put their lives back on track.

THE MAGDALENE SISTERS

(MIRAMAX) Producer, Frances Higson; Executive Producers, Ed Guiney, Paul Trijbits; Director/Screenplay, Peter Mullan; Inspired by the documentary *Sex in a Cold Climate* produced and directed by Steve Humphries; Photography, Nigel Willoughby; Designer, Mark Leese; Costumes, Trisha Biggar; Music, Craig Armstrong; Editor, Colin Monie; Co-Producer, Alan J. "Willy" Wands; Line Producer, Paddy Higson; Casting, Lenny Mullan; a Scottish Screen, the Film Council and Irish Film Board/Bord Scannán na hÉireann presentation in association with Momentum Pictures, of a PFP Films, Temple Films production; British-Irish, 2002; Dolby; Color; Rated R; 120 minutes; American release date: August 1, 2003

Cast

Sister Bridget **Geraldine McEwan**
Margaret **Anne-Marie Duff**
Bernadette **Nora-Jane Noone**
Rose Dunne (Patricia) **Dorothy Duffy**
"Crispina" (Harriet) **Eileen Walsh**
Una O'Connor **Mary Murray**
Katy **Britta Smith**
Sister Jude **Frances Healy**
Sister Clementine **Eithne McGuinness**
Sister Augusta **Phyllis McMahon**
Josephine **Rebecca Walsh**

Geraldine McEwan

Nora-Jane Noone, Eileen Walsh

Nora-Jane Noone

and Eamonn Owens (Eamonn, Margaret's Brother), Chris Simpson (Brendan), Sean Colgan (Seamus), Daniel Costello (Father Fitzroy), Alison Goldie, Jemma Heath, Anita Hyslop, Leonna McGilligan, Claire McKenzie, Claire Murray, Lynsey Robson, Mariann Taylor (Dormitory Girls), Maureen Allan (Rose's Mother), Julie Austin (Theresa), Fran Brennan (Garda Sergeant), Ashley Conroy (Sonia), Deirdre Davis (Margaret's Mother), Pauline Goldsmith (Mrs. Barton), Ian Hanmore (Margaret's Father), Leanne Henderson (Amy), Tracy Kearney (Crispina's Sister), Paul McAdam, David Muldrew, Kevin Shields (Band Members at Wedding), Stephen McCole (Young Man in Car), Sean McDonough (Kevin, Margaret's Cousin), Sean Mackin (Priest at Wedding), Stephen Mallon, Jim Murray, Christopher Sheridan (Orphanage Boys), Peter

Mullan (Mr. O'Connor), Julie Nimmo (Girl with Baby), Ciaran Owen (Young Eamonn), Allan Sharpe (Archbishop), Callum Smith, McCauley Smith, Fynn Turner (Crispina's Sons), Laurie Ventry (Father Doonigan), Jim Walsh (Rose's Father)

In 1964 Ireland, three young girls, believed to be sinners, are unjustly sent to the Magdalene Asylum, where they are subjected to the harsh conditions imposed upon them by the self-righteous sisters in charge.

Dorothy Duffy, Nora-Jane Noone, Anne-Marie Duff PHOTOS COURTESY OF MIRAMAX

AND NOW...LADIES AND GENTLEMEN

(PARAMOUNT CLASSICS) Producers, Claude Lelouch, Paul Hickcock, Rick Senat; Executive Producers, Tania Zazulinsky, Jean-Paul De Vidas; Director/Screenplay, Claude Lelouch; Adaptation and Dialogue, Claude Lelouch, Pierre Leroux, Pierre Uytterhoeven; Photography, Pierre-William Glenn; Art Director, Johann George; Costumes, Pierre Béchir; Music, Michel Legrand; Lyrics, Boris Bergman, Paul Ives; Editors, Hélne de Luze, Vanessa Basté; Associate Producer, Martine Kampf-Dussart; Casting, Arlette Gordon; an L&G Productions LTD, Films 13, Gemka, France 2 Cinema, with the participation of Canal+ production; British-French 2002; Dolby; Fujicolor; Rated PG-13; 125 minutes; American release date: August 1, 2003

Cast

Valentin Valentin **Jeremy Irons**
Jane Lester **Patricia Kaas**
Thierry **Thierry Lhermitte**
Françoise **Alessandra Martines**
Madame Falconetti **Claudia Cardinale**
Dr. Larry, Pharmacist **Jean-Marie Bigard**

and Ticky Holgado (Boubou), Yvan Attal (David), Amidou (Police Inspector), Sylvie Loeillet (Soleil), Constantin Alexandrov (Monsieur Falconetti), Stéphane Ferrara (Sam Hernandez), Samuel Labarthe (Trumpet Player), Paul Freeman (English Customer), Souad Amidou (Chambermaid), Laure Mayne-Kerbrat (Jane's Friend), Grégory Reznik (Bartender), Charles Gérard (Bateay-Mouche Director), Nicholas Jones (London Jeweller), Nabil Massad (Director Jamai), Mouna Fettou (Receptionist), Patrick Braoudé (Bulgari Jeweller), Simon Bakinde (Boxing Opponent), Géraldine Danon (American Dream Waitress), Matyelok Gibbs (Old Woman, London), Adam Godley (Son of London Jeweller), David Gulliford (Young Valentin), Mehdi Elouazani (TV Journalist), Driss Faceh (Associate Inspector), Fatima Harrandi (Healer), Xavier Lecoeur (Xavier), Bernard Montiel (Bernard), Luchino Visconit di Modrone (Italian Tourist), Romula Walker (Jenny), Henry Wyndham (Auctioneer), Mohamed Bensouda (Taxi Driver), Daniela Lumbroso (Herself), Pierre-William Glenn, Boris Bergman (Motards)

A British jewel thief and a French cabaret singer, both of whom are suffering from the same potentially fatal neurological condition, are thrown together by fate.

Jeremy Irons, Patricia Kaas PHOTO COURTESY OF PARAMOUNT CLASSICS

Victoria Abril, Penelope Cruz PHOTO COURTESY OF FIRST LOOK PICTURES

DON'T TEMPT ME

(FIRST LOOK PICTURES) Producers, Eduardo Campoy, Edmundo Gil, Gerardo Herrero; Executive Producer, Edmundo Gil; Director/Screenplay, Agustín Díaz Yanes; Photography, Paco Feminina; Designer, Javier Fernández; Costumes, Sonia Grande; Editor, Jose Salcedo; Music, Bernardo Bonezzi; Spanish, 2001; Dolby; Color; Rated R; 108 minutes; American release date: August 22, 2003

Cast

Lola Nevado **Victoria Abril**
Carmen Ramos **Penélope Cruz**
Manny **Demián Bichir**
Marina D'Angelo **Fanny Ardant**
Supermarket Manager **Juan Echanove**
Davenport **Gael García Bernal**
Police Chief **Emilio Gutiérrez**
Police Officer **Cristina Marcos**
Nancy **Gemma Jones**
Eduardo **Bruno Bichir**
Pili **Elena Anaya**
Henry **Peter McDonald**

and Alicia Sánchez (Checkout Girl), Luis Tosar (Police Officer), Elsa Pataky (Waitress in Hell), Ángel Alcázar (Encargado Supemercado), Paz Gómez (Cajera Joven), Mercedes Arbizu (Cajera #1), Vincenta N'Dongo (Checkout Girl), Monstre Garcia Romeu (Cajera Embarazada), Peter Yapp (Inferno Man), Charlie Lázaro (Police), Pilar Bardem (Manny's Mother), Javier Bardem

An angel from Heaven and an operative from Hell are sent to earth to win over the soul of a punch-drunk prizefighter.

THE MEDALLION

(SCREEN GEMS/TRISTAR) Producer/Story/Original Characters, Alfred Cheung; Director, Gordon Chan; Screenplay, Bennett Joshua Davlin, Alfred Cheung, Gordon Chan, Paul Wheeler, Bey Logan; Executive Producers, Jackie Chan, Albert Yeung, Willie Chan; Co-Producers, Candy Leung, Tim Kwok; Co-Executive Producer, Bill Borden; Action Director, Sammo Hung; Line Producer, Rick Nathanson; Photography, Arthur Wong; Designer, Joseph C. Nemec III; Costumes, Grania Preston; Editor, Don Brochu; Music, Adrian Lee; a Golden Port Production Limited production, a Jackie Chan production, presented in association with Emperor Multimedia Group; Hong Kong-U.S.; Dolby; Super 35 Widescreen; Color; Rated PG-13; 88 minutes; American release date: August 22, 2003

Lee Evans, Jackie Chan

Claire Forlani, Jackie Chan PHOTOS COURTESY OF SCREEN GEMS/TRISTAR

Cast

Eddie Yang **Jackie Chan**
Arthur Watson **Lee Evans**
Nicole James **Claire Forlani**
Snakehead **Julian Sands**
Commander Hammerstock-Smythe **John Rhys-Davies**
Lester **Anthony Wong**
Charlotte Watson **Christy Chung**
Giscard **Johann Myers**
Jai **Alexander Bao**
Antiquerium Dealer **Lau Siu Ming**
Undercover Woman **Diana Weng**

and Chow Pok Fu (High Priest), Chan Tat Kwong (Monk), Anthony Carpio (Guard Monk), Bruce Khan (Snakehead Thug), Nicholas Tse, Edison Chen (Waiters), Scott Adkins, Matthew James Routledge, Reuben Christopher Langdon, Michael Strange, Hiroyoshi Komuro, Han Guan Hua (Henchmen), Neili Conroy (Interpol Receptionist), Billy Hill (Miles Watson), Tara Leniston (Jai's Nurse), Nikki Berwick (Kidnap Nurse), Paul Andreovski (Kidnap Porter), Howard Gibbins (Professor of Archeology), Rick Nathanson (Physician), Alfred Cheung (Chinese Professor), Mon Lynn (Astrologer), Kirk Trutner (Hippie Scientist)

Hong Kong detective Eddie Yang sets out to find a child who possesses a mysterious medallion whose powers are coveted by the villainous Snakehead.

AUTUMN SPRING

(FIRST LOOK PICTURES) Producers, Jirí Bartoska, Jaroslav Boucek, Jaroslav Kucera; Director, Vladimír Michálek; Screenplay, Jirí Hubac; Photography, Martin Strba; Designer, Jirí Sternwald; Music, Michal Lorenc; Editor, Jirí Brozek; BKP Film, Buc-Film, Czech TV productions; Czech Republic, 2002; Dolby; Color; Rated PG-13; 95 minutes; American release date: August 22, 2003

Cast

Frantisek Hána **Vlastimil Brodsky**
Emílie Hánová **Stella Zázvorková**
Eda **Stanislav Zindulka**
Jára Hána **Ondrej Vetchy**
Králová **Petra Spalková**
Estate Agent **Jirí Lábus**
Maruska Grulichová **Zita Kabátová**
Judge **Katerina Pindejová**

and Lubomir Kostelka (Vondrácek), Juraj Johanides (Dr. Rysavy), Zuzana Fialová (Erna), Simona Stasová (Marcela), Vlastimil Zavrel (Hlavaty), Martin Sitta (Král)

An incorrigible senior citizen takes great delight in playing pranks until he and his wife are faced with a mound of bills derived from his various deceptions.

Vlastimil Brodsky, Stella Zazvorkova PHOTO COURTESY OF FIRST LOOK PICTURES

Rhys Ifans, Shirley Henderson PHOTO COURTESY OF SONY CLASSICS

ONCE UPON A TIME IN THE MIDLANDS

(SONY CLASSICS) Producer, Andrea Calderwood; Executive Producers, Paul Webster, Paul Trijbits, Hanno Huth; Director, Shane Meadows; Screenplay, Paul Fraser, Shane Meadows; Photography, Brian Tufano; Designer, Crispian Sallis; Costumes, Robin Fraser Paye; Music, John Lunn; Editors, Peter Beston, Trevor Waite; Co-Producers, Louise Knight, James Wilson; Line Producer, Claire Hunt; Casting, Julia Duff; a FilmFour in association with the Film Council and Senator Films presentation of EMMI; a Slate Films production in association with Big Arty; British-German, 2002; Dolby; Super 35 Widescreen; Deluxe color; Rated R; 104 minutes; American release date: August 29, 2003

Cast
Jimmy **Robert Carlyle**
Dek **Rhys Ifans**
Carol **Kathy Burke**
Shirley **Shirley Henderson**
Charlie **Ricky Tomlinson**
Marlene **Finn Atkins**
Vanessa **Vanessa Feltz**
Audience Guest **Vicki Patterson**
Donna **Kelly Thresher**
Donut **Andrew Shim**
Emerson **Ryan Bruce**
Lake **Elliot Otis Brown Walters**
Jumbo **Anthony Strachan**

and David McKay (Dougy), James Cosmo (Billy), Vic Reeves (Plonko the Clown), Bob Mortimer (Kung Fu Clown), Richard Garfoot (Wrestilng Clown), Justin Brady (Eugene), Tony Nyland (Big Al), Anthony Clarke (YTS Dave), Ladene Hall (Bingo Woman), Shane Meadows (Bingo Caller), Paul Fraser (Bingo Checker)

When Jimmy sees his ex-girlfriend accept a proposal of marriage on television, he returns to the Midlands with some stolen cash, hoping to win her back.

CARNAGE

(WELLSPRING) a.k.a. *Carnages*; Producer, Jérôme Dopffer; Director, Delphine Gleize; Photography, Crystel Fourneir; Designer, André Fonsny; Music, Éric Neveux; Editor, François Quiqueré; Casting, Antoinette Boulat; a Balthazar Productions presentation of a Need Productions/Oasis Producciones/PCT Cinema Television/Studio Canal France/France 3 Cinema/RTBF/TSR/CRRAV production; French-Belgian-Spanish-Swiss, 2002; Dolby; Color; Not rated; 133 minutes; American release date: September 5, 2003

Cast
Winnie **Raphaël Molinier**
Carlotta **Chiara Mastroianni**
Betty **Lio**
Jeanne **Lucia Sanchez**
Rosy **Esther Gorintin**
Lucy **Maryline Even**
Alexis **Clovis Cornillac**
Luc **Bernard Sens**

and Pascal Bongard (Henry), Féodor Atkine (Paco), Julien Lescarret (Victor), Ángela Molina (Alice), Jacques Gamblin (Jacques), Ramón Arenillas Llorente (Pedro the Agent), Dominique Vache (Trusted Peasant), Michel Malmoustier (Sword Valet), Stéphane Touitou (Voice at the Audition), Armen Godel (Partner at the Audition), Sandrine Laroche (Jacques' Mistress), Rodolfo De Souza (Journalist), Begonna Martinez Cezon (Young Woman at Airport), Jean-Michel Gouffrant (Surgeon), Perrine Ferret (Young Girl Skating), Juliette Noureddine (Monica), Mike Koumi (Kebab Seller), Irène Dafonte (Victor's Nurse), Pascal Nzonzi (Cow Man), Nicolas Challal (Jérémy), Fabienne Mainquet (Jérémy's Mother), Alexandre Von Sivers (Professor), Jorge Rodriguez (Youth Leader), Luc Delhumeau (Luc's Father), Alexis Smolen, Antoni Valiante (Pizza Delivery Guys), Michel Cordes (Man at Restaurant), Noham Cochenet (Waiter), Bernard Gleize (TV Show Guest), Bénédicte Martin (TV Presenter), Michèle Dorge (Alice's Nurse), Marie Landfried (Singer), Jorge Cabezas Moreno (Betty's Doctor)

After a bull is killed in the arena, its parts are distributed throughout Europe where they have an effect on each of the people who receive them.

Chiara Mastroianni PHOTO COURTESY OF WELLSPRING

TAKING SIDES

(NEW YORKER) Producer, Yves Pasquier; Co-Producers, Jacques Rousseau, Michael von Wolkenstein, Rainer Schaper, Rainer Mockert, Jeremy Isaacs, Maureen McCabe; Line Producer, Udo Happel; Supervising Producer, Michel Nicolini; Director, István Szabó; Screenplay, Ronald Harwood, based on his play; Photography, Lajos Koltai; Designer, Ken Adam; Costumes, Györgyi Szakács; Editor, Sylvie Landra; Casting, Gillian Hawser, Caroline Hutchings, Heta Mantscheff; an Enterprise Films—France 2 Cinema—Great British Films— Jeremy Isaacs Prods.—Le Studio Canal+—Little Big Bear—Filmproduktion GmbH production; British-French-German-Austrian, 2002; Dolby; Color; Not rated; 108 minutes; American release date: September 5, 2003

Cast

Major Steve Arnold **Harvey Keitel**
Dr. Wilhelm Furtwängler **Stellan Skarsgård**
Lt. David Wills **Moritz Bleibtreu**
Emmi Straube **Birgit Minichmayr**
Helmut Rode, 2nd Violinist **Ulrich Tukur**
Colonel Dymshitz **Oleg Tabakov**
Rudolf Werner, Oboist **Hanns Zischler**
Schlee, Timpanist **Armin Rohde**
General Wallace **R. Lee Ermey**
Captain Ed Martin **August Zirner**
Sergeant Adams **Daniel White**
Reichminister **Thomas Thieme**
Colonel Green **Jed Curtis**
Major Richards **Garrick Hagon**
Captain Vernay **Robin Renucci**

and Markus Heinicke (Attendant), Aleksander Tesla (Projectionist), Jarreth J. Merz (US Soldier), Holger Schober (Steve's Driver), Frank Leboeuf (French Aide), Philip Bowen (US Aide), Thomas Morris (British Sergeant), Peter Doering (British Officer), Rinat Shaham (Jazz Singer), Werner Armelin (Remer), Matthias Wilke (Schmidt), Holger Jahn, Werner Zwosta (Aides), Thomas Rösicke, Marco Riccardi (Barkeepers), Jouri Babalikachvili (Russian Aide), Henry Schindler (U.K. Aide), Chris Martin (U.S. Soldier), Benno Wirth (Stallholder), Ron Hermann, Vanetin Tornow (Boys)

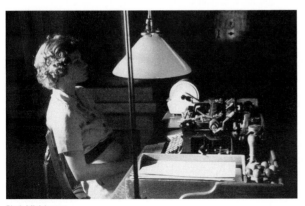

Birgit Minichmayr PHOTOS COURTESY OF NEW YORKER

Moritz Bleibtreu, Harvey Keitel

Harvey Keitel, Moritz Bleibtreu, Stellan Skarsgård

The true story of German conductor Wilhelm Furtwängler, who despite his efforts to save Jewish musicians, was accused of collaboration with the Nazis.

Stellan Skarsgård

MILLENNIUM ACTRESS

(GO FISH PICTURES) Producer, Chiyoko Committee; Director/Story, Satoshi Kon; Screenplay, Satoshi Kon, Sadyuki Murai; Executive Producer, Taro Maki; Character Design, Takeshi Honda, Satoshi Kon; Animation Directors, Takeshi Honda, Toshiyuki Inoue, Hideki Hamasu, Kenichi Noinshi, Shogo Furuya; Editor, Takeshi Honda; Art Director, Nobutaka Ike; Photography, Hisao Shirai; Music, Susumu Hirasawa; Animation Studio, Mad House; Animation Production, Genco, Inc.; a Chiyoko Committee production; Japanese; Dolby; Color/Black and White; Rated PG; 87 minutes; American release date: September 12, 2003

Voice Cast

Chiyoko Fujiwara in Her 70s **Miyoko Shoji**
Chiyoko Fujiwara in Her Mid-20s to 40s **Mami Koyama**
Chiyoko Fujiwara in Her Teenage Years to Early 20s **Fumiko Orikasa**
Genya Tachibana **Shozo Iizuka**
Kyoji Ida **Masaya Onosaka**
Eiko Shimao **Syouko Tsuda**
The Man with the Scar **Masane Tsukayama**
The Man of the Key **Kohichi Yamadera**
Otaki **Hirotaka Suzuoki**
Mother **Hisako Kyoda**

A filmmaker presents a long retired and reclusive actress with a special key she had believed to be lost, which magically unlocks long-held secrets of her life.

Chiyoko Fujiwara, Genya Tachibana PHOTO COURTESY OF GO FISH PICTURES

UNDERWORLD

(SCREEN GEMS) Producers, Tom Rosenberg, Gary Lucchesi, Richard Wright; Executive Producers, Terry A. McKay, Henry Winterstein, Skip Williamson, James McQuaide, Robert Bernacchi; Diretor, Len Wiseman; Screenplay, Danny McBride; Story, Len Wiseman, Danny McBride, Kevin Grevioux; Photography, Tony Pierce-Roberts; Designer, Burton Jones; Costumes, Wendy Partridge; Music, Paul Haslinger; Editor, Martin Hunter; Special Effects Supervisor, Nick Allder; Casting, Deborah Aquila, Tricia Wood, Celestia Fox; Stunts, Brad Martin; British-German-Hungarian-U.S.; a Lakeshore Entertainment production; Dolby; Super 35 Widescreen; Color; Rated R; 121 minutes; American release: September 19, 2003

Cast

Selene **Kate Beckinsale**
Michael Corvin **Scott Speedman**
Lucian **Michael Sheen**
Kraven **Shane Brolly**
Viktor **Bill Nighy**
Singe **Erwin Leder**
Erika **Sophia Myles**
Kahn **Robby Gee**
Dr. Adam Lockwood **Wentworth Miller**
Raze **Kevin Grevioux**

and Zita Görög (Amelia), Dennis Kozeluh (Dignitary), Scott McElroy (Soren), Todd Schneider (Trix), Sándor Bolla (Rigel), Hank Amos (Nathaniel), Zsuzsa Barsi (Gunshot Girl), Rich Cetrone (Pierce), Mike Mukatis (Taylor), Sándor Boros, János Oláh (Candidates), Andreas Patton (Death Dealer Captain), Danny McBride (Mason), Jazmín Damak (Sonja), Atilla Pinke (Wolfgang), Judit Kuchta (Zsuzsa), Vanessa Nagy (Timea), Ildiko Kovacs (Michael's Old Girlfriend), Brian Steele, Kurt Carley (Werewolves)

A group of werewolves ensnare the human love interest of vampire Selene in order to create a hybrid species in hope of gaining power from their bloodsucking enemies.

Kate Beckinsale in *Underworld* PHOTO COURTESY OF SCREEN GEMS

MAMBO ITALIANO

(SAMUEL GOLDWYN FILMS) Producers, Denise Robert, Daniel Louis; Director, Émile Gaudreault; Screenplay, Émile Gaudreault, Steve Galluccio; Based on the play by Steve Galluccio; Photography, Serge Ladouceur; Art Director, Patricia Christie; Costumes, Francesca Chamberland; Editor, Richard Comeau; Music, FM Le Sieur; an Equinoxe Films and Cinemaginaire presentation of a Denise Robert, Daniel Louis production; Canadian; Dolby; Color; Rated R; 88 minutes; American release date: September 19, 2003

Luke Kirby, Peter Miller

Paul Sorvino, Ginette Reno

Luke Kirby, Claudia Ferri

Cast

Angelo Barberini **Luke Kirby**
Gino Barberini **Paul Sorvino**
Maria Barberini **Ginette Reno**
Anna Barberini **Claudia Ferri**
Nino Paventi **Peter Miller**
Lina Paventi **Mary Walsh**
Pina Lunetti **Sophie Lorain**
Peter **Tim Post**
Rosetta **Pierrette Robitaille**
Giorgio **Dino Tavarone**
Father Carmignani **Michel Perron**
Marco **Lou Vani**
Beer-Bellied Man **Gordon Masten**
Johnny Cristofaro **Mark Camacho**
Melanie **Diane Lavallée**
Angelo **Michael Romano**
Nino **Mathieu Major-Langevin**
Gino **Stephen Perreault**
Anna **Grace Bush-Vineberg**

The Barberinis' sensitive son Angelo worries that he must break the news to his very traditional Italian family that his roommate, Nino, is also his lover.

Peter Miller, Mary Walsh, Pierrette Robitaille PHOTOS COURTESY OF SAMUEL GOLDWYN FILMS

Georges Lopez (right) PHOTO COURTESY OF NEW YORKER

TO BE AND TO HAVE

(NEW YORKER) Producer, Gilles Sandoz; Director/Editor, Nicolas Philibert; Photography, Laurent Didier, Nicolas Philibert, Katell Djian, Hugues Gemignani; Music, Philippe Hersant; a Centre National de Documentation Pédagogique, Centre National de la Cinématographie, Gimages 4, Le Studio Canal+, Les Films d'Ici, Maïa Films, ARTE France Cinéma; French, 2002; Dolby; Color; Not rated; 104 minutes; American release date: September 19, 2003. Documentary about French teacher, Georges Lopez, and his one-room school house.

This film received an Oscar nomination for feature documentary.

Jamal Udin Torabi in *In This World*

Enayatullah, Jamal Udin Torabi PHOTOS COURTESY OF SUNDANCE CHANNEL PICTURES

IN THIS WORLD

(SUNDANCE CHANNEL PICTURES) Producers, Andrew Eaton, Anita Overland; Executive Producers, Chris Auty, David M. Thompson; Co-Producer, Behrooz Hashemian; Director, Michael Winterbottom; Screenplay, Tony Grisoni; Photography, Marcel Zyskind; Music, Dario Marianelli; Editor, Peter Christelis; Casting, Wendy Brazington; The Film Consortium and BBC Films in association with The Film Council and The Works presentation of a Revolution Films production; British; Dolby; Widescreen; Deluxe color; DV-to-35mm; Rated R; 90 minutes; American release date: September 19, 2003

Cast
Jamal **Jamal Udin Torabi**
Enayat **Enayatullah**
PAKISTAN
Travel Agent **Imran Paracha**
Enayat's Brother **Hiddayatullah**
Enayat's Father **Jamau**
Enayat's Uncles **Wakeel Khan, Lal Zarin**
Money Changer **Ahsan Raza**
Jamal's Older Brother **Mirwais Torabi**
Groom **Abdul Ahmad**
Jamal's Younger Brother **Amanullah Torabi**
Drivers **Ramzan Ali, Chaman Ali**
Soldier Shaheen **Rasheed**
Farid **Allah Bauhsh**
IRAN
Behrooz **Hossain Baghaeian**
Kurdish Father **Yaaghoob Nosraj Poor**
Kurdish Mother **Ghodrat Poor**
Kurdish Baby **Mehdi Poor**
2nd Kurdish Father **Ahmad Azami**
Kurdish Son **Yusef Zaami**
Bus Drivers **Mr. Eghdame, Mr. Dehghame, Mr. Yusuf**
Truck Driver **Bayram Arjangi**
4WD Driver **Jaffa Eghbali**
TURKEY
Policeman **Kerem Atabeyoglu**
Factor Boss **Erham Sekizcan**
EUROPE
Yusif **Nabil Elouhabi**
Voice **Paul Popplewell**

Two Afghan cousins living in a refugee camp in Pakistan attempt to smuggle themselves out of the country and make their way to London.

Connie Nielsen

DEMONLOVER

(PALM PICTURES) Producers, Xavier Giannoli, Edouard Weil; Executive Producers, Claude Davy, Jean Coulon; Line Producer, Sylvie Barthet; Director/Screenplay, Olivier Assayas; Photography, Denis Lenoir; Designer, François-Renaud Labarthe; Costumes, Anaïs Romand; Music, Jim O'Rourke, Sonic Youth; Editor, Luc Barnier; Casting, Antoinette Boulat, Kerry Barden; Visual Effects, François Dumoulin; a Citizen Films, Cofimage, Elizabeth Films, Group Datacine, La Sofica Gimages 2, M6 Gfilms, Procirep, TPS Cinema production; French; Dolby; Super 35 Widescreen; Color; Rated R; 129 minutes; American release date: September 19, 2003

Cast
Diane de Monx **Connie Nielsen**
Hervé La Millinec **Charles Berling**
Elise Lipsky **Chloë Sevigny**
Elaine Si Gibril **Gina Gershon**
Henri-Pierre Volf **Jean-Baptiste Malarte**
Karen **Dominique Reymond**
Edward Gomez **Edwin Gerard**
American Lawyer **Thomas M. Pollard**
Kaori **Abi Sakamoto**
Gina **Julie Brochen**

Chloë Sevigny PHOTOS COURTESY OF PALM PICTURES

and Jorgen Doering (Styliste), Jean-Charles Dumay (Henri), Jean-Pierre Gos (Verkamp), Randal Holden (Ray), Alexandre Lachaux (Erwan), Gilles Masson (Man at the Villa), Mathias Mlekuz (Mr. X), Nao Ohmori (Shoji), Alexis Pivot (Frankie), Ludovic Schoendoerffer (Luis), Taro Suwa, Ikko Suzuki (Lawyers), Naoki Yamazaki (Eiko)

Two rival media companies both hope to take control of the cutting edge technology of a Japanese corporation that produces pornographic comic books and anime.

Ohad Knoller, Yehuda Levi PHOTO COURTESY OF STRAND

YOSSI & JAGGER

(STRAND) Producers, Amir Harel, Gal Uchovsky; Director, Eytan Fox; Screenplay, Avner Bernheimer; Photography, Yaron Scharf; Art Director, Amir Pick; Costumes, Natan Elkanovich; Music, Ivri Lider; Editor, Yosef Grunfeld; Casting, Yael Aviv; from Israel Cable Programming, Lama Productions; Israeli, 2002; Dolby; Color; DV-to-35mm; Not rated; 67 minutes; American release date: September 24, 2003

Cast
Yossi **Ohad Knoller**
Jagger **Yehuda Levi**
Ofir **Assi Cohen**
Yaeli **Aya Steinovitz**
Goldie **Hani Furstenberg**
The Colonel **Sharon Raginiano**
Psycho **Yuval Semo**
Samoncha **Yaniv Moyal**
Adams **Hanan Savyon**
Yaniv the Cook **Erez Kahana**
Jagger's Mother **Yael Perl Becker**
Jagger's Father **Shmulik Bernheimer**

Two young soldiers fall in love while stationed at an Israeli outpost near the Lebanese border.

Scott Speedman, Sarah Polley

Sarah Polley, Mark Ruffalo PHOTOS COURTESY OF SONY CLASSICS

MY LIFE WITHOUT ME

(SONY CLASSICS) Producers, Esther Garcia, Gordon McLennan; Executive Producers, Pedro Almodovar, Agustin Almodovar, Ogden Gavanski; Director/Screenplay, Isabel Coixet; Based on the novel *Pretending the Bed Is a Raft* by Nanci Kincaid; Photography, Jean Claude Larrieu; Designer, Carol Lavallee; Costumes, Katia Stano; Music, Alfonso de Villallonga; Editor, Lisa Jane Robison; Line Producer, Jordi Torrent; Associate Producer, Michel Ruben; Casting, Heidi Levitt, Monika Mikkelsen (US), Coreen Mayrs, Heike Brandstatter; Spanish-Canadian, 2002; Dolby; Color; Rated R; 106 minutes; American release date: September 26, 2003

Cast
Ann **Sarah Polley**
Laurie **Amanda Plummer**
Don, Ann's Husband **Scott Speedman**
Ann, Ann's Neighbor **Leonor Watling**
Ann's Mother **Deborah Harry**

and Maria de Medeiros (The Hairdresser), Mark Ruffalo (Lee), Julian Richings (Doctor Thompson), Kenya Jo Kennedy (Patsy), Jessica Amlee (Penny), Alfred Molina (Ann's Father), Sonja Bennett (Sarah)

After a 23-year-old wife and mother is diagnosed with terminal cancer, she sets out to do all of the things she has wanted to do before she dies.

LUTHER

(R.S. ENTERTAINMENT) Producers, Brigitte Rochow, Christian P. Stehr, Alexander Thies; Executive Producers, Dennis Clauss, Kurt Rittig, Gabriela Pfandner, J. Daniel Nichols; Director, Eric Till; Screenplay, Camille Thomasson, Bart Gavigan; Photography, Robert Fraisse; Designer, Rolf Zehetbauer; Costumes, Ulla Gothe; Music, Richard Harvey; Editor, Clive Barrett; Casting, Brigitte Rochow; an NFP and R.S. Entertainment presentation of an NFP Teleart production; German; Dolby; Color; Rated PG-13; 113 minutes; American release date: September 26, 2003

Peter Ustinov PHOTO COURTESY OF R.S. ENTERTAINMENT

Cast
Martin Luther **Joseph Fiennes**
Johann Tetzel **Alfred Molina**
Johann von Staupitz **Bruno Ganz**
Girolamo Aleander **Jonathan Firth**
Prince Frederick the Wise **Sir Peter Ustinov**
Katharina von Bora **Claire Cox**
Pope Leo X **Uwe Ochsenknecht**
Georg Spalatin **Benjamin Sadler**
Prof. Andreas Karlstadt **Jochen Horst**
Emperor Charles V **Torben Liebrecht**
Cardinal Jakob Cajetan **Mathieu Carrière**
Ulrich **Marco Hofschneider**
Hanna **Maria Simon**

and Lars Rudolph (Philip Melanchthon), James Babson (Dominican Monk), Christopher Buchholz (Von der Eck), Jeff Caster (Matthew), Cesare Cremonini (Guardian Monk), Doris Prusova (Grete), Anatole Taubman (Otto), Jens Winter (Fugger Auditor), Timothy Peach (Karl von Miltitz), Tom Strauss (Georg von Brandenburg), Gene Reed (Johann von Sachsen), Anian Zollner (Philip von Hessen), Johannes Lang (Albrecht Erzbischof von Mainz).

The true story of how a monk rebelled against the religious and political authorities of 16th-century Europe and paved the way for the establishment of Protestantism. Previous movie on the subject was the 1973 British film *Luther* (American Film Theatre) starring Stacy Keach.

CONCERT FOR GEORGE

(ARENA PLEX) Producers, Ray Cooper, Olivia Harrison, Jon Kame; Director, David Leland; Photography, Chris Menges; Designer, Eve Stewart; Editor, Claire Ferguson; Songs, George Harrison; Line Producer, James Bradley; @radical Media Inc.; British-U.S.; Dolby; Color; Rated PG-13; 146 minutes; American release date: October 3, 2003. Documentation of a memorial concert for musician George Harrison held at London's Royal Albert Hall in November of 2002.

Jeff Lynne, Eric Clapton, Ringo Starr, Dhani Harrison, Marc Mann

Ravi Shankar PHOTOS COURTESY OF ARENA PLEX

With

Gary Brooker, Joe Brown, Sam Brown, Eric Clapton, Carol Cleveland, Ray Cooper, Andy Fairweather-Low, Terry Gilliam, Tom Hanks, Dhani Harrison, Olivia Harrison, Jools Holland, Eric Idle, Neil Innes, Terry Jones, Albert Lee, Jeff Lynne, Paul McCartney, Michael Palin, Tom Petty, Billy Preston, Anoushka Shankar, Ravi Shankar, Ringo Starr, Klaus Voormann

Concert for George

BUS 174

(THINKFILM) Producer, José Padilha, Marcos Prado; Director, José Padhila; Producer, Rodrigo Pimentel; Photography, Cesar Moraes, Marcelo "Guru" Duarte; Editor, Felipe Lacerda; Music, Joao Nabuco, Sasha Ambak; a Zazen Produções production; Brazilian, 2002; Black and white/color; Not rated; 122 minutes; American release date: October 8, 2003. Documentary about the June 12, 2000, hijacking of a Rio de Janeiro bus; featuring Yvonne Bezerra de Mello, Rodrigo Pimentel, Luiz Eduardo Soares.

Bus 174 PHOTO COURTESY OF THINKFILM

THE FLOWER OF EVIL

(PALM PICTURES) Producer, Marin Karmitz; Executive Producer, Yvon Crenn; Director, Claude Chabrol; Screenplay, Claude Chabrol, Louis L. Lambrichs, Caroline Eliacheff; Photography, Eduardo Serra; Designer, Françoise Benoît-Fresco; Costumes, Mic Cheminal; Music, Matthieu Chabrol; Editor, Monique Fardoulis; a Marin Karmitz presentation of an MK2, France 3 Cinema production with the participation of Canal+, Aquitaine Regional Council and the support of Procirep; French; Dolby; Color; Rated R; 104 minutes; American release date: October 3, 2003

Suzanne Flon, Benoît Magimel, Melanie Doutey

Nathalie Baye, Benoît Magimel

Cast

François Vasseur **Benoît Magimel**
Anne Charpin-Vasseur **Nathalie Baye**
Michèle Charpin-Vasseur **Mélanie Doutey**
Aunt Line **Suzanne Flon**
Gérard Vasseur **Bernard Le Coq**
Matthieu Lartigue **Thomas Chabrol**
Fanny's Father-in-Law **Henri Attal**
First Kid **Kevin Ahyi**
Volunteer **Jérôme Bertin**
Thérèse **Françoise Bertin**
Fanny **Caroline Baehr**
Brissot **Didier Bénureau**
Yves Pouët **Yvon Crenn**

and Jean-Marc Druet (Lab Assistant), Michel Herbault (Mayor), Edmond Kastelnik, Jean-Pierre Marin (Election Officials), Marius de Laage (Second Kid), Isabelle Mamère (Journalist), Juliette Meyniac (Hélène), François Maistre (Jules), Michèle Dascain (Marthe), Dominique Pivain (Dominique), Léa Pellpaut (Drugstore Saleswoman), Valérie Rojan (Gérard's Secretary)

Benoît Magimel, Melanie Doutey

Just as Anne Charpin-Vasseur is about to venture into local politics, a long dormant scandal from her family's past explodes after a corpse shows up on the eve of the election.

Nathalie Baye, Bernard Le Coq, Suzanne Flon, Benoît Magimel, Melanie Doutey

PHOTOS COURTESY OF PALM PICTURES

Daniel Craig, Amira Casar

Gwyneth Paltrow

The true story of poet and author Sylvia Plath and how her troubled marriage to British Poet Laureate Ted Hughes brought out both her creative energy and mental instability.

SYLVIA

(FOCUS FEATURES) Producer, Alison Owen; Executive Producers, David M. Thompson, Tracey Scoffield, Robert Jones, Jane Barclay, Sharon Harel; Director, Christine Jeffs; Screenplay, John Brownlow; Co-Producer, Neris Thomas; Photography, John Toon; Designer, Maria Djurkovic; Costumes, Sandy Powell; Editor, Tariq Anwar; Music, Gabriel Yared; Associate Producers, Phil Rymer; Line Producer, Mary Richards; Casting, Karen Lindsay Stewart; a Ruby Films production, presented in association with BBC Films, Capitol Films and the UK Film Council; British; Dolby; Color; Rated R; 110 minutes; American release date: October 17, 2003

Cast

Sylvia Plath **Gwyneth Paltrow**
Ted Hughes **Daniel Craig**
Al Alvarez **Jared Harris**
Aurelia Plath **Blythe Danner**
Professor Thomas **Michael Gambon**
Assia Wevill **Amira Casar**
David Wevill **Andew Havill**
Morecambe **David Birkin**
Elizabeth **Alison Bruce**
Doreen **Lucy Davenport**
James Michie **Julian Firth**
Mr. Robinson **Jeremy Fowlds**
Ted's Cambridge Girlfriend **Sarah Guyler**
Martha Bergstrom **Liddy Holloway**
Charles Langridge **Michael Mears**
Vicar **Derek Payne**
Midwife **Sonia Ritter**

Daniel Craig, Gwyneth Paltrow

and Robyn Malcolm, Tandi Wright, Theresa Healey (Women at Ted's Lecture), Siobhan Page (Young American Student), Billie Seymour (Telegraph Boy), Antony Strachan (Michael Boddy), Katherine Tozer (Myra Norris), Sam Troughton (Tom Hadley-Clarke), Eliza Wade (Infant Frieda), Ben & Joel Want (Baby Nicholas), Hannah Watkins (Tom's Girlfriend)

Jared Harris PHOTOS COURTESY OF FOCUS FEATURES

VERONICA GUERIN

(TOUCHSTONE) Producer, Jerry Bruckheimer; Executive Producers, Chad Oman, Mike Stenson, Ned Dowd; Director, Joel Schumacher; Screenplay, Carol Doyle, Mary Agnes Donoghue; Story, Carol Doyle; Photography, Brendan Galvin; Designer, Nathan Crowley; Costumes, Joan Bergin; Editor, David Gamble; Music, Harry Gregson-Williams; Casting, Nuala Moiselle, Frank Moiselle; a Jerry Bruckheimer presentation; Irish-British; Dolby; Panavision; Technicolor; Rated R; 98 minutes; American release date: October 17, 2003

Cate Blanchett, Don Wycherley

Cast

Veronica Guerin **Cate Blanchett**
John Gilligan **Gerard McSorley**
John Traynor **Ciarán Hinds**
Bernie Guerin **Brenda Fricker**
Chris Mulligan **Don Wycherley**
Graham Turley **Simon O'Driscoll**
Aengus Fanning **Emmet Bergin**
Anne Harris **Charlotte Bradley**
Willie Kealy **Mark Lambert**
Tony Gregory **Garrett Keogh**
Geraldine Gilligan **Maria McDermottroe**
Brian Meehan **Paudge Behan**
Eugene "Dutchie" Holland **Joe Hanley**
Charles Bowden **David Murray**
Tattooed Boy (Spanky McSpank) **Colin Farrell**

and Karl Shiels, Barry McEvoy (Gilligan Gang Members), Gina Costigan (Traynor's Girlfriend), Alan Devine (Gerry Hutch), Gerry O'Brien (Martin Cahill), Gabrielle Reidy (Frances Cahill), Paul Roe (Tommy Mullen), David Herlihy (Peter "Fatso" Mitchell), Darragh Kelly (Terry Fagan), Laurence Kinlan (Timmy, 14-year-old Junkie), Danielle Fox-Clarke, Sarah O'Reilly-Maloney (Junkies), Paul Ronan (Jimmy Guerin), Philip O'Sullivan (Solicitor), Niall Tobin (Judge Ballaugh), Kevin McHugh (Judge at Assault Trial), Joe Taylor (Priest, Bernadette's Church), Vincent McCabe (Priest at Funeral), Des Cave (Police Spokesman), Luke Hayden, Joe Gallagher (Protection Gardas), Ned Dennehy (Jamey the Tout), Tommy O'Neill,

Barry Barnes, Cate Blanchett, Simon O'Driscoll

Shane McCabe, Brian McGuinness (Cahill Thugs), Sally Ann Doddy (Mrs. Hutch), Aaron Harris, Jonathan White (Press Conference Reporters), Maggie Wade (Coleen the Parole Clerk), Ann Cassin, Elizabeth Moynihan, Jimmy Greeley, Brian Dobson (Newscasters), Kevin Reynolds, Gerry Ryan (Studio Interviewers), Barbara Brennan, Gary Lilburn, Jane Brennan, Frank Smith (Jealous Journalists), Malachy McKenna, Kieran Hurley (Officers), Terry Byrne (Man in Registry Office), Mick Nolan (Tax Assessor), Barbara Ryan (Aengus' Secrertary), Enda Oates, Martin Dunne (Warehouse Workers), Helen Norton, Noelle Brown (Witness Nurses), Veronica Hduffy (ICU Attendant), Brian Munn, Cathy White (Elegant Equestrians), Amy Shiels (Gililgan's Mistress), Fiona Glascott (Meehan's Girlfriend), Shelly Smith, Grainne Debuitlear, Emily Kelly (Gang Girlfriends), Vanessa Keogh (Hooker No. 1)

The true story of how journalist Veronica Guerin's crusade against exposing the underworld behind Dublin's heroin trade led to tragedy.

Ciaran Hinds, Gerard McSorley PHOTOS COURTESY OF TOUCHSTONE

IN MY SKIN

(WELLSPRING) Producer, Laurence Farenc; Director/Screenplay, Marina de Van; Photography, Pierre Barougier; Designer, Baptiste Glaymann; Costumes, Marielle Robaut; Music, Esbjorn Svensson; Editor, Mike Fromentin; Casting, Brigitte Moidon; Associate Producers, Alain Rocca, Stephanie Carreras, Laurent Soregaroli; a co-production of Canal+, Centre National de la Cinematographie, Lazennc Films, Les Productions Lazennec, Natexis Banques Populaires Images 2; French, 2002; Dolby; Color; Not rated; 93 minutes; American release date: November 7, 2003

Laurent Lucas, Marina de Van

Laurent Lucas, Marina de Van

Cast
Esther **Marina de Van**
Vincent **Laurent Lucas**
Sandrine **Léa Drucker**
Daniel **Thibault de Montalembert**
Clients **Dominique Reymond, Bernard Alane**

and Marc Rioufol (Henri), François Lamotte (Pierre), Adrien de Van (Intern), Alain Rimoux (Pharmacist), Thomas de Van (Servant)

Following an injury, Esther becomes obsessed with her own torn flesh and begins cutting away at her body in a desperate effort to produce some kind of feeling.

Marina de Van PHOTOS COURTESY OF WELLSPRING

LOVE FORBIDDEN

(STRAND) Producer/Director/Screenplay, Rodolphe Marconi; Photography, Duccio Cimatti; Music, Bruno Alexiu; Editor, Isabelle Devinck; Co-Producer, Eric Landau; a Centre National de la Cinématographie production; French, 2002; Color; Not rated; 96 minutes; American release date: November 7, 2003

Cast
Bruce **Rodolphe Marconi**
Matteo **Andrea Necci**
Aston **Echo Danon**
Orietta **Orietta Gianjorio**
Germain **Hervé Brunon**
Maria Teresa **Marie Teresa de Belis**
Irene **Irene D'Agostino**
Tomaso **Tomazo D'Ulisia**

A young filmmaker, recovering from a breakup with his girlfriend, arrives in Rome where he befriends Matteo, who wants to take their relationship beyond friendship.

Andrea Necci in *Love Forbidden* PHOTO COURTESY OF STRAND

LOVE ACTUALLY

(UNIVERSAL) Producers, Duncan Kenworthy, Tim Bevan, Eric Fellner; Director/Screenplay, Richard Curtis; Co-Producers, Debra Hayward, Liza Chasin; Photography, Michael Coulter; Designer, Jim Clay; Costumes, Joanna Johnston; Editor, Nick Moore; Music, Craig Armstrong; Music Supervisor, Nick Angel; Song: "Christmas is All Around" ("Love Is All Around")/performed by Bill Nighy; Line Producer, Chris Thompson; Casting, Mary Selway; a Studiocanal presentation of a Working Title production in association with DNA Films; British; Dolby; Super 35 Widescreen; Color; Rated R; 135 minutes; American release date: November 7, 2003

Bill Nighy

Hugh Grant, Martine McCutcheon

Alan Rickman, Laura Linney

Colin Firth, Lúcia Moniz

Cast

Harry **Alan Rickman**
Billy Mack **Bill Nighy**
Jamie Bennett **Colin Firth**
Karen **Emma Thompson**
The Prime Minister **Hugh Grant**
Sarah **Laura Linney**
Daniel **Liam Neeson**
Natalie **Martine McCutcheon**
Juliet **Keira Knightley**
Rufus, Jewelry Salesman **Rowan Atkinson**
Mark **Andrew Lincoln**
The U.S. President **Billy Bob Thornton**
Just Judy **Joanna Page**
Colin Frissell **Kris Marshall**
Aurelia **Lúcia Moniz**
John **Martin Freeman**
Sam **Thomas Sangster**

Andrew Lincoln

and Gregor Fisher (Joe), Rory MacGregor (Engineer), Sienna Guillory (Jamie's Girlfriend), Lulu Popplewell (Daisy, Karen's Daughter), Heike Makatsch (Mia), Chiwetel Ejiofor (Peter), Nina Sosanya (Annie), Frank Moorey (Terence, Who's in Charge), Jill Freud (Pat the Housekeeper), Tim Hatwell (Vicar), Lyndon David Hall (The Wedding Singer), The Big Blue (Church Musicians), Jont Wittington (Guitarist), Dan Fredenburgh (Jamie's Bad Brother), Julia Davis (Nancy the Caterer), Abdul Salis (Tony), Alan Barnes (Movie Director), Shaughan Seymour (Movie Cameraman),

Helen Murton (Funeral Priest), Edward Hardwicke (Sam's Grandfather), Caroline John (Sam's Grandmother), Gemma Aston, Matt Harvey, Adrian Preater, Joanna Thaw (Family Mourners), Junior Simpson (Wedding DJ), Rodrigo Santoro (Karl), Brian Bovell (Radio Watford DJ), Sarah McDougall (Receptionist), Marcus Brigstocke (Mikey, DJ Interviewer), Richard Hawley (Alex, Deputy Prime Minister), Wyllie Longmore (Jeremy), Gillian Barge, Richard Wills-Cotton, Kate Bowes Renna, Kate Glover, Nicola McRoy (Cabinet Members), Anthony McPartlin (Ant), Declan Donnelly (Dec), Elizabeth Margoni (Eleonore), Peter Marinker (U.S. Expert), Keir Charles, Doraly Rosen (Press Conference Reporters), Meg Wynn Owen (PM's Secretary), Carol Carey (Natalie's Replacement), Jo Whiley (Radio DJ), Sarah Atkinson, Clare Bennett, Sarah Holland, Vicki Murdoch, Meredith Ostrom, Katherine Poulton, Tuuli (Billy's Video Vixens), Michael Parkinson (Parky), Michael Fitzgerald (Michael, Sarah's Brother), Ciaran O'Driscoll (Hospital Patient), William Wadham (Bernie, Karen's Son), Catia Duarte, Igor Urdenko, Nat Udom, Ines Boughanmi, Yuk Sim Yau (Language Students), John Sharian (Wisconsin Taxi Driver), Glenn Conroy (Barman), Ivana Milicevic (Stacey, American Dreamgirl), January Jones (Jeannie, American Angel), Elisha Cuthbert (Carol-Anne, American Goddess), Wes Butters (Radio 1 Chart Show DJ), Laura Rees (Record Company Executive), Emma Buckley (Jamie's Sister), Sheila Allen (Jamie's Mum), Terry Reece (PM's Chauffeur, Terry), Colin Coull (PM's Bodyguard, Gavin), Margery Mason (Harris Street Old Lady), Katharine Bailey (Harris Street Little Girl), Tiffany Boysell, Georgia Flint (Her Friends), Joanna Bacon (Natalie's Mum), Bill Moody (Natalie's Dad), Billy Campbell (Natalie's Octopus Brother, Keith), Paul Slack (John's Brother), Adam Godley (Mr. Trench), Olivia Olson (Joanna Anderson), Ruby Turner (Mrs. Jean Anderson), Amanda Garwood (Backing-singer Teacher), Arturo Venegas (Mr. Anderson), Claudia Schiffer (Carol), Patrick Delaney (Tommy, Carol's Son), Helder Costa (Mr. Barros), Carla Vasconcelos (Sophia Barros), Stewart Howson (Airport Gate Man), Jamie Edgell, Dave Fisher, Paul Heasman, Tony Lucken (Airport Guards), Raul Atalaia (Restaurant Proprietor), Nancy Sorrell (Greta), Shannon Elizabeth (Harriet, the Sexy One), Denise Richards (Carla, the Real Friendly One), Richard Curtis (Trombone Player)

In the weeks leading up to Christmas a batch of Londoners find themselves falling in love and hoping to sort out the chaos of it all.

Thomas Sangster, Liam Neeson

Elisha Cuthbert, January Jones, Kris Marshall, Ivana Milicevic

William Wadham, Emma Thompson

Heike Makatsch, Alan Rickman PHOTOS COURTESY OF UNIVERSAL

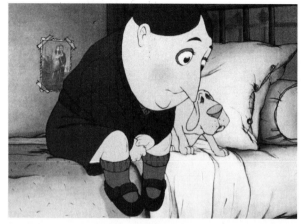

Champion, Bruno

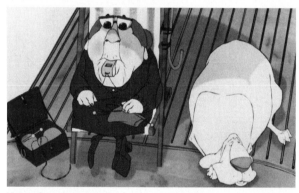

Madame Souza, Bruno

Bruno, Champion

Madame Souza

THE TRIPLETS OF BELLEVILLE

(SONY CLASSICS) a.k.a *Belleville Rendez-vous*; Producers, Didier Brunner (Les Armateurs), Paul Cadieux (Production Champion); Associate Producers, Viviane Vanfleteren (Vivi Film), Régis Gheselbash (RGP France), Colin Rose (BBC Bristol); Director/Screenplay/Storyboard/Graphic Design/Animation Director/Character Graphic Design, Sylvain Chomet; Production Design and Execution, Evgeni Tomov; Music, Benoît Charest; Colors, Art Direction, Thierry Million; Character Color Research, Carole Roy; Animation Supervision, Jean-Christophe Lie; 3D Animation Direction/Special Effects/Compositing Design, Pieter Van Houte; Editor, Chantal Colibert Brunner; Anmiation Studios, Studio Les Triplettes, Artdog, Walking the Dog, Rija Films, 2D3D; a Les Armateurs/Production Champion/Vivi Film/France 3 Cinéma/RGP France co-production; French-Belgian-Canadian; Dolby; Color; Rated PG-13; 80 minutes; American release date: November 26, 2003

Voices

Michèle Caucheteux, Jean-Claude Donda, Michel Robin, Monica Viegas, Béatrice Bonifassi, Lina Boudreault, Mari-Lou Gauthier, Charles Prévost Linton

Madame Souza and her faithful dog Bruno set out to rescue her bicyclying grandson, Champion, after he and two other cyclists are kidnapped during a race.

This film received Oscar nominations for animated feature and original song ("Belleville Rendez-vous")

Madame Souza

The Triplets

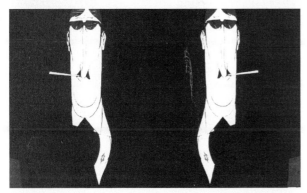

Mafioso

Triplets, Madame Souza, Bruno

Mafioso, Champion

Triplets, Madame Souza   PHOTOS COURTESY OF SONY CLASSICS

IN AMERICA

(FOX SEARCHLIGHT) Producers, Jim Sheridan, Arthur Lappin; Director, Jim Sheridan; Screenplay, Jim Sheridan, Naomi Sheridan, Kirsten Sheridan; Co-Producer, Paul Myler; Photography, Declan Quinn; Designer, Mark Geraghty; Costumes, Eimer Ni Mhaoldomhnaigh; Music, Gavin Friday, Maurice Seezer; Editor, Naomi Geraghty; Casting, Nuala Moiselle, Frank Moiselle (Ireland), Avy Kaufman (U.S.), Joyce Gallie (U.K.), Sally Osoba; a Hell's Kitchen production; British-Irish; Dolby; Color; Rated PG-13; 103 minutes; American release date: November 26, 2003

Emma Bolger, Sarah Bolger

Paddy Considine, Emma Bolger, Sarah Bolger, Samantha Morton

Cast

Sarah Sullivan **Samantha Morton**
Johnny Sullivan **Paddy Considine**
Mateo **Djimon Hounsou**
Christy Sullivan **Sarah Bolger**
Ariel Sullivan **Emma Bolger**
Immigration Officers **Neal Jones, Randall Carlton**
Frankie **Ciaran Cronin**
Papo **Juan Hernandez**
Blind Man **Nye Heron**
Tony **Jason Salkey**
Steve **Rene Millan**
Papo's Girlfriend **Sara James**
Theatre Director **Bob Gallico**
Assistant Theatre Director **Jason Killalee**
Mexican Woman with Child **Chary O'Dea**
Shopkeeper **Adrian Martinez**
Marina **Merrina Millsapp**
Barker **David Wike**
Man at Fair **Guy Carleton**
Nun on School Steps **Elaine Grollman**
Gynecologist **Nick Dunning**
Frank **Michael Sean Tighe**
Angela **Jennifer Seifert**
Prize Giving Nun **Kathleen King**
Nun Playing Piano **Eilish Scanlon**

Emma Bolger, with director Jim Sheridan

Emma Bolger, Paddy Considine

and Tom Murphy (Actor in Queue), Des Bishop (Stockbroker in Taxi), Bernadette Quigley (Hospital Administrator), Frank Wood (Pediatrician), Molly Glynn (Sarah Mateo), Jer O'Leary (Thomas Bakewell), Regina Roe (Administrator/Nurse), Tamla Clarke (Hospital Receptionist), Carmen Regan (Doctor), Nisha Nayar (Hospice Nurse), Rodrigo Pineda Sanchez, Gabriela Quintero Lopez (Mexican Guitarists)

Samantha Morton, Paddy Considine

Emma Bolger PHOTOS COURTESY OF FOX SEARCHLIGHT

Sarah Bolger, Paddy Considine, Samantha Morton, Emma Bolger

Johnny and Sarah arrive in New York City with their two young girls to establish a new life there and try to overcome their grief over the loss of their son.

This film received Oscar nominations for actress (Samantha Morton), supporting actor (Djimon Hounsou), and original screenplay.

Paddy Considine, Sarah Bolger, Samantha Morton, Emma Bolger

MONSIEUR IBRAHIM

(SONY CLASSICS) a.k.a. *Monsieur Ibrahim and the Flowers of the Koran;* Producers, Michèle & Laurent Pétin; Director/Adaptation, François Dupeyron; Dialogue, François Dupeyron, Eric-Emmanuel Schmitt; Based on the play *Monsieur Ibrahim and the Flowers of the Koran* by Eric-Emmanuel Schmitt; Photography, Rémy Chevrin; Designer, Katia Wyszkop; Costumes, Catherine Bouchard; Editor, Dominique Faysse; Casting, Brigitte Moidon; an ARP Production co-production with France 2 Cinema, with the participation of Canal+; French; Dolby; Color; Rated R; 94 minutes; American release date: December 5, 2003

Pierre Boulanger, Omar Sharif

Pierre Boulanger, Mata Gavin

Cast
Monsieur Ibrahim **Omar Sharif**
Momo (Moïse) **Pierre Boulanger**
Momo's Father **Gilbert Melki**
Momo's Mother **Isabelle Renauld**
Myriam **Lola Naynmark**
Sylvie **Anne Suarez**
Fatou **Mata Gavin**
Eva **Celine Samie**
"La Star" **Isabelle Adjani**
The Car Salesman **Guillaume Gallienne**
The Director **Guillane Rannou**
Driving School Instructor **Manuel Lelievre**
The Policeman **Daniel Znyk**
The Schoolmistress **Françoise Armelle**
The Testgiver **Sylvie Herbert**
The Notary **Claude Merline**

and Pascal Vincent (The Bouquiniste), Tessa Volkine (Myriam's Mother), Marie-Sophie Ahmadi (Nadia), Maryse Deol, Gerard Bole du Chaumont, François Toumaarkine, Sylvie Debrun (Administrative Workers), Jeremy Sitbon (Momo at eight years old), Eric Caravaca (Momo at thirty years old)

Anne Suarez, Pierre Boulanger PHOTOS COURTESY OF SONY CLASSICS

In early 1960s Paris a young Jewish boy and an elderly Muslim shopkeeper form an unlikely friendship.

Scarlett Johansson

GIRL WITH A PEARL EARRING

(LIONS GATE) Producers, Andy Paterson, Anand Tucker; Executive Producers, François Ivernel, Cameron McCracken, Duncan Reid, Tom Ortenberg, Peter Block, Daria Jovici, Philip Erdoes, Nick Drake; Co-Producers, Jimmy de Brabant, Matthew T. Gannon, Jason Constantine; Director, Peter Webber; Screenplay, Olivia Hetreed; Based on the novel by Tracy Chevalier; Photography, Eduardo Serra; Designer, Ben van Os; Costumes, Dien van Straalen; Editor, Kate Evans; Music, Alexandre Desplat; Line Producer, Guy Tannahill; Associate Producer, Anna Campeau; Make Up & Hair Designer, Jenny Shircore; Casting, Leo Davis, Valerie Schiel; a Pathé Pictures presentation in association with UK Film Council of an Archer Street/Delux production, produced with Inside Track and Film Fund Luxembourg; British-Luxembourg-U.S.; Dolby; Super 35 Widescreen; Technicolor; Rated PG-13; 99 minutes; American release date: December 13, 2003

Cast

Johannes Vermeer **Colin Firth**
Griet **Scarlett Johansson**
Van Ruijven **Tom Wilkinson**
Maria Thins **Judy Parfitt**
Pieter **Cillian Murphy**
Catharina Vermeer **Essie Davis**
Tanneke **Joanna Scanlan**
Cornelia Vermeer **Alakina Mann**

and Chris McHallem (Griet's Father), Gabrielle Reidy (Griet's Mothe), Rollo Weeks (Frans), Anna Popplewell (Maertge), Anais Nepper (Lisbeth), Melanie Meyfroid (Aleydis), Nathan Nepper (Johannes), Lola Carpentier, Charlotte Carpentier, Olivia Chauveau (Baby Franciscus), Geoff Bell (Paul the Butcher), Virginie Colin (Emilie van Ruijven), Sarah Drews (Van

Ruijven's Daughter), Christelle Buickaen (Wet Nurse), John McEnery (Apothecary), Gintare Parulyte (Model), Claire Johnston (White-Haired Woman), Marc Maes (Old Gentleman), Pere Robert Sibernaler (Priest), Dustin James, Joe Reavis (Servants), Martin Serene (Sergeant), Chris Kelly (Gay Blade)

In 1665 Holland, a lowly servant girl begins work at the house of the great artist Johannes Vermeer, who is inspired by her beauty to create one of his most masterful paintings.

Cillian Murphy, Scarlett Johansson

Scarlett Johansson, Colin Firth

This film received Oscar nominations for cinematography, costume design, and art direction.

Scarlett Johansson   PHOTOS COURTESY OF LIONS GATE

THE STATEMENT

(SONY CLASSICS) Producers, Robert Lantos, Norman Jewison; Executive Producers, David T. Thompson, Mark Musselman, Jason Piette, Michael Cowan; Line Producer, Sandra Cunningham; Director, Norman Jewison; Screenplay, Ronald Harwood, based on the novel by Brian Moore; Photography, Kevin Jewison; Designer, Jean Rabase; Costumes, Carine Sarfati; Music, Normand Cobrell; Editors, Stephen Rivkin, Andrew S. Eisen; Associate Producer, Julia Rosenberg; Co-Producers, Sandra Cunningham, Yannick Bernard, Robyn Slovo; Casting, Nina Gold; a Serendipity Point Films, Odessa Films, Copmany Pictures co-production; Canadian-French-British-U.S.; Dolby; Deluxe color; Rated R; 120 minutes; American release date: December 13, 2003

Cast

Pierre Brossard **Michael Caine**
Judge Annemarie Livi **Tilda Swinton**
Colonel Roux **Jeremy Northam**
Armand Bertier **Alan Bates**
Father Leo **John Boswell**
David Manenbaum **Matt Craven**
Commissaire Vionnet **Frank Finlay**
Pochon **Ciarán Hinds**
Monsignor Le Moyne **William Hutt**
Michael Levy **Noam Jenkins**
Dom Andre **David De Keyser**
Old Man **John Neville**
Dom Vladimir **Edward Petherbridge**
Nicole **Charlotte Rampling**
Father Patrice **Colin Salmon**
Inspector Cholet **Peter Wight**
Father Joseph **Christian Erickson**
Captain Durand **Dominic Gould**
Professor Valentin **Peter Hudson**
Max **Joseph Malerba**
Clotilde **Irene Palko**
Young Brossard **George Williams**

Jeremy Northam, Tilda Swinton

and, Simon Gregor (Father Rozier), James Greene (Dom Olivier), Joseph Long (Bishop), Helen Later (Marianne), Jürgen Zwingel (SS Officer), Alain Morel (Milice Captain), Jörg Schnass (German Sergeant), Wolfgang Pissors (German Soldier), Benjamin Euvrard (Photographer), Catherine van Hecke (Mme. Vionnet), Annette Milsom (Sister Dominique), Edward Hamilton Clark (Father Thiers), Shelly De Vito (Forensics Officer), Thierry Obaika (Legal Clerk), Daniel Lundh (Bertier's Secretary), Renaud Calvet (Bartender Montana), Frederic Pellegeay (Janitor), Jean-Jacques Boullay (Manservant), Michael Berreby (Interrogation Officer), Christophe Deslandes, Guy Germody, Kostia Gouzic, Aranud Rosenblatt, Rolland Safrana, Jean-Claude Subiro (Dombey Victims)

Michael Caine, Charlotte Rampling

Pierre Brossard, a former Nazi war criminal, long protected by a sympathetic Catholic group called the Chevaliers, finds himself running for his life from both a mysterious group determined to hunt him down and execute him and a war crimes judge eager to bring him to trial.

John Neville, Tilda Swinton PHOTOS COURTESY OF SONY CLASSICS

CALENDAR GIRLS

(TOUCHSTONE) Producers, Suzanne Mackie, Nick Barton; Director, Nigel Cole; Screenplay, Juliette Towhidi, Tim Firth; Co-Producer, Steve Clark-Hill; Photography, Ashley Rowe; Designer, Martin Childs; Costumes, Frances Tempest; Music, Patrick Doyle; Music Supervisor, Liz Gallacher; Editor, Michael Parker; a Harbour Pictures production; British; Dolby; Panavision; Technicolor; Rated PG-13; 107 minutes; American release date: December 19, 2003

Linda Bassett, Julie Walters, Celia Imrie, Annette Crosby, Helen Mirren, Penelope Wilton

Cast

Chris	**Helen Mirren**
Annie	**Julie Walters**
John	**John Alderton**
Cora	**Linda Bassett**
Jessie	**Annette Crosbie**
Lawrence	**Philip Glenister**
Rod	**Ciaran Hinds**
Celia	**Celia Imrie**
Marie	**Geraldine James**
Ruth	**Penelope Wilton**
Eddie	**George Costigan**
Richard	**Graham Crowden**
Frank	**John Fortune**
Kathy	**Georgie Glen**
May	**Angela Curran**
Trudy	**Rosalind March**
Jem	**John-Paul MacLeod**
Gaz	**Marc Pickering**

and John Sharian (Danny), Belinda Everett (Maya), Harriet Thorpe (Brenda Mooney), Gillian Wright (Eddie's Woman), Ian Embleton (Andy), Janet Howd (Julia), Lesley Staples (Policeman), Maggie McCarthy, Diana Marchment (W.I. Administrators), Celia Henebury (Check-In Stewardess), Ted Robbins (Bike Man), Arthur Kelly (Bookshop Owner), Alison Pargeter (Chemist's Assistant), Tim Barker (Holiday Speaker), Angus Barnett (Orchid Photographer), Frank Barrie (Lecherous Photographer), John Sparkes (Welsh Photographer), Merryn Owen (Student Photographer),

Julie Walters, Helen Mirren

Richard Ashton, Shameer Madarbakus (Policemen), Elizabeth Bennett (W.I. Judge), Simon Ludders (Waiter), Darren Southworth (Sofa Salesman), Sharon Thomas (TV Reporter), Christa Ackroyd (News Presenter), Geoffrey Wilkinson (Seed Company Manager), Bob Flag (Alan Rathbone), Mark Hayford (Charity Chicken Worker), Geoffrey Banks, Wilfred Harrison (Lycra Cyclists), Adil Hussain, Waqas Altaf (Jem's Friends), Paul McLeary, Peter Lorenzelli (Husbands), Jay Leno (Himself), Matt Malloy (Hotel Manager), Patton Oswalt (Larry), Craig Kirkwood (Bellboy), Frank Bello, John Bush, Scott Ian Rosenfeld (Anthrax), Ashley Niles (Hotel Registration), Angela Baker, Beryl Bamforth, Christine Clancy, Ros Fawcett, Lynda Logan, Tricia Stewart (Highgyll W.I. Ladies), Roy the Postman (Himself)

Helen Mirren, Julie Walters PHOTOS COURTESY OF TOUCHSTONE

The true story of how a group of middle-aged women from the small English village of Napley came up with the outrageous idea of posing naked for a calendar in order to raise money for a local hospital.

Claire Bouanich

THE BUTTERFLY

(FIRST RUN FEATURES) Producer, Patrick Godeau; Executive Producer, Francoise Galfre; Director/Screenplay, Philippe Muyl; Photography, Nicholas Herdt; Designer, Nikos Meletopoulos; Costumes, Sylvie de Segonzac, Francoise Dubois; Music, Nicolas Errera; Editor, Mireille Leroy; an Aliceleo, France 2 Cinema, Rhone-Aples Cinema, Gimages Films production; French, 2002; Dolby; Color; Not rated; 80 minutes; American release date: December 19, 2003

Cast
Julien **Michel Serrault**
Elsa **Claire Bouanich**
Elsa' Mother **Nade Dieu**
Cafe Waitress **Françoise Michaud**
Marguerite, the Concierge **Helen Hily**
Police Commissioner **Pierre Poirot**
The Other Police Officer **Jacky Nercessian**
Sebastien's Father **Jacques Bouanich**
Sebastien's Mother **Catherine Cyler**
Sebastien **Jerry Lucas**

Claire Bouanich, Michel Serrault PHOTOS COURTESY OF FIRST RUN FEATURES

Sebastien's Grandmother **Dominique Marcas**
Entomologist **Idwig Stephane**
Geometrician **Francis Frappat**

A lonely eight-year-old girl strikes up a friendship with a curmudgeonly neighbor who shares her passion for butterfly collecting.

Toni Collette, Gotaro Tsunashima PHOTO COURTESY OF GOLDWYN

JAPANESE STORY

(GOLDWYN) Producer, Sue Maslin; Director, Sue Brooks; Screenplay, Alison Tilson; Photography, Ian Baker; Designer, Paddy Reardon; Costumes, Margot Wilson; Editor, Jill Bilcock; Music, Elizabeth Drake; Line Producer, David Lightfoot; Casting, Dina Mann; an Austrlian Film Finance Corp. presentation of a Gecko Films production; Australian; Dolby; Super 35 Widescreen; Color; Rated R; 105 minutes; American release date: December 31, 2003

Cast
Sandy Edwards **Toni Collette**
Tachibana Hiromitsu **Gotaro Tsunashima**
Bill Baird **Matthew Dyktynski**
Mum **Lynette Curran**
Yukiko Hiromitsu **Yumiko Tanaka**
Jackie **Kate Atkinson**
Richards **John Howard**
Jimmy Smithers **Bill Young**
Bloke in Row Boat **Reg Evans**
James **George Shevtsov**
Jane **Justine Clarke**

and Heath Bergersen (Petrol Bloke), Mike Frencham (Blake), Kuni Hashimoto (Translator), Dean Vince (Karaoke Singer)

Geologist Sandy Edwards finds herself falling into an unlikely relationship with Japanese businessman Hiromitsu while taking him on a field trip through Australia's remote Pilbara desert.

WXIII: PALTABOR THE MOVIE 3

(PIONEER ENTERTAINMENT) Producer, Takuji Endo; Executive Producer, Fumihiko Takayama; Directors, Takuji Endo, Fumihiko Takayama; Screenplay, Tori Miki; Story, Yuuki Masami; Music, Kenji Kawai; an Emotion, Headgear, Mad House Ltd., TFC production; Japanese, 2002; Stereo; Color; Rated R; 102 minutes; American release date: January 10, 2003. Voices: Richard Cansino, Richard Epcar, Saeko Misaki, Steve Kramer, Julie Maddalena, Jake Martin, Bob Thomas, Tony Oliver, Simon Isaacson, David Umansky, Michelle Ruff, Helen Storm, Alfred Thor, Ron Allen, Dave Lelyveld.

KIRA'S REASON: A LOVE STORY

(FIRST RUN FEATURES) Producers, Morten Kaufmann, Bo Ehrhardt; Director, Ole Christian Madsen; Screenplay, Ole Christian Madsen, Mogens Rukov; Photography, Jørgen Johansson; Editor, Søren B. Ebbe; Music, Øyvind Ougaard, César Berti; Casting, Kompagniet V. Rie Hedegaard; Danish, 2001; Color; Not rated; 94 minutes; American release date: January 17, 2003. Cast: Stine Steingade (Kira), Lars Mikkelsen (Mdas), Sven Wollter (Kira's Father), Peacheslatrice Petersen (Kay), Camilla Bendix (Charlotte), Lotte Bergstrøm (Michelle), Thomas W. Gabrielsson (Gustav), Ronnie Hiort Lorenzen (Mikkel), Oliver Appelt Nielsen (Julius), Klaus Pagh (Mads' Boss), Claus Strandberg, Henrik Birch, Michael Hasselflug (Suppliers), Helee Herete Sørensen (Wife of 1st Supplier), Nicolas Bro (John), Jesper Hyldegaard (Erik), Michael Zuckow Mardorf (Waiter at Suppliers Party), Søren Poppel (Worker), Øyvind Ougaard, César Berti, Mads Vinding, Klaus Menzer (Orchestra)

DIVINE INTERVENTION

(AVATAR FILMS) Producer, Humbert Balsan; Director/Screenplay/Co-Producer, Elia Suleiman; Photography, Marc-Andre Batigne; Sets, Miguel Markin, Denis Renault; Editor, Véronique Lange; Line Producer, Avi Kleinberger; a co-production of Ognon Pictures/Arte France Cinema/Gimages Films/Soread 2M/Litchblick/Filmstiftung NRW; French-Palestine, 2002; Dolby; Color; Not rated; 89 minutes; American release date: January 17, 2003. Cast: Elia Suleiman (E.S.), Manal Khader (The Woman), Nayef Fahoum Daher (The Father), Amer Daher (Auni), Jamel Daher (Jamel), George Ibrahim (Santa Claus), George Khleifi (Jerusalem Neighbor), Avi Kleinberger (Trainer & Tax Collector), Salman Nattor (Uncle's Friend), Menashe Noy (Soldier at Checkpoint), Nazira Suleiman (Mother)

BIG SHOT'S FUNERAL

(SONY CLASSICS) Producers, Yang Buting, Wang Zhongiun, Chen Kuo Fu; Executive Producers, Tong Gang, Wang Zhonglei, He Ping; Line Producer, Lu Guoqiang; Director, Feng Xiaogang; Screenplay, Li Shaoming, Shi Kang, Feng Xiaogang; Photography, Zhang Li; Deisgner, Liu Xingang; Costumes, Duan Xiaoli; Editor, Zhou Ying; Music, San Bao; a China Film Group, Hua Yi Brothers & Taihe Film Investment Corporation, Columbia Pictures Film Production (Asia) Ltd. presentation in association with China Film Co-Production Company; Hong Kong-China, 2001; Dolby; Color; Rated PG; 101 minutes; American release date: January 17, 2003. Cast: Ge You (Yo Yo), Donald Sutherland (Don Tyler), Rosamund Kwan (Lucy), Ying Da (Louis Wang), Paul Mazursky (Tony), Christopher Barden, Fu Biao, Li Chengru, He Ping, Zhang Hanyu, Niu Piao, Tianian Wuren, Paul Duke, Li Xiaogeng, Liu Yiwei, Xu Xiaoli, Ye Hong, Yuan

Lars Mikkelsen, Stine Stengade in *Kira's Reason* PHOTO COURTESY OF FIRST RUN FEATURES

Dewang, Xhang Xilin, Yang Xin, Ji Mi, Li Weijia, Zhang Qingning, Shang Rong, Zhang Danlu, Niu Zifan, Ge Lei, Yan Mingshi, Ye Jun, Yang Chunlin, Ban Zan, Li Qing, Hu Kexin, Zhao Yan, Wang Ying, Li Ke, Li Jiandong, Duan Duan, Yuan Weidon, Chu Xingyi, Chen Dazhong, Wang Hongwu, Qiu Yingsan, Zhang Weiguo, Rui Lirong, Wang Suda, Wang Liyun, Wang Shigui, Dal Jinfeng, Xu Baofeng, Luo Yangfang, Xing Jun, Zhong Zongyin, Liu Xiugie, Deng Guangxun

IN THE MIRROR OF MAYA DEREN

(ZEITGEIST) Director/Screenplay, Martina Kudlácek; Photography, Wolfgang Lehner; Music, John Zorn; Editor, Henry Hills; a co-production of the Austrian Film Institute, Dschoint Ventschr Filmproduktion AG, Navigator Film, TAG/TRAUM Filmproduktion, Vienna Film Foundation, arte; Austrian-Czech-Swiss-German, 2002; Black and white/color; Not rated; 103 minutes; American release date: January 24, 2003. Documentary on one of the leading figures of the underground film movement, Maya Deren.

Maya Deren in *In the Mirror of Maya Deren* PHOTO COURTESY OF ZEITGEIST

THE LAST LETTER

(ZIPPORAH) Producers, Frederick Wiseman, Pierre-Olivier Bardet; Director/Screenplay, Frederick Wiseman; Based on the novel and play *Zhizn I sudba* by Vasili Grossman; Photography, Yorgos Arvanitis; Editor, Frederick Wiseman, Luc Barnier; a co-production of Centre National de La Cinématographie, Idéale Audience, La Comédie-Francaise, Le Studio Canal+, Zipporah Films, arte France Cinema; French-U.S.; Dolby; Black and white; 61 minutes; American release date: January 29, 2003. Catherine Samie (Anna Semyonovna)

KEDMA

(KINO) Producers, Amos Gitai, Laurent Truchot; Director, Amos Gitai; Screenplay, Amos Gitai, Marie-José Sanelme, with the collaboration of Marc Weitzmann, Mordechai Goldhecht, Haim Hazaz, Taufik Zayad; Photography, Yorgos Arvanitis; Set Decoration, Eitan Levi; Costumes, Laura Dinulescu; Line Producer, Shuki Friedman; Editor, Kobi Netanel; Music, David Darling, Manfred Eicher; Casting, Ilan Moscovitch; a co-production of Agav Films, Arte France Cinéma, MP Productions, Agav Hafakot, BIM Distribuzione; Israeli-French, 2002; Dolby; Color; Not rated; 100 minutes; American release date: February 7, 2003. Cast: Andrei Kashkar (Janusz), Helena Yaralova (Rosa), Yussef Abu Warda (Yussuf), Moni Moshonov (Klibanov), Juliano Merr (Mussa), Menachem Lang (Menahem), Sandy Bar (Yardena), Tomer Ruso (Milek), Veronica Nicole (Hanka), Liron Levo (Gideon), Roman Hazanowski (Roman), Dalia Shachaf (Dalia), Keren Ben Raphaël (Isha), Sacha Tchernichovsky (Sacha), Rawda Suleiman (Jaffra), Gal Altsculer (Yigal)

Kedma PHOTO COURTESY OF KINO

CHIHWASEON: PAINTED FIRE

(KINO) Producer, Lee Tae-won; Executive Producer, Kang Woo-seok; Director, Im Kwon-taek; Screenplay, Kim Yong-oak, Im Kwon-taek; Story, Min Byung-sam; Photography, Jung Il-sung; Music, Kim Young-dong; Editor, Park Soon-duk; Production Designer, Joo Byung-doh; Costumes, Lee Hye-ran; South Korean, 2002; Dolby; Color; Not rated; 117 minutes; American release date: February 14, 2003. Cast: Choi Min-sik (Jang Seung-ub), Yoo Ho-jung (Mae-hyang), Ahn Sung-ki (Kim Byung-moon), Kim Yeo-jin (Jin-hong), Son Yae-jin (So-woon), Han Myung-goo (Lee Eung-heon), Jung Tae-woo (Teenage Seung-up), Choi Jong-sung (Boy Seung-up), Gi Jung-soo (Master Yook-sook), Park Jee-il (Scholar Kwak), Park Bum-gyoo (Gaettong), Hwang Choon-ha (Pan-soi)

Catherine Samie in *The Last Letter* PHOTO COURTESY OF ZIPPORAH

Yoo Ho-jung, Choi Min-sik in *Chihwaseon* PHOTO COURTESY OF KINO

LOVE AT TIMES SQUARE

(MEDIA PARTNERS) Producer/Director/Screenplay, Dev Anand; Photography, Chaman K. Basu, David Tumblety; Designer, B.D. Jadhav; Editor, Ashok Bandekar; an Navketan International Films production; Indian; Color; Not rated; 155 minutes; American release date: February 14, 2003. Cast: Dev Anand (Mr. Shaan), Heenee Kaushik (Sweety), Chaitanya Chaudhry (Bobby), Shoeb Khan (Raj), Siya Rana (Angela), Salman Khan (Himself), Rishi Kapoor (CEO), Satish Shah, Ketki Dave (Motel Owners)

FROM THE OTHER SIDE

(FIRST RUN/ICARUS) Producers, Fabrice Puchault, Luciano Rigolini, Marilyn Watelet, Xavier Carniaux, Brigitte De Villepoix, Thierry Garrel, Elisabeth Marliangeas, Christiane Philippe; Director/Screenplay, Chantal Akerman; Photography, Chantal Akerman, Robert Fenz, Raymond Fromont; Editor, Claire Atherton; a co-production of AMIP, Carré-Noir RTBF, Chemah I.S., Paradise Films, SBS Television, Yleisradio (YLE), arte France Cinéma; French-Belgian-Australian-Finnish, 2002; Dolby; Color; Not rated; 99 minutes; American release date: February 20, 2003. Documentary on illegal Mexican immigrants hoping to cross the border into the United States.

From the Other Side PHOTO COURTESY OF FIRST RUN/ICARUS

THE NAVIGATORS

(FIRST LOOK) Producer, Rebecca O'Brien; Line Producer, Peter Gallagher; Director, Ken Loach; Screenplay Ron Dawber; Photography, Mike Eley, Barry Ackroyd; Designer, Martin Johnson; Costumes, Theresa Hughes; Music, George Fenton; Editor, Jonathan Morris; an Atta Films, Parallax Pictures, Road Movie Filmproduktion, Tornasol Films production; British-German-Spanish, 2001; Dolby; Color; Rated R; 92 minutes; American release date: February 21, 2003. Cast: Dean Andrews (John), Tom Craig (Mick), Joe Duttine (Paul), Steve Huison (Jim), Venn Tracey (Gerry), Andy Swallow (Len), Sean Glenn (Harpic), Charlie Brown (Jack), Juliet Bates (Fiona), John Aston (Bill Walters), Graham Heptinstall (Owen), Angela Saville (Tracy), Clare McSwain (Lisa), Megan Topham (Chloe), Abigail Pearson (Eve), Charlotte Hukin (Rose), Jamie Widowson (Michael), Andy Oldham (PICOP), Nigel Harrison (Will Hemmings), Charles Armstrong (John Wilson), Charlie Wathen (Manager of Chip Shop), John Roy (Installation Man), Kevin Carroll, Tim Cooper, Max Lemon, Tony Nyland (Company Reps), Gerry McMahon, Tony Maskell (Essex Builders), Mike Wattam (Supervisor)

Freddy Flores in *Bolivia* PHOTO COURTESY OF CINEMA TROPICAL

BOLIVIA

(CINEMA TROPICAL) Producer, Roberto Ferro; Executive Producer, Matias Mosteirin; Director/Screenplay, Israel Adrián Caetano; Based on a story by Romina Lafranchini; Photography, Julián Apezteguía; Art Director/Costumes, María Eva Duarte; Editors, Lucas Scavino, Santiago Ricci; Music, Los Kjarkas; Instituto Nacional de Cinematografia y Artes Audiovisuales de la Argentina; Argentine, 2001; Dolby; Black and white; Not rated; 75 minutes; American release date: February 26, 2003. Cast: Freddy Flores (Freddy), Rosa Sánchez (Rosa), Oscar Bertea (Oso), Enrique Liporace (Jefe), Marcelo Videla (Marcelo), Héctor Anglada (Vendedor), Alberto Mercado (Mercado)

FOREIGN SISTER

(INDEPENDENT) Producer/Director/Screenplay, Dan Wolman; Photography, Itamar Hadar; Editor, Shoshana Wolman; Music, Slava Ganelin; a Film Project, Israeli Film Fund, Reshet Communication production; Israeli. 2000; Color; Not rated; 124 minutes; American release date: February 28, 2003. Cast: Tamar Yerushalmi (Naomi), Askala Markos (Negist), Zvi Salton (Binyamin), Miriam Nevo (Miriam), Neli Tagar (Noga), Yossi Wassa (Andarge), Nir Ben Zion (Tom), Titina Asafa (Titina), Ilan Shani (Boss), Doron Abrahami (Lawyer), Shai Facado (Andarge's Friend), Alabacho Teka (Ethiopian Worker), Eva Takatz (Miriam's Friend), Jacob Zigler (Policeman), Rasam Jaraban, Rifat Amash (Doctors), Shlomo Chatina (Taxi Driver), Naga Ishte (Foreign Worker)

Askala Markos, Tamar Yerushalmi, Titine Asafa in *Foreign Sister* PHOTO COURTESY OF INDEPENDENT

TEN

(ZEITGEIST) Producers, Abbas Kiarostami, Marin Karmitz; Director/Screenplay/Photography, Abbas Kiarostami; Associate Producer, Caley Thomas; Music, Howard Blake; Editors, Abbas Kiarostami, Bahman Kiarostami, Vahid Ghazi; a co-production of Abbas Kiarostami Productions, Key Lime Productions, MK2 Productions; French-Iranian, 2002; Color; Not rated; 94 minutes; American release date: March 5, 2003. Cast: Mania Akbari (Driver), Amin Maher (Amin), Kamran Adl, Roya Arabashi, Roya Arabashi, Amene Moradi, Mandana Sharbaf, Katayoun Taleidzadeh

Mania Akbari in *Ten* PHOTO COURTESY OF ZEITGEIST

CHAOS

(KINO) Producers, Kimio Hara, Satoshi Kanno, Takeo Kodero; Executive Producer, Naoki Kai; Director, Hideo Nakata; Screenplay, Hisashi Saito, based on the novel by Shogo Utano; Photography, Tokusho Kikumura; Music, Kenji Kawai; Tidepoint Pictures; Japanese, 2000; Color; Not rated; 90 minutes; American release date: March 7, 2003. Cast: Masato Hagiwara (Goro Kuroda), Miki Nakatani (Satomi Tsushima), Ken Mitsuishi (Takayuki Komiyama), Jun Kunimura (Detective Hamaguchi)

Miki Nakatani, Masato Hagiwara in *Chaos* PHOTO COURTESY OF KINO

Mohammada Reza Foroutan, Golab Adineh in *Under the Skin of the City*
PHOTO COURTESY OF MAGNOLIA

UNDER THE SKIN OF THE CITY

(MAGNOLIA) Producers, Rakhshan Bani-Etemad, Jahangir Kowsari; Director, Rakhshan Bani-Etemad; Screenplay, Rakhshan Bani-Etemad, Jahangir Kowsari; Photography, Hassein Jafarian; Designer, Omid Mohit; Editor, Mastafa Kherghehpoush; Iranian, 2001; Color; Not rated; 93 minutes; American release date: March 14, 2003. Cast: Golab Adineh (Tuba), Mohammada Reza Foroutan (Abbas), Baran Kowsari (Mahboubeh), Ebraheem Sheibani (Ali), Mohsen Ghazi Moradi (Mahmoud, the Father), Mahraveh Sharifi-Nia (Masoumeh), Homeira Riazi (Hamideh), Ali Ossivand (Nasser Khan), Mehrdad Falahatgar (Marandi), Mariam Boubani (Masoumeh's Mother), Nazanin Farahani (Nahid)

PLATFORM

(EMPIRE) Producers, Kit Ming Li, Shozo Ichiyama; Executive Producer, Masayuki Mori; Director/Screenplay, Zhang Ke Jia; Photography, Yu Lik Wai; Art Director, Sheng Qiu; Costumes, Lei Qi, Xiafei Zhao; Music, Yoshihiro Hanno; Editor, Jing Lei Kong; a co-production of Artcam International, Bandai Entertainment, Hu Tong Communications, Office Kitano, T-Mark; Hong Kong-Chinese-Japanese-French, 2001; Stereo; Color; Not rated; 154 minutes; American release date: March 14, 2003. Cast: Hong Wei Wang (Minliang), Tao Zhao (Ruijuan), Jing Dong Liang (Chang Jun), Tian Yi Yang (Zhong Pin), Bo Wang (Yao Eryong)

JAPON

(VITAGRAPH FILMS) Producer/Director/Screenplay, Carlos Reygadas; Photography, Diego Martinez Vignatti; Associate Producer, Carlos Serrano Azcona; Art Director, Alejandro Reygadas; Music, Arvo Part; Editors, Daniel Melguizo, Carlos Serrano Azcona, David Torres Labansat; a co-production of Mantarraya Proudcciones, NoDream Cinema, Solaris Film; German-Mexican-Dutch-Spanish, 2002; Color; Not rated; 122 minutes; American release date: March 19, 2003. Cast: Alejandro Ferretis (The Man), Magdalena Flores (Ascen), Yolanda Villa (Sabina), Martin Serrano (Juan Luis), Rolando Hernandez (The Judge), Bernabe Perez (The Singer), Fernando Benitez (Fernando), Carlos Reygadas Barquin (The Hunter), Pablo Gil Sanchez Mejorada, Alejandro Sanchez Mejorada (Hunting Boys), Ernesto Velazquez (Hunter Unloading), Pablo Tamariz (Puzzled Hunter), Alex Ezpeleta (Hunter with Beer), Fran Castillo (Walking Hunter), Diego Martinez Vignatti (Sitting Hunter), Carlos Reygadas

Alejandro Ferretis (left), Carlos Reygadas Barquin (center) in *Japon* PHOTO COURTESY OF VITAGRAPH FILMS

Castillo (Hunter Handing Over Gun), Luis Amador (The Butcher), Noe Barranco (Fat Boy at Butcher's), Angel Flores (Boy with a Slingshot/Football Boy), Jesus Escamilla (Boy's Father), Paz Perez (Vicente), Fernando Tellez (Fernando, Man Without the Use of His Hands), Jazmin Acosta (Fernando's Daughter), Eugenio (Peasant with Hoe), Maria Flores (Old Woman Having a Stroll), Matias Serrano (Old Man Having a Stroll), Claudia Rodriguez (Woman in Dream), Juan Octavio Serrano (Juan Luis' Son), Jose Luis Najera (Juan Luis' Thin Son), Alejandro Reygadas (Priest)

GAUDI AFTERNOON

(FIRST LOOK PICTURES) Producer, Andres Vicente Gomez; Executive Producer/Director, Susan Seidelman; Screenplay, James Myhre, based on the novel by Barbara Wilson; Photography, Josep M. Civit; Costumes, Antxon Gomez; Music, Bernardo Bonezzi; Editor, Deidre Slevin; Casting, Pep Armengol, Kerry Barden; a co-production of Antena 3 TV, Lola Films, Via Digital; Spanish; Dolby; Color; Rated R; 88 minutes; American release date: March 21, 2003. Cast: Judy Davis (Cassandra Reilly), Marcia Gay Harden (Frankie Stevens), Lili Taylor (Ben), Juliette Lewis (April), Courtney Jines (Delilah), Maria Barranco (Carmen), Christopher Bowen (Hamilton), Sergi Ruiz (Carlos), Gloria Casas (Elisa), Aitor Extravizz (Esteban), Pep Molina (Paco), Victor Alvaro (Juan)

Judy Davis, Marcia Gay Harden in *Gaudi Afternoon* PHOTO COURTESY OF FIRST LOOK PICTURES

FULLTIME KILLER

(PALM PICTURES) Producers, Wai Ka Fai, Andy Lau, Johnnie To; Executive Producers, Catherine Chan, Shirley Lau; Directors, Johnnie To, Wai Ka Fai; Screenplay, Wai Ka Fai, Joseph O'Bryan, based on the novel by Edmond Pang; Photography, Cheng Siu Keung; Art Directors, Jerome Fung, Silver Cheung; Editor, David Richardson; Music, Alex Khaskin, Guy Zerafa; a co-production of

CMC Magnetics Corporation, Milkyway Image, Team Work Motion Pictures Ltd.; Hong Kong, 2002; Color; Not rated; 102 minutes; American release date: March 21, 2003. Cast: Andy Lau (Tok), Takashi Sorimachi (O), Simon Yam (Lee), Kelly Lin (Chin), Cherrie Ying (Gigi), Teddy Lin (C7), Suet Lam (Fat Ice)

Kelly Lin, Andy Lau in *Fulltime Killer* PHOTO COURTESY OF PALM PICTURES

THE GIRL FROM PARIS

(FILMS PHILOS) Producer, Christophe Rossignon; Director, Christian Carion; Screenplay, Eric Assous, Christian Carion; Photography, Antoine Heberle; Designer, Jean-Michel Simonet; Costumes, Francoise Dubois, Virginie Montel; Editor, Andrea Sedlackova; Music, Philippe Rombi; Casting, Richard Rousseau; a co-production of Artemis Productions, Mars Films, MS Productions, Nord-Quest, Rhone-Alpes Cinema Productions, Studio Canal; Belgian-French, 2001; Color; Not rated; 103 minutes; American release date: March 21, 2003. Cast: Michel Serrault (Adrien Rochas), Mathilde Seigner (Sandrine Dumez), Jean-Paul Roussillon (Jean), Frederic Pierrot (Gerard), Marc Berman (Stephanie), Francoise Bette (Sandrine's Mother), Christophe Rossignon (Owner), Roland Chalosse (Barman), Achilles Francisco Varas dell'Aquilla (Barfly), Henri Pasquale, Paul Courat, Bernard Gerland, Ramon Bertrand (Card Players), Grazziela Horens (Dark-Haired Girl), Vincent Borei (Dark-Haired Boy), Nathalie Villard (Fair-Haired Girl), Joel Paparella (Fair-Haired Boy), Stephanie Ittel (Schoolteacher), Noel Martin (Priest), Christian Carion (Man with Portable), Mickey Dedaj (Man with Walkman), Yves Rochas, Eric Rochas (Pig Breeders)

Mathilde Seigner, Michel Serrault in *The Girl from Paris* PHOTO COURTESY OF FILMS PHILOS

THE GOOD OLD NAUGHTY DAYS

(STRAND) Producer/Director, Michel Reilhac; Based on an idea by Michel Reilhac, Sébastien Marnier; Inspired by Pascal Greggory; Executive Director, Xénia Maingot; Music, Eric Le Guen; Editor, Olivier Lupczynsky; French, 2002; Black and white; Not rated; 67 minutes; American release date: March 28, 2003. Compilation of French "blue movies" shorts from the silent era.

COWBOY BEBOP: THE MOVIE

(SAMUEL GOLDWYN CO.) Producers, Masudo Ueda, Masahiko Minami, Minoru Takanashi; Executive Producers, Takayuki Yoshii (Sunrise), Ryohei Tsunoda (Bandai Visual); Director, Shinichiro Watanabe; Action Animation Director, Yutaka Nakamura; Mechanical Animation Director, Masami Goto; Co-Director, Yoshiyuki Takei; Screenplay, Keiko Nobumoto; Based on the story by Hajme Yatate; Photography, Yoichi Ogami; Art Director, Atsushi Morikawa; Set Designer, Shiho Takeichi; Music, Yoko Kanno; Music Performed by Seatbelts; Editor, Shuichi Kakesu; Character Design & Animation Director, Toshihio Kawamoto; a Destination Films presentation of a Bandai Visual Co., Sunrise Inc. production; Japanese, 2001; Dolby; Color; Rated R; 116 minutes; American release date: April 4, 2003. Voice Cast: Steve Blum (Spike Spiegel), Beau Billingslea (Jet Black), Wendee Lee (Faye Valentine), Melissa Fahn (Edward), Jennifer Hale (Elektra), Mickey Curtis, Nicholas Guest (Rasheed), Grant J. Albrecht (Hoffman), Kirk Bailey (Robber D), Fred Toma, Said Faraj, Michael Desante (Moroccan Villagers), Murphy Dunne (Captain), Michael Forest (Ticket), Crispin Freeman (Operator), Jerry Gelb (Shadkins), Barbara Goodson (Old Woman), Michael Gregory (Laughing Bull), William Knight (Vandamme), Steve Kramer (Carlos), Michael Lindsay (Taxi Driver), Mary Elizabeth McGlynn (Chris Riley), Daran Norris (Vincent Volaju), Bob Papenbrook (Antique Dealer), Jamieson Price (Analyzer B, Spy B), Mike Reynolds (Colonel), Ron Roggie (Soldier/Weather 2), Michelle Ruff (Cashier), Lia Sargent (Judy), John Snyder (Bob), Peter Spellos (Duvchenko/Queen), Doug Stone (Analyzer), Paul St. Peter (Punch/Mark Rather), Kirk Thornton (Steve), Mirron E. Willis (Harris), Dave Wittenberg (Lee Sampon), Tom Wyner (Rengle)

THE HERO: LOVE STORY OF A SPY

(VIDEO SOUND) Producers, Dhirajlal Shah, Pravin Shah, Hasmukh Shah; Executive Producer, Asif Sheikh; Director, Anil Sharma; Photography, Kabir Lal; Art Director, Sanjay Dhabade; Music, Uttam Singh; Editor, Suresh Urs; Indian; Color; Not rated; 185 minutes; American release date: April 11, 2003. Cast: Sunny Deol (Major Arun Khanna), Preity Zinta (Reshma), Priyanka Chopra (Shine Zakaria), Amrish Puri (Isaq Khan), Kabir Bedi (Zakaria), Deep Dhillon (Col. Hidayatulla), Khalid Mohammad (Maulana Azhar), Arif Zakaria (Muhazir Karimuddin), Ashwani Pandey (RAW Agent Meelma), Vallabh Vyas (Reshma's Father), Rajpal Yadav (Dorji), Pradeep Rawat (RAW Chief Kapoor), Shahbaz Khan (Inderjeet), Rajat Bedi (Wasim Khan)

SHARK SKIN MAN AND PEACH HIP GIRL

(KINO) Producer, Kazuto Takida; Executive Producer, Hilo Iizumi; Director/Screenplay, Katsuhito Ishii; Based on the comics by Minetaro Mochizuki; Photography, Hiroshi Machida; Designer, Tomoyuki Maruo; Editor, Yumiko Doi; a Tohohashinsha Film Company Ltd. production; Japanese, 1998; Color; Rated R; 108 minutes; American release date: April 16, 2003. Cast:

Faye in *Cowboy Bebop* PHOTO COURTESY OF SAMUEL GOLDWYN CO.

Sie Kohinata in *Shark Skin Man and Peach Hip Girl* PHOTO COURTESY OF KINO

Tadanobu Asano (Kuroo Samehada), Ittoku Kishibe (Tanuki), Sie Kohinata (Toshiko Momojiri), Kimie Shingyoji (Mitsuko Fukuda), Susumu Terajima (Sawada), Shingo Tsurumi (Mitsuru Fukuda), Daigaku Sekine (Sakaguchi), Koh Takasugi (Sorimachi), Shingoro Yamada (Taniguchi), Hitoshi Kiyokawa (Maruo), Boba (Asahina), Keisuke Horibe (Inuzuka), Yoshiyuki Morishita (Hidari), Kanji Tsuda (Fukazume), Youhachi Shimada (Michio Sonezaki), Tatsuya Gashuin (Yamada), Hisaji Yamamo (Shiota)

MARION BRIDGE

(FILM MOVEMENT) Producer, Julia Sereny, Bill Niven, Jennifer Kawaja; Director, Wiebke von Carolsfeld; Screenplay, Daniel MacIvor; Photography, Stefan Ivanov; Designer, Bill Fleming; Costumes, Martha Currie; Music, Lesley Barber; Editor, Dean Soltys; Casting, Jenny Lewis; an Idlewild Films, Sienna Films production; Canadian, 2002; Color; Not rated; 90 minutes; American release date: April 18, 2003. Cast: Molly Parker (Agnes), Stacy Smith (Louise), Marguerite McNeil (Rose), Ellen Page (Joanie), Hollis McLaren (Chrissy), Emmy Alcorn (Dory), Joseph Rutten (Ken), Nicola Lipman (Valerie), Jackie Torrens (Marlene), Kevin Curran (Sandy), Ashley MacIsaac (Mickey), Heather Rankin (Sue), Linda Busby (Evie), Stephen Manuel (Tavern Bartender), Jim Swansburg (Airport Bartender), Rebecca Jenkins (Theresa)

ALI ZAOUA: PRINCE OF THE STREETS

(ARAB FILM DISTRIBUTION) Producers, Jean Cottin, Antoine Voituriez; Director, Nabil Ayouch; Screenplay, Nabil Ayouch, Nathalie Saugeon; Photography, Vincent Mathias; Art Director, Saïd Raïs; Costumes, Nezha Dakil; Music, Krishna Levy; Editor, Jean-Robert Thomann; Casting, Fayçal Boughrine; a co-production of 2M, Ace Editing, Alexis Films, Ali'n Productions, Gimages 3, Le Studio Canal+, Playtime, TF1 International, TPBS Cinema; Morrocan-Tunisian-French-Belgian, 2001; Dolby; Color; 90 minutes; American release date: April 18, 2003. Cast: Mounïm Kbab (Kwita), Mustapha Hansali (Omar), Hicham Hansali (Omar), Hicham Moussoune (Boubker), Abdelhak Zhayra (Ali Zaoua), Saïd Taghmaoui (Dib), Amal Ayouch (Ali Zaoua's Mother), Mohamed Majd (The Fisherman), Hicham Ibrahimi (The Sailor), Nadia Ould Hajjaj (Schoolgirl), Abdelkader Lofti (Hardware Store Owner), Khalil Essaadi (Khalid), Abdessamad Tourab Seddam (Noureddine), Ahmed Lahlil (Man in Bar), Karim Merzak (The Marabout's Son), Halima Frizi (Old Woman), Khalid Ghanimi (Shita), Mohamed Ajmil (Barrito), Mohamed Ezzanati (Menss), Tarik El Hichou (Chino), Jalila Boulhimez (Journalist)

Ali Zaoua: Prince of the Streets PHOTO COURTESY OF ARAB FILM DISTRIBUTION

VENUS & MARS

(ZENPIX/INNOVATION FILM GROUP) Producers, Emmo Lempert, Bernd F. Lunkewitz, Uwe Schott; Executive Producers, Daniela Amavia, Nelson Woss; Director, Harry Mastrogeorge; Screenplay, Ben Taylor; Photography, Martin Fuhrer; Designer, Boerries Hahn-Hoffmann; Costumes, Barbara Baum; Editor, Darcy Worsham; Music, Nathan Barr; Casting, Marion Dougherty, Doug Wright; an Atlantis Film and Mitteldeutches Filmkontor production; German, 2001; Dolby; Color; Rated R; 94 minutes; American release date: April 18, 2003. Cast: Lynn Redgrave (Emily Vogel), Daniela Lunkewitz (Kay Vogel), Ryan Hurst (Roberto), Fay Masterson (Celeste), Julia Sawalha (Marie), Julie Bowen (Lisa), Michael Weatherly (Cody Battle Vandermeer), Michael Brandoner (Ernst), Sebastian Ggosch (Patrick, Kay's Brother), Manou Lubowski (Andre), Jens Neuhaus (Denis), Hedda Oledzki ("Crazy" Lady), Hella von Sinnen (Bertha), Frank Behnke (Willhelm), Harry Weber (Celeste's Trashman), Ramona Kunze-Libnow (Carmen), Dieter Haubold (Father Brown), Stephan Menzel Gehrke (Manager at Restaurant), Anne Germann, Kristin Germann ("Martian" Twins), Eric Hansen (Coach Frank Firscher), Eden (Sharon), Niklas Papst, Olivia Anschtz, Jessica Schuch (Marie's Kids), Monique Schuldt (Juliet), Stephan Rochelt (Romeo), Richard Reizleien (Baby in Shop), Johanna Libeneiner (Doris), Heike Ronniger (Lisa's Assistant), Michael Kohn (Bus Driver), Borries Hahn-Hoffman (Funeral Director), Detlef Kapplisch, Manfred Erwe (Local Boy), Harry Mastrogeorge (Host)

Daniela Amavia, Michael Weatherly in *Venus & Mars* PHOTO COURTESY OF ZENPIX/INNOVATION FILM GROUP

ONMYOJI: THE YIN YANG MASTER

(PIONEER ENTERTAINMENT) Producers, Kazuya Hamana, Nobuyuki Tohya, Tetusji Hayashi; Executive Producer, Banjiro Uemura; Director, Yojiro Takita; Screenplay, Baku Yumemakura, Itaru Era, Yasushi Fukuda; Based on the book by Baku Yumemakura; Photography, Naoki Kayano; Designer, Kyoko Heya; Editor, Isao Tomita; Music, Shigeru Umebayashi; a Dentsu Inc., Kadokawa Shoten Publishing Co., TBS Inc., Toho Co., Tohokushina Film Corporation production; Japanese, 2001; Color; Rated R; 112 minutes; American release date: April 25, 2003. Cast: Mansai Nomura (Abe no Seimei), Hideaki Ito (Hiromasa no Hiromasa), Hiroyuki Sanda (Doson), Kyoko Koizumi (Aone), Eriko Imai (Mitsumushi), Yui Natsukawa (Suke Hime), Mai Hosho (Ghost Woman), Kenichi Yajima (Fujiwarano Morosuke), Kenichi Ishii (Fujiwarano Kaneie), Kenjio Ishimaru (Head of Onmyoji), Sachiko Kokubu (Toko), Yukijiro Hotaru (Minamotono Tadamasa), Shiro Shinomoto (Onono Kiyomaro), Kenji Yamaki (Tachibanano Ukon), Hoka Kinoshita (Emperor Kanmu), Hitomi Tachihara (Ayako), Masato Hagiwara (Sawara Shinno), Akira Emoto (Fujiwarano Motokata), Ittoku Kishibe (Mikado, Emperor)

Molly Parker in *Marion Bridge* PHOTO COURTESY OF FILM MOVEMENT

MAROONED IN IRAQ

(WELLSPRING MEDIA) Producer/Director/Screenplay, Bahman Ghobadi; Photography, Saed Nikzat; Editor, Haydeh Safi-Yari; a Mij Film Co. production; Iranian, 2002; Color; Not rated; 108 minutes; American release date: April 25, 2003. Cast: Shahab Ebrahimi (Mirza), Faegh Mohamadi (Barat), Allah-Morad Rashtian (Audeh), Rojan Hosseini (Rojan), Iran Ghobadi (Hanareh), Saeed Mohamadi (The Teacher)

MR. & MRS. IYER

(MADHU/TIPS EXPORT) Producer, N. Vankatesan; Executive Producer, Rupali Mehta; Director/Screenplay, Aparna Sen; Based on a story by Aparna Sen and Dulal Dey; Photography, Ghoutam Gose; Art Director, Ustad Zakir Hussain; Costumes, Saborni Das; Editor, Rabiranjan Maitra; a Triplecom Media production; Indian, 2002; Color; Not rated; 120 minutes; American release date: April 25, 2003. Cast: Konkona Sensharma (Meenakshi Iyer), Rahul Bose (Jehangir "Raja" Chowdhury), Vijaya Subramanium (Meenakshi's Mother), A.V. Iyenger (Meenakshi's Father), Rabiranjan Maitra (Mr. Chatterjee), Niharika Seth (Khushbu), Riddhi Basu (Mala), Arnab Moitra (Suhel), Richa Vayas (Sonali), Oden Das (Amrita), Jishnu Songupta (Akaash), Jagpal Singh (Elderly Sikh Gentleman), K. Deep (Young Sikh Gentleman), Kaushik Bose (Mr. Dubey), Bidipta Chakraborty (Mrs. Dubey), Punam Singh (Lady Next to Meenakshi), Masud Akhtar (Her Brother), Veena Hichiu (His Wife), Arnab Dutta (Disabled Boy), Rwita Dutta Chakrabofty (His Mother)

OWNING MAHOWNY

(SONY CLASSICS) Producers, Andras Hamori, Seaton McLean, Alessandro Camon; Executive Producers, Edward R. Pressman, Sean Furst; Co-Producers, Victoria Hirst, Damon Bryant, Bradley Adams; Director, Richard Kwietniowski; Screenplay, Maurice Chauvet, Richard Kwietniowski; Based on the book *Stung* by Gary Ross; Photography, Oliver Curtis; Deisgner, Taavo Soodor; Costumes, Gersha Phillips; Music, The Insects, Richard Grassby-Lewis, Jon Hassell; Editor, Mike Munn; Casting, Deirdre Bowen; an Alliance Atlantis presentation of an Alliance Atlantis, Andras Hamori production in association with Natural Nylon Entertainment; Canadian-British; Dolby; Super 35 Widescreen; Deluxe color; Rated R; 104 minutes; American release date: May 2, 2003. Cast: Philip Seymour Hoffman (Dan Mahowny), Minnie Driver (Belinda), Maury Chaykin (Frank Perlin), John Hurt (Victor Foss), Sonja Smits (Dana Selkirk), Ian Tracey (Det. Ben Lock), Roger Dunn (Bill Gooden), Jason Blicker (Dave Quinson), Chris

Shahab Ebrahimi, Faegh Mohamadi, Allan-Morad Rashtian in *Marooned in Iraq*
PHOTO COURTESY OF WELLSPRING MEDIA

Collins (Bernie), Eric Fink (Psychologist), Mike "Nug" Nahrgang (Parking Attendant), Tanya Henley, Brona Brown (Tellers), Philip Craig (Briggs), Alex Retsnor (Michael Caruna), Gary Brennan (Man in Ice Rink), Matthew Ferguson (Martin), Tannis Burnett (Mary the Teller), Steve Cumyn, Tony Munch (Observers), Lorn Eisen (Blackjack Dealer), M.J. Kang (Secretary), Janine Theriault (Maggie), Lina Felice (Hot Date Teller), Jim Aldridge (Customs Officer), Karen Robinson (Cage Woman), Conrad Dunn (Edgar), Lani Billard (Tori the Teller), Judah Katz (Broker), Carol Anderson (Securities Clerk), Sherry Hilliard (Prostitute), Nicco Lorenzo Garcia (New Observer Recruit), Carmela Albero (Quinson's Mother), Keith Knight (Surveillance Operator), Matthew MacFadzean (Office Cop), Paul Hubbard (Vegas Casino Manager), Dennis Mirkovic (Vegas Floorman), David Collins (Private Investigator), Tony Stellisano (Vegas Stickman), Ted Ludzik (Vegas Security Guard), James McGrath (Old Man on the Piano), Darren McGuire (Guy Pulled by Zamboni), Russell Yuen (Auditor), Linda Goranso (Belinda's Mother), Stan Coles (Belinda's Father), Daniel Schneiderman (Security Official), Demetrius Joyette (Boy), R. Carson Durven (Shifty Driver), Michael Tait (Mr. Selkirk), Marvin Karon (Atlantic City Accountant), Frank Moore (Atlantic City CFO), Bob Zidel (Atlantic City Chief Executive), Joe Pingue (Plain Clothes Cop), Makyla Smith (Car Rental Girl), Claudio Masciulli, Robbie Rox (Detectives), Angelo Pedari (Craps Table Man), Troy Skog (Atlantic City Floorman), Scott Wickware (Uniformed Cop), Alex Poch-Goldin, Joseph Scoren (Investigators)

DRACULA: PAGES FROM A VIRGIN'S DIARY

(ZEITGEIST) Producer, Vonnie von Helmot; Director, Guy Maddin; Based on the *Dracula* ballet by Mark Godden, from the novel by Bram Stoker; Photography, Paul Suderman; Designer, Deanne Rohde; Costumes, Paul Daigle; Editor, Deco Dawson; Music, Gustav Mahler; Canadian Broadcasting Corporation; Canadian, 2002; Black and white/color; Not rated; 73 minutes; American release date: May 14, 2003. Cast: Wei-Qiang Zhang (Dracula), Tara Birtwhistle (Lucy Westenra), David Moroni (Dr. Van Helsing), Cindy Marie Small (Mina), Johnny A. Wright (Jonathan Harker), Stephanie Leonard (Arthur Holmwood), Matthew Johnson (Jack Seward), Keir Knight (Quincy Morris), Brent Neale (Renfield), Stephanie Ballard (Mrs. Westenra), Sarah Murphy-Dyson (Maid/Nun/Vampiress), Carrie Broda (Maid/Nun), Gail Stefanek (Maid/Vampiress), Janet Sartore (Maid/Nun), Jennifer Weisman, Emily Grizzell, Chalnessa Eames, Vanessa Lawson (Gargoyles/Nuns), Michelle Lack (Nun), Kerrie Souster (Vampiress)

John Hurt, Philip Seymour Hoffman in *Owning Mahowny* PHOTO COURTESY OF SONY CLASSICS

CINEMANIA

(WELLSPRING) Producer, Gunter Hanfgarn; Directors/Editors, Angela Christlieb, Stephen Kijak; Photography, Angela Christlieb; Music, Robert Drasnin, Stereo Total; Theme Song, Stereo Total; Co-Producer (NYC), Stephen Kijak; a Hanfgarn & Ufer Film-U. TV-Produktion (Berlin) presentation; German, 2002; Color; Not rated; 80 minutes; American release date: May 16, 2003. Documentary on a group of obsessive, avid New York filmgoers; featuring Jack Angstreich, Eric Chadbourne, Bill Heidbreder, Roberta Hill, Harvey Schwartz ("Cinemaniacs"), Richard Aidala (Projectionist), Tia Bonacore (Usher), David Schwartz (Curator), Michael Slipp (Neighbor)

Jack Angstreich in *Cinemania* PHOTO COURTESY OF WELLSPRING

POKÉMON HEROES

(MIRAMAX) Producers, Kathryn A. Borland, Choji Yoshikawa, Yukako Matsusako, Takemoto Mori; Executive Producers, Alfred Kahn, Norman J. Grossfeld, Takashi Kawaguchi, Masakazu Kubo; Directors, Kunihiko Yuyama, Jim Malone; Screenplay, Hideki Sonoda, Jim Malone; 4 Kids Entertainment; Japanese; Dolby; Color; Rated G; 80 minutes; American release date: May 16, 2003. Voice Cast: Addie Blaustein (Meowth/Additional Voices), Rachael Lillis (Misty/Jessie/Jigglypuff), Eric Stuart (Brock/James/Squirtle), Veronica Taylor (Ash Ketchum)

Wei-Qiang Zhang, Tara Birtwhistle in *Dracula: Pages from a Virgin's Diary*
PHOTO COURTESY OF ZEITGEIST

Tadanobu Asano in *Ichi the Killer* PHOTO COURTESY OF MEDIA BLASTERS

ICHI THE KILLER

(MEDIA BLASTERS) a.k.a. *Koroshiya Ichi*; Producers, Akiko Funatsy, Dai Miyazaki; Executive Producers, Toyoyuki Yokohama, Sumiji Miyake, Albert Yeung; Director, Takashi Miike; Screenplay, Sakichi Sato; Based on the magna by Hideo Yamamoto; Photography, Hideo Yamamoto; Designer, Takashi Sasaki; Costumes, Michiko Kitamura; Editor, Yasushi Shimamura; Music, Karera Musication; a co-production of Alpha Group, Emperor Mulitmedia Group, Excellent Gilm, Omega Micott, Omega Project, Spike Co., Starmax; Japanese, 2001; Dolby; Color; Not rated; 127 minutes; American release date: May 19, 2003. Cast: Tadanobu Asano (Kakihara), Nao Omori (Ichi), Shinya Tsukamoto (Jijii), Alien Sun (Karen), Sabu (Kaneko), Susumu Terajima (Suzuki), Shun Sugata (Takayama), Toru Tezuka (Fujiwara), Yoshiki Arizono (Nakazawa), Kee (Ryu), Satoshi Matsuo (Inoue), Hiroshi Kobayashi (Takeshi), Mai Goto (Sailor), Houka Kinoshita (Sailor's Lover), Rio Aoki (Miyuki)

Museum Caretaker, Nurse Joy, Latias, Pikachu, Ash in *Pokémon Heroes*
PHOTO COURTESY OF MIRAMAX

TSUI HARK'S VAMPIRE HUNTERS

(DESTINATION) Producer/Screenplay, Tsui Hark; Director, Wellson Chin; Executive Producers, Nansun Shi, Satoru Iseki, Wouter Barenorecht, Michael J. Werner; Photography, Joe Chan Kwong Hung, Sunny Tsang Tat Sze, Herman Yau Lai To; Music, J.M. Logan; Editor, Marco Hak Chi Sin; a Film Workshop Co. Ltd., Hark & Co. in association with Fortissimo Film Sales presentation of The Vampires Co. Ltd. production; Hong Kong-Japanese-Dutch, 2002; Dolby; Color; Rated R; 90 minutes; American release date: May 23, 2003. Voice Cast: Steven Blum (Hei), Richard Cansino (Dragon Tang)

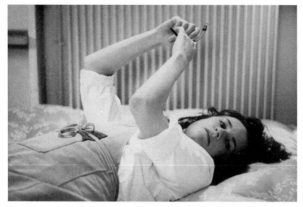

Valerie Lemercier in *Friday Night* PHOTO COURTESY OF WELLSPRING

FRIDAY NIGHT

(WELLSPRING) Producer, Bruno Pesery; Director/Screenplay, Claire Denis; Based on the novel *Vendredi Sori* by Emmanuele Bernheim; Photography, Agnes Godard; Art Director, Katia Wyszkop; Costumes, Catherine Leterrier; Music, Dickon Hinchliffe; Editor, Nelly Quettier; an Arena Films, France 2 Cinema, France Television Images production; French; Color; Not rated; 86 minutes; American release: May 23, 2003. Cast: Valerie Lemercier (Laure), Vincent Lindon (Jean), Helene de Saint Pere (Marie), Hélène Filliéres (Woman in the Pizzeria), Florence Loiret Caille (Girl Playing Pinball), Gregoire Colin (Passer-by in a Parka), Gilles D'Ambra (Tired Woman's Husband), Micha Lescot (Receptionist), Gianfranco Poddighe (Hotel Maitre d'), Nordine Barour (Walter), Lionel Goldstein (Buyer), Didier Woldemard (Driver of the Van), Nicolas Struve, Jerome Pouly (Repair Men), Nausicaa Meyer (Repair Woman)

BHOOT

(SPARK MEDIA) Producer/Director, Ram Gopal Varma; Screenplay, Lalit Marathe, Sameer Sharma; Photography, Vishal Sinha; Music, Salim-Sulaiman; Editor, Shimit Amin; a Varna Corporation Limited production; Indian; Color; Not rated; 113 minutes; American release date: May 30, 2003. Cast: Ajay Devgan (Vishal), Urmila Matondkar (Swati), Rekha (Witch Doctor), Victor Banerjee (Dr. Rajan), Nana Patekar (Inspector Liyacat), Tanuja (Mrs. Khosla), Seema Biswas (Maid), Fardeen Khan (Sanjay Thakker), Sabir Masani (Watchman)

THE THREE MARIAS

(EMPIRE) Producers, Eva Mariani, Aluizio Abranches; Director, Aluizio Abranches; Screenplay, Heitor Dhalia, Wilson Freire; Photography, Marcelo Durst; Art Director/Costumes, Bruno Schmidt; Music, André Abujamra; Editors, Aluizio Abranches, Karen Harley; a Lama Filmes, Teodora Films production; Brazilian-Italian, 2002; Dolby; Color; Not rated; 90 minutes; American release date: May 30, 2003. Cast: Marieta Severo (Filomena Capadócio), Julia Lemmertz (Maria Francisa), Maria Luisa Mendonça (Maria Rosa), Luiza Mariani (Maria Pia), Carlos Vereza (Firmino Santos Guerra), Enrique Diaz (Zé das Cobras), Tuca Andeada (Chief Tenório), Wagner Moura (Jesuíno Cruz), Lázaro Ramos (Catrevagem), Cassiano Carneiro (José Tranquilo Santos Guerra), Fábio Limma (Arcanjo Santos Guerra), André Barros (João Capadócio)

AMERICA SO BEAUTIFUL

(B GOOD FILMS) Producer/Director, Babak Shokrian; Screenplay, Babak Shokrian, Brian Horiuchi; Executive Producer, Jane Reardon; Photography, Thom Ryan; Designer, Leora Lutz; Costumes, Chris Kreiling; Music, Ramin Torkian; Editor, Andrew M. Somers, Mary Stephen; Casting, John Cato; Corey Tong, Epicentre Films, Filmmakers Alliance productions; Color; Not rated; 91 minutes; Release date: May 30, 2003. Cast: Mansour (Houshang), Alan De Satti (Hamid), Houshang Touzie (Sahmi), Diane Gaidry (Lucy), David Fairborz Davoodian (Parviz), Atossa Leoni (Maryam), Shohreh Aghdashloo (Exiled Actress), Belinda Waymouth (Kathy), Steven Zlotnick (Club Door Manager)

STARKISS: CIRCUS GIRLS IN INDIA

(WILDERELL) Directors/Screenplay, Chris Relleke, Jascha de Wilde; Photography, Chris Relleke; Music, Marcel Boudewijn; Netherlands; Color; Not rated; 77 minutes; American release date: June 11, 2003. Documentary about children who are sold to the circus to be performers.

PISTOL OPERA

(MEDIA BLASTERS) Producers, Satoru Ogura, Ikki Katashima; Director, Seijun Suzuki; Screenplay, Kazunroi Itô, Takeo Kimura; Photography, Yonezo Maeda; Designer, Takeo Kimura; Music, Kodama Kzufumi; Editor, Akira Suzuki; a Dentus Inc., Eisei Gekijo, Oguara Jimusyo, Shochiku Films, TV Tokyo, Victor Company of Japan production; Japanese, 2001; Dolby; Color; Not rated; 112 minutes; American release date: June 13, 2003. Cast: Makiko Esumi (Miyuki Minazuki), Sayoko Yamaguchi (Sayoko Uekyo), Masatoshi Nagase (Man Dressed in Black), Mikijiro Hira (Goro Hanada), Kenji Sawada (Man at Tokyo Station), Yeong-he Han (Girl Sayoko), Yoshiyuki Morishita (Killer No. 9), Jan Woudstra (Painless Surgeon)

TYCOON: A NEW RUSSIAN

(NEW YORKER) Producers, Vladimir Grigoriev, Catherine Dussart, Sergei Selyanov; Director/Designer, Pavel Lungin; Screenplay, Pavel Lungin, Aleksandr Borodyansky, Yuli Dubov; Based on the novel *Bolshaya pajka* by Yuli Dubov; Photography, Aleksei Fyodorov; Editor, Sophie Brunet; Music, Leonid Desyatnikov; a co-production of CDP, CTB Film Company, France 2 Cinema,

Julia Lemmertz, Luiza Mariani, Marieta Severo, Maria Mendonça in *Three Marias*
PHOTO COURTESY OF EMPIRE

Miyuki Minazuki in *Pistol Opera* PHOTO COURTESY OF MEDIA BLASTERS

Levani Outchaneichvili, Vladimir Mashkov in *Tycoon* PHOTO COURTESY OF NEW YORKER

Gimages, Kinokompaniya STV, Kominter, Magnat, Network Movie Filmproduktion GmbH & Co., Zweitest Deutsches Fernsehen, arte France Cinema; French-German-Russian; Dolby; Color; Not rated; 123 minutes; American release date: June 13, 2003. Cast: Vladimir Mashkov (Platon), Mariya Mironova (Masha), Levani Outchaneichvili (Larry), Aleksandr Baluyev (Koretsky), Andrei Krasko (Shmakov), Marat Basharov (Koshkin), Mikhail Vasserbaum (Mark), Sergei Yushkevich (Viktor), Natalya Kolyakanova (Nina), Aleksandr Samojlenko (Musa), Vladimir Steklov (Belenky), Vladimir Kashpur (Captain), Vladimir Golovin (Akhmet)

THE LEGEND OF SURIYOTHAI

(SONY CLASSICS) Producer, Kamla Yukol; Executive Producers, Francis Ford Coppola, Kim Aubry; Director, Chatri Chalerm Yukol; Screenplay, Chatri Chalerm Yukol, Sunait Chutintaranond; Photography, Igor Luther, Stanislav Dorsic, Anupap Boachan; Art Directors, Prasopcok Trhanasetvirai, Prasert Posrirat, Chetsada Prunarakard; Editors, Chatri Chalerm Yukol, Pattamanadda Yukol; Music, Richard Harvey; Thailand; Dolby; Color; Rated R; 142 minutes; American release date: June 20, 2003. Cast: M.L. Piyapas Bhirombhakdi (Queen Suriyothai), Sarunyoo Wongkrchang (King Thienracha), Pongpat Wachirabunjong (King Chairacha), Chatchai Plengpanich (Lord Pirenthorathep),

Johnny Anfone (Lord Warawongsa), Mai Charoenpura (Lady Srisudachan), Sinjai Plengoanich (Lady Srichulalak), Sorapong Chatri (Captain Rajseneha), Ampol Lampoon (Lord Intrathep), Suppakorn Kitsuwan (Sir Sriyod), Penpak Sirikul (Queen Jiraprapa), Wannasa Thongwiset (Akrachaya), Ronrittchai Khanket (King of Prae), Saharat Sangkapricha (Lord Buyinnaung), Varuth Waratham (Lord Sihatu), Suppakit Tangthatswasd (Tabinshwehti), Sombati Medhanee (Lord Minyesihatu), Akekaphan Bunluerit (Chan), Saad Peampongsanta (Lord Mahasena), Manop Ausawatep (Lord Sawankalok), Krung Srivilai (Lord Pichai), Atthep Chodhoy (Lt. Thepruksa), Suchao Pongvilai (King Norputthanukul), Aranya Namvong (Thongsuk), Naiyana Chanruang (Pudkrong), Pawanrat Narksuriya (Kayoon), Jiravadee Israngura (Prik), Yani Tramod (Lord Rajpakdee), Meesak Nakkarat (Lord Yommaraj)

My Terrorist PHOTO COURTESY OF WOMEN MAKE MOVIES

MY TERRORIST

(WOMEN MAKE MOVIES) Producers, Yulie Gerstel, Esther van Messel; Director/Screenplay, Yulie Gerstel; Photography, Moshe Gerstel, Yulie Gerstel, Oded Kirma; Music, Tal Segev; Editor, Boaz Leon; a Gohen Gerstel Productions, BBC, TV Ontario, TV2 Denmark, Yleisradio co-production; Israeli-Canadian-Danish-Finish-British; Black and white/color; Not rated; 60 minutes; American release date: June 25, 2003. Documentary in which Yulie Gerstel chronicles her efforts to get parole for the terrorist who was responsible for the death of her friend in 1978.

M.L. Piyapas Bhirombhakdi in *The Legend of Suriyothi* PHOTO COURTESY OF SONY CLASSICS

WAR AND PEACE

(FIRST RUN FEATURES) Producer/Director/Screenplay/Photography/Editor/-Narrator, Anand Patwardhan; Indian; Black and white/color; Not rated; 148 minutes; American release date: June 25, 2003. Documentary about the development of nuclear weapons in India and Pakistan.

War and Peace PHOTO COURTESY OF FIRST RUN FEATURES

GASOLINE

(STRAND) Producer, Galliano Juso; Director, Monica Lisa Stambrini; Screenplay, Monica Lisa Stambrini, Elena Stancanelli, Anneritte Ciccone; Based on the novel *Benzina* by Elena Stancanelli; Photography, Fabio Cianchetti; Art Director, Alessandro Rosa; Costumes, Antonella Cannarozzi; Music, Massimo Zamboni, Luca Rossi, Simone Filippi; Editor, Paola Freddi; Casting, Marina Alpi, Stefania Incagnoli; a Galliano Uso presentation with the participation of Tele+; Italian, 2001; Dolby; Fotocinema color; Not rated; 89 minutes; American release date: July 2, 2003. Cast: Maya Sansa (Stella), Regina Oriolli (Lenni), Mariella Valentini (Mamma), Chiara Conti (Pippi), Marco Quaglia (Sandro), Pietro Ragusa (Filippo), Osvaldo Livio Alzari (Cashier), Luigi Maria Burruano (Gabriele, Priest), Pasquale Zurlin (Taxi Driver), Giovanni Mastrangelo , Gina Larocca (Police)

LA COMMUNE (PARIS, 1871)

(FIRST RUN ICARUS) Director/Editor, Peter Watkins; Screenplay, Peter Watkins, Agathe Bluysen; Photography, Odd-Geir Sæther; a co-production of 13 Productions, La Sept-Arte, Le Musée d'Orsay; French; Black and white; 345 minutes; American release date: July 3, 2003. Documentary examining the poorest section of Paris.

CONFUSION OF GENDERS

(PICTURE THIS!) Producer, Didier Boujard; Director/Associate Producer, Ilan Duran Cohen; Screenplay, Ilan Duran Cohen, Philippe Lasry; Photography, Jeanne Lapoirie; Designer, Françpose Dupertuis; Costumes, Barbara Kraft; Music, Jay Jay Johnson; Editor, Fabrice Rouaud; Casting, Marie-Sylvie Caillierez, Stéphanie Foenkinos; a co-production of Alta Loma Films, Centre National de la Cinématographie, Fugitive Productions, Le Studio Canal+, UGC International; French, 2000; Dolby; Color; Not rated; 94 minutes; American release date: July 9, 2003. Cast: Pascal Greggory (Alain Bauman), Nathalie Richard (Lauren

Julie Gayet, Pascal Greggory, Vincent Martinez in *Confusion of Genders*
PHOTO COURTESY OF PICTURE THIS!

Albertini), Julie Gayet (Babette), Alain Bashung (Etienne), Vincent Martinez (Marc), Cyrille Thouvenin (Christophe), Marie Saint-Dizier (Marlene), Bulle Ogier (Laurence's Mother), Pierre Barrat (Laurence's Father), Nelly Borgeaud (Alain's Mother), Michel Betray (Alain's Father), Valérie Stroh (Patricia), Vincent Gauthier (Christophe's Father), Malik Faraoun (Karim), Michèle Brousse (Boss), Emmanuelle Bougerol (Sylvie), Dominique Bernardi (Deputy Mayor), Denis Lachaud (Laurence's Client), Julien Féret (Nurse), Emmanuel Vieilly (Prison Warden), Catherine Giron (Hairdresser's Client), Christophe Perrier (Accountant), Chloé Mons (Blond Girl), Samuel Perche (Young Adonis), Arnaud Vallens (Smoothie Man), Fedronio Saaro (Brazilian), Frédéric Haddou (Small Dark-Haired Man), Christophe Lebeslour (Highbrow Man), Guylaine Lemire (Androgynous Girl), Serge Feuillard (Fifty-Year-Old Man), Jacqueline Chambon (Woman at the Bus Stop), David Gilbert (Adolescent Kevin), Franck Magnier (Franck), Renaud Sherpa (Adolescent Julien)

La Commune (Paris, 1871) PHOTO COURTESY OF FIRST RUN ICARUS

TATTOO

(AMERICAN VITAGRAPH) Producers, Jan Hinter, Roman Kuhn; Executive Producer, Verena Herfurth; Director/Screenplay, Robert Schwentke; Photography, Jan Fehse; Designer, Josef Sanktjohanser; Costumes, Peri de Bragança; Music,

Martin Todsharow; Editor, Peter Przygodda; Casting, Anja Dihrberg; a B.A. Produktion, Lounge Entertainment GmbH, Studio Canal production; German, 2002; Dolby; Color; Not rated; 108 minutes; American release date: July 11, 2003. Cast: August Diehl (Marc Schrader), Christian Redl (Minks), Nadesha Brennicke (Maya Kroner), Johan Leysen (Frank Schoubya), Faith Cevillkollu (Dix), Monika Bleibtreu (Kommissarin Roth), Ilknur Bahadir (Meltem), Joe Bausch (Günzel), Florian Panzer (Poscher), Jasmin Schwiers (Marie Minks), Gustav-Peter Wöhler (Scheck), Ingo Naujkos (Stefan Kreiner), Christiane Scheda (Lynn Wilson)

THE SEA IS WATCHING

(TRISTAR) Producer, Naoto Sarukawa; Director, Kei Kumai; Screenplay, Akira Kurosawa; Based on the novel by Shugoro Yamamoto; Photography, Kazuo Okuhara; Art Director, Takeo Kimura; Costumes, Kazuko Kurosawa; Music, Teizo Matsumura; Editor, Osamu Inoue; a Nikkatsu Corporation, Sony Pictures Entertainment, Sony/PCL, TV Tokyo production; Japanese; Dolby; Black and white/color; Rated R; 119 minutes; American release date: July 18, 2003. Cast: Misa Shimizu (Kikuno), Nagiko Tono (Oshin), Mastaoshi Nagase (Ryosuke), Hidetaka Yoshioka (Fusanosuke), Eiji Okuda (Ginji), Renji Ishibashi (Zenbei), Miho Tsumiki (Okichi), Michiko Kawai (Osono), Yumiko Nogawa (Omine), Tenshi Kamogawa (Umekichi), Yukiya Kitamura (Kenta), Kumiko Tsuchiya (Prostitute)

BALSEROS

(SEVENTH ART) Producer, Marcos Loris Omedes Regas; Executive Producers, Tom Roca, Maria Jose Solera; Directors, José María Doménech; Screenplay, Carlos Bosch, David Trueba; Photography, José María Doménech; Music, Lucrecia Pérez; Editor, Ernest Blasi; a Buasan Films, Buenavida Producciones, Tevisión de Catalunya production; Spanish, 2002; Dolby; Color; Not rated; 120 minutes; American release date: July 23, 2003. Documentary on Cuban refugees and their efforts to reach the United States; featuring Guillermo Armas, Rafael Cano, Miriam Hernandez.

LUCÍA, LUCÍA

(FOX SEARCHLIGHT) a.k.a. *The Cannibal's Daughter*; Producer, Matthias Ehrenberg; Director/Screenplay, Antonio Serrano; Based on the novel *The Cannibal's Daughter* by Rosa Montero; Line Producer, Sandra Solares;

Cecilia Roth, Kuno Becker, Carlos Alvarez-Novoa in *Lucía, Lucía* PHOTO COURTESY OF FOX SEARCHLIGHT

Photography, Xavier Pérez Grobet; Designer, Brigitte Broch; Costumes, María Estela Fernández; Music, Nacho Mastretta; Editor, Jorge García; Casting, Ana Urquidi; a Conaculta/Foprocine/Instituto Mexicano de Cinematografica/Fondo Ibermedia presentation of a Titan Prods., Argo Communications Picture in co-production with Lola Films, Total Films; Mexican-Spanish; Dolby; Widescreen; Azteca Color; Rated R; 109 minutes; American release date: July 25, 2003. Cast: Cecilia Roth (Lucía), Carlos Álvarez-Novoa (Félix), Kuno Becker (Adrián), Manuel Blejerman (Suspect), Socorro de la Campa (Cashier), Itatí Cantoral (Airline Saleswoman #1), Javier Díaz Dueñas (Inspector García), Margarita Isabel (Lucía's Mom), Max Kerlow (Old Wehner), Enoc Leaño (El Ruso), Mario Iván Martínez (Mr. Wehner), Adela Micha (Anchor Woman), Héctor Ortega (The Cannibal), Vivian Pierce (Estrella), Jorge Salinas (Security Guard), Mónika Sánchez (Actress), Enrique Singer (Undersecretary Ortiga), Luis Felipe Tovar (Drunk), Jorge Zárate (Blanco)

Salma Hayek in *Hotel* PHOTO COURTESY OF INNOVATION

HOTEL

(INNOVATION) Producers, Mike Figgis, Etchie Stroh, Annie Stewart; Executive Producer, Andrea Calderwood; Director/Screenplay, Mike Figgis; Photography, Mike Figgis, Patrick Alexander Stewart; Designer, Franco Fumagalli; Costumes, Catherine Byse Dian; Music, Mike Figgis, Anthony Marinelli; Casting, Celestia Fox; a co-production of Cattleya, Hotel Productions, Moonstone Entertainment, Red Mullet Productions; British-Italian, 2001; Dolby; Color; Not rated; 93 minutes; American release date: July 25, 2003. Cast: Max Beesley (Antonio), Fabrizio Bentivoglio (Very Important Doctor), Brian Bovell (Cardinal), Saffron Burrows (Duchess of Malfi), Elisabetta Cavallotti (Abducted Hotel Guest), Valentina Cervi (Hotel Maid), George DiCenzo (Boris), Andrea Di Stefano (Assassin), Nicola Farron (Hotel Guest), Christopher Fulford (Steve Hawk), Valeria Golino (Italian Actress), Jeremy Hardy (Flamenco Troupe Administrator), Salma Hayek (Charlee Boux), Danny Huston (Hotel Manager), Rhys Ifans (Trent Stoken), Jason Isaacs (Australian Actor), Paco Jarana (Flamenco Guitarist), Lucy Liu (Kawika), Mark Long (Hotel Kitchen Manager), Mia Maestro (Cariola), John Malkovich (Omar Johnson), Chiara Mastroianni (Hotel Nurse), Laura Morante (Greta), Ornella Muti (Flamenco Spokesperson), Burt Reynolds (Flamenco Manager), Stefania Roccca (Sophie), Julian Sands (Tour Guide), Danny Sapani (AJ), David Schwimmer (Jonathan Danderfine), Alexandra Staden (Film PA), Mark Strong (Ferdinand), Heathcote Williams (Bosola), Eva La Yerba Buena (Flamenco Dancer)

SEASIDE

(FIRST RUN) Producer, Alain Benguigui; Director, Julie Lopes-Curval; Screenplay, Julie Lopes-Curval, François Favrat; Photography, Stephan Massis; Designer, Philippe van Herwijnen; Music, Christophe Chevalier, Nicolas Gerber; Editor, Anne Weil; Casting, Nathalie Esther; a co-production of Centre National de la Cinematographie, La Sofica Sofinergie 5, Le Studio Canal+, Procirep, Sombrero Productions; French; Dolby; Color; Not rated; 90 minutes; American release date: August 6, 2003. Cast: Bulle Ogier (Rose), Hélène Fillières (Marie), Ludmila Mikaël (Anne), Jonathan Zaccaï (Paul), Patrick Lizana (Albert), Liliane Rovère (Odette), Jean-Michel Noirey (Robert), Jauris Casanova (Pierre), Audrey Bonnet (Lilas), Emmanuelle Lepoutre (Angélique), Fabien Orcier (Jacquot)

THE PRINCESS BLADE

(ADV FILMS) Producer, Taka Ichise; Director, Shinsuke Sato; Screenplay, Shinsuke Sato, Kei Kunii; Based on the comic by Kazuo Koike, Kazuo Kamimura; Photography, Taro Kawazu; Art Director, Tomoyuki Maruo; Music, Kenji Kawai; Editor, Hirohide Abe; Special Effects, Shinji Higuchi; Stunts, Kenji Tanigaki; from GAGA Communications and Oz Productions; Japanese; Dolby; Color; Rated R; 92 minutes; American release date: August 8, 2003. Cast: Hideaki Ito (Takashi), Yumiko Shaku (Yuki), Shiro Sano (Kidokoro), Yoichi Numata (Kuka), Kyusaku Shimada (Byakurai), Yoko Maki (Aya)

Yumiko Shaku in *The Princess Blade* PHOTO COURTESY OF ADV FILMS

KOI...MIL GAYA

(YASH RAJI FILMS) a.k.a. *I Found Someone*; Producer/Director/Story, Rakesh Roshan; Screenplay, Rakesh Roshan, Robin Bhatt, Sachin Bhowmick, Honey Irani; Dialogue, Javed Siddiqi; Photography, Sameer Arya, Ravi K. Chandran; Art Director, Sharmishta Roy; Costumes, Rocky S; Music, Rajesh Roshan; Editor, Sanjay Verma; Film Kraft productions; Indian-Canadian; Dolby; Widescreen; Color; Not rated; 172 minutes; American release date: August 8, 2003. Cast: Hrithik Roshan (Rohit Mehra), Preity Zinta (Nisha), Rakesh Roshan (Sanjay Mehra), Rekha (Sonia Mehra), Prem Chopra (Harbans Saxena), Rajat Bedi (Raj Saxena), Johnny Lever (Chelaram Sukhwani), Mukesh Rishi (Inspector Khurshid Khan), Anuj Pandit, Mohit Makkad, Jai Choksi, Omkar Purohit, Hansika Motwani, Pranita Bishnoi (The Super Six)

Jauris Casanova, Audrey Bonnet in *Seaside* PHOTO COURTESY OF FIRST RUN

VENUS BOYZ

(FIRST RUN FEATURES) Producers, Kurt Maeder, Gabriel Baur; Co-Producers, Nina Froriep, Andea Hanke, Heike Hempel; Director/Screenplay, Gabriel Baur; Photography, Sophie Maintigneux; Music, David Shiller; Editors, Salome Pitschen, Jean Vites, Daniel Roderer; a co-production of Clock Wise Productions (NY), Nina Froriep WDR, Koln, Heike Hempel, Andrea Hanke; Swiss-U.S., 2001; Dolby; Color; Not rated; 104 minutes; American release date: August 22, 2003. Documentary on drag kings, female masculinity, and gender performance in New York and London; featuring Dréd Gerestant, Diane Torr, Del LaGrace Volcano, Bridge Markland, Mo Fischer, Storme Webber, Queen Bee Luscious, Mistress Formika, Judith Haberstam

RANA'S WEDDING

(ARAB FILM) a.k.a. *Another Day in Jerusalem*; Producers, George Ibrahim, Bero Beyer; Director, Hany Abu-Assad; Screenplay, Liana Badr, Ihab Lamey; Photography, Brigit Hillenius; Costumes, Hamada Atallah; Music, Bashar Abd Rabbou, Mariecke van der Linden; Editor, Denise Janzee; a co-production of Augustus Film, Palestinian Film Foundation; Palestine, 2002; American release date: August 22, 2003. Cast: Clara Khoury (Rana), Khalifa Natour (Khalil), Ismael Dabbag (Ramzy), Walid Abed Elsalam (Marriage Official), Zuher Fahoum

Clara Khoury in *Rana's Wedding* PHOTO COURTESY OF ARAB FILM

(Father), Bushra Karaman (Grandmother), Georgina Asfour (Mary), Manal Awad (Alia), Nasrin Buqa'i (Samira), Sami Metwasi (Friend)

DOG DAYS

(LEISURE TIME FEATURES) Producers, Helmut Grasser, Philippe Bober; Director, Ulrich Seidl; Screenplay, Ulrich Seidl, Veronika Franz; Photography, Wolfgang Thaler; Designer, Andreas Donhauser; Costumes, Sabine Volz; Editors, Andrea Wagner, Christof Schertenleib; German; Color; Not rated; 120 minutes; American release date: August 22, 2003. Cast: Maria Hofstatter (Hitchhiker), Christine Jirku (Teacher), Victor Hennemann (Teacher's Lover), George Friedrich (Lucky), Alfred Mrva (Alarm Salesman), Erich Finsches (Old Man), Gerti Lehner (Housekeeper), Franziska Weiss (Klaudia), Rene Wanko (Mario), Claudia Martini (Ex-Wife), Victor Rathbone (Ex-Husband)

Queen Bee Luscious, Drèd Gerestant *Venus Boyz* PHOTO COURTESY OF FIRST RUN FEATURES

DUST

(LIONS GATE) Producers, Chris Auty, Vesna Jovanoska, Domenico Procacci; Supervising Line Producer, Steve Clark-Hall; Director/Screenplay, Milcho Manchevski; Photography, Barry Ackroyd; Designer, David Munns; Costumes, Anne Jendritzko; Music, Kiril Dzajkovski; Editor, Nic Gaster; a History Deams, Ena Film, Fandango production, with Shadow Films in association with South Fork Pictures, of a presentation of The Film Consortium; British-German-Italian-Macedonian, 2001; Dolby; Deluxe color; Rated R; 127 minutes; American release date: August 22, 2003. Cast: Joseph Fiennes (Elijah), David Wenham (Luke), Adrian Lester (Edge), Anne Brochet (Lilith), Nikolina Kujaca (Neda), Rosemary Murphy (Angela), Vlado Jovanovski (Teacher), Salaetin Bilal (The Major), Vera Farmiga (Amy), Matt Ross (Stitch), Meg Gibson (Bone), Tamer Ibrahim (Kemal), Vladimir Jacev (Spase), Vladimir Gjorgjijoski (Enver), Zora Georgieva (Maslina), Jordan Simonov (Iorgo), Josif Josifovski (Priest), Joe Mosso (Church Bell), Saundra McClain (Nurse), Nick Sandow (White Trash), Bruce MacVittie (Paramedic), Tom Strauss (Catholic Priest), Milica Stojanova (Dosta), Stanko Stoilkov (Godfather), Petar Mircevski (Foreign Priest), Mladen Krstevski (Mirko), Stojan Arev (Slavejko), Pavle Dameski (Krste), Martin Mircevski (Simeon), Danilo Mandic (Flute Boy), Krste Jovanovski (Mace Man), Rubens Muratovski (Sailor), Judith Windsor (The Madam), Randy Duke (Sheriff),

Franziska Weiss in *Dog Days* PHOTO COURTESY OF LEISURE TIME FEATURES

Afrodita Atanasova (Catherine), Jon Ivanovski (Sigmund Freud), Blagoja Micevski (Painter), Elena Mosevska (Sam), Jordanka Todorova (Judy), Boris Corevski (Sharpshooter), Blagoja Spirkovski-Dzumerko (Perus)

SUDDENLY

(EMPIRE) Producers, Diego Lerman, Sebastián Ariel, Lita Stantic, Nicolás Martínez Zemborian; Director, Diego Lerman; Screenplay, Diego Lerman, María Meira; Based on the novel *La Prueba* by César Aira; Photography, Luciano Zito, Diego del Piano; Art Director, Mauro Do Porto, Luciana Kohn; Music, Juan Ignacio Bouscayrol Murciélago; Editors, Alberto Ponce, Benjamín Ávila; a Hubert Bals Fund, Lita Stantic Producciones, Nylon Cine production; Argentine-Dutch, 2002; Dolby; Black and white; 90 minutes; American release date: August 29, 2003. Cast: Tatiana Saphire (Marcia), Carla Crespo (Mao), Veronica Hassan (Lenin), Beatriz Thibaudin (Blanca), María Merlino (Delia), Marcos Ferrante (Felipe), Ana María Martínez (Ramona), Susana Pampin (Woman in Car), Luis Herrera (Truck Driver)

Joseph Fiennes, David Wenham in *Dust* PHOTO COURTESY OF LIONS GATE

Guillermo Toledo, Paz Vega in *The Other Side of the Bed* PHOTO COURTESY OF SUNDANCE FILM SERIES

THE OTHER SIDE OF THE BED

(SUNDANCE FILM SERIES) Producer, Tomás Cimadevilla, José Antonio Sáinz de Vicuña; Director, Emilio Martínez Lázaro; Screenplay, David Serrano; Photography, Juan Molina Temboury; Art Director, Juilo Torrecilla; Music, Roque Baños; Editor, Ángel Hernández Zoido; an Impala, Telecino, Telespan 2000, Via Digital production; Spanish; Dolby; Color; Rated R; 114 minutes; American release date: August 29, 2003. Cast: Ernesto Alterio (Javier), Paz Vega (Sonia), Guillermo Toledo (Pedro), Natalia Verbeke (Paula), Alberto San Juan (Rafa), María Esteve (Pilar), Ramón Barea (Sagaz), Nathalie Poza (Lucia), Secun de la Rosa (Carlos), Carol Salvador (Victoria), Geli Albaladejo (Professor), Blanca Marsillach (Monica), Leticia Dolera (Jennifer), Cote Soler, Luis Bermejo (Tennis Players), Curro Iglesias (Julio), Javier Gutiérrez (Fernando), Mohamed Khashoggi (Waiter), Daniel González (Daniel), Roma Alfaro (Marilyn Monroe), Coral Ortega, Dacia González, Mercedes del Castillo, Julio Viero, Julio Reches (Dancers)

WARRIOR OF LIGHT

(NEW YORKER) Producer/Director/Screenplay, Monika Treut; Photography, Elfi Mikesch; Music, Jack Motta; Editors, Monika Treut, Andrew Bird; German, 2001; Color; Not rated; 91 minutes; American release date: September 12, 2003. Documentary about Brazilian artist and human rights activist Yvonne Bezerra de Mello.

SO CLOSE

(COLUMBIA) Producer, Po Chu Chui; Director, Corey Yuen; Screenplay, Jeff Lau; Photography, Kwok-Man Keung; Designer, Eddy Wong; Costumes, Jesie Dai, Chung Man Yee; Music, Sam Kao, Kenji Tan; Editor, Ka-Fai Cheung; Action Choreographers, Corey Yuen, Jianyong Gao; a Columbia Pictures Film Production Asia, Eastern Productions; Hong Kong, 2002; Dolby; Color; Rated R; 110 minutes; American release date: September 12, 2003. Cast: Qi Shu (Lynn), Zhao Wei (Sue), Karen Wok (Hong Yat Hong), Song Seung Hun (Yen), Yasuaki Kurata, Derek Wan (Masters), Michael Wai (Ma Siu Ma), Siu-Lun Wan (Chow Nunn), Shek Sau (Chow Lui), Ki Yan Lam (Alice), Josephine Ho (Ching), Sheung Mo Lam (Lai Kai-joe), May Kwong (May), Fong Ping (Dad), Hee Ching Paw

(Mom), Lau Yee Tat (Secret King), Hing Ying Kam (Captain), So Pik Wong (May), Ben Lam (Ben), Ricardo Mamood (Peter), Jude Poyer (Flashback Killer)

EMERALD COWBOY: ESMERALDERO

(INDICAN) Producers/Directors, Andrew Molina, Eva Hayata; Editor, Andrew Molina; Screenplay/Executive Producer, Eishy Hayata; Co-Producer, Efrain Gamba; Photography, Byron Werner; Art Director, Eva Hayata; Music, Joe Kraemer; Casting, Manuel Cabral; a Burn Pictures production, presented in association with Andes Art Films; Colombian; Dolby; Color; Rated R; 117 minutes; American release date: September 19, 2003. Cast: Eishy Hayata (Himself), Eva Hayata (Esmeraldero), J.K. Anderson (Reporter)

THE PETERSBURG-CANNES EXPRESS

(MIRACLE FILM DISTRIBUTION) Producer, Bill Chamberlain; Director/Screenplay/Executive Producer, John Daly; Designer, David Endley; Music, Igor Khoroshev; Editor, Gregory Plotkin; an Entertech Releasing, Parallel Pictures, Russian Entertainment Group production; Color; Rated PG-13; 100 minutes; American release date: September 19, 2003. Cast: Nolan Hemmings (Alexie), Ksenia Alpherova (Anna), Jay Benedict (Zidkin), Svetlana Lunkina (Sophie), Andris Lielais (Drascovitch)

Warrior of Light PHOTO COURTESY OF NEW YORKER

Zhao Wei, Karen Wok in *So Close* PHOTO COURTESY OF COLUMBIA

Eishy Hayato (front) in *Emerald Cowboy* PHOTO COURTESY OF INDICAN

Nolan Hemmings, Ksenia Alpherova in *Petersburg-Cannes Express*
PHOTO COURTESY OF MIRACLE FILM DISTRIBUTION

CRIME SPREE

(INNOVATION FILM GROUP) Producers, Gary Howsam, Jamie Brown, Richard Rionda Del Castro; Director/Screenplay, Brad Mirman; Photography, Matthew Williams, Derek Rogers; Designer, Gordon Barnes; Costumes, Gersha Phillips; Music, Rupert Gregson-Williams; Editor, Eddie Hamilton; Casting, Marjorie Lecker; a co-production of GFT Entertainment, Hannibal Pictures, Studio Eight Productions, Vision View Entertainment; Canadian-British; Dolby; Color; Rated R; 98 minutes; American release date: September 19, 2003. Cast: Gerard Depardieu (Daniel Foray), Harvey Keitel (Frankie Zammeti), Johnny Hallyday (Marcel Burot), Renaud (Zero), Saïd Taghmaoui (Sami), Stéphane Freisss (Julien Labesse), Shawn Lawrence (Agent Pogue), Albert Dray (Raymond Gayet), Joanne Kelly (Sophie Nicols), Richard Bohringer (Bastaldi), Abe Vigoda (Angelo Giancarlo), Gino Marrocco (Joey Two Tons), Sal Figliomeni (Nicky the Rake), Diego Chambers (Raphael), Carlos Diaz (Hector), Chris Collins (Lamar), Michel Perron (Vinny), Louis Di Bianco (Bobby Vee), Jeff Geddis (Wayne), Joyce Gordon (Waitress), Dwayne McLean (Old Man Caretaker), Rick Sood (Store Clerk), Cam Natale (Half Tooth Tony), Philip Mackenzie (FBI Agent), Lory Wajnberg (Joey's Wife), Ron Kennell (Felix), Scott Watson (Motel Clerk), Lyriq Bent (Ellwood), P.J. Ingram (Deaf Guy), Garnet Harding, Plato Fountidakis, Ḥakan Coskuner (Gang Members), Geoffrey Coulter (Car Rental Clerk), Reginald Doresa (Eddie the Hare), Billy Khoury (Freddy O), Richard Bauer (Man on Phone), Kiera Belley (Little Girl), Liz Gordon (Receptionist), Philip Marshall (Judge), Patrick Ezerzer (French Mobster)

BOUNCE KO GALS

(MEDIA BLASTERS) a.k.a. *Leaving;* Producer, Masakatsu Suzuki; Co-Producer, Hilo Iizumi; Director/Screenplay, Masato Harada; Photography, Yoshitaka Sakamoto; Art Director, Hiroshi Maruyama; Music, Masahiro Kawasaki; Editor, Hirohide Abe; Shochiku Films; Japanese, 1997; Dolby; Color; Not rated; 110 minutes; American release date: October 3, 2003. Cast: Hitomi Sato (Jonko), Yasue Sato (Raku), Yukiko Okamoto (Lisa), Jun Murakami (Sap), Shin Yazawa (Maru), Kaori Momoi (Saki), Koji Yakusho (Oshima), Kazuki Kosakai (Salaryman)

Hitomi Sato, Yasue Sato, Yukiko Okamoto in *Bounce KO Gals* PHOTO COURTESY OF MEDIA BLASTERS

THE EVENT

(THINKFILM) Producers, Bryan Hofbauer, Thom Fitzgerald; Executive Producers, Robert Flutie, Vicki McCarty, Jeff Sackman, Chris Zimmer; Co-Producers, Steven Hillyer, Tim Marback; Director, Thom Fitzgerald; Screenplay, Tim Marback, Steven Hillyer, Thom Fitzgerald; Photography, Thomas M. Harting; Designer, D'Arcy Poultney; Costumes, Mia Morgan, Sian Morris Ross; Music, Christophe Beck; Editor, Christopher Cooper; Casting, John Comerford, Leonard Finger; a Covington Intl. and Flutie Entertainment presentation of an Arkanjel and Emotion Pictures production; Canadian-U.S.; Dolby; Color; HD-to-35mm; Not rated; 110 minutes; American release date: October 3, 2003. Cast: Parker Posey (Nick), Olympia Dukakis (Lila), Don McKellar (Matt), Sarah Polley (Dana), Brent Carver (Brian), Jane Leeves (Mona), Joanna P. Adler (Gaby), Rejean J. Cournoyer (Rory), Christina Zorich (Judy), Richard Latessa (Uncle Leo), Cynthia Preston (Amy)

Don McKellar, Joanna P. Adler, Sarah Polley in *The Event* PHOTO COURTESY OF THINKFILM

PORN THEATRE (LA CHATTE À DEUX TÊTES)

(STRAND) Producer, Pauline Duhault; Director/Screenplay, Jacques Nolot; Photography, Germain Desmoulins; Art Director, Patrick Durand; Music, Nino; Editor, Sophie Reine; Casting, Brigitte Moidon; French, 2002; Color; Not rated; 90 minutes; American release date: October 10, 2003. Cast: Jacques Nolot (50-Year-Old Man), Vittoria Scognamiglio (Cashier), Sébastien Viala (Projectionist), Olivier Torres (Ingrid Craven), Lionel Goldstein (The Transsexual), Frédéric Longbois (Glowing Eyes), Fouad Zeraoui (Transvestite), Jean-Louis Coquery (Nana Mouskouri)

HOUSE OF THE DEAD

(ARTISAN) Producers, Uwe Boll, Wolfgang Herold, Shawn Williamson; Executive Producers, Daniel S. Kletzky, Mark Gottwald, Dan Bates, Mark A. Altman; Director, Uwe Boll; Screenplay, Dave Parker, Mark A. Altman; Photography, Mathias Neumann; Designer, Tink; Costumes, Lorraine Carson; Music, Reinhard Besser; Editor, David M. Richardson; Special Effects Makeup, WCT Productions; Casting, Maureen Webb; a Brightlight Pictures-Herold and Besser Studios-Mindfire Entertainment production; Canadian-U.S.-German; Dolby; Color; Rated R; 90 minutes; American release date: October 10, 2003. Cast: Jonathan Cherry (Rudy), Tyron Leitso (Simon), Clint Howard (Salish), Ona Grauer (Alicia), Ellie Cornell (Casper), Will Sanderson (Greg), Enuka Okuma (Karma), Kira Clavell (Liberty), Sonya Salomaa (Cynthia), Michael Eklund (Hugh), David Palffy (Castillo), Jurgen Prochnow (Capt. Victor Kirk), Steve Byers (Matt), Erica Parker (Johanna), Birgit Stein (Lena), Jay Brazeau (Captain), Adam Harrington (Rogan), Colin Lawrence (G), Ben Derrick (McGivers), Elisabeth Rosen (Skye), Bif Naked (DJ), Penny Phang (Tyranny), Kris Pope (Raver), Mashiah Vaughn-Hulbert (Flashing Woman)

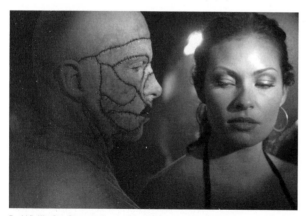

David Palffy, Ona Grauer in *House of the Dead* PHOTO COURTESY OF ARTISAN

SMALL VOICES

(SKY ISLAND FILMS) Producers, Gil Portes, Ray Cuerdo; Executive Producers, Cresencio Bendijo, Marissa Dames; Director, Gil Portes; Screenplay, Gil Portes, Adolfo Alix Jr., Senedy Que; Photography, Ely Cruz; Designer, Art Nicado ;Music, Jay Marfil; Editor, George Jarlego; from Teamwork Productions; Philippines, 2002; Color; Not rated; 109 minutes; American release date: October 10, 2003. Cast: Alessandra de Rossi (Melinda), Dexter Doria (Mrs. Pantalan), Gina Alajar

Vittoria Scognamiglio (left), Sébastien (right) in *Porn Theatre* PHOTO COURTESY OF STRAND

(Chayong), Amy Austria (Luz), Bryan Homecillo (Popoy), Pierro Rodriguez (Obet), Sining Blanco (Gela), Noni Buencamino (Fidel), Mhalouh Crisologo (Solita), Nanding Josef (Adong's Father), Tony Mabesa (Mr. Tibayan), Lailani Navarro (Pilar)

RETURNER

(SAMUEL GOLDWYN CO.) Producers, Akifumi Takuma, Toru Horibe, Chikahiro Ando; DIrector/Special Visual Effects, Takashi Yamazaki; Screenplay, Takashi Yamazaki, Kenya Hirata; Photography, Kozo Shibazaki, Akira Sako; Designer, Anri Johjo; Editor, Takuya Taguchi; Muisc, Akihiko Matsumoto; a Fuji Television Network/Toho/Amuse Pictures/Robot/Shirogumi/Imagica presentation; Japanese; Dolby; Color; Rated R; 118 minutes; American release date: October 17, 2003. Cast: Takeshi Kaneshiro (Miyamoto), Anne Suzuki (Milly), Goro Kishitani (Mizoguchi), Kirin Kiki (Zie), Yukiko Okamoto (Dr. Yagi), Kisuke Iida (Karasawa), Kazuya Shimizu (Murakami), Mitsura Murata (Mizoguchi's

Anne Suzuki, Goro Kishitani in *Returner* PHOTO COURTESY OF SAMUEL GOLDWYN CO.

Henchman), Chiharu Kawai (Liu's Interpreter), Dean Harrington (Dr. Brown), Xiaoqun Zhao (Slave Merchant), Masay Takahashi (Liu Laoban)

9 DEAD GAY GUYS

(TLA RELEASING) Producer, Lamia Nayeb-St. Hilaire; Executive Producers, Amanda Coombes, Amit Barooah, Robert Bevan, Keith Hayley, Charlie Savill; Director/Screenplay, Lab Ky Mo; Photography, Damien Elliott; Designer, Nik Callan; Costumes, Jane Spicer; Editors, Christopher Blunde, Jonathon Braman; Music, Stephen W. Parsons; Co-Producer, Colin McKeown; a Little Wing Films presentation in association with 9 Films; British; Dolby; Widescreen; Color; Not rated; 83 minutes; American release date: October 17, 2003. Cast: Glenn Mulhern (Kenny), Brendan Mackey (Byron), Steven Berkoff (Jeff), Michael Praed (The Queen), Vas Blackwood (Donkey-Dick Dark), Fish (Old Nick), Simon Godley (Golders Green), Carol Decker (Jeff's Wife), Raymond Griffiths (The Desperate Dwarf), Abdala Keserwani (Dick-Cheese Deepak), Karen Sharman (Margaret, The Iron Lady), Leon Herbert (Nev), Steven Woodhouse (Father Ted), John Michaels, Rickardo Beckles-Burrowes, Deban Aderemi (West African Brothers), Bryan Lawrence (Cop), Barry Martin (A Very Camp Man Indeed), Peter Lochburn (Moaning Man), Bill Hayes (Dirty Ole Irish Tramp), Wayne Crompton, Mark Gardner, Neil Howarth, Peter Keswick (Gay Gossips), Harry Harris (Other Cop), Yvonne Fisher (Blind Old Bat), Janice Frost, Cordelia Thomas, Laura Hazell (Old Grannies), Martin Collins, Karen Coppins (Breeders), Nicolas Chinardet, Adrian Flack, Mark Joyce, Jason Daly (Orthodox Jews)

THE LEGEND OF JOHNNY LINGO

(INNOVATION FILM GROUP) Producers, Gerald R. Molen, John Gabrett; Executive Producers, Tim Coddington, Brad Pelo; Director/Editor, Steven Ramirez; Screenplay, John Garbett, Riwia Brown; Based on the story *Johnny Lingo's Eight Cow Wife* by Patricia McGerr; Photography, Allen Guilford; Designer, Rob Gillies; Costumes, Jane Holland; Music, Kevin Kiner; Casting, Christina Asher; a Morinda Inc. and Tahitian Noni presentation of a Molen/Garbett production in association with the Stable Moving Image; New Zealand; Dolby; Panavision; Color; Rated G; 91 minutes; American release date: October 31, 2003. Cast: Rawiri Paratene (Chief), Joe Falou (Tama), Alvin Fitisemanu (Chief Steward), Kayte Ferguson (Old Mahana), Hori Ahipene (Pioi), Sima Urale (Hoku), Fokikovi Soakimi (Young Mahana), Tausani Simei-Barton (Young Tama), George Henare (Johnny Lingo), Pete Smith (Island Chief)

THE REVOLUTION WILL NOT BE TELEVISED

(VITAGRAPH) a.k.a. *Chavez: Inside the Coup*; Producer, David Power; Executive Producers, Rod Stoneman, Cees van Ede, Kevin Dawson, Nick Fraser, Leena Pasanen; Directors/Photography, Kim Bartley, Donnacha O'Briain; Editor, Ángel Hernández Zoido; a Palm Pictures 2002 production in association with the Irish Film Board; Irish-Dutch-German-British; Color; Not rated; 74 minutes; American release date: November 5, 2003. Documentary on the April 11, 2002, Venezuelan uprising that toppled President Hugo Chavez from power.

GLOOMY SUNDAY

(MENEMSHA) Producers, Richard Schöps; Executive Producer, Martin Rohrbeck; Director, Rolf Schübel; Screenplay, Rolf Schübel, Ruth Toma; Based on the novel by Nick Barkow; Photography, Edward Klosinski; Designer, Csaba Stork, Volker

Schäfer; Costumes, Andrea Flesch; Music, Rezsö Seress, Detlef Petersen; Editor, Ursula Höf; Casting, Tina Böckenhauer; a Studio Hamburg Filmproduktion, Dom Film, Focufilm, PolyGram Filmproduktion, Westdeutscher Rundfunk Premiere production; German-Hungarian, 1999; Dolby; Color; Not rated; 112 minutes; American release date: November 7, 2003. Cast: Erika Marozsán (Ilona), Joachim Król (László), Ben Becker (Hans Wieck), Stefano Dionisi (András), András Bálint (Ilonas Sohn), Géza Boros (Geigenspierl), Rolf Becker (Der Alte Wieck), Ilse Zielstorff (Frau Wieck), Ferenc Bács (Botschafter), Julia Zsolinai (Frau Botschafter), Aron Sipos (Arzt)

MANGO YELLOW

(INDEPENDENT) Producers, Paulo Sacramento, Cláudio Assis; Director, Cláudio Assis; Screenplay, Hilton Lacerda; Photography, Walter Carvalho; Designer/Costumes, Renata Pinheiro; Editor, Paulo Sacramento; Music, Jorge Du Peixe, Lúcio Maia; an Olhos de Cao Filmworks production; Brazilian, 2002; Dolby; Widescreen; Color; Not rated; 103 minutes; American release date: November 13, 2003. Cast: Matheus Machtergaele (Dunga), Jonas Bloch (Isaac), Leona Cavalli (Lígia), Dira Paes (Kika), Chico Díaz (Wellinton Kanibal), Conceição Camaroti (Aurora), Magdale Alves (Dayse), Jones Melo (Padre), Taveira Júnior (Taxi Driver)

Hugo Chavez in *The Revolution Will Not Be Televised*

Hugo Chavez in *The Revolution Will Not Be Televised* PHOTOS COURTESY OF VITAGRAPH

HUKKLE

(SHADOW DISTRIBUTION) Producers, András Böhm, Csaba Bereczki; Director/Screenplay, György Pálfi; Photography, Gergely Pohárnok; Music, Balázs Barna, Samu Gryllus; Editor, Ágnes Mógor; a Mokép production; Hungarian; Color; Not rated; 75 minutes; American release date: November 14, 2003. Cast: Ferenc Bandi (Cesklik Bácsi), Józsefné Rácz (Bába), József Forkas (Rendõr), Ferenc Nagy (Méhész), Ferencné Virág (A Méhész Felesége), Mihályné Király (Nagymama), Mihály Király (Nagypapa), Eszter Ónodi (Városi Anya), Attila Kaszás (Városi Papa), Szimonetta Koncz (Városi Kislány), Jánosné Gyõri (Postás)

Jósef Forkasin *Hukkle* PHOTO COURTESY OF SHADOW DISTRIBUTION

Henry Ian Cusick in *The Gospel of John* PHOTO COURTESY OF THINKFILM

THE GOSPEL OF JOHN

(THINKFILM) Producers, Garth H. Drabinsky, Chris Chrisafis; Executive Producer, Joel B. Michaels, Martin Katz, Sandy Pearl; Director, Philip Saville; Screenplay, John Goldsmith; Photography, Miroslav Baszak; Designer, Don Taylor; Costumes, Debra Hanson; Music, Jeff Danna; Editor, Michel Arcand, Ron Wisman Jr.; a Toronto Film Studios, Visual Bible International production; Canadian-British; Dolby; Color; Rated PG-13; 180 minutes; American release date: November 14, 2003. Cast: Henry Ian Cusick (Jesus Christ), Stuart Bunce (John), Daniel Kash (Simon Peter), Steven Russell (Pontius Pilate), Diana Berriman (Virgin Mary), Alan Van Spring (Judas Iscariot), Richard Lintern (Leading Pharisee), Scott Hand (John the Baptist), Lynsey Baxter (Mary Magdalene), Diego Matamoros (Nicodemus), Nancy Palk (Samaritan) Elliot Levey (Nathanael), Andrew Pifko (Philip), Cedric Smith (Caiaphas), Tristan Gemmill (Andrew), Stuart Fox (Blind Man), David Meyer (Lame Man), Nicolas Van Burek (Young Levite), William Pappas (Elderly Levite), Mark Brighton (Malchus), Miriam Brown (Martha), Greg Bryk, Alex Karzis, Gregory Meyers, Alex Poch-Golden (Disciples), Inga Cadranel (Adulterous Woman), Donald Ewer (Annas), Jan Filips (Joseph of Arimathea), Lisa Marcos (Bride), Paul Nolan (Bridegroom), Tim Progosh (The Master of the Feast), Nitzan Sharron (Lazarus), Andy Velasquez (Thomas the Twin)

TICKET TO JERUSALEM

(GLOBAL FILM INITIATIVE) Producers, Rashid Masharawai, Peter van Vogelpoel; Executive Producer, Areen Omari; Director/Screenplay, Rashid Masharawi; Photography, Baudoin Koenig; Designers, Ala'Abu Ghoush, Barbara Wijnveld;

Music, Samir Jubran; Editors, Jan Hendricks, Nestor Sanz; an Argus Film Produktie, Cinema Production Center, SBS Independent, Silkroad Production, Arte France Cinema production; Dutch-Palestinian-French-Australian; Color; Not rated; 85 minutes; American release date: November 19, 2003. Cast: Gassan Abbas (Jaber), Areen Omari (Sana), Reem Ilo (Rabab), George Ibrahim, Imad Farageen, Naja Abu al-Hejah

BLUE GATE CROSSING

(STRAND) Producers, Hsiao-ming Hsu, Peggy Chiao; Executive Producer, Wang Toon; Director/Screenplay, Chin-yen Yee; Photography, Hsiang Chienn; Designer, Shao-yu Hsia; Music, Chris Hou; Editor, Ching-Song Liao; from Arc Light Films, Pyramide Productions; Taiwanese-French; Dolby; Color; Not rated; 85 minutes; American release date: November 21, 2003. Cast: Bo-lin Chen (Zhang Shihao), Shu-hui Liang (Lin Yuezhen), Lun-mei Guey (Meng Kerou), Joanna Chou (Mrs. Meng)

EL BONARENSE

(MENEMSHA) Producer/Director, Pablo Trapero; Screenplay, Pablo Trapero, Nicolas Gueilburt, Ricardo Ragendorfer, Daniel Valenzuela, Dodi Shoeur; Photography, Guillermo Nieto; Art Director, Sebastián Roses; Costumes, Marisa Urruti; Music, Pablo Lescano; Editor, Nicolás Golbart; Andrés Wood Producciones, Centre National de la Cinématographie, Ibermedia European Community Program, Instituto European Community Program, Insituto Nacional de Cine y Atres Audiovisuales, Ministry of Culture and Communications, Pablo Trapero Productions, Pol-Ka Producciones; Argentine-Chilean-French-Dutch, 2002; Dolby; Color; Not rated; 105 minutes; American release date: November 26, 2003. Cast: Jorge Román (Zapa), Mimí Ardú (Mabel), Darío Levy (Gallo), Víctor Hugo Carrizo (Molinari), Hugo Anganuzzi (Polaco), Graciana Chironi (Zapa's Mother), Luis Viscat (Pellegrino), Roberto Posse (Ismael), Aníbal Barengo (Caneva), Lucas Olivera (Abdala), Gastón Polo (Lanza), Jorge Luis Giménez (Berti)

KAL HO NAA HO

(YASH RAJ FILMS) a.k.a. *Tomorrow May Never Come*; Producer, Karan Johar; Executive Producer, Yash Johar; Director, Nikhil Advani; Screenplay, Nikhil Advani, Karan Johar, Niranjan Iyengar; Photography, Anil Mehta; Art Director, Sharmishta Roy; Costumes, Manish Malhotra; Editor, Sanjay Sankla; a Yash & Karan Johar presentation of a Dharma Prods. production; Indian; Dolby; Widescreen; Color; 186 minutes; American release date: November 27, 2003. Cast: Shahrukh Khan (Aman Mathur), Saif Ali Khan (Rohit Patel), Preity Zinta (Naina Catherine Kapur), Jaya Machchan (Jennifer Kapur), Lillete Dubey (Jaswinder Kapoor), Daniela De Almeida (Gia Kapur), Sonali Bendre (Dr. Priya), Sushma Seth (Lajjo Kapur), Dara Singh (Chaddha Uncle), Satish Shah (Kurzon bhai Patel), Reema Lagoo (Aman's Mother), Shoma Anand (Lajjo Kapur's Sister), Sulabha Arya (Kanta Bhen), Ketki Dave (Rohit's Mother), Kamini Khanna (Lajjo Kapur's Sister), Simone Singh (Camilla), Rajpal Yadav (Guru), Sanjay Kapoor (Abhay)

Jorge Roman (center) in *El Bonarense* PHOTO COURTESY OF MENEMSHA

THE LEGEND OF LEIGH BOWERY

(PALM PICTURES) Director, Charles Atlas; Editor, Jens Tang; an INA, Atlas Films (NY), Arte France production in association with BBC, Centre National de la Cinematographie; French-British-U.S.; Color; Not rated; 82 minutes; Release date: November 28, 2003. Documentary on flamboyant performance artist and London club denizen Leigh Bowery; featuring Boy George, Damien Hirst, Bella Freud, Michael Clark, Rifat Ozbek, Cerith Wyn Evans, Norman Rosenthal, Nicola Bowery, Sue Tilley, Rachel Auburn, Bronwyn Bowery, Tom Bowery, Michael Bracewell, Les Child, Sophie Fiennes, David Holah, Lorcan O'Neill, Richard Torry, Donald Urquhart.

FORGET BAGHDAD

(AFD THEATRICALS) Producers, Samir, Karin Koch, Gerd Haag; Director/Screenplay, Samir; Photography, Nurith Aviv, Philippe Bellaiche; Music, Rabih Abou-Khalil; Editors, Samir, Nina Schneider; a Dschoint Ventschr Filmproduktion AG/TAG/TRAUM Filmproduktion; German-Swiss, 2002; Dolby; Color; Not rated; 111 minutes; American opening: December 5, 2003.

Ella Habiba Shohat in *Forget Bagdad* PHOTO COURTESY OF AFD THEATRICALS

Documentary on Iraqi-born Jews living in Israeli; featuring Shimon Ballas, Moshe Houri, Sami Michael, Samir Naqqash, Ella Shohat.

AKA

(EMPIRE) Producer, Richard West; Executive Producers, Duncan Roy, Julian Hayward; Director/Screenplay, Duncan Roy; Photography, Scott Taylor, Steve Smith, Claire Vinson, Ingrid Domeij; Designer, Philip Robinson; Costumes, David Thomas; Editors, Lawrence Catford, Jackie Ophir, Jon Cross; Casting, Gary Davy; a Third Rock production in association with Bard Entertainments; British, 2002; Dolby; Color; Not rated; 124 minutes; American release date: December 12, 2003. Cast: Matthew Leitch (Dean Page), Diana Quick (Lady Francine Gryffoyn), George Asprey (David Glendenning), Lindsey Coulson (Georgie Page), Blake Ritson (Alexander Gryffoyn), Peter Youngblood Hills (Ben), Geoff Bell (Brian Page), Camille Sturton (Hannah Yelland), Daniel Lee (Jamie Page), Bill Nighy (Uncle Louis Gryffoyn), David Kendall (Lee Page), Fenella Woolgar (Sarah), Sean Gilder (Tim Lyttleton), Robin Soans (Neil Forst), Stephen Boxer (Dermot), Neil Maskell (Marcus), Reginald S. Bundy (Jeremy), Kathryn Pogson (Freddy Furnish), Sue Douglas (Shop Assistant), Martin Wimbush (Reed Furnish), Harry Gostelow (Restaurant Customer), Kenny Gibson (Derek), Christopher Luscombe (Sandy), Georgina Hale (Elizabeth of Lithuania), Paul Roseby (George), Faith Brook (Contessa de la Reche), John Quayle (Lord John Choat), Brian Bovell, Shaun Prendergast (Prison Officers), Graham Seed (Bank Manager), Jane How (Cosima van Badon), Brian Lawrence (Perry), Sophie Clarke (Selina Hoyland-Jones), Anders Price (Piers), Rachel Pickup (Stella Primrose), Sonya Leite (Sonya), Hannah Yelland (Camille)

Peter Youngblood Hills, Matthew Leitch in *AKA* PHOTO COURTESY OF EMPIRE

PRISONER OF PARADISE

(MENEMSHA) Producers, Karl-Eberhard Schaefer, Malcolm Clarke; Executive Producer, Stuart Sender, Jake Eberts; Directors, Malcolm Clarke, Stuart Sender; Screenplay, Malcolm Clarke; Photography, Michael Hammon; Music, Luc St. Pierre; Editors, Susan Shanks, Glenn Berman; Narrator, Ian Holm; PBS-Alliance Atlantis Communications-BBC-Cafe Productions-Canadian Audio-Visual Certification Officer-History Television-Media Verite-Societe de Developpement des Entreprises; Black and white/color; Not rated; 96 minutes; Canadian-U.S.-German-British; American release date: December 12, 2003. Documentary about German-Jewish actor-entertainer Kurt Gerron, who was recruited by the Nazis to make a propaganda documentary to deceive the Red Cross about the true nature of their concentration camps; featuring Robby Lantz, Ela Weissberger, Lore Moos, Coco Schumann.

Kurt Gerron in *Prisoner of Paradise* PHOTO COURTESY OF MENEMSHA

HOTEL ROOM

(HOLLYWOOD INDEPENDENTS) Producers, Ferran Viladevall, Marta Figueras; Directors, Cesc Gay, Daniel Gimelberg; Screenplay, Cesc Gay; Photography, Nicholas Hoffman; Art Director, Daniel Gimelberg; Music, Joan Diaz, Jordi Prats; Editors, Larry Walkin, Frank Gutierrez; a co-production of Bailando con Todos S.L., The Film Machine; Spanish-Argentine-U.S.; Black and white; Not rated; 86 minutes; American release date: December 12, 2003. Cast: Barbara Boudon, Eric Kraus, Paris Kiely, Xavier Domingo, Keidi Wolfe, David Jacob Ryder, Gary Dennis, Nicholas Devine, Raul Quintana, Lourdes Delgado, Barry Papick, Mike Kimmel, Montse Catala.

CHILDREN OF LOVE

(CINE-INTERNATIONAL) Producers, Mariano Vanhoof, C. Buchet-Charlet; Director/Screenplay/Editor, Geoffrey Enthoven; Photography, Gerd Schelfhout; Art Director, Jean-Pierre Temmerman; Costumes, Mie Van Daele; Music, Das Pop, Louis Devos; Editor, Geoffrey Enthoven; an Atelier de Production de la Cambre ASBL, Fobic Films, L'Arbre de la Vie, Les Choeurs de Luis Mariano production; Belgian, 2002; Color; Not rated; 90 minutes; American release date: December 24, 2003. Cast: Nathalie Stas (Nathalie), Winnie Vigilante (Winnie), Michael Philpot (Michel), Olivier Ythier (Olivier), Fauve De Loof (Aurelie), Jean-Louis Leclerq (Renaud)

MILLENNIUM MAMBO

(PALM PICTURES) Producer/Designer, Hwarng Wern-ying; Director, Hou Hsiao-hsien; Screenplay, Chu Tien-wen; Photography, Lee Ping-bing; Music, Lim Giong, Hanno Yoshihiro; Editor, Hsiao Ju-kuan; a co-production of 3H Productions, Orly Films, Paradis Films, Sinomovie; French-Taiwan, 2001; Color; Not rated; 119 minutes; American release date: December 31, 2003. Cast: Shu Qi (Vicky), Jack Kao (Jack), Tuan Chun-hao (Tuan Chun-hao), Jun Takeuchi (Jun), Niu Chen-er (Doze), Kao Kuo Guang (Godi), Chen Yi-hsuan (Xuan), Jenny Tseng (Jenny), Tramy Wat (Tramy), Jo Jo Huang (Jo Jo), Huang Hsiu (Jessie X), Peng Kang-yu (Dao), Chang Pro (Pro), Ting Chine-chung (Ding), Hsu Huei-ni (Kitty)

Shu Qi, Tuan Chun-hao in *Millennium Mambo* PHOTO COURTESY OF PALM PICTURES

PROMISING NEW ACTORS OF 2003

Bobby Cannavale (*The Station Agent*)

Jennifer Garner (*Daredevil*)

Paddy Considine (*In America*)

Keira Knightley (*Bend It Like Beckham, Love Actually, Pirates of the Caribbean*)

Peter Dinklage (*Elf, The Station Agent*)

Lindsay Lohan (*Freaky Friday*)

Shia LaBeouf (*The Battle of Shaker Heights, Holes*)

Bridget Moynahan (*The Recruit*)

Jimi Mistry (*The Guru*)

Parminder Nagra (*Bend It Like Beckham*)

Cillian Murphy (*Cold Mountain, Girl with a Pearl Earring, 28 Days Later...*)

Nikki Reed (*Thirteen*)

ACADEMY AWARD WINNERS & NOMINEES

BEST PICTURE
THE LORD OF THE RINGS: THE RETURN OF THE KING

(NEW LINE CINEMA) Producers, Barrie M. Osborne, Peter Jackson, Fran Walsh; Executive Producers, Mark Ordesky, Bob Weinstein, Harvey Weinstein, Robert Shaye, Michael Lynne; Director, Peter Jackson; Screenplay, Fran Walsh, Philippa Boyens, Peter Jackson; Based on the novel by J.R.R. Tolkien; Photography, Andrew Lesnie; Designer, Grant Major; Costumes, Ngila Dickson, Richard Taylor; Music, Howard Shore; Song: "Into the West" performed by Annie Lennox; Editors, Jamie Selkirk, Annie Collins; Special Makeup, Creatures, Armour and Miniatures, Richard Taylor; Makeup & Hair Design, Peter Owen, Peter King; Visual Effects Supervisor, Jim Rygiel; Co-Producers, Rick Porras, Jamie Selkirk; Casting, John Hubbard, Amy MacLean (UK), Victoria Burrows (US), Liz Mullane (New Zealand), Ann Robinson (Australia); Stunts, George Marshall Ruge; a Wingnut Films production; Dolby; Arriflex Widescreen; Deluxe color; Rated PG-13; 200 minutes; Release date: December 17, 2003

Cast

Frodo Baggins **Elijah Wood**
Gandalf **Ian McKellen**
Arwen **Liv Tyler**
Aragorn (Strider) **Viggo Mortensen**
Sam (Samwise Gamgee) **Sean Astin**
Galadriel **Cate Blanchett**
Gimli **John Rhys-Davies**
King Theoden of Rohan **Bernard Hill**
Pippin (Peregrin Took) **Billy Boyd**
Merry (Meriadoc Brandbuck) **Dominic Monaghan**
Legolas **Orlando Bloom**
Elrond **Hugo Weaving**
Éowyn of Rohan **Miranda Otto**
Faramir **David Wenham**
Éomer **Karl Urban**

Viggo Mortensen, Ian McKellen

Sean Astin

Denethor **John Noble**
Gollum/Smeagol **Andy Serkis**
Bilbo Baggins **Ian Holm**
Boromir **Sean Bean**
Witchking/Gothmog **Lawrence Makoare**
King of the Dead **Paul Norell**
Celeborn **Marton Csokas**
Everard Proudfoot **Noel Appleby**
Eleanor Gamgee **Alexandra Astin**
Gondorian Soldiers **Richard Edge, David Aston**
Madril **John Bach**
Eldarion **Sadwyn Brophy**
Damrod **Alistair Browning**
Uruk 2 **Jason Fitch**
Gamling **Bruce Hopkins**
Irolas **Ian Hughes**
Elf Escort **Bret McKenzie**
Rosie Cotton **Sarah McLeod**
Baby Gamgee **Maisie McLeod-Riera**
Grimold **Bruce Phillips**
Harad Leaders **Todd Rippon, Shane Rangi**
Deagol **Thomas Robins**
Isildur **Harry Sinclair**
Shagrat **Peter Tait**
Orc Lieutenant 1 **Joel Tolbeck**
Gorbag **Stephen Ure**

Dominic Monaghan

Miranda Otto

Bernard Hill

John Rhys-Davies

King Theoden and his warriors head to Minas Tirith to help fend off the on-coming forces of the evil Orcs, while Hobbits Frodo and Sam come closer to Mount Doom where they hoped to at last destroy the ring that will put an end to Sauron's attempt to destroy mankind. Third installment in the New Line Cinema trilogy, following *The Lord of the Rings: The Fellowship of the Rings* (2001) and *The Lord of the Rings: The Two Towers* (2002), with most of the principals continuing in their roles.

2003 Academy Award winner for Best Picture, Best Director, Best Screenplay (Adaptation), Best Art Direction, Best Costume Design, Best Sound, Best Editing, Best Original Score, Best Original Song ("Into the West"), Best Makeup, and Best Visual Effects.

Andy Serkis

Billy Boyd

Elijah Wood, Sean Astin

Hugo Weaving, Liv Tyler

Orlando Bloom PHOTOS COURTESY OF NEW LINE CINEMA

BEST FEATURE DOCUMENTARY
THE FOG OF WAR

(SONY CLASSICS) Producers, Errol Morris, Michael Williams, Julie Ahlberg; Executive Producers, Jon Kamen, Jack Lechner, Frank Scherma, Robert May, John Sloss; Co-Producer, Robert Fernandez; Photography, Peter Donahue, Robert Chappell; Designers, Ted Bafaloukos, Steve Hardy; Music, Philip Glass; Editors, Karen Schmeer, Doug Abel, Chyld King; a @Radical.Media & Senart Films production in association with The Globe Department Store; Dolby; Color; Rated PG-13; 105 minutes; Release date: December 19, 2003. Documentary in which former defense secretary Robert S. McNamara discusses his feeling about the United States' involvement in the Vietnam War.

2003 Academy Award winner for Best Feature Documentary

Robert S. McNamara

Robert S. McNamara, Errol Morris

Robert S. McNamara PHOTOS COURTESY OF SONY CLASSICS

Errol Morris

Rémy Girard, Marie-Josée Croze

BEST FOREIGN LANGUAGE FEATURE
THE BARBARIAN INVASIONS

(MIRAMAX) Producers, Denise Robert, Daniel Louis; Director/Screenplay, Denys Arcand; Photography, Guy Dufaux; Designer, François Séguin; Costumes, Denis Sperdouklis; Music, Pierre Aviat; Editor, Isabelle Dedieu; Casting, Lucie Robitaille; a Cinemaginaire, Inc. (Quebec)/Pyramide (France) co-production with the participation of Telefilm Canada Quebec, Sodec Quebec, Radio-Canada Television, Astral Media, the Harold Greenburg Fund, Canal+, CNC; Canadian-French; Dolby; Super 35 Widescreen; Color; Rated R; 99 minutes; American release date: November 21, 2003

Cast
Rémy **Rémy Girard**
Sébastien **Stéphane Rousseau**
Louise **Dorothée Berryman**
Diane **Louise Portal**
Dominique **Dominique Michel**
Claude **Yves Jacques**
Pierre **Pierre Curzi**
Nathalie **Marie-Josée Croze**
Gaëlle **Marina Hands**
Alessandro **Toni Cecchinato**
Ghislaine **Mitsou Gélinas**
First Lover **Sophie Lorain**
Sister Constance **Johanne-Marie Tremblay**
Duhamel **Denis Bouchard**
Nurse Carole **Micheline Lanctôt**
Nurse Suzanne **Markita Boies**
Sylvaine **Isabelle Blais**
Second Lover **Sylvie Drapeau**
Olivier **Yves Desgagnés**
Unionist **Denys Arcand**
Alain Lussier **Daniel Brière**
Maxime **Dominic Darceuil**
Gilles Levac **Roy Dupuis**
Student **Rose-Maïté Erkoreka**
Arielle **Macha Grenon**

Vincent **Sébastien Huberdeau**
Security Guard **Gaston Lepage**
Pharmacist **Sean Lu**
Nurse **Bonnie Mak**
Dr. Dubé **Jean-René Ouellet**
Ronald the Syndicalist **Jean-Marc Parent**
Priest **Gilles Pelletier**
Jérôme **Sébastien Ricard**
Mme. Jonas-Pelletier **Lise Roy**
Bulgarian Nurse **Anna-Marie Sutherland**

Sebastien, an international financier, attempts to come to some understanding with his father, a history professor and free-spirited '60s radical suffering from terminal cancer who requests that his closest friends come to bid him farewell. A sequel to the 1986 film *The Decline of the American Empire*.

2003 Academy Award winner for Best Foreign Language Film. This film received an additional nomination for original screenplay.

Toni Cecchinato, Louise Portal, Marina Hands, Rémy Girard, Yves Jacques, Pierre Curzi, Dorothée Berryman, Stéphane Rousseau, Dominique Michel

Dominique Michel, Yves Jacques

Stéphane Rousseau, Rémy Girard PHOTOS COURTESY OF MIRAMAX

BEST ANIMATED FEATURE
FINDING NEMO

(WALT DISNEY PICTURES) Producer, Graham Walters; Executive Producer, John Lasseter; Director/Story, Andrew Stanton; Screenplay, Andrew Stanton, Bob Peterson, David Reynolds; Co-Director, Lee Unkrich; Associate Producer, Jinko Gotoh; Music, Thomas Newman; Story Supervisors, Ronnie del Carmen, Dan Jeup, Jason Katz; Editor, David Ian Salter; Supervising Technical Director, Oren Jacob; Designer, Ralph Eggleston; Photography, Sharon Calahan, Jeremy Lasky; Supervising Animator, Dylan Brown; Art Directors: Characters, Ricky Vega Nierva; Shading, Robin Cooper; Enviorments, Anthony Christov, Randy Berrett; Casting, Mary Hidalgo, Kevin Reher, Matthew Jon Beck; a Pixar Animation Studios film; Dolby; Technicolor; Rated PG; 100 minutes; Release date: May 30, 2003

Marlin, Dory

Marlin, Dory

Voice Cast

Marlin **Albert Brooks**
Dory **Ellen DeGeneres**
Nemo **Alexander Gould**
Gill **Willem Dafoe**
Bloat **Brad Garrett**
Peach **Allison Janney**
Gurgle **Austin Pendleton**
Bubbles **Stephen Root**
Deb (& Flo) **Vicki Lewis**
Jacques **Joe Ranft**
Nigel **Geoffrey Rush**
Crush **Andrew Stanton**
Coral **Elizabeth Perkins**
Squirt **Nicholas Bird**
Mr. Ray **Bob Peterson**
Bruce **Barry Humphries**
Anchor **Eric Bana**
Chum **Bruce Spence**

and Bill Hunter (Dentist), LuLu Ebeling (Darla), Jordy Ranft (Tad), Erica Beck (Pearl), Erik Per Sullivan (Sheldon), John Ratzenberger (Fish School)

Marlin, Anchor, Chum, Dory, Bruce

Nemo, Gill

Squirt, Crush, Dory, Marlin

Dory, Marlin, Angler fish

Clown fish and single parent Marlin frantically searches for his son Nemo after his offspring is captured by a diver.

2003 Academy Award winner for Best Animated Feature. This film received additional Oscar nominations for original score and original screenplay.

Dory, Marlin PHOTOS COURTESY OF WALT DISNEY PICTURES

ACADEMY AWARD FOR BEST ACTOR
SEAN PENN in *Mystic River*

ACADEMY AWARD FOR BEST ACTRESS
CHARLIZE THERON in *Monster*

ACADEMY AWARD FOR BEST SUPPORTING ACTOR
TIM ROBBINS in *Mystic River*

ACADEMY AWARD FOR SUPPORTING BEST ACTRESS
RENÉE ZELLWEGER in *Cold Mountain*

ACADEMY AWARD NOMINEES FOR BEST ACTOR

Johnny Depp in *Pirates of the Caribbean: The Curse of the Black Pearl*

Ben Kingsley in *House of Sand and Fog*

Jude Law in *Cold Mountain*

Bill Murray in *Lost in Translation*

ACADEMY AWARD NOMINEES FOR BEST ACTRESS

Keisha Castle-Hughes in *Whale Rider*

Diane Keaton in *Something's Gotta Give*

Samantha Morton in *In America*

Naomi Watts in *21 Grams*

ACADEMY AWARD NOMINEES FOR BEST SUPPORTING ACTOR

Alec Baldwin in *The Cooler*

Benicio Del Toro in *21 Grams*

Djimon Hounsou in *In America*

Ken Watanabe in *The Last Samurai*

ACADEMY AWARD NOMINEES FOR BEST SUPPORTING ACTRESS

Shohreh Aghdashloo in *House of Sand and Fog*

Patricia Clarkson in *Pieces of April*

Marcia Gay Harden in *Mystic River*

Holly Hunter in *Thirteen*

TOP BOX OFFICE STARS & FILMS OF 2003

TOP BOX OFFICE STARS OF 2003

(Clockwise from top left corner)

1. Jim Carrey
2. Nicole Kidman
3. Jack Nicholson
4. Tom Cruise
5. Julia Roberts
6. Johnny Depp
7. Russell Crowe
8. Tom Hanks
9. Will Ferrell
10. Renée Zellweger

TOP 100 BOX OFFICE FILMS OF 2003

1. **The Lord of the Rings: The Return of the King** (NL) $375,210,000
2. **Finding Nemo** (BV) $339,600,000
3. **Pirates of the Caribbean** (BV) $305,420,000
4. **The Matrix Reloaded** (WB) $281,500,000
5. **Bruce Almighty** (Univ) $242,500,000
6. **X2** (20th) $214,820,000
7. **Elf** (New Line) $173,400,000
8. **Terminator 3: Rise of the Machines** (WB) $149,320,000
9. **The Matrix Revolutions** (WB) $138,470,000
10. **Bad Boys II** (Col) $139,100,000
11. **Cheaper by the Dozen** (20th) $137,890,000
12. **Anger Management** (Col) $133,600,000
13. **Bringing Down the House** (BV) $132,550,000
14. **Hulk** (Univ) $131,770,000
15. **2 Fast 2 Furious** (Univ) $126,100,000
16. **Something's Gotta Give** (Col/WB) $124,600,000
17. **Seabiscuit** (Univ/DW) $120,150,000
18. **Spy Kids 3-D: Game Over** (Mir) $111,710,000
19. **The Last Samurai** (WB) $111,100,000
20. **Freaky Friday** (BV) $110,230,000
21. **Scary Movie 3** (Miramax) $108,720,000
22. **S.W.A.T.** (Columbia) $108,630,000
23. **The Italian Job** (Par) $106,120,000
24. **How to Lose a Guy in 10 Days** (Par) $105,240,000

Elijah Wood in *The Lord of the Rings: Return of the King* PHOTOS COURTESY OF NEW LINE CINEMA

Jack Black in *The School of Rock* PHOTOS COURTESY OF PARAMOUNT

25. **American Wedding** (Univ) $104,220,000
26. **Daddy Day Care** (Col) $104,100,000
27. **Daredevil** (20th) $102,460,000
28. **Charlie's Angels: Full Throttle** (Col) $100,790,000
29. **Dr. Seuss's The Cat in the Hat** (Univ) $99,880,000
30. **Cold Mountain** (Mir) $95,280,000
31. **Master and Commander:**
    The Far Side of the World (20th/Univ/Mir) $93,710,000
32. **Mystic River** (WB) $88,960,000
33. **Legally Blonde 2: Red, White and Blonde** (MGM) $87,100,000
34. **Brother Bear** (BV) $85,240,000
35. **Freddy vs. Jason** (NL) $81,940,000
36. **The School of Rock** (Par) $81,100,000
37. **The Texas Chainsaw Massacre** (NL) $80,150,000
38. **The Haunted Mansion** (BV) $75,800,000
39. **Old School** (DW) $74,610,000
40. **Kill Bill Vol. 1** (Mir) $69,710,000
41. **Holes** (BV) $67,100,000
42. **Kangaroo Jack** (WB) $66,740,000
43. **The League of Extraordinary Gentlemen** (20th) $66,470,000
44. **Big Fish** (Col) $66,260,000
45. **Lara Croft: Tomb Raider: The Cradle of Life** (Par) $65,660,000
46. **Mona Lisa Smile** (Col) $63,700,000
47. **Shanghai Knights** (BV) $60,480,000
48. **Bad Santa** (Mir) $60,100,000
49. **Gothika** (WB) $59,540,000

Shawn Ashmore, Anna Paquin in *X2* PHOTO COURTESY OF 20TH CENTURY FOX

Alison Lohman, Ewan McGregor in *Big Fish* PHOTO COURTESY OF COLUMBIA

50. **Love Actually** (Univ) $59,100,000
51. **Open Range** (BV) $58,300,000
52. **Just Married** (20th) $55,730,000
53. **Once Upon a Time in Mexico** (Col) $55,850,000
54. **Paycheck** (Par/DW) $53,690,000
55. **The Recruit** (BV) $52,790,000
56. **Radio** (Col) $51,990,000
57. **Identity** (Col) $51,330,000
58. **Underworld** (Scr Gems) $51,000,000
59. **Runaway Jury** (20th) $49,370,000
60. **Peter Pan** (Univ/Col) $48,420,000
60. **Agent Cody Banks** (MGM) $47,670,000
61. **The Rundown** (Univ/Col) $47,600,000
63. **The Jungle Book 2** (BV) $46,890,000
64. **Phone Booth** (20th) $45,830,000
65. **Final Destination 2** (NL) $45,330,000
66. **28 Days Later...** (Fox Search) $45,100,000
67. **Lost in Translation** (Focus) $44,570,000
68. **Under the Tuscan Sun** (BV) $43,460,000
69. **The Lizzie McGuire Movie** (BV) $42,340,000
70. **Tears of the Sun** (Col) $41,440,000
71. **Secondhand Lions** (NL) $41,410,000
72. **Out of Time** (MGM) $41,100,000
73. **Rugrats Go Wild** (Par) $39,380,000
74. **Head of State** (DW) $37,850,000
75. **Good Boy!** (MGM) $37,660,000
77. **Matchstick Men** (WB) $36,830,000

Lúcia Moniz, Colin Firth in *Love Actually* PHOTO © PETER MOUNTAIN/UNIVERSAL

Parminder Nagra (center) in *Bend It Like Beckham* PHOTOS COURTESY OF FOX SEARCHLIGHT

78. **What a Girl Wants** (WB) $35,960,000
79. **National Security** (Col) $35,770,000
80. **Intolerable Cruelty** (Univ) $35,000,000
81. **Cradle 2 the Grave** (WB) $34,510,000
82. **Monster** (Newmarket) $34,190,000
83. **Jeepers Creepers 2** (UA) $34,150,000
84. **The Hunted** (Par) $34,110,000
85. **Malibu's Most Wanted** (WB) $33,900,000
86. **Stuck on You** (20th) $33,770,000
87. **Dreamcatcher** (WB) $33,630,000
88. **Bend It Like Beckham** (Fox Search) $32,450,000
89. **Darkness Falls** (Col) $32,140,000
90. **Calendar Girls** (BV) $30,940,000
91. **The Core** (Par) $30,860,000
92. **The Fighting Temptations** (Par) $30,240,000
93. **Hollywood Homicide** (Col) $30,100,000
94. **Honey** (Univ) $30,000,000
95. **Johnny English** (Univ) $27,890,000
96. **The Missing** (Col) $26,700,000
97. **Basic** (Col) $26,410,000
98. **A Man Apart** (New Line) $26,190,000
99. **Sinbad: Legend of the Seven Seas** (DW) $25,940,000
100. **Dumb & Dumberer: When Harry Met Lloyd** (NL) $25,910,000

Haley Joel Osment, Michael Caine, Robert Duvall in *Secondhand Lions*
PHOTOS COURTESY OF NEW LINE CINEMA

David Moscow, Missy Elliott in *Honey* PHOTOS COURTESY OF UNIVERSAL

BIOGRAPHICAL DATA

Ben Affleck

Jennifer Aniston

Patricia Arquette

Rowan Atkinson

Aames, Willie: (William Upton): Los Angeles, CA, July 15, 1960.

Aaron, Caroline: Richmond, VA, Aug. 7, 1954. Catholic U.

Abbott, Diahnne: NYC, 1945.

Abbott, John: London, June 5, 1905.

Abraham, F. Murray: Pittsburgh, PA, Oct. 24, 1939. UTx.

Ackland, Joss: London, Feb. 29, 1928.

Adams, Brooke: NYC, Feb. 8, 1949. Dalton.

Adams, Catlin: Los Angeles, Oct. 11, 1950.

Adams, Don: NYC, Apr. 13, 1923.

Adams, Edie (Elizabeth Edith Enke): Kingston, PA, Apr. 16, 1927. Juilliard, Columbia.

Adams, Jane: Washington, DC, Apr. 1, 1965.

Adams, Joey Lauren: Little Rock, AR, Jan. 6, 1971.

Adams, Julie (Betty May): Waterloo, IA, Oct. 17, 1926. Little Rock, Jr. College.

Adams, Mason: NYC, Feb. 26, 1919. UWi.

Adams, Maud (Maud Wikstrom): Lulea, Sweden, Feb. 12, 1945.

Adjani, Isabelle: Germany, June 27, 1955.

Affleck, Ben: Berkeley, CA, Aug. 15, 1972.

Affleck, Casey: Falmouth, MA, Aug. 12, 1975.

Aghdashloo, Shohreh: Tehran, Iran, May 11, 1952.

Agutter, Jenny: Taunton, England, Dec. 20, 1952.

Aiello, Danny: NYC, June 20, 1933.

Aiken, Liam: NYC, Jan. 7, 1990.

Aimee, Anouk (Dreyfus): Paris, France, Apr. 27, 1934. Bauer Therond.

Akers, Karen: NYC, Oct. 13, 1945, Hunter College.

Alberghetti, Anna Maria: Pesaro, Italy, May 15, 1936.

Albert, Eddie (Eddie Albert Heimberger): Rock Island, IL, Apr. 22, 1908. U of Minn.

Albert, Edward: Los Angeles, Feb. 20. 1951. UCLA.

Albright, Lola: Akron, OH, July 20, 1925.

Alda, Alan: NYC, Jan. 28, 1936. Fordham.

Aleandro, Norma: Buenos Aires, Dec. 6, 1936.

Alejandro, Miguel: NYC, Feb. 21, 1958.

Alexander, Jane (Quigley): Boston, MA, Oct. 28, 1939. Sarah Lawrence.

Alexander, Jason (Jay Greenspan): Newark, NJ, Sept. 23, 1959. Boston U.

Alice, Mary: Indianola, MS, Dec. 3, 1941.

Allen, Debbie (Deborah): Houston, TX, Jan. 16, 1950. Howard U.

Allen, Joan: Rochelle, IL, Aug. 20, 1956. EastIllU.

Allen, Karen: Carrollton, IL, Oct. 5, 1951. UMd.

Allen, Nancy: NYC, June 24, 1950.

Allen, Tim: Denver, CO, June 13, 1953. W. MI. Univ.

Allen, Woody (Allan Stewart Konigsberg): Brooklyn, Dec. 1, 1935.

Alley, Kirstie: Wichita, KS, Jan. 12, 1955.

Allyson, June (Ella Geisman): Westchester, NY, Oct. 7, 1917.

Alonso, Maria Conchita: Cuba, June 29, 1957.

Alt, Carol: Queens, NY, Dec. 1, 1960. HofstraU.

Alvarado, Trini: NYC, Jan. 10, 1967.

Ambrose, Lauren: New Haven, CT, Feb. 20, 1978.

Amis, Suzy: Oklahoma City, OK, Jan. 5, 1958. Actors Studio.

Amos, John: Newark, NJ, Dec. 27, 1940. Colo. U.

Anderson, Anthony: Los Angeles, Aug. 15, 1970.

Anderson, Gillian: Chicago, IL, Aug. 9, 1968. DePaul U.

Anderson, Kevin: Waukegan, IL, Jan. 13, 1960.

Anderson, Loni: St. Paul, MN, Aug. 5, 1946.

Anderson, Melissa Sue: Berkeley, CA, Sept. 26, 1962.

Anderson, Melody: Edmonton, Canada, Dec. 3, 1955. Carlton U.

Anderson, Michael, Jr.: London, England, Aug. 6, 1943.

Anderson, Richard Dean: Minneapolis, MN, Jan. 23, 1950.

Andersson, Bibi: Stockholm, Sweden, Nov. 11, 1935. Royal Dramatic Sch.

Andes, Keith: Ocean City, NJ, July 12, 1920. Temple U., Oxford.

Andress, Ursula: Bern, Switzerland, Mar. 19, 1936.

Andrews, Anthony: London, Dec. 1, 1948.

Andrews, Julie (Julia Elizabeth Wells): Surrey, England, Oct. 1, 1935.

Anglim, Philip: San Francisco, CA, Feb. 11, 1953.

Aniston, Jennifer: Sherman Oaks, CA, Feb. 11, 1969.

Ann-Margret (Olsson): Valsjobyn, Sweden, Apr. 28, 1941. Northwestern U.

Ansara, Michael: Lowell, MA, Apr. 15, 1922. Pasadena Playhouse.

Anspach, Susan: NYC, Nov. 23, 1945.

Anthony, Lysette: London, Sept. 26, 1963.

Anthony, Tony: Clarksburg, WV, Oct. 16, 1937. Carnegie Tech.

Anton, Susan: Yucaipa, CA, Oct. 12, 1950. Bemardino College.

Antonelli, Laura: Pola, Italy, Nov. 28, 1941.

Anwar, Gabrielle: Lalehaam, England, Feb. 4, 1970.

Applegate, Christina: Hollywood CA, Nov. 25, 1972.
Archer, Anne: Los Angeles, Aug. 25, 1947.
Archer, John (Ralph Bowman): Osceola, NB, May 8, 1915. USC.
Ardant, Fanny: Monte Carlo, Mar 22, 1949.
Arkin, Adam: Brooklyn, NY, Aug. 19, 1956.
Arkin, Alan: NYC, Mar. 26, 1934. LACC.
Armstrong, Bess: Baltimore, MD, Dec. 11, 1953.
Arnaz, Desi, Jr.: Los Angeles, Jan. 19, 1953.
Arnaz, Lucie: Hollywood, July 17, 1951.
Arness, James (Aurness): Minneapolis, MN, May 26, 1923. Beloit College.
Arquette, David: Winchester, VA, Sept. 8, 1971.
Arquette, Patricia: NYC, Apr. 8, 1968.
Arquette, Rosanna: NYC, Aug. 10, 1959.
Arthur, Beatrice (Frankel): NYC, May 13, 1924. New School.
Asher, Jane: London, Apr. 5, 1946.
Ashley, Elizabeth (Elizabeth Ann Cole): Ocala, FL, Aug. 30, 1939.
Ashton, John: Springfield, MA, Feb. 22, 1948. USC.
Asner, Edward: Kansas City, KS, Nov. 15, 1929.
Assante, Armand: NYC, Oct. 4, 1949. AADA.
Astin, John: Baltimore, MD, Mar. 30, 1930. U Minn.
Astin, MacKenzie: Los Angeles, May 12, 1973.
Astin, Sean: Santa Monica, Feb. 25, 1971.
Atherton, William: Orange, CT, July 30, 1947. Carnegie Tech.
Atkins, Christopher: Rye, NY, Feb. 21, 1961.
Atkins, Eileen: London, June 16, 1934.
Atkinson, Rowan: England, Jan. 6, 1955. Oxford.
Attenborough, Richard: Cambridge, England, Aug. 29, 1923. RADA.
Auberjonois, Rene: NYC, June 1, 1940. Carnegie Tech.
Audran, Stephane: Versailles, France, Nov. 8, 1932.
Auger, Claudine: Paris, France, Apr. 26, 1942. Dramatic Cons.
Aulin, Ewa: Stockholm, Sweden, Feb. 14, 1950.
Auteuil, Daniel: Alger, Algeria, Jan. 24, 1950.
Avalon, Frankie (Francis Thomas Avallone): Philadelphia, PA, Sept. 18, 1939.
Aykroyd, Dan: Ottawa, Canada, July 1, 1952.
Azaria, Hank: Forest Hills, NY, Apr. 25, 1964. AADA, Tufts Univ.
Aznavour, Charles (Varenagh Aznourian): Paris, France, May 22, 1924.
Azzara, Candice: Brooklyn, NY, May 18, 1947.

Bacall, Lauren (Betty Perske): NYC, Sept. 16, 1924. AADA.
Bach, Barbara: Queens, NY, Aug. 27, 1946.
Bach, Catherine: Warren, OH, Mar. 1, 1954.
Backer, Brian: NYC, Dec. 5, 1956. Neighborhood Playhouse.
Bacon, Kevin: Philadelphia, PA, July 8, 1958.
Bain, Barbara: Chicago, IL, Sept. 13, 1934. U Ill.
Baio, Scott: Brooklyn, NY, Sept. 22, 1961.
Baker, Blanche: NYC, Dec. 20, 1956.
Baker, Carroll: Johnstown, PA, May 28, 1931. St. Petersburg, Jr. College.
Baker, Diane: Hollywood, CA, Feb. 25, 1938. USC.
Baker, Dylan: Syracuse, NY, Oct. 7, 1959.
Baker, Joe Don: Groesbeck, TX, Feb. 12, 1936.
Baker, Kathy: Midland, TX, June 8, 1950. UC Berkley.
Bakula, Scott: St. Louis, MO, Oct. 9, 1955. KansasU.
Balaban, Bob: Chicago, IL, Aug. 16, 1945. Colgate.
Baldwin, Adam: Chicago, IL, Feb. 27, 1962.

Baldwin, Alec: Massapequa, NY, Apr. 3, 1958. NYU.
Baldwin, Daniel: Massapequa, NY, Oct. 5, 1960.
Baldwin, Stephen: Massapequa, NY, May 12, 1966.
Baldwin, William: Massapequa, NY, Feb. 21, 1963.
Bale, Christian: Pembrokeshire, West Wales, Jan. 30, 1974.
Balk, Fairuza: Point Reyes, CA, May 21, 1974.
Ballard, Kaye: Cleveland, OH, Nov. 20, 1926.
Bana, Eric: Melbourne, Australia, Aug. 9, 1968.
Bancroft, Anne (Anna Maria Italiano): Bronx, NY, Sept. 17, 1931. AADA.
Banderas, Antonio: Malaga, Spain, Aug. 10, 1960.
Banerjee, Victor: Calcutta, India, Oct. 15, 1946.
Banes, Lisa: Chagrin Falls, OH, July 9, 1955. Juilliard.
Baranski, Christine: Buffalo, NY, May 2, 1952. Juilliard.
Barbeau, Adrienne: Sacramento, CA, June 11, 1945. Foothill College.
Bardem, Javier: Gran Canaria, Spain, May 1, 1969.
Bardot, Brigitte: Paris, France, Sept. 28, 1934.
Barkin, Ellen: Bronx, NY, Apr. 16, 1954. Hunter College.
Barnes, Christopher Daniel: Portland, ME, Nov. 7, 1972.
Barr, Jean-Marc: Bitburg, Germany, Sept. 27, 1960.
Barrault, Jean-Louis: Vesinet, France, Sept. 8, 1910.
Barrault, Marie-Christine: Paris, France, Mar. 21, 1944.
Barren, Keith: Mexborough, England, Aug. 8, 1936. Sheffield Playhouse.
Barrett, Majel (Hudec): Columbus, OH, Feb. 23, 1939. Western Reserve U.
Barrie, Barbara: Chicago, IL, May 23, 1931.
Barry, Gene (Eugene Klass): NYC, June 14, 1919.
Barry, Neill: NYC, Nov. 29, 1965.
Barrymore, Drew: Los Angeles, Feb. 22, 1975.
Barrymore, John Drew: Beverly Hills, CA, June 4, 1932. St. John's Military Academy.
Baryshnikov, Mikhail: Riga, Latvia, Jan. 27, 1948.
Basinger, Kim: Athens, GA, Dec. 8, 1953. Neighborhood Playhouse.
Bassett, Angela: NYC, Aug. 16, 1958.
Bateman, Jason: Rye, NY, Jan. 14, 1969.
Bateman, Justine: Rye, NY, Feb. 19, 1966.
Bates, Jeanne: San Francisco, CA, May 21, 1918. RADA.
Bates, Kathy: Memphis, TN, June 28, 1948. S. Methodist U.
Bauer, Steven (Steven Rocky Echevarria): Havana, Cuba, Dec. 2, 1956. U Miami.
Baxter, Keith: South Wales, England, Apr. 29, 1933. RADA.
Baxter, Meredith: Los Angeles, June 21, 1947. Intelochen Acad.
Baye, Nathalie: Mainevile, France, July 6, 1948.
Beach, Adam: Winnipeg, Canada, Nov. 11, 1972.
Beacham, Stephanie: Casablanca, Morocco, Feb. 28, 1947.
Beals, Jennifer: Chicago, IL, Dec. 19, 1963.
Bean, Orson (Dallas Burrows): Burlington, VT, July 22, 1928.
Bean, Sean: Sheffield, Yorkshire, England, Apr. 17, 1958.
Béart, Emmanuelle: Gassin, France, Aug. 14, 1965.
Beatty, Ned: Louisville, KY, July 6, 1937.
Beatty, Warren: Richmond, VA, Mar. 30, 1937.
Beck, John: Chicago, IL, Jan. 28, 1943.
Beck, Michael: Memphis, TN, Feb. 4, 1949. Millsap College.
Beckinsale, Kate: England, July 26, 1974.
Bedelia, Bonnie: NYC, Mar. 25, 1946. Hunter College.
Begley, Ed, Jr.: NYC, Sept. 16, 1949.

Kate Beckinsale

Annette Bening

Jason Biggs

Jack Black

Belafonte, Harry: NYC, Mar. 1, 1927.

Bel Geddes, Barbara: NYC, Oct. 31, 1922.

Bell, Tom: Liverpool, England, Aug. 2, 1933.

Beller, Kathleen: NYC, Feb. 10, 1957.

Bellucci, Monica: Citta di Castello, Italy, Sept. 30, 1964.

Bellwood, Pamela (King): Scarsdale, NY, June 26, 1951.

Belmondo, Jean Paul: Paris, France, Apr. 9, 1933.

Belushi, James: Chicago, IL, June 15, 1954.

Belzer, Richard: Bridgeport, CT, Aug. 4, 1944.

Benedict, Dirk (Niewoehner): White Sulphur Springs, MT, March 1, 1945. Whitman Col.

Benedict, Paul: Silver City, NM, Sept. 17, 1938.

Benigni, Roberto: Tuscany, Italy, Oct. 27, 1952.

Bening, Annette: Topeka, KS, May 29, 1958. SFSt. U.

Benjamin, Richard: NYC, May 22, 1938. Northwestern U.

Bennent, David: Lausanne, Sept. 9, 1966.

Bennett, Alan: Leeds, England, May 9, 1934. Oxford.

Bennett, Bruce (Herman Brix): Tacoma, WA, May 19, 1909. U Wash.

Bennett, Hywel: Garnant, So. Wales, Apr. 8, 1944.

Benson, Robby: Dallas, TX, Jan. 21, 1957.

Bentley, Wes: Jonesboro, AR, Sept. 4, 1978.

Berenger, Tom: Chicago, IL, May 31, 1950, U Mo.

Berenson, Marisa: NYC, Feb. 15, 1947.

Berg, Peter: NYC, March 11, 1964. Malcalester College.

Bergen, Candice: Los Angeles, May 9, 1946. U PA.

Bergen, Polly: Knoxville, TN, July 14, 1930. Compton, Jr. College.

Berger, Helmut: Salzburg, Austria, May 29, 1942.

Berger, Senta: Vienna, Austria, May 13, 1941. Vienna Sch. of Acting.

Berger, William: Austria, Jan. 20, 1928. Columbia.

Bergerac, Jacques: Biarritz, France, May 26, 1927. Paris U.

Bergin, Patrick: Dublin, Feb. 4, 1951.

Berkley, Elizabeth: Detroit, MI, July 28, 1972.

Berkoff, Steven: London, England, Aug. 3, 1937.

Berlin, Jeannie: Los Angeles, Nov. 1, 1949.

Berlinger, Warren: Brooklyn, Aug. 31, 1937. Columbia.

Bernal, Gael García: Guadalajara, Mexico, Oct. 30, 1978.

Bernhard, Sandra: Flint, MI, June 6, 1955.

Bernsen, Corbin: Los Angeles, Sept. 7, 1954. UCLA.

Berri, Claude (Langmann): Paris, France, July 1, 1934.

Berridge, Elizabeth: Westchester, NY, May 2, 1962. Strasberg Inst.

Berry, Halle: Cleveland, OH, Aug. 14, 1968.

Berry, Ken: Moline, IL, Nov. 3, 1933.

Bertinelli, Valerie: Wilmington, DE, Apr. 23, 1960.

Best, James: Corydon, IN, July 26, 1926.

Bettany, Paul: London, May 27, 1971.

Bey, Turhan: Vienna, Austria, Mar. 30, 1921.

Beymer, Richard: Avoca, IA, Feb. 21, 1939.

Bialik, Mayim: San Diego, CA, Dec. 12, 1975.

Biehn, Michael: Anniston, AL, July 31, 1956.

Biggerstaff, Sean: Glasgow, Mar. 15, 1983.

Biggs, Jason: Pompton Plains, NJ, May 12, 1978.

Bikel, Theodore: Vienna, May 2, 1924. RADA.

Billingsley, Peter: NYC, Apr. 16, 1972.

Binoche, Juliette: Paris, France, Mar. 9, 1964.

Birch, Thora: Los Angeles, Mar. 11, 1982.

Birkin, Jane: London, Dec. 14, 1947.

Birney, David: Washington, DC, Apr. 23, 1939. Dartmouth, UCLA.

Birney, Reed: Alexandria, VA, Sept. 11, 1954. Boston U.

Bishop, Joey (Joseph Abraham Gotllieb): Bronx, NY, Feb. 3, 1918.

Bishop, Julie (Jacqueline Wells): Denver, CO, Aug. 30, 1917. Westlake School.

Bishop, Kevin: Kent, Eng., June 18, 1980.

Bisset, Jacqueline: Waybridge, England, Sept. 13, 1944.

Black, Jack: Edmonton, Alberta, Canada, Apr. 7, 1969.

Black, Karen (Ziegler): Park Ridge, IL, July 1, 1942. Northwestern.

Black, Lucas: Speake, AL, Nov. 29, 1982.

Blackman, Honor: London, Aug. 22, 1926.

Blades, Ruben: Panama City, July 16, 1948. Harvard.

Blair, Betsy (Betsy Boger): NYC, Dec. 11, 1923.

Blair, Janet (Martha Jane Lafferty): Blair, PA, Apr. 23, 1921.

Blair, Linda: Westport, CT, Jan. 22, 1959.

Blair, Selma: Southfield, MI, June 23, 1972.

Blake, Robert (Michael Gubitosi): Nutley, NJ, Sept. 18, 1933.

Blakely, Susan: Frankfurt, Germany, Sept. 7, 1950. U TX.

Selma Blair

Neve Campbell

George Clooney

Jennifer Connelly

Blakley, Ronee: Stanley, ID, 1946. Stanford U.

Blanchett, Cate: Melbourne, Australia, May 14, 1969.

Bledel, Alexis: Houston, TX, Sept. 16, 1981.

Blethyn, Brenda: Ramsgate, Kent, Eng., Feb. 20, 1946.

Bloom, Claire: London, Feb. 15, 1931. Badminton School.

Bloom, Orlando: Canterbury, Eng., Jan. 13, 1977.

Bloom, Verna: Lynn, MA, Aug. 7, 1939. Boston U.

Blount, Lisa: Fayettville, AK, July 1, 1957. UAk.

Blum, Mark: Newark, NJ, May 14, 1950. UMinn.

Blyth, Ann: Mt. Kisco, NY, Aug. 16, 1928. New Waybum Dramatic School.

Bochner, Hart: Toronto, Canada, Oct. 3, 1956. U San Diego.

Bochner, Lloyd: Toronto, Canada, July 29, 1924.

Bogosian, Eric: Woburn, MA, Apr. 24, 1953. Oberlin College.

Bohringer, Richard: Paris, France, Jan. 16, 1941.

Bolkan, Florinda (Florinda Soares Bulcao): Ceara, Brazil, Feb. 15, 1941.

Bologna, Joseph: Brooklyn, NY, Dec. 30, 1938. Brown U.

Bond, Derek: Glasgow, Scotland, Jan. 26, 1920. Askes School.

Bonet, Lisa: San Francisco, CA, Nov. 16, 1967.

Bonham-Carter, Helena: London, England, May 26, 1966.

Boone, Pat: Jacksonville, FL, June 1, 1934. Columbia U.

Boothe, James: Croydon, England, Dec. 19, 1930.

Boothe, Powers: Snyder, TX, June 1, 1949. So. Methodist U.

Borgnine, Ernest (Borgnino): Hamden, CT, Jan. 24, 1917. Randall School.

Bosco, Philip: Jersey City, NJ, Sept. 26, 1930. CatholicU.

Bosley, Tom: Chicago, IL, Oct. 1, 1927. DePaul U.

Bostwick, Barry: San Mateo, CA, Feb. 24, 1945. NYU.

Bottoms, Joseph: Santa Barbara, CA, Aug. 30, 1954.

Bottoms, Sam: Santa Barbara, CA, Oct. 17, 1955.

Bottoms, Timothy: Santa Barbara, CA, Aug. 30, 1951.

Boulting, Ingrid: Transvaal, So. Africa, 1947.

Boutsikaris, Dennis: Newark, NJ, Dec. 21, 1952. CatholicU.

Bowie, David (David Robert Jones): Brixton, South London, England, Jan. 8, 1947.

Bowker, Judi: Shawford, England, Apr. 6, 1954.

Boxleitner, Bruce: Elgin, IL, May 12, 1950.

Boyd, Billy: Glasgow, Scotland, Aug. 28, 1968.

Boyle, Lara Flynn: Davenport, IA, Mar. 24, 1970.

Boyle, Peter: Philadelphia, PA, Oct. 18, 1933. LaSalle College.

Bracco, Lorraine: Brooklyn, NY, Oct. 2, 1949.

Bradford, Jesse: Norwalk, CT, May 27, 1979.

Braeden, Eric (Hans Gudegast): Kiel, Germany, Apr. 3, 1942.

Braga, Sonia: Maringa, Brazil, June 8, 1950.

Branagh, Kenneth: Belfast, No. Ireland, Dec. 10, 1960.

Brandauer, Klaus Maria: Altaussee, Austria, June 22, 1944.

Brando, Jocelyn: San Francisco, Nov. 18, 1919. Lake Forest College, AADA.

Brando, Marlon: Omaha, NB, Apr. 3, 1924. New School.

Brandon, Clark: NYC, Dec. 13, 1958.

Brandon, Michael (Feldman): Brooklyn, NY, Apr. 20, 1945.

Brantley, Betsy: Rutherfordton, NC, Sept. 20, 1955. London Central Sch. of Drama.

Bratt, Benjamin: San Francisco, Dec. 16, 1963.

Brennan, Eileen: Los Angeles, CA, Sept. 3, 1935. AADA.

Brenneman, Amy: Glastonbury, CT, June 22, 1964.

Brialy, Jean-Claude: Aumale, Algeria, 1933. Strasbourg Cons.

Bridges, Beau: Los Angeles, Dec. 9, 1941. UCLA.

Bridges, Jeff: Los Angeles, Dec. 4, 1949.

Brimley, Wilford: Salt Lake City, UT, Sept. 27, 1934.

Brinkley, Christie: Malibu, CA, Feb. 2, 1954.

Britt, May (Maybritt Wilkins): Stockholm, Sweden, Mar. 22, 1936.

Brittany, Morgan (Suzanne Cupito): Los Angeles, Dec. 5, 1950.

Britton, Tony: Birmingham, England, June 9, 1924.

Broadbent, Jim: Lincoln, England, May 24, 1959.

Broderick, Matthew: NYC, Mar. 21, 1962.

Brody, Adrien: NYC, Dec. 23, 1976,

Brolin, James: Los Angeles, July 18, 1940. UCLA.

Brolin, Josh: Los Angeles, Feb. 12, 1968.

Bromfield, John (Farron Bromfield): South Bend, IN, June 11, 1922. St. Mary's College.

Bron, Eleanor: Stanmore, England, Mar. 14, 1934.

Brookes, Jacqueline: Montclair, NJ, July 24, 1930. RADA.

Brooks, Albert (Einstein): Los Angeles, July 22, 1947.

Brooks, Mel (Melvyn Kaminski): Brooklyn, NY, June 28, 1926.

Brosnan, Pierce: County Meath, Ireland. May 16, 1952.

Brown, Blair: Washington, DC, Apr. 23, 1947. Pine Manor.

Brown, Bryan: Panania, Australia, June 23, 1947.
Brown, Gary (Christian Brando): Hollywood, CA, 1958.
Brown, Georg Stanford: Havana, Cuba, June 24, 1943. AMDA.
Brown, James: Desdemona, TX, Mar. 22, 1920. Baylor U.
Brown, Jim: St. Simons Island, NY, Feb. 17, 1935. Syracuse U.
Browne, Leslie: NYC, 1958.
Browne, Roscoe Lee: Woodbury, NJ, May 2, 1925.
Buckley, Betty: Big Spring, TX, July 3, 1947. TxCU.
Bujold, Genevieve: Montreal, Canada, July 1, 1942.
Bullock, Sandra: Arlington, VA, July 26, 1964.
Burghoff, Gary: Bristol, CT, May 24, 1943.
Burgi, Richard: Montclair, NJ, July 30, 1958.
Burke, Paul: New Orleans, July 21, 1926. Pasadena Playhouse.
Burnett, Carol: San Antonio, TX, Apr. 26, 1933. UCLA.
Burns, Catherine: NYC, Sept. 25, 1945. AADA.
Burns, Edward: Valley Stream, NY, Jan. 28, 1969.
Burrows, Darren E.: Winfield, KS, Sept. 12, 1966.
Burrows, Saffron: London, Jan. 1, 1973.
Burstyn, Ellen (Edna Rae Gillhooly): Detroit, MI, Dec. 7, 1932.
Burton, LeVar: Los Angeles, CA, Feb. 16, 1958. UCLA.
Buscemi, Steve: Brooklyn, NY, Dec. 13, 1957.
Busey, Gary: Goose Creek, TX, June 29, 1944.
Busfield, Timothy: Lansing, MI, June 12, 1957. E. Tenn. St. U.
Buttons, Red (Aaron Chwatt): NYC, Feb. 5, 1919.
Buzzi, Ruth: Westerly, RI, July 24, 1936. Pasadena Playhouse.
Bygraves, Max: London, Oct. 16, 1922. St. Joseph's School.
Bynes, Amanda: Thousand Oaks, CA, Apr. 3, 1986.
Byrne, David: Dumbarton, Scotland, May 14, 1952.
Byrne, Gabriel: Dublin, Ireland, May 12, 1950.
Byrnes, Edd: NYC, July 30, 1933.

Caan, James: Bronx, NY, Mar. 26,1939.
Caesar, Sid: Yonkers, NY, Sept. 8, 1922.
Cage, Nicolas (Coppola): Long Beach, CA, Jan. 7, 1964.
Cain, Dean (Dean Tanaka): Mt. Clemens, MI, July 31, 1966.
Caine, Michael (Maurice Micklewhite): London, Mar. 14, 1933.
Caine, Shakira (Baksh): Guyana, Feb. 23, 1947. Indian Trust College.
Callan, Michael (Martin Calinieff): Philadelphia, Nov. 22, 1935.
Callow, Simon: London, June 15, 1949. Queens U.
Cameron, Kirk: Panorama City, CA, Oct. 12, 1970.
Camp, Colleen: San Francisco, CA, June 7, 1953.
Campbell, Bill: Chicago, IL, July 7, 1959.
Campbell, Glen: Delight, AR, Apr. 22, 1935.
Campbell, Neve: Guelph, Ontario, Canada, Oct. 3, 1973.
Campbell, Tisha: Oklahoma City, OK, Oct. 13, 1968.
Canale, Gianna Maria: Reggio Calabria, Italy, Sept. 12, 1927.
Cannon, Dyan (Samille Diane Friesen): Tacoma, WA, Jan. 4, 1937.
Capers, Virginia: Sumter, SC, Sept. 25, 1925. Juilliard.
Capshaw, Kate: Ft. Worth, TX, Nov. 3, 1953. UMo.
Cara, Irene: NYC, Mar. 18, 1958.
Cardinale, Claudia: Tunis, N. Africa. Apr. 15, 1939. College Paul Cambon.
Carey, Harry, Jr.: Saugus, CA, May 16, 1921. Black Fox Military Academy.
Carey, Philip: Hackensack, NJ, July 15, 1925. U Miami.
Cariou, Len: Winnipeg, Canada, Sept. 30, 1939.

Carlin, George: NYC, May 12, 1938.
Carlyle, Robert: Glasgow, Scotland, Apr. 14, 1961.
Carmen, Julie: Mt. Vernon, NY, Apr. 4, 1954.
Carmichael, Ian: Hull, England, June 18, 1920. Scarborough College.
Carne, Judy (Joyce Botterill): Northampton, England, 1939. Bush-Davis Theatre School.
Caron, Leslie: Paris, France, July 1, 1931. Nat'l Conservatory, Paris.
Carpenter, Carleton: Bennington, VT, July 10, 1926. Northwestern.
Carradine, David: Hollywood, Dec. 8, 1936. San Francisco State.
Carradine, Keith: San Mateo, CA, Aug. 8, 1950. Colo. State U.
Carradine, Robert: San Mateo, CA, Mar. 24, 1954.
Carrel, Dany: Tourane, Indochina, Sept. 20, 1936. Marseilles Cons.
Carrera, Barbara: Managua, Nicaragua, Dec. 31, 1945.
Carrere, Tia (Althea Janairo): Honolulu, HI, Jan. 2, 1965.
Carrey, Jim: Jacksons Point, Ontario, Canada, Jan. 17, 1962.
Carriere, Mathieu: Hannover, West Germany, Aug. 2, 1950.
Carroll, Diahann (Johnson): NYC, July 17, 1935. NYU.
Carroll, Pat: Shreveport, LA, May 5, 1927. Catholic U.
Carson, John David: California, Mar. 6, 1952. Valley College.
Carson, Johnny: Corning, IA, Oct. 23, 1925. U of Neb.
Carsten, Peter (Ransenthaler): Weissenberg, Bavaria, Apr. 30, 1929. Munich Akademie.
Cartwright, Veronica: Bristol, England, Apr 20, 1949.
Caruso, David: Forest Hills, NY, Jan. 7, 1956.
Carvey, Dana: Missoula, MT, Apr. 2, 1955. SFST.Col.
Casella, Max: Washington D.C, June 6, 1967.
Casey, Bernie: Wyco, WV, June 8, 1939.
Cassavetes, Nick: NYC, 1959, Syracuse U, AADA.
Cassel, Jean-Pierre: Paris, France, Oct. 27, 1932.
Cassel, Seymour: Detroit, MI, Jan. 22, 1935.
Cassel, Vincent: Paris, Nov. 23, 1966.
Cassidy, David: NYC, Apr. 12, 1950.
Cassidy, Joanna: Camden, NJ, Aug. 2, 1944. Syracuse U.
Cassidy, Patrick: Los Angeles, CA, Jan. 4, 1961.
Cates, Phoebe: NYC, July 16, 1962.
Cattrall, Kim: Liverpool, England, Aug. 21, 1956. AADA.
Caulfield, Maxwell: Glasgow, Scotland, Nov. 23, 1959.
Cavani, Liliana: Bologna, Italy, Jan. 12, 1937. U Bologna.
Cavett, Dick: Gibbon, NE, Nov. 19, 1936.
Caviezel, Jim: Mt. Vernon, WA, Sept. 26, 1968.
Chakiris, George: Norwood, OH, Sept. 16, 1933.
Chamberlain, Richard: Beverly Hills, CA, March 31, 1935. Pomona.
Champion, Marge (Marjorie Belcher): Los Angeles, Sept. 2, 1923.
Chan, Jackie: Hong Kong, Apr. 7, 1954.
Channing, Carol: Seattle, WA, Jan. 31, 1921. Bennington.
Channing, Stockard (Susan Stockard): NYC, Feb. 13, 1944. Radcliffe.
Chapin, Miles: NYC, Dec. 6, 1954. HB Studio.
Chaplin, Ben: London, July 31, 1970.
Chaplin, Geraldine: Santa Monica, CA, July 31, 1944. Royal Ballet.
Chaplin, Sydney: Los Angeles, Mar. 31, 1926. Lawrenceville.
Charisse, Cyd (Tula Ellice Finklea): Amarillo, TX, Mar. 3, 1922. Hollywood Professional School.
Charles, Josh: Baltimore, MD, Sept. 15, 1971.
Charles, Walter: East Strousburg, PA, Apr. 4, 1945. Boston U.

Chase, Chevy (Cornelius Crane Chase): NYC, Oct. 8, 1943.
Chaves, Richard: Jacksonville, FL, Oct. 9, 1951. Occidental College.
Chaykin, Maury: Canada, July 27, 1954.
Cheadle, Don: Kansas City, MO, Nov. 29, 1964.
Chen, Joan (Chen Chung): Shanghai, Apr. 26, 1961. CalState.
Cher (Cherilyn Sarkisian): El Centro, CA, May 20, 1946.
Chiles, Lois: Alice, TX, Apr. 15, 1947.
Chong, Rae Dawn: Vancouver, Canada, Feb. 28, 1962.
Chong, Thomas: Edmonton, Alberta, Canada, May 24, 1938.
Christian, Linda (Blanca Rosa Welter): Tampico, Mexico, Nov. 13, 1923.
Christie, Julie: Chukua, Assam, India, Apr. 14, 1941.
Christopher, Dennis (Carrelli): Philadelphia, PA, Dec. 2, 1955. Temple U.
Christopher, Jordan: Youngstown, OH, Oct. 23, 1940. Kent State.
Cilento, Diane: Queensland, Australia, Oct. 5, 1933. AADA.
Clark, Candy: Norman, OK, June 20, 1947.
Clark, Dick: Mt. Vernon, NY, Nov. 30, 1929. Syracuse U.
Clark, Matt: Washington, DC, Nov. 25, 1936.
Clark, Petula: Epsom, England, Nov. 15, 1932.
Clark, Susan: Sarnid, Ont., Canada, Mar. 8, 1943. RADA.
Clarkson, Patricia: New Orleans, Dec. 29, 1959.
Clay, Andrew Dice (Andrew Silverstein): Brooklyn, NY, Sept. 29, 1957, Kingsborough College.
Clayburgh, Jill: NYC, Apr. 30, 1944. Sarah Lawrence.
Cleese, John: Weston-Super-Mare, England, Oct. 27, 1939, Cambridge.
Close, Glenn: Greenwich, CT, Mar. 19, 1947. William & Mary College.
Cody, Kathleen: Bronx, NY, Oct. 30, 1953.
Coffey, Scott: HI, May 1, 1967.
Cole, George: London, Apr. 22, 1925.
Coleman, Dabney: Austin, TX, Jan. 3, 1932.
Coleman, Gary: Zion, IL, Feb. 8, 1968.
Coleman, Jack: Easton, PA, Feb. 21, 1958. Duke U.
Colin, Margaret: NYC, May 26, 1957.
Collet, Christopher: NYC, Mar. 13, 1968. Strasberg Inst.
Collette, Toni: Sydney, Australia, Nov. 1, 1972.
Collins, Joan: London, May 21, 1933. Francis Holland School.
Collins, Pauline: Devon, England, Sept. 3, 1940.
Collins, Stephen: Des Moines, IA, Oct. 1, 1947. Amherst.
Colon, Miriam: Ponce, PR., 1945. UPR.
Coltrane, Robbie: Ruthergien, Scotland, Mar. 30, 1950.
Combs, Sean "Puffy": NYC, Nov. 4, 1969.
Comer, Anjanette: Dawson, TX, Aug. 7, 1942. Baylor, Tex. U.
Conant, Oliver: NYC, Nov. 15, 1955. Dalton.
Conaway, Jeff: NYC, Oct. 5, 1950. NYU.
Connelly, Jennifer: NYC, Dec. 12, 1970.
Connery, Jason: London, Jan. 11, 1963.
Connery, Sean: Edinburgh, Scotland, Aug. 25, 1930.
Connick, Harry, Jr.: New Orleans, LA, Sept. 11, 1967.
Connolly, Billy: Glasgow, Scotland, Nov. 24, 1942.
Connors, Mike (Krekor Ohanian): Fresno, CA, Aug. 15, 1925. UCLA.
Conrad, Robert (Conrad Robert Falk): Chicago, IL, Mar. 1, 1935. Northwestern U.
Constantine, Michael: Reading, PA, May 22, 1927.
Conti, Tom: Paisley, Scotland, Nov. 22, 1941.
Converse, Frank: St. Louis, MO, May 22, 1938. Carnegie Tech.

Conway, Gary: Boston, Feb. 4, 1936.
Conway, Kevin: NYC, May 29, 1942.
Conway, Tim (Thomas Daniel): Willoughby, OH, Dec. 15, 1933. Bowling Green State.
Coogan, Keith (Keith Mitchell Franklin): Palm Springs, CA, Jan. 13, 1970.
Cook, Rachael Leigh: Minneapolis, MN, Oct. 4, 1979.
Cooper, Ben: Hartford, CT, Sept. 30, 1930. Columbia U.
Cooper, Chris: Kansas City, MO, July 9, 1951. UMo.
Cooper, Jackie: Los Angeles, Sept. 15, 1921.
Copeland, Joan: NYC, June 1, 1922. Brooklyn College, RADA.
Corbett, Gretchen: Portland, OR, Aug. 13, 1947. Carnegie Tech.
Corbett, John: Wheeling, WV, May 9, 1961.
Corbin, Barry: Dawson County, TX, Oct. 16, 1940. Texas Tech. U.
Corcoran, Donna: Quincy, MA, Sept. 29, 1942.
Cord, Alex (Viespi): Floral Park, NY, Aug. 3, 1931. NYU, Actors Studio.
Corday, Mara (Marilyn Watts): Santa Monica, CA, Jan. 3, 1932.
Cornthwaite, Robert: St. Helens, OR, Apr. 28, 1917. USC.
Corri, Adrienne: Glasgow, Scot., Nov. 13, 1933. RADA.
Cort, Bud (Walter Edward Cox): New Rochelle, NY, Mar. 29, 1950. NYU.
Cortesa, Valentina: Milan, Italy, Jan. 1, 1924.
Cosby, Bill: Philadelphia, PA, July 12, 1937. Temple U.
Coster, Nicolas: London, Dec. 3, 1934. Neighborhood Playhouse.
Costner, Kevin: Lynwood, CA, Jan. 18, 1955. CalStaU.
Courtenay, Tom: Hull, England, Feb. 25, 1937. RADA.
Courtland, Jerome: Knoxville, TN, Dec. 27, 1926.
Cox, Brian: Dundee, Scotland, June 1, 1946. LAMDA.
Cox, Courteney: Birmingham, AL, June 15, 1964.
Cox, Ronny: Cloudcroft, NM, Aug. 23, 1938.
Coyote, Peter (Cohon): NYC, Oct. 10, 1941.
Craig, Daniel: Chester, England, 1968.
Craig, Michael: Poona, India, Jan. 27, 1929.
Craven, Gemma: Dublin, Ireland, June 1, 1950.
Crawford, Michael (Dumbel-Smith): Salisbury, England, Jan. 19, 1942.
Cremer, Bruno: Saint-Mande, Val-de-Varne, France, Oct. 6, 1929.
Cristal, Linda (Victoria Moya): Buenos Aires, Feb. 25, 1934.
Cromwell, James: Los Angeles, CA, Jan. 27, 1940.
Crosby, Denise: Hollywood, CA, Nov. 24, 1957.
Crosby, Harry: Los Angeles, CA, Aug. 8, 1958.
Crosby, Mary Frances: Los Angeles, CA, Sept. 14, 1959.
Cross, Ben: London, Dec. 16, 1947. RADA.
Cross, Murphy (Mary Jane): Laurelton, MD, June 22, 1950.
Crouse, Lindsay: NYC, May 12, 1948. Radcliffe.
Crowe, Russell: New Zealand, Apr. 7, 1964.
Crowley, Pat: Olyphant, PA, Sept. 17, 1932.
Crudup, Billy: Manhasset, NY, July 8, 1968. UNC/Chapel Hill.
Cruise, Tom (T. C. Mapother, IV): July 3, 1962, Syracuse, NY.
Cruz, Penélope (P.C. Sanchez): Madrid, Spain, Apr. 28, 1974.
Cruz, Wilson: Brooklyn, Dec. 27, 1973.
Cryer, Jon: NYC, Apr. 16, 1965, RADA.
Crystal, Billy: Long Beach, NY, Mar. 14, 1947. Marshall U.
Culkin, Kieran: NYC, Sept. 30, 1982.
Culkin, Macaulay: NYC, Aug. 26, 1980.
Culkin, Rory: NYC, July 21, 1989.
Cullum, John: Knoxville, TN, Mar. 2, 1930. U Tenn.

Billy Crudup

John Cusack

Matt Damon

Charles Dance

Cullum, John David: NYC, Mar. 1, 1966.
Culp, Robert: Oakland, CA, Aug. 16, 1930. U Wash.
Cumming, Alan: Perthshire, Scotland, Jan. 27, 1965.
Cummings, Constance: Seattle, WA, May 15, 1910.
Cummings, Quinn: Hollywood, Aug. 13, 1967.
Cummins, Peggy: Prestatyn, N. Wales, Dec. 18, 1926. Alexandra School.
Curry, Tim: Cheshire, England, Apr. 19, 1946. Birmingham U.
Curtin, Jane: Cambridge, MA, Sept. 6, 1947.
Curtis, Jamie Lee: Los Angeles, CA, Nov. 22, 1958.
Curtis, Tony (Bernard Schwartz): NYC, June 3, 1924.
Cusack, Joan: Evanston, IL, Oct. 11, 1962.
Cusack, John: Chicago, IL, June 28, 1966.
Cusack, Sinead: Dalkey, Ireland, Feb. 18, 1948.

Dafoe, Willem: Appleton, WI, July 22, 1955.
Dahl, Arlene: Minneapolis, Aug. 11, 1928. U Minn.
Dale, Jim: Rothwell, England, Aug. 15, 1935.
Dallesandro, Joe: Pensacola, FL, Dec. 31, 1948.
Dalton, Timothy: Colwyn Bay, Wales, Mar. 21, 1946. RADA.
Daltrey, Roger: London, Mar. 1, 1944.
Daly, Tim: NYC, Mar. 1, 1956. Bennington College.
Daly, Tyne: Madison, WI, Feb. 21, 1947. AMDA.
Damon, Matt: Cambridge, MA, Oct. 8, 1970.
Damone, Vic (Vito Farinola): Brooklyn, NY, June 12, 1928.
Dance, Charles: Plymouth, England, Oct. 10, 1946.
Danes, Claire: New York, NY, Apr. 12, 1979.
D'Angelo, Beverly: Columbus, OH, Nov. 15, 1953.
Dangerfield, Rodney (Jacob Cohen): Babylon, NY, Nov. 22, 1921.
Daniels, Jeff: Athens, GA, Feb. 19, 1955. EMichSt.
Daniels, William: Brooklyn, NY, Mar. 31, 1927. Northwestern.
Danner, Blythe: Philadelphia, PA, Feb. 3, 1944. Bard College.
Danning, Sybil (Sybille Johanna Danninger): Vienna, Austria, May 4, 1949.
Danson, Ted: San Diego, CA, Dec. 29, 1947. Stanford, Carnegie Tech.
Dante, Michael (Ralph Vitti): Stamford, CT, 1935. U Miami.
Danza, Tony: Brooklyn, NY, Apr. 21, 1951. UDubuque.
D'arbanville-Quinn, Patti: NYC, May 25, 1951.
Darby, Kim (Deborah Zerby): North Hollywood, CA, July 8, 1948.

Darcel, Denise (Denise Billecard): Paris, France, Sept. 8, 1925. U Dijon.
Darren, James: Philadelphia, PA, June 8, 1936. Stella Adler School.
Darrieux, Danielle: Bordeaux, France, May 1, 1917. Lycee LaTour.
Davenport, Nigel: Cambridge, England, May 23, 1928. Trinity College.
David, Keith: NYC, June 4, 1954. Juilliard.
Davidovich, Lolita: Toronto, Ontario, Canada, July 15, 1961.
Davidson, Jaye: Riverside, CA, 1968.
Davidson, John: Pittsburgh, Dec. 13, 1941. Denison U.
Davies, Jeremy (Boring): Rockford, IA, Oct. 28, 1969.
Davis, Clifton: Chicago, IL, Oct. 4, 1945. Oakwood College.
Davis, Geena: Wareham, MA, Jan. 21, 1957.
Davis, Hope: Tenafly, NJ, Mar. 23, 1964.
Davis, Judy: Perth, Australia, Apr. 23, 1955.
Davis, Mac: Lubbock, TX, Jan. 21,1942.
Davis, Nancy (Anne Frances Robbins): NYC, July 6, 1921. Smith College.
Davis, Ossie: Cogdell, GA, Dec. 18, 1917. Howard U.
Davis, Sammi: Kidderminster, Worcestershire, England, June 21, 1964.
Davison, Bruce: Philadelphia, PA, June 28, 1946.
Dawber, Pam: Detroit, MI, Oct. 18, 1954.
Day, Doris (Doris Kappelhoff): Cincinnati, Apr. 3, 1924.
Day, Laraine (Johnson): Roosevelt, UT, Oct. 13, 1917.
Day-Lewis, Daniel: London, Apr. 29, 1957. Bristol Old Vic.
Dayan, Assi: Israel, Nov. 23, 1945. U Jerusalem.
Deakins, Lucy: NYC, 1971.
Dean, Jimmy: Plainview, TX, Aug. 10, 1928.
Dean, Loren: Las Vegas, NV, July 31, 1969.
DeCarlo, Yvonne (Peggy Yvonne Middleton): Vancouver, B.C., Canada, Sept. 1, 1922. Vancouver School of Drama.
Dee, Frances: Los Angeles, Nov. 26, 1907. Chicago U.
Dee, Joey (Joseph Di Nicola): Passaic, NJ, June 11, 1940. Patterson State College.
Dee, Ruby: Cleveland, OH, Oct. 27, 1924. Hunter College.
Dee, Sandra (Alexandra Zuck): Bayonne, NJ, Apr. 23, 1942.
DeGeneres, Ellen: New Orleans, LA, Jan. 26, 1958.
DeHaven, Gloria: Los Angeles, July 23, 1923.
DeHavilland, Olivia: Tokyo, Japan, July 1, 1916. Notre Dame Convent School.

Minnie Driver

Kirsten Dunst

Colin Farrell

Morgan Freeman

Delair, Suzy (Suzanne Delaire): Paris, France, Dec. 31, 1916.
Delany, Dana: NYC, March 13, 1956. Wesleyan U.
Delon, Alain: Sceaux, France, Nov. 8, 1935.
Delorme, Daniele: Paris, France, Oct. 9, 1926. Sorbonne.
Delpy, Julie: Paris. Dec, 21, 1969.
Del Toro, Benicio: Santurce, Puerto Rico, Feb. 19, 1967.
DeLuise, Dom: Brooklyn, NY, Aug. 1, 1933. Tufts College.
DeLuise, Peter: NYC, Nov. 6, 1966.
Demongeot, Mylene: Nice, France, Sept. 29, 1938.
DeMornay, Rebecca: Los Angeles, Aug. 29, 1962. Strasberg Inst.
Dempsey, Patrick: Lewiston, ME, Jan. 13, 1966.
DeMunn, Jeffrey: Buffalo, NY, Apr. 25, 1947. Union College.
Dench, Judi: York, England, Dec. 9, 1934.
Deneuve, Catherine: Paris, France, Oct. 22, 1943.
De Niro, Robert: NYC, Aug. 17, 1943. Stella Adler.
Dennehy, Brian: Bridgeport, CT, Jul. 9, 1938. Columbia.
Denver, Bob: New Rochelle, NY, Jan. 9, 1935.
Depardieu, Gérard: Chateauroux, France, Dec. 27, 1948.
Depp, Johnny: Owensboro, KY, June 9, 1963.
Derek, Bo (Mary Cathleen Collins): Long Beach, CA, Nov. 20, 1956.
Dern, Bruce: Chicago, IL, June 4, 1936. UPA.
Dern, Laura: Los Angeles, Feb. 10, 1967.
DeSalvo, Anne: Philadelphia, Apr. 3, 1949.
Deschanel, Zooey: Los Angeles, Jan. 17, 1980.
Devane, William: Albany, NY, Sept. 5, 1939.
DeVito, Danny: Asbury Park, NJ, Nov. 17, 1944.
Dey, Susan: Pekin, IL, Dec. 10, 1953.
DeYoung, Cliff: Los Angeles, CA, Feb. 12, 1945. Cal State.
Diamond, Neil: NYC, Jan. 24, 1941. NYU.
Diaz, Cameron: Long Beach, CA, Aug. 30, 1972.
DiCaprio, Leonardo: Hollywood, CA, Nov. 11, 1974.
Dickinson, Angie (Angeline Brown): Kulm, ND, Sept. 30, 1932. Glendale College.
Diesel, Vin (Mark Vincent): NYC, July 18, 1967.
Diggs, Taye (Scott Diggs): Rochester, NY, Jan. 2, 1972.
Diller, Phyllis (Driver): Lima, OH, July 17, 1917. Bluffton College.
Dillman, Bradford: San Francisco, Apr. 14, 1930. Yale.

Dillon, Kevin: Mamaroneck, NY, Aug. 19, 1965.
Dillon, Matt: Larchmont, NY, Feb. 18, 1964. AADA.
Dillon, Melinda: Hope, AR, Oct. 13, 1939. Goodman Theatre School.
Dixon, Donna: Alexandria, VA, July 20, 1957.
Dobson, Kevin: NYC, Mar. 18, 1944.
Dobson, Tamara: Baltimore, MD, May 14, 1947. MD Inst. of Art.
Doherty, Shannen: Memphis, TN, Apr. 12, 1971.
Dolan, Michael: Oklahoma City, OK, June 21, 1965.
Donat, Peter: Nova Scotia, Jan. 20, 1928. Yale.
Donnelly, Donal: Bradford, England, July 6, 1931.
D'Onofrio, Vincent: Brooklyn, NY, June 30, 1959.
Donohoe, Amanda: London, June 29 1962.
Donovan, Martin: Reseda, CA, Aug. 19, 1957.
Donovan, Tate: NYC, Sept. 25, 1963.
Doohan, James: Vancouver, BC, Mar. 3, 1920. Neighborhood Playhouse.
Dooley, Paul: Parkersburg WV, Feb. 22, 1928. U WV.
Dorff, Stephen: Atlanta, GA, July 29, 1973.
Doug, Doug E. (Douglas Bourne): Brooklyn, NY, Jan. 7, 1970.
Douglas, Donna (Dorothy Bourgeois): Baywood, LA, Sept. 26, 1935.
Douglas, Illeana: MA, July 25, 1965.
Douglas, Kirk (Issur Danielovitch): Amsterdam, NY, Dec. 9, 1916. St. Lawrence U.
Douglas, Michael: New Brunswick, NJ, Sept. 25, 1944. U Cal.
Douglass, Robyn: Sendai, Japan, June 21, 1953. UCDavis.
Dourif, Brad: Huntington, WV, Mar. 18, 1950. Marshall U.
Down, Lesley-Anne: London, Mar. 17, 1954.
Downey, Robert, Jr.: NYC, Apr. 4, 1965.
Drake, Betsy: Paris, France, Sept. 11, 1923.
Drescher, Fran: Queens, NY, Sept. 30, 1957.
Dreyfuss, Richard: Brooklyn, NY, Oct. 19, 1947.
Drillinger, Brian: Brooklyn, NY, June 27, 1960. SUNY/Purchase.
Driver, Minnie (Amelia Driver): London, Jan. 31, 1971.
Duchovny, David: NYC, Aug. 7, 1960. Yale.
Dudikoff, Michael: Torrance, CA, Oct. 8, 1954.
Duff, Hilary: Houston, TX, Sept. 28, 1987.
Dugan, Dennis: Wheaton, IL, Sept. 5, 1946.
Dukakis, Olympia: Lowell, MA, June 20, 1931.

Duke, Bill: Poughkeepsie, NY, Feb. 26, 1943. NYU.
Duke, Patty (Anna Marie): NYC, Dec. 14, 1946.
Dullea, Keir: Cleveland, NJ, May 30, 1936. SF State College.
Dunaway, Faye: Bascom, FL, Jan. 14, 1941, Fla. U.
Duncan, Sandy: Henderson, TX, Feb. 20, 1946. Len Morris College.
Dunne, Griffin: NYC, June 8, 1955. Neighborhood Playhouse.
Dunst, Kirsten: Point Pleasant, NJ, Apr. 30, 1982.
Duperey, Anny: Paris, France, June 28, 1947.
Durbin, Deanna (Edna): Winnipeg, Canada, Dec. 4, 1921.
Durning, Charles S.: Highland Falls, NY, Feb. 28, 1923. NYU.
Dushku, Eliza: Boston, Dec. 30, 1980.
Dussollier, André: Annecy, France, Feb. 17, 1946.
Dutton, Charles: Baltimore, MD, Jan. 30, 1951. Yale.
DuVall, Clea: Los Angeles, Sept. 25, 1977.
Duvall, Robert: San Diego, CA, Jan. 5, 1931. Principia College.
Duvall, Shelley: Houston, TX, July 7, 1949.
Dysart, Richard: Brighton, ME, Mar. 30, 1929.
Dzundza, George: Rosenheim, Germ., July 19, 1945.

Easton, Robert: Milwaukee, WI, Nov. 23, 1930. U Texas.
Eastwood, Clint: San Francisco, May 31, 1931. LACC.
Eaton, Shirley: London, 1937. Aida Foster School.
Eckemyr, Agneta: Karlsborg, Sweden, July 2. Actors Studio.
Edelman, Gregg: Chicago, IL, Sept. 12, 1958. Northwestern U.
Eden, Barbara (Huffman): Tucson, AZ, Aug. 23, 1934.
Edwards, Anthony: Santa Barbara, CA, July 19, 1962. RADA.
Edwards, Luke: Nevada City, CA, Mar. 24, 1980.
Eggar, Samantha: London, Mar. 5, 1939.
Eichhorn, Lisa: Reading, PA, Feb. 4, 1952. Queens Ont. U RADA.
Eikenberry, Jill: New Haven, CT, Jan. 21, 1947.
Eilber, Janet: Detroit, MI, July 27, 1951. Juilliard.
Ekberg, Anita: Malmo, Sweden, Sept. 29, 1931.
Ekland, Britt: Stockholm, Sweden, Oct. 6, 1942.
Eldard, Ron: Long Island, NY, Feb. 20, 1965.
Elfman, Jenna (Jennifer Mary Batula): Los Angeles, Sept. 30, 1971.
Elizondo, Hector: NYC, Dec. 22, 1936.
Elliott, Alison: San Francisco, CA, May 19, 1970.
Elliott, Chris: NYC, May 31, 1960.
Elliott, Patricia: Gunnison, CO, July 21, 1942. UCol.
Elliott, Sam: Sacramento, CA, Aug. 9, 1944. U Ore.
Elwes, Cary: London, Oct. 26, 1962.
Ely, Ron (Ronald Pierce): Hereford, TX, June 21, 1938.
Embry, Ethan (Ethan Randall): Huntington Beach, CA, June 13, 1978.
Englund, Robert: Glendale, CA, June 6, 1949.
Epps, Omar: Brooklyn, July 23, 1973.
Erbe, Kathryn: Newton, MA, July 2, 1966.
Erdman, Richard: Enid, OK, June 1, 1925.
Ericson, John: Dusseldorf, Ger., Sept. 25, 1926. AADA.
Ermey, R. Lee (Ronald): Emporia, KS, Mar. 24, 1944.
Esmond, Carl (Willy Eichberger): Vienna, June 14, 1906. U Vienna.
Esposito, Giancarlo: Copenhagen, Denmark, Apr. 26, 1958.
Estevez, Emilio: NYC, May 12, 1962.
Estrada, Erik: NYC, Mar. 16, 1949.
Evans, Josh: NYC, Jan. 16, 1971.

Evans, Linda (Evanstad): Hartford, CT, Nov. 18, 1942.
Everett, Chad (Ray Cramton): South Bend, IN, June 11, 1936.
Everett, Rupert: Norfolk, England, May 29, 1959.
Evigan, Greg: South Amboy, NJ, Oct. 14, 1953.

Fabares, Shelley: Los Angeles, Jan. 19, 1944.
Fabian (Fabian Forte): Philadelphia, Feb. 6, 1943.
Fabray, Nanette (Ruby Nanette Fabares): San Diego, Oct. 27, 1920.
Fahey, Jeff: Olean, NY, Nov. 29, 1956.
Fairchild, Morgan (Patsy McClenny): Dallas, TX, Feb. 3, 1950. UCLA.
Falco, Edie: Brooklyn, July 5, 1963.
Falk, Peter: NYC, Sept. 16, 1927. New School.
Fanning, Dakota: Conyers, GA, Feb. 23, 1994.
Farentino, James: Brooklyn, NY, Feb. 24, 1938. AADA.
Fargas, Antonio: Bronx, NY, Aug. 14, 1946.
Farina, Dennis: Chicago, IL, Feb. 29, 1944.
Farina, Sandy (Sandra Feldman): Newark, NJ, 1955.
Farr, Felicia: Westchester, NY, Oct. 4. 1932. Penn State College.
Farrell, Colin: Castleknock, Ireland, Mar. 31, 1976.
Farrow, Mia (Maria): Los Angeles, Feb. 9, 1945.
Faulkner, Graham: London, Sept. 26, 1947. Webber-Douglas.
Favreau, Jon: Queens, NY, Oct. 16, 1966.
Fawcett, Farrah: Corpus Christie, TX, Feb. 2, 1947. TexU.
Feinstein, Alan: NYC, Sept. 8, 1941.
Feldman, Corey: Encino, CA, July 16, 1971.
Feldon, Barbara (Hall): Pittsburgh, Mar. 12, 1941. Carnegie Tech.
Feldshuh, Tovah: NYC, Dec. 27, 1953, Sarah Lawrence College.
Fellows, Edith: Boston, May 20, 1923.
Fenn, Sherilyn: Detroit, MI, Feb. 1, 1965.
Ferrell, Conchata: Charleston, WV, Mar. 28, 1943. Marshall U.
Ferrell, Will: Irvine, CA, July 16, 1968.
Ferrer, Mel: Elbeton, NJ, Aug. 25, 1912. Princeton U.
Ferrer, Miguel: Santa Monica, CA, Feb. 7, 1954.
Ferrera, America: Los Angeles, Apr. 18, 1984.
Ferris, Barbara: London, July 27, 1942.
Fiedler, John: Plateville, WI, Feb. 3, 1925.
Field, Sally: Pasadena, CA, Nov. 6, 1946.
Field, Shirley-Anne: London, June 27, 1938.
Field, Todd (William Todd Field): Pomona, CA, Feb. 24, 1964.
Fiennes, Joseph: Salisbury, Wiltshire, England, May 27, 1970.
Fiennes, Ralph: Suffolk, England, Dec. 22, 1962. RADA.
Fierstein, Harvey: Brooklyn, NY, June 6, 1954. Pratt Inst.
Finch, Jon: Caterham, England, Mar. 2, 1941.
Finlay, Frank: Farnworth, England, Aug. 6, 1926.
Finney, Albert: Salford, Lancashire, England, May 9, 1936. RADA.
Fiorentino, Linda: Philadelphia, PA, Mar. 9, 1960.
Firth, Colin: Grayshott, Hampshire, England, Sept. 10, 1960.
Firth, Peter: Bradford, England, Oct. 27, 1953.
Fishburne, Laurence: Augusta, GA, July 30, 1961.
Fisher, Carrie: Los Angeles, CA, Oct. 21, 1956. London Central School of Drama.
Fisher, Eddie: Philadelphia, PA, Aug. 10, 1928.
Fisher, Frances: Milford-on-the-Sea, Eng., May 11, 1952.
Fitzgerald, Geraldine: Dublin, Ireland, Nov. 24, 1914. Dublin Art School.

Fitzgerald, Tara: London, Sept. 17, 1968.
Flagg, Fannie: Birmingham, AL, Sept. 21, 1944. UAl.
Flanagan, Fionnula: Dublin, Dec. 10, 1941.
Flannery, Susan: Jersey City, NJ, July 31, 1943.
Fleming, Rhonda (Marilyn Louis): Los Angeles, Aug. 10, 1922.
Flemyng, Robert: Liverpool, England, Jan. 3, 1912. Haileybury College.
Fletcher, Louise: Birmingham, AL, July 22 1934.
Flockhart, Calista: Stockton, IL, Nov. 11, Rutgers U.
Foch, Nina: Leyden, Holland, Apr. 20, 1924.
Foley, Dave: Toronto, Canada, Jan. 4, 1963.
Follows, Megan: Toronto, Canada, Mar. 14, 1968.
Fonda, Bridget: Los Angeles, Jan. 27, 1964.
Fonda, Jane: NYC, Dec. 21, 1937. Vassar.
Fonda, Peter: NYC, Feb. 23, 1939. U Omaha.
Fontaine, Joan: Tokyo, Japan, Oct. 22, 1917.
Foote, Hallie: NYC, 1953. UNH.
Ford, Glenn (Gwyllyn Samuel Newton Ford): Quebec, Canada, May 1, 1916.
Ford, Harrison: Chicago, IL, July 13, 1942. Ripon College.
Forest, Mark (Lou Degni): Brooklyn, NY, Jan. 1933.
Forlani, Claire: London, July 1, 1972.
Forrest, Frederic: Waxahachie, TX, Dec. 23, 1936.
Forrest, Steve: Huntsville, TX, Sept. 29, 1924. UCLA.
Forslund, Connie: San Diego, CA, June 19, 1950. NYU.
Forster, Robert (Foster, Jr.): Rochester, NY, July 13, 1941. Rochester U.
Forsythe, John (Freund): Penn's Grove, NJ, Jan. 29, 1918.
Forsythe, William: Brooklyn, NY, June 7, 1955.
Fossey, Brigitte: Tourcoing, France, Mar. 11, 1947.
Foster, Ben: Boston, MA, Oct. 29, 1980.
Foster, Jodie (Ariane Munker): Bronx, NY, Nov. 19, 1962. Yale.
Foster, Meg: Reading, PA, May 14, 1948.
Fox, Edward: London, Apr. 13, 1937. RADA.
Fox, James: London, May 19, 1939.
Fox, Michael J.: Vancouver, BC, June 9, 1961.
Fox, Vivica A.: Indianapolis, July 30, 1964.
Foxworth, Robert: Houston, TX, Nov. 1, 1941. Carnegie Tech.
Foxx, Jamie: Terrell, TX, Dec. 13, 1967.
Frain, James: Leeds, England, Mar. 14, 1969.
Frakes, Jonathan: Bethlehem, PA, Aug. 19, 1952. Harvard.
Franciosa, Anthony (Papaleo): NYC, Oct. 25, 1928.
Francis, Anne: Ossining, NY, Sept. 16, 1932.
Francis, Arlene (Arlene Kazanjian): Boston, Oct. 20, 1908. Finch School.
Francis, Connie (Constance Franconero): Newark, NJ, Dec. 12, 1938.
Francks, Don: Vancouver, Canada, Feb. 28, 1932.
Franklin, Pamela: Tokyo, Feb. 4, 1950.
Franz, Arthur: Perth Amboy, NJ, Feb. 29, 1920. Blue Ridge College.
Franz, Dennis: Chicago, IL, Oct. 28, 1944.
Fraser, Brendan: Indianapolis, IN, Dec. 3, 1968.
Frazier, Sheila: NYC, Nov. 13, 1948.
Frechette, Peter: Warwick, RI, Oct. 1956. URI.
Freeman, Al, Jr.: San Antonio, TX, Mar. 21, 1934. CCLA.
Freeman, Mona: Baltimore, MD, June 9, 1926.
Freeman, Morgan: Memphis, TN, June 1, 1937. LACC.
Frewer, Matt: Washington, DC, Jan. 4, 1958, Old Vic.
Fricker, Brenda: Dublin, Ireland, Feb. 17, 1945.

Friels, Colin: Glasgow, Sept. 25, 1952.
Fry, Stephen: Hampstead, London, Eng., Aug. 24, 1957.
Fuller, Penny: Durham, NC, 1940. Northwestern U.
Funicello, Annette: Utica, NY, Oct. 22, 1942.
Furlong, Edward: Glendale, CA, Aug. 2, 1977.
Furneaux, Yvonne: Lille, France, May 11, 1928. Oxford U.

Gable, John Clark: Los Angeles, Mar. 20, 1961. Santa Monica College.
Gabor, Zsa Zsa (Sari Gabor): Budapest, Hungary, Feb. 6, 1918.
Gail, Max: Derfoil, MI, Apr. 5, 1943.
Gaines, Boyd: Atlanta, GA, May 11, 1953. Juilliard.
Galecki, Johnny: Bree, Belgium, Apr. 30, 1975.
Gallagher, Peter: NYC, Aug. 19, 1955. Tufts U.
Galligan, Zach: NYC, Feb. 14, 1963. ColumbiaU.
Gallo, Vincent: Buffalo, NY, Apr. 11, 1961.
Gam, Rita: Pittsburgh, PA, Apr. 2, 1928.
Gamble, Mason: Chicago, IL, Jan. 16, 1986.
Gambon, Michael: Dublin, Ireland, Oct. 19, 1940.
Gandolfini, James: Westwood, NJ, Sept. 18, 1961.
Ganz, Bruno: Zurich, Switzerland, Mar. 22, 1941.
Garber, Victor: Montreal, Canada, Mar. 16, 1949.
Garcia, Adam: Wahroonga, New So. Wales, Australia, June 1, 1973.
Garcia, Andy: Havana, Cuba, Apr. 12, 1956. FlaInt.
Garfield, Allen (Allen Goorwitz): Newark, NJ, Nov. 22, 1939. Actors Studio.
Garfunkel, Art: NYC, Nov. 5, 1941.
Garland, Beverly: Santa Cruz, CA, Oct. 17, 1926. Glendale College.
Garner, James (James Baumgarner): Norman, OK, Apr. 7, 1928. Okla. U.
Garner, Jennifer: Houston, TX, Apr. 17, 1972.
Garofalo, Janeane: Newton, NJ, Sept. 28, 1964.
Garr, Teri: Lakewood, OH, Dec. 11, 1949.
Garrett, Betty: St. Joseph, MO, May 23, 1919. Annie Wright Seminary.
Garrison, Sean: NYC, Oct. 19, 1937.
Gary, Lorraine: NYC, Aug. 16, 1937.
Gavin, John: Los Angeles, Apr. 8, 1935. Stanford U.
Gaylord, Mitch: Van Nuys, CA, Mar. 10, 1961. UCLA.
Gaynor, Mitzi (Francesca Marlene Von Gerber): Chicago, IL, Sept. 4, 1930.
Gazzara, Ben: NYC, Aug. 28, 1930. Actors Studio.
Geary, Anthony: Coalsville, UT, May 29, 1947. UUt.
Gedrick, Jason: Chicago, IL, Feb. 7, 1965. Drake U.
Geeson, Judy: Arundel, England, Sept. 10, 1948. Corona.
Gellar, Sarah Michelle: NYC, Apr. 14, 1977.
Geoffreys, Stephen (Miller): Cincinnati, OH, Nov. 22, 1959. NYU.
George, Susan: West London, England, July 26, 1950.
Gerard, Gil: Little Rock, AR, Jan. 23, 1940.
Gere, Richard: Philadelphia, PA, Aug. 29, 1949. U Mass.
Gerroll, Daniel: London, Oct. 16, 1951. Central.
Gershon, Gina: Los Angeles, June 10, 1962.
Gertz, Jami: Chicago, IL, Oct. 28, 1965.
Getty, Balthazar: Los Angeles, CA, Jan. 22, 1975.
Getty, Estelle: NYC, July 25, 1923. New School.
Gholson, Julie: Birmingham, AL, June 4, 1958.
Ghostley, Alice: Eve, MO, Aug. 14, 1926. Okla U.
Giamatti, Paul: NYC, June 6, 1967.
Giannini, Giancarlo: Spezia, Italy, Aug. 1, 1942. Rome Acad. of Drama.

Gibb, Cynthia: Bennington, VT, Dec. 14, 1963.
Gibson, Henry: Germantown, PA, Sept. 21, 1935.
Gibson, Mel: Peekskill, NY, Jan. 3, 1956. NIDA.
Gibson, Thomas: Charleston, SC, July 3, 1962.
Gift, Roland: Birmingham, England, May 28 1962.
Gilbert, Melissa: Los Angeles, CA, May 8, 1964.
Giles, Nancy: NYC, July 17, 1960, Oberlin College.
Gillette, Anita: Baltimore, MD, Aug. 16, 1938.
Gilliam, Terry: Minneapolis, MN, Nov. 22, 1940.
Gillis, Ann (Alma O'Connor): Little Rock, AR, Feb. 12, 1927.
Ginty, Robert: NYC, Nov. 14, 1948. Yale.
Girardot, Annie: Paris, France, Oct. 25, 1931.
Gish, Annabeth: Albuquerque, NM, Mar. 13, 1971. DukeU.
Givens, Robin: NYC, Nov. 27, 1964.
Glaser, Paul Michael: Boston, MA, Mar. 25, 1943. Boston U.
Glass, Ron: Evansville, IN, July 10, 1945.
Gleason, Joanna: Winnipeg, Canada, June 2, 1950. UCLA.
Gleason, Paul: Jersey City, NJ, May 4, 1944.
Gleeson, Brendan: Belfast, Nov. 9, 1955.
Glenn, Scott: Pittsburgh, PA, Jan. 26, 1942. William and Mary College.
Glover, Crispin: NYC, Sept 20, 1964.
Glover, Danny: San Francisco, CA, July 22, 1947. SFStateCol.
Glover, John: Kingston, NY, Aug. 7, 1944.
Glynn, Carlin: Cleveland, Oh, Feb. 19, 1940. Actors Studio.
Goldberg, Whoopi (Caryn Johnson): NYC, Nov. 13, 1949.
Goldblum, Jeff: Pittsburgh, PA, Oct. 22, 1952. Neighborhood Playhouse.
Golden, Annie: Brooklyn, NY, Oct. 19, 1951.
Goldstein, Jenette: Beverly Hills, CA, Feb. 4, 1960.
Goldthwait, Bob: Syracuse, NY, May 1, 1962.
Goldwyn, Tony: Los Angeles, May 20, 1960. LAMDA.
Golino, Valeria: Naples, Italy, Oct. 22, 1966.
Gonzales-Gonzalez, Pedro: Aguilares, TX, Dec. 21, 1926.
Gonzalez, Cordelia: Aug. 11, 1958, San Juan, PR. UPR.
Goodall, Caroline: London, Nov. 13, 1959. BristolU.
Gooding, Cuba, Jr.: Bronx, N.Y., Jan. 2, 1968.
Goodman, Dody: Columbus, OH, Oct. 28, 1915.
Goodman, John: St. Louis, MO, June 20, 1952.
Gordon, Keith: NYC, Feb. 3, 1961.
Gordon-Levitt, Joseph: Los Angeles, Feb. 17, 1981.
Gorshin, Frank: Pittsburgh, PA, Apr. 5, 1933.
Gortner, Marjoe: Long Beach, CA, Jan. 14, 1944.
Gosling, Ryan: London, Ontario, Nov. 12, 1980.
Goss, Luke: London, Sept. 28, 1968.
Gossett, Louis, Jr.: Brooklyn, NY, May 27, 1936. NYU.
Gould, Elliott (Goldstein): Brooklyn, NY, Aug. 29, 1938. Columbia U.
Gould, Harold: Schenectady, NY, Dec. 10, 1923. Cornell.
Gould, Jason: NYC, Dec. 29, 1966.
Goulet, Robert: Lawrence, MA, Nov. 26, 1933. Edmonton.
Graf, David: Lancaster, OH, Apr. 16, 1950. OhStateU.
Graff, Todd: NYC, Oct. 22, 1959. SUNY/ Purchase.
Graham, Heather: Milwauke, WI, Jan. 29, 1970.
Granger, Farley: San Jose, CA, July 1, 1925.
Grant, David Marshall: Westport, CT, June 21, 1955. Yale.
Grant, Hugh: London, Sept. 9, 1960. Oxford.

Grant, Kathryn (Olive Grandstaff): Houston, TX, Nov. 25, 1933. UCLA.
Grant, Lee: NYC, Oct. 31, 1927. Juilliard.
Grant, Richard E: Mbabane, Swaziland, May 5, 1957. Cape Town U.
Graves, Peter (Aurness): Minneapolis, Mar. 18, 1926. U Minn.
Graves, Rupert: Weston-Super-Mare, England, June 30, 1963.
Gray, Coleen (Doris Jensen): Staplehurst, NB, Oct. 23, 1922. Hamline.
Gray, Linda: Santa Monica, CA, Sept. 12, 1940.
Gray, Spalding: Barrington, RI, June 5, 1941.
Grayson, Kathryn (Zelma Hedrick): Winston-Salem, NC, Feb. 9, 1922.
Green, Kerri: Fort Lee, NJ, Jan. 14, 1967. Vassar.
Green, Seth: Philadelphia, PA, Feb. 8, 1974.
Greene, Ellen: NYC, Feb. 22, 1950. Ryder College.
Greene, Graham: Six Nations Reserve, Ontario, June 22, 1952.
Greenwood, Bruce: Quebec, Canada, Aug. 12, 1956.
Greer, Michael: Galesburg, IL, Apr. 20, 1943.
Greist, Kim: Stamford, CT, May 12, 1958.
Grey, Jennifer: NYC, Mar. 26, 1960.
Grey, Joel (Katz): Cleveland, OH, Apr. 11, 1932.
Grey, Virginia: Los Angeles, Mar. 22, 1917.
Grieco, Richard: Watertown, NY, Mar. 23, 1965.
Griem, Helmut: Hamburg, Germany, Apr. 6, 1932. HamburgU.
Grier, David Alan: Detroit, MI, June 30, 1955. Yale.
Grier, Pam: Winston-Salem, NC, May 26, 1949.
Griffin, Eddie: Kansas City, MO, July 15, 1968.
Griffith, Andy: Mt. Airy, NC, June 1, 1926. UNC.
Griffith, Melanie: NYC, Aug. 9, 1957. Pierce Col.
Griffith, Thomas Ian: Hartford, CT, Mar. 18, 1962.
Griffiths, Rachel: Melbourne, Australia, 1968.
Griffiths, Richard: Tornaby-on-Tees, England, July 31, 1947.
Grimes, Gary: San Francisco, June 2, 1955.
Grimes, Scott: Lowell, MA, July 9, 1971.
Grimes, Tammy: Lynn, MA, Jan. 30, 1934. Stephens College.
Grizzard, George: Roanoke Rapids, NC, Apr. 1, 1928. UNC.
Grodin, Charles: Pittsburgh, PA, Apr. 21, 1935.
Groh, David: NYC, May 21, 1939. Brown U, LAMDA.
Gross, Mary: Chicago, IL, Mar. 25, 1953.
Gross, Michael: Chicago, IL, June 21, 1947.
Gruffud, Ioan: Cardiff, Wales, Oct. 6, 1973.
Guest, Christopher: NYC, Feb. 5, 1948.
Guest, Lance: Saratoga, CA, July 21, 1960. UCLA.
Guillaume, Robert (Williams): St. Louis, MO, Nov. 30, 1937.
Guiry, Thomas: Trenton, NJ, Oct. 12, 1981.
Gulager, Clu: Holdenville, OK, Nov. 16 1928.
Guttenberg, Steve: Massapequa, NY, Aug. 24, 1958. UCLA.
Guy, Jasmine: Boston, Mar. 10, 1964.
Gyllenhaal, Jake: Los Angeles, Dec. 19, 1980.
Gyllenhaal, Maggie: Los Angeles, Nov. 16, 1977.

Haas, Lukas: West Hollywood, CA, Apr. 16, 1976.
Hack, Shelley: Greenwich, CT, July 6, 1952.
Hackman, Gene: San Bernardino, CA, Jan. 30, 1930.
Hagerty, Julie: Cincinnati, OH, June 15, 1955. Juilliard.
Hagman, Larry (Hageman): Weatherford, TX, Sept. 21, 1931. Bard.
Haid, Charles: San Francisco, June 2, 1943. CarnegieTech.

Harold Gould

Heather Graham

Salma Hayek

Philip Seymour Hoffman

Haim, Corey: Toronto, Canada, Dec. 23, 1972.
Hale, Barbara: DeKalb, IL, Apr. 18, 1922. Chicago Academy of Fine Arts.
Haley, Jackie Earle: Northridge, CA, July 14, 1961.
Hall, Albert: Boothton, AL, Nov. 10, 1937. Columbia.
Hall, Anthony Michael: Boston, MA, Apr. 14, 1968.
Hall, Arsenio: Cleveland, OH, Feb. 12, 1959.
Hamel, Veronica: Philadelphia, PA, Nov. 20, 1943.
Hamill, Mark: Oakland, CA, Sept. 25, 1952. LACC.
Hamilton, George: Memphis, TN, Aug. 12, 1939. Hackley.
Hamilton, Linda: Salisbury, MD, Sept. 26, 1956.
Hamlin, Harry: Pasadena, CA, Oct. 30, 1951.
Hampshire, Susan: London, May 12, 1941.
Hampton, James: Oklahoma City, OK, July 9, 1936. NTexasStU.
Han, Maggie: Providence, RI, 1959.
Handler, Evan: NYC, Jan. 10, 1961. Juilllard.
Hanks, Colin: Sacramento, CA, Nov. 24, 1977.
Hanks, Tom: Concord, CA, Jul. 9, 1956. CalStateU.
Hannah, Daryl: Chicago, IL, Dec. 3, 1960. UCLA.
Hannah, Page: Chicago, IL, Apr. 13, 1964.
Harden, Marcia Gay: LaJolla, CA, Aug. 14, 1959.
Hardin, Ty (Orison Whipple Hungerford, II): NYC, June 1, 1930.
Harewood, Dorian: Dayton, OH, Aug. 6, 1950. U Cinn.
Harmon, Mark: Los Angeles, CA, Sept. 2, 1951. UCLA.
Harper, Jessica: Chicago, IL, Oct. 10, 1949.
Harper, Tess: Mammoth Spring, AK, 1952. SWMoState.
Harper, Valerie: Suffern, NY, Aug. 22, 1940.
Harrelson, Woody: Midland, TX, July 23, 1961. Hanover College.
Harrington, Pat: NYC, Aug. 13, 1929. Fordham U.
Harris, Barbara (Sandra Markowitz): Evanston, IL, July 25, 1935.
Harris, Ed: Tenafly, NJ, Nov. 28, 1950. Columbia.
Harris, Jared: UK, Aug. 24, 1961.
Harris, Julie: Grosse Point, MI, Dec. 2, 1925. Yale Drama School.
Harris, Mel (Mary Ellen): Bethlehem, PA, 1957. Columbia.
Harris, Neil Patrick: Albuquerque, NM, June 15, 1973.
Harris, Rosemary: Ashby, England, Sept. 19, 1930. RADA.
Harrison, Gregory: Catalina Island, CA, May 31, 1950. Actors Studio.
Harrison, Noel: London, Jan. 29, 1936.

Harrold, Kathryn: Tazewell, VA, Aug. 2, 1950. Mills College.
Harry, Deborah: Miami, IL, July 1, 1945.
Hart, Ian: Liverpool, England, Oct. 8, 1964.
Hart, Roxanne: Trenton, NJ, July 27, 1952, Princeton.
Hartley, Mariette: NYC, June 21, 1941.
Hartman, David: Pawtucket, RI, May 19, 1935. Duke U.
Hartnett, Josh: San Francisco, July 21, 1978.
Hassett, Marilyn: Los Angeles, CA, Dec. 17, 1947.
Hatcher, Teri: Sunnyvale, CA, Dec. 8, 1964.
Hatosy, Shawn: Fredrick, MD, Dec. 29, 1975.
Hauer, Rutger: Amsterdam, Holland, Jan. 23, 1944.
Hauser, Cole: Santa Barbara, CA, Mar. 22, 1975.
Hasuer, Wings (Gerald Dwight Hauser): Hollywood, CA, Dec. 12, 1947.
Haver, June: Rock Island, IL, June 10, 1926.
Havoc, June (Hovick): Seattle, WA, Nov. 8, 1916.
Hawke, Ethan: Austin, TX, Nov. 6, 1970.
Hawn, Goldie: Washington, DC, Nov. 21, 1945.
Hayek, Salma: Coatzacoalcos, Veracruz, Mexico, Sept. 2, 1968.
Hayes, Isaac: Covington, TN, Aug. 20, 1942.
Hays, Robert: Bethesda, MD, July 24, 1947, SD State College.
Haysbert, Dennis: San Mateo, CA, June 2, 1954.
Headly, Glenne: New London, CT, Mar. 13, 1955. AmCollege.
Heald, Anthony: New Rochelle, NY, Aug. 25, 1944. MIStateU.
Heard, John: Washington, DC, Mar. 7, 1946. Clark U.
Heatherton, Joey: NYC, Sept. 14, 1944.
Heche, Anne: Aurora, OH, May 25, 1969.
Hedaya, Dan: Brooklyn, NY, July 24, 1940.
Hedison, David: Providence, RI, May 20, 1929. Brown U.
Hedren, Tippi (Natalie): Lafayette, MN, Jan. 19, 1931.
Hegyes, Robert: Metuchen, NJ, May 7, 1951.
Helmond, Katherine: Galveston, TX, July 5, 1934.
Hemingway, Mariel: Ketchum, ID, Nov. 22, 1961.
Hemsley, Sherman: Philadelphia, PA, Feb. 1, 1938.
Henderson, Florence: Dale, IN, Feb. 14, 1934.
Hendry, Gloria: Winter Have, FL, Mar. 3, 1949.
Henner, Marilu: Chicago, IL, Apr. 6, 1952.
Henriksen, Lance: NYC, May 5, 1940.

Henry, Buck (Henry Zuckerman): NYC, Dec. 9, 1930. Dartmouth.
Henry, Justin: Rye, NY, May 25, 1971.
Henstridge, Natasha: Springdale, Newfoundland, Canada, Aug. 15, 1974.
Herrmann, Edward: Washington, DC, July 21, 1943. Bucknell, LAMDA.
Hershey, Barbara (Herzstein): Hollywood, CA, Feb. 5, 1948.
Hesseman, Howard: Lebanon, OR, Feb. 27, 1940.
Heston, Charlton: Evanston, IL, Oct. 4, 1922. Northwestern U.
Hewitt, Jennifer Love: Waco, TX, Feb. 21, 1979.
Hewitt, Martin: Claremont, CA, Feb. 19, 1958. AADA.
Heywood, Anne (Violet Pretty): Birmingham, England, Dec. 11, 1932.
Hickman, Darryl: Hollywood, CA, July 28, 1933. Loyola U.
Hickman, Dwayne: Los Angeles, May 18, 1934. Loyola U.
Hicks, Catherine: NYC, Aug. 6, 1951. Notre Dame.
Higgins, Anthony (Corlan): Cork City, Ireland, May 9, 1947. Birmingham Dramatic Arts.
Higgins, Michael: Brooklyn, NY, Jan. 20, 1921. AmThWing.
Hill, Arthur: Saskatchewan, Canada, Aug. 1, 1922. U Brit. College.
Hill, Bernard: Manchester, England, Dec. 17, 1944.
Hill, Steven: Seattle, WA, Feb. 24, 1922. U Wash.
Hill, Terrence (Mario Girotti): Venice, Italy, Mar. 29, 1941. U Rome.
Hillerman, John: Denison, TX, Dec. 20, 1932.
Hinds, Ciaran: Belfast, No. Ireland, Feb. 9, 1953.
Hines, Gregory: NYC, Feb. 14, 1946.
Hingle, Pat: Denver, CO, July 19, 1923. Tex. U.
Hirsch, Emile: Topanga Canyon, CA, Mar. 13, 1985.
Hirsch, Judd: NYC, Mar. 15, 1935. AADA.
Hobel, Mara: NYC, June 18, 1971.
Hodge, Patricia: Lincolnshire, England, Sept. 29, 1946. LAMDA.
Hoffman, Dustin: Los Angeles, Aug. 8, 1937. Pasadena Playhouse.
Hoffman, Philip Seymour: Fairport, NY, July 23, 1967.
Hogan, Jonathan: Chicago, IL, June 13, 1951.
Hogan, Paul: Lightning Ridge, Australia, Oct. 8, 1939.
Holbrook, Hal (Harold): Cleveland, OH, Feb. 17, 1925. Denison.
Holliman, Earl: Tennesas Swamp, Delhi, LA, Sept. 11, 1928. UCLA.
Holm, Celeste: NYC, Apr. 29, 1919.
Holm, Ian: Ilford, Essex, England, Sept. 12, 1931. RADA.
Holmes, Katie: Toledo, OH, Dec. 18, 1978.
Homeier, Skip (George Vincent Homeier): Chicago, IL, Oct. 5, 1930. UCLA.
Hooks, Robert: Washington, DC, Apr. 18, 1937. Temple.
Hopkins, Anthony: Port Talbot, So. Wales, Dec. 31, 1937. RADA.
Hopper, Dennis: Dodge City, KS, May 17, 1936.
Horne, Lena: Brooklyn, NY, June 30, 1917.
Horrocks, Jane: Rossendale Valley, England, Jan. 18, 1964.
Horsley, Lee: Muleshoe, TX, May 15, 1955.
Horton, Robert: Los Angeles, July 29, 1924. UCLA.
Hoskins, Bob: Bury St. Edmunds, England, Oct. 26, 1942.
Houghton, Katharine: Hartford, CT, Mar. 10, 1945. Sarah Lawrence.
Hounsou, Djimon: Benin, West Africa, Apr. 24, 1964.
Houser, Jerry: Los Angeles, July 14, 1952. Valley, Jr. College.
Howard, Arliss: Independence, MO, 1955. Columbia College.
Howard, Ken: El Centro, CA, Mar. 28, 1944. Yale.
Howard, Ron: Duncan, OK, Mar. 1, 1954. USC.
Howell, C. Thomas: Los Angeles, Dec. 7, 1966.
Howells, Ursula: London, Sept. 17, 1922.

Howes, Sally Ann: London, July 20, 1930.
Howland, Beth: Boston, MA, May 28, 1941.
Hubley, Season: NYC, May 14, 1951.
Huddleston, David: Vinton, VA, Sept. 17, 1930.
Hudson, Ernie: Benton Harbor, MI, Dec. 17, 1945.
Hudson, Kate: Los Angeles, Apr. 19, 1979.
Hughes, Barnard: Bedford Hills, NY, July 16, 1915. Manhattan College.
Hughes, Kathleen (Betty von Gerkan): Hollywood, CA, Nov. 14, 1928. UCLA.
Hulce, Tom: Plymouth, MI, Dec. 6, 1953. N.C. Sch. of Arts.
Hunnicut, Gayle: Ft. Worth, TX, Feb. 6, 1943. UCLA.
Hunt, Helen: Los Angeles, June 15, 1963.
Hunt, Linda: Morristown, NJ, Apr. 1945. Goodman Theatre.
Hunt, Marsha: Chicago, IL, Oct. 17, 1917.
Hunter, Holly: Atlanta, GA, Mar. 20, 1958. Carnegie-Mellon.
Hunter, Tab (Arthur Gelien): NYC, July 11, 1931.
Huppert, Isabelle: Paris, France, Mar. 16, 1955.
Hurley, Elizabeth: Hampshire, Eng., June 10, 1965.
Hurt, John: Lincolnshire, England, Jan. 22, 1940.
Hurt, Mary Beth (Supinger): Marshalltown, IA, Sept. 26, 1948. NYU.
Hurt, William: Washington, DC, Mar. 20, 1950. Tufts, Juilliard.
Hussey, Ruth: Providence, RI, Oct. 30, 1917. U Mich.
Huston, Anjelica: Santa Monica, CA, July 9, 1951.
Hutton, Betty (Betty Thornberg): Battle Creek, MI, Feb. 26, 1921.
Hutton, Lauren (Mary): Charleston, SC, Nov. 17, 1943. Newcomb College.
Hutton, Timothy: Malibu, CA, Aug. 16, 1960.
Hyer, Martha: Fort Worth, TX, Aug. 10, 1924. Northwestern U.

Ice Cube (O'Shea Jackson): Los Angeles, June 15, 1969.
Idle, Eric: South Shields, Durham, England, Mar. 29, 1943. Cambridge.
Ingels, Marty: Brooklyn, NY, Mar. 9, 1936.
Ireland, Kathy: Santa Barbara, CA, Mar. 8, 1963.
Irons, Jeremy: Cowes, England, Sept. 19, 1948. Old Vic.
Ironside, Michael: Toronto, Canada, Feb. 12, 1950.
Irving, Amy: Palo Alto, CA, Sept. 10, 1953. LADA.
Irwin, Bill: Santa Monica, CA, Apr. 11, 1950.
Isaak, Chris: Stockton, CA, June 26, 1956. UofPacific.
Ivanek, Zeljko: Lujubljana, Yugo., Aug. 15, 1957. Yale, LAMDA.
Ivey, Judith: El Paso, TX, Sept. 4, 1951.
Izzard, Eddie: Aden, Yemen, Feb. 7, 1962.

Jackson, Anne: Alleghany, PA, Sept. 3, 1926. Neighborhood Playhouse.
Jackson, Glenda: Hoylake, Cheshire, England, May 9, 1936. RADA.
Jackson, Janet: Gary, IN, May 16, 1966.
Jackson, Kate: Birmingham, AL, Oct. 29, 1948. AADA.
Jackson, Michael: Gary, IN, Aug. 29, 1958.
Jackson, Samuel L.: Atlanta, Dec. 21, 1948.
Jackson, Victoria: Miami, FL, Aug. 2, 1958.
Jacobi, Derek: Leytonstone, London, Oct. 22, 1938. Cambridge.
Jacobi, Lou: Toronto, Canada, Dec. 28, 1913.
Jacobs, Lawrence-Hilton: Virgin Islands, Sept. 14, 1953.
Jacoby, Scott: Chicago, IL, Nov. 19, 1956.
Jagger, Mick: Dartford, Kent, England, July 26, 1943.
James, Clifton: NYC, May 29, 1921. Ore. U.
Janney, Allison: Dayton, OH, Nov. 20, 1960. RADA.

Jarman, Claude, Jr.: Nashville, TN, Sept. 27, 1934.
Jason, Rick: NYC, May 21, 1926. AADA.
Jean, Gloria (Gloria Jean Schoonover): Buffalo, NY, Apr. 14, 1927.
Jeffreys, Anne (Carmichael): Goldsboro, NC, Jan. 26, 1923. Anderson College.
Jeffries, Lionel: London, June 10, 1926. RADA.
Jergens, Adele: Brooklyn, NY, Nov. 26, 1922.
Jillian, Ann (Nauseda): Cambridge, MA, Jan. 29, 1951.
Johansen, David: Staten Island, NY, Jan. 9, 1950.
John, Elton (Reginald Dwight): Middlesex, England, Mar. 25, 1947. RAM.
Johns, Glynis: Durban, S. Africa, Oct. 5, 1923.
Johnson, Don: Galena, MO, Dec. 15, 1950. UKan.
Johnson, Page: Welch, WV, Aug. 25, 1930. Ithaca.
Johnson, Rafer: Hillsboro, TX, Aug. 18, 1935. UCLA.
Johnson, Richard: Essex, England, July 30, 1927. RADA.
Johnson, Robin: Brooklyn, NY, May 29, 1964.
Johnson, Van: Newport, RI, Aug. 28, 1916.
Jolie, Angelina (Angelina Jolie Voight): Los Angeles, June 4, 1975.
Jones, Christopher: Jackson, TN, Aug. 18, 1941. Actors Studio.
Jones, Dean: Decatur, AL, Jan. 25, 1931. Actors Studio.
Jones, Grace: Spanishtown, Jamaica, May 19, 1952.
Jones, Jack: Bel-Air, CA, Jan. 14, 1938.
Jones, James Earl: Arkabutla, MS, Jan. 17, 1931. U Mich.
Jones, Jeffrey: Buffalo, NY, Sept. 28, 1947. LAMDA.
Jones, Jennifer (Phyllis Isley): Tulsa, OK, Mar. 2, 1919. AADA.
Jones, L.Q. (Justice Ellis McQueen): Aug 19, 1927.
Jones, Orlando: Mobile, AL, Apr. 10, 1968.
Jones, Sam J.: Chicago, IL, Aug. 12, 1954.
Jones, Shirley: Smithton, PA, March 31, 1934.
Jones, Terry: Colwyn Bay, Wales, Feb. 1, 1942.
Jones, Tommy Lee: San Saba, TX, Sept. 15, 1946. Harvard.
Jourdan, Louis: Marseilles, France, June 19, 1920.
Jovovich, Milla: Kiev, Ukraine, Dec. 17, 1975.
Joy, Robert: Montreal, Canada, Aug. 17, 1951. Oxford.
Judd, Ashley: Los Angeles, CA, Apr. 19, 1968.

Kaczmarek, Jane: Milwaukee, WI, Dec. 21, 1955.
Kane, Carol: Cleveland, OH, June 18, 1952.
Kaplan, Marvin: Brooklyn, NY, Jan. 24, 1924.
Kapoor, Shashi: Calcutta, India, Mar. 18, 1938.
Kaprisky, Valerie (Cheres): Paris, France, Aug. 19, 1962.
Karras, Alex: Gary, IN, July 15, 1935.
Kartheiser, Vincent: Minneapolis, MN, May 5, 1979.
Karyo, Tcheky: Istanbul, Oct. 4, 1953.
Kassovitz, Mathieu: Paris, Aug. 3, 1967.
Katt, William: Los Angeles, CA, Feb. 16, 1955.
Kattan, Chris: Mt. Baldy, CA, Oct. 19, 1970.
Kaufmann, Christine: Lansdorf, Graz, Austria, Jan. 11, 1945.
Kavner, Julie: Burbank, CA, Sept. 7, 1951. UCLA.
Kazan, Lainie (Levine): Brooklyn, NY, May 15, 1942.
Kazurinsky, Tim: Johnstown, PA, March 3, 1950.
Keach, Stacy: Savannah, GA, June 2, 1941. U Cal., Yale.
Keaton, Diane (Hall): Los Angeles, CA, Jan. 5, 1946. Neighborhood Playhouse.

Keaton, Michael: Coraopolis, PA, Sept. 9, 1951. KentStateU.
Keegan, Andrew: Los Angeles, Jan. 29, 1979.
Keel, Howard (Harold Leek): Gillespie, IL, Apr. 13, 1919.
Keener, Catherine: Miami, FL, Mar. 26, 1960.
Keeslar, Matt: Grand Rapids, MI, Oct. 15, 1972.
Keitel, Harvey: Brooklyn, NY, May 13, 1939.
Keith, David: Knoxville, TN, May 8, 1954. UTN.
Keller, Marthe: Basel, Switzerland, 1945. Munich Stanislavsky Sch.
Kellerman, Sally: Long Beach, CA, June 2, 1936. Actors Studio West.
Kelly, Moira: Queens, NY, Mar. 6, 1968.
Kemp, Jeremy (Wacker): Chesterfield, England, Feb. 3, 1935. Central Sch.
Kennedy, George: NYC, Feb. 18, 1925.
Kennedy, Leon Isaac: Cleveland, OH, 1949.
Kensit, Patsy: London, Mar. 4, 1968.
Kerr, Deborah: Helensburg, Scotland, Sept. 30, 1921. Smale Ballet School.
Kerr, John: NYC, Nov. 15, 1931. Harvard, Columbia.
Kerwin, Brian: Chicago, IL, Oct. 25, 1949.
Keyes, Evelyn: Port Arthur, TX, Nov. 20, 1919.
Kidder, Margot: Yellow Knife, Canada, Oct. 17, 1948. UBC.
Kidman, Nicole: Hawaii, June 20, 1967.
Kiel, Richard: Detroit, MI, Sept. 13, 1939.
Kier, Udo: Koeln, Germany, Oct. 14, 1944.
Kilmer, Val: Los Angeles, Dec. 31, 1959. Juilliard.
Kincaid, Aron (Norman Neale Williams, III): Los Angeles, June 15, 1943. UCLA.
King, Alan (Irwin Kniberg): Brooklyn, NY, Dec. 26, 1927.
King, Perry: Alliance, OH, Apr. 30, 1948. Yale.
Kingsley, Ben (Krishna Bhanji): Snaiton, Yorkshire, England, Dec. 31, 1943.
Kinnear, Greg: Logansport, IN, June 17, 1963.
Kinski, Nastassja: Berlin, Ger., Jan. 24, 1960.
Kirby, Bruno: NYC, Apr. 28, 1949.
Kirk, Tommy: Louisville, KY, Dec. 10 1941.
Kirkland, Sally: NYC, Oct. 31, 1944. Actors Studio.
Kitt, Eartha: North, SC, Jan. 26, 1928.
Klein, Chris: Hinsdale, IL, March 14, 1979.
Klein, Robert: NYC, Feb. 8, 1942. Alfred U.
Kline, Kevin: St. Louis, MO, Oct. 24, 1947. Juilliard.
Klugman, Jack: Philadelphia, PA, Apr. 27, 1922. Carnegie Tech.
Knight, Michael E.: Princeton, NJ, May 7, 1959.
Knight, Shirley: Goessel, KS, July 5, 1937. Wichita U.
Knox, Elyse: Hartford, CT, Dec. 14, 1917. Traphagen School.
Koenig, Walter: Chicago, IL, Sept. 14, 1936. UCLA.
Kohner, Susan: Los Angeles, Nov. 11, 1936. U Calif.
Korman, Harvey: Chicago, IL, Feb. 15, 1927. Goodman.
Korsmo, Charlie: Minneapolis, MN, July, 20, 1978.
Koteas, Elias: Montreal, Quebec, Canada, 1961. AADA.
Kotto, Yaphet: NYC, Nov. 15, 1937.
Kozak, Harley Jane: Wilkes-Barre, PA, Jan. 28, 1957. NYU.
Krabbe, Jeroen: Amsterdam, The Netherlands, Dec. 5, 1944.
Kretschmann, Thomas: Dessau, E. Germany, Sept. 8, 1962.
Kreuger, Kurt: St. Moritz, Switzerland, July 23, 1917. U London.
Krige, Alice: Upington, So. Africa, June 28, 1955.
Kristel, Sylvia: Amsterdam, The Netherlands, Sept. 28, 1952.
Kristofferson, Kris: Brownsville, TX, June 22, 1936, Pomona College.

Angelina Jolie

Tommy Lee Jones

Greg Kinnear

Martin Lawrence

Kruger, Hardy: Berlin, Germany, April 12, 1928.
Krumholtz, David: NYC, May 15, 1978.
Kudrow, Lisa: Encino, CA, July 30, 1963.
Kurtz, Swoosie: Omaha, NE, Sept. 6, 1944.
Kutcher, Ashton (Christopher Ashton Kutcher.): Cedar Rapids, IA, Feb. 7, 1978.
Kwan, Nancy: Hong Kong, May 19, 1939. Royal Ballet.

LaBelle, Patti: Philadelphia, PA, May 24, 1944.
LaBeouf, Shia: Los Angeles, June 11, 1986.
Lacy, Jerry: Sioux City, IA, Mar. 27, 1936. LACC.
Ladd, Cheryl (Stoppelmoor): Huron, SD. July 12, 1951.
Ladd, Diane (Ladner): Meridian, MS, Nov. 29, 1932. Tulane U.
Lahti, Christine: Detroit, MI, Apr. 4, 1950. U Mich.
Lake, Ricki: NYC, Sept. 21, 1968.
Lamas, Lorenzo: Los Angeles, Jan. 28, 1958.
Lambert, Christopher: NYC, Mar. 29, 1958.
Landau, Martin: Brooklyn, NY, June 20, 1931. Actors Studio.
Landrum, Teri: Enid, OK, 1960.
Lane, Abbe: Brooklyn, NY, Dec. 14, 1935.
Lane, Diane: NYC, Jan. 22, 1963.
Lane, Nathan: Jersey City, NJ, Feb. 3, 1956.
Lang, Stephen: NYC, July 11, 1952. Swarthmore College.
Lange, Jessica: Cloquet, MN, Apr. 20, 1949. U Minn.
Langella, Frank: Bayonne, NJ, Jan. 1, 1940. SyracuseU.
Lansbury, Angela: London, Oct. 16, 1925. London Academy of Music.
LaPaglia, Anthony: Adelaide, Australia. Jan 31, 1959.
Larroquette, John: New Orleans, LA, Nov. 25, 1947.
Lasser, Louise: NYC, Apr. 11, 1939. Brandeis U.
Lathan, Sanaa: NYC, Sept. 19, 1971.
Latifah, Queen (Dana Owens): East Orange, NJ, 1970.
Laughlin, John: Memphis, TN, Apr. 3.
Laughlin, Tom: Minneapolis, MN, 1938.
Lauper, Cyndi: Astoria, Queens, NYC, June 20, 1953.
Laure, Carole: Montreal, Canada, Aug. 5, 1951.
Laurie, Hugh: Oxford, Eng., June 11, 1959.
Laurie, Piper (Rosetta Jacobs): Detroit, MI, Jan. 22, 1932.

Lauter, Ed: Long Beach, NY, Oct. 30, 1940.
Lavin, Linda: Portland, ME, Oct. 15 1939.
Law, John Phillip: Hollywood, CA, Sept. 7, 1937. Neighborhood Playhouse, U Hawaii.
Law, Jude: Lewisham, Eng., Dec. 29, 1972.
Lawrence, Barbara: Carnegie, OK, Feb. 24, 1930. UCLA.
Lawrence, Carol (Laraia): Melrose Park, IL, Sept. 5, 1935.
Lawrence, Martin: Frankfurt, Germany, Apr. 16, 1965.
Lawrence, Vicki: Inglewood, CA, Mar. 26, 1949.
Lawson, Leigh: Atherston, England, July 21, 1945. RADA.
Leachman, Cloris: Des Moines, IA, Apr. 30, 1930. Northwestern U.
Leary, Denis: Boston, MA, Aug. 18, 1957.
Léaud, Jean-Pierre: Paris, France, May 5, 1944.
LeBlanc, Matt: Newton, MA, July 25, 1967.
Ledger, Heath: Perth, Australia, Apr. 4, 1979.
Lee, Christopher: London, May 27, 1922. Wellington College.
Lee, Jason: Huntington Beach, CA, Apr. 25, 1970.
Lee, Mark: Sydney, Australia, 1958.
Lee, Michele (Dusiak): Los Angeles, June 24, 1942. LACC.
Lee, Sheryl: Augsburg, Germany, Arp. 22, 1967.
Lee, Spike (Shelton Lee): Atlanta, GA, Mar. 20, 1957.
Legros, James: Minneapolis, MN, Apr. 27, 1962.
Leguizamo, John: Columbia, July 22, 1965. NYU.
Leibman, Ron: NYC, Oct. 11, 1937. Ohio Wesleyan.
Leigh, Janet (Jeanette Helen Morrison): Merced, CA, July 6, 1926. College of Pacific.
Leigh, Jennifer Jason: Los Angeles, Feb. 5, 1962.
Le Mat, Paul: Rahway, NJ, Sept. 22, 1945.
Lemmon, Chris: Los Angeles, Jan. 22, 1954.
Leno, Jay: New Rochelle, NY, Apr. 28, 1950. Emerson College.
Lenz, Kay: Los Angeles, Mar. 4, 1953.
Lenz, Rick: Springfield, IL, Nov. 21, 1939. U Mich.
Leonard, Robert Sean: Westwood, NJ, Feb. 28, 1969.
Leoni, Téa (Elizabeth Téa Pantaleoni): NYC, Feb. 25, 1966.
Lerner, Michael: Brooklyn, NY, June 22, 1941.
Leslie, Joan (Joan Brodell): Detroit, Jan. 26, 1925. St. Benedict's.
Lester, Mark: Oxford, England, July 11, 1958.

Heath Ledger

Eugene Levy

Alison Lohman

Jennifer Lopez

Leto, Jared: Bossier City, LA, Dec. 26, 1971.
Levels, Calvin: Cleveland. OH, Sept. 30, 1954. CCC.
Levin, Rachel (Rachel Chagall): NYC, Nov. 24, 1954. Goddard College.
Levine, Jerry: New Brunswick, NJ, Mar. 12, 1957, Boston U.
Levy, Eugene: Hamilton, Canada, Dec. 17, 1946. McMasterU.
Lewis, Charlotte: London, Aug. 7, 1967.
Lewis, Geoffrey: San Diego, CA, Jan. 1, 1935.
Lewis, Jerry (Joseph Levitch): Newark, NJ, Mar. 16, 1926.
Lewis, Juliette: Los Angeles CA, June 21, 1973.
Li, Jet: Beijing, China, Apr. 26, 1963.
Ligon, Tom: New Orleans, LA, Sept. 10, 1945.
Lillard, Matthew: Lansing, MI, Jan. 24, 1970.
Lincoln, Abbey (Anna Marie Woolridge): Chicago, IL, Aug. 6, 1930.
Linden, Hal: Bronx, NY, Mar. 20, 1931. City College of NY.
Lindo, Delroy: London, Nov. 18, 1952.
Lindsay, Robert: Ilketson, Derbyshire, England, Dec. 13, 1951, RADA.
Linn-Baker, Mark: St. Louis, MO, June 17, 1954, Yale.
Linney, Laura: New York, NY, Feb. 5, 1964.
Liotta, Ray: Newark, NJ, Dec. 18, 1955. UMiami.
Lisi, Virna: Rome, Nov. 8, 1937.
Lithgow, John: Rochester, NY, Oct. 19, 1945. Harvard.
Liu, Lucy: Queens, NY, Dec. 2, 1967.
LL Cool J (James Todd Smith): Queens, NY, Jan. 14, 1968.
Lloyd, Christopher: Stamford, CT, Oct. 22, 1938.
Lloyd, Emily: London, Sept. 29, 1970.
Locke, Sondra: Shelbyville, TN, May, 28, 1947.
Lockhart, June: NYC, June 25, 1925. Westlake School.
Lockwood, Gary: Van Nuys, CA, Feb. 21, 1937.
Loggia, Robert: Staten Island, NY, Jan. 3, 1930. UMo.
Lohan, Lindsay: NYC, July 2, 1986.
Lohman, Alison: Palm Springs, CA, Sept. 18, 1979.
Lollobrigida, Gina: Subiaco, Italy, July 4, 1927. Rome Academy of Fine Arts.
Lom, Herbert: Prague, Czechoslovakia, Jan. 9, 1917. Prague U.
Lomez, Celine: Montreal, Canada, May 11, 1953.
Lone, John: Hong Kong, Oct 13, 1952. AADA.
Long, Nia: Brooklyn, NY, Oct. 30, 1970.
Long, Shelley: Ft. Wayne, IN, Aug. 23, 1949. Northwestern U.

Lopez, Jennifer: Bronx, NY, July 24, 1970.
Lopez, Perry: NYC, July 22, 1931. NYU.
Lords, Tracy (Nora Louise Kuzma): Steubenville, OH, May 7, 1968.
Loren, Sophia (Sophia Scicolone): Rome, Italy, Sept. 20, 1934.
Louis-Dreyfus, Julia: NYC, Jan. 13, 1961.
Louise, Tina (Blacker): NYC, Feb. 11, 1934, Miami U.
Love, Courtney (Love Michelle Harrison): San Francisco, July 9, 1965.
Lovett, Lyle: Klein, TX, Nov. 1, 1957.
Lovitz, Jon: Tarzana, CA, July 21, 1957.
Lowe, Chad: Dayton, OH, Jan. 15, 1968.
Lowe, Rob: Charlottesville, VA, Mar. 17, 1964.
Löwitsch, Klaus: Berlin, Apr. 8, 1936, Vienna Academy.
Lucas, Lisa: Arizona, 1961.
Luckinbill, Laurence: Fort Smith, AK, Nov. 21, 1934.
Luft, Lorna: Los Angeles, Nov. 21, 1952.
Luke, Derek: Jersey City, NJ, Apr. 24, 1974.
Lulu (Marie Lawrie): Glasgow, Scotland, Nov. 3, 1948.
Luna, Barbara: NYC, Mar. 2, 1939.
Luna, Diego: Mexico City, Dec. 29, 1979.
Lundgren, Dolph: Stockolm, Sweden, Nov. 3, 1959. Royal Inst.
LuPone, Patti: Northport, NY, Apr. 21, 1949, Juilliard.
Lydon, James: Harrington Park, NJ, May 30, 1923.
Lynch, Kelly: Minneapolis, MN, Jan. 31, 1959.
Lynley, Carol (Jones): NYC, Feb. 13, 1942.
Lyon, Sue: Davenport, IA, July 10, 1946.
Lyonne, Natasha (Braunstein): NYC, Apr. 4, 1979.

Mac, Bernie (Bernard Jeffrey McCollough): Chicago, Oct. 5, 1958.
MacArthur, James: Los Angeles, Dec. 8, 1937. Harvard.
Macchio, Ralph: Huntington, NY, Nov. 4, 1961.
MacCorkindale, Simon: Cambridge, England, Feb. 12, 1953.
Macdonald, Kelly: Glasgow, Feb. 23, 1976.
MacDowell, Andie (Rose Anderson MacDowell): Gaffney, SC, Apr. 21, 1958.
MacFadyen, Angus: Scotland, Oct. 21, 1963.
MacGinnis, Niall: Dublin, Ireland, Mar. 29, 1913. Dublin U.
MacGraw, Ali: NYC, Apr. 1, 1938. Wellesley.
MacLachlan, Kyle: Yakima, WA, Feb. 22, 1959. UWa.

Frances McDormand   Malcolm McDowell   Demi Moore   Brittany Murphy

MacLaine, Shirley (Beaty): Richmond, VA, Apr. 24, 1934.
MacLeod, Gavin: Mt. Kisco, NY, Feb. 28, 1931.
MacNaughton, Robert: NYC, Dec. 19, 1966.
Macnee, Patrick: London, Feb. 1922.
MacNicol, Peter: Dallas, TX, Apr. 10, 1954. UMN.
MacPherson, Elle: Sydney, Australia, 1965.
MacVittie, Bruce: Providence, RI, Oct. 14, 1956. BostonU.
Macy, W. H. (William): Miami, FL, Mar. 13, 1950. Goddard College.
Madigan, Amy: Chicago, IL, Sept. 11, 1950. Marquette U.
Madonna (Madonna Louise Veronica Cicone): Bay City, MI, Aug. 16, 1958. UMi.
Madsen, Michael: Chicago, IL, Sept. 25, 1958.
Madsen, Virginia: Winnetka, IL, Sept. 11, 1963.
Magnuson, Ann: Charleston, WV, Jan. 4, 1956.
Maguire, Tobey: Santa Monica, CA, June 27, 1975.
Maharis, George: Astoria, NY, Sept. 1, 1928. Actors Studio.
Mahoney, John: Manchester, England, June 20, 1940, WUIII.
Mailer, Stephen: NYC, Mar. 10, 1966. NYU.
Majors, Lee: Wyandotte, MI, Apr. 23, 1940. E. Ky. State College.
Makepeace, Chris: Toronto, Canada, Apr. 22, 1964.
Mako (Mako Iwamatsu): Kobe, Japan, Dec. 10, 1933. Pratt.
Malden, Karl (Mladen Sekulovich): Gary, IN, Mar. 22, 1914.
Malkovich, John: Christopher, IL, Dec. 9, 1953, IllStateU.
Malone, Dorothy: Chicago, IL, Jan. 30, 1925.
Mann, Terrence: KY, 1945. NCSchl Arts.
Manoff, Dinah: NYC, Jan. 25, 1958. CalArts.
Mantegna, Joe: Chicago, IL, Nov. 13, 1947. Goodman Theatre.
Manz, Linda: NYC, 1961.
Marais, Jean: Cherbourg, France, Dec. 11, 1913, St. Germain.
Marceau, Sophie (Maupu): Paris, Nov. 17, 1966.
Marcovicci, Andrea: NYC, Nov. 18, 1948.
Margulies, Julianna: Spring Valley, NY, June 8, 1966.
Marin, Cheech (Richard): Los Angeles, July 13, 1946.
Marin, Jacques: Paris, France, Sept. 9, 1919. Conservatoire National.
Marinaro, Ed: NYC, Mar. 31, 1950. Cornell.
Mars, Kenneth: Chicago, IL, Apr. 14, 1936.
Marsden, James: Stillwater, OK, Sept. 18, 1973.

Marsh, Jean: London, England, July 1, 1934.
Marshall, Ken: NYC, June 27, 1950. Juilliard.
Marshall, Penny: Bronx, NY, Oct. 15, 1942. UN. Mex.
Martin, Andrea: Portland, ME, Jan. 15, 1947.
Martin, Dick: Battle Creek, MI Jan. 30, 1923.
Martin, George N.: NYC, Aug. 15, 1929.
Martin, Millicent: Romford, England, June 8, 1934.
Martin, Pamela Sue: Westport, CT, Jan. 15, 1953.
Martin, Steve: Waco, TX, Aug. 14, 1945. UCLA.
Martin, Tony (Alfred Norris): Oakland, CA, Dec. 25, 1913. St. Mary's College.
Martinez, Olivier: Paris, Jan. 12, 1966.
Mason, Marsha: St. Louis, MO, Apr. 3, 1942. Webster College.
Massen, Osa: Copenhagen, Denmark, Jan. 13, 1916.
Masters, Ben: Corvallis, OR, May 6, 1947. UOr.
Masterson, Mary Stuart: Los Angeles, June 28, 1966, NYU.
Masterson, Peter: Angleton, TX, June 1, 1934. Rice U.
Mastrantonio, Mary Elizabeth: Chicago, IL, Nov. 17, 1958. UIll.
Masur, Richard: NYC, Nov. 20, 1948.
Matheson, Tim: Glendale, CA, Dec. 31, 1947. CalState.
Mathis, Samantha: NYC, May 12, 1970.
Matlin, Marlee: Morton Grove, IL, Aug. 24, 1965.
Matthews, Brian: Philadelphia, Jan. 24. 1953. St. Olaf.
May, Elaine (Berlin): Philadelphia, Apr. 21, 1932.
Mayo, Virginia (Virginia Clara Jones): St. Louis, MO, Nov. 30, 1920.
Mayron, Melanie: Philadelphia, PA, Oct. 20, 1952. AADA.
Mazursky, Paul: Brooklyn, NY, Apr. 25, 1930. Bklyn College.
Mazzello, Joseph: Rhinebeck, NY, Sept. 21, 1983.
McCallum, David: Scotland, Sept. 19, 1933. Chapman College.
McCambridge, Mercedes: Jolliet, IL, Mar. 17, 1918. Mundelein College.
McCarthy, Andrew: NYC, Nov. 29, 1962, NYU.
McCarthy, Kevin: Seattle, WA, Feb. 15, 1914. Minn. U.
McCartney, Paul: Liverpool, England, June 18, 1942.
McClanahan, Rue: Healdton, OK, Feb. 21, 1934.
McClure, Marc: San Mateo, CA, Mar. 31, 1957.
McClurg, Edie: Kansas City, MO, July 23, 1950.
McCormack, Catherine: Alton, Hampshire, Eng., Jan. 1, 1972.
McCowen, Alec: Tunbridge Wells, England, May 26, 1925. RADA.

Eddie Murphy

Jack Nicholson

Jeremy Northam

Clive Owen

McCrane, Paul: Philadelphia, PA, Jan. 19. 1961.
McCrary, Darius: Walnut, CA, May 1, 1976.
McDermott, Dylan: Waterbury, CT, Oct. 26, 1962. Neighborhood Playhouse.
McDonald, Christopher: NYC, Feb. 15, 1955.
McDonnell, Mary: Wilkes Barre, PA, Apr. 28, 1952.
McDormand, Frances: Illinois, June 23, 1957.
McDowell, Malcolm (Taylor): Leeds, England, June 19, 1943. LAMDA.
McElhone, Natascha (Natasha Taylor): London, Mar. 23, 1971.
McEnery, Peter: Walsall, England, Feb. 21, 1940.
McEntire, Reba: McAlester, OK, Mar. 28, 1955. SoutheasternStU.
McGavin, Darren: Spokane, WA, May 7, 1922. College of Pacific.
McGill, Everett: Miami Beach, FL, Oct. 21, 1945.
McGillis, Kelly: Newport Beach, CA, July 9, 1957. Juilliard.
McGinley, John C.: NYC, Aug. 3, 1959. NYU.
McGoohan, Patrick: NYC, Mar. 19, 1928.
McGovern, Elizabeth: Evanston, IL. July 18, 1961. Juilliard.
McGovern, Maureen: Youngstown, OH, July 27, 1949.
McGregor, Ewan: Perth, Scotland, March 31, 1971.
McGuire, Biff: New Haven, CT, Oct. 25. 1926. Mass. Stale College.
McHattie, Stephen: Antigonish, NS, Feb. 3. Acadia U AADA.
McKean, Michael: NYC, Oct. 17, 1947.
McKee, Lonette: Detroit, MI, July 22, 1955.
McKellen, Ian: Burnley, England, May 25, 1939.
McKenna, Virginia: London, June 7, 1931.
McKeon, Doug: Pompton Plains, NJ, June 10, 1966.
McKuen, Rod: Oakland, CA, Apr. 29, 1933.
McLerie, Allyn Ann: Grand Mere, Canada, Dec. 1, 1926.
McMahon, Ed: Detroit, MI, Mar. 6, 1923.
McNair, Barbara: Chicago, IL, Mar. 4, 1939. UCLA.
McNamara, William: Dallas, TX, Mar. 31, 1965.
McNichol, Kristy: Los Angeles. CA, Sept. 11, 1962.
McQueen, Armelia: North Carolina, Jan. 6, 1952. Bklyn Consv.
McQueen, Chad: Los Angeles, CA, Dec. 28, 1960. Actors Studio.
McRaney, Gerald: Collins, MS, Aug. 19, 1948.
McShane, Ian: Blackburn, England, Sept. 29, 1942. RADA.
McTeer, Janet: York, England, May 8, 1961.

Meadows, Jayne (formerly Jayne Cotter): Wuchang, China, Sept. 27, 1924. St. Margaret's.
Meaney, Colm: Dublin, May 30, 1953.
Meara, Anne: Brooklyn, NY, Sept. 20, 1929.
Meat Loaf (Marvin Lee Aday): Dallas, TX, Sept. 27, 1947.
Medwin, Michael: London, 1925. Instut Fischer.
Mekka, Eddie: Worcester, MA, June 14, 1952. Boston Cons.
Melato, Mariangela: Milan, Italy, Sept. 18, 1941. Milan Theatre Acad.
Meredith, Lee (Judi Lee Sauls): Oct. 22, 1947. AADA.
Merkerson, S. Epatha: Saganaw, MI, Nov. 28, 1952. Wayne St. Univ.
Merrill, Dina (Nedinia Hutton): NYC, Dec. 29, 1925. AADA.
Messing, Debra: Brooklyn, NY, Aug. 15, 1968.
Metcalf, Laurie: Edwardsville, IL, June 16, 1955., IIIStU.
Metzler, Jim: Oneonda, NY, June 23, 1955. Dartmouth.
Meyer, Breckin: Minneapolis, May 7, 1974.
Michell, Keith: Adelaide, Australia, Dec. 1, 1926.
Midler, Bette: Honolulu, HI, Dec. 1, 1945.
Milano, Alyssa: Brooklyn, NY, Dec. 19, 1972.
Miles, Joanna: Nice, France, Mar. 6, 1940.
Miles, Sarah: Ingatestone, England, Dec. 31, 1941. RADA.
Miles, Sylvia: NYC, Sept. 9, 1934. Actors Studio.
Miles, Vera (Ralston): Boise City, OK, Aug. 23, 1929. UCLA.
Miller, Ann (Lucille Ann Collier): Chireno, TX, Apr. 12, 1919. Lawler Professional School.
Miller, Barry: Los Angeles, CA, Feb. 6, 1958.
Miller, Dick: NYC, Dec. 25, 1928.
Miller, Jonny Lee: Surrey, England, Nov. 15, 1972.
Miller, Linda: NYC, Sept. 16, 1942. Catholic U.
Miller, Penelope Ann: Santa Monica, CA, Jan. 13, 1964.
Miller, Rebecca: Roxbury, CT, 1962. Yale.
Mills, Donna: Chicago, IL, Dec. 11, 1945. UII.
Mills, Hayley: London, Apr. 18, 1946. Elmhurst School.
Mills, John: Suffolk, England, Feb. 22, 1908.
Mills, Juliet: London, Nov. 21, 1941.
Milner, Martin: Detroit, MI, Dec. 28, 1931.
Mimieux, Yvette: Los Angeles, Jan. 8, 1941. Hollywood High.
Minnelli, Liza: Los Angeles, Mar. 19, 1946.

Miou-Miou (Sylvette Henry): Paris, France, Feb. 22, 1950.
Mirren, Helen (Ilynea Mironoff): London, July 26, 1946.
Mistry, Jimi: Scarborough, England, 1973.
Mitchell, James: Sacramento, CA, Feb. 29, 1920. LACC.
Mitchell, John Cameron: El Paso, TX, Apr. 21, 1963. NorthwesternU.
Mitchum, James: Los Angeles, CA, May 8, 1941.
Modine, Matthew: Loma Linda, CA, Mar. 22, 1959.
Moffat, Donald: Plymouth, England, Dec. 26, 1930. RADA.
Moffett, D. W.: Highland Park, IL, Oct. 26, 1954. Stanford U.
Mohr, Jay: New Jersey, Aug. 23, 1971.
Mokae, Zakes: Johannesburg, So. Africa, Aug. 5, 1935. RADA.
Molina, Alfred: London, May 24, 1953. Guildhall.
Moll, Richard: Pasadena, CA, Jan. 13, 1943.
Monaghan, Dominic: Berlin, Dec. 8, 1976.
Monk, Debra: Middletown, OH, Feb. 27, 1949.
Montalban, Ricardo: Mexico City, Nov. 25, 1920.
Montenegro, Fernada (Arlete Pinheiro): Rio de Janiero, Brazil, 1929.
Montgomery, Belinda: Winnipeg, Canada, July 23, 1950.
Moody, Ron: London, Jan. 8, 1924. London U.
Moor, Bill: Toledo, OH, July 13, 1931. Northwestern.
Moore, Constance: Sioux City, IA, Jan. 18, 1919.
Moore, Demi (Guines): Roswell, NM, Nov. 11, 1962.
Moore, Dick: Los Angeles, Sept. 12, 1925.
Moore, Julianne (Julie Anne Smith): Fayetteville, NC, Dec. 30, 1960.
Moore, Kieron: County Cork, Ireland, 1925. St. Mary's College.
Moore, Mandy: Nashua, NH, Apr. 10, 1984.
Moore, Mary Tyler: Brooklyn, NY, Dec. 29, 1936.
Moore, Roger: London, Oct. 14, 1927. RADA.
Moore, Terry (Helen Koford): Los Angeles, Jan. 7, 1929.
Morales, Esai: Brooklyn, NY, Oct. 1, 1962.
Moranis, Rick: Toronto, Canada, Apr. 18, 1954.
Moreau, Jeanne: Paris, France, Jan. 23, 1928.
Moreno, Rita (Rosita Alverio): Humacao, P.R., Dec. 11, 1931.
Morgan, Harry (Henry) (Harry Bratsburg): Detroit, Apr. 10, 1915. U Chicago.
Morgan, Michele (Simone Roussel): Paris, France, Feb. 29, 1920. Paris Dramatic School.
Moriarty, Cathy: Bronx, NY, Nov. 29, 1960.
Moriarty, Michael: Detroit, MI, Apr. 5, 1941. Dartmouth.
Morison, Patricia: NYC, Mar. 19, 1915.
Morita, Noriyuki "Pat": Isleton, CA, June 28, 1932.
Morris, Garrett: New Orleans, LA, Feb. 1, 1937.
Morris, Howard: NYC, Sept. 4, 1919. NYU.
Morrow, Rob: New Rochelle, NY, Sept. 21, 1962.
Morse, David: Hamilton, MA, Oct. 11, 1953.
Morse, Robert: Newton, MA, May 18, 1931.
Mortensen, Viggo: New York, NY, Oct. 20, 1958.
Morton, Joe: NYC, Oct. 18, 1947. Hofstra U.
Morton, Samantha: Nottingham, England, May 13, 1977.
Mos Def (Dante Beze): Brooklyn, Dec. 11, 1973.
Moses, William: Los Angeles, Nov. 17, 1959.
Moss, Carrie-Anne: Vancouver, BC, Canada, Aug. 21, 1967.
Mostel, Josh: NYC, Dec. 21, 1946. Brandeis U.
Mouchet, Catherine: Paris, France, 1959. Ntl. Consv.
Moynahan, Bridget: Binghamton, NY, Sept. 21, 1972.

Mueller-Stahl, Armin: Tilsit, East Prussia, Dec. 17, 1930.
Muldaur, Diana: NYC, Aug. 19, 1938. Sweet Briar College.
Mulgrew, Kate: Dubuque, IA, Apr. 29, 1955. NYU.
Mulhern, Matt: Philadelphia, PA, July 21, 1960. Rutgers Univ.
Mull, Martin: N. Ridgefield, OH, Aug. 18, 1941. RISch. of Design.
Mulroney, Dermot: Alexandria, VA, Oct. 31, 1963. Northwestern.
Mumy, Bill (Charles William Mumy, Jr.): San Gabriel, CA, Feb. 1, 1954.
Muniz, Frankie: Ridgewood, NJ, Dec. 5, 1985.
Murphy, Brittany: Atlanta, GA, Nov. 10, 1977.
Murphy, Cillian: Douglas, Ireland, March 13, 1974.
Murphy, Donna: Queens, NY, March 7, 1958.
Murphy, Eddie: Brooklyn, NY, Apr. 3, 1961.
Murphy, Michael: Los Angeles, CA, May 5, 1938. UAz.
Murray, Bill: Wilmette, IL, Sept. 21, 1950. Regis College.
Murray, Don: Hollywood, CA, July 31, 1929.
Musante, Tony: Bridgeport, CT, June 30, 1936. Oberlin College.
Myers, Mike: Scarborough, Canada, May 25, 1963.

Nabors, Jim: Sylacauga, GA, June 12, 1932.
Nader, Michael: Los Angeles, CA, 1945.
Namath, Joe: Beaver Falls, PA, May 31, 1943. UAla.
Naughton, David: Hartford, CT, Feb. 13, 1951.
Naughton, James: Middletown, CT, Dec. 6, 1945.
Neal, Patricia: Packard, KY, Jan. 20, 1926. Northwestern U.
Neeson, Liam: Ballymena, Northern Ireland, June 7, 1952.
Neff, Hildegarde (Hildegard Knef): Ulm, Germany, Dec. 28, 1925. Berlin Art Acad.
Neill, Sam: No. Ireland, Sept. 14, 1947. U Canterbury.
Nelligan, Kate: London, Ont., Canada, Mar. 16, 1951. U Toronto.
Nelson, Barry (Robert Nielsen): Oakland, CA, Apr. 16, 1920.
Nelson, Craig T.: Spokane, WA, Apr. 4, 1946.
Nelson, David: NYC, Oct. 24, 1936. USC.
Nelson, Judd: Portland, ME, Nov. 28, 1959, Haverford College.
Nelson, Lori (Dixie Kay Nelson): Santa Fe, NM, Aug. 15, 1933.
Nelson, Tim Blake: Tulsa, OK, 1964.
Nelson, Tracy: Santa Monica, CA, Oct. 25, 1963.
Nelson, Willie: Abbott, TX, Apr. 30, 1933.
Nemec, Corin: Little Rock, AK, Nov. 5, 1971.
Nero, Franco (Francisco Spartanero): Parma, Italy, Nov. 23, 1941.
Nesmith, Michael: Houston, TX, Dec. 30, 1942.
Nettleton, Lois: Oak Park, IL, 1931. Actors Studio.
Neuwirth, Bebe: Princeton, NJ, Dec. 31, 1958.
Newhart, Bob: Chicago, IL, Sept. 5, 1929. Loyola U.
Newman, Barry: Boston, MA, Nov. 7, 1938. Brandeis U.
Newman, Laraine: Los Angeles, Mar. 2, 1952.
Newman, Nanette: Northampton, England, 1934.
Newman, Paul: Cleveland, OH, Jan. 26, 1925. Yale.
Newmar, Julie (Newmeyer): Los Angeles, Aug. 16, 1933.
Newton, Thandie: Zambia, Nov. 16, 1972.
Newton-John, Olivia: Cambridge, England, Sept. 26, 1948.
Nguyen, Dustin: Saigon, Vietnam, Sept. 17, 1962.
Nicholas, Denise: Detroit, MI, July 12, 1945.
Nicholas, Paul: Peterborough, Cambridge, Eng., Dec. 3, 1945.
Nichols, Nichelle: Robbins, IL, Dec. 28, 1933.

Nicholson, Jack: Neptune, NJ, Apr. 22, 1937.
Nickerson, Denise: NYC, Apr. 1, 1959.
Nicol, Alex: Ossining, NY, Jan. 20, 1919. Actors Studio.
Nielsen, Brigitte: Denmark, July 15, 1963.
Nielsen, Connie: Elling, Denmark, July 3, 1965.
Nielsen, Leslie: Regina, Saskatchewan. Canada, Feb. 11, 1926. Neighborhood Playhouse.
Nighy, Bill: Caterham, England, 1949.
Nimoy, Leonard: Boston, MA, Mar. 26, 1931. Boston College, Antioch College.
Nixon, Cynthia: NYC, Apr. 9, 1966. Columbia U.
Noble, James: Dallas, TX, Mar. 5, 1922, SMU.
Noiret, Philippe: Lille, France, Oct. 1, 1930.
Nolan, Kathleen: St. Louis, MO, Sept. 27, 1933. Neighborhood Playhouse.
Nolte, Nick: Omaha, NE, Feb. 8, 1940. Pasadena City College.
Norris, Bruce: Houston, TX, May 16, 1960. Northwestern.
Norris, Christopher: NYC, Oct. 7, 1943. Lincoln Square Acad.
Norris, Chuck (Carlos Ray): Ryan, OK, Mar. 10, 1940.
North, Heather: Pasadena, CA, Dec. 13, 1950. Actors Workshop.
North, Sheree (Dawn Bethel): Los Angeles. Jan. 17, 1933. Hollywood High.
Northam, Jeremy: Cambridge, Eng., Dec. 1, 1961.
Norton, Edward: Boston, MA, Aug. 18, 1969.
Norton, Ken: Jacksonville, Il, Aug. 9, 1945.
Noseworthy, Jack: Lynn, MA, Dec. 21, 1969.
Nouri, Michael: Washington, DC, Dec. 9, 1945.
Novak, Kim (Marilyn Novak): Chicago, IL, Feb. 13, 1933. LACC.
Novello, Don: Ashtabula, OH, Jan. 1, 1943. UDayton.
Nuyen, France (Vannga): Marseilles, France, July 31, 1939. Beaux Arts School.

O'Brian, Hugh (Hugh J. Krampe): Rochester, N,. Apr. 19, 1928. Cincinnati U.
O'Brien, Clay: Ray, AZ, May 6, 1961.
O'Brien, Margaret (Angela Maxine O'Brien): Los Angeles, Jan. 15, 1937.
O'Connell, Jerry (Jeremiah O'Connell): New York, NY, Feb. 17, 1974.
O'Connor, Carroll: Bronx, NY, Aug. 2, 1924. Dublin National Univ.
O'Connor, Glynnis: NYC, Nov. 19, 1955. NYSU.
O'Donnell, Chris: Winetka, IL, June 27, 1970.
O'Donnell, Rosie: Commack, NY, March 21, 1961.
O'Hara, Catherine: Toronto, Canada, Mar. 4, 1954.
O'Hara, Maureen (Maureen Fitzsimons): Dublin, Ireland, Aug. 17, 1920.
O'Herlihy, Dan: Wexford, Ireland, May 1, 1919. National U.
O'Keefe, Michael: Larchmont, NY, Apr. 24, 1955. NYU, AADA.
Oldman, Gary: New Cross, South London, England, Mar. 21, 1958.
Olin, Ken: Chicago, IL, July 30, 1954. UPa.
Olin, Lena: Stockholm, Sweden, Mar. 22, 1955.
Olmos, Edward James: Los Angeles, Feb. 24, 1947. CSLA.
O'Loughlin, Gerald S.: NYC, Dec. 23, 1921. U Rochester.
Olson, James: Evanston, IL, Oct. 8, 1930.
Olson, Nancy: Milwaukee, WI, July 14, 1928. UCLA.
Olyphant, Timothy: HI, May 20, 1968.
O'Neal, Griffin: Los Angeles, 1965.
O'Neal, Ron: Utica, NY, Sept. 1, 1937. Ohio State.
O'Neal, Ryan: Los Angeles, Apr. 20, 1941.
O'Neal, Tatum: Los Angeles, Nov. 5, 1963.

O'Neil, Tricia: Shreveport, LA, Mar. 11, 1945. Baylor U.
O'Neill, Ed: Youngstown, OH, Apr. 12, 1946.
O'Neill, Jennifer: Rio de Janeiro, Feb. 20, 1949. Neighborhood Playhouse.
Ontkean, Michael: Vancouver, B.C., Canada, Jan. 24, 1946.
O'Quinn, Terry: Newbury, MI, July 15, 1952.
Orbach, Jerry: Bronx, NY, Oct. 20, 1935.
Ormond, Julia: Epsom, England, Jan. 4, 1965.
O'Shea, Milo: Dublin, Ireland, June 2, 1926.
Osment, Haley Joel: Los Angeles, Apr. 10, 1988.
O'Toole, Annette (Toole): Houston, TX, Apr. 1, 1953. UCLA.
O'Toole, Peter: Connemara, Ireland, Aug. 2, 1932. RADA.
Overall, Park: Nashville, TN, Mar. 15, 1957. Tusculum College.
Owen, Clive: Keresley, Eng., Oct. 3, 1964.
Oz, Frank (Oznowicz): Hereford, England, May 25, 1944.

Pacino, Al: NYC, Apr. 25, 1940.
Pacula, Joanna: Tamaszow Lubelski, Poland, Jan. 2, 1957. Polish Natl. Theatre Sch.
Paget, Debra (Debralee Griffin): Denver, Aug. 19, 1933.
Paige, Janis (Donna Mae Jaden): Tacoma, WA, Sept. 16, 1922.
Palance, Jack (Walter Palanuik): Lattimer, PA, Feb. 18, 1920. UNC.
Palin, Michael: Sheffield, Yorkshire, England, May 5, 1943, Oxford.
Palmer, Betsy: East Chicago, IN, Nov. 1, 1926. DePaul U.
Palmer, Gregg (Palmer Lee): San Francisco, Jan. 25, 1927. U Utah.
Palminteri, Chazz (Calogero Lorenzo Palminteri): New York, NY, May 15, 1952.
Paltrow, Gwyneth: Los Angeles, Sept. 28, 1973.
Pampanini, Silvana: Rome, Sept. 25, 1925.
Panebianco, Richard: NYC, 1971.
Pankin, Stuart: Philadelphia, Apr. 8, 1946.
Pantoliano, Joe: Jersey City, NJ, Sept. 12, 1954.
Papas, Irene: Chiliomodion, Greece, Mar. 9, 1929.
Paquin, Anna: Winnipeg, Manitoba, Canada, July, 24, 1982.
Pare, Michael: Brooklyn, NY, Oct. 9, 1959.
Parker, Corey: NYC, July 8, 1965. NYU.
Parker, Eleanor: Cedarville, OH, June 26, 1922. Pasadena Playhouse.
Parker, Fess: Fort Worth, TX, Aug. 16, 1925. USC.
Parker, Jameson: Baltimore, MD, Nov. 18, 1947. Beloit College.
Parker, Jean (Mae Green): Deer Lodge, MT, Aug. 11, 1912.
Parker, Mary-Louise: Ft. Jackson, SC, Aug. 2, 1964. Bard College.
Parker, Nathaniel: London, May 18, 1962.
Parker, Sarah Jessica: Nelsonville, OH, Mar. 25, 1965.
Parker, Trey: Auburn, AL, May 30, 1972.
Parkins, Barbara: Vancouver, Canada, May 22, 1943.
Parks, Michael: Corona, CA, Apr. 4, 1938.
Parsons, Estelle: Lynn, MA, Nov. 20, 1927. Boston U.
Parton, Dolly: Sevierville, TN, Jan. 19, 1946.
Patinkin, Mandy: Chicago, IL, Nov. 30, 1952. Juilliard.
Patric, Jason: NYC, June 17, 1966.
Patrick, Robert: Marietta, GA, Nov. 5, 1958.
Patterson, Lee: Vancouver, Canada, Mar. 31, 1929. Ontario College.
Patton, Will: Charleston, SC, June 14, 1954.
Paulik, Johan: Prague, Czech., 1975.
Paulson, Sarah: Tampa, FL, Dec. 17, 1975.

Al Pacino

Amanda Peet

Bernadette Peters

Sarah Polley

Pavan, Marisa (Marisa Pierangeli): Cagliari, Sardinia, June 19, 1932. Torquado Tasso Col.

Paxton, Bill: Fort Worth, TX, May. 17, 1955.

Paymer, David: Long Island, NY, Aug. 30, 1954.

Pays, Amanda: Berkshire, England, June 6, 1959.

Peach, Mary: Durban, S. Africa, Oct. 20, 1934.

Pearce, Guy: Ely, England, Oct. 5, 1967.

Pearson, Beatrice: Dennison, TX, July 27, 1920.

Peet, Amanda: NYC, Jan. 11, 1972.

Peña, Elizabeth: Cuba, Sept. 23, 1961.

Pendleton, Austin: Warren, OH, Mar. 27, 1940. Yale U.

Penhall, Bruce: Balboa, CA, Aug. 17, 1960.

Penn, Sean: Burbank, CA, Aug. 17, 1960.

Pepper, Barry: Campbell River, BC, Canada, Apr. 4, 1970.

Perez, Jose: NYC, 1940.

Perez, Rosie: Brooklyn, NY, Sept. 6, 1964.

Perkins, Elizabeth: Queens, NY, Nov. 18, 1960. Goodman School.

Perkins, Millie: Passaic, NJ, May 12, 1938.

Perlman, Rhea: Brooklyn, NY, Mar. 31, 1948.

Perlman, Ron: NYC, Apr. 13, 1950. UMn.

Perreau, Gigi (Ghislaine): Los Angeles, Feb. 6, 1941.

Perrine, Valerie: Galveston, TX, Sept. 3, 1943. U Ariz.

Perry, Luke (Coy Luther Perry, III): Fredricktown, OH, Oct. 11, 1966.

Pesci, Joe: Newark, NJ. Feb. 9, 1943.

Pescow, Donna: Brooklyn, NY, Mar. 24, 1954.

Peters, Bernadette (Lazzara): Jamaica, NY, Feb. 28, 1948.

Peters, Brock: NYC, July 2, 1927. CCNY.

Petersen, Paul: Glendale, CA, Sept. 23, 1945. Valley College.

Petersen, William: Chicago, IL, Feb. 21, 1953.

Peterson, Cassandra: Colorado Springs, CO, Sept. 17, 1951.

Pettet, Joanna: London, Nov. 16, 1944. Neighborhood Playhouse.

Petty, Lori: Chattanooga, TN, Mar. 23, 1963.

Pfeiffer, Michelle: Santa Ana, CA, Apr. 29, 1958.

Phifer, Mekhi: NYC, Dec. 12, 1975.

Phillippe, Ryan (Matthew Phillippe): New Castle, DE, Sept. 10, 1975.

Phillips, Lou Diamond: Phillipines, Feb. 17, 1962, UTx.

Phillips, MacKenzie: Alexandria, VA, Nov. 10, 1959.

Phillips, Michelle (Holly Gilliam): Long Beach, CA, June 4, 1944.

Phillips, Sian: Bettws, Wales, May 14, 1934. UWales.

Phoenix, Joaquin: Puerto Rico, Oct. 28, 1974.

Picardo, Robert: Philadelphia, PA, Oct. 27, 1953. Yale.

Picerni, Paul: NYC, Dec. 1, 1922. Loyola U.

Pidgeon, Rebecca: Cambridge, MA, 1963.

Pierce, David Hyde: Saratoga Springs, NY, Apr. 3, 1959.

Pigott-Smith, Tim: Rugby, England, May 13, 1946.

Pinchot, Bronson: NYC, May 20, 1959. Yale.

Pine, Phillip: Hanford, CA, July 16, 1920. Actors' Lab.

Piscopo, Joe: Passaic. NJ, June 17, 1951.

Pisier, Marie-France: Vietnam, May 10, 1944. U Paris.

Pitillo, Maria: Mahwah, NJ, 1965.

Pitt, Brad (William Bradley Pitt): Shawnee, OK, Dec. 18, 1963.

Piven, Jeremy: NYC, July 26, 1965.

Place, Mary Kay: Tulsa OK, Sept. 23, 1947. U Tulsa.

Platt, Oliver: Windsor, Ontario, Can., Oct. 10, 1960.

Playten, Alice: NYC, Aug. 28, 1947. NYU.

Pleshette, Suzanne: NYC, Jan. 31, 1937. Syracuse U.

Plimpton, Martha: NYC, Nov. 16, 1970.

Plowright, Joan: Scunthorpe, Brigg, Lincolnshire, England, Oct. 28, 1929. Old Vic.

Plumb, Eve: Burbank, CA, Apr. 29, 1958.

Plummer, Amanda: NYC, Mar. 23, 1957. Middlebury College.

Plummer, Christopher: Toronto, Canada, Dec. 13, 1927.

Podesta, Rossana: Tripoli, June 20, 1934.

Poitier, Sidney: Miami, FL, Feb. 27, 1927.

Polanski, Roman: Paris, France, Aug. 18, 1933.

Polito, Jon: Philadelphia, PA, Dec. 29, 1950. Villanova U.

Polito, Lina: Naples, Italy, Aug. 11, 1954.

Pollack, Sydney: South Bend, IN, July 1, 1934.

Pollak, Kevin: San Francisco, Oct. 30, 1958.

Pollan, Tracy: NYC, June 22, 1960.

Pollard, Michael J.: Passaic, NJ, May 30, 1939.

Polley, Sarah: Toronto, Ontario, Can., Jan. 8, 1979.

Portman, Natalie: Jerusalem, June 9, 1981.

Posey, Parker: Baltimore, MD, Nov. 8, 1968.

Ving Rhames

Giovanni Ribisi

Christina Ricci

Julia Roberts

Postlethwaite, Pete: London, Feb. 7, 1945.
Potente, Franka: Dulmen, Germany, July 22, 1974.
Potter, Monica: Cleveland, OH, June 30, 1971.
Potts, Annie: Nashville, TN, Oct. 28, 1952. Stephens College.
Powell, Jane (Suzanne Burce): Portland, OR, Apr. 1, 1928.
Powell, Robert: Salford, England, June 1, 1944. Manchester U.
Power, Taryn: Los Angeles, CA, Sept. 13, 1953.
Power, Tyrone, IV: Los Angeles, CA, Jan. 22, 1959.
Powers, Mala (Mary Ellen): San Francisco, CA, Dec. 29, 1921. UCLA.
Powers, Stefanie (Federkiewicz): Hollywood, CA, Oct. 12, 1942.
Prentiss, Paula (Paula Ragusa): San Antonio, TX, Mar. 4, 1939. Northwestern U.
Presle, Micheline (Micheline Chassagne): Paris, France, Aug. 22, 1922. Rouleau Drama School.
Presley, Priscilla: Brooklyn, NY, May 24, 1945.
Presnell, Harve: Modesto, CA, Sept. 14, 1933. USC.
Preston, Kelly: Honolulu, HI, Oct. 13, 1962. USC.
Preston, William: Columbia, PA, Aug. 26, 1921. PaStateU.
Price, Lonny: NYC, Mar. 9, 1959. Juilliard.
Priestley, Jason: Vancouver, Canada, Aug, 28, 1969.
Primus, Barry: NYC, Feb. 16, 1938. CCNY.
Prince (P. Rogers Nelson): Minneapolis, MN, June 7, 1958.
Principal, Victoria: Fukuoka, Japan, Jan. 3, 1945. Dade, Jr. College.
Prinze, Freddie, Jr.,: Los Angeles, March 8, 1976.
Prochnow, Jurgen: Berlin, June 10, 1941.
Prosky, Robert: Philadelphia, PA, Dec. 13, 1930.
Proval, David: Brooklyn, NY, May 20, 1942.
Provine, Dorothy: Deadwood, SD, Jan. 20, 1937. U Wash.
Pryce, Jonathan: Wales, UK, June 1, 1947, RADA.
Pryor, Richard: Peoria, IL, Dec. 1, 1940.
Pullman, Bill: Delphi, NY, Dec. 17, 1954. SUNY/Oneonta, UMass.
Purcell, Lee: Cherry Point, NC, June 15, 1947. Stephens.
Purdom, Edmund: Welwyn Garden City, England, Dec. 19, 1924. St. Ignatius College.

Quaid, Dennis: Houston, TX, Apr. 9, 1954.
Quaid, Randy: Houston, TX, Oct. 1, 1950. UHouston.

Qualls, DJ (Donald Joseph): Nashville, TN, June 12, 1978.
Quinlan, Kathleen: Mill Valley, CA, Nov. 19, 1954.
Quinn, Aidan: Chicago, IL, Mar. 8, 1959.

Radcliffe, Daniel: London, July 23, 1989.
Rafferty, Frances: Sioux City, IA, June 16, 1922. UCLA.
Raffin, Deborah: Los Angeles, Mar. 13, 1953. Valley College.
Ragsdale, William: El Dorado, AK, Jan. 19, 1961. Hendrix College.
Railsback, Steve: Dallas, TX, 1948.
Rainer, Luise: Vienna, Austria, Jan. 12, 1910.
Ramis, Harold: Chicago, IL, Nov. 21, 1944. WashingtonU.
Rampling, Charlotte: Surmer, England, Feb. 5, 1946. U Madrid.
Ramsey, Logan: Long Beach, CA, Mar. 21, 1921. St. Joseph.
Randall, Tony (Leonard Rosenberg): Tulsa, OK, Feb. 26, 1920. Northwestern U.
Randell, Ron: Sydney, Australia, Oct. 8, 1920. St. Mary's College.
Rapaport, Michael: March 20, 1970.
Rapp, Anthony: Chicago, Oct. 26, 1971.
Rasche, David: St. Louis, MO, Aug. 7, 1944.
Rea, Stephen: Belfast, No. Ireland, Oct. 31, 1949.
Reagan, Ronald: Tampico, IL, Feb. 6, 1911. Eureka College.
Reason, Rex: Berlin, Ger., Nov. 30, 1928. Pasadena Playhouse.
Reddy, Helen: Melbourne, Australia, Oct. 25, 1942.
Redford, Robert: Santa Monica, CA, Aug. 18, 1937. AADA.
Redgrave, Corin: London, July 16, 1939.
Redgrave, Lynn: London, Mar. 8, 1943.
Redgrave, Vanessa: London, Jan. 30, 1937.
Redman, Joyce: County Mayo, Ireland, 1919. RADA.
Reed, Pamela: Tacoma, WA, Apr. 2, 1949.
Reems, Harry (Herbert Streicher): Bronx, NY, 1947. U Pittsburgh.
Rees, Roger: Aberystwyth, Wales, May 5, 1944.
Reese, Della: Detroit, MI, July 6, 1932.
Reeve, Christopher: NYC, Sept. 25, 1952. Cornell, Juilliard.
Reeves, Keanu: Beiruit, Lebanon, Sept. 2, 1964.
Regehr, Duncan: Lethbridge, Canada, Oct. 5, 1952.
Reid, Elliott: NYC, Jan. 16, 1920.
Reid, Tara: Wyckoff, NJ, Nov. 8, 1975.

Paul Rudd

Mark Ruffalo

Kurt Russell

Tom Skerritt

Reid, Tim: Norfolk, VA, Dec, 19, 1944.
Reilly, Charles Nelson: NYC, Jan. 13, 1931. UCt.
Reilly, John C.: Chicago, IL, May 24, 1965.
Reiner, Carl: NYC, Mar. 20, 1922. Georgetown.
Reiner, Rob: NYC, Mar. 6, 1947. UCLA.
Reinhold, Judge (Edward Ernest, Jr.): Wilmington, DE, May 21, 1957. NC
Reinking, Ann: Seattle, WA, Nov. 10, 1949.
Reiser, Paul: NYC, Mar. 30, 1957.
Remar, James: Boston, MA, Dec. 31, 1953. Neighborhood Playhouse.
Renfro, Brad: Knoxville, TN, July 25, 1982.
Reno, Jean (Juan Moreno): Casablanca, Morocco, July 30, 1948.
Reubens, Paul (Paul Reubenfeld): Peekskill, NY, Aug. 27, 1952.
Revill, Clive: Wellington, NZ, Apr. 18, 1930.
Rey, Antonia: Havana, Cuba, Oct. 12, 1927.
Reynolds, Burt: Waycross, GA, Feb. 11, 1935. Fla. State U.
Reynolds, Debbie (Mary Frances Reynolds): El Paso, TX, Apr. 1, 1932.
Rhames, Ving (Irving Rhames): NYC, May 12, 1959.
Rhoades, Barbara: Poughkeepsie, NY, Mar. 23, 1947.
Rhodes, Cynthia: Nashville, TN, Nov. 21, 1956.
Rhys, Paul: Neath, Wales, Dec. 19, 1963.
Rhys-Davies, John: Salisbury, England, May 5, 1944.
Rhys-Meyers, Jonathan: Cork, Ireland, July 27, 1977.
Ribisi, Giovanni: Los Angeles, CA, Dec. 17, 1974.
Ricci, Christina: Santa Monica, CA, Feb. 12, 1980.
Richard, Cliff (Harry Webb): India, Oct. 14, 1940.
Richards, Denise: Downers Grove, IL, Feb. 17, 1972.
Richards, Michael: Culver City, CA, July 14, 1949.
Richardson, Joely: London, Jan. 9, 1965.
Richardson, Miranda: Southport, England, Mar. 3, 1958.
Richardson, Natasha: London, May 11, 1963.
Rickles, Don: NYC, May 8, 1926. AADA.
Rickman, Alan: Hammersmith, England, Feb. 21, 1946.
Riegert, Peter: NYC, Apr. 11, 1947. U Buffalo.
Rifkin, Ron: NYC, Oct. 31, 1939.
Rigg, Diana: Doncaster, England, July 20, 1938. RADA.
Ringwald, Molly: Rosewood, CA, Feb. 16, 1968.
Ritter, John: Burbank, CA, Sept. 17, 1948. US. Cal.

Rivers, Joan (Molinsky): Brooklyn, NY, NY, June 8, 1933.
Roache, Linus: Manchester, England, 1964.
Robards, Sam: NYC, Dec. 16, 1963.
Robbins, Tim: NYC, Oct. 16, 1958. UCLA.
Roberts, Eric: Biloxi, MS, Apr. 18, 1956. RADA.
Roberts, Julia: Atlanta, GA, Oct. 28, 1967.
Roberts, Ralph: Salisbury, NC, Aug. 17, 1922. UNC.
Roberts, Tanya (Leigh): Bronx, NY, Oct. 15, 1954.
Roberts, Tony: NYC, Oct. 22, 1939. Northwestern U.
Robertson, Cliff: La Jolla, CA, Sept. 9, 1925. Antioch College.
Robertson, Dale: Oklahoma City, July 14, 1923.
Robinson, Chris: West Palm Beach, FL, Nov. 5, 1938. LACC.
Robinson, Jay: NYC, Apr. 14, 1930.
Robinson, Roger: Seattle, WA, May 2, 1940. USC.
Rochefort, Jean: Paris, France, 1930.
Rock, Chris: Brooklyn, NY, Feb. 7, 1966.
Rockwell, Sam: Daly City, CA, Nov. 5, 1968.
Rodriguez, Michelle: Bexar County, TX, July 12, 1978.
Rogers, Mimi: Coral Gables, FL, Jan. 27, 1956.
Rogers, Wayne: Birmingham, AL, Apr. 7, 1933. Princeton.
Romijn-Stamos, Rebecca: Berkeley, CA, Nov. 6, 1972.
Ronstadt, Linda: Tucson, AZ, July 15, 1946.
Rooker, Michael: Jasper, AL, Apr. 6, 1955.
Rooney, Mickey (Joe Yule, Jr.): Brooklyn, NY, Sept. 23, 1920.
Rose, Reva: Chicago, IL, July 30, 1940. Goodman.
Roseanne (Barr): Salt Lake City, UT, Nov. 3, 1952.
Ross, Diana: Detroit, MI, Mar. 26, 1944.
Ross, Justin: Brooklyn, NY, Dec. 15, 1954.
Ross, Katharine: Hollywood, Jan. 29, 1943. Santa Rosa College.
Rossellini, Isabella: Rome, June 18, 1952.
Rossovich, Rick: Palo Alto, CA, Aug. 28, 1957.
Roth, Tim: London, May 14, 1961.
Roundtree, Richard: New Rochelle, NY, Sept. 7, 1942. Southern Ill.
Rourke, Mickey (Philip Andre Rourke, Jr.): Schenectady, NY, Sept. 16, 1956.
Rowe, Nicholas: London, Nov. 22, 1966, Eton.
Rowlands, Gena: Cambria, WI, June 19, 1934.
Rubin, Andrew: New Bedford, MA, June 22, 1946. AADA.

Rubinek, Saul: Fohrenwold, Germany, July 2, 1948.
Rubinstein, John: Los Angeles, CA, Dec. 8, 1946. UCLA.
Ruck, Alan: Cleveland, OH, July 1, 1960.
Rucker, Bo: Tampa, FL, Aug. 17, 1948.
Rudd, Paul: Boston, MA, May 15, 1940.
Rudd, Paul: Passaic, NJ, Apr. 6, 1969.
Rudner, Rita: Miami, FL, Sept. 17, 1955.
Ruehl, Mercedes: Queens, NY, Feb. 28, 1948.
Ruffalo, Mark: Kenosha, WI, Nov. 22, 1967.
Rule, Janice: Cincinnati, OH, Aug. 15, 1931.
Rupert, Michael: Denver, CO, Oct. 23, 1951. Pasadena Playhouse.
Rush, Barbara: Denver, CO, Jan. 4, 1927. U Calif.
Rush, Geoffrey: Toowoomba, Queensland, Australia, July 6, 1951. Univ. of Queensland.
Russell, Jane: Bemidji, MI, June 21, 1921. Max Reinhardt School.
Russell, Kurt: Springfield, MA, Mar. 17, 1951.
Russell, Theresa (Paup): San Diego, CA, Mar. 20, 1957.
Russo, James: NYC, Apr. 23, 1953.
Russo, Rene: Burbank, CA, Feb. 17, 1954.
Rutherford, Ann: Toronto, Canada, Nov. 2, 1920.
Ryan, John P.: NYC, July 30, 1936. CCNY.
Ryan, Meg: Fairfield, CT, Nov. 19, 1961. NYU.
Ryan, Tim (Meineslschmidt): Staten Island, NY, 1958. Rutgers U.
Ryder, Winona (Horowitz): Winona, MN, Oct. 29, 1971.

Sacchi, Robert: Bronx, NY, 1941. NYU.
Sägebrecht, Marianne: Starnberg, Bavaria, Aug. 27, 1945.
Saint, Eva Marie: Newark, NJ, July 4, 1924. Bowling Green State U.
Saint James, Susan (Suzie Jane Miller): Los Angeles, Aug. 14, 1946. Conn. College.
St. John, Betta: Hawthorne, CA, Nov. 26, 1929.
St. John, Jill (Jill Oppenheim): Los Angeles, Aug. 19, 1940.
Sala, John: Los Angeles, CA, Oct. 5, 1962.
Saldana, Theresa: Brooklyn, NY, Aug. 20, 1954.
Salinger, Matt: Windsor, VT, Feb. 13, 1960. Princeton, Columbia.
Salt, Jennifer: Los Angeles, Sept. 4, 1944. Sarah Lawrence College.
Samms, Emma: London, Aug. 28, 1960.
San Giacomo, Laura: Orange, NJ, Nov. 14, 1961.
Sanders, Jay O.: Austin, TX, Apr. 16, 1953.
Sandler, Adam: Bronx, NY, Sept. 9, 1966. NYU.
Sands, Julian: Yorkshire, England, Jan 15, 1958.
Sands, Tommy: Chicago, IL, Aug. 27, 1937.
San Juan, Olga: NYC, Mar. 16, 1927.
Sara, Mia (Sarapocciello): Brooklyn, NY, June 19, 1967.
Sarandon, Chris: Beckley, WV, July 24, 1942. U WVa., Catholic U.
Sarandon, Susan (Tomalin): NYC, Oct. 4, 1946. Catholic U.
Sarrazin, Michael: Quebec City, Canada, May 22, 1940.
Sarsgaard, Peter: Scott Air Force Base, Illinois, Mar. 7, 1971.
Savage, Fred: Highland Park, IL, July 9, 1976.
Savage, John (Youngs): Long Island, NY, Aug. 25, 1949. AADA.
Saviola, Camille: Bronx, NY, July 16, 1950.
Savoy, Teresa Ann: London, July 18, 1955.
Sawa, Devon: Vancouver, BC, Canada, Sept. 7, 1978.
Saxon, John (Carmen Orrico): Brooklyn, NY, Aug. 5, 1935.

Sbarge, Raphael: NYC, Feb. 12, 1964.
Scacchi, Greta: Milan, Italy, Feb. 18, 1960.
Scalia, Jack: Brooklyn, NY, Nov. 10, 1951.
Scarwid, Diana: Savannah, GA, Aug. 27, 1955, AADA. Pace U.
Scheider, Roy: Orange, NJ, Nov. 10, 1932. Franklin-Marshall.
Scheine, Raynor: Emporia, VA, Nov. 10. VaCommonwealthU.
Schell, Maria: Vienna, Jan. 15, 1926.
Schell, Maximilian: Vienna, Dec. 8, 1930.
Schlatter, Charlie: Englewood, NJ, May 1, 1966. Ithaca College.
Schneider, John: Mt. Kisco, NY, Apr. 8, 1960.
Schneider, Maria: Paris, France, Mar. 27, 1952.
Schreiber, Liev: San Francisco, CA, Oct. 4, 1967.
Schroder, Rick: Staten Island, NY, Apr. 13, 1970.
Schuck, John: Boston, MA, Feb. 4, 1940.
Schultz, Dwight: Milwaukee, WI, Nov. 10, 1938. MarquetteU.
Schwartzman, Jason: Los Angeles, June 26, 1980.
Schwarzenegger, Arnold: Austria, July 30, 1947.
Schwimmer, David: Queens, NY, Nov. 12, 1966.
Schygulla, Hanna: Katlowitz, Germany, Dec. 25, 1943.
Sciorra, Annabella: NYC, Mar. 24, 1964.
Scofield, Paul: Hurstpierpoint, England, Jan. 21, 1922. London Mask Theatre School.
Scoggins, Tracy: Galveston, TX, Nov. 13, 1959.
Scolari, Peter: Scarsdale, NY, Sept. 12, 1956. NYCC.
Scott, Campbell: South Salem, NY, July 19, 1962. Lawrence.
Scott, Debralee: Elizabeth, NJ, Apr. 2, 1953.
Scott, Gordon (Gordon M. Werschkul): Portland, OR, Aug. 3, 1927. Oregon U.
Scott, Lizabeth (Emma Matso): Scranton, PA, Sept. 29, 1922.
Scott, Seann William: Cottage Grove, MN, Oct. 3, 1976.
Scott Thomas, Kristin: Redruth, Cornwall, Eng., May 24, 1960.
Seagal, Steven: Detroit, MI, Apr. 10, 1951.
Sears, Heather: London, Sept. 28, 1935.
Sedgwick, Kyra: NYC, Aug. 19, 1965. USC.
Segal, George: NYC, Feb. 13, 1934. Columbia.
Selby, David: Morganstown, WV, Feb. 5, 1941. UWV.
Sellars, Elizabeth: Glasgow, Scotland, May 6, 1923.
Selleck, Tom: Detroit, MI, Jan. 29, 1945. USCal.
Serbedzija, Rade: Bunic, Yugoslavia, July 27, 1946.
Sernas, Jacques: Lithuania, July 30, 1925.
Serrault, Michel: Brunoy, France. Jan. 24, 1928. Paris Consv.
Seth, Roshan: New Delhi, India. Aug. 17, 1942.
Sewell, Rufus: Twickenham, Eng., Oct. 29, 1967.
Seymour, Jane (Joyce Frankenberg): Hillingdon, England, Feb. 15, 1952.
Shalhoub, Tony: Green Bay, WI, Oct. 9, 1953.
Shandling, Garry: Chicago, IL, Nov. 29, 1949.
Sharif, Omar (Michel Shalhoub): Alexandria, Egypt, Apr. 10, 1932. Victoria College.
Shatner, William: Montreal, Canada, Mar. 22, 1931. McGill U.
Shaver, Helen: St. Thomas, Ontario, Canada, Feb. 24, 1951.
Shaw, Fiona: Cork, Ireland, July 10, 1955. RADA.
Shaw, Stan: Chicago, IL, 1952.
Shawn, Wallace: NYC, Nov. 12, 1943. Harvard.
Shea, John: North Conway, NH, Apr. 14, 1949. Bates, Yale.
Shearer, Harry: Los Angeles, Dec. 23, 1943. UCLA.

Shearer, Moira: Dunfermline, Scotland, Jan. 17, 1926. London Theatre School.
Sheedy, Ally: NYC, June 13, 1962. USC.
Sheen, Charlie (Carlos Irwin Estevez): Santa Monica, CA, Sept. 3, 1965.
Sheen, Martin (Ramon Estevez): Dayton, OH, Aug. 3, 1940.
Sheffer, Craig: York, PA, Apr. 23, 1960. E. StroudsbergU.
Sheffield, John: Pasadena, CA, Apr. 11, 1931. UCLA.
Shelley, Carol: London, England, Aug. 16, 1939.
Shepard, Sam (Rogers): Ft. Sheridan, IL, Nov. 5, 1943.
Shepherd, Cybill: Memphis, TN, Feb. 18, 1950. Hunter, NYU.
Sher, Antony: England, June 14, 1949.
Sheridan, Jamey: Pasadena, CA, July 12, 1951.
Shields, Brooke: NYC, May 31, 1965.
Shire, Talia: Lake Success, NY, Apr. 25, 1946. Yale.
Short, Martin: Toronto, Canada, Mar. 26, 1950. McMasterU.
Shue, Elisabeth: S. Orange, NJ, Oct. 6, 1963. Harvard.
Siemaszko, Casey: Chicago, IL, March 17, 1961.
Sikking, James B.: Los Angeles, Mar. 5, 1934.
Silva, Henry: Brooklyn, NY, 1928.
Silver, Ron: NYC, July 2, 1946. SUNY.
Silverman, Jonathan: Los Angeles, CA, Aug. 5, 1966. USC.
Silverstone, Alicia: San Francisco, CA, Oct. 4, 1976.
Silverstone, Ben: London, Eng, Apr. 9, 1979.
Simmons, Jean: London, Jan. 31, 1929. Aida Foster School.
Simon, Paul: Newark. NJ, Nov. 5, 1942.
Simon, Simone: Bethune, France, Apr. 23, 1910.
Simpson, O. J. (Orenthal James): San Francisco, CA, July 9, 1947. UCLA.
Sinbad (David Adkins): Benton Harbor, MI, Nov. 10, 1956.
Sinclair, John (Gianluigi Loffredo): Rome, Italy, 1946.
Sinden, Donald: Plymouth, England, Oct. 9, 1923. Webber-Douglas.
Singer, Lori: Corpus Christi, TX, May 6, 1962. Juilliard.
Sinise, Gary: Chicago, Mar. 17. 1955.
Sizemore, Tom: Detroit, MI, Sept. 29, 1964.
Skarsgård, Stellan: Gothenburg, Vastergotland, Sweden, June 13, 1951.
Skerritt, Tom: Detroit, MI, Aug. 25, 1933. Wayne State U.
Skye, Ione (Leitch): London, England, Sept. 4, 1971.
Slater, Christian: NYC, Aug. 18, 1969.
Slater, Helen: NYC, Dec. 15, 1965.
Smith, Charles Martin: Los Angeles, CA, Oct. 30, 1953. CalState U.
Smith, Jaclyn: Houston, TX, Oct. 26, 1947.
Smith, Jada Pinkett: Baltimore, MD, Sept. 18, 1971.
Smith, Kerr: Exton, PA, Mar. 9, 1972.
Smith, Kevin: Red Bank, NJ, Aug. 2, 1970.
Smith, Kurtwood: New Lisbon, WI, Jul. 3, 1942.
Smith, Lane: Memphis, TN, Apr. 29, 1936.
Smith, Lewis: Chattanooga, TN, 1958. Actors Studio.
Smith, Lois: Topeka, KS, Nov. 3, 1930. U Wash.
Smith, Maggie: Ilford, England, Dec. 28, 1934.
Smith, Roger: South Gate, CA, Dec. 18, 1932. U Ariz.
Smith, Will: Philadelphia, PA, Sept. 25, 1968.
Smithers, William: Richmond, VA, July 10, 1927. Catholic U.
Smits, Jimmy: Brooklyn, NY, July 9, 1955. Cornell U.
Snipes, Wesley: NYC, July 31, 1963. SUNY/Purchase.
Snodgress, Carrie: Chicago, IL, Oct. 27, 1946. UNI.

Sobieksi, Leelee (Liliane Sobieski): NYC, June 10, 1982.
Solomon, Bruce: NYC, 1944. U Miami, Wayne State U.
Somers, Suzanne (Mahoney): San Bruno, CA, Oct. 16, 1946. Lone Mt. College.
Sommer, Elke (Schletz): Berlin, Germany, Nov. 5, 1940.
Sommer, Josef: Greifswald, Germany, June 26, 1934.
Sordi, Alberto: Rome, Italy, June 15, 1920.
Sorvino, Mira: Tenafly, NJ, Sept. 28, 1967.
Sorvino, Paul: NYC, Apr. 13, 1939. AMDA.
Soto, Talisa (Miriam Soto): Brooklyn, NY, Mar. 27, 1967.
Soul, David: Chicago, IL, Aug. 28, 1943.
Spacek, Sissy: Quitman, TX, Dec. 25, 1949. Actors Studio.
Spacey, Kevin: So. Orange, NJ, July 26, 1959. Juilliard.
Spade, David: Birmingham, MS, July 22, 1964.
Spader, James: Buzzards Bay, MA, Feb. 7, 1960.
Spall, Timothy: London, Feb. 27, 1957.
Spano, Vincent: Brooklyn, NY, Oct. 18, 1962.
Spenser, Jeremy: London, July 16, 1937.
Spinella, Stephen: Naples, Italy, Oct. 11, 1956. NYU.
Springfield, Rick (Richard Spring Thorpe): Sydney, Australia, Aug. 23, 1949.
Stadlen, Lewis J.: Brooklyn, NY, Mar. 7, 1947. Neighborhood Playhouse.
Stahl, Nick: Dallas, TX, Dec. 5, 1979.
Stallone, Frank: NYC, July 30, 1950.
Stallone, Sylvester: NYC, July 6, 1946. U Miami.
Stamp, Terence: London, July 23, 1939.
Stanford, Aaron: Westford, MA, Dec. 18, 1977.
Stang, Arnold: Chelsea, MA, Sept. 28, 1925.
Stanton, Harry Dean: Lexington, KY, July 14, 1926.
Stapleton, Jean: NYC, Jan. 19, 1923.
Stapleton, Maureen: Troy, NY, June 21, 1925.
Starr, Ringo (Richard Starkey): Liverpool, England, July 7, 1940.
Staunton, Imelda: UK, Jan. 9, 1956.
Steele, Barbara: England, Dec. 29, 1937.
Steele, Tommy: London, Dec. 17, 1936.
Steenburgen, Mary: Newport, AR, Feb. 8, 1953. Neighborhood Playhouse.
Sterling, Jan (Jane Sterling Adriance): NYC, Apr. 3, 1923. Fay Compton School.
Sterling, Robert (William Sterling Hart): Newcastle, PA, Nov. 13, 1917. UPittsburgh.
Stern, Daniel: Bethesda, MD, Aug. 28, 1957.
Sternhagen, Frances: Washington, DC, Jan. 13, 1932.
Stevens, Andrew: Memphis, TN, June 10, 1955.
Stevens, Connie (Concetta Ann Ingolia): Brooklyn, NY, Aug. 8, 1938. Hollywood Professional School.
Stevens, Fisher: Chicago, IL, Nov. 27, 1963. NYU.
Stevens, Stella (Estelle Eggleston): Hot Coffee, MS, Oct. 1, 1936.
Stevenson, Juliet: Essex, Eng., Oct. 30, 1956.
Stevenson, Parker: Philadelphia, PA, June 4, 1953. Princeton.
Stewart, Alexandra: Montreal, Canada, June 10, 1939. Louvre.
Stewart, Elaine (Elsy Steinberg): Montclair, NJ, May 31, 1929.
Stewart, French (Milton French Stewart): Albuquerque, NM, Feb. 20, 1964.
Stewart, Jon (Jonathan Stewart Liebowitz): Trenton, NJ, Nov. 28, 1962.
Stewart, Martha (Martha Haworth): Bardwell, KY, Oct. 7, 1922.
Stewart, Patrick: Mirfield, England, July 13, 1940.

Will Smith

Julia Stiles

Hilary Swank

Charlize Theron

Stiers, David Ogden: Peoria, IL, Oct. 31, 1942.

Stiles, Julia: NYC, Mar. 28, 1981.

Stiller, Ben: NYC, Nov. 30, 1965.

Stiller, Jerry: NYC, June 8, 1931.

Sting (Gordon Matthew Sumner): Wallsend, England, Oct. 2, 1951.

Stockwell, Dean: Hollywood, Mar. 5, 1935.

Stockwell, John (John Samuels, IV): Galveston, TX, Mar. 25, 1961. Harvard.

Stoltz, Eric: Whittier, CA, Sept. 30, 1961. USC.

Stone, Dee Wallace (Deanna Bowers): Kansas City, MO, Dec. 14, 1948. UKS.

Storm, Gale (Josephine Cottle): Bloomington, TX, Apr. 5, 1922.

Stowe, Madeleine: Eagle Rock, CA, Aug. 18, 1958.

Strassman, Marcia: New Jersey, Apr. 28, 1948.

Strathairn, David: San Francisco, Jan. 26, 1949.

Strauss, Peter: NYC, Feb. 20, 1947.

Streep, Meryl (Mary Louise): Summit, NJ, June 22, 1949 Vassar, Yale.

Streisand, Barbra: Brooklyn, NY, Apr. 24, 1942.

Stritch, Elaine: Detroit, MI, Feb. 2, 1925. Drama Workshop.

Stroud, Don: Honolulu, HI, Sept. 1, 1937.

Struthers, Sally: Portland, OR, July 28, 1948. Pasadena Playhouse.

Studi, Wes (Wesley Studie): Nofire Hollow, OK, Dec. 17, 1947.

Summer, Donna (LaDonna Gaines): Boston, MA, Dec. 31, 1948.

Sutherland, Donald: St. John, New Brunswick, Canada, July 17, 1935. U Toronto.

Sutherland, Kiefer: Los Angeles, CA, Dec. 18, 1966.

Suvari, Mena: Newport, RI, Feb. 9, 1979.

Svenson, Bo: Goreborg, Sweden, Feb. 13, 1941. UCLA.

Swank, Hilary: Bellingham, WA, July 30, 1974.

Swayze, Patrick: Houston, TX, Aug. 18, 1952.

Sweeney, D. B. (Daniel Bernard Sweeney): Shoreham, NY, Nov. 14, 1961.

Swinton, Tilda: London, Nov. 5, 1960.

Swit, Loretta: Passaic, NJ, Nov. 4, 1937, AADA.

Sylvester, William: Oakland, CA, Jan. 31, 1922. RADA.

Symonds, Robert: Bistow, AK, Dec. 1, 1926. TexU.

Syms, Sylvia: London, June 1, 1934. Convent School.

Szarabajka, Keith: Oak Park, IL, Dec. 2, 1952. UChicago.

T, Mr. (Lawrence Tero): Chicago, IL, May 21, 1952.

Tabori, Kristoffer (Siegel): Los Angeles, Aug. 4, 1952.

Takei, George: Los Angeles, CA, Apr. 20, 1939. UCLA.

Talbot, Nita: NYC, Aug. 8, 1930. Irvine Studio School.

Tamblyn, Russ: Los Angeles, Dec. 30, 1934.

Tambor, Jeffrey: San Francisco, July 8, 1944.

Tarantino, Quentin: Knoxville, TN, Mar. 27, 1963.

Tate, Larenz: Chicago, IL, Sept. 8, 1975.

Tautou, Audrey: Beaumont, France, Aug. 9, 1978.

Taylor, Elizabeth: London, Feb. 27, 1932. Byron House School.

Taylor, Lili: Glencoe, IL, Feb. 20, 1967.

Taylor, Noah: London, Sept. 4, 1969.

Taylor, Renee: NYC, Mar. 19, 1935.

Taylor, Rod (Robert): Sydney, Aust., Jan. 11, 1929.

Taylor-Young, Leigh: Washington, DC, Jan. 25, 1945. Northwestern.

Teefy, Maureen: Minneapolis, MN, Oct. 26, 1953, Juilliard.

Temple, Shirley: Santa Monica, CA, Apr. 23, 1927.

Tennant, Victoria: London, England, Sept. 30, 1950.

Tenney, Jon: Princeton, NJ, Dec. 16, 1961.

Terzieff, Laurent: Paris, France, June 25, 1935.

Tewes, Lauren: Braddock, PA, Oct. 26, 1954.

Thacker, Russ: Washington, DC, June 23, 1946. Montgomery College.

Thaxter, Phyllis: Portland, ME, Nov. 20, 1921. St. Genevieve.

Thelen, Jodi: St. Cloud, MN, 1963.

Theron, Charlize: Benoni, So. Africa, Aug. 7, 1975.

Thewlis, David: Blackpool, Eng., 1963.

Thomas, Henry: San Antonio, TX, Sept. 8, 1971.

Thomas, Jay: New Orleans, July 12, 1948.

Thomas, Jonathan Taylor (Weiss): Bethlehem, PA, Sept. 8, 1981.

Thomas, Marlo (Margaret): Detroit, Nov. 21, 1938. USC.

Thomas, Philip Michael: Columbus, OH, May 26, 1949. Oakwood College.

Thomas, Richard: NYC, June 13, 1951. Columbia.

Thompson, Emma: London, England, Apr. 15, 1959. Cambridge.

Thompson, Fred Dalton: Sheffield, AL, Aug. 19, 1942.

Thompson, Jack (John Payne): Sydney, Australia, Aug. 31, 1940.

Thompson, Lea: Rochester, MN, May 31, 1961.

Thompson, Rex: NYC, Dec. 14, 1942.

Stephen Tobolowsky

Marisa Tomei

John Travolta

Liv Tyler

Thompson, Sada: Des Moines, IA, Sept. 27, 1929. Carnegie Tech.
Thornton, Billy Bob: Hot Spring, AR, Aug. 4, 1955.
Thorson, Linda: Toronto, Canada, June 18, 1947. RADA.
Thulin, Ingrid: Solleftea, Sweden, Jan. 27, 1929. Royal Drama Theatre.
Thurman, Uma: Boston, MA, Apr. 29, 1970.
Ticotin, Rachel: Bronx, NY, Nov. 1, 1958.
Tierney, Lawrence: Brooklyn, NY, Mar. 15, 1919. Manhattan College.
Tiffin, Pamela (Wonso): Oklahoma City, OK, Oct. 13, 1942.
Tighe, Kevin: Los Angeles, Aug. 13, 1944.
Tilly, Jennifer: Los Angeles, CA, Sept. 16, 1958.
Tilly, Meg: Texada, Canada, Feb. 14, 1960.
Tobolowsky, Stephen: Dallas, TX, May 30, 1951. So. Methodist U.
Todd, Beverly: Chicago, IL, July 1, 1946.
Todd, Richard: Dublin, Ireland, June 11, 1919. Shrewsbury School.
Tolkan, James: Calumet, MI, June 20, 1931.
Tomei, Marisa: Brooklyn, NY, Dec. 4, 1964. NYU.
Tomlin, Lily: Detroit, MI, Sept. 1, 1939. Wayne State U.
Topol (Chaim Topol): Tel-Aviv, Israel, Sept. 9, 1935.
Torn, Rip: Temple, TX, Feb. 6, 1931. UTex.
Torres, Liz: NYC, Sept. 27, 1947. NYU.
Totter, Audrey: Joliet, IL, Dec. 20, 1918.
Towsend, Robert: Chicago, IL, Feb. 6, 1957.
Townsend, Stuart: Dublin, Dec. 15, 1972.
Travanti, Daniel J.: Kenosha, WI, Mar. 7, 1940.
Travis, Nancy: Astoria, NY, Sept. 21, 1961.
Travolta, Joey: Englewood, NJ, Oct. 14, 1950.
Travolta, John: Englewood, NJ, Feb. 18, 1954.
Trintignant, Jean-Louis: Pont-St. Esprit, France, Dec. 11, 1930. DullinBalachova Drama School.
Tripplehorn, Jeanne: Tulsa, OK, June 10, 1963.
Tsopei, Corinna: Athens, Greece, June 21, 1944.
Tubb, Barry: Snyder, TX, 1963. AmConsv Th.
Tucci, Stanley: Katonah, NY, Jan. 11, 1960.
Tucker, Chris: Decatur, GA, Aug. 31, 1972.
Tucker, Jonathan: Boston, May 31, 1982.
Tucker, Michael: Baltimore, MD, Feb. 6, 1944.
Tune, Tommy: Wichita Falls, TX, Feb. 28, 1939.

Tunney, Robin: Chicago, June 19, 1972.
Turner, Janine (Gauntt): Lincoln, NE, Dec. 6, 1963.
Turner, Kathleen: Springfield, MO, June 19, 1954. UMd.
Turner, Tina (Anna Mae Bullock): Nutbush, TN, Nov. 26, 1938.
Turturro, John: Brooklyn, NY, Feb. 28, 1957. Yale.
Tushingham, Rita: Liverpool, England, Mar. 14, 1940.
Twiggy (Lesley Hornby): London, Sept. 19, 1949.
Twomey, Anne: Boston, MA, June 7, 1951. Temple U.
Tyler, Beverly (Beverly Jean Saul): Scranton, PA, July 5, 1928.
Tyler, Liv: Portland, ME, July 1, 1977.
Tyrrell, Susan: San Francisco, Mar. 18, 1945.
Tyson, Cathy: Liverpool, England, June 12, 1965. Royal Shake. Co.
Tyson, Cicely: NYC, Dec. 19, 1933. NYU.

Uggams, Leslie: NYC, May 25, 1943. Juilliard.
Ullman, Tracey: Slough, England, Dec. 30, 1959.
Ullmann, Liv: Tokyo, Dec. 10, 1938. Webber-Douglas Acad.
Ulrich, Skeet (Bryan Ray Ulrich): North Carolina, Jan. 20, 1969.
Umeki, Miyoshi: Otaru, Hokaido, Japan, Apr. 3, 1929.
Underwood, Blair: Tacoma, WA, Aug. 25, 1964. Carnegie-Mellon U.
Unger, Deborah Kara: Victoria, British Columbia, May 12, 1966.
Union, Gabrielle: Omaha, NE, Oct. 29, 1973.
Ustinov, Peter: London, Apr. 16, 1921. Westminster School.

Vaccaro, Brenda: Brooklyn, NY, Nov. 18, 1939. Neighborhood Playhouse.
Valli, Alida: Pola, Italy, May 31, 1921. Academy of Drama.
Van Ark, Joan: NYC, June 16, 1943. Yale.
Van Damme, Jean-Claude (J-C Vorenberg): Brussels, Belgium, Apr. 1, 1960.
Van De Ven, Monique: Zeeland, Netherlands, July 28, 1952.
Van Der Beek, James: Chesire, CT, March 8, 1977.
Van Devere, Trish (Patricia Dressel): Englewood Cliffs, NJ, Mar. 9, 1945. Ohio Wesleyan.
Van Dien, Casper: Ridgefield, NJ, Dec. 18, 1968.
Van Doren, Mamie (Joan Lucile Olander): Rowena SD, Feb. 6, 1933.
Van Dyke, Dick: West Plains, MO, Dec. 13, 1925.
Vanity (Denise Katrina Smith): Niagara, Ont., Can, Jan. 4, 1959.
Van Pallandt, Nina: Copenhagen, Denmark, July 15, 1932.

Mark Wahlberg

Paul Walker

Sigourney Weaver

Rachel Weisz

Van Patten, Dick: NYC, Dec. 9, 1928.
Van Patten, Joyce: NYC, Mar. 9, 1934.
Van Peebles, Mario: NYC, Jan. 15, 1958. Columbia U.
Van Peebles, Melvin: Chicago, IL, Aug. 21, 1932.
Vance, Courtney B.: Detroit, MI, Mar. 12, 1960.
Vardalos, Nia: Winnipeg, Manitoba, Can., Sept. 24, 1962.
Vaughn, Robert: NYC, Nov. 22, 1932. USC.
Vaughn, Vince: Minneapolis, MN, Mar. 28, 1970.
Vega, Isela: Hermosillo, Mexico, Nov. 5, 1940.
Veljohnson, Reginald: NYC, Aug. 16, 1952.
Vennera, Chick: Herkimer, NY, Mar. 27, 1952. Pasadena Playhouse.
Venora, Diane: Hartford, CT, 1952. Juilliard.
Vereen, Ben: Miami, FL, Oct. 10, 1946.
Vernon, John: Montreal, Canada, Feb. 24, 1932.
Victor, James (Lincoln Rafael Peralta Diaz): Santiago, D.R., July 27, 1939. Haaren HS/NYC.
Vincent, Jan-Michael: Denver, CO, July 15, 1944. Ventura.
Violet, Ultra (Isabelle Collin-Dufresne): Grenoble, France, Sept. 6, 1935.
Vitale, Milly: Rome, Italy, July 16, 1928. Lycee Chateaubriand.
Vohs, Joan: St. Albans, NY, July 30, 1931.
Voight, Jon: Yonkers, NY, Dec. 29, 1938. Catholic U.
Von Bargen, Daniel: Cincinnati, OH, June 5, 1950. Purdue.
Von Dohlen, Lenny: Augusta, GA, Dec. 22, 1958. UTex.
Von Sydow, Max: Lund, Sweden, July 10, 1929. Royal Drama Theatre.

Wagner, Lindsay: Los Angeles, June 22. 1949.
Wagner, Natasha Gregson: Los Angeles, CA, Sept. 29, 1970.
Wagner, Robert: Detroit, Feb. 10, 1930.
Wahl, Ken: Chicago, IL, Feb. 14, 1953.
Wahlberg, Mark: Dorchester, MA, June. 5, 1971.
Waite, Genevieve: South Africa, 1949.
Waite, Ralph: White Plains, NY, June 22, 1929. Yale.
Waits, Tom: Pomona, CA, Dec. 7, 1949.
Walken, Christopher: Astoria, NY, Mar. 31, 1943. Hofstra.
Walker, Clint: Hartfold, IL, May 30, 1927. USC.
Walker, Paul: Glendale, CA, Sept. 12, 1973.
Wallach, Eli: Brooklyn, NY, Dec. 7, 1915. CCNY, U Tex.

Wallach, Roberta: NYC, Aug. 2, 1955.
Wallis, Shani: London, Apr. 5, 1941.
Walsh, M. Emmet: Ogdensburg, NY, Mar. 22, 1935. Clarkson College, AADA.
Walter, Jessica: Brooklyn, NY, Jan. 31, 1944 Neighborhood Playhouse.
Walter, Tracey: Jersey City, NJ, Nov. 25, 1942.
Walters, Julie: London, Feb. 22, 1950.
Walton, Emma: London, Nov. 1962. Brown U.
Wanamaker, Zoë: NYC, May 13, 1949.
Ward, Burt (Gervis): Los Angeles, July 6, 1945.
Ward, Fred: San Diego, CA, Dec. 30, 1942.
Ward, Rachel: London, Sept. 12, 1957.
Ward, Sela: Meridian, MS, July 11, 1956.
Ward, Simon: London, Oct. 19, 1941.
Warden, Jack (Lebzelter): Newark, NJ, Sept. 18, 1920.
Warner, David: Manchester, England, July 29, 1941. RADA.
Warner, Malcolm-Jamal: Jersey City, NJ, Aug. 18, 1970.
Warren, Jennifer: NYC, Aug. 12, 1941. U Wisc.
Warren, Lesley Ann: NYC, Aug. 16, 1946.
Warren, Michael: South Bend, IN, Mar. 5, 1946. UCLA.
Warrick, Ruth: St. Joseph, MO, June 29, 1915. U Mo.
Washington, Denzel: Mt. Vernon, NY, Dec. 28, 1954. Fordham.
Wasson, Craig: Ontario, OR, Mar. 15, 1954. UOre.
Watanabe, Ken: Koide, Japan, Oct. 21, 1959.
Waterston, Sam: Cambridge, MA, Nov. 15, 1940. Yale.
Watson, Emily: London, Jan. 14, 1967.
Watson, Emma: Oxford, England, Apr. 15, 1990.
Watts, Naomi: Shoreham, Eng., Sept. 28, 1968.
Wayans, Damon: NYC, Sept. 4, 1960.
Wayans, Keenen Ivory: NYC, June 8, 1958. Tuskegee Inst.
Wayne, Patrick: Los Angeles, July 15, 1939. Loyola.
Weathers, Carl: New Orleans, LA, Jan. 14, 1948. Long Beach CC.
Weaver, Dennis: Joplin, MO, June 4, 1924. U Okla.
Weaver, Fritz: Pittsburgh, PA, Jan. 19, 1926.
Weaver, Sigourney (Susan): NYC, Oct. 8, 1949. Stanford, Yale.
Weaving, Hugo: Nigeria, Apr. 4, 1960. NIDA.
Weber, Steven: Queens, NY, March 4, 1961.
Wedgeworth, Ann: Abilene, TX, Jan. 21, 1935. U Tex.

Bruce Willis

Henry Winkler

Kate Winslet

Reese Witherspoon

Weisz, Rachel: London, Mar. 7, 1971.

Welch, Raquel (Tejada): Chicago, IL, Sept. 5, 1940.

Weld, Tuesday (Susan): NYC, Aug. 27, 1943. Hollywood Professional School.

Weldon, Joan: San Francisco, Aug. 5, 1933. San Francisco Conservatory.

Weller, Peter: Stevens Point, WI, June 24, 1947. AmThWing.

Welling, Tom: NYC, Apr. 26, 1977.

Wendt, George: Chicago, IL, Oct. 17, 1948.

West, Adam (William Anderson): Walla Walla, WA, Sept. 19, 1929.

West, Shane: Baton Rouge, LA, June 10, 1978.

Westfeldt, Jennifer: Guilford, CT, Feb. 2, 1971.

Wettig, Patricia: Cincinatti, OH, Dec. 4, 1951. TempleU.

Whaley, Frank: Syracuse, NY, July 20, 1963. SUNY/Albany.

Whalley-Kilmer, Joanne: Manchester, England, Aug. 25, 1964.

Wheaton, Wil: Burbank, CA, July 29, 1972.

Whitaker, Forest: Longview, TX, July 15, 1961.

Whitaker, Johnny: Van Nuys, CA, Dec. 13, 1959.

White, Betty: Oak Park, IL, Jan. 17, 1922.

White, Charles: Perth Amboy, NJ, Aug. 29, 1920. Rutgers U.

Whitelaw, Billie: Coventry, England, June 6, 1932.

Whitman, Stuart: San Francisco, Feb. 1, 1929. CCLA.

Whitmore, James: White Plains, NY, Oct. 1, 1921. Yale.

Whitney, Grace Lee: Detroit, MI, Apr. 1, 1930.

Whitton, Margaret: Philadelphia, PA, Nov, 30, 1950.

Widdoes, Kathleen: Wilmington, DE, Mar. 21, 1939.

Widmark, Richard: Sunrise, MN, Dec. 26, 1914. Lake Forest.

Wiest, Dianne: Kansas City, MO, Mar. 28, 1948. UMd.

Wilby, James: Burma, Feb. 20, 1958.

Wilcox, Colin: Highlands, NC, Feb. 4, 1937. U Tenn.

Wilder, Gene (Jerome Silberman): Milwaukee, WI, June 11, 1935. Uiowa.

Wilkinson, Tom: Leeds, England, Dec. 12, 1948. Univ.of Kent.

Willard, Fred: Shaker Heights, OH, Sept. 18, 1939.

Williams, Billy Dee: NYC, Apr. 6, 1937.

Williams, Cara (Bernice Kamiat): Brooklyn, NY, June 29, 1925.

Williams, Cindy: Van Nuys, CA, Aug. 22, 1947. KACC.

Williams, Clarence, III: NYC, Aug. 21, 1939.

Williams, Esther: Los Angeles, Aug. 8, 1921.

Williams, Jobeth: Houston, TX, Dec 6, 1948. Brown U.

Williams, Michelle: Kalispell, MT, Sept. 9, 1980.

Williams, Olivia: London, Jan. 1, 1968.

Williams, Paul: Omaha, NE, Sept. 19, 1940.

Williams, Robin: Chicago, IL, July 21, 1951. Juilliard.

Williams, Treat (Richard): Rowayton, CT, Dec. 1, 1951.

Williams, Vanessa L.: Tarrytown, NY, Mar. 18, 1963.

Williamson, Fred: Gary, IN, Mar. 5, 1938. Northwestern.

Williamson, Nicol: Hamilton, Scotland, Sept. 14, 1938.

Willis, Bruce: Penns Grove, NJ, Mar. 19, 1955.

Willison, Walter: Monterey Park, CA, June 24, 1947.

Wilson, Demond: NYC, Oct. 13, 1946. Hunter College.

Wilson, Elizabeth: Grand Rapids, MI, Apr. 4, 1925.

Wilson, Lambert: Neuilly-sur-Seine, France, Aug. 3, 1958.

Wilson, Luke: Dallas, TX, Sept. 21, 1971.

Wilson, Owen: Dallas, TX, Nov. 18, 1968.

Wilson, Scott: Atlanta, GA, Mar. 29, 1942.

Wincott, Jeff: Toronto, Canada, May 8, 1957.

Wincott, Michael: Toronto, Canada, Jan. 6, 1959. Juilliard.

Windom, William: NYC, Sept. 28, 1923. Williams College.

Winfield, Paul: Los Angeles, May 22, 1940. UCLA.

Winfrey, Oprah: Kosciusko, MS, Jan. 29, 1954. TnStateU.

Winger, Debra: Cleveland, OH, May 17, 1955. Cal State.

Winkler, Henry: NYC, Oct. 30, 1945. Yale.

Winn, Kitty: Washington, D.C., Feb, 21, 1944. Boston U.

Winningham, Mare: Phoenix, AZ, May 6, 1959.

Winslet, Kate: Reading, Eng., Oct. 5, 1975.

Winslow, Michael: Spokane, WA, Sept. 6, 1960.

Winter, Alex: London, July 17, 1965. NYU.

Winters, Jonathan: Dayton, OH, Nov. 11, 1925. Kenyon College.

Winters, Shelley (Shirley Schrift): St. Louis, Aug. 18, 1922. Wayne U.

Withers, Googie: Karachi, India, Mar. 12, 1917. Italia Conti.

Withers, Jane: Atlanta, GA, Apr. 12, 1926.

Witherspoon, Reese (Laura Jean Reese Witherspoon): Nashville, TN, Mar. 22, 1976.

Wolf, Scott: Newton, MA, June 4, 1968.

Wong, B.D.: San Francisco, Oct. 24,1962.

Wong, Russell: Troy, NY, Mar. 1, 1963. SantaMonica College.

Elijah Wood

Chow Yun-Fat

Renée Zellweger

Catherine Zeta-Jones

Wood, Elijah: Cedar Rapids, IA, Jan 28, 1981.
Wood, Evan Rachel: Raleigh, NC, Sept. 7, 1987.
Woodard, Alfre: Tulsa, OK, Nov. 2, 1953. Boston U.
Woodlawn, Holly (Harold Ajzenberg): Juana Diaz, PR, 1947.
Woods, James: Vernal, UT, Apr. 18, 1947. MIT.
Woodward, Edward: Croyden, Surrey, England, June 1, 1930.
Woodward, Joanne: Thomasville, GA, Feb. 27, 1930. Neighborhood Playhouse.
Woronov, Mary: Brooklyn, NY, Dec. 8, 1946. Cornell.
Wray, Fay: Alberta, Canada, Sept. 15, 1907.
Wright, Amy: Chicago, IL, Apr. 15, 1950.
Wright, Max: Detroit, MI, Aug. 2, 1943. WayneStateU.
Wright-Penn, Robin: Dallas, TX, Apr. 8, 1966.
Wright, Teresa: NYC, Oct. 27, 1918.
Wuhl, Robert: Union City, NJ, Oct. 9, 1951. UHouston.
Wyatt, Jane: NYC, Aug. 10, 1910. Barnard College.
Wyle, Noah: Los Angeles, June 2, 1971.
Wyman, Jane (Sarah Jane Fulks): St. Joseph, MO, Jan. 4, 1914.
Wymore, Patrice: Miltonvale, KS, Dec. 17, 1926.
Wynn, May (Donna Lee Hickey): NYC, Jan. 8, 1930.
Wynter, Dana (Dagmar): London, June 8. 1927. Rhodes U.

York, Michael: Fulmer, England, Mar. 27, 1942. Oxford.
York, Susannah: London, Jan. 9, 1941. RADA.
Young, Alan (Angus): North Shield, England, Nov. 19, 1919.
Young, Burt: Queens, NY, Apr. 30, 1940.
Young, Chris: Chambersburg, PA, Apr. 28, 1971.
Young, Sean: Louisville, KY, Nov. 20, 1959. Interlochen.
Yulin, Harris: Los Angeles, Nov. 5, 1937.
Yun-Fat, Chow: Lamma Island, Hong Kong, May 18, 1955.

Zacharias, Ann: Stockholm, Sweden, Sweden, Sept. 19, 1956.
Zadora, Pia: Hoboken, NJ, May 4, 1954.
Zahn, Steve: Marshall, MN, Nov. 13, 1968.
Zellweger, Renée: Katy, TX, Apr. 25, 1969.
Zerbe, Anthony: Long Beach, CA, May 20, 1939.
Zeta-Jones, Catherine: Swansea, Wales, Sept. 25, 1969.
Zimbalist, Efrem, Jr.: NYC, Nov. 30, 1918. Yale.
Zuniga, Daphne: Berkeley, CA, Oct. 28, 1963. UCLA

OBITUARIES
2003

Alan Bates

Lyle Bettger

Charles Bronson   Horst Buchholz

Lewis M. Allen, 81, Virginia-born movie and theatre producer died of pancreatic cancer on Oct. 8, 2003 in New York. His films include Lord of the Flies (1963, as well as the 1990 remake), *The Balcony, Fahrenheit 451, Fortune and Men's Eyes,* and *Swimming to Cambodia.* He is survived by his wife, writer Jay Presson Allen; a daughter; two brothers; and two grandchildren.

Rod Amateau, 79, New York City–born television and film director, died of a cerebral hemorrhage on June 29, 2003 in Los Angeles. His movies include *Pussycat Pussycat I Love You, The Statue, Where Does It Hurt?, Drive-In,* and *The Garbage Pail Kids Movie.* He is survived by his wife; two sons; two daughters; and four grandchildren.

Hy Anzel, 79, New York City–born character actor died on Aug. 23, 2003 in Fresno, CA, of natural causes. He appeared in such movies as Bengal Brigade, Bananas, The Taking of Pelham One Two Three, Annie Hall, Radio Days, Ironweed, Crimes and Misdemeanors, Pacific Heights, The Cemetery Club, and Deconstructing Harry. Survivors include four children.

George Axelrod, 81, New York City–born writer-director-producer, who received an Oscar nomination for his adaptation of *Breakfast at Tiffany's,* died in his sleep in Los Angeles on June 21, 2003, of heart failure. His other credits include *Phffft* (writer), *Bus Stop* (writer), *The Manchurian Candidate* (writer, producer), *How to Murder Your Wife* (writer, producer), *Lord Love a Duck* (writer, director, producer), *The Secret Life of an American Wife* (writer, director, producer), and *The Fourth Protocol* (writer). His best-known Broadway credit was the comedy *The Seven Year Itch.* Survivors include a daughter; three sons; a sister; and seven grandchildren.

Alan Bates, 69, motion picture, stage and television actor, who became one of the key figures of British cinema during the 1960s, in movies like *A Kind of Loving* and *Georgy Girl,* died in London on Dec. 27, 2003 of pancreatic cancer. Following his 1960 debut in *The Entertainer,* he was seen in such films as *Whistle Down the Wind, The Caretaker, Zorba the Greek, Nothing But the Best, King of Hearts, Far From the Madding Crowd, The Fixer* (Oscar nomination), *Women in Love, The Go-Between, A Day in the Death of Joe Egg, Butley, An Unmarried Woman, The Shout, The Rose, Nijinsky, Quartet, The Return of the Soldier, Duet for One, We Think the World of You, Hamlet* (1990), *Silent Tongue, Gosford Park, The Mothman Prophecies, The Sum of All Fears, Evelyn,* and *The Statement.* Survived by two sons, one of whom is actor Benedict Bates; two brothers; and a granddaughter.

Early Bellamy, 86, Minneapolis-born director died on Nov. 30, 2003 in Albuquerque, NM, of a heart attack. Although he worked principally on television he directed a handful of theatrical features including *Fluffy, Munster Go Home, Incident at Phantom Hill,* and *Sidecar Racers.*

Lyle Bettger, 88, Philadelphia-born screen and television actor, perhaps best known for his villainous role in the 1952 Oscar-winner *The Greatest Show on Earth,* died on Sept. 24, 2003 at his son's home in Atascadero, CA. He was seen in such other pictures as *No Man of Her Own, Union Station, Hurricane Smith, The Great Sioux Uprising, Carnival Story, Gunfight at the O.K. Corral, Town Tamer, Nevada Smith, The Fastest Guitar Alive,* and *The Seven Minutes.* He is survived by two sons; a daughter; a sister; and three grandchildren.

Jonathan Brandis, 27, Connecticut-born movie and television actor, who starred on the series *SeaQuest DSV,* died on Nov. 12, 2003 in Los Angeles after hanging himself. Among his movie credits were *Ladybugs, Sidekicks, Outside Providence, Ride with the Devil,* and *Hart's War.* Survived by his parents.

Jack Brodsky, 69, motion picture publicist and producer, died of a heart attack on Feb. 18, 2003 in Los Angeles. His credits include *Little Murders, Everything You Always Wanted to Know About Sex, Summer Wishes Winter Dreams, Romancing the Stone, King Ralph,* and *Daddy Day Care.* He is survived by his mother; his wife; two sons; and two grandchildren.

Charles Bronson (Charles Buchinsky), 81, Pennsylvania-born motion picture and television actor, who rose from supporting player to the star of such action movies as *Once Upon a Time in the West, The Valachi Papers,* and his signature film, *Death Wish,* died of pneumonia on Aug. 30, 2003 in Los Angeles. Following his debut in 1951 (as Charles Buchinsky) in *U.S.S. Teakettle,* he was seen in such movies as *The Marrying Kind, Pat and Mike, House of Wax, Miss Sadie Thompson, Vera Cruz, Drum Beat* (his first as Charles Bronson, in 1954), *Big House USA, Jubal, Machine Gun Kelly, Never So Few, The Magnificent Seven, Master of the World, The Great Escape, 4 for Texas, The Sandpiper, Battle of the Bulge, The Dirty Dozen, Red Sun, Chato's Land, The Mechanic, Mr. Majestyk, Hard Times, Breakheart Pass, From Noon Till Three, St. Ives, Telefon, Caboblanco, Borderline, Death Hunt, The Evil That Men Do, Murphy's Law, Messenger of Death,* and *The Indian Runner.* He is survived by his third wife; three daughters; a son; two stepsons; and two grandchildren.

Norman Burton

Art Carney

Nell Carter

Anthony Caruso

Rand Brooks, 84, Los Angeles–born film actor, best known for playing Scarlet O'Hara's first husband, Charles, in the 1939 classic *Gone with the Wind*, died of cancer on Sept. 1, 2003 at his home in Santa Ynez, CA. His other movies include *Babes in Arms*, *The Old Maid*, *Northwest Passage*, *Cheers for Miss Bishop*, *Lady Scarface*, *The Cimarron Kid*, *The Charge at Feather River*, and several Hopalong Cassidy westerns, as "Lucky Jenkins." Survived by his wife; two children; five grandchildren; and two great-grandchildren.

Robert Brown, 72, British character actor, who played the role of "M" in four James Bond films, died in Swanage, Dorset, England on Nov. 11, 2003. His films include *Helen of Troy*, *A Hill in Korea (Hell in Korea)*, *The Abominable Snowman of the Himalayas*, *The Steel Bayonets*, *The 300 Spartans*, *Billy Budd*, *Operation Crossbow*, *Lion of the Desert*, *Octopussy*, *A View to a Kill*, *The Living Daylights*, and *License to Kill*. Survived by his wife and his daughter.

Horst Buchholz, 69, German actor who starred in such American films as *The Magnificent Seven* and *Fanny*, died in Berlin on March 3, 2003 of pneumonia while recovering from a broken thighbone. Among his other pictures are *Teenage Wolfpack*, *Confessions of Felix Krull*, *Tiger Bay* (his English-language debut), *One Two Three*, *Nine Hours to Rama*, *The Empty Canvas*, *Marco the Magnificent*, *That Man in Istanbul*, *The Great Waltz* (1972), *Code Name: Emerald*, *Faraway So Close*, and *Life is Beautiful*. He is survived by his wife, former actress Myriam Bru; and two children.

Norman Burton, 79, New York City–born character actor died in a car accident on Nov. 29, 2003 near the California-Arizona border. He appeared in such movies as *Pretty Boy Floyd*, *Planet of the Apes*, *R.P.M.*, *Diamonds Are Forever* (as Felix Leiter), *Save the Tiger*, *The Towering Inferno*, *The Reincarnation of Peter Proud*, *The Gumball Rally*, *Fade to Black*, and *Crimes of Passion*. He is survived by a daughter.

Art Carney (William Matthew Carney), 85, New York–born screen, television, and stage actor, who won an Academy Award for playing a lonely senior citizen in the 1974 film *Harry and Tonto*, died in Chester, CT, on Nov. 9, 2003. Best known for playing sewer worker Ed Norton on the classic 1950s sitcom *The Honeymooners*, Carney would later appear in such movies as *The Yellow Rolls-Royce*, *A Guide for the Married Man*, *W.W. and the Dixie Dancekings*,

Won Ton Ton the Dog Who Saved Hollywood, *The Late Show*, *House Calls*, *Movie Movie*, *Sunburn*, *Going in Style*, *Roadie*, *The Muppets Take Manhattan*, and *Last Action Hero*. Survivors include his wife and three children.

Nell Carter, 54, Alabama-born singer-actress, who won a Tony Award for the musical *Ain't Misbehavin'*, died of complications from diabetes at her Beverly Hills home on Jan. 23, 2003. In addition to starring on the TV series *Gimme a Break*, she was seen in such films as *Hair*, *Modern Problems*, *The Grass Harp*, and *The Proprietor*. Survived by a daughter and two sons.

Anthony Caruso, 86, Indiana-born character actor died at his Los Angeles home on Apr. 4, 2003. His films include *Johnny Apollo*, *Watch on the Rhine*, *To the Victor*, *Song of India*, *The Undercover Man*, *The Asphalt Jungle*, *Boots Malone*, *The Iron Mistress*, *Blackbeard the Pirate*, *Phantom of the Rue Morgue*, *Saskatchewan*, *Cattle Queen of Montana*, *Never Steal Anything Small*, *Where Love Has Gone*, *Sylvia*, *Never a Dull Moment* (1968), and *Mean Johnny Barrows*. Survived by his wife of 63 years, former actress Tonia Valente; and his son.

Johnny Cash, 71, Arkansas-born singer-musician-actor, one of the most famous names in country music, whose hit songs include "I Walk the Line" and "Ring of Fire," died on Sept. 12, 2003 in Nashville, of complications from diabetes. He made a handful of film appearances including *Door-to-Door Maniac (Five Minutes to Live)*, *Hootenanny Hoot*, and *A Gunfight*. His wife, singer June Carter Cash, had died on May 15, 2003. Survived by his five children.

Leslie Cheung, 46, Hong Kong actor-singer, best known for the film *Farewell My Concubine*, died in Hong Kong on Apr. 1, 2003 after jumping from his hotel room. His other movies include *A Better Tomorrow* and *Happy Together*. No reported survivors.

Suzanne Cloutier, 80, Canadian actress, best known for playing Desdemona in Orson Welles' film of *Othello*, died of liver cancer on Dec. 2, 2003 in Montreal. Her small list of movies includes *Temptation*, *Doctor in the House*, and *Romanoff and Juliet*, in the last appearing opposite Peter Ustinov to whom she was married from 1954 to 1971. Survivors include their three children.

Jeanne Crain

Richard Crenna

Hume Cronyn

Ellen Drew

Fielder Cook (James Fielder Cook), 80, Atlanta-born director of such television dramas as *Patterns* and *The Price* (for which he received an Emmy), died of a stroke on June 20, 2003 in Charlotte, NC. His theatrical motion picture credits include the 1956 film of *Patterns*, as well as *A Big Hand for the Little Lady*, *How to Save a Marriage (and Ruin Your Life)*, and *Prudence and the Pill*. Survived by his wife; two daughters; a sister; and four grandchildren.

Jeanne Crain, 78, California-born screen and television actress, who earned an Oscar nomination for her performance in the 1949 film *Pinky*, died of a heart attack on Dec. 14, 2003 in Santa Barbara, CA. Following her 1943 debut in *The Gang's All Here*, she was seen in such movies as *Home in Indiana*, *Winged Victory*, *State Fair* (1945), *Leave Her to Heaven*, *Centennial Summer*, *Margie*, *Apartment for Peggy*, *A Letter to Three Wives*, *The Fan* (1949), *Cheaper by the Dozen* (1950), *People Will Talk*, *The Model and the Marriage Broker*, *Vicki*, *Gentlemen Marry Brunettes*, *Man without a Star*, *The Tattered Dress*, *The Joker Is Wild*, *Madison Avenue*, *Hot Rods to Hell*, and *Skyjacked*. She is survived by two sons and three daughters.

Richard Crenna, 76, Los Angeles–born screen and television actor, who was seen in such movies as *The Sand Pebbles*, *Wait Until Dark*, and *The Flamingo Kid*, died of heart failure on Jan. 17, 2003 in Los Angeles. His other pictures include *Red Skies of Montana*, *Our Miss Brooks* (repeating his role from the TV series), *John Goldfarb Please Come Home*, *Made in Paris*, *Star!*, *Midas Run*, *Marooned*, *Red Sky at Morning*, *Breakheart Pass*, *Body Heat*, *First Blood*, *Table for Five*, *Summer Rental*, *Jade*, *Sabrina* (1995), and *Wrongfully Accused*. On television he won an Emmy Award for the movie *The Rape of Richard Beck*. Survived by two daughters; a son; and three grandchildren.

Hume Cronyn, 91, Canadian-born actor, best known for his many appearances opposite his wife of 52 years, Jessica Tandy, died at his home in Fairfield, CT, on June 15, 2003 of prostate cancer. Following his 1943 debut in *Shadow of a Doubt*, he was seen in such films as *Phantom of the Opera* (1943), *The Cross of Lorraine*, *The Seventh Cross* (Oscar nomination), *Lifeboat*, *The Sailor Takes a Wife*, *Ziegfeld Follies*, *The Green Years*, *The Postman Always Rings Twice* (1946), *The Beginning or the End*, *Brute Force*, *Top o' the Morning*, *People Will Talk*, *Sunrise at Campobello*, *Cleopatra* (1963), *Gaily Gaily*, *There Was a Crooked Man...*, *Conrack*, *The Parallax View*, *Honky Tonk Freeway*, *The World According to Garp*, *Cocoon*, *Batteries Not Included*, *The Pelican Brief*, *Camilla*,

and *Marvin's Room*. He is also credit as co-writer on the Alfred Hitchcock films *Rope* and *Under Capricorn*. Survivors include his second wife; three children from his marriage to Tandy; eight grandchildren; and five great-grandchildren.

Dick Cusack, 77, New York City–born character actor died in Evanston, IL, on June 2, 2003 of pancreatic cancer. His film credits include *My Bodyguard*, *Class*, *Eight Men Out*, *The Package*, *The Fugitive* (1993), *While You Were Sleeping*, *High Fidelity*, and *Return to Me*. He is survived by his wife; his five children, which include actors John and Joan Cusack; and two grandchildren.

Ellen Drew, 89, Kansas City–born screen and television actress, best known for her appearances in such Paramount films as *Christmas in July* and *The Monster and the Girl*, died of liver trouble on Dec. 3, 2003 in Palm Desert. CA. Starting under the name Terry Ray she did small roles in such movies as *Yours for the Asking*, *Internes Can't Take Money*, and *Hotel Haywire*, first appearing as Ellen Drew in *Sing You Sinners*, which was followed by movies like *The Gracie Allen Murder Case*, *Buck Benny Rides Again*, *The Mad Doctor*, *Reaching for the Sun*, *The Parson of Panamint*, *Night of January 16th*, *The Remarkable Andrew*, *Star Spangled Rhythm*, *Isle of the Dead*, *Johnny O'Clock*, *The Baron of Arizona*, *Stars in My Crown*, and *The Great Missouri Raid*. Survived by her son and several grandchildren.

John Gregory Dunne, 71, Connecticut-born author, whose works include *The Studio*, about the inner workings of 20th Century-Fox in the late 1960s, died of a heart attack at his Manhattan apartment on Dec. 30, 2003. He wrote (in collaboration with his wife of 39 years, Joan Didion) the screenplays for the films *The Panic in Needle Park*, *Play It As It Lays*, *A Star is Born* (1976), *True Confessions* (from his novel), and *Up Close and Personal*. Survivors include Didion; two brothers, one of whom is writer-producer Dominick Dunne; and a daughter.

Buddy Ebsen

Buddy Hackett

David Hemmings

Katharine Hepburn

Buddy Ebsen (Christian Rudolph Ebsen, Jr.), 95, Illinois-born actor-dancer, perhaps best known for playing Jed Clampett on the long-running series *The Beverly Hillbillies,* died in Torrance, CA, on July 6, 2003 of complications from pneumonia. Part of a one-time dance act with his sister, Vilma, he made his movie debut alongside her in the film *Broadway Melody of 1936.* His other pictures include *Born to Dance, Captain January, Broadway Melody of 1938, The Girl of the Golden West, My Lucky Star, Sing Your Worries Away, Night People, Attack, Breakfast at Tiffany's, The Interns, Mail Order Bride,* and *The One and Only Genuine Original Family Band.* His second hit television series was *Barnaby Jones.* Survived by his wife; his sister; six children; and six grandchildren.

Anthony Eisley (Frederick Eisley), 78, Philadelphia-born screen and television actor, best known for starring in the series *Hawaiian Eye,* died on Jan. 20, 2003 in Woodland Hills, CA, of heart failure. Among his motion pictures were *The Young Philadelphians, The Wasp Woman, The Naked Kiss, Frankie and Johnny* (1966), *The Navy vs. the Night Monsters,* and *Star!* No reported survivors.

Jack Elam, 85, Arizona-born character actor, best known for his western roles in such movies as *Gunfight at the O.K. Corral* and *Support Your Local Sheriff!,* died on Oct. 20, 2003 at his home in Ashland, OR. His many other films include *Rawhide, Rancho Notorious, High Noon, Kansas City Confidential, Ride Vaquero!, Appointment in Honduras, Vera Cruz, The Far Country, Cattle Queen of Montana, Kismet, Pardners, Jubal, Night Passage, Baby Face Nelson, The Comancheros, 4 for Texas, The Way West, Firecreek, Dirty Dingus Magee, Hannie Caulder, Pat Garrett and Billy the Kid, The Cannonball Run,* and *Suburban Commando.* Survived by his wife; a daughter; and two sons.

Mary Ellis, 105, New York City–born stage star and occasional film actress, died in London on Jan. 30, 2003. She could be seen in such pictures as *All the King's Horses, Paris in Spring, The Magic Box,* and *The 3 Worlds of Gulliver.* No immediate survivors.

Jinx Falkenberg (Eugenia Lincoln Falkenberg), 84, Barcelona-born model-turned-actress and radio host, best known for the show *Breakfast with Tex and Jinx,* which she co-hosted with her husband Tex McCrary, died on Aug. 27, 2003 in Manhasset, NY. McCrary had passed away only a few weeks earlier, on July 29th, at age 92. Falkenberg was seen in such movies as *Nothing Sacred, Song of the Buckaroo, Sweethearts of the Fleet, Sing for Your Supper, Nine Girls, The Gay Senorita,* and *Cover Girl.* Survived by two sons.

Erin Fleming (Marilyn Fleming), 61, Canadian actress who was best known as comedian Groucho Marx's guardian in the final years of his life, died in Los Angeles on Apr. 15, 2003 of unspecified causes. She was seen in such movies as *Everything You Always Wanted to Know About Sex* and *Sheila Levine Is Dead and Living in New York.*

Herb Gardner, 68, Brooklyn-born writer-director, best known for the comedy *A Thousand Clowns,* which he adapted for the screen in 1965, earning an Oscar nomination, died of lung disease on Sept. 24, 2003 at his Manhattan home. His other film credits (all adaptations of his own work) are *Who is Harry Kellerman and Why Is He Saying Those Terrible Things About Me?, Thieves, The Goodbye People* (also director), and *I'm Not Rappaport* (also director; based on his Tony Award–winning play). Survived by his wife and two sons.

Massimo Girotti, 84, Italian film actor died on Jan. 5, 2003 in Rome, of a heart attack. He was seen in such films as *The Cossacks, Duel of the Titans, Marco the Magnificent, Teorema, The Red Tent, Last Tango in Paris,* and *Mr. Klein.*

Trevor Goddard, 40, British screen and television actor, who appeared as Lt. Mic Brumby on the series *JAG,* died on June 7, 2003 in North Hollywood of an apparent drug overdose. His movies include *Mortal Kombat, Deep Rising,* and *Pirates of the Caribbean.* Survivors include two children.

Alex Gordon, 80, London-born "B" movie producer died of cancer on June 24, 2003 in Los Angeles. His films include *Day the World Ended, Girls in Prison, The She-Creature, Wonder Woman, Dragstrip Girl, Atomic Submarine,* and *The Underwater City.*

David Greene, 82, British motion picture and television director, who helmed the 1973 film version of the stage musical *Godspell*, died on Apr. 7, 2003 in Ojai, CA, of pancreatic cancer. His other theatrical features include *The Shuttered Room*, *Sebastian*, *The Strange Affair*, and *Gray Lady Down*. His work was principally on television where he received Emmy Awards for *Rich Man Poor Man*, *Roots*, and *Friendly Fire*. Survived by his wife; and four children from his first marriage.

Anne Gwynne, 84, Texas-born screen and television actress, best known for appearing in such Universal films as *Black Friday*, *Ride 'em Cowboy*, and *House of Frankenstein*, died of a stroke following surgery on Mar. 31, 2003, in the Woodland Hills section of Los Angeles. Her other motion picture credits include *Spring Parade*, *The Strange Case of Doctor Rx*, *Weird Woman*, *Babes on Swing Street*, *Murder in the Blue Room*, *Dick Tracy Meets Gruesome*, *Men of Texas*, *The Blazing Sun*, and *Adam at 6 A.M.* Survived by her daughter; a son; and two grandchildren.

Buddy Hackett (Leonard Hacker), 78, Brooklyn-born comedian-actor, who appeared in such notable 1960s films as *The Music Man*, *It's a Mad Mad Mad Mad World*, and *The Love Bug*, died on June 30, 2003 at his home in Malibu, CA. His other films include *Walking My Baby Back Home* (his debut in 1953), *Fireman Save My Child*, *God's Little Acre*, *All Hands on Deck*, *Everything's Ducky*, *The Wonderful World of the Brothers Grimm*, *Muscle Beach Party*, *Scrooged*, *The Little Mermaid* (voice of Scuttle), and *Paulie*. He is survived by his wife; his son; two daughters; and two grandchildren.

Conrad L. Hall, 76, Tahiti-born cinematographer, who won Academy Awards for his work on *Butch Cassidy and the Sundance Kid*, *American Beauty*, and (posthumously), *Road to Perdition*, died in Santa Monica of complications from bladder cancer on Jan. 4, 2003. He received additional Oscar nominations for *Morituri*, *The Professionals*, *In Cold Blood*, *The Day of the Locust*, *Tequila Sunrise*, *Searching for Bobby Fischer*, and *A Civil Action*. He is survived by his son, cinematographer Conrad W. Hall; two daughters; and a sister.

Marion Hargrove (Edward Thomas Marion Hargrove, Jr.), 83, North Carolina–born writer, whose bestseller, *See Here, Private Hargrove*, was turned into a hit film in 1944, died of complications from pneumonia on Aug. 23, 2003 in Long Beach, CA. He would later write the scripts for such movies as *Joe Butterfly*, *Cash McCall*, *The Music Man*, and *The Brothers O'Toole*. Survivors include his second wife.

David Hemmings, 62, British screen, stage and television actor, who became a star with the cryptic 1966 release *Blowup*, died of a heart attack on Dec. 3, 2003 while filming the movie *Samantha's Child* in Bucharest, Romania. His other movies include *The Girl-Getters (The System)*, *Eye of the Devil*, *Camelot*, *The Charge of the Light Brigade* (1968), *Only When I Larf*, *Barbarella*, *Alfred the Great*, *The Best House in London*, *Unman Wittering and Zigo*, *The Love Machine*, *Juggernaut*, *Islands in the Stream*, *Crossed Swords* (*The Prince and the Pauper*), *Murder by Decree*, *Man Woman and Child*, *The Rainbow*, *Gladiator* (2000), *Last Orders*, *Gangs of New York*, and *The League of Extraordinary Gentlemen*. Survived by his third wife, their two sons; a daughter from his first marriage; and a son from his second.

Katharine Hepburn, 96, Connecticut-born screen, stage, and television actress, one of the most admired and brilliant of all film stars, whose work earned her 12 Oscar nominations and a record four wins, died at her home in Old Saybrook, CT, on June 29, 2003. With her 1932 debut in *A Bill of Divorcement*, she was instantly acclaimed as one of the most exciting and unique performers in film. Over the next 62 years she would become perhaps the most famous of all motion picture actresses, earning Academy Awards for *Morning Glory*, *Guess Who's Coming to Dinner*, *The Lion in Winter*, and *On Golden Pond*, plus nominations for *Alice Adams*, *The Philadelphia Story*, *Woman of the Year*, *The African Queen*, *Summertime* (*Summer Madness*), *The Rainmaker*, *Suddenly Last Summer*, and *Long Day's Journey Into Night*. Her other movies are *Christopher Strong*, *Little Women* (1933), *Spitfire*, *The Little Minister*, *Break of Hearts*, *Sylvia Scarlett*, *Mary of Scotland*, *A Woman Rebels*, *Quality Street*, *Stage Door*, *Bringing Up Baby*, *Holiday* (1938), *Keeper of the Flame*, *Stage Door Canteen*, *Dragon Seed*, *Without Love*, *Undercurrent*, *The Sea of Grass*, *Song of Love*, *State of the Union*, *Adam's Rib*, *Pat and Mike*, *The Iron Petticoat*, *Desk Set*, *The Madwoman of Chaillot*, *The Trojan Women*, *A Delicate Balance*, *Rooster Cogburn*, *Olly Olly Oxen Free* (*The Great Balloon Adventure*), *Grace Quigley*, *George Stevens: A Filmmaker's Journey*, and *Love Affair*. She is survived by a brother, a sister; four nieces, one of whom, Katharine Houghton, appeared with her in *Guess Who's Coming to Dinner*; and nine nephews.

Wendy Hiller, 90, British screen, stage and television actress, who won an Academy Award for the 1958 film *Separate Tables*, died at her home in Beaconsfield, England on May 14, 2003. One of the most admired of all British actresses, she made her motion picture debut in 1937 in *Lancashire Luck*, followed by her Oscar-nominated performance in *Pygmalion*. Her other films include *Major Barbara*, *I Know Where I'm Going*, *Outcast of the Islands*, *Something of Value*, *How to Murder a Rich Uncle*, *Sons and Lovers*, *Toys in the Attic*, *A Man for All Seasons* (Oscar nomination), *Murder on the Orient Express*, *Voyage of the Damned*, *The Elephant Man*, *Making Love*, and *The Lonely Passion of Judith Hearne*. Survivors include her son and daughter, from her marriage to writer Ronald Gow (who died in 1993).

Earl Hindman, 61, Arizona-born screen and television actor, best known for playing the barely-seen neighbor on the hit TV series *Home Improvement*, died of lung cancer in Stamford, CT, on Dec. 29, 2003. His movies include *The Parallax View*, *The Taking of Pelham One Two Three*, *The Brink's Job*, *Taps*, *Silverado*, and *The Ballad of the Sad Café*. He is survived by his wife; his mother; a brother; and a sister.

Gregory Hines, 57, New York City–born actor-tap dancer, who won a Tony Award for his performance in *Jelly's Last Jam*, died in Los Angeles on Aug. 9, 2003 of liver cancer. He was seen in such movies as *History of the World Part 1*, *White Nights*, *Running Scared*, *Tap*, *Eve of Destruction*, and *The Preacher's Wife*. He is survived by his father and brother with whom he used to dance as Hines, Hines and Dad; his fiancée; a daughter; a son; a stepdaughter; and a grandson.

Thora Hird, 91, British actress died on March 15, 2003 in Twickenham, England following a stroke. Her long career included appearances in such films as *The Magic Box*, *The Quatermass Experiment*, *The Entertainer*, *A Kind of Loving*, *Term of Trial*, *The Nightcomers*, and *Consuming Passions*. She is survived by her daughter, former actress Janette Scott; and her grandchildren.

Wendy Hiller

Gregory Hines

Al Hirschfeld

Bob Hope

Al Hirschfeld, 99, beloved artist, whose instantly recognizable caricatures of famous celebrities appeared in the *New York Times* for over seventy years, died at his Manhattan home on Jan. 20, 2003. He was the subject of the 1996 Oscar-nominated documentary *The Line King*. He is survived by his third wife; his daughter, Nina, whose name was frequently hidden in her father's drawings; a grandson; a granddaughter; and two stepsons.

David Holt, 76, Jacksonville-born child actor, died of congestive heart failure on Nov. 15, 2003 in San Juan Capistrano, CA. His films include *The Big Broadcast of 1936*, *The Last Days of Pompeii*, *The Adventures of Tom Sawyer*, *Beau Geste* (1939), *Pride of the Yankees*, *The Human Comedy*, and *Courage of Lassie*. He later became a jazz musician and songwriter.

Bob Hope (Leslie Townes Hope), 100, legendary American comedian (born in England) who became one of the key show business figures of the 20th century in movies, on television and radio, and by performing for U.S. troops overseas during several wars, died at his home in Toluca Lake, CA, on July 27, 2003. He made his 1938 feature film debut in *The Big Broadcast of 1938*, where he introduced what was to become his theme song, "Thanks for the Memory." His many other films included *College Swing*, *Never Say Die*, *The Cat and the Canary*, *The Ghost Breakers*, *Road to Singapore* (his first of many teamings with Bing Crosby), *Road to Zanzibar*, *Caught in the Draft*, *Nothing But the Truth*, *Louisiana Purchase*, *My Favorite Blonde*, *Road to Morocco*, *Let's Face It*, *The Princess and the Pirate*, *Road to Utopia*, *Monsieur Beaucaire* (1946), *My Favorite Brunette*, *Variety Girl*, *Where There's Life*, *Road to Rio*, *The Paleface*, *Sorrowful Jones*, *The Great Lover*, *Fancy Pants*, *The Lemon Drop Kid* (1951), *Son of Paleface*, *Road to Bali*, *Off Limits*, *Casanova's Big Night*, *The Seven Little Foys*, *The Iron Petticoat*, *Beau James*, *Paris Holiday* (also producer, co-writer), *Alias Jesse James* (also executive producer), *The Facts of Life*, *Bachelor in Paradise*, *The Road to Hong Kong*, *Critic's Choice*, *A Global Affair*, *I'll Take Sweden*, *Boy Did I Get a Wrong Number!*, *Eight on the Lam*, *How to Commit Marriage*, *Cancel My Reservation*, and *The Muppet Movie*. His many honors include 4 special Academy Awards. He is survived by his wife of 69 years; his four children; and four grandchildren.

Victoria Horne, 91, New York City–born character actress, perhaps best known for playing Myrtle Mae Simmons in the classic 1950 comedy *Harvey*, died on Oct. 10, 2003 in Beverly Hills of natural causes. Her other films include *To Each His Own*, *Suddenly It's Spring*, *The Ghost and Mrs. Muir*, *The Snake Pit*, *The Life of Riley*, *Abbott and Costello Meet the Killer—Boris Karloff*, and *Scandal Sheet*. She was married to actor Jack Oakie from 1950 to his death in 1978.

Robert Ivers, 68, Seattle-born screen and television actor, who appeared opposite Elvis Presley in the 1960 film *G.I. Blues*, died of cancer of the esophagus on Feb. 13, 2003 in Yakima, WA. Among his other credits are *The Delicate Delinquent*, *I Married a Monster from Outer Space*, *Cattle King*, and *The Errand Boy*.

Graham Jarvis, 72, Toronto-born actor, perhaps best known for playing Charlie Haggers on the TV series *Mary Hartman, Mary Hartman*, died on April 16, 2003 in Los Angeles, of multiple myeloma. His movie appearances include *Alice's Restaurant*, *The Out-of-Towners*, *The Traveling Executioner*, *Cold Turkey*, *What's Up Doc?*, *Mr. Mom*, *Silkwood*, *One Magic Christmas*, *Tough Guys*, *Misery*, and *Son in Law*.

Michael Jeter, 50, Tennessee-born film, stage and television character actor, was found dead of complications from HIV on March 30, 2003 in Los Angeles. He was seen in such movies as *Hair*, *Ragtime*, *The Money Pit*, *Tango & Cash*, *Miller's Crossing*, *The Fisher King*, *Waterworld*, *Air Bud*, *Patch Adams*, *Mouse Hunt*, *The Green Mile*, and *Welcome to Collinwood*. Jeter won a Tony Award for *Grand Hotel* and an Emmy for the series *Evening Shade*. He is survived by his partner; his parents; a brother; and four sisters.

Gordon Jump, 71, Ohio-born screen, television and stage character actor, best known for his role on the series *WKRP in Cincinnati*, died at his home in Los Angeles on Sept. 22, 2003 of pulmonary fibrosis. Among his film appearances are *Conquest of the Planet of the Apes*, *Trouble Man*, *The Fury*, *House Calls*, *Making the Grade*, and *Moving*. Survived by his wife; four daughters; a son; and a brother.

Michael Jeter

Eli Kazan

Hope Lange

William Marshall

Michael Kamen, 55, New York City–born composer died of a heart attack at his home in London on Nov. 18, 2003. He wrote scores for such films as *Polyester, The Dead Zone, Brazil, Mona Lisa, Lethal Weapon, Die Hard, Road House, Mr. Holland's Opus, The Winter Guest, The Iron Giant, Frequency,* and *Open Range,* and received Oscar nominations for the songs "(Everything I Do) I Do It for You" from *Robin Hood: Prince of Thieves* and "Have You Ever Really Loved a Woman?" from *Don Juan DeMarco.* He is survived by his wife; two daughters; and three brothers.

Eli Kazan (Elia Kazanjolous), 94, Constantinople-born director, one of the greatest and most influential directors of the postwar years, who received Academy Awards for his work on *Gentleman's Agreement* and *On the Waterfront,* died at his Manhattan home on Sept. 28, 2003. He received additional nominations for directing *A Streetcar Named Desire* and *East of Eden,* and direction, writing and producing nominations for his autobiographical *America, America.* His other films are *A Tree Grows in Brooklyn, The Sea of Grass, Boomerang!, Pinky, Panic in the Streets, Viva Zapata!, Man on a Tightrope, Baby Doll, A Face in the Crowd, Wild River, Splendor in the Grass, The Arrangement, The Visitors,* and *The Last Tycoon.* He received a special Academy Award in 1999. Survivors include three children from his first marriage; a son from his second marriage; six grandchildren; two great-grandchildren; and three stepchildren.

Andrea King, 84, Paris-born screen and television actress died on Apr. 22, 2003 in Woodland Hills, CA, of natural causes. She was seen in such movies as *God is My Co-Pilot, The Beast with Five Fingers, Ride the Pink Horse, My Wild Irish Rose, Mr. Peabody and the Mermaid, I Was a Shoplifter, The Lemon Drop Kid* (1951), *Red Planet Mars,* and *Band of Angels.* Survived by a daughter; three grandchildren; and a sister.

Hope Lange, 70, Connecticut-born screen, stage and television actress, who received an Oscar nomination for portraying Selena Cross in the 1957 film *Peyton Place,* died on Dec. 19, 2003 in Santa Monica, CA, of an intestinal infection brought on by a bout of diverticulitis. She appeared in such other films as *Bus Stop* (debut, 1956), *The True Story of Jesse James, The Young Lions, The Best of Everything, Wild in the Country, Pocketful of Miracles, Love is a Ball, Death Wish, Blue Velvet, Tune in Tomorrow..., Clear and Present Danger,* and *Just Cause.* On television she won 2 Emmy Awards for the series *The Ghost and Mrs. Muir.* She is survived by her third husband; and two children from her marriage to actor Don Murray.

Sydney Lassick, 80, Chicago-born character actor, best known for playing mental patient Charlie Cheswick in the 1975 Oscar-winner *One Flew Over the Cuckoo's Nest,* died in Los Angeles of complications from diabetes on April 12, 2003. He appeared in such movies as *Carrie, Happy Hooker Goes to Washington, Hot Stuff, Alligator, History of the World Part 1, Ratboy, Lady in White, Sonny Boy, Cool as Ice, Shakes the Clown, Johns,* and *Man on the Moon.*

Dorothy Loudon, 70, Boston-born actress and singer, who won a Tony Award for playing Miss Hannigan in the musical *Annie,* died of cancer on Nov. 15, 2003 in New York. She was seen in the films *Garbo Talks* and *Midnight in the Garden of Good and Evil.* She is survived by two stepchildren.

William Marshall, 78, Indiana-born character actor, who had the title role in the 1972 horror film *Blacula,* died on June 11, 2003 in Los Angeles of a heart attack. His other films include *Lydia Bailey, Demetrius and the Gladiators, Something of Value, Scream Blacula Scream, The Boston Strangler, Skullduggery, Amazon Women on the Moon, The Fisher King,* and *Maverick.* Survived by his partner; a daughter; and three sons.

Sean McClory, 79, Dublin-born screen and television actor died on Dec. 10, 2003 in Hollywood. His movie credits include *The Daughter of Rosie O'Grady, The Quiet Man, Les Miserables* (1952), *Niagara, Island in the Sky, Them!, I Cover the Waterfront, Moonfleet, Cheyenne Autumn, Follow Me Boys!, The Happiest Millionaire, The Gnome-Mobile,* and *The Dead.* Survived by his wife; two sons; a daughter; and seven grandchildren.

Donald O'Connor

Suzy Parker

Gregory Peck

Vera Ralston

Gordon Mitchell (Charles Pendleton), 80, Denver-born actor-body-builder, who starred in such Italian spectacles as *The Giant of Metropolis* and *Fury of Achilles*, died of a heart attack on Sept. 20, 2003 in Marina del Rey, CA. His other credits include *Li'l Abner, The Centurion, Reflections in a Golden Eye,* and *Fellini Satyricon.* No immediate survivors.

Paul Monash, 85, New York City–born writer-producer died on Jan. 14, 2003 in Los Angeles. Although principally connected with television his film credits include executive producing *Butch Cassidy and the Sundance Kid,* writing *The Safecracker* and *The Friends of Eddie Coyle* (which he also produced), and producing such movies as *Slaughterhouse-Five, The Front Page* (1974), and *Carrie.* He is survived by his wife; two children; and two stepchildren.

Karen Morley, 93, Iowa-born motion picture actress, who appeared in such notable films from the early 1930s as *Scarface* and *Dinner at Eight,* died of pneumonia on March 8, 2003 in the Woodland Hills section of Los Angeles. Her other films include *The Sin of Madelon Claudet, Arsene Lupin, Mata Hari, The Mask of Fu Manchu, Gabriel Over the White House, Our Daily Bread, Black Fury, The Littlest Rebel, The Last Train from Madrid, Kentucky,* and *Pride and Prejudice.* She was married to actor Lloyd Gough from 1943 until his death in 1984. Survivors include two grandsons; a granddaughter; and two great-grandchildren.

David Newman, 66, New York City–born screenwriter, who earned an Oscar nomination for *Bonnie and Clyde,* died of a stroke on Oct. 27, 2003 in Manhattan. His other film credits include *Superman, There Was a Crooked Man..., What's Up Doc?, Bad Company* (1972), *Still of the Night, Jinxed,* and *Santa Claus.* Survived by his wife; two children; two grandchildren; and a brother.

N!xau, 59, Kalahari Bushman who was selected to star in the 1984 sleeper hit *The Gods Must Be Crazy,* died on July 5, 2003 of natural causes in Tsumkwe in the Namibian part of the Kalahari. He appeared in a sequel and a few other films designed to cash in on his fame from the first picture. No reported survivors.

Cliff Norton, 84, Chicago-born screen, stage, and television character actor, died on Jan. 25, 2003 at his home in Studio City, CA. Among his movies are *It's a Mad Mad Mad Mad World, Kiss Me Stupid, Munster Go Home, The Russians Are Coming The Russians Are Coming, Harry and Tonto, Funny Lady,* and *Won Ton Ton the Dog Who Saved Hollywood.* Survived by his three children, and four grandchildren.

Donald O'Connor, 78, Chicago-born actor-dancer, who starred in a series of "Francis the Talking Mule" films as well as one of the great musicals of all time, *Singin' in the Rain,* died on Sept. 27, 2003 of heart failure in Calabasas, CA. Starting as a child performer he was seen in such movies as *Sing You Sinners, Tom Sawyer Detective, Beau Geste* (1939), *Boy Trouble, On Your Toes, Private Buckaroo, What's Cookin'?, When Johnny Comes Marching Home, Top Man, Chip Off the Old Block, Bowery to Broadway, The Merry Monahans, Patrick the Great, Something in the Wind, Feudin' Fightin' and a-Fussin', Yes Sir That's My Baby, Double Crossbones, Curtain Call at Cactus Creek, The Milkman, I Love Melvin, Walking My Baby Back Home, There's No Business Like Show Business, Anything Goes* (1956), *The Buster Keaton Story, The Wonders of Aladdin, That Funny Feeling, Ragtime, Toys,* and *Out to Sea.* Survivors include his second wife and three children.

Norman Panama, 88, Chicago-born writer-director-producer, who received Oscar nominations for his scripts for *Road to Utopia, Knock on Wood* (which he also produced and directed), and *The Facts of Life* (which he also produced), all written in collaboration with his long-time partner, Melvin Frank, died on Jan. 13, 2003 in Los Angeles of complications from Parkinson's disease. He was also director-writer-producer of *The Reformer and the Redhead, Callaway Went Thataway, Above and Beyond, The Court Jester, The Road to Hong Kong, Not With My Wife You Don't!;* writer of such movies as *Thank Your Lucky Stars, Monsieur Beaucaire,* and *White Christmas,* and producer-writer of films like *Mr. Blandings Builds His Dream House* and *Li'l Abner.*

Suzy Parker (Cecilia Ann Renee Parker), 69, San Antonio–born actress-turned-model, died on May 3, 2003 at her home in Montecito, CA, after a series of illnesses. Her handful of movies include *Funny Face, Ten North Frederick, Kiss Them for Me, The Best of Everything,* and *The Interns.* She is survived by her husband of forty years, actor Bradford Dillman; her daughter; two sons; four grandchildren; and two sisters.

Julie Parrish, 62, Kentucky-born screen and television actress died of ovarian cancer on Oct. 1, 2003 in Los Angeles. She was seen in such movies as *The Nutty Professor* (1963), *Winter A-Go-Go, Fireball 500, Paradise Hawaiian Style, The Doberman Gang,* and *The Devil and Max Devlin.* Survived by two sisters and two brothers.

Madlyn Rhue

John Ritter

Guy Rolfe

Janice Rule

Gregory Peck (Eldred Gregory Peck), 87, California-born screen, stage and television actor, a top star for over fifty years, who won an Academy Award for portraying lawyer Atticus Finch in the 1962 classic *To Kill a Mockingbird*, died at his Los Angeles home on June 12, 2003. He received additional Oscar nominations for *The Keys of the Kingdom*, *The Yearling*, *Gentleman's Agreement*, and *Twelve O'Clock High*. His other movies include *Day of Glory* (debut, 1944), *Spellbound*, *Valley of Decision*, *Duel in the Sun*, *The Macomber Affair*, *Yellow Sky*, *The Great Sinner*, *The Gunfighter*, *Captain Horatio Hornblower*, *David and Bathsheba*, *The Snows of Kilimanjaro*, *Roman Holiday*, *Night People*, *The Man in the Grey Flannel Suit*, *Moby Dick*, *Designing Woman*, *The Big Country*, *Pork Chop Hill*, *Beloved Infidel*, *On the Beach*, *The Guns of Navarone*, *Cape Fear* (1962 and 1991 remake), *How the West Was Won*, *Captain Newman M.D.*, *Behold a Pale Horse*, *Mirage*, *Arabesque*, *Mackenna's Gold*, *Marooned*, *I Walk the Line*, *The Omen*, *MacArthur*, *The Boys from Brazil*, *The Sea Wolves*, *Old Gringo*, and *Other People's Money*. Among his honors are the Jean Hersholt Humanitarian Award and the American Film Institute Lifetime Achievement Award. He is survived by his second wife; two sons from his first marriage; a son and a daughter from his second marriage; and six grandchildren.

Louise Platt, 88, Connecticut-born actress, best known for playing Lucy Mallory in the 1939 classic *Stagecoach*, died on Sept. 6, 2003 in Greenport, NY. Her handful of other movies include *I Met My Love Again*, *Spawn of the North*, *Forgotten Girls*, and *Street of Chance* (1942).

George Plimpton, 76, New York City–born journalist, editor and actor, best known for his exploits placing himself in unsuitable jobs and writing about the experience, died on Sept. 26, 2003 of a heart attack at his Manhattan home. Perhaps his most famous amateur position was playing third-string quarterback for the Detroit Lions, which formed the basis for the 1968 film *Paper Lion*, in which he was portrayed by Alan Alda. Plimpton himself was seen in such movies as *Rio Lobo*, *Reds*, *L.A. Story*, *Little Man Tate*, *Nixon*, and *Good Will Hunting*. He is survived by his second wife and their two children.

Denis Quilley, 75, London-born stage, screen and television actor died of liver cancer on Oct. 5, 2003 in London. Among his film credits are *Life at the Top*, *Anne of the Thousand Days*, *Murder on the Orient Express*, *Evil Under the Sun*, *Privates on Parade*, *Memed My Hawk*, *King David*, and *Mister Johnson*.

Vera (Hruba) Ralston, 79, Czech-born figure skater-turned-actress, died of cancer on Feb. 9, 2003 at her home in Santa Barbara, CA. Signed by Republic Pictures she appeared in such movies as *Ice-Capades*, *Ice-Capades Revue*, *Lake Placid Serenade*, *Storm Over Lisbon*, *I Jane Doe*, *Dakota*, *The Fighting Kentuckian*, *The Plainsman and the Lady*, and *Fair Wind to Java*. She was married to the head of Republic, Herbert J. Yates, from 1952 to his death in 1966. She is survived by her second husband.

Maurice Rapf, 88, New York City–born screenwriter died on Apr. 15, 2003 in Hanover, NH of natural causes. Among his films are *They Gave Him a Gun*, *The Bad Man of Brimstone*, *Winter Carnival*, *Song of the South*, *So Dear to My Heart*, and *Father Brown*. Survived by his wife of 56 years; his brother; two daughters; a son; and four grandchildren.

Anthony Ray, 64, British actor who played the title role in the 1950 film *The Mudlark*, died of a heart attack on Aug. 20, 2003 in London. His other movies include *A Prize of Gold*, *Gideon of Scotland Yard*, *The Girl-Getters (The System)*, and *Rough Cut*. Survived by his wife and two children.

Paula Raymond, 79, San Francisco–born actress died on Dec. 31, 2003 in West Hollywood of a respiratory ailment. Her films include *Adam's Rib*, *Duchess of Idaho*, *Devil's Doorway*, *The Tall Target*, *The Sellout*, *Story of Three Loves*, *The Beast from 20,000 Fathoms*, *King Richard and the Crusaders*, and *Five Bloody Graves*. Survived by her granddaughter.

Madlyn Rhue, 68, D.C.-born screen and television actress died of pneumonia on Dec. 16, 2003 in Los Angeles. She was seen in such films as *Operation Petticoat*, *The Ladies Man*, *A Majority of One*, *It's a Mad Mad Mad Mad World*, and *Stand Up and Be Counted*. Survived by a sister.

Leni Riefenstahl, 101, German filmmaker whose documentaries *Olympiad* and *Triumph of the Will* were looked upon both as masterful works of art and blatant Nazi propaganda, died on Sept. 8, 2003 at her home in Pöcking, Germany. She would spend the rest of her life denounced as a Nazi sympathizer, a controversial figure because of her involvement with Hitler and his film unit. No reported survivors.

John Ritter, 54, screen and television actor, perhaps best known for his Emmy Award–winning role on the sitcom *Three's Company*, died of an aortic dissection in Burbank, CA, on Sept. 11, 2003. He had become ill while on the set of his latest series, *8 Simple Rules for Dating My Teenage Daughter*. He appeared in such motion pictures as *The Barefoot Executive*, *The Other*, *Nickelodeon*, *Hero at Large*, *They All Laughed*, *Skin Deep*, *Problem Child*, *Noises Off*, *Stayed Tuned*, *North*, *Sling Blade*, and *Tadpole*. He is survived by his wife, actress Amy Yasbeck, their daughter; and three children from his first marriage, one of whom is actor Jason Ritter.

Carlos Rivas, 74, Texas-born actor, best known for playing Lun Tha in the 1956 film adaptation of *The King and I*, died of prostate cancer on June 16, 2003 in Los Angeles. Among his other films are *The Beast of Hollow Mountain*, *The Big Boodle*, *The Deerslayer*, *The Black Scorpion*, *The Unforgiven*, *Pepe*, *They Saved Hitler's Brain*, *True Grit*, *Topaz*, and *Mi Vida Loca*. He is survived by his wife, daughter, and granddaughter.

Guy Rolfe, 91, British screen, stage and television actor, died on Oct. 19, 2003 in London. His films include *Saraband for Dead Lovers*, *Ivanhoe*, *Young Bess*, *King of the Khyber Rifles*, *The Barbarians*, *Snow White and the Three Stooges*, *Mr. Sardonicus* (in the title role), *King of Kings* (as Caiaphas), *Taras Bulba*, *The Alphabet Murders*, and *Nicholas and Alexandra*.

Janice Rule, 72, Ohio-born screen, stage and television actress died of a cerebral hemorrhage on Oct. 17, 2003 at her Manhattan home. Following her 1951 debut in *Goodbye My Fancy*, she appeared in such movies as *Starlift*, *Holiday for Sinners*, *Gun for a Coward*, *Bell Book and Candle*, *The Subterraneans*, *Invitation to a Gunfighter*, *Alvarez Kelly*, *The Chase*, *The Swimmer*, *The Ambushers*, *Doctors' Wives*, *Gumshoe*, *3 Women*, *Missing*, and *American Flyers*. She is survived by two daughters, one from her third marriage, to actor Ben Gazzara, and three sisters.

Bing Russell (Neil Russell), 76, Vermont-born actor who specialized in westerns and appeared as Deputy Clem Foster on the hit series *Bonanza*, died of cancer on Apr. 8, 2003 in Thousand Oaks, CA. Among his credits are *Kiss Me Deadly*, *Tarantula*, *Gunfight at the O.K. Corral*, *Suicide Battalion*, *The Horse Soldiers*, *Last Train from Gun Hill*, *The Magnificent Seven*, *The Stripper*, *The Hallelujah Trail*, *The Computer Wore Tennis Shoes* (first appearance in a film starring his son, Kurt Russell), *$1,000,000 Duck*, *Overboard*, *Sunset*, and *Tango & Cash*. Survivors include Kurt Russell.

John Schlesinger, 77, British filmmaker, who won the Academy Award for directing the 1969 classic *Midnight Cowboy*, died on July 25, 2003 in Palm Springs, CA. He had been in poor health after suffering a stroke. He received additional Oscar nominations for *Darling* and *Sunday Bloody Sunday*. His other movies include *A Kind of Loving*, *Billy Liar*, *Far from the Madding Crowd*, *The Day of the Locust*, *Marathon Man*, *Yanks*, *Honky Tonk Freeway*, *Madame Sousatzka*, *Pacific Heights*, *Eye for an Eye*, *Cold Comfort Farm*, and *The Next Best Thing*. He is survived by his companion; a brother; and a sister.

Bernard Schwartz, 85, New York City–born film producer, who received an Oscar nomination for *Coal Miner's Daughter*, died of complications from a stroke on Oct. 17, 2003 in Los Angeles. His other movies include *Eye of the Cat*, *Bucktown*, *Road Games*, and *Sweet Dreams*. Survivors include his wife, two sons, and a grandson.

Martha Scott, 88, Missouri-born screen, stage, and television actress, who earned an Oscar nomination for recreating her role of Emily from the original Broadway production of Thornton Wilder's classic *Our Town*, died on May 28, 2003 in Los Angeles of natural causes. She was seen in such other films as *The Howards of Virginia*, *Cheers for Miss Bishop*, *One Foot in Heaven*, *In Old Oklahoma*, *So Well Remembered*, *The Desperate Hours*, *The Ten Commandments*, *Sayonara*, *Ben-Hur*, *Airport 1975*, *The Turning Point*, and *Doin' Time on Planet Earth*. She is survived by her son, two daughters, and her brother.

Raymond Serra, 71, New York City–born film and television character actor died on June 20, 2003. He was seen in such movies as *Marathon Man*, *Manhattan*, *Wolfen*, *Alphabet City*, *The Purple Rose of Cairo*, *Forever Lulu*, *Teenage Mutant Ninja Turtles*, *Sugar Hill*, and *Safe Men*.

Dick Simmons, 89, St. Paul–born actor, best known for starring in the title role of the series *Sergeant Preston of the Yukon*, died on Jan. 11, 2003 in Oceanside, CA of Alzheimer's disease. His movie credits include *Seven Sweethearts*, *The Youngest Profession*, *Pilot#5*, *Thousands Cheer*, *Lady in the Lake*, *This Time for Keeps*, *On an Island with You*, *Duchess of Idaho*, *The Well*, *Above and Beyond*, *Battle Circus*, and *Sergeants 3*. Survived by his wife, a daughter, a son, two grandchildren, and two great-grandchildren.

Penny Singleton (Dorothy McNulty), 95, Philadelphia-born screen and television actress, best remembered for playing Blondie Bumstead in the 1938 film *Blondie* and its follow-up series of 27 other movies based on the Chic Young comic strip, died on Nov. 12, 2003 in Los Angeles. She was billed under her real name in such films as *Good News* (1930), *After the Thin Man*, and *Vogues of 1938*, then appeared as Penny Singleton in pictures like *Swing Your Lady*, *Boy Meets Girl*, *The Mad Miss Manton*, and *The Best Man*. In later years she did the voice of Jane Jetson on the animated series *The Jetsons* and its later specials and movies. Survived by two daughters, two grandchildren, and a great-grandchild.

Michael Small, 64, New York City–born film composer died of prostate cancer on Nov. 25, 2003 in Manhattan. His movie scores include *Out of It*, *Klute*, *The Drowning Pool*, *The Stepford Wives* (1975), *Marathon Man*, *The China Syndrome*, *The Star Chamber*, *Firstborn*, *Black Widow*, and *Mountains of the Moon*. He is survived by his wife, and two sons.

Jack Smight, 78, Minneapolis-born screen and television director died of cancer on Sept. 1, 2003 in Los Angeles. Among his motion picture credits are *I'd Rather Be Rich*, *Harper*, *The Secret War of Harry Frigg*, *The Illustrated Man*, *The Traveling Executioner*, *Airport 1975*, *Midway*, *Fast Break*, and *Loving Couples*. On television he won an Emmy Award for directing the "Alcoa Theater" presentation *Eddie*. He is survived by two sons, four grandchildren, and his sister.

Alberto Sordi, 82, Italian film star died on Feb. 25, 2003 in Rome of a heart attack. Among his many motion pictures are *The White Sheik*, *I Vitelloni*, *Nero's Mistress*, *...and the Wild Wild Women*, *The Great War*, *The Last Judgment*, *To Bed...or Not to Bed*, *Those Magnificent Men in Their Flying Machines*, *The Queens*, *The Witches* (1969), *The Conspirators*, and *Traffic Jam*. Survived by a sister.

John Schlesinger

Martha Scott

Penny Singleton

Robert Stack

Robert Stack, 84, Los Angeles–born film and television actor, who won an Emmy Award for the series *The Untouchables* and an Oscar nomination for *Written on the Wind*, died of heart failure on May 14, 2003 at his Los Angeles home. Following his 1939 debut as Deanna Durbin's love interest in *First Love*, he appeared in such movies as *The Mortal Storm, Nice Girl?, To Be or Not to Be* (1942), *Eagle Squadron, A Date with Judy, Miss Tatlock's Millions, Mr. Music, Bullfighter and the Lady, My Outlaw Brother, Bwana Devil, Conquest of Cochise, The High and the Mighty, Good Morning Miss Dove, The Tarnished Angels, John Paul Jones, The Last Voyage, The Caretakers, Is Paris Burning?, Story of a Woman, 1941, Airplane!, Uncommon Valor,* and *Joe Versus the Volcano.* Survivors include his wife and two children.

Florence Stanley (Florence Schwartz), 79, Chicago-born screen, television and stage character actress, perhaps best known for the series *Barney Miller*, died of a stroke on Oct. 3, 2003 in Los Angeles. Among her film appearances were *Up the Down Staircase, The Prisoner of Second Avenue* (repeating her Broadway role), *The Fortune, Outrageous Fortune, Bulworth,* and *Down with Love.* Survived by her husband, two children, and two grandchildren.

Peter Stone, 73, Los Angeles–born writer, who won an Academy Award for his screenplay for *Father Goose*, died on Apr. 26, 2003 in Manhattan of pulmonary fibrosis. His other credits include *Charade, Mirage, Arabesque* (as "Pierre Marton"), *Sweet Charity, 1776, Skin Game* (as "Pierre Marton"), *The Taking of the Pelham One Two Three,* and *Who is Killing the Great Chefs of Europe?* He won Tony Awards for his scripts for the musicals *1776, Woman of the Year,* and *Titanic.* Survived by his wife and a brother.

Daniel Taradash, 90, Kentucky-born screenwriter, who won an Academy Award for his adaptation of *From Here to Eternity*, died on Feb. 22, 2003 in Los Angeles of pancreatic cancer. His other credits include *Golden Boy, Knock on Any Door, Don't Bother to Knock, Picnic, Storm Center* (which he also directed), *Bell Book and Candle, Morituri, Hawaii,* and *The Other Side of Midnight.* Survived by his wife of 58 years, two daughters, a son, and two grandchildren.

Peter Tewksbury (Henry Peter Tewksbury), 79, Cleveland-born director-writer, best known for his work on the series *My Three Sons*, died on Feb. 20, 2003 in Brattelboro, VT. He also directed the theatrical features *Sunday in New York, Emil and the Detectives* (1965), *Doctor You've Got to Be Kidding, Stay Away Joe,* and *The Trouble with Girls.* Survived by his wife and six children.

Lynne Thigpen, 54, Illinois-born screen, stage and television actress, who won a Tony Award for *American Daughter*, died of a circulatory ailment on March 12, 2003 at her home in Los Angeles. She was working on the series *The District* at the time of her death. Her motion pictures include *Godspell, Tootsie, Sweet Liberty, Running on Empty, Lean on Me, Bob Roberts, The Paper, The Insider, Novocaine,* and *Anger Management.* No reported survivors.

Les Tremayne, 90, England-born screen, television and radio actor, perhaps best known for the radio series *The First Nighter*, died of heart failure on Dec. 19, 2003 in Santa Monica, CA. Among his movie credits were *The Blue Veil, I Love Melvin, It Grows on Trees, The War of the Worlds, A Man Called Peter, Susan Slept Here, The Unguarded Moment, The Monolith Monsters, Say One for Me, North by Northwest, The Gallant Hours, The Story of Ruth, The Slime People,* and *The Fortune Cookie.* Survived by his wife and a brother.

Leon Uris, 78, Baltimore-born author, perhaps best known for the novel *Exodus*, which was adapted into a film in 1960, died on June 21, 2003 at his home on Shelter Island, NY, of renal failure. He adapted another of his books, *Battle Cry*, to the screen and wrote the screenplay for *Gunfight at the O.K. Corral.* Survived by three children from his first marriage and a sister.

Skip Ward, 70, Cleveland-born screen and television actor died on June 27, 2003 in Calabasas, CA, of natural causes. Among his films were *Voyage to the Bottom of the Sea, The Nutty Professor* (1963), *The Night of the Iguana, Kiss Me Stupid, Is Paris Burning?, Hombre, The Mad Room,* and *Myra Breckinridge.* He later became a producer, his credits in this field including the series *The Dukes of Hazzard.* Survivors include his father.

Sheb Wooley (Shelby F. Wooley), 82, Oklahoma-born western actor and singer, best known for his 1958 hit record *The Purple People Eater*, died of leukemia on Sept. 16, 2003 in Nashville, TN. He acted in such movies as *Distant Drums, High Noon* (as one of the killers), *Sky Full of Moon, The Boy from Oklahoma, Man without a Star, Giant, Ride a Violent Mile, Hootenanny Hoot, The War Wagon, The Outlaw Josey Wales, Silverado, Hoosiers,* and *Purple People Eater.* Survivors include his wife.

Les Tremayne   Vera Zorina

Philip Yordan, 88, Chicago-born screenwriter-producer, who won an Oscar for writing *Broken Lance*, died on March 24, 2003 in La Jolla, CA, of pancreatic cancer. His other writing credits include *Dillinger* (Oscar nomination), *Bad Men of Tombstone*, *Detective Story* (Oscar nomination), *Houdini*, *Johnny Guitar*, *The Big Combo*, *The Harder They Fall* (which he also produced), *Anna Lucasta* (1958; also producer), *King of Kings*, *El Cid*, *55 Days at Peking*, *Circus World*, and *Battle of the Bulge* (also producer). He is survived by his fourth wife, two sisters, and five children.

Paul Zindel, 66, Staten Island–born writer, best known for adapting his award-winning play *The Effect of Gamma Rays on Man-in-the-Moon Marigolds* to film in 1972, died of cancer on March 27, 2003 in Manhattan. In addition to his many books he also worked on the scripts for *Up the Sandbox*, *Mame*, *Maria's Lovers*, and *Runaway Train*. He is survived by a daughter, a son, and a sister.

Vera Zorina (Eva Brigitta Hartwig), 86, Berlin-born dancer-actress, best known for the ballets she appeared in that were choreographed by her first husband, George Balanchine, died on April 9, 2003 at her home in Santa Fe, NM, of natural causes. She appeared in a handful of movies including *The Goldwyn Follies*, *On Your Toes* (repeating her role from the London stage production), *Louisiana Purchase*, *Star Spangled Rhythm*, and *Follow the Boys*. She is survived by a son from her marriage to CBS records president Goddard Lieberson; her third husband; and three granddaughters.

INDEX

A

Aagard, Heather 169
Aalbaek, Peter 217
Aames, Willie 112
Aaseng, Jay 117
Abbadie, Axelle 238
Abbas, Gassan 292
Abbate, Allison 152
Abbate, Joe 190
Abbé, Michèle 214, 234
Abbott, Annie 199
Abdul-Jillil, Aminah 43
Abe, Hirohide 286, 289
Abel, Dieudonne S. 95
Abel, Doug 302
Abela, Albertino 198
Abell, Alistair 107, 198
Abella, Diego 181
Abello, Pere 228
Abercromby, Michelle 229
Aberle, Matt 129
Abernathy, Donzaleigh Avis 38
Abernathy, Lewis 60
Able, Charles 51
Ableson, Andrew 184
Abma, Marie 117
Abou-Khalil, Rabih 293
Abraham, Marc 123
Abrahami, Doron 275
Abrahams, Jon 193
Abramowitz, Richard 195
Abrams, Aaron 80
Abrams, Patsy Grady 51
Abranches, Aluizio 282
Abril, Victoria 248
Abruzzo, Ray 166
Abu-Assad, Hany 286
Abujamra, André 282
Aceron, Susan 80
Acheson, James 35, 60
Acheson, Mark 149

Acheson, Matt 55
Achille, Felix 73
Achorn, John 198
Ackerman, Thomas E. 109, 112
Ackland, Joss 196
Ackroyd, Barry 229, 275, 287
Ackroyd, Christa 271
Acogny, George 83
Acord, Lance 114, 197
Acosta, Jazmin 277
Acovone, Jay 89, 104
Acts of Worship 204
Adair, Sandra 126
Adair-Rios, Mark 79
Adalsteinsson, Bjarni 230
Adam, Jory 190
Adam, Ken 251
Adam, Marie-Christine 103
Adamickij, Stanislav 93
Adams, Dean 185
Adams, Abigail 140
Adams, Amy 174
Adams, Bradley 280
Adams, Bryan 226
Adams, Cecily 196
Adams, Dave 156
Adams, Enid-Raye 174, 176
Adams, Joe 117
Adams, Keith 134
Adams, Lillian 78
Adams, Lloyd 60
Adams, Lynne 144, 205
Adams, Patrick 40
Adams, Polly 67, 107
Adams, Ryan 81
Adams, Samantha 176
Adams, Therond Justin 139
Adams, Timothy 95
Adams, Yolanda 118
Adamson, Swede 182
Addison, Walter 43

Addy, Mark 195
Ade, Herbert 100
Adefarasin, Remi 156, 242
Adelson, Gary 173
Adelstein, Paul 133
Aderemi, Deban 291
Adineh, Golab 276
Adini, Alket 190
Adjani, Isabelle 268
Adkins, Scott 249
Adl, Kamran 276
Adlah, Taleb 244
Adler, Brian 177
Adler, Charlie 83
Adler, Joanna P. 127, 289
Adler, Lauren 165
Adoskin, Anatoly 226
Adsit, Scott 81
Advani, Nikhil 293
Affleck, Ben 35, 99, 109, 168
Affleck, Casey 176
Afflerbach, Veronica 21, 126
Afghan Stories 183
Afterman, Peter 95, 137
Agapova, Ljubov 225
Agent Cody Banks 45, 319
Age of Grief, The 100
Aghdashloo, Shohreh 166, 187, 282, 313
Agie, Awaovieyi 44
Agnello, Tom 176
Agoglia, John Steven 86
Agosto, Limary L. 83
Agranov, David 27
Aguilan, Alejandra 205
Aguilar, Daniel 71
Aguilar, David 71
Aguilar, Mario 104
Aguilar, Paulina 71
Aguilar, Ricardo 85
Aguirre, Carmen 193

Ahdout, Jackie 166
Ahdout, Jonathan 166
Ahern, Lloyd 101
Ahi, Elton 166
Ahipene, Hori 291
Ahl, Michael 51
Ahlberg, Julie 302
Ahlert, Eve 74, 89
Ahmad, Abdul 254
Ahmad, Maher 62
Ahmadi, Marie-Sophie 268
Ahmed, Kamal 176, 204
Ahren, Richard 200
Ahrens, Robert 191
Ahyi, Kevin 258
Aida, Shigekazu 115
Aidala, Richard 281
Aidem, Betsy 67
Aiello, Danny 204
Aiken, Liam 132
Aileen, Tricia 236
Aim, Pierre 216
Ainge, Michelle 179
Ainouz, Karim 237
Aira, César 287
Airlie, Andrew 41, 144, 176
Aisbett, Mark 193
Ajmil, Mohamed 279
Ajuala, Hezron 95
AKA 293
Akbari, Mania 276
Akel, Jason 183
Åkerlund, Jonas 179
Akerman, Chantal 275
Akhtar, Masud 280
Akin, Philip 94
Akinfemi, Bayo 60
Akinshina, Oksana 225
Akram, Hajaz 95
Alailima, Faleolo 39
Alajar, Gina 290

Álamo, Roberto 239
Alane, Bernard 261
Alane, Dawn 57
Alaskey, Joe 83, 152
Alba, Jessica 158
Albaladejo, Geli 288
Alban, Carlo 153
Albanese, Kelly 164
Albeck, Bruria 237
Alberda, Tristan 169
Alberg, Tom 177
Alberghetti, Anna Maria 186
Albero, Carmela 280
Albert, Marv 33
Albert, Otis Walter 164
Albert, Trevor 93
Alberts, Jonathan 191
Albo, Mike 191
Albrecht, Grant J. 278
Alcaine, José Luis 71
Alcázar, Ángel 248
Alcorn, Emmy 278
Aldag, Edward 161
Alden, John 81
Alderson, Linda 218
Alderton, John 271
Aldredge, Tom 133, 170
Aldrich, Evan 139
Aldrich, Mark 38
Aldridge, Jim 280
Aleong, Aki 166
Alexander, Aaron 80
Alexander, Elle 65
Alexander, Jason 45
Alexander, Khandi 39
Alexander, Michelle 33
Alexander, Rosemary 185
Alexander, Scott 45
Alexander, Sean 59
Alexander, Thomas 81
Alexandre, Laurent 27

Gaster, Nic 287
Gatewood, Charles 197
Gatica, René 116
Gatto, Tony 101
Gauchy, Araud 219
Gaudioso, Massimo 243
Gaudi Afternoon 277
Gaudreault, Émile 253
Gaudry, Yvonne 187
Gault, Willie 104
Gausden, John 140
Gauthier, Adella 137
Gauthier, Chris 45, 107
Gauthier, Mari-Lou 264
Gauthier, Vincent 284
Gautier, Eric 238
Gavanski, Ogden 256
Gavigan, Bart 256
Gavin, Bill 232
Gavin, Madeleine 182
Gavin, Mata 268
Gaviria, Fernando 95
Gavois-Kahn, Emilie 236
Gavreau, Rick 95
Gawtti, Peter 81
Gay, Cesc 294
Gaydos, Joey, Jr. 126
Gaye, Nona 77, 146
Gayet, Julie 284
Gaylord, E.K., II 55, 174, 192
Gaynes, George 27
Gazzola, Aaron 29
Geddis, Jeff 289
Gedigier, Francois 238
Gee, Christopher 36
Gee, Robby 252
Geer, Kevin 188
Gehr, Rocky 138
Gehrke, Stephan Menzel 279
Gehry, Frank O. 147
Geiben, Carrie 35
Geissbuhler, Luke 204
Gejera, Kal 196
Gelb, Jerry 278
Gelber, Jeffrey 89
Geleng, Rinaldo 222
Gelfond, Cathy Sandrich 62, 117, 122, 155
Gélinas, Mitsou 303
Geljo, Jasmin 140
Gellis, Barry 191
Gellman, Yani 69
Gemignani, Hugues 254
Gemmill, Tristan 292
Genaro, Tony 58
Genest, Edmond 107
Gennaro, Domenico 124
Gentil, Dominique 226
Gentry, Cecil 204
Gentry, Mojo 51

Gentry, Simon 202
Georgalis, Rob 82
Georgaris, Dean 95, 168
George, Boy 293
George, Christian 86
George, J. Patrick 192
George, Johann 248
George, Melissa 74
George, Nicole 141
George, Sarah 193
George, Tom 245
Georgieva, Zora 287
Geovandekou, Evangelia 180
Geraci, Dan 164
Geraghty, Mark 266
Geraghty, Naomi 266
Gerald, Matt 89
Gérard, Almaric 238
Gerard, Anne 211
Gérard, Charles 248
Gerard, Edwin 255
Gerard, Kurt 179
Gerard, Lisa 232
Gerardi, Michael 190
Gerber, Bill 55, 80, 192
Gerber, Nicolas 286
Gerestant, Dréd 286
Gerety, Peter 67
Gerhson, Gina 199
Geringas, Alexander 213
Gerini, Claudia 124
Gerlach, Brad 202
Gerland, Bernard 277
Germain, Paul 83
German, Laura 138
Germann, Anne 279
Germann, Kristin 279
Germano, Elio 230
Germody, Guy 270
Gerner, Pete 200
Gerrard, Matthew 69
Gerrior, Dawn M. 189
Gerron, Kurt 294
Gerry 176
Gershon, Gina 199, 255
Gerstel, Moshe 283
Gerstel, Yulie 283
Gerston, Randy 60, 181, 187
Gertsch, Didier 188
Gertz, Michelle Morris 158
Gervais, Phillip Collete 143
Gesner, Zen 180
Getas, Marilyn 51
Gethers, Amani 245
Getz, Ileen 128
Geurs, Karl 36
Ggosch, Sebastian 279
Ghafori, Ebrahim 244
Ghani, Tanveer 221
Ghanimi, Khalid 279

Ghazi, Vahid 276
Gheselbash, Régis 264
Ghir, Kulvinder 221
Ghobadi, Bahman 280
Ghobadi, Iran 280
Ghosts of the Abyss 60
Ghoush, Ala'Abu 292
Giacomo-Carbone, Franco 117
Giaimo, Anthony 95
Giaimo, Anthony 95
Giamatti, Paul 15, 65, 105, 168
Giambalvo, Louis 122
Gianjorio, Orietta 261
Giannini, Adriano 88
Giannoli, Xavier 255
Giannone, Jay 65
Gianola, Jeff 47
Gianzero, Annunziata 178
Giarraputo, Jack 58, 112
Gibb, Don 192
Gibb, Steve 95
Gibbins, Howard 249
Gibbons, Blake 84
Gibbons, Tommy 190
Gibbs, Christina 206
Gibbs, Greg 181
Gibbs, Jeff 37
Gibbs, Matyelok 248
Gibbs, Nicholas 243
Gibbs, Nigel 39, 113
Gibbs, Richard 191, 207
Gibson, Channing 41
Gibson, John 28
Gibson, Kenny 293
Gibson, Laurie Ann 158
Gibson, Meg 287
Gibson, Mel 202
Gibson, Noelle 165
Gibson, Ryan 28
Gidley, Pamela 197
Giebenhain, Todd 99
Gifford, Barry 68
Gigantic (A Tale of Two Johns) 187
Gigli 99
Gil, Adriana 198
Gil, Arturo 152
Gil, Edmundo 248
Gil, Silvia 239
Gilbert, Brian 187
Gilbert, David 82, 284
Gilbert, Jennifer 51
Gilbert, Mickey 29
Gilbert, Peter 180
Gilbert, Stephen 46
Gilbert, Troy 29, 56
Gilbreth, Frank Bunker, Jr. 172
Gilchrist, Jason 233
Gildea, Sean P. 164
Gilder, Sean 293
Gilinski, Julia 237

Gilkman, Charlotte 178
Gill, Andy 94
Gill, Chris 235
Gill, Mark 124
Gill, Scott J. 198
Gillan, Lisa Roberts 165
Gillen, Aidan 32
Gillespie, Jay 191
Gillet, Randall J. 44
Gillette, Anita 31
Gilliam, Terry 215, 257
Gillies, Andrew 94
Gillies, Isabel 190
Gillies, Matthew 97
Gillies, Rob 291
Gilliland, Richard 196
Gillis, Mary 133
Gillum, Britney 205
Gilmore, Patrick 88
Gilroy, Grace 140
Gimelberg, Daniel 294
Gimenez, Jennifer 88
Giménez, Jorge Luis 292
Gimpel, Erica 102
Ginat, NaAma 183
Ginori, Tanya 243
Ginsberg, Janice 36, 204
Ginsberg, Shani 108
Ginter, Lindsey 104
Ginuwine 158
Giobbe, Anney 136
Giola, T.J. 155
Giong, Lim 294
Giovannucci, Paolo 69
Girard, Michael 83
Girard, Rémy 22, 303
Girard, Simone-Elise 144
Girau, Maria Vicens 165
Girlhood 202
Girls Will Be Girls 200
Girl from Paris, The 277
Girl with a Pearl Earring 269
Giro, Ivelin 95
Giroday, Francois 87
Giron, Catherine 284
Girotti, Massimo 358
Gish, Annabeth 186
Gísladóttir, Gudrún 230
Gíslason, Erlingur 230
Gispert, Joan 37
Gitai, Amos 244, 274
Gitlin, Todd 82
Giulianetti, Stefano 69
Giuliani, Rudy 58
Given, Andy 29, 53, 181
Givens, Robin 51
Givens, Samuel Luis 99
Gjorgjijoski, Vladimir 287
Gladstein, Richard N. 122, 181
Glascott, Fiona 260

Glaser, Paul Michael 162
Glass, Ira 187
Glass, Kate 165
Glass, Philip 302
Glass, Ted 100
Glass, Terry 93
Glasser, David C. 45
Glasser, Karen 123
Glasser, Phillip 179
Glasser, Richard 178
Glave, Karen 122
Glaymann, Baptiste 261
Glazer, Alan G. 60
Glazer, Larry 169
Glazer, Mitch 30, 114
Gleason, Brendan 170
Gleason, Mary Pat 78, 133
Glebas, Francis 48
Gleeson, Brendan 39, 235
Gleeson, Sean 170
Gleize, Bernard 250
Gleize, Delphine 250
Glen, Georgie 271
Glenday, Benjamin 72
Glenister, Philip 271
Glenn, Pierre-William 244, 248
Glenn, Scott 245
Glenn, Sean 275
Glennon, James 132
Glicker, Danny 92
Glickman, Jonathan 30, 32
Glienna, Greg 174
Glo, Frank 52
Gloomy Sunday 291
Glover, Crispin 46, 88
Glover, Kate 263
Gluckman, John 169
Gluhar, Martin 205
Glynn, Molly 267
Goberman, Karen 38
Godard, Agnes 282
Godbold, J.K. 117
Godboldo, Dale 181, 184
Goddard, Trevor 91, 358
Godden, Mark 280
Godeau, Patrick 272
Godel, Armen 250
Godenir, Mike 168
Godfrey, Joe 61
Godfrey, Wyck 73
Godin, Maurice 180
Godley, Adam 248, 263
Godley, Simon 291
Godoy, Lucio 246
Godrèche, Judith 228
Godshall, Ray, Sr. 159
Gods and Generals 38
God Has a Rap Sheet 176
Goede, Don 178
Goggins, Walton 181

Salter, Ben 63
Salter, David Ian 304
Salter, Loyd Keith 153
Salton, Zvi 275
Salus, Gale 185
Salva, Victor 194
Salvador, Carol 288
Salvano, Gino 95
Salvatore, Richard 191
Salvay, Bennett 194
Salvidar, Gilbert 86
Sama, Francine 199
Samaha, Elie 80, 87
Samaroo, Dennison 166
Sambrell, Aldo 200
Sambucci, Pierluigi 69
Same River Twice, The 196
Samie, Catherine 103, 274
Samie, Celine 268
Samir 293
Sammarco, Charles 204
Samojlenko, Aleksandr 283
Samovitz, Todd 129
Sampath, Srinath 193
Samper, Kristjana 230
Sampson, Angus 29
Sampson, Paul 191
Sams, Russell 129
Samuel, Peter 100
Samuels, Jeremiah 166
Samuelson, Camilla Millican 98
San-Giacomo, Laura 203
Sanada, Hiroyuki 159
Sánchez, Alicia 248
Sanchez, Jonathan 86
Sanchez, Kiele 164, 199
Sanchez, Lauren 84
Sanchez, Lisa 153
Sanchez, Lucia 250
Sánchez, Mónika 285
Sanchez, Otto 95
Sanchez, Roberto 185
Sanchez, Roberto "Sanz" 83
Sanchez, Rodrigo Pineda 267
Sánchez, Rosa 275
Sanchez, Roselyn 53, 180, 182
Sanda, Hiroyuki 279
Sandberg, Francine 228
Sande, Theo Van de 125
Sandell, William 150, 168
Sanderlin, Ann Marie 102
Sanders, Amanda 51
Sanders, Charles 37, 119
Sanders, Jackie 165
Sanders, Tim 232
Sanders, Tom 205
Sanderson, Will 174, 290
Sanderson, William 38
Sandeval, David 206
Sandiford, Hadley 60

Sandler, Adam 58, 112
Sandow, Nick 287
Sandoz, Gilles 254
Sandro, Ivan 207
Sands, Julian 179, 249, 285
Sands, Rico 205
Sands, Stark 145
Sanelme, Marie-José 274
Sanes, Camillia 96
Sangkapricha, Saharat 283
Sangster, Thomas 262
Sanheim, Kurtis 106
Sankhavesa, Chalee 68
Sankla, Sanjay 293
Sanktjohanser, Josef 284
Sano, Dana 57
Sano, Shiro 286
Sanping, Han 231
Sansa, Maya 284
Sanselme, Marejos 244
Sansom, Ken 48
Sansone, Angelina 169
Santana, Alexandre 212
Santana, Cynthia 67
Santana, Marcos 182
Santana, Reginaldo 123
Santaolalla, Gustavo 153, 244
Santelli, Heidi 73
Santesmases, Rosario 239
Santiago, Flora 200
Santiago, Saundra 188
Santiago, Susan 73
Santoro, Kristina 179
Santoro, Rodrigo 88, 263
Santos, Al 194
Santos, Albert P. 79
Santos, Bianca 105
Santoyo, Silivia 116
Santy, Charles 188
Sanville, Guy 175
Sanz, Horatio 180
Sanz, Nestor 292
San Juan, Alberto 239, 288
San Luis, Laura 176
San Nicholas, Theresa 86
Sapani, Danny 285
Saphire, Tatiana 287
Sarafian, Richard 191
Sarafian, Tedi 89
Saran, Andrea 124
Sarandon, Susan 189
Saravia, Joey 156
Sarchielli, Massimo 124
Sarde, Alain 214, 223, 234
Sarfati, Carine 270
Sargent, Lia 278
Sarkissian, Hamlet 198
Sarnataro, Patricia 198
Sarnof, Vivian 110
Sarnoff, Elizabeth 182

Sarpong, Sam 191, 207
Sarsgaard, Peter 14, 144
Sartore, Janet 280
Sarukawa, Naoto 285
Sasaki, Takashi 281
Sasse, Ernst 226
Sassine, Jackline 243
Sather, Joe 174
Satiani, Smita 59
Sato, Hitomi 289
Sato, Sakichi 134, 281
Sato, Shinsuke 286
Sato, Yasue 289
Sattanathan, Satish 193
Satterfield, Paul 78
Saturnin, Milla S. 244
Sau, Shek 288
Sauber, Patrick 61
Saugeon, Nathalie 279
Sauli, Anneli 225
Saun, Kara 199
Saunders, Cliff 106
Saunders, Katy 69
Saunders, Lee-Anna 51
Sauphanor, Stanislas 223
Saux, Stephen 164
Savage, Barbara 206
Savage, Jason R. 198
Savage, John 190
Savaria, Ellen 93
Savides, Harris 141, 176
Savill, Charlie 291
Saville, Angela 275
Saville, Philip 292
Savin, Eric 216
Savoca, Nancy 184
Savoy, David 51
Savoy, Sharon 51
Savyon, Hanan 255
Sawada, Kenji 282
Sawada, Masamishi 244
Sawadogo, Justine 244
Sawalha, Julia 279
Sawyer, Connie 49, 162, 185
Sawyer, Timothy 178
Saxton, Charlie 204
Sayer, William 243
Sayles, John 120
Sayres, Amy 119
Sbarge, Raphael 196
Sbragia, Mattia 195
Scalia, Pietro 181, 190
Scalise, Scot 205
Scallan, Paul 157
Scandal 132
Scanlan, Joanna 269
Scanlon, Caitlin 139
Scanlon, Eilish 266
Scanlon, Pat 199
Scanlon, Patti 197

Scantlebury, Glen 138
Scar 194
Scarabelli, Michele 144
Scarborough, Adrian 241
Scarborough, Margaret 189
Scariano, Sandro 211
Scarlatos, Terry J. 149
Scarlett, Jane 200
Scarpa, Fabio 81
Scarpa, Margaret 183
Scarpato, Beatrice 230
Scarry, Rick 74
Scarwid, Diana 111, 174
Scary Movie 3 140, 318
Scavino, Lucas 275
Schaefer, Karl-Eberhard 294
Schäfer, Volker 291
Schaffer, Jeff 154
Schamburg, Wolfgang 80
Schamus, James 85, 245
Schaper, Rainer 251
Scharf, William S. 196
Scharf, Yaron 255
Schatzberg, Andrew 96
Schatzberg, Jerry 183
Schawn, Josephine 157
Scheda, Christiane 285
Scheelar, Darryl 168
Scheide, Jon C. 244
Scheider, Roy 183
Scheingross, Jaime 70
Scheinman, Catherine 175
Schelfhout, Gerd 294
Schepisi, Fred 66, 181
Scheppler, Tony 165
Scherer, Ralph 207
Scherick, Jay 29
Scherma, Frank 302
Schertenleib, Christof 287
Scherzinger, Nicole 182, 207
Scheuring, Paul 57
Schiel, Valerie 269
Schiff, Paul 165
Schiff, Richard 67
Schiff, Steven 183
Schiffer, Claudia 263
Schiffer, Michael 103
Schiffner, Travis 194
Schifrin, Lalo 43
Schimdt, Antje 213
Schina, Massimo 27
Schindler, Deborah 165
Schindler, Henry 251
Schlei, Brad L. 179
Schlesinger, John 364
Schlesinger, Sherril 189
Schletter, Eban 189
Schliessler, Tobias 123
Schlissel, Charles J.D. 113
Schlosser, Greg 106

Schmahl, Hildegard 220
Schmeer, Karen 196, 302
Schmid, Andreas 167
Schmiderer, Othmar 214
Schmidt, Adele 189
Schmidt, Anthony 29
Schmidt, Arne L. 160
Schmidt, Arthur 90
Schmidt, Bruno 282
Schmidt, Gerhard 180
Schmidt, Jeff 153
Schmidt, John 111, 155, 207
Schmidt, Kevin G. 172
Schmidt, Rob 187
Schmidt-Hambrock, Jochen 220
Schmitt, Eric-Emmanuel 268
Schmitz, Eric 60
Schnack, AJ 187
Schnass, Jörg 270
Schneider, Ernst-August 80
Schneider, Nina 293
Schneider, Paul 36
Schneider, Todd 252
Schneiderman, Daniel 280
Schober, Holger 251
Schock, Colton 107
Schoenberg, Sarah 183
Schoendoerffer, Ludovic 255
Schofield, Ben 55
Schofield, Paul 149
Scholey, Michael 206
Scholfield, Olivia 221
Scholte, Tom 50
Schonherr, Albrecht 189
Schoof, Aimee 59, 204
School of Rock, The 21, 126, 318
Schoot, Slava 188, 204
Schöps, Richard 291
Schott, Uwe 279
Schotte, Anne 228
Schrader, Paul 183
Schrick, Galen 164
Schroder, Rick 179
Schroeder, Adam 110
Schroeder, Carly 69
Schroth, Sabine 188
Schroud, Nicole L. 177
Schübel, Rolf 291
Schuch, Jessica 279
Schudlova, Hanka 32
Schuldt, Monique 279
Schulman, Roger S.H. 36
Schultz, Peter V. 189
Schultz, Robert 99
Schultz, Ronald 207
Schumacher, Joel 56, 260
Schuman, Melissa 207
Schumann, Coco 294
Schunter, Bettina 68
Schuster, Julie 70